BEWARE OF SMALL STATES

Lebanon, Battleground of the Middle East

Also by David Hirst

Oil and Public Opinion in the Middle East

Sadat

The Gun and the Olive Branch

BEWARE OF SMALL STATES

Lebanon, Battleground of the Middle East

DAVID HIRST

NATION BOOKS
New York

Copyright © 2010 by David Hirst
Published in the United States by Nation Books,
A Member of the Perseus Books Group
116 East 16th Street, 8th Floor
New York, NY 10003

Nation Books is a co-publishing venture of the Nation Institute
and the Perseus Books Group

Published in Great Britain in 2010 by Faber and Faber Ltd
British ISBN: 978–0-571–23741–8

Books published by Nation Books are available at special discounts for
bulk purchases in the United States by corporations, institutions, and other
organizations. For more information, please contact the Special Markets
Department at the Perseus Books Group, 2300 Chestnut Street, Suite
200, Philadelphia, PA 19103, or call (800) 810-4145, ext. 5000, or e-mail
special.markets@perseusbooks.com.

A CIP catalog record for this book is available from the Library of
Congress.
ISBN: 978-1-56858-422-5
LCCN: 2009942493

10 9 8 7 6 5 4 3 2 1

For Ted and Mimi

The people are all charming to me. They are not really Eastern, or anything: just a poor fringe of a people between Islam and the sea, doomed to be pawns in whatever politics are played here ... I haven't yet come across one spark of national feeling: it is all sects and hatreds and religions. I read the Maronite mass book the other day, and felt the prayer 'to be saved from bloodshed' take on a particular meaning in this country of massacres. And it is a grand country, too.

Freya Stark, *Letters from Syria* (John Murray, London, 1942) p. 59

Contents

Maps

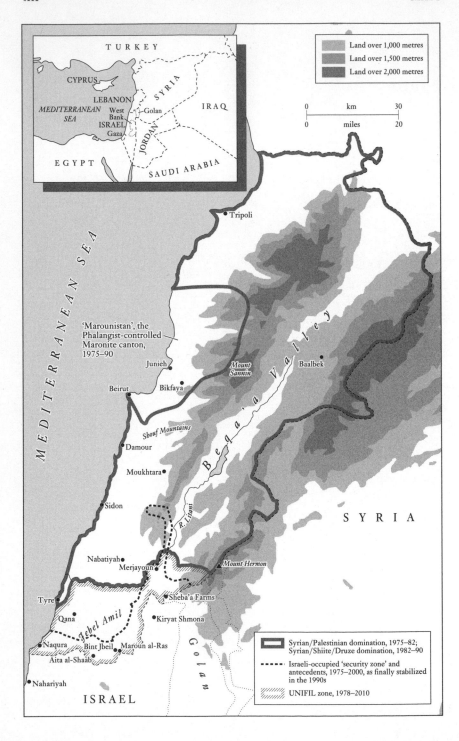

Land over 1,000 metres
Land over 1,500 metres
Land over 2,000 metres

TURKEY

CYPRUS

LEBANON

MEDITERRANEAN SEA

Golan

West Bank.

ISRAEL

Gaza

SYRIA

IRAQ

JORDAN

EGYPT

SAUDI ARABIA

km 30
0
miles 20
0

Tripoli

MEDITERRANEAN SEA

'Marounistan', the
Phalangist-controlled
Maronite canton,
1975–90

Junieh

Mount
Sannin

Baalbek

Beirut

Bikfaya

Shouf Mountains

Damour

Moukhtara

Sidon

R. Litani

Beqa'a Valley

S Y R I A

Nabatiyah

Merjayoun

Mount Hermon

Tyre

Jebel Amil

Sheba'a Farms

Qana

Kiryat Shmona

Golan

Naqura

Bint Jbeil

Maroun al-Ras

Aita al-Shaab

Nahariyah

ISRAEL

Syrian/Palestinian domination, 1975–82;
Syrian/Shiite/Druze domination, 1982–90

Israeli-occupied 'security zone' and
antecedents, 1975–2000, as finally stabilized
in the 1990s

UNIFIL zone, 1978–2010

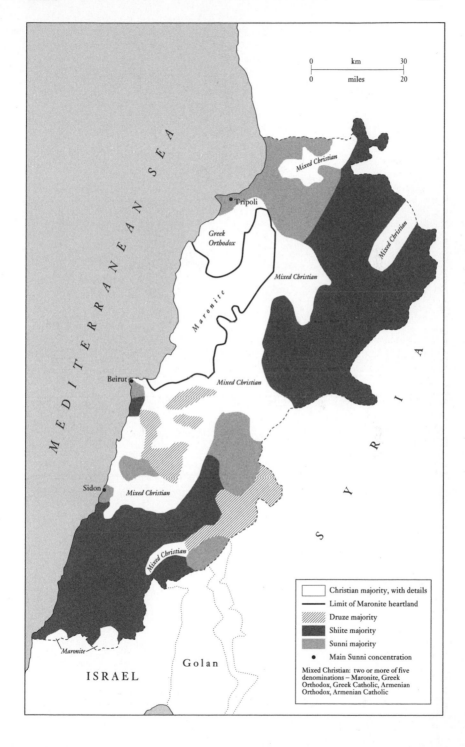

0   km   30
0   miles   20

Mixed Christian

Tripoli

Greek
Orthodox

Mixed Christian

Mixed Christian

Maronite

Mixed Christian

Beirut

Mixed Christian

S

Y

R

I

A

Sidon

Mixed Christian

Mixed Christian

Maronite

Golan

ISRAEL

M E D I T E R R A N E A N   S E A

	Christian majority, with details
	Limit of Maronite heartland
	Druze majority
	Shiite majority
	Sunni majority
●	Main Sunni concentration

Mixed Christian: two or more of five
denominations – Maronite, Greek
Orthodox, Greek Catholic, Armenian
Orthodox, Armenian Catholic

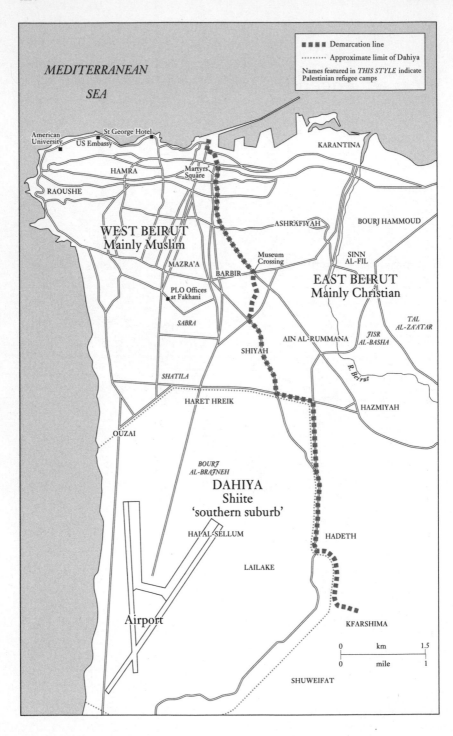

MEDITERRANEAN

SEA

Demarcation line

Approximate limit of Dahiya

Names featured in *THIS STYLE* indicate
Palestinian refugee camps

American University

St George Hotel

US Embassy

KARANTINA

HAMRA

Martyrs' Square

RAOUSHE

ASHRAFIYAH

BOURJ HAMMOUD

WEST BEIRUT
Mainly Muslim

MAZRA'A

Museum Crossing

SINN AL-FIL

BARBIR

PLO Offices at Fakhani

EAST BEIRUT
Mainly Christian

SABRA

TAL AL-ZA'ATAR

AIN AL-RUMMANA

JISR AL-BASHA

SHIYAH

SHATILA

R. Beirut

HARET HREIK

HAZMIYAH

OUZAI

BOURJ AL-BRAJNEH

DAHIYA
Shiite
'southern suburb'

HAI AL-SELLUM

HADETH

LAILAKE

Airport

KFARSHIMA

0   km   1.5
0   mile   1

SHUWEIFAT

Acknowledgements

Among those who helped me with this book, I would particularly like to thank the Institute for Palestine Studies, its staff and library, in Beirut, and two other excellent institutions: the London-based *Middle East Mirror*, source of many of the newspaper quotations in Arabic, Farsi and Hebrew, and the *Middle East Reporter*, Beirut. In addition I owe a very special debt to Karsten Tveit, and Peter Scott-Hansen, who translated Tveit's book *Nederlag: Israel's Krig i Libanon*, from the Norwegian on my behalf.

CHAPTER ONE

The Seeds of Conflict

1860–1923

LEBANON: THE SMALL, SECTARIAN STATE OF THE MIDDLE EAST

Lebanon, a mountainous country on the Eastern Mediterranean no bigger than Wales or the American state of Connecticut, has long attracted an international attention disproportionate to its size and, one might at first think, its importance. The attention has generally come in dramatic spasms provoked by crises apt to subside as quickly as they erupt, but whose underlying causes never go away. Rarely, however, did it reach such a pitch of sustained intensity as during the event that inspired the writing of this history – those thirty-three days in July and August 2006, which Arabs have called the 'Sixth [Arab–Israeli] War'. And rarely have pundits and partisans ascribed such great, such well-nigh cosmic significance to a war that was limited in scope and, in any immediate military sense at least, inconclusive in its outcome.

On the one hand, so passionate a devotee of Israel as the controversial American celebrity lawyer Alan Dershowitz could say that it was 'the first major battle of a third world war between terrorist armies and democracies, the first instance since the Holocaust in which Jews, as Jews, are targeted by an international organization that seeks recognition as a legitimate power, by Islamic extremists who want to "liberate" all Islamic land, which includes all of Israel proper, including Tel Aviv, from the "crusaders."'[1] On the other, the Islamic Republic of Iran, Dershowitz's polar opposite and chief sponsor of Hizbullah, found it richly meaningful too. 'Those people and groups,' said the newspaper

Kayhan, 'who are trying to scare Tehran out of its support for the Lebanese people, Hizbullah and Hamas, are like a little kid who is trying to create a big wave in the ocean by throwing a small stone into it. The evil triangle of America, Israel and reactionary Arabs has been defeated in the four weeks since the crisis began, and this triangle will cease to exist in the Middle East that lies ahead.'[2]

Pronouncements of the kind did at least, in their very grandiloquence, serve to dramatize what had long established itself as Lebanon's pre-eminent role in the world. 'Beware of small states', wrote Mikhail Bakunin, the Russian anarchist, to a friend in 1870. What he meant, in that era of European war and geopolitical upheaval, was not only that such diminutive polities were peculiarly vulnerable to the machinations of greater ones, but that they were a source of trouble for their tormentors too.[3] He had in mind Belgium, for example, or Latvia, trapped on the Baltic between the rival ambitions of Czarist Russia and a Germany undergoing its unification and aggrandizement at the hand of Prussia and its Iron Chancellor, Otto von Bismarck. Lebanon, by this geopolitical criterion, undoubtedly qualifies as the 'small state' of the Middle East. Not for nothing have its ancient, biblical name, and that of its capital, Beirut, now entered the world's political vocabulary as bywords for a certain type of modern conflict. Not for nothing has the term *libanisation* ('Lebanonization') become an official part of the French language, defined in the latest editions of Larousse as 'a process of fragmentation of a state, as a result of confrontation between diverse communities', and 'tending to replace "balkanisation"'.

But it is not simply Lebanon's small size, sensitive location between East and West, or the special interest European powers have always taken in this largely Christian country, which accounts for its susceptibility to outside interference. It is, above all, its unique internal composition. For as an amalgam of religious communities and their myriad sub-divisions, with a constitutional and political order to match, Lebanon is the sectarian state *par excellence*. The condition from which it suffers is chronic; or, at the very least, it is surely bound to endure so long as the whole Middle East also remains what it is: the most endemically unstable region in the world. Lebanon, it seems, was almost *designed* to be the everlasting battleground for others' political, strategic and ideological conflicts, conflicts which sometimes escalate into their proxy wars. These others are first and foremost, of course, the larger states of the region. But they are also America, Europe, Russia, or any great power, actual or aspiring, that takes an interest in the region's affairs. And great powers always have taken such an interest, on account of its importance, historically, as a hub of international politics, and, in recent times, as the repository of vast reserves of oil, life-blood of the modern world, and the *locus* of its longest-running, most implacable and dangerous conflict, the struggle between Arab and Jew. If the Middle East habitually interferes in Lebanon's affairs, the outside world habitually does so in those of the Middle East.

Nor is it just states, and their official agencies, to whose designs, public or clandestine, Lebanon is uniquely exposed. It is no less exposed, at the popular level, to every new idea or ideology, every religious, political or cultural current that arises and spreads across the region. That is because it is, and always has been, a more open, liberal and democratic society than any of its Arab neighbours. In this respect, its vulnerability to domestic dissension, its chief flaw, has become, as it were, its chief of virtues. For the sectarian state just could not function at all unless its constituent parts agreed, at least in principle, that respecting the rights, interests and sensibilities of each was indispensable to the welfare of all. That amounted to a built-in prophylactic against the dictatorship of one group, usually ethnic or sectarian, over others that has blighted the rest of the Arab world.

So, although Lebanon has undoubtedly been the object and victim of others' actions and ambitions, on the plane of ideas it has not only been an object, but an agent too. Thus, in its own, idiosyncratic and, of course, frequently sectarian way, it has been a reflector of, or major contributor to, all the broad historical experiences of the modern Middle East: the transition from Ottoman Turkish rule to European colonial domination; the rise of the pan-Arab nationalist idea and the advent of independence; the post-independence, revolutionary seizures of power – in all their variously secular, socialist, unionist, 'anti-imperialist' guises – which, with President Nasser as their great champion, the nationalist idea spawned; and finally, with the failure of

nationalism, or at least of the decadent regimes that presumed to
embody it, the rise of the fundamentalist Islam which is pre-eminent
today. Indeed, could it even be said that Lebanon – the eternal victim
– has now become the perpetrator too, posing no less a threat to greater
states than they habitually posed to it? Was it mere braggadocio, or was
it a serious, credible proposition that Hassan Nasrallah, the Hizbullah
leader, advanced in his first public appearance after 'the divine victory'
which God had bestowed on his jihadist warriors – the proposition that
the 'small state' of the Middle East had now been transformed into one
of its 'great powers'?[4] His enraptured followers clearly thought so. And
could anyone, amid the shocks and tumult of the times, confidently
pronounce them wrong?

Several states, from inside the region and beyond, have impinged on
Lebanon – wooed, bullied or sought to subvert it from within, attacked,
invaded, occupied or otherwise maltreated it – in its nearly ninety-year
existence in its modern form. But none has done so more strenuously
and disruptively than the state of Israel – or, to be more precise, Israel
preceded by the pre-state Zionist movement out of which it grew. For,
however familiar the existence and characteristic activities of the
Jewish state may now have come to seem in the eyes of the world, it is
an historically remarkable fact that when Lebanon as we know it first
arose, in 1920, no such thing existed. Not only was there no Jewish state,
there were not even the basic prerequisites of one – a distinct and
recognized people inhabiting a distinct and recognized territory of its
own – as there had been prior to the formation of the smaller nation-
states of Europe. Latvia, for example, finally achieved statehood after
the First World War, upon the dissolution of the last of the successive
empires within which it had hitherto been subsumed. In Palestine,
where Israel eventually did arise, there was only a very small community of Jews, no more than six per cent of the total population,
owning no more than two per cent of the land.[5] Of those only a
minority, natives born and bred, were as truly indigenous as the Arabs
among whom they lived; the majority were recent immigrants from
Eastern Europe. Nor did these immigrants possess any conceivable
right, under international law or custom, to create an exclusively Jewish
state, or any reasonable expectation that they ever could, given the

seemingly insuperable obstacles which stood in their path, not just legal
ones of course, but moral, diplomatic, political and demographic too.
Yet not only did they achieve that – mainly, and inevitably, through
force – within the space of thirty years, they eventually turned their
state, militarily and diplomatically, into the most powerful in the
region. No less inevitably, given the manner of its birth, this new-born
state was from the outset predisposed to use its power in an aggressive,
domineering and violent fashion. That was to be felt throughout the
region, but – after Palestine itself – nowhere more than it was by the
smallest and weakest of its neighbours, Lebanon. And when one speaks
of Israeli power, one cannot but speak of the Western power that was
always integral to it. In its embryonic, pre-state days, the Zionist enterprise in Palestine was utterly dependent on Great Britain, the dominant
imperial state of the age, which had sponsored it. But even now, the
regional superpower into which it eventually grew remains no less
dependent for its ultimate survival on the global superpower, or, rather,
on its unique ability – directly or via the 'friends of Israel' inside the US
itself – to enlist American power on its own behalf.

SYKES–PICOT: FRANCE AND BRITAIN SHARE THE SPOILS

Modern Lebanon, like Latvia, was born out of the cataclysm of the
First World War, when the Ottoman Empire, the 'Sick Man of Europe',
finally expired. It was a part of the new Middle Eastern order which
Britain and France, the war's victors, imposed on the empire's former
Arab provinces.

That order represented a betrayal of the Arab peoples – of their
hopes and expectations for a renewal of mastery in their own house
which had not been theirs for centuries. The last time it had been, they
ranked for a while as a standard-bearer of human progress. That was
when, with Europe still sunk in the Dark Ages, they created a brilliant
civilization inextricably associated with the religion, Islam, which their
Prophet, Muhammad, had founded. From Damascus, seat of the first,
Omayyad Caliphate, they carried it in an extraordinary succession of
imperial conquests to India in the east, while their westerly advance,
through North Africa and Spain, was only checked, beyond the

Pyrenees, by the Frankish chief, Charles Martel, in the battle of Tours in 732. Other peoples shared in this enterprise, but it was the original Arab conquerors who, as its ruling class, bound the vast empire together. In time, however, their unifying ascendancy crumbled beneath a combination of internal convulsions and external challenges, and eventually the empire's Arabian heartlands themselves fell prey to foreign, albeit – Crusader kingdoms apart – Muslim rulers. During the four hundred years that the last of them, the Ottomans, held sway, the Arab decline accelerated disastrously in relation to a European Christendom forging triumphantly ahead in all fields of human endeavour. It was in response to Europe's supremacy, and its invasion or outright annexation of parts of the Arab homeland, that in the later years of the nineteenth century Arab thinkers began to reflect on the reasons why their once pre-eminent civilization had fallen so far behind. They studied and sought to profit not only from those most obvious and outwardly impressive manifestations of Europe's progress – its scientific and technological achievements – but from those larger, less tangible concepts – the nation state, constitutional government, individual liberties, secularism, democracy – that underlay them. At first it had been primarily as Muslims that they reacted. But by the turn of the twentieth century, in a movement known as the Arab Awakening – a great debate about Arab identity, history, language, culture, religion – they tended more and more to look upon themselves primarily as Arabs. The central idea was that of nationhood. There *was* an Arab nation; however diverse its component parts might be, these had certain basic aspirations in common. The more closely each worked with the other the stronger all would be.

In 1915, early in the war, Britain effectively acknowledged the force and justice of the pan-Arab nationalist ideal when it solemnly pledged its support for a free, sovereign and potentially united Arab state encompassing all, or at least the vast bulk, of those liberated Ottoman provinces. It had entered into a protracted correspondence with Sherif Hussein of Mecca, the Ottoman-appointed governor of the province of Hijaz in what is now Saudi Arabia. Long bent on the establishment of an independent Arab kingdom, with himself and his Hashemite dynasty at its head, he was the most representative spokesman of the

Arab cause. In return for his collaboration with the Allies in their military campaign against the Ottomans, Britain undertook to 'recognize and support the independence of the Arabs' in all their domains except for 'portions of Syria [i.e. principally Lebanon] lying to the west of Damascus, Homs, Hama and Aleppo that could not be said to be purely Arab'. The Sherif did not agree to this exception – which Britain had introduced in deference to France – reserving the right to contest it later.

In fulfilment of their part of the bargain, the Sherif and his sons, the amirs Faisal and Abdullah, launched the Arab Revolt. Its climax came with the capture of Damascus in 1918. That historic city should then have become, for the first time in more than a thousand years, the capital of the 'Arab Kingdom' which he proclaimed there. But this was not to be – or at least not for more than a few weeks. French troops marched from Lebanon – where Faisal had already surrendered an even briefer, week-long tenure[6] – defeated his army, and added Damascus and the whole of Syria to France's existing array of colonial possessions.

It did so with British connivance. For, six months after its negotiations with Sherif Hussein, the British government had concluded a secret understanding between itself, France and Czarist Russia. This, the Sykes–Picot agreement, was one of the two key documents that shaped the modern history of the Middle East. Under its terms, made public in 1917, to the Arabs' immense consternation, by the newly installed Bolshevik government, Russia and Italy were to take control of essentially Turkish parts of the former Ottoman domains, while France and Britain were to divide the Arab provinces between them, with Syria and Lebanon going to France, and Iraq, Palestine and Transjordan to Britain.

It was unrepentant, old-fashioned imperialism. But it was dressed up in philanthropic guise. Britain and France were obliged to pay lip-service of sorts to the principles which, with its promises to the Arabs, Britain had effectively endorsed. They did so in the shape of the so-called Mandates. According to these, assigned to them as 'a sacred trust of civilization' by the League of Nations, their charges had formally speaking become 'independent states'; at the same time, however, they were 'subject to the rendering of administrative advice and assistance by a Mandatory until such time as they [were] able to stand alone'.

The newly subordinate Arabs owed this at least ostensible concession to the United States. Declaring war on Germany in 1917, President Woodrow Wilson had called for a post-war world 'made safe for democracy'; and in his Fourteen Points, enunciated in January 1918, he decreed that this post-war world should also be an anti-colonial one which banished 'force' and 'aggression' from the affairs of nations, replacing them with 'self-determination', 'justice', 'fair dealing' and 'open covenants openly arrived at'. As for the Middle East itself, its peoples should be 'assured of undoubted security of life and absolutely unmolested opportunity of development'. At the Versailles peace conference in 1919, Wilson refused even to consider the secret wartime agreements of the European powers. Furthermore, in response to pleas that came, most forcefully, from fellow Americans resident in the Middle East – such as Daniel Bliss, president of the American University of Beirut – he resolved that the conference should dispatch a mission of inquiry to ascertain the true desire of the people 'directly concerned', the Arabs themselves. The 'King– Crane Commission', as it came to be known after the names of its exclusively American participants, found that what the Arabs almost unanimously desired was full independence. The inhabitants of Syria – and Palestine, then considered to be a part of it – insisted on a sovereign and united state embracing not only the whole of what is now the *state* of Syria, but Lebanon, Palestine and Transjordan too. The Commission also determined that if these people really needed a period of foreign tutelage at all 'the Mandate should certainly go to America'. But then Wilson, losing interest, left the field to the recalcitrant Europeans.

THE MARONITES AND THE BIRTH OF GREATER LEBANON

Under Sykes–Picot France was entitled to set up whatever kind of administration, 'direct or indirect', it saw fit in those Mediterranean coastal regions which Britain had sought to exclude from an 'Arab Kingdom'. It proceeded with the creation of Greater Lebanon, so called because, though still a small state, it was very substantially larger than the historical entity, Mount Lebanon, out of which it grew.

Under the Ottomans, these rugged highlands had long enjoyed a special, autonomous status as the ancestral home of two religious communities, the Maronite Christians and the Druzes. In search of a refuge from Muslim conquests, the Maronites, offspring of the early Church's Monothelite controversy as to the dual or single nature of Christ, first established a foothold there in the seventh century. They drew close to Catholic Europe during the Crusades and entered into full union with Rome in 1736. They developed a very special relationship with their so-called 'tender mother', France. The Druzes, an esoteric, sub-Shiite sect, took root there in the eleventh century.

The two communities fluctuated between cooperation and bitter conflict. But in the nineteenth century relations between them became inextricably entwined with Mount Lebanon's emergence, adumbrating the 'small state' role to come, as the focal point of both regional and international competition – between an Ottoman Empire striving to preserve a grip on its restive province, an Egypt which had invaded it, a France backing the Maronites, and Britain the Druzes. 'If one man hits another,' a local chieftain complained, 'the incident becomes an Anglo-French affair, and there might even be trouble between the two countries if a cup of coffee gets spilt on the ground.'[7] Civil war came to a head in 1860, when the Druzes inflicted horrible massacres on the Maronites. It ended with French military intervention on the Maronites' behalf and the creation of a new autonomous order under European protection.

Despite their defeat, however, the Maronites emerged stronger than the Druzes. They had long been gaining ground demographically, territorially, educationally and economically, and now they secured a clear political primacy too. Under the new order, and the stability, prosperity and self-confidence that came with it, they developed the larger communal ambitions that were to come to fruition with the formation of Greater Lebanon.

The Christians of Mount Lebanon, of Beirut and coastal regions then part of Syria had played a dominant and pioneering role in the intellectual ferment of the Arab Awakening. They owed that very largely to their long-standing association with the West, and to seats of learning, such as the American University of Beirut, which missionaries and philanthropists, both European and American, had established among them. They had thereby contributed much to the growth of the pan-Arab nationalist idea. Ironically, however, that idea was now about to collide with a more local nationalism of their own. At first, when the imperial Turk had been perceived, by Muslims and Christians alike, as the common adversary, this had only been latent within the larger pan-Arab one. But with the prospect of liberation from the Ottomans improving, and Arab nationalism seemingly never quite able to shed its Islamic character in favour of a truly secular one, it took a more concrete and assertive form. It was essentially Maronite nationalism in Lebanese guise. Its roots lay in the Maronites' historical fear of, and antipathy for, Islam, in their self-perception as an embattled outpost of Christendom, the largest, most compact and pugnacious in the Middle East, which, secure in its mountain fastnesses, had never submitted to the officially protected, but subordinate, so-called *dhimmi* status endured by Greek Orthodox and other Christian denominations, as scattered islands in a Muslim sea. Lebanon, in their estimation, was essentially 'their' country. Indeed, according to a mythology clerics and ideologues promoted, they were not really Arabs at all.[8] They were heirs to the Phoenicians, the merchant, sea-faring nation of antiquity; they were a Mediterranean people, honorary Europeans, with Rome as their spiritual Mecca, Paris their cultural one.[9] Whereas the Arab nationalists wanted to absorb Lebanon into a greater Arab state, they wanted a small and separate one, with themselves in charge. And with French help they got it.

The state which France conjured into being in August 1920 more than doubled the dimensions of Mount Lebanon with the annexation of the coastal cities of Beirut, Tyre, Sidon and Tripoli, as well as the Beqa'a valley in the interior. This, for the Maronites, was the restoration of the 'historic frontiers', well beyond the Mountain, to which the writ of powerful (though mostly non-Christian) rulers had once in practice run. The Maronite patriarch, exercising temporal as well as spiritual authority, was the leading champion of this expansionist dream come true. Economic as well as ideological motives lay behind it: only with the addition of the Mediterranean ports, vital for commerce, and the fertile inland plain, ensuring a measure of self-sufficiency in agriculture, could their new Lebanon be a truly viable one. The trouble with this arrangement was that the new territories, thus arbitrarily acquired, were actually Syrian, and, though they included scattered Maronite communities, their great majority, mainly Muslim, considered themselves Syrian too; they mostly identified with the pan-Arab nationalism of which Syria was the heart. For the orthodox, largely city-dwelling Sunnis, members of the Arab nation's largest religious community and its traditional ruling class, the prospect of sub-ordination by local Christians was if anything worse than European colonialism; an 'almost unimaginable inversion of the natural order in their world'.[10]

For the Maronites were resolved to perpetuate the dominance, over this Greater Lebanon, which they formerly exerted over the lesser one of the Mountain. For a variety of reasons, they believed they could manage that. In a country of well under a million people they still constituted the largest single community, if no longer the absolute majority they had been; twelve years later, according to the only official census ever conducted, they numbered 351,197, or 33.57 per cent out of a total population of 1,046,164.[11] They were also relatively well-educated, prosperous, and persuaded of the inherent superiority of their Westernized ways. Their beloved France, for colonial reasons, stood four-square behind them. With Lebanon's independence in 1943, their ascendancy was formally consecrated in the so-called National Pact. This unwritten agreement enshrined an historic compromise: the Maronites, recognizing Lebanon's Arab character and membership of the Arab family, agreed to renounce any protective links to European powers and the Muslims, acknowledging the finality of its independent statehood, shed their pan-Arab nationalist dream of re-integration into the Syria from which they had been severed. The Pact also presumed to regulate the share and status of every religious community in the whole. There were a full seventeen of these; they were all crammed cheek by jowl into the narrow confines, some 200 kilometres long by 80 broad, of the multi-confessional state, all more or less identified with their own particular, yet rarely homogeneous, segment – be it a precipitous mountain domain or a compact city quarter – in the crazy patchwork of separate entities that was its territorial expression. The Maronites, taking the presidency, command of the army and other key posts, came out firmly at the apex of the hierarchy. The Sunnis, numbering 194,305, or 18.57 per cent of the population, at the time of the 1932 census, took the premiership. The least favoured were the 166,545 Shiites, at 15.92 per cent.[12]

Once upon a time, back in the tenth century, when Shiite dynasties still ruled most of the Middle East and North Africa, they had been dominant, possibly even the majority, in the territories now part of the new-born Lebanese state. But, oppressed and persecuted under orthodox Sunni Mamluks and Ottomans, they were driven out of the Tripoli region of northern Lebanon. With the rise and expansion of the Maronites and Druzes, they were then driven from Mount Lebanon, until, apart from a pocket here and there, they were territorially reduced to Jebel Amil – the hill country inland from Tyre and Sidon – and part of the Beqa'a Valley, with which they are immemorially associated. In 1919, loyal to Syria and Amir Faisal, and suspicious of a French-ruled, Maronite-dominated Lebanon, they were attacked by French troops, assisted by local Maronites, who constituted the second, if very much smaller community of Jebel Amil. Their towns and villages came under artillery and aerial bombardment. They formally submitted to the new order with the enforced signature, by their notables and *ulema* (religious leaders), of an admission of responsibility for their own plight.[13] Their situation did improve somewhat, when the Mandatory authority began to favour – besides the Maronites – non-Sunni sects as a counterweight to the troublesome Sunnis, who were agitating against both their separation from Syria and the Maronite hegemony under which they chafed in the embryonic, pre-independence state.[14] But by the time of the National Pact, they still felt themselves to be the 'despised stepchildren' of a Maronite–Sunni condominium.[15] Mostly poor peasants, mainly represented, politically, by the great Shiite landowners who exploited them socially and economically, they remained Lebanon's most backward community, remote, peripheral victims of official neglect and discrimination. But this was a state of affairs for which, before very long and in the most unforeseeable of ways, history would exact its retribution.

Even at the time, some, both French and Maronite, saw great trouble in the making. Robert Caix, secretary-general of the French high commission, warned that, in their 'megalomania', the Maronites were sowing the seeds of their own eventual adversity.[16] To enlarge Christian Lebanon, said a newspaper editor, George Samne, was to attempt 'the squaring of the circle'. And, in truth, the contradiction at its heart became its abiding curse. The Lebanese themselves, left to their own devices, might eventually have overcome it, but citizens of the 'small state' that they were, they were never going to be left to them. The contradiction forever nourished, and was nourished by, the influence and interferences of more powerful states. Chief of these was one whose creation amounted to a vastly more arbitrary example of late-imperial arrogance, geopolitical caprice and perniciously misguided philanthropy than Lebanon's could ever have done – the Jewish state-to-be.

'DON'T WORRY, DOCTOR WISE; PALESTINE IS YOURS'

The Balfour Declaration of 1917, the other key document to have shaped the modern history of the Middle East, grew out of Sykes–Picot, but, in retrospect, its importance outweighs it. Under it, the British government pledged itself to 'view with favour the establishment in Palestine of a national home for the Jewish people, it being clearly understood that nothing shall be done which may prejudice the civil and religious rights' of the country's 'existing non-Jewish' inhabitants.

It seemed on the face of it to have been a wholly British initiative, but in reality the Zionists themselves both inspired the Declaration and framed its text.[17] And in their scheme of things it did not, nor ever could, have anything to do with the high ideals that Wilson had promulgated. In Palestine, the philanthropic principles which the Mandatory system supposedly embodied were to be honoured more flagrantly in the breach than they were anywhere else. Wilson's own King–Crane Commission had been categoric: if the Zionist project went forward, it warned, that would constitute 'a gross violation of the principle of self-determination and the peoples' rights'. But Wilson, a devout bible-reading Presbyterian and self-professed Zionist,[18] chose to ignore the warning. He assured the American Zionist leader, 'don't worry, Dr Wise, Palestine is yours',[19] thereby inaugurating, at the highest level, the Western double standards without which the Zionist enterprise would have very quickly come to naught.

Theirs, in the fullest sense, the Zionists always intended that Palestine should be. It was not merely a 'home' they sought there, but a fully-fledged state. Nor were they planning to respect the Palestinians' 'civil and religious rights', for, in the fullness of time, there would be no Palestinians in Palestine with rights to respect. To be sure, it was always official Zionist policy publicly to deny any such intentions; anyone who said otherwise was 'suffering from gross ignorance, or actuated by malice'.[20] But that was merely the wilful dissimulation which, from the earliest days, had established itself as a basic tenet of Zionist theory and practice. Inevitably, however, enthusiasm sometimes got the better of discretion. Thus Chaim Weizmann, the Russian-born British citizen who became the great statesman of pre-state Zionism, went to Palestine in 1918 to assure the Arabs that it was not 'our objective to seize control of the higher policy of the province of Palestine', or 'to turn anyone out of his property'.[21] But two years later he told a London Jewish audience: 'I trust to God that a Jewish state will come about', and that 'we can finally establish such a society in Palestine that Palestine shall be as Jewish as England is English or America is American'.[22]

What were to be the dimensions of this state? 'As great', said Weizmann, 'as Jewish energy in getting Palestine'.[23] The ultimate rationale for locating it in that already inhabited land – as opposed to other places which Theodor Herzl, the founder of Zionism, had seriously considered – was biblical: this was to be a restoration of the Jews to 'the land of their ancestors'. No one actually knew where the frontiers of ancient Israel had been. But the wider the bounds of the new one were to be set the better.[24] And Jewish scholars down the ages had developed a whole range of possibilities. According to the maximalist view, the Land of Israel should cover the whole of Sinai, Jordan, Lebanon, Syria, and the southern part of Turkey. In practice, however, the mainstream, 'political' Zionists, without renouncing larger, theoretical aims, were to concentrate on securing the most that they considered realistically possible in the political and diplomatic conditions of the time. They would basically confine their ambitions within the boundaries of the British Mandate for Palestine, which, at the time, meant not just Palestine proper, but the whole of Transjordan (now Jordan) too.

Zionism's other basic tenet – not publicized either – was the role that force would play in the creation of this state. It was to be applied, above all, to the solving of what the early pioneers discreetly called 'the Arab problem', the problem that Palestine was not, as Weizmann used to say, 'a country without a people' awaiting a people which 'has no country'.[25] Whatever interpretation Western audiences to which he said this might have put upon his words, he himself could not literally have meant that Palestine really was an uninhabited land. After all, even another such prominent British Zionist as himself, Israel Zangwill, had publicly acknowledged that it was 'already twice as thickly populated as the United States'. No, what Weizmann really meant was that those 'existing non-Jewish' inhabitants of the promised land need not con- stitute a serious impediment to Zionist purposes. 'The British told us', he confided to a colleague, 'that there are some hundred thousands of negroes and for those there is no value';[26] they were like 'the rocks of Judea, obstacles that had to be cleared on a difficult path'.[27] Embold- ened by the Balfour Declaration, leading Zionists became increasingly convinced of the need for the Palestinians' 'forcible removal'.[28] Zangwill, who had once opined that 'we should drive [the Arabs] out by the sword as our forefathers did', now began to campaign quite openly on the subject. In his book, *The Voice of Jerusalem*, he argued that 'an Arab exodus', which he saw as 'race redistribution' or a 'trek like that of the Boers from Cape Colony', was 'literally the only way out of the difficulty of creating a Jewish State in Palestine'. 'After all', he added, 'they [had] all of Arabia with its million square miles' to 'trek' to and 'no particular reason to cling to these few kilometres [of Palestine]. "To fold their tents" and "silently steal away" is their pro- verbial habit: let them exemplify it now.'[29] But of all the Arab countries to which the Palestinians might be transferred, the one which – before the transfer actually came to pass – the Zionists always most favoured was Iraq,[30] not merely because it was fertile, and far away, but because, as Baron Edmond-James de Rothschild, a would-be financier of such schemes, said, more immediate neighbours like Syria (which, in those days, meant mostly what is now Lebanon) or Transjordan were already 'part of the Land of Israel'.[31]

THE PALESTINIANS ARE ARABS TOO

Self-evidently, the Palestinians were to be the most directly – and ultimately disastrously – affected by this Jewish state-in-the-making. They certainly were not privy to the precise nature and full extent of the Zionists' project, or of the methods they had in mind, but they had already seen, heard and experienced enough to sense what was afoot. Their hostility was already an established fact; their opposition was set to grow. But what about the Arabs – and Muslims – at large?

The Zionists recognized that, second only to the Palestinians themselves, the Arabs were always bound to constitute a vital factor in their calculations. They entertained no less disparaging opinions of them than they did of the Palestinians; culturally, socially, temperamentally, they made little distinction between the two. That was implicit in the fact that they always referred to Palestinians as 'Arabs' anyway; so when they said of one or the other that they were, for example, 'backward', 'primitive', 'nomads', or – in the choice terminology of Revisionist leader Vladimir Jabotinsky – a mere 'yelling rabble dressed up in gaudy, savage rags',[32] these descriptions automatically applied with equal force to both. Nevertheless, they did give credence to the reality of Arab nationalism. They did so begrudgingly, however, because of the potentially adverse implications its very existence would have as a rival to their own. And, not surprisingly, their view of it was always an expedient one. When it served their purposes, they would stress the Arabism, or certain useful aspects of it, which their neighbours, Syrians, Jordanians, Iraqis, might have in common. When it did not, they would stress its inherent flaws.

From the outset they faced a basic choice: to seek the Arabs' friendship or, realizing that this was impossible, to resign themselves to their enduring hostility. Given the potentialities inherent in the Arabs' large population, vast territories, abundance of natural resources, and strategic centrality in the world's affairs, their friendship would clearly be as great an asset as their hostility would be a liability. And in whichever direction the Arabs chose to respond, the more united they were in making that choice, the more decisive its consequences would be for the Zionists.

So, naturally enough, they began by seeking Arab friendship and co-operation. Naturally, too, they sought to secure it through whichever Arab leaders they deemed most representative and influential. No one at the time better fitted that prescription than Amir Faisal. And he it was in whom Weizmann discerned his Arab counterpart. Indeed, he concluded a formal, written agreement with him. It was partly due to heavy pressure from the British, as well as the naïve bewilderment of an Arabian prince untutored in the arts and wiles of European diplomacy, that he signed what he signed. But partly it came from a genuine spirit of openness and goodwill towards the Jews. To be sure, there was a history and tradition of anti-Semitism in the Arab and Muslim worlds, but it never approached the systematic virulence and cruelty that it did in Christian Europe.[33] The Hashemites, descendants of the Prophet, considered it their obligation to respect the Jews, a 'people of the Book', as the Koran enjoined.[34] Faisal and his father were not averse, and neither were many politically minded Arabs of the time, to some kind of Jewish settlement in Palestine.[35] But that, Faisal insisted, was subject to two conditions: that it should not impinge on the general welfare and the political and economic rights of the existing inhabitants – not just Balfour's 'civil and religious' ones – and that Palestine should form part of the independent state originally promised by Britain. He believed that, if those conditions were met, there would be no fundamental incompatibility between Arab and Zionist aspirations in Palestine. And he had had plentiful assurances, albeit more from Britain than the Zionists, that they would be.[36]

However, it soon became clear that they would not, that what the Zionists sought, via friendship with the Arabs, was what no Arabs could give. Not merely were they expected to accept a concept of Jewish nationhood at odds with the terms of the agreement Faisal had lent himself to, they were to persuade the Palestinians to do so too. And, according to the Zionists, it was pan-Arab nationalism itself that dictated such a course. A fundamental reason why they themselves had a national claim to Palestine so incontestably superior to that of the Palestinians was because the Palestinians were simply 'not a nation', as David Ben-Gurion, the leader of the *Yishuv*, the Jewish community in Palestine, later put it.[37] It was in the greater Arab world, not a segment of it called Palestine, where their identity and sense of belonging lay. 'Palestine', wrote Moshe Bellinson, a close associate of Ben-Gurion, 'is not needed by the [Palestinians] from the national point of view. They are bound to other centres. There, in Syria, in Iraq, in the Arabian Peninsula, lies the homeland of the Arab people.'[38] It followed, therefore, that the Palestinians would suffer no great wrong, no great cultural shock upon their enforced 'transfer' to the territories of their Arab brethren, especially as these were so 'many' and so 'spacious' in comparison with the 'few kilometres' of Palestine. Carrying their interpretation of Arab nationalism to its logical conclusion, the Zionist leadership decided that there was really no point in dealing directly with so subsidiary a community as the Palestinians at all. To be sure, they could develop local economic, social and administrative relations with them, but for the higher political, the truly destiny-shaping issues, other Arabs should settle those on the Palestinians' behalf. And if, said Ben-Gurion, they persuaded the 'Arabs of Palestine to come to terms', the Zionists could, in return, offer them all the modern skills, the capital, the political connections which they brought with them from the West. They could help them make their deserts bloom.[39]

For the Arabs this Zionist reading of their own interests and emotions embodied a curious and contrary logic. It required no new-fangled, pan-Arab nationalist credo for them to identify with the Palestinians against the Zionists, rather than the precise opposite which the Zionists were asking of them, but it did add a strong, ideological element to the natural sympathy which, as fellow Arabs, they already felt in this regard. In this they were merely reacting as the British would surely have reacted had the Zionists induced some rival imperial power to inflict on them what Britain was planning to inflict on the Arabs; had Czarist Russia, for example, suddenly decided that a portion of their 'scepter'd isle, other Eden, demi-paradise' should, *à la* Weizmann,

become as Jewish as Russia is Russian. And not just some remote
extremity of it, but its very heartland, containing a city as historically
important to them as Jerusalem is to Arabs and Muslims. The Arabs
were as quickly, instinctively and almost universally hostile to Zionism
as were the Palestinians. Even if the Zionists themselves had not
violated the terms of the historic Weizmann–Faisal agreement, Faisal
would have soon enough repudiated it in the face of his people's
overwhelming disapproval.

The Zionists nonetheless persisted, through much of their pre-state
years, in periodic efforts to find a representative Arab interlocutor with
whom to deal, but – with the dubious exception of Faisal's brother,
King Abdullah of Transjordan – they never succeeded. And the more
the Zionists realized that Arabism was to become a permanently hostile
force, and that preserving Palestine as an integral part of the Arab
homeland from the fate they had in store for it was to become its
central, indeed sacred cause, the more they began to turn against it.
They feared and reviled it. It was the enemy, the anti-Christ; it schooled
its followers in anti-Zionist, anti-Semitic fanaticism. What in others'
nationalisms might have been quite normal and legitimate, became, in
the Arabs', something illegitimate, suspect, malignant. Thus the Arab
quest for unity, be it in the ultimate form of common statehood, or
lesser expressions of collective will, was anathema to the Zionists,
because unity meant strength, and strength, when added to hostility,
meant danger, possibly existential danger, to themselves. So they soon
developed another theory about the natural order in the region, that of
the Middle East as a 'mosaic'. This laid down that the Arabs were by no
means the only, or even the dominant, ethnic group in the region.
There were Turks, Iranians, Kurds as well. Furthermore, the Arabs
themselves were far from being the single, cohesive, organic whole
which only Sykes–Picot, in its arbitrary malevolence, had divided up.
The imperialist carve-up might indeed have been wanton, destructive
and deeply unnatural; but there were other, more 'naturally' divisive
forces at work in Arab society, regional, dynastic, sectarian, tribal, on
which it had been superimposed.

Whatever the objective merits of this theory – and it can hardly be
denied that the Arab 'nation' did add up to a fractious lot – it was

nonetheless expediency that caused the Zionists to promote it, and they failed, not surprisingly, to draw one very obvious and fundamental conclusion from it. This was that, in their very promotion of it, they were effectively ceding to the Palestinians that legitimate claim to Palestine which, with their other, 'Palestinians-are-Arabs-only' theory, they sought to take away. For if – like Syrians, Iraqis or Lebanese – the Palestinians, too, were one of this 'plurality' of distinct communities, as they surely had to be, then they must also have had at least something akin to a national feeling to match. And that in fact was the case. Undoubtedly, nothing has subsequently contributed more to the growth and intensification of Palestinian nationalism than Zionism itself, and the long, bitter and often lonely struggle the Palestinians have waged against it. But, in fact, as dissident Israeli as well as Palestinian scholarship has amply demonstrated, it had always been there – a local nationalism, yes, but entirely compatible with the larger, pan-Arab nationalism which, faced with the Zionist threat, it sought to enlist on its behalf.[40]

Heedless of this contradiction, the Zionists reasoned that the more 'pluralist' the Middle East was seen to be, the more numerous the states, nationalities, ethnicities or sects of which it was composed, the more easily it could accommodate yet another one, in the shape of their Jewish state-to-be. And from this reasoning it was but a short step to actively seeking to promote the 'pluralist' Middle East. Thus was born the alliance-building, the hegemony-seeking, the interference in the domestic affairs of neighbouring states that became abiding features of Zionist foreign policy – from the discreet, suppliant, experimental overtures of the embryonic, pre-state movement to the relentless violence, the 'chosen' wars, the geopolitical grand designs of the full-grown military superpower. Directly or indirectly, one key objective always remained the same: to weaken and undermine the mainstream, pan-Arabist centres of power and influence with which, because they were so representative, they would originally have preferred to deal, but which, being rebuffed, they now felt bound to combat. The strategy had two main components. One was to seek the collaboration of outlying, non-Arab states, like Turkey, Iran or Ethiopia, in a policy that eventually blossomed into the so-called 'alliance of the periphery' –

against the Arab centre. The other was to encourage and support, within that centre, all those forces that feared or rejected pan-Arabism, and its single most important practical consequence, the quest for pan-Arab unity. In other words, where diversity and division, rifts and rivalries, already existed within the putative whole, the Zionists sought to deepen them, and where they did not they sought to create them. Thus would they keep the Arabs fighting one another instead of uniting against themselves. Their principal tool was what foreign-policy experts call the 'minority alliance': that is to say, the support and encouragement, generally clandestine, not of a state – as in the case of 'the alliance of the periphery' – but of individuals, factions or whole communities, usually ethnic or religious, within a state.[41] And their favourite candidate for this, the one which they repeatedly, but erroneously hoped would yield the greatest results, was the 'small state' of Lebanon, and the Maronite Christians who dominated it.

CHAPTER TWO

Zionists and Maronites

An inadmissible affair: 1923–1948

EARLY DESIGNS ON LEBANON

The Zionists were none too happy about the new-born state of Greater Lebanon, not, at least, about its dimensions. They regarded those as one of two major encroachments on their own future domain. In its original form the British mandate had been intended to incorporate the east as well as the west bank of the River Jordan. But in 1923 the British government decided that Transjordan should lead a separate existence as a British-controlled emirate under the aegis of Amir Abdullah, who had already established a *de facto* authority there; and, as such, it would fall beyond the compass of the Balfour Declaration. So, at a stroke, the Zionists lost some three-quarters of the territory on which their 'national home' would theoretically have arisen. Much of it was a barren waste. But that could not be said of the smaller piece of real estate, in the nebulous, contested border lands of Palestine, Lebanon and Syria, on which they had also set their sights. At the Versailles peace conference they had staked a formal claim for the inclusion within mandatory Palestine of (in addition to Syria's Golan Heights) a swathe of southern Lebanon running from the southern Beqa'a Valley in the interior to a point north of Tyre and Sidon on the Mediterranean coast. This amounted to nearly a third of the country. Their interests in it were three-fold.

The first was historical. In ancient times this area had supposedly been home to the Jewish tribes of Asher and Naftali. On the strength of that, a Zionist leader, Menahem Ussishkin, was able to claim that Lebanon, not Palestine, was where the very first colony of the renascent Land of Israel arose.[1] It was located in Sidon; and its members came from the city's indigenous Jewish community. Originally the protégé of the 'Lovers of Zion', a nationalist movement of Russian Jews, the colony preceded Herzl's 'political' Zionism proper, but was subsequently adopted by it. The 'Lovers of Zion' had maintained an office in Beirut for buying land to be settled by Russian Jews. In 1908 they became very excited about another potential acquisition, a very large, Christian-owned farm for sale between Sidon and the inland town of Nabatiyah. They wanted it to be the first in a chain of settlements reaching down into Palestine proper. In the end, nothing came of this, nor of Weizmann's plans to buy several small industries in the Sidon area, including an olive oil factory through which, he believed, the Zionists could eventually control the entire oil industry of the country. But clearly, despite this disappointment, great potentialities still beckoned.

Their second interest was strategic and military: a border situated so much further to the north, and the kind of terrain through which it would have run, would have much enhanced the defences of the future state. And their third was economic: control of, and assured access to, the Litani river, Lebanon's most abundant, as well as the Lebanese– Syrian headwaters and tributaries of the Jordan, were deemed indispensable for the irrigation of Palestine's fertile northern plains.[2] But, along with Transjordan, the Zionists had to forego this prize too. Despite the intense and partisan passions it aroused, the demarcation of the border, destined to become one of the world's most dangerous flashpoints, ended up as an arbitrary, pointless and obstructionist line on the map. In truth, it represented little more than just another cold-blooded geographic trade-off between Britain and France in the distribution of their post-war Middle East spoils. The French insisted – and the British did not strenuously demur – that the Litani and territories to its south should go to Lebanon. The basic imperial impulse aside, they did so because many of them found the very idea of a 'Zionist state' in Palestine distasteful, even smacking of an Anglo-Jewish-Bolshevik conspiracy against themselves and the Catholic church,[3] and because they wanted to gratify the expansionist ambitions of the Maronites.

THE FIRST CONTACTS

The anti-Zionist, not to say anti-Semitic, motives that inspired the French were definitely not shared by their Lebanese protégés. Between Maronites and Zionists it could not be called love at first sight, because they knew each other already. It was, rather, the flowering of a mutual attraction that had lain dormant since that last great Maronite tragedy, the massacres of 1860. Moved to pity by those, Sir Moses Montefiori, a wealthy British Jew, and Adolphe Cremieux, a distinguished French one, had been among the first Europeans to respond to desperate Maronite appeals for help, one by ensuring prominent coverage of their plight in the London *Times* and setting up a fund for the survivors, and the other by urging the French government to send troops to save them from further slaughter. They had been acting as philanthropists only, not as Jews, still less as 'Zionists'.[4] But their charitable action firmly lodged itself in the collective Maronite memory. It contributed not a little to the welcome which early Zionists received when, in the years before the Balfour Declaration, they first made contact with Maronite leaders. Indeed, to their surprise, these seemed, if anything, at least as keen on cultivating a friendship as they were themselves. It was an emotionally gratifying discovery that generated a host of extravagant clichés about Lebanon as 'an island in the vast Muslim sea', or 'window in the wall of Arab enmity'. One of them wrote at the time:

> Not only did they want the Jews to come to Palestine and Syria, but they hoped that the influx of settlers would be large and quick, because it matched their own political and economic interests as Christian Arabs. The Arab Christians were a minority and so were the Jews. If both these minorities increased in numbers they could form a bloc that would counterbalance the overwhelming numerical superiority of the Muslims, which the Christians feared. The intellectual superiority of the Jews and Christians could balance the Muslims' numerical supremacy ... The Christians ... realized that [Jewish] capital, modern industrial plants and up-to-

date production methods would create a climate of prosperity, not only for those who introduced them to the Middle East, but also for the indigenous population.[5]

Foreshadowed here were some of the core beliefs and sentiments which, in years to come, would justify and inspire the 'minority alliance' which the Zionists and then, on a far more ambitious scale, the Zionists-turned-Israelis sought to establish with their Maronite neighbours. There was, they argued, a 'natural harmony of interests' between them, a common destiny shaped by history, geography, by obvious similarities both of circumstance and outlook on the world.[6] Both were small peoples or 'nations' seeking either to safeguard – or to construct from scratch – their separate status and identity in a vast and populous region which, impelled by theology, temperament and historical memory, would always seek to deny it to them. Both sought their *raison d'être* in a real or imagined past; the 'Phoenicianism' of the Maronites, sometimes called 'Lebanese Zionism', was matched by the 'Hebrew' revivalism of the Zionists, whose poets and theoreticians would invoke the relations between King Solomon and the Phoenician King Hiram as ancient justification for a renewed, contemporary friendship between the two peoples. The Zionists were pleased to discern in the Maronites something of the 'European' qualities they considered themselves to possess: modern, sophisticated, superior to other Arabs, and Muslims, in general. They were, Weizmann assured a Maronite archbishop, 'the two progressive peoples of the Middle East'.[7] It was only to be expected that, with their innate, historical disposition to seek a distant European protector, the Maronites should turn, in the same spirit, to this potential new one, so suddenly, so providentially arising on their doorstep. If ever there were a natural partnership against a common adversary it would surely be theirs.

'Not the western edge of the Arabic Muslim world but the eastern edge of Western Christendom' – maybe, in their hearts, most Maronites really did feel like that about themselves.[8] But even if they did, that did not necessarily mean that they, or more importantly their leaders, all automatically followed their hearts where the Zionists were concerned. In fact, from the outset, Maronite leaders fell, by and large, into two opposing camps. There were those, whom we shall call the 'pro-Zionists', led by the clergy and the political ideologues, who, immediately and enthusiastically, empathized with them. They saw them as a potential bulwark against Arabs and Muslims, and ally in the preservation of their own ascendancy within multi-confessional Greater Lebanon or, should it ever fall apart, in the resurrection of that older, smaller, predominantly Christian Lebanon to which they would then revert. Opposing them were those, whom we shall call the 'Arabists', who contended that the Maronites' status and security lay, not in befriending the newcomers, but in jealously guarding the *modus vivendi* they had achieved with the Lebanese Muslims, and, beyond them, with the Arabs and Muslims at large. This would, after all, be no more than a logical continuation, in the field of contemporary politics and diplomacy, of the intellectual and cultural role the Christians had earlier played in the Arab Awakening and the pan-Arab nationalist movement to which it gave rise. Intra-community conflict between the two camps was endemic.[9] The 'Arabists' might have the upper hand one moment, the 'pro-Zionists' the next; it largely depended on external circumstances, and not least, of course, on the conduct of the Zionists themselves.

To begin with, the Zionists had no clearly defined or systematic strategy with regard to the Maronites, or any other Middle Eastern minority. There were only tendencies, exploratory probings and personal relationships.[10] Already discernible in these, however, were two basic schools of thought that reflected, and interacted with, the Maronites' own. Both, of course, valued whatever degree of Arab recognition, goodwill or cooperation they might succeed in eliciting, but neither could ever really be sure whether, in the final analysis, cultivating the 'minority alliance' with the Maronites was to help or hinder them in that task. The hope of one school, the 'interventionists', was, of course, that it helped. They believed in actively encouraging and supporting the 'pro-Zionists' wherever and whenever the opportunity arose. Naturally, it would have been better to win over the Arab and Muslim mainstream. But 'beggars couldn't be choosers', and the probability of achieving agreement with a minority, however small and unrepresentative, should not be sacrificed for the improbability of ever achieving one with the majority. Besides, it might actually pay off in the end, and encourage other, less likely quarters to follow in the Maronites' footsteps. The fear of the non-interventionist school, by contrast, was that too active a courtship of the 'pro-Zionists', and too ardent a response from them, would merely alarm the 'Arabists', and then turn *all* the Muslims against *all* the Maronites. In the 'small state' of Lebanon, any position anyone took automatically generated its own antithesis, between the rival sects internally, and between the rival states, to which the sects were invariably linked, regionally and internationally. Carried too far, such a cycle of action and reaction would threaten the very foundations of the state itself, and the crucial, but always fragile, National Pact which secured the Maronites' preeminence in it. Not surprisingly, then, however exalted the interventionists' 'pro-Zionist' friends might be – a patriarch, a president, or both – however ardent their convictions, they could never carry the whole Maronite community with them, let alone the country at large. In their dealings with the Zionists, and later the Israelis, they would forever swear in private what they dared not support in public; they would promise, but rarely deliver. Although this happened again and again, the interventionists never gave up. Decades on, they would finally triumph – but only to have their triumph quickly turn to disaster.

In these early days, it didn't much matter what this or that Maronite might propose to this or that Zionist, or vice versa. It didn't much matter, for example, that, in 1920, even before Greater Lebanon had officially come into being, a land-purchaser called Yehoshua Hankin, professing to represent the Zionist Organization in Palestine, rushed to sign a treaty with an extreme, freebooting 'pro-Zionist' called Najib Sfeir, and two colleagues, professing to represent something called the Nationalist Group in Syria and Lebanon. Under this pact, the Maronites recognized the Jews' right to a 'national home' in the Land of Israel, and unlimited immigration into it, while the Zionists recognized the Christians' right to an independent Lebanon separate from Muslim Syria and pledged assistance in developing it.[11]

It might have been profoundly significant as a harbinger of things to come, embodying as it did the basic principles of the 'minority alliance' idea; and it did at least prove that 'the Zionists had something to talk about with the Lebanese and someone with whom to talk'.[12] But nothing much was going to come of it at the time. For, at this embryonic stage, the Zionist movement simply lacked the intrinsic weight and resources for serious political and diplomatic – let alone military – intervention anywhere in the region. Moreover, its principal leaders, both in Palestine and London, were heavily engaged in their central task, the 'up-building' of the 'national home' in Palestine itself, and the higher strategies and calculations which that required. Maronite friendship and its potentialities, however pleasant and gratifying, still occupied a small place in those. And finally it didn't much matter because of the whole Arab temper of the times.

ARABS FEAR THE LOSS OF PALESTINE TO THE ZIONISTS, BUT STILL DO BUSINESS WITH ITS JEWS

To be sure, what the Zionists were doing to the land and people of Palestine was disturbing to Arabs everywhere, but it had yet to acquire that centrality in their affairs, that extraordinary ability to stir region-wide passions, contention and upheaval, which it later would. Neither did the Palestinians, still less the Arabs in general, know much about the precise strategies, the modes of operation, which Zionist leaders and theoreticians were already developing and discussing among themselves. They probably did not know, for example, about the 'Iron Wall'. This was the brainchild of Vladimir Jabotinsky, the founder of the right-wing Revisionist school of Zionism, ancestor of the present-day Likud, who, as early as 1923, had written:

> Every indigenous people will resist alien settlers as long as they
> see any hope of ridding themselves of the danger of foreign
> settlement. This is how the [Palestinians] will behave and go
> on behaving so long as they possess a gleam of hope that they
> can prevent 'Palestine' from becoming the Land of Israel ... A
> voluntary agreement with them is unattainable ... And so ...
> we must either suspend our settlement efforts or continue them
> without paying attention to the mood of the natives. Settlement
> can thus develop under the protection of a force that is not

dependent on the local population behind an iron wall which they will be powerless to break down.[13]

Ben-Gurion and the left-wing Labour Zionists, who led the *Yishuv*, officially disdained the Revisionists as extremists, visionaries or even – given their early admiration for, and associations with, Benito Mussolini[14] – as fascists. But in practice, beneath an outward veneer of moderation, the methods they were to adopt were nothing if not Jabotinskian. In effect, Jabotinsky's Iron Wall became Ben-Gurion's too.

What the Palestinians – and doubtless a good many Arabs – certainly did know, or at least strongly sensed, was that worse was sure to come, and that with the Jewish immigrants 'coming up', the land being 'redeemed' and labour 'conquered', with an alien, ethnocentric and self-segregating society arising in their midst, dispossession was likely to be their ultimate fate. They could not but sense, too, that, if this went on, force – or counter-force as they considered it – would be their only means of preventing it. For legitimate constitutional means were being systematically denied them. True, there was to have been democracy, and its offspring, self-determination, in Palestine; had not the great powers decreed it? Unfortunately for the Palestinians, however, these blessings of civilization were to be for the newcomers only, the aliens from overseas, not for them, the original inhabitants of the land. 'The democratic principle', said Weizmann, 'which reckons with the relative numerical strength and brutal numbers, operates against us, for there are five Arabs [actually there were about ten] to one Jew',[15] and the 'treacherous Arabs' could not be allowed to manipulate this circumstance in their own favour. The Zionists would brook no representative government until, their majority assured through immigration, they could outvote the natives they were preparing to displace. And thus it came to pass; the British Mandatory authorities, resisting all Palestinian appeals and petitions, duly obliged them in that. So, at one remove, did the United States. For, in Washington's corridors of power, a Jewish lobby was already giving an impressive adumbration of the mighty machine it would eventually become. By 1922, under its persuasions, Congress had already made up its mind. For it, supporting the Zionists, 'one of those oppressed smaller nationalities which must have an opportunity to assert themselves', was 'in line with the principles of self-determination'; supporting the Palestinians, who – 'backward, poor and ignorant' – had reduced the biblical 'land of milk and honey' to 'a ravaged and spoiled land', was not.[16]

But, sense it though Palestinians and Arabs did, that worse-to-come still lay in the inscrutable future. And – who knows? – given what, in Arab eyes, would have been the sheer, the scarcely credible, enormity of it, perhaps it might never have been suffered to come at all. So it was that the general temper, between Arabs and Jews, was still, relatively speaking, casual and relaxed. Indeed, it is hard nowadays to imagine the ease and freedom with which Palestinian Jews could travel around the Arab world. Only the desert kingdom of Saudi Arabia, primitive, impoverished, and steeped in Wahhabite xenophobia, looked askance at Jews and Christians alike. Elsewhere, Jews might get lectures on their politics, but they would be hospitably received in their persons. Their officials and journalists routinely met with Arab leaders of every political persuasion. Their students patronized Arab universities.[17] Their businessmen and tourists filled Arab hotels. They exported their manufactures through much of the region.

AND LEBANON EVEN WELCOMES THEM

What was true of the Arab world was particularly true of Lebanon and its capital, Beirut, one of the great Levantine cities, gregarious, polyglot, dedicated to commerce and the good life. There, on the political level, Zionist officials lived and worked quite openly, enjoyed regular access to religious and political leaders and influential members of society. On the non-political level, Palestinian Jews were active in many fields.

The perverse and capricious border demarcation had done little to deter Jewish or Zionist interest or activity in the country. Inhabitants on both sides of it sought to go about their affairs as if the border did not exist, buying and selling, pursuing business and social relations, across it. Residents of some of the remoter Galilee settlements would as soon go to Beirut, for medical or other services, as to Tel Aviv.[18] Most of the Lebanese border villages were Shiite, but the settlers enjoyed as uniformly good relations with them as with the few Maronite ones. They received and reciprocated invitations to weddings, feasts and other gatherings. Students went on trips to Beaufort Castle, played football against Lebanese schools, and made family outings to Tyre, Sidon and Beirut. The Lebanese went down to Haifa and Tel Aviv.

Inevitably – with its scenic beauty and summer mountain cool, its sea, rivers and greenery, conviviality and superb cuisine – Lebanon had long since established itself as the tourist Mecca of the driest, hottest region on earth. And the rapidly swelling ranks of immigrant Palestinian Jewry were quick to join Arab vacationers in its coastal towns and hill resorts. They became a veritable bulwark of the Lebanese economy. Local hoteliers went to great lengths to allure them. They hired kosher cooks and subscribed to Hebrew newspapers. The government even produced a tourist manual in Hebrew, whose preface proclaimed that 'Anyone who wants to lengthen his days, taste paradise and feel the world to come should spend some time in Lebanon beneath the shade of its splendid cedars, breathing its healthy air, drinking its good waters, and pampering himself with its glorious visions of nature."[19]

For the Jewish visitors, at least the active Zionists among them – and who could tell who was or wasn't one of those? – tourism was not just tourism. It exemplified the function that Lebanon was earmarked to play in their wider, political and strategic scheme of things: that of listening post and propaganda platform for the whole Arab world. The array of Arab ministers, journalists and businessmen he came across at the resorts so impressed one such visitor that he proposed to the Zionist executive that it 'plant' staff members with every one of them in order to cultivate and befriend these influential Arabs – relationships which, he contended, would eventually help achieve an amicable settlement in Palestine. It was of a piece with another Zionist activity to which Lebanon particularly lent itself. As the region's most open society, it also had its most flourishing – and venal – newspaper industry. Zionist representatives tried to win more favourable, or at least less hostile, coverage for their cause. At least one newspaper, *la Syrie*, was permanently on their payroll. They paid for the publication of pro-Zionist articles in others.[20]

Lebanese property-owners were no less interested in Zionist money, especially given the high prices, often in European currencies, they were ready to pay. Weizmann marvelled at the way the Zionist Organization was being 'inundated with the most attractive offers from landowners in Syria and Lebanon'.[21] Lebanese entrepreneurs sought Jewish capital, or participation in joint ventures. Occasionally the Jews set up an enterprise on their own, such as a match factory in the coastal town of Damur.[22] Jewish business delegations would be warmly received in Beirut; the Lebanese sponsored a pavilion at the trade fair in Tel Aviv. By the mid-thirties imports and exports between Palestine and Lebanon (and Syria) far exceeded those between Palestine and any other Arab country. There were cultural, scholarly and literary exchanges too.

Maronites, by virtue of their politics and their sometimes greater means, were foremost in these affairs. But they were certainly not alone. Many Arabs were unwilling to sell land or property directly to the Jews, so a group of Sunni Muslim merchants in Beirut offered to buy it themselves, and then sell it on, making a handsome profit in the process.[23] Some Sunnis even engaged the Zionists politically, without the genuine enthusiasm of the Maronites no doubt, but in quite far-reaching ways nonetheless. Riad Sulh, scion of one of Muslim Beirut's great political families and a future prime minister, presented himself as an influential figure within the Arab nationalist movement. That made it all the more remarkable that he should have proposed the bargain that he did. If, he said, the Zionists would throw their financial and political weight behind the pan-Arab cause in French-ruled 'Greater Syria', he could conjure up an 'Arab Balfour Declaration' and get the Palestinians to honour it.[24]

But within two decades of the original Declaration, accommodating attitudes like that, always exceptional, were to become heroic and heretical indeed. The Arab temper was changing. For the long-feared worse-to-come was by now manifestly at hand.

THE GREAT REBELLION

One night in November 1935, a sexagenarian Muslim cleric, Sheikh Izzeddin Qassam, and a small band of followers, having pledged to give their lives for Palestine, took to the wooded hills of Jenin with the intention of waging guerilla war on the British and the Jews. Detected and hunted down before they had even begun their campaign, he and three or four companions died in their first encounter. With this self-immolation, however militarily futile in itself, they ushered in a three-year insurgency. The Great Rebellion, as it was called, was the largest of the kind which the British Empire had to face in the twentieth century. It was a truly popular movement. The peasantry constituted the vast majority of Palestinian society. They had been the first and most grievously affected by loss of land and livelihood to the settlers from overseas, and it was they who responded to the insurrectional flame that Sheikh Qassam, ever after the original, iconic martyr of the Palestinian cause, had lit. Exacerbating their despair was what the Zionist media hailed as 'a great Jewish victory' – the sabotaging, achieved via Jewish influence on the 'mother of parliaments' at Westminster, of yet another Palestinian bid for at least a partially representative legislature.[25]

For the Zionists Qassam was a kind of freak, the product of unnatural fanaticism, and the movement he inspired banditry and murder, a reversion to what Weizmann called the 'barbarism of the desert'. The *Manchester Guardian*, whose editor, C. P. Scott, was a friend of Weizmann and devout and influential supporter of his cause, greatly admired the *havlaga* – or 'self-restraint' – which the Zionists exhibited in the face of continual terrorism 'organized from outside'.[26] 'Self-restraint' and its inseparable companion, *tahar haneshek*, or 'purity of arms', were concepts rooted in Jewish ethics by which the Zionist 'self-defence' organizations had always professed to set great store. In the United States Secretary of the Interior Harold Ickes told the Zionists that 'the enemy against whom you are forced to contend are ... the enemies of all human progress'.[27] Americans, wrote a historian of the period, were in general so ignorant of the realities on the ground that 'when the Palestinians rose up in resistance they were able to see the Zionists' increasingly aggressive, colonialist behaviour as a defence of democracy and other progressive Western ideals', while this 'Palestinian resistance to imperialist invasion became a form of unwarranted offense against civilization'.[28] The British put down the

Rebellion, often with such cruel and brutal methods that, as one of their doctors confided to his diary, they could 'probably [have] taught Hitler something he didn't know about running concentration camps'.[29] And the Zionists joined in: the Arabs may have begun the violence, but they imitated and, with their much improved techniques, far outdid them. All of them – not just the 'terrorist' undergrounds, the Irgun and the Stern Gang of future prime ministers Menachem Begin and Yitzhak Shamir, but the official, mainstream Hagana – abandoned 'self-restraint', if they had ever really practised it. A policy of indiscriminate 'reprisals' took its place. These, wrote the official historian of the Irgun, 'did not aim at those who had perpetrated acts of violence against the Jews, and had no geographic connection with the places where they had done so. The principal consideration in the choice of target was first accessibility, and then the [maximum] number of Arabs that could be hit.'[30] At the climax of their anti-Arab rampage, with bombs in market-places or mosques, grenades hurled into buses or the machine-gunning of trains, they killed more Palestinians, 140, in the space of three weeks than the Palestinians had killed Jews in the year and a half since the Rebellion began – an achievement over which the Irgun's *National Bulletin* openly exulted.[31]

Palestinian violence was 'terror', an evil which, in and of itself, nullified the legitimacy of any cause it might have claimed to promote. Zionist violence, though no less terroristic in nature, was 'self-defence' against it. That, at its baldest, became the moral antithesis by which the Zionists would ever after seek to define the conflict. The Great Rebellion was the first really sustained and systematic instance of it, and – what with the rise of Hitler and the racist legislation, violence and spoliation he was already unleashing on German Jewry – of the emotionally understandable, but undiscriminating, sympathy it commanded in Britain, America, and Western democracies in general. It was not, of course, a view shared by the Arabs.

It was with the Rebellion, in fact, that the struggle for Palestine first became truly 'Arabized', and has remained so ever since. Which is not to say – *pace* the *Manchester Guardian* – that it was 'organized from outside', that argument being then, even more than it is today, a characteristic way of disparaging the authenticity of Palestinian resistance. But many Arabs did swell the ranks of the Palestinian guerilla bands. They were moved not merely by solidarity with the Palestinians, but, on pan-Arab grounds, by outrage at the kind of solutions the British were now proposing for an intractable problem of their own, utterly foreseeable making: the partition of Palestine into an Arab and a Jewish state, and the consequent, irrevocable loss, to the Arabs, of an inalienable part of their ancestral homeland. There were riots and demonstrations around the Arab world. Popular congresses told Arab rulers that they should treat the Palestinian cause as their own. Not just the Zionists were reviled, but their Western supporters too. Arab governments collectively warned Britain that it 'must choose between our friendship and the Jews'.[32]

LEBANON LEADS THE ARABS IN SUPPORT

It fell to the 'small state' of Lebanon to play a more real and tangible, though not intolerably burdensome, part in the Great Rebellion than any of the larger states of the region, and, as a uniquely sectarian one, to suffer the most disturbing internal consequences too. For it was there that the Palestinians, under crippling attack and siege in their own land, found a sanctuary and a political centre. Forewarned that, along with other Palestinian leaders, he was about to be deported to the Seychelles Islands, Haj Amin Husseini, the Mufti of Jerusalem, escaped by boat to Lebanon.

The French grudgingly granted him asylum. In spite of the promise they extracted from him not to engage in political activities, he continued to do so. In fact, Weizmann bitterly complained, he turned Lebanon into nothing less than the 'the centre of a far-flung net of political conspiracy against [Jewish] Palestine'. From the little coastal village of Zouk, in the heart of Maronite Christendom, to which the French had ostensibly confined him, he continued to direct the Rebellion as he had formerly done from the al-Aqsa compound in Jerusalem. He maintained almost daily contact, via intermediaries, with its military leaders. He enlisted the services of a devoted network of followers from among the exiles, fleeing the British or rival Palestinian factions, who had poured into the country. He conferred with prominent personalities from all over the Arab world. As well as a logistical base for rebels, Beirut became the chief centre of pan-Arab propaganda for the cause – a department in which the rival Zionist effort suffered a veritable rout. His public relations bureau circulated a daily bulletin about Palestine to 10,000 Arab subscribers. Partly out of genuine conviction, partly in return for financial inducements, the Lebanese press mounted a fierce campaign against the British and the Zionists which neither, for all their strenuous representations with France, was able to do anything about.

But it was in the deep south of the country, in the Jebel Amil adjacent to Palestine, that Lebanon most dramatically became the very opposite of what the Zionists, and their 'pro-Zionist' Maronite friends, fondly imagined that it should have been: not the bridge, the physical and symbolic meeting point, between the two like-minded societies of the region, but the place where its adversaries came to blows. The politically dominant Maronites had originally secured the Jebel Amil's attachment to Greater Lebanon, supposedly an accretion of their strength. But they had so neglected what they acquired that it became a source of weakness instead – the small, sectarian state at its most vulnerable to the subversion and penetration of greater ones. Discriminated against because it was largely Shiite, impoverished, retarded, resentful and unruly, it became the perfect vacuum for any outsider to fill. The same lack of government authority that had enabled, and indeed still did, Jews and Arabs to do friendly business across the border now enabled hostile business too. The political immunity the Mufti enjoyed at the centre was matched by the military immunity his men acquired at its extremities. Arab, not just Palestinian, fighters were recruited, based, armed, trained and dispatched on raids from there. Acting on the pan-Arab call for the economic boycott of Jewish Palestine, its goods and markets, they waylaid Lebanese trucks that violated it, destroying their contents and threatening reprisals if the trade continued. Not merely were Lebanese civil and military authorities – and French, for that matter – unable to control the guerillas, the Mufti was able to hire *them* to protect the guerillas, supply them with weapons, and facilitate their passage across the frontier, sometimes even in government vehicles.[33]

The boundary which the British and French empires had interposed between their new Middle Eastern possessions proved so inept and indefensible that, in the later stages of the Rebellion, the British had to construct a barbed-wire entanglement, the 'Tegart Line', which, two metres high and two deep, and strung on stakes set in concrete, ran its entire length from Lake Tiberias to the Mediterranean. An obstacle to the commerce on which both Jews and Arabs so much depended, it angered everyone, peaceable traders and guerillas alike; it came under constant assault, and Lebanese market-places were soon inundated with wiring pilfered from it.[34] Then, lacking manpower, the British authorized the formation of a Jewish auxiliary police force and put it under the command of one of their own officers, Orde Wingate, who, unbeknown to them, had become a fanatical devotee of Zionism. He devised the 'special night squads', units in which he inculcated those principles of offensive daring, surprise, deep penetration and high mobility which Israel later developed to the full. Some of their operations carried them over the border – and thus it was that Jews who used to slip casually across it for social or business reasons now found themselves doing so at dead of night, with guns, on very different missions. In one such operation, the sergeant of a British company whom Wingate had enlisted to take part in it, shouted at them: 'I think you are totally ignorant in your Ramat Yochanan [Hagana training base] since you do not even know the elementary use of bayonets when attacking dirty Arabs: how can you put your left foot in front!'[35] So, at least in part, it was in the remote and rugged hills and valleys of South Lebanon that these special night squads 'gradually became what Wingate secretly intended, the beginnings of a Jewish army'.[36]

As for the Lebanese people at large, it was naturally among its Muslim half that the Mufti and his cause won the most ardent support. Indeed, even before he arrived, a Zionist representative in the country had complained of a 'Palestinian atmosphere' the like of which was 'not even to be found in Palestine' itself.[37] Palestine was of greater interest to the Lebanese than their own, forthcoming elections, in which it was a highly emotive issue. 'The most abusive accusation', said a Jewish Agency report, 'which the rival parties can find to hurl at one another is to pretend that the other clique is the friend of the Jews. In short, for one and all we are the undesirables and we compromise those who have sympathy for us or who aid our cause.'[38] It was because of such a climate, in addition to their traditional rivalry with, and resentment of, the British, that the French were so reluctant to rein in the Mufti or police the southern frontier; they feared that it might touch off some kind of Lebanese rebellion too.[39] Peculiarly disturbing to British and Zionists was the fact that Christian Lebanese were becoming notably hostile as well. 'They have not the same religious and racial affinities with the Palestinian Arabs as have the Muslims', wrote the British consul in Beirut, 'but they feel quite genuinely that a great wrong is being done to a neighbouring people with whom they have much in common.' With Palestinian refugees 'pouring in daily', lamented a Zionist representative, Lebanese feelings, 'including those of the Christians', now inclined to Arabism.[40]

THE MARONITES DIVIDED BETWEEN ARABS AND ZIONISTS: THEIR 'ARABISTS' PREVAIL

It was not, of course, only Lebanon's Muslims, or those Christians, such as the Greek Orthodox, traditionally closest to them, who were affected by this 'Arabization' of the Palestinian struggle, it was the Maronites too. The self-same Great Rebellion, or rather the British/Zionist response to it, that so alienated the rest, had the very opposite effect on them – or, at least, it did on those of them who had been resolved to throw in their lot with the Zionists from the outset.[41] The cleavage was now to deepen between these, the 'pro-Zionists', and the 'Arabists', who considered that, whatever their inner feelings might be, the Maronites should be all the more careful to respect the pan-Arab, anti-Zionist sentiments of their Muslim compatriots, not to mention those of their Christian, but non-Maronite, ones too.

Similarly, on the Zionist side, as general Arab and Muslim hostility increased, so did the appeal of achieving some kind of 'minority alliance' with at least someone, somewhere. And where more appealing than the very country which the Mufti had turned into a Palestinian stronghold, and whose frontier regions were a staging post for attacks on the Jews?[42] Besides, should not the increasing difficulties of

Lebanon's Christians propel them towards partnership with other, non-Muslim communities like themselves? So reasoned the 'interventionist' school. The non-interventionists, while not averse to such a goal, feared that they might propel them from, not toward, it.

To begin with, on the face of it at least, 'pro-Zionism' had the upper hand. No institution was more susceptible to it than the Maronite Church, and in the person of the current patriarch, Antoine Arida, it had a particularly strong champion. Among the politicians, Emile Eddé, an urbane Francophile more at home in the salons of Paris than the *diwans* of Beirut, had always been a fervent devotee; and he was now the president.

For the likes of these, the Rebellion was less a natural response to what the British and Zionists had been doing to the Palestinians than it was a reminder of the melancholic warning a Lebanese Christian proverb – 'After Saturday, Sunday' – conveys: once the Muslims have done away with the Jews the Christians' turn will come.[43] One of their Zionist confidants reported that, in their eyes, it was 'proof of what rule by a Muslim majority would mean'; and they were 'terribly afraid lest the Arabs win this war'. Apostles of a famously mercantile society, they told him how 'vitally interested they were in the safety and prosperity of the Jews in Palestine'.[44] They were alarmed at the losses their traders were already incurring, and perhaps even more so at a Zionist press campaign calling for a Jewish counter-boycott of Lebanon – and especially of its greatest pride, its lucrative, substantially Maronite, tourist industry.[45] The Mufti's influence on, and penetration of, the Lebanese state and body politic was deeply disturbing to them – and very personally galling to Eddé, in that, whenever his government did try to stop the traffic of men and arms across the frontier, Beirut newspapers would immediately accuse him of connivance with the enemy.[46] And in the background there lurked a variety of kindred fears. They worried that when Lebanon achieved its independence, as other Arab states were doing, France would no longer be there to defend its Maronite protégés, that nationalist Syria would press an irredentist claim to its lost, now Lebanese provinces, or that the Muslim inhabitants who had come with them would, with their much higher birthrate, soon overtake the Christians' already much reduced majority of the total population.

Hardly had Eddé become president than an emissary of Weizmann laid before him a fully-fledged, draft 'treaty of friendship'. The most advanced step yet in the formalization of a Lebanese–Zionist relationship, it recognized the future Jewish state in Palestine – before the British or Zionists were even talking openly about such a thing – and foresaw a political and military alliance between it and an independent Lebanon. In private, at least, Eddé enthusiastically endorsed it. It was only to be aborted by the French high commissioner, who correctly estimated that such open encouragement of Zionist aspirations in Palestine would be anathema to all Muslims, most Christians, and many an 'Arabist' Maronite too.[47] On the very day that, in July 1937, a British commission of inquiry issued its long-awaited report on the situation in Palestine, and, in the course of it, proposed – to the fury of the Arabs – that it be partitioned into a Jewish and an Arab state, Eddé met Weizmann in Paris and declared: 'Now that the Peel Report is an official document, I have the honour of congratulating the first President of the future Jewish state.'[48]

As Weizmann eagerly – though in the end unsuccessfully – promoted a scheme for the resettlement in Lebanon of Jewish refugees from Hitler's Germany, and many Lebanese, mainly Maronite, eagerly acclaimed the business opportunities this would bring, Patriarch Arida called on all Maronite churches to pray for European Jewry – and offered patriarchal property near Beirut for sale to the Zionist Organization. From Beirut's synagogue in Wadi Abu Jamil, the Archbishop of Beirut, Ignace Mubarak, the most intrepid 'pro-Zionist' of them all, announced that Lebanon had plenty of room for all those Jews who had not been 'amicably received by the Arabs of Palestine ... We want to say to you: be welcome, Jews ... I now declare myself the archbishop of the Jews.'[49] It was not so much as Zionists, or even as Jews, that he and others would have welcomed them, but simply as non-Muslims, and 'high-quality', European ones to boot, who would tilt the inter-communal, demographic balance back in favour of shrinking Christian Lebanon.

But what the Aridas, Eddés and Mubaraks represented did not endure; it was, in fact, no more than the high-water mark, for an entire generation, of the Zionists' influence in Lebanon, of any prospect of their securing a 'minority alliance' within the Arab country that had always held out most promise of one. For the rest of the pre-state period – and indeed for a long way into Israeli statehood – they had to contend with the 'Arabists' of the Maronite community who, aided in part by the Middle Eastern consequences of French defeat in the Second World War, were soon to establish, and then consolidate, their ascendancy over the 'pro-Zionists'.[50] The Arabists' decisive break-through came in 1943, with Lebanon's formal independence, the accession to the presidency of Eddé's great rival, Bishara al-Khouri, and the adoption of the National Pact, the inter-communal, power-sharing compromise which, by its very nature, virtually ordained a pan-Arab nationalist, anti-Zionist vocation for the new-born state.

Khouri was no less concerned about his community's status under the Pact than Eddé. In contrast with Eddé, however, Khouri, French-educated but steeped in Arabic culture, looked on France not as the guarantor of this independent, Maronite-dominated Lebanon, but as an obstacle to the Christian–Muslim cooperation which alone could ensure it. So under Khouri Lebanon now formally adopted anti-Zionism. Anti-Zionist Christian and Maronite officials applied it. State-endorsed anti-Zionist sentiment spread unhindered, promoting opposition not merely to the Zionist project in Palestine, but to its possible designs on Lebanon as well. New laws were passed which, with the Zionists as their real and principal target, severely restricted the purchase of land by foreigners. Lebanon became a founding member of the Arab League. In 1946, it co-chaired the first of those Arab summits which, for decades to come, were almost always to place Palestine, the 'permanent emergency' of Palestine, at the top of their agenda. In 1946, appearing before an Anglo-American Committee of Inquiry, all Lebanese witnesses, Christian as well as Muslim, were described as expressing a 'violent opposition to Zionism, a deter-mination to resist it at all costs, and an unwillingness to consider the immigration of one single Jew to Palestine'. Lebanon's official delegate in the US, the Greek Orthodox Charles Malik, effectively established himself as 'the unofficial annunciator in the West of Arab opposition to the creation of the state of Israel'.[51] In sum, wrote Laura Zittrain Eisenberg, a historian of Zionist–Maronite relations, "'Christian

Lebanon", the notion which guided the Jewish Agency's policy towards Lebanon, was acting very much like an "Arab" country.'[52]

Not that the 'pro-Zionists' didn't fight back. So frightened were they at the prospect of Lebanon's absorption into an enlarged Arab state, despite Arab assurances to the contrary, that they sought to undermine its first, independent, and democratically elected administration. Eddé repeatedly tried to persuade the Jewish Agency that with its financial support he could reclaim the presidency in the next elections and that this time he would finally be able to sign an open treaty of friendship with it. Some in the Agency seemed to have had as unrealistic a view of his capabilities as he did himself. Its leading Lebanon expert, long-time resident of the country and regular emissary to the 'pro-Zionists', went so far as to assert that 'the bulk of Lebanese opinion regards with misgivings and anxiety the beginnings of an Arab imperialism that threatens Lebanon's territorial integrity' – a very considerable exaggeration even had he been referring to the country's Christians only.[53] Some urged Lebanon to cast off 'the artificial mask of pan-Arabism which had been bound on to it from without'.[54]

Others in the Agency did note, however, that the more ground the 'pro-Zionists' lost the more extravagant, even hysterical, their ideas were apt to become. One of these was that the Maronites should now retreat from Greater Lebanon, handing back to Syria at least some of those predominantly Muslim territories which they had formerly wrested from it.[55] And Eddé – who, to be fair, had never believed in Greater Lebanon in the first place – had an even more novel and explosive fancy than that. It was not to Syria, he suggested, that a Christian Lebanon reduced to something like its former dimensions should relinquish some portions of the no longer wanted territory, but to the Jewish state-in-the-making. It could have Tyre and Sidon and the 100,000 Muslims living there. But when he put the matter to Weizmann, even he balked at what he called 'a gift which bites'.[56]

It was, however, to be the Maronite Church, in the person of Patriarch Arida, which carried this Maronite–Zionist bonding in the pre-state period to its apogee. In 1946 he went to Jerusalem, where, on behalf of the Church and the Maronite community, he signed an agreement with Weizmann on behalf of the Jewish community.[57] The agreement embodied reciprocal recognitions: of a sovereign Jewish statehood in Palestine and of the independent, Christian character of Lebanon. The Church pledged – with extraordinary presumption – that, once it had achieved political control of the country, it would make the treaty an integral part of Lebanese state policy; it would also, among other things, facilitate the immigration of Jews to Palestine via Lebanon.[58]

It may have been a 'splendid' treaty, as one of its Zionist drafters called it, but its very splendour, from his point of view, made it literally horrendous from an Arab one. So horrendous, in fact, that its Maronite sponsors, above all the Patriarch himself, knew very well that, barring a fundamental change of circumstances, it could never be implemented, or even see the light of day. They knew what obloquy their initiative, if exposed, would bring down upon them. So they did not even admit that it existed and utterly denied it if anyone suggested that it did. Indeed, that it be kept 'strictly confidential' was a condition of the agreement itself.[59] For Zionists, then, this treaty – however gratifying in itself, or as an earnest of possible future intent – was in practice all but useless. For their central objective in Lebanon – to impress on the world that they did have important friends and influence in the region – hinged precisely on such a public demonstration of what the Maronites privately felt.[60] The very desperation that had propelled Arida towards such an extreme position caused him to withdraw from it.

Yet the Zionists, especially the 'interventionists' among them, were not to be deterred. Their leaders were predisposed to discern a 'natural harmony of interests' between the two communities, and to believe that it was only Arab pressure and propaganda that disturbed it. For such a leadership all those years of personal, social and political dalliance, those early alliance proposals, then the draft treaties, and finally the formal accord, did create at least a sense of progress; and they did so especially, of course, when set against the almost total, dispiriting rejection they ran into everywhere else. Furthermore, they had learned to accept that public denials and private assurances were 'standard operating procedure for [their] skittish Maronite friends'.[61] When circumstances changed, so would the Maronites, their 'pro-Zionists' coming to the fore again. Eventually, in fact, they did.

But, more than mere changing circumstances, great upheavals were required to convulse the region *before* they did. The Arab Rebellion had put great strain on the small, sectarian state of Lebanon; in the end, however, it had if anything served to unite rather than divide it. But now, a decade on, there was worse, very much worse, to come. And the first of those upheavals was to be *al-Nakba*, 'the Catastrophe', itself.

CHAPTER THREE

The Reckoning Delayed

Lebanon escapes the consequences of the catastrophe: 1948–1967

THE ETHNIC CLEANSING OF THE PALESTINIANS

The Catastrophe is what, quite simply, the Palestinians have ever afterwards called their dispossession and dispersal before and during the first Arab–Israeli war of 1948. Hailing the new-born Jewish state which arose in their place, Weizmann called it a 'miraculous clearing of the land; a miraculous simplification of Israel's task'.[1] In fact, it could hardly have been more premeditated, being nothing less, for Ilan Pappe, than 'the final act in a plot written in 1880'.[2] And in his latest book, *The Ethnic Cleansing of Palestine*,[3] this most unflinching of Israel's 'new historians' strips away the last, tattered remnants of all the myths which Israelis have sedulously cultivated about their 'War of Independence', from the earliest and most implausible of them – that the Palestinians fled the country on the orders of their leaders – to the latest and least implausible – which was actually endorsed by the first of the 'new historians' himself[4] – that their flight was the unplanned consequence of war. In fact, Pappe says, it was the other way round; the original objective was the removal of the Palestinians, and 'the war was the *consequence*, the *means*, to carry it out'.[5]

It was during the Great Rebellion that Zionist officials had begun work on converting the theoretical schemes of their predecessors into concrete plans of action. 'The only way', said the most important of these, Joseph Weitz, in charge of colonization and settlement, 'is to cut and eradicate [the Arabs] from the roots; not a single village or a single tribe must be left.'[6] Under Weitz's auspices, and with 'ant-like' thoroughness, staff of the Jewish Agency went about their meticulous preparations for the ethnic cleansing of urban and rural Palestine.[7] They secretly compiled data on just about everything – and more – that anyone could possibly want to know about every town and village in the country. In addition to maps, photographs, names and ages of everyone between sixteen and fifty, sociopolitical composition, best means of attack, they drew up an 'index of hostility' towards Zionism, and, in this connection, lists of 'suspects' or 'wanted' persons. Masquerading in front of the villagers as mere casual visitors, they had accomplished much of this research by exploiting the traditional codes of Arab hospitality.

With Weitz's mission all but complete, his chief, David Ben-Gurion, the leader of the *Yishuv*, was able to say that all he needed was 'the opportune moment for making it happen, such as a war'.[8] That came in the shape of the Second World War and the all-surpassing atrocity, the Nazis' attempt to exterminate an entire people, that accompanied it. Some six million Jews died in local, Nazi or Nazi-instigated massacres, or in the concentration camps and gas chambers to which they were transported from every European country – from the Arctic to the Mediterranean, the Atlantic to the Volga – that had fallen under Nazi conquest or control. Ben-Gurion could not possibly have imagined the price his people were to pay for this opportunity, this emergence of a combination of local and international conditions, political, diplomatic and military, that now strongly favoured his cause. For one thing, in response to the Hitlerian genocide, climax of centuries of Christian anti-Semitism, Europe was now 'prepared to compensate the Jewish people for the Holocaust ... with a state in Palestine'.[9] For another, the Zionists were imbued with a whole new, overwhelming sense of the righteousness of their enterprise and determination that it would triumph. Holocaust survivors enlisted in the Jewish militias which were soon to ensure that it did.

The only real obstacle now left in their path was the imperial Britain to which they owed so much. The British Labour Party had always been pro-Zionist, even to the point of formally supporting 'transfer' for the Palestinians.[10] But, with the responsibilities of office, the post-war

Labour government, notably its foreign minister, Ernest Bevin, made an Archimedean discovery: the Balfour Declaration and Zionist interpretations of it were, and always had been, utterly incompatible with the Palestinian-dominated realities on the ground. On the strength of that discovery, Bevin was struggling to achieve as impartial, as democratic a solution as this whole, wretched, British-created mess would allow, to meet the wishes and the interests of the people actually living in Palestine, not just of those whom the Zionist leaders desired to bring there, and to bequeath an independent state that was neither Jewish nor Arab, but a marriage, in conditions of mutual respect and equality, of both. It was a solution to which, once more, the Zionists, with their very different plans, took the most furious exception. So the terror and the violence which they were preparing to use against the Palestinians they first directed against the British, with bombs, bullets and sabotage. Eighty-eight people, Jews and Arabs as well as British, died in the blowing up of their military and civilian headquarters in Palestine. Unable and unwilling, in the wake of the Holocaust, to tackle the Jewish rebellion with anything like the harshness they had the Arab one in the 1930s, war-weary and at their diplomatic wits' end, the British duly announced that they had had enough. In November 1947, the United Nations, in whose lap they had dumped their problem, called, in a non-binding General Assembly recommendation, for the creation, within a partitioned Palestine, of a Jewish state alongside an Arab one.

Ethnic cleansing operations, conducted under cover of the collapse of law and order which, despite the continued British presence, the UN recommendation had provoked, began immediately. Then, in March 1948, Ben-Gurion activated the master plan, Plan Dalet, for the Palestinians' 'systematic and total expulsion' from their homeland.[11] Every Hagana commander received a list of villages and neighbourhoods in his zone and precise operational instructions about how and when to attack, occupy and destroy them, and evict their inhabitants.[12] Much of the plan had already been carried out by 15 May, when the British pulled out, and the Arab armies began to move in, in their futile, fore-doomed bid to check it.

MASSACRES IN GALILEE, FLIGHT TO LEBANON

The 'large chunk of Palestine' to which – in Ben-Gurion's words – the plan was to apply was, in fact, precisely that 78 per cent of the country, instead of the mere 56 per cent allotted to it by the UN, on which the Israeli state eventually arose.[13] That included most of the Galilee region, adjoining Lebanon, which the UN had assigned to the Arab state. Here, the Palestinians – and some Lebanese too – learned, more systematically than anywhere else, to what new, brutal and far-reaching purposes those 'punitive missions', first taught by Orde Wingate, would be put in the hands of the Zionist militia shortly to become the army of the new-born state. For up here, thanks in part to the (pathetically inadequate) arms they managed to acquire from Lebanon and the (pathetically ineffectual) presence of the volunteer, non-state Arab Liberation Army, Palestinian resistance was generally stronger, if ultimately unavailing, than anywhere else. Stronger, in consequence, were the characteristic modes of Zionist attack: exemplary terror, preliminary siege and 'softening up' by aerial and artillery bombardment, psychological warfare, expulsions at gunpoint, collective executions of 'wanted' men in village after village – and outright massacres. Of these, that of Deir Yassin, on the edge of Jerusalem, was to become the most infamous of the whole, six-month ethnic cleansing campaign. It was carried out by the underground Irgun organization; but it was the very official Hagana, supposedly committed to 'purity of arms', which carried out the bulk of more than thirty other, Deir Yassin-type mass killings. A goodly portion of them took place in Galilee – and even in Lebanon too. For there, in Operation Hiram, their last great, cleansing sweep, the Zionists, spilling across the frontier, had captured thirteen villages. In one of them, Houle, they assembled residents in two houses, then blew these up over their heads, killing eighty; in another, Saliha, ninety-four people, packed into a single abode, perished similarly.[14]

But, in retrospect, it can be said that the principal aggression, or at least the most enduring and fateful in its consequences, which the Zionists – now of course Israelis – carried out against Lebanon was to push the refugees they had created across its border. Lebanon was in any case the place to which, being closest, the Galilean villagers had been bound to turn for ultimate, if deeply reluctant, refuge after the kind of ordeal, repeated a hundred-fold, which Muhammad Hassan Furhan and Abdul Raman Furhan, from the village of Majd el Kurum, recounted to a researcher twenty-five years later:

> We knew they [the Arab Liberation Army] were not coming back ... A few villagers and I went to see Officer Turki, commander of the ALA in the village, to find out the real reason for their retreat. Speaking to the villagers outside the *mukhtar*'s house, he told us that he had been informed by the ALA High Command that the Jews had occupied most of the Upper Galilee and he was ordered to retreat to Lebanon before the Jews blocked all the roads ...
> He concluded, saying that those were the orders of our Arab leaders and not his ... As he departed, he advised all our young men and women to leave the village, while the elderly people stayed and carried white flags to avoid a Jewish attack ... We knew we would be killed if caught with our arms ... We did not want to take any risks and decided to leave to Lebanon while we still had the chance. About 100 to 120 families left that night ... The roads were filled with people fleeing to Lebanon. The villagers we left behind on our way were worried. They said: 'you have a head start, but our turn is next ... we will catch up with you later.'

Umm Abd al-Qiblawi was among the villagers who resolved to stay behind:

> During the morning of October 30, a few villagers decided to carry white flags and then meet the Jews west of the village. They were to tell the Jewish soldiers that the villagers had gotten rid of the ALA and that the village was safe and prepared to surrender. We were surprised when suddenly another Jewish force approached the village from the east. The Jews joined up at the village and soon after ordered us to assemble ... in the centre of the village. Jewish soldiers picked twelve of our men at random, blindfolded them, and shot them in front of us. I kept praying that my husband would not return to the village. One night, I joined

about 60 families who had decided to leave to Lebanon where I
met my husband ... The Jews did not stop us from leaving ...[15]

By early 1949, the Palestinian exodus was complete. Anything
between 700,000 and a million of the country's 1,300,000 inhabitants
had left for neighbouring Arab countries or those portions of
Palestine – Gaza and the West Bank – which, for tactical and pragmatic
reasons, fell outside that 'large chunk' of Palestine on which Ben-
Gurion had originally set his sights. Overland, or by sea from Haifa
and the coastal regions, about 110,000 of them fetched up in Lebanon.

ISRAEL LEAVES LEBANON IN PEACE

In the armistice talks that followed the war, those with Lebanon
proceeded more easily than with any other Arab country. It was due in
part to Ben-Gurion's belief that, in joining other Arabs in their bid to
'save' Palestine, it had done so 'without enthusiasm and with limited
forces'. And that was undoubtedly the case. Its recently created, 3,000-
man army – more like a police force really – was chaotically
disorganized, confessionally fractured and primitively equipped;
furthermore, it so happened that in the critical period of 1948 its meagre
resources were already heavily stretched by anti-bandit operations
in the Beqa'a Valley and by a potential military threat from Syria,
deemed serious enough for it to dig in anti-tank artillery as a precaution against possible incursions across the frontier. But if it lacked
the means to make much of a contribution, Maronite-controlled and
overwhelmingly Maronite-officered, it lacked the will too. Indeed – or
so the Israelis themselves believed – not a single Maronite participated
in the fighting, such as it was, at all.

From the outset, the army commander, Fuad Chehab – a future
president – spurned the joint Arab plan of action, in which his forces
were supposed to advance down the Mediterranean coast, forbidding
them to 'cross into Palestine' or even to 'use their arms from Lebanese
territory against persons in Palestine'. His army's only involvement in
the war lasted four days, during which it mounted an attack on the
strategically important Palestinian border village of Malakiyya, at a
moment when it was very poorly defended, and then handed it over to

the Arab Liberation Army. Essentially, this was a 'symbolic battle' designed to impress the Lebanese Muslim, and wider Arab, public that Lebanon was 'doing its bit' for Palestine. Amid hugely exaggerated accounts of the hard-fought nature of the campaign, of territory captured and casualties inflicted, President Khouri and an array of dignitaries toured the battlefield and handed out medals at a 'victory' parade in the southern town of Bint Jbeil. Thereafter Chehab ordered his troops to stay on their side of the border and 'to fight only if forced to reply to Jewish attacks'. But when the Israelis did cross the frontier, his troops did nothing at all. In fact, the Israelis had reached the Litani river before Ben-Gurion ordered them to stop – and only then over the protests of local commanders who wanted to go all the way to Beirut, and thought they would get there in twelve hours.[16] Lebanon's was the only non-Palestinian territory which Israel conquered in the war – but also the only one from which it withdrew.

Indeed, from the armistice on, Israel's relationship with Lebanon, so fertile in pre-state days, was to turn into the most static, the most uneventful, of its relationships with any of its neighbours in its first two decades of statehood. It was not that Ben-Gurion had suddenly lost interest in it. On the contrary, he clearly believed that the war, and Israel's prowess in it, opened up new and grander opportunities there. The havoc he wished upon its Arab co-'aggressors', he did not wish on it, or at least not its Christian citizens. 'We will break Transjordan,' he had told his cabinet in the exultation of early military triumphs, 'bomb Amman and destroy its army; then Syria falls; and if Egypt continues to fight, we will bombard Port Said, Alexandria and Cairo. This will be in revenge for what they [the Egyptians, the Arabs and Assyrians] did to our forefathers during Biblical times.'[17] As for Lebanon, however, 'We will establish a Christian state, whose southern border will be the Litani river.' And in three places in his wartime diaries he recorded his conviction that such a state – and a stronger one the better – would be a logical outcome of the conflict. In years to come he repeatedly raised the idea of a 'minority alliance' – yet never, in the end, did he seriously try to make it operational.[18]

Nor was there a lack of interest from the Maronites, or at least the 'pro-Zionists' among them. These were pleased with the emergence of the Jewish state. Its borders were now sealed, all dealings with it strictly forbidden by pan-Arab fiat. But the 'pro-Zionists' kept up their contacts of the pre-war era, apparently believing, like Ben-Gurion, that, with Jewish statehood, grander opportunities now awaited them too. In their meetings with Israeli foreign ministry officials, Emile Eddé and a representative of Pierre Gemayel's right-wing Phalange party, now emerging as a pole of opposition to the 'Arabist' regime of Bishara al-Khouri, spoke of staging a Christian 'rebellion' in Beirut; Israel should help it, among other things by linking up with the rebels through an invasion of the south. However, the Israeli foreign ministry, where non-interventionist thinking was dominant, felt that, even if the Maronites were psychologically ready for such a drastic action, in practical terms they definitely were not. And, apparently without much dissent from the interventionist camp, which nonetheless did give consideration to the idea, it was the foreign ministry's view that prevailed.[19]

What saved Lebanon from the Israelis' attentions was that, in the early years of statehood, they turned them elsewhere, to their other, larger neighbours, Egypt, Jordan and Syria. It was to these that, in their 'Arab policy', they first applied the new means that statehood brought with it. A reason why, in pre-state days, they had devoted so much attention to the small, sectarian state of Lebanon was not merely because, by its very nature, it was so promising an arena for external intervention, but because it was the only country where they could have achieved *anything* at all by the means then available to them – essentially the non-violent, political and diplomatic. But now, with state-hood, they had force, and vastly superior force, at their disposal too. The leap which that represented, though huge, had always been foreseen. Zionism, it had always been understood, would be advanced by this means above all others. Its founder, Theodor Herzl, had first expounded that; his disciples, Jabotinsky on the right, Ben-Gurion on the left, had enlarged upon it. Now, with the 'War of Independence', and that ancient dream, statehood itself, fulfilled, force had just furnished the most spectacular demonstration of its efficacy. Never Again – the slogan that, in the wake of the Holocaust, embodied what the new-born state perhaps above all reckoned to stand for – played its part as well: never again, that is to say, would Jews go like lambs to the slaughter.

ISRAEL'S BORDER WARS WITH ITS OTHER ARAB NEIGHBOURS

The Zionists-as-Israelis were resolved from the outset to make full use of their new asset. For it almost goes without saying that, in the conflict between the interventionist and non-interventionist schools of thought, the interventionists now secured the upper hand. With their ascendancy came that of the institutions where force would find its natural home: the army and the security and intelligence services. Force became the instinctive, automatic remedy for every problem, more effective than diplomacy, negotiation or the mediation of out-siders, and 'security' became the great shibboleth in whose name it was applied. It was a state of mind perhaps best summed up in Ben-Gurion's celebrated dictum that the business of the foreign ministry was not to make foreign policy but to explain the policy of the defence ministry to the rest of the world.[20] Its leading lights were Ben-Gurion himself, famous generals such as Moshe Dayan, and – already a rising star – the most reckless, ruthless and ambitious interventionist of them all, Ariel Sharon. Their leading opponent was Moshe Sharett, Israel's first foreign minister; his never-ending conflict with them was symp-tomatic of the fundamental choice that faced the new-born state, the choice, as he himself once put it, between making itself 'a state of law' or 'a state of piracy'.[21] In his posthumously published diaries, he lamented the moral corruption that reliance on force engendered, and the subordination of 'purity of arms' to a policy of 'revenge' elevated into a 'sacred principle' of state. Yet even he, while opposing these things, did not oppose them enough. For in the end – lamented Livia Rokach, the translator of his diaries – 'his unflagging Zionist faith' meant that 'he was as fascinated as he was repelled by the strategy, as envious of its immediate success as he was worried over its longer range consequences ... for Zionism and Israel.'[22] The chief of these conse-quences was that with brief interludes – the first of them being his own, much-contested two-year premiership – the interventionist school became the more or less permanently dominant one, that a nation born by the sword was forever going to live by it.

In those early years, however alluring the potentialities it might have offered the interventionists, Lebanon did not pose a serious, immediate challenge or threat. In their eyes, Egypt, Syria and Jordan did. The armistice agreements had helped set off a chain of violent upheaval in the Arab world. New revolutionary movements were sweeping the region and, in some places, seizing power. The Catastrophe fuelled them. For the revolutionaries attributed the Arab defeat to the rotten-ness of the old order – the monarchies, the regimes of the beys and the pashas, the great landowners and feudalists, selfish, frivolous, reactionary, subservient to the Western creators of Israel. The revolutionaries came in various guises, but above all they were pan-Arabist, secular nationalists, the offspring – two or three generations on – of the Arab Awakening to which Lebanese Christians had contrib-uted much. By the end of the Second World War, most Arab countries had achieved at least a formal independence, but they still laboured under various forms of neo-colonial influence. The new revolutionary regimes were bent on throwing these off, adopting truly independent foreign policies, forging new relationships with whomsoever they pleased, the Soviet Union or other emergent Third World nations like themselves, striving to unify the Arab 'nation' that Sykes–Picot had sundered, and turning to radical, socialist or even communist agendas for the reform and modernization of their societies. And they were to make of Palestine the pan-Arab cause *par excellence.*

Among Israel's neighbours, Syria and Egypt became members of this new order. Syria had always been the so-called 'beating heart' of pan-Arabism, but Egypt was now set to become its 'great power'. In 1952 President Nasser and his Free Officers had overthrown King Farouk and the monarchy. At first the Israelis had entertained the hope that, under them, Egypt – which, with its sense of separate identity reaching back to Pharaonic antiquity, was less beguiled by pan-Arabism than other Arab states – would be the first to make peace with them. Just as, in an earlier generation, Weizmann had sought a deal with Amir Faisal as the most representative of Arabs, so now they had similar expec-tations of Nasser, not perhaps as the most representative of them, but the most powerful. And, to begin with, in his secret dealings with Israel, Nasser was indeed very reasonable and restrained.[23] These expectations were quickly dashed, however. Pan-Arabism was 'a role wandering aimlessly about in search of an actor to play it'.[24] Thus had Nasser, the disgruntled officer who had fought and been wounded in Palestine, mused to himself in the wake of Egypt's wretched performance and defeat. It was not very long before he himself became that actor, indeed – very much more than that – the great Arab champion, the idol of the masses from the Atlantic to the Gulf. And nothing had more helped him do it than – with all their bluster and belligerence – Ben-Gurion and the interventionists themselves.

The other neighbour, Jordan (formerly Transjordan), was not part of this revolutionary new order. Its problem lay in the fact that it was situated, geopolitically, in the very cockpit of the regional turbulence which the Arab–Israeli conflict, in its new dimensions, was now to engender. Its regime, indeed its very existence as a state, was threatened by both Arabs and Israelis. For the new revolutionaries, the Hashemite monarchy was precisely the kind of 'imperialist lackey' they abhorred, and all the more so because it had gone to war less to save Palestine for the Palestinians than to expand its own territory at their expense. Its British-trained and British-officered army was the best in the Arab world, and Ben-Gurion had been reluctant to take it on. So, instead, he had done a secret deal with King Abdullah, who was to annex the West Bank, some 22 per cent of Palestine, to his original Transjordanian domain as his reward for doing nothing to prevent Ben-Gurion from securing the other 78 per cent which he wanted for the Jewish state. But Israel still coveted that missing 22 per cent, and it could be pretty sure that one day, out of the turbulence, the opportunity would arise to get it.

TERRITORIAL EXPANSION AND REGIONAL HEGEMONY
THE OBJECTIVE

There were two principal, and intimately related, purposes to which, in the interventionists' hands, force would be put. The first was the territorial expansion of the new-born state. So far, said Ben-Gurion, this had been set up in only 'a portion of the Land of Israel'; and 'to maintain the status quo will not do'.[25] After all, it had long been his conviction that if Zion were to rise again, it would have to do so in stages; so first 'we build up a strong force following the establishment of the state', and then 'we will abolish the partition of the country and ... expand to the whole Land of Israel'. And this would be achieved not by 'moralizing and "preaching sermons on the mount" but by machine-guns, which we will need'.[26] For the Palestinians, of course, expansion meant more of the same: expulsion for some, or most, and expro-priation, colonization, oppression and racial discrimination for others who managed to stay behind.

The precise limits of the expansion were not defined. For the right-wing Revisionists and others yet more extreme, they should have incorporated the whole of Jordan and substantial tracts of Egypt, Syria and Lebanon. For the mainstream, ruling Labour, the least they should comprise were those parts of historic Palestine which had eluded Israeli control in 1948. But wherever expansion, direct physical possession, ended, the establishing of regional hegemony began. For this was the second purpose to which force would be put. That is to say its use, not for the further 'up-building' of the Jewish state itself, but for its defence through attacking, fighting, intimidating, dominating and deterring all those Arabs beyond the borders who might threaten or destroy it from without. At the core of Ben-Gurion's philosophy lay the conviction that the Arabs were quite simply incapable of accepting peaceful co-existence with the intruder in their midst; and he was ready for decades of their hostility until Israel's superior strength, and vigorous and repeated demonstrations of it, finally persuaded them that they had no choice but to do so. Forever spurned by its neighbours, Israel was to be a beleaguered state, but, for that very reason, it had to be an invincible one too. It was the doctrine of the Iron Wall, first applied to the Palestinians, now extended to the entire Arab world.[27]

MAKING WAR TO MAKE PEACE

The official version of Israel's early years was that it earnestly strove for peace with the Arab neighbours which it had defeated in the epic, David-versus-Goliath struggle of its birth, but stood no chance of achieving it in the face of ongoing, unprovoked Palestinian terror and Arab aggression. This version did have a certain outward plausibility. The first Arab–Israeli war had set a pattern. By any serious reckoning, the Zionists themselves had been the real aggressors, yet they had been remarkably successful in portraying the Arabs in that guise. And the Arabs helped them do so, because, as losers, it was now they who had to take the initiative, to undo the *faits accomplis* the Zionists had achieved at their expense. Israel was probably right: the Arab governments would, if they could, have destroyed it. After all, under pressure from their publics, they were officially committed to the 'liberation' of the usurped Arab province, and *al-'Awda*, 'the Return', had become the great rallying-cry of the Palestinians themselves. But whatever their real intentions or capabilities, the Arabs were in any case almost bound to *look* like aggressors, or would-be aggressors, once again. And, as inept in public relations as they had been in war, their own, often belligerent rhetoric only reinforced the impression. It is true that this came less from Arab governments, actually rather cautious in their public utterances, than from the press or politicians, forever sounding off about the 'second round', the 'vengeance' that would surely come. But these were distinctions to which, not surprisingly perhaps, the outside world paid scant regard.[28]

By contrast, to achieve virtue, all the Israelis had to do was to stand still, to hold what they had. They called their army the Israel Defence Forces and all its actions were ostensibly defensive in nature. The West in general exhibited very little scepticism about this new Israeli narrative, least of all the United States. There, heavily influenced – where they were not frankly suborned – by the increasingly powerful Jewish lobby, press and politicians strongly supported – where they did not openly idolize – an Israel which, as well as supposedly battling valiantly for its young life, very quickly acquired another inestimable merit in their eyes. The state that would never even have been born without the systematic, pre-state sabotage of democracy and self-determination for the people it supplanted – almost overnight this self-same state earned the title it so profitably boasts till this day: 'the only democracy in the Middle East'.[29]

The official Israeli narrative was not merely a deformation of reality, it was, as the 'new historians' discovered, so very far removed from it that one of them, Avi Shlaim, professed himself 'astonished' at the disparity:

I believed in Israel's purity of arms ... that Israel was the victim
... I knew that in every country there's a gap between rhetoric
and practice, but I don't know of any country where the gap is as
great as in Israel ... Golda Meir used to say that she was willing to
travel anywhere in the world to make peace. But these were not
truthful words. In the archive ... I found that all the Arab leaders
were practical people, people who wanted peace.[30]

The files of the Israeli foreign ministry burst at the seams with
evidence of Arab peace feelers and Arab readiness to negotiate
with Israel from September 1948.[31]

By far the boldest of these feelers came – it seems amazing now –
from Syria. This most Arab of Arab countries has always appeared to
be the most patriotically intransigent on Palestine's behalf. Yet at the
time, in the person of General Husni Zaim, it had a very conciliatory
ruler indeed. His motives might not have been the purest, but there is
no doubt about the facts: nearly thirty years, and three Arab–Israeli
wars, before President Sadat made his historic pilgrimage to Jerusalem,
and then concluded the first, seminal peace agreement between Israel
and an Arab country, Zaim was offering to meet Ben-Gurion face to
face, and, as part of a Syrian–Israeli peace agreement, permanently to
settle 300,000 refugees in the fertile Jazira plain – enough, that is, to
absorb not merely the 100,000 who, in their flight from Palestine, had
fetched up in Syria itself, but all of Lebanon's, and a further 100,000
from anywhere else as well. But Ben-Gurion spurned this extraordinary offer, and the overtures of other Arab countries too, in
accordance with the celebrated and quintessentially hard-line Zionist
grounds of *ein brera* – of 'no choice'. No choice, that is to say, because
there was allegedly 'no one to talk to', no Arab leader willing even to
consider a peaceful settlement. This was obduracy that quite 'dumb-
founded' the American secretary of state, Dean Acheson.[32]

It was not that Ben-Gurion did not want peace. That was ever the
ultimate goal. It was just that, for the foreseeable future, he considered
that there was more to be gained without it. Peace *now* would have
shackled Zionism, arrested its growth, both territorially and in other
ways, long before it had acquired the stature and the strength it would

need to hold its own, come what may, in a world made hostile ... by no one more than Ben-Gurion himself. Peace with Syria would *inter alia* have left Israel without control over most of its water resources; with Jordan, it would forever have saddled it with 'ridiculous borders' that deprived it of the rest of Palestine and – a strategist's nightmare – militarily imperilled it;[33] with Egypt, it would have thwarted the expansionist designs it had on that front too. And, in addition, Ben-Gurion wanted to establish Israel's incontestable strategic and military dominance over all three countries. Another war, the 'second round' which was the incessant – but infinitely more serious – talk of Israelis too, was the way to get it.

THE ROAD TO SUEZ

This could have come, depending on opportunity, against any one – or more – of the three. And, by 1953, it had been more or less determined which that one would be. 'How wonderful it would be if the Egyptians started an offensive which we could defeat and follow with an invasion of that [Sinai] desert.' Thus, in October of that year, did the first Israeli president, Ben Zvi, give succinct utterance to the yearnings of the interventionists – and the method by which they would fulfil them.[34] This was to profit from the endless cycle of violence, the so-called 'border wars', already under way. Since 1948, Palestinian refugees, rotting and resentful in squalid camps that had sprung up all around the new-born state, had been sneaking across its frontiers; at first it had been simply, and typically, to retrieve some possessions from their homes or fields; but later, though even then on a very small scale, they came with hostile intent – to attack and sometimes kill the settlers who had usurped them. The cross-border raids the Israelis mounted in response – if, that is, they could be said to have had any credible justification at all, which they often did not – were monstrously disproportionate. They were expressly designed by Ariel Sharon, commander of the special forces – Unit 101 – that carried them out, 'to kill as many civilians as possible'. So wilfully murderous were they, in fact, that on one occasion even his own, highly indoctrinated and anything but squeamish men were moved to protest the slaughter of women in a Gaza refugee camp; what business was it of theirs, he retorted, to concern themselves with these 'whores of the Arab infiltrators?'[35] The reprisals were primarily about 'revenge, punishment and deterrence'.[36] But in their other, their war-provoking strategic purpose, they were, as General Dayan, their most influential advocate, put it, the very 'elixir of life for us'.[37]

To begin with at least, most of the Palestinian 'infiltrations' came from Jordanian territory, because, for geographical and other reasons, they were the more tempting, and the more easily carried out, from there than from anywhere else. But against whichever of Israel's neighbours Ben-Gurion and his interventionists unleashed the battle-hungry Sharon, it was always Egypt, and the goading of it down the road to war, that they had primarily in mind.[38] Their critical break-through came in February 1955, when, in a surprise attack on an Egyptian position in Gaza, they slaughtered thirty-nine soldiers 'in their beds'.[39] Nasser, who had hitherto restrained Palestinian 'infiltrations' from Gaza, now allowed them free rein. At the same time, responding to his commanders' clamour for weapons, he negotiated the famous Czech arms deal, a landmark in the Soviet Union's drive to undermine Western influence in the Middle East. It was just what Ben-Gurion wanted; the 'hosts of Amalek' were re-arming in Egypt, he said, and the 'grave and dangerous' arms deal had been concluded for 'one reason and one reason only – to destroy the state and people of Israel'; in the name of pan-Arabism, Nasser was bent on establishing an Arab empire, eliminating all Western influence from it, and turning Egypt into a forward base for Soviet power.[40] Ben-Gurion resolved to topple him. It was, he proclaimed, 'a *mitzvah* [sacred duty] to do so ... Who [was] he anyway, this Shmasser-Nasser?'[41] Just as he had considered Egypt, as the 'great power' of the Arab world, to be the only neighbour really worth making peace with when once it had seemed so potentially friendly, so he resolved to make war on it now that he had caused it to become so *un*friendly.

Thereafter, said an Israeli military history of the period, it was only a short step from the 'hidden war' of border skirmishing to the 'open war' of October 1956.[42] But, in the event, the full-scale Israeli invasion of Egypt, known to history as the 'Suez War', did not come about in response to any Egyptian 'offensive' of the Israeli president's wishing, let alone any evidence – for there was none – that Egypt was bent on an all-out war to destroy the Jewish state.[43] It came about, unprovoked, when Britain and France, angered by Nasser's nationalization of the Suez Canal, another blow to their fraying, neo-colonial position in the Middle East, decided that they too must attack Egypt and overthrow its obstreperous, upstart ruler. Israel was secretly invited to start a war on Egypt that would give them the pretext to intervene themselves. Israel duly obliged, and, in a week-long *Blitzkrieg*, seized the whole of the Sinai Peninsula.

The objectives of Ben-Gurion and his interventionists were both expansionist and hegemonic. They wanted to keep Gaza, Sinai and its newly discovered oilfields,[44] or, failing that, Sharm al-Sheikh and the Straits of Tiran linked by a land corridor to Israel. As for the hegemony, the grand design which Ben-Gurion had in mind was indeed quite as 'fantastic' as he himself conceded it to be – nothing less than a thorough-going re-arrangement of the whole Middle East, Sykes–Picot fashion, with Israel in the role of regional overlord on the West's behalf.[45] On the expansionist front, he did secure the opening of the Straits of Tiran to Israeli shipping, and, on the hegemonic one, he did establish Israel as the pre-eminent military power of the region; and that, for a nation forever doomed to put its trust in force, was very important. But of his grand design – nothing.

It was above all President Eisenhower who frustrated him. Then, as now, Israel could command the automatic support, sympathy or extravagant applause of the 'friends of Israel' in the United States. On this occasion Senator Jacob Javits rushed to Israel to declare that 'the American people fully understand the self-defense motives' that lay behind the invasion of Sinai, while Rabbi Louis Newman of New York said that 'America must aid, not hurt, the three democracies of Britain, France and Israel.'[46] But Israel held no special charm for Eisenhower, who had previously warned its ambassador to Washington that his administration would do everything in its power to 'prevent the settlement of international issues by force', and that if he thought that 'Jewish sympathy' for Israel 'would have any influence on [him]', he 'should disabuse his mind about it'. In those days, the American commitment to the well-being and survival of Israel was offset by the conviction that too close an identification with it, and with its treatment of Palestinians and Arabs, would undermine all America's efforts to keep the strategically vital Middle East on the Western side in the struggle against Soviet communism. Far from regarding it as a strategic asset, his secretary of state, Foster Dulles, once confided that it was a 'millstone round our necks'.[47] Eisenhower enforced Israel's humiliating, all but unconditional withdrawal. But it was the last time any American president was to take so resolute, so moral a stand, or anything approaching it, against Israel and 'the Lobby'. That was a deficiency from which, in the fullness of time, Lebanon was to suffer more painfully than any other Arab state. Meanwhile, however, it was spared.

BEN-GURION PUSHES FOR A 'CHRISTIAN LEBANON'

But Lebanon was never out of Ben-Gurion and the interventionists' thoughts. Indeed, in principle at least, they had greater ambitions for Lebanon than they did for anywhere else. But, in the event, whatever form these ambitions took, they were to remain in the realm of theory, of 'ideas to be played around' with.[48] A number of times they looked like going into effect, but in the end they did not. That was partly because Ben-Gurion, the supreme pragmatist, believed that, in the resort to force, opportunity was all, or at least highly desirable. And in his judgement what often promised to become a configuration of sufficiently favourable circumstances never quite did so. It was also because Lebanon was one place where Sharett and the non-interventionists did manage to stay the interventionists' hand. That was usually because of the sheer scale, audacity and illegality of what they had in mind; they were made to see that they just couldn't get away with it. There was a paradox here as well. It was the Maronites who so tempted them to act – yet simultaneously deterred them. It was the 'pro-Zionist' Maronites out of whom they might have fashioned their instrument for turning multi-sectarian Lebanon into that 'Christian state', and Israel's 'natural ally', of their dreams. But it was the 'Arabist' Maronites who would never let them do it. And the 'Arabists' now held power. And what they did with power, in the spirit of the National Pact, was to strike all the right pan-Arab attitudes that they possibly could, yet never quite aggressively or provocatively enough to give Israel the pretext to do to Lebanon – through 'border wars' and the 'open wars' to which they led – what it was doing to Syria, Jordan and Egypt.

From the outset, the Lebanese authorities opposed all 'infiltration' across their southern frontier, and set up an apparatus for the surveillance of it. Wherever they could without antagonizing the Muslim half of the population, they transferred refugees who had fetched up near the border northwards to camps in Tyre, Sidon and Beirut. By 1952 infiltration was almost non-existent. It did revive a little in 1953 when the Mufti sponsored a bout of trans-frontier terrorism from Lebanon at the same time as he was doing so, on a larger scale, from Jordan; a guerilla band calling itself the Servants of the Merciful suddenly came into being, killed two Israeli settlers in what was once the village of Saffuriya, from which all the band's members had been driven in 1948 – and just as suddenly disappeared. In 1955, in response to Israel's bloody Gaza ambush, it was President Nasser's turn to lay on some *fedayeen* incursions from Lebanon as well as from Gaza. Whereupon, the Lebanese army stepped up its border controls, declaring a ten-kilometre-deep 'security zone' and granting 'freedom of fire' to troops encountering infiltrators inside it. As a result, throughout this period, and to the annoyance of the interventionists, the Lebanese frontier was the only one that witnessed no large-scale Israeli retaliatory attacks.[49]

SEARCHING FOR THE CASUS BELLI THAT NEVER QUITE COMES

Sharett's diaries furnish the most authoritative and revealing insights into what the interventionists would actually have liked to be doing, into their 'ideas' for the use of force against the smallest and most peaceable of Israel's neighbours, and the 'opportunities' for putting them into effect. These opportunities lay outside Lebanon altogether. Typically, they had to do with Iraq. In the region-wide power struggle then taking shape between the 'revolutionary' new order, led by President Nasser, and the old, traditionalist one which it sought to overthrow, Iraq, under its British-backed Hashemite monarchy, was chief contender for the leadership of the traditionalist camp. Syria, racked by instability and domestic political conflicts that mirrored the regional ones, was the great prize over which the rival camps competed for ascendancy. Lebanon's destiny was, in turn, intimately linked to that of Syria, which, of all Arab states, was bound, through the ties of history and geographic proximity, to have both the strongest impulse to bring it under its sway, and the greatest capacity to do so.

It was hardly an accident, therefore, that when their opportunity arose to intervene by force in Syria, the interventionists automatically thought of doing the same – and more – in Lebanon too. In early 1954, as the pro-Egyptian regime of Colonel Adib Shishakli tottered on the point of collapse, the region was agog with expectations that Iraq would send its army across the Syrian frontier in a bid to install a pro-Iraqi regime in its place. This was enough, for a while at least, for Ben-Gurion and his faithful lieutenant, Moshe Dayan, then plotting war on Egypt, to 'concentrate on action against Syria' instead.[50] The moment Iraq went in, urged Dayan, Israel should 'advance [into Syria] and realize a series of *faits accomplis*'. Another ardent interventionist, Pinhas Lavon, told a deeply sceptical Sharett, then prime minister, that now was 'the time to move forward and occupy Syrian border positions beyond the demilitarized zones ... Syria is disintegrating. A state with whom we signed an armistice agreement exists no more. This is a historic opportunity; we shouldn't miss it.'[51] All this was being urged against a neighbour which, for all its nationalist pretensions, had actually given Israel hardly more trouble, across its frontiers, than had diminutive, inoffensive Lebanon; in fact, if there had been trouble it had almost always been of Israel's making. When Shishakli finally fell, he did so without any interference from Iraq; yet Lavon asserted that it added up to 'a typical Iraqi action' anyway, and that Israel should proceed regardless.[52] An 'electrified' Ben-Gurion agreed with him – then turned to his favourite, Lebanese obsession. The manner in which he did so was striking in its disregard for international law or morality. If, when making their case for action against Syria, he and his interventionists would don at least a fig leaf of 'security' or 'defence' justifications, where Lebanon was concerned, he didn't bother even with that.[53] Sharett recorded in his diary:

This is the time, [Ben-Gurion] said, to push Lebanon, that is, the Maronites in that country, to proclaim a Christian state. I said that this was nonsense. The Maronites are divided. The partisans of Christian separatism are weak and will dare do nothing. A Christian Lebanon would mean their giving up Tyre, Tripoli, the Beqa'a. There is no force that could bring Lebanon back to its pre-World War I dimensions ... Ben-Gurion reacted furiously. He began to enumerate the historical justifications for a restricted Christian [i.e. Christian only] Lebanon. If such a development were to take place, the Christian Powers would not dare oppose it. I claimed that there was no factor ready to create such a situation, and that if we were to push and encourage it on our own we would get ourselves into an adventure that [would] place shame on us. Here came a wave of insults regarding my lack of daring and my narrow-mindedness ... I got tired of struggling against a whirlwind.[54]

The next day Sharett received a letter from Ben-Gurion in his Negev retreat:

It is clear that Lebanon is the weakest link in the Arab League ... [The Christians] are a majority in historical Lebanon and this majority has a tradition and a culture different from those other components of the Arab League ... The creation of a Christian state is therefore a natural act; it has historical roots and will find support in wide circles in the Christian world, both Catholic and Protestant. In normal times this would be impossible. First and foremost because of the lack of initiative and courage of the Christians. But at times of confusion, or revolution or civil war, things take on another aspect, and even the weak declares himself to be a hero. It seems to me that this is the *central duty* ... of our foreign policy. We must act in all possible ways to bring about a radical change in Lebanon ... this is an historic opportunity. Missing it will be unpardonable.[55]

On this occasion Sharett prevailed: there was no attack on Lebanon, and none, at least for a while, on Syria. But the idea of one would not go away. In May of the following year, 1955, Ben-Gurion once again demanded that something be done about Lebanon. And once again it was trouble inside Syria and the possibility of an Iraqi invasion that was to furnish the pretext. Dayan leapt to his support and, going beyond a mere general advocacy of intervention as such, outlined a plan by which it should actually be carried out:

> According to him, the only thing that's necessary is to find an officer, even just a Major. We should either win his heart or buy him with money, to make him agree to declare himself the saviour of the Maronite population. Then the Israeli army will enter Lebanon, will occupy the necessary territory, and will create a Christian regime which will ally itself with Israel. The territory from the Litani southward will be totally annexed to Israel and everything will be all right. If we were to accept the advice of the Chief of Staff [Dayan] we would do it tomorrow, without awaiting a signal from Baghdad, but under the circumstances the government of Iraq will do our will and will occupy Syria.[56]

Once again the opportunity never arose. But then, after repeatedly looking northward, to Iraq and Syria, for at least a semblance of the *casus belli* Israel required to intervene in Lebanon, only to be repeatedly frustrated, Ben-Gurion finally found it elsewhere – in the maturing of his plans to wage war on Egypt, and, above all, in the undreamt-of bonus of waging it in partnership with Western Europe's two leading military powers. For even via an offensive on Israel's southern front, Lebanon, on its northern one, was still to be a key component, the linchpin even, of his scheme for the geopolitical restructuring of the whole region. It could hardly have been otherwise, given his Lebanese obsession, as well as the fact that the interventionists had actually been putting it about – to the Lebanese themselves and, through them, to the Americans, British and French – that 'an attack on Lebanon', rather than on Syria, Jordan or Egypt, '[offered] chances of the greatest results'.[57]

SUEZ TO THE RESCUE: BEN-GURION'S 'FANTASTIC' PLAN
FOR THE MIDDLE EAST

It had been only a week before his Sinai *Blitzkrieg* that he laid his grand
design before the conference which, in the words of 'new historian'
Avi Shlaim, 'hatched not just the most famous but also the best-
documented war plot in modern history'.[58] That took place in a private
villa in Sèvres, on the outskirts of Paris, where, in the deepest secrecy,
Ben-Gurion, Dayan and other members of his delegation had closeted
themselves for two days with their co-conspirators, led by French
prime minister Guy Mollet and British foreign secretary Selwyn Lloyd.
His 'general plan', he said, was to 'oust Nasser' and 'partition' Jordan,
this being a country which, he considered, had 'no right to exist'. Its
eastern part (Transjordan) would go to Iraq 'so that it [would] make
peace with Israel', thereby enabling the refugees to settle there with
the aid of American money. Its territories west of the Jordan river
would be 'annexed to Israel as an autonomous region'. As for Lebanon,
its borders would be 'reduced' and it would 'become a Christian state';
its predominantly Muslim territories would go 'part to Syria and part –
as far as the Litani – to us'.[59] To his somewhat astonished or embarrassed
listeners, he conceded that his plan might indeed, at first hearing, seem
'fantastic'; but, to his diary, he confided that he was in deadly earnest.
With the destruction of the Nasser regime, he believed, the nationalist
movement whose leadership it had seized would suffer body blows from
one end of the Arab world to the other, and in the power struggle
between it and all those rival forces in the region – be they secular-
modernist, traditionalist, pro-Western, ethnic or sectarian – the
nationalists' enemies would regain the upper hand. In these conditions
his plan, or something like it, would automatically fulfil itself.

DEBACLE AT SUEZ: ANY PLAN WOULD NOW BE NASSER'S,
NOT BEN-GURION'S

But the opposite happened. If any plan, or vision, were going to impose
itself on the region it would now be Nasser's, not Ben-Gurion's. In the
second Arab–Israeli war, Nasser had indeed suffered a great, but not,
in the circumstances, very dishonourable, military defeat. Politically,

however, he had won a huge victory. Overnight, the hero had become virtually synonymous with the pan-Arab role he had made his own.

After Suez, Nasserism, now inscribed in the hearts of millions as nationalism's other name, became more confident, more strident, more hostile to all who stood in its path. That meant Israel first of all. Nasser's worst fears about Israel had been confirmed. Whereas, in his former, relatively moderate self, he had talked mainly about finding a solution to the problem of the Palestinian refugees, he now began to talk about the liberation of their usurped homeland as the principal goal of nationalism, and the need, under the banner of Arab unity, to mobilize all Arab resources to that end. Then it meant the European powers which, having planted this intruder in their midst, were now using it as a stick to beat the newly independent Arabs down; they too must be fought. Finally, it meant all those Arab regimes, 'reactionary, imperialist lackeys', led by Iraq, who looked for their security in pacts and alliances with their former Western masters. Arabs, Nasserism decreed, must unite only with other Arabs. Nothing less than total self-reliance, total freedom from foreign tutelage, would do.

On top of all this, and growing out of it, the Middle East now became a key arena of the Cold War. Profiting from Europe's blunders, pro-Israeli partisanship, and persistent neo-colonial designs, the Soviet Union was mounting a very serious challenge to the West's exclusive pre-eminence in the region. With the rival superpower for friend and backer, the nationalists were further emboldened. The US promulgated the Eisenhower Doctrine, promising military aid to any Middle Eastern state 'threatened by International Communism'; in effect, in spite of Suez, Arab states were now being urged to band together, under Western auspices, in the conviction that the Russians were greater enemies than the Israelis. Nasser declared war on all such Western schemes. So did Syria, which, ever in the van of pan-Arab radicalism, was ahead, even of him, in the deepening Arab embrace of the Soviet Union. Then it entered into a fully-fledged, organic merger with Egypt, a seminal event, acclaimed as the first great breakthrough on the road to all-encompassing Arab unity. In July 1958, the Iraqi monarchy was overthrown in a military coup. It looked as though more pro-Western bastions, such as Jordan, might fall too. British paratroopers hastened

to the rescue of that other embattled Hashemite throne. Where, if anywhere, was the Nasserist tide to be turned? Not long before, in a
regional and international contest such as this, Syria, still divided on
itself, would have been the battleground on which the traditionalists
struck back. But now that Syria itself had plunged so deeply into what
Ben-Gurion called the 'Nasserist-Soviet torrent',[60] that role inevitably
fell to the only, but most congenitally fitting, candidate left, the small,
sectarian state of Lebanon. It was there, in the shape of a mini civil war,
that Nasserism reached its high-water mark.

MINI CIVIL WAR, 1958

It would be going too far to say that this fratricidal strife had come
about because, after years of 'Arabist' ascendancy within the Maronite
establishment, the 'pro-Zionists' were once again in command. Israel,
and the Maronites' relations with it, was certainly an issue, but it was
subsidiary to the principal one. This was the eruption, to the point
where it threatened the very integrity of the state, of that most basic,
most existential, of Lebanon's internal conflicts, between its predominantly Christian, Westward-looking self and its predominantly
Muslim, Eastward-looking one. President Camille Chamoun was the
focus of it. In earlier years, he had, on the face of it at least, been very
much an 'Arabist'; as Lebanon's representative at the UN, he had rallied
unreservedly to the universal Arab rejection of a Jewish state in
Palestine. But, as president, he became an anti-Nasserist, and although
that did not automatically make him a 'pro-Zionist', it placed him
firmly in company to which, in the eyes of the nationalists, Israel
certainly belonged. Nasser had revived the Maronites' atavistic fear of
the Arab hinterland. Instead of seeking to accommodate him, as the
'Arabists' would have sought to do, Chamoun turned more impor-
tunately to 'Christian Lebanon's' traditional Western protectors,
notably its 'tender mother', France. During the Suez crisis, he rejected
the nationalists' clamour for the breaking of diplomatic relations with
France and Britain. Soon after that he announced his support for the
Eisenhower Doctrine. At the same time, on the home front, he sought,
through gerrymandering, vote-buying and tinkering with the

constitution, to perpetuate himself in office at the apex of a system now institutionally tilted in favour of Lebanon's Westward-looking self.

The conflict became violent. Inevitably, as it did so, it took an increasingly sectarian turn; inevitably, too, the internal and the external became inextricably intertwined. Muslim and Druze rebels, notable among them unsuccessful candidates in the elections Chamoun had rigged in his favour, took up arms, seizing control of much of the countryside. Syria – or, strictly speaking, the United Arab Republic which, after the union with Egypt, it had now become – helped to recruit, train and arm them. The predominantly Sunni Muslim north, swept by unionist fervour, announced its secession from Lebanon and applied to join the new-born, pan-Arab state. Damascus denounced official, loyalist Lebanon as 'imperialist and Zionist'.[61] Palestinian fighters were shipped to rebel-held Lebanon from Egyptian-controlled Gaza.

In the loyalist camp, Christians, mainly Maronites, and a few dissident Muslims and Druzes, rallied to the defence of 'their' Lebanon against the pan-Arab suzerainty, or even outright take-over, which they believed Nasser had in store for it. Chamoun's Maronite rivals, the right-wing Phalangists, fielded a militia of their own.[62] Iraq and Jordan responded to Chamoun's request for troops, who made their way to Lebanon across Israeli territory. The foreign minister, Charles Malik, a former 'Arabist' too, openly asserted that his government needed 7,000 men to seal off its porous border (with Syria), and that it had 'no objection to anybody in any way sealing that border' on its behalf.[63] Israel hastened to become that 'anybody', intercepting a group of infil-trators and supplying arms and artillery support to loyalist forces confronting rebels in the south. It was no less anxious than the United States to keep Lebanon in 'the free world'. Chastened by Suez, Israel's interventionists were still in cautious mode; but they made it known that if, *in extremis*, the US let 'Christian Lebanon' down, they themselves would not.

By the summer of 1958, after fighting that had cost some 2,500 lives, government authority was basically reduced to the old 'Mount Lebanon' of Ottoman times plus the eastern, Christian side of Beirut. The rest of the country was essentially under rebel control. It looked as though the Greater Lebanon the French had created in 1920 might break asunder, the 'Mountain' and East Beirut re-constituting themselves as a Christian mini-state and the former Syrian provinces returning whence they had come. The US, suspicious of Chamoun's personal ambitions and unconstitutional practices, at first spurned his appeals for intervention under the aegis of the Eisenhower Doctrine. In the end, it was great events elsewhere – revolution in Iraq and the fall of its pro-Western monarchy – that spurred the Americans into action. Within hours, as British paratroopers descended on Amman, US Marines were coming ashore off Beirut, in the first such direct American military intervention in the Arab world since early in the nineteenth century, when, with the Barbary Pirates sowing terror on the high seas, the fledgling republic had built a fleet to combat them. An American trouble-shooter, Robert Murphy, shouldered the mediatory role to which a local, Lebanese 'third force' had proved unequal. He swiftly devised a compromise, to which the army, ultimate bulwark of national unity, was the key. Its commander, General Fuad Chehab, was of course a Maronite, but as a Maronite of the 'Arabist' persuasion he had made it his business, throughout the crisis, to keep the army above, and out of, the fray. He had not thereby endeared himself to many in his own community, but, as the only figure who commanded a broad acceptance on both sides, he had become the only possible candidate for the presidency. Under him, the equilibrium of the sectarian state was restored, and 'no victor no vanquished' became the hallowed maxim that should henceforth guide it. On the one hand, Lebanon remained a plausibly independent, essentially pro-Western, Maronite-dominated state, determined to keep itself out of any kind of conflict with Israel. On the other hand – to please the Muslims – it observed all the rites and pieties of pan-Arabism; in practice, that meant deferring so far as possible to Nasser – or to his ambassador in Beirut, of whom it used to be said that he was really his 'high commissioner', interfering as he did in the very minutiae of domestic politics.[64]

LEBANON STAYS OUT OF TWO MORE ARAB–ISRAELI WARS

Cohesion thus restored, Lebanon managed – just – to preserve itself unscathed by the developments that led to the next, and third, Arab–

Israeli war. These were Israel's diversion of a major part of the River
Jordan for its own exclusive use, and the collective, but unsuccessful,
Arab attempts to prevent that by a counter-diversion of the Jordan's
tributaries, which lay in Syrian and Jordanian territory, and its
headwaters, which lay in Lebanon's. Then it emerged intact from the
war itself. Some in the Israeli leadership had actually wanted to attack
Lebanon too, and then annex those southern regions, Litani river
included, which the interventionists had so long coveted.[65] But once
again their ambitions were thwarted: after all, what possible pretext
could Israel invoke against this weakest and – thanks mainly to the
Maronites it so hankered to befriend – most peaceable of its
neighbours? Instead, in those six astonishing days of June 1967, Israel
contented itself with destroying the armies of its three other
neighbours and acquiring territories – the West Bank and Gaza which
had eluded it in 1948, the whole of Sinai from which it had been forced
to withdraw in 1956, and the Golan Heights – several times its own size.
It was the apogee of force – and, perhaps most disconcertingly, of the
world's tolerance, indeed approval, of it. For this time, under President
Lyndon Johnson, the US deemed that Israel had sufficient *casus belli* in
Nasser's ostensible closure of the Straits of Tiran to Israeli shipping; in
any case, even before the war broke out, Johnson had already rejected
his predecessors' attempts to come to terms with Arab nationalist
regimes, and anti-Arab – especially anti-Nasser – sentiment pervaded
Washington. As for Western, particularly American, public opinion, it
was by and large literally entranced by Israel's smashing victory, and by
the Jewish people's deliverance from a second Holocaust which it was
widely perceived to have wrought.[66]

   Second only to Israel's military prowess, it had been the folly and
incompetence of the Arab regimes and, above all, a boastful and
bellicose rhetoric unaccompanied by the intention, let alone the
capacity, to live up to it, which yielded this result.[67] Coming in the wake
of other reverses – chief among them the break-up of the
Syrian–Egyptian union – which Nasser and the nationalist cause had
suffered since they reached their high-water mark in the Lebanese
settlement of nine years before, this was indeed their lowest ebb. Nasser
himself called it *al-Naksa*, 'the Setback', but in reality it was another

Nakba, another Catastrophe, and, in a sense, a worse one than before. For if, as the Arab nationalists contended, the struggle for Palestine was eventually to have furnished the ultimate proof of nationalism's success, it had now become the opposite: the damning measure of its failure.

NASSER'S DEFEAT, MARONITES' DELIGHT

There was outright rejoicing in Kesrouan, doughtiest of Maronite provinces, not simply because Lebanon had been spared again, but because, after such a defeat, Nasser and his nationalists would surely never pose a threat to it again.[68] But the rejoicing was singularly out of place. It could not have been known at the time, of course, or even truly apprehended for years to come, but the fact was that if any one event would one day come to qualify, in retrospect, as Lebanon's nemesis, it was surely the Six-Day War. At any rate, the adversities it was to suffer in its wake were to prove greater, and certainly more enduring, than those of any other Arab state. To be sure, Lebanon – or its true believers – managed for a while yet to sustain its faith, despite growing reasons for not doing so, in its own, felicitous exceptionality, its difference from the region of which it was nonetheless inescapably a part. And it was to be spared any involvement in yet another Middle Eastern war, the fourth, which, in October 1973, Egypt and Syria unleashed on Israel in retaliation for their defeat in the third. Yet whatever Lebanon uniquely was or reckoned itself to be – Switzerland of the Orient, meeting place of East and West, oasis of freedom and democracy, high place of culture, commerce and the good life – one thing was becoming steadily clearer: in its geopolitical self, it was definitely coming into its own as Mikhail Bakunin's 'small state' of the Middle East, the battleground for other people's wars. And it has remained so ever since. So much so, in fact, that from 1973 till this day it has (apart from Palestine itself) furnished the only militarily active front in the Arab–Israeli struggle; in other words, well over half the time – thirty-five years out of more than sixty – that struggle has so far endured since 1948. And that is not to mention what, Lebanon being the quintessential sectarian state it also is, all but inevitably came with that proxy role: its own, internal, *civil* war, compared with which, in duration and intensity, the brief affray of 1958 had been a mere prologue. In the fullness of time, of course, Islam – militant, political, fundamentalist Islam – was to become the region's great new universal credo, which filled the yawning void left by the decline and disrepute of secular-modernist nationalism. And, with the coming of Hizbullah, Lebanon would, in its peculiarly Lebanese way, feel the full impact of that. But before Hizbullah came the Palestinians.

CHAPTER FOUR

Lebanon and the Palestinians

The road to civil war: 1967–1975

THE ONLY PASSION OF THE REFUGEES

For two decades, in the wake of their expulsion, the Palestinians barely registered on the Lebanese political landscape. Virtually overnight they had come to represent a good 12 per cent of the local population. Yet, leaderless, fragmented, prostrate, they lacked the collective will or means to organize and speak for themselves as a community – and for the single aim, the return to their homeland, that instantly possessed them. They fell into two distinct categories. A minority, with the skills, means and connections to do so, more or less successfully integrated themselves into the society of their host country, and even went on to acquire its fully-fledged citizenship. About 20,000 in number, they came essentially from Palestine's middle classes. The rest, a little over 100,000, fetched up in some seventeen refugee camps dispersed around the country. These were essentially Palestine's peasantry. Inevitably, it was in the camps that the idea of *al-'Awda*, 'the Return', put down strongest roots. Separate from the society around them, virtual ghettoes, they became the foremost preservers of the Palestinian national identity in exile, the most visible, living reminders of the Catastrophe that had produced them, and the most fertile breeding-grounds of the determination that it be reversed. Their inhabitants made of the Return a virtual obsession. It shaped their rituals and regalia. Children were steeped in it from birth. Their schoolday would begin with their standing to attention and taking the oath:

> Palestine is our country,
> Our aim is to return,
> Death does not frighten us,
> Palestine is ours,
> We shall never forget her,
> Another homeland we shall never accept.[1]

FROM THE ENEMY'S OPPRESSION TO THE BROTHER'S

The Return was a passionate ideal in its own right. But it was reinforced by something else – the conditions of exile itself. Driven out by the Jews from their own country, the Palestinians had become, some of them lamented, 'the Jews of the Arab world'. It had begun, this replacement of one kind of oppression, the enemy's, by another, the brother's, as soon as they crossed the frontier. In Lebanon, conditions were in some ways worse than anywhere else. To be sure, they got an official welcome. President Bishara al-Khouri had gone in person to Tyre to tell them: 'Enter your country.' And in later years refugees were to recall the help, the acts of kindness and compassion, which they did encounter from many Lebanese, Christian and Muslim alike.[2] But the negative memories dominated, some of the most painful stemming from the period of maximum adversity, shock and bewilderment, as the newly made refugees trekked through the dirt-poor, mainly Shiite villages of the south. 'They even wanted to sell us the weeds in their fields,' recalled a mother who was refused a glass of water for her five children because she could only muster two and a half of the three pence cruelly demanded for it.[3] But even settled into their camps, they were to find that many ordinary people, not just government officials, habitually looked upon them as somehow different, threatening, or even contemptible. Merely to venture out of them was to risk taunts and mockery. A characteristic jibe was that they themselves were to blame for their plight because they had sold their land or fled it in cowardice. Lebanese children would ask their parents to buy a Palestinian to play with.[4] It has often been noted that while Arabs may be abstractly passionate for Palestine the cause, they often display little such passion for Palestinians as persons. But whereas in other host countries the refugees found the people more friendly than their governments, that was very much less the case in Lebanon. 'Perhaps', wrote Rosemary Sayigh in her moving account of refugee life in the country, 'this was because Lebanon's peculiar combination of religious divisions and class polarization sharpens inter-group aggression far beyond that of any other Arab country.'[5]

Alone among their host countries, and in violation of agreements with international organizations, Lebanon placed severe restrictions on the refugees' basic right to work. They were formally excluded from all public and a wide range of private employment. They had to apply for work permits for any formal occupation, and, as a matter of deliberate policy, these became harder and harder to acquire; and even when, under law, they should have been issued, they were often not, owing to the tortuous political processes, the discrimination and corruption involved. The only employment outside the camps from which they were unlikely to be debarred if it were available was casual menial labour. That brought extreme exploitation. In the early fifties it earned an average annual income of $60 a worker; a middle-class compatriot in private business would make $2,000.

Physically, camps like Sabra and Shatila on the outskirts of Beirut were dismal places, barely fit for animals, but their human residents were forbidden to make any improvement in them because that could smack of permanent residence. It is true that, to begin with, the refugees themselves, in their determined belief that their exile was only temporary, often connived in this, even to the point of protesting against any officially permitted alleviations of their own misery. Eventually they wearied of such masochistic zeal. Yet the few tents they boasted on their arrival barely evolved, over twenty years, into anything more than diminutive hovels, puny contraptions of stones, boards, zinc sheeting and canvas. Concrete, or any structure solid enough to require nails to hold it together, was forbidden. 'Anyone banging a nail, of course, would be heard right through the place, and everybody would ask: who's that? Why's he nailing? What's he nailing? And you had to say you were nailing the zinc: that was the only thing allowed.'[6]

And where politics and security were concerned, Lebanon was for its own special reasons every bit as afraid of these intruders as another main host country, Jordan, was of its. It was not merely because their numbers were so high in relation to the local population, but because they were liable to disturb the delicate mechanisms of the sectarian state, and especially the Maronites' pride of place within it. They were mostly Sunnis, and though in class terms there was a wide gulf fixed between these mainly untutored peasants and their typically city-dwelling co-religionists of Lebanon, it was feared that, politically, each might reinforce the other in domestic and regional causes; the pan-Arab nationalism that so alarmed the Maronites and other minorities was a Sunni credo *par excellence.* Small wonder, then, that with the rise of Nasser the other bitter grievance of the camp-dwellers – the harassment and humiliation they endured at the hands of the Maronite-led state security services – was greatly intensified. Small wonder, even, that the man chiefly responsible for that was none other than the 'Arabist' president, General Fuad Chehab, who, in 1958, had 'saved' Lebanon by what in spirit was a precisely opposite course – his accommodation with Nasser himself. Under his rule particularly, the security services, mainly the Deuxième Bureau, or military intelligence, dominated and blighted the refugees' lives. The Deuxième Bureau's sole concern was surveillance and repression. 'The Palestinian is like a spring,' said Joseph Kaylani, one of its notoriously harsh officers, 'if you step on him he stays quiet, but if you take your foot off he hits you in the face.'[7] At its most basic their policy was to isolate the refugees in their camps; residents of one could not visit another without permission, and that was hard to obtain; even to drop in on neighbours in one's own could lead to trouble after nightfall. But there were also continuous threats and intimidations, haphazard imprisonment without trial, mass punishments, fines on ludicrous grounds, random or systematic brutality, and occasional murder. Any Palestinian association with Lebanese political parties was particularly frowned upon. Thus, the moment any demonstration, entirely Lebanese in character, began in any part of any city, security men would immediately rush to arrest this or that presumed Palestinian sympathizer in the camps, aware though they were that it would have been physically impossible for him to have joined it. Such arrests were routine, and routinely accompanied by torture and interrogation lasting for days, weeks and months.[8]

WHAT WAS TAKEN BY FORCE COULD ONLY BE RESTORED BY FORCE

But how, in practice, was the Return to be accomplished? Of one thing most Palestinians were sure from the outset: that what had been taken from them by force could only be recovered by force. That was the instinctive view of the camp-dwellers. It was also that of the first Palestinian political movement to come into being in the wake of the Catastrophe. That it did so in Lebanon was not mere chance. The Arab Nationalist Movement (ANM) was a beneficiary of what, for Palestinians as well as for the Lebanese themselves, was the positive side of the sectarian state: its relatively democratic nature, its pluralism, and its intellectual freedoms. Although, as its name indicates, it was a pan-Arab organization, its founders were predominantly Palestinian, and Palestine was its principal *raison d'être*. Several of them were graduates of the American University of Beirut; they came from the typically middle-class component of the Palestinian diaspora. The most prominent was George Habash, who subsequently achieved international renown as head of the Popular Front for the Liberation of Palestine (PFLP) and pioneer of aerial hijacking. While never to become a mass movement, the ANM commanded a popular base in the refugee camps of Lebanon and Jordan. It argued that counter-force, or 'vengeance', was 'the only solution for the Palestine question'. The Zionist challenge could only be met on the terms which the Zionists themselves had laid down: expulsion or extermination.[9]

But whose force? However much its advocates, camp-dwellers or middle-class intellectuals, might originally have intended otherwise, it was to be the Arabs' force rather than their own. A convergence of circumstance and ideology dictated that. For one thing, the refugees, indispensable foot-soldiers of any such endeavour, were to begin with simply too crushed by the mundane struggle of day-to-day existence to think about the higher, national one. For another, even when, in due course, they could think about it, they ran into the determination of the Arab regimes to prevent them from converting their thoughts into action, or at least any action over which the regimes themselves exerted no control. Lebanon was implacable in this respect. However ardent it might have been in its rhetorical support for Palestine, it was no less ardent, and sometimes violent, in its suppression of 'Palestinianism' on its own soil. 'They beat us', said a militant of the time, 'so that we would feel it is dangerous even to talk about Palestine.' 'All you have to do is eat and sleep,' refugees would often be told, 'the Arab armies will get your country back for you.'[10]

However insincere in the mouths of Arab government officials, however little trusted by ordinary Palestinians, that promise was nonetheless, formally speaking at least, in impeccable accord with the pan-Arab nationalism that was the dominant ideology of the times, and with the ANM's conviction that 'the Battle of Vengeance' would be 'the battle of the whole Arab people', with the refugees as 'the vanguard of the Arab nation'. But – the ANM also believed – that battle could not take place before the Arab 'nation' had undergone a fundamental, revolutionary process of reform, modernization and unification, eliminating the 'backwardness' which had been responsible for its defeat in the Catastrophe. For the ANM, then, though Israel would always be the primary enemy, during the period of reform it was Arab governments, every single one of them, which bore the brunt of its hostility. At least it was until Nasser came along. For in him, after initial hesitation, it discerned the man of destiny who would unite the Arabs and harness their strength for the decisive struggle to banish Western imperialism from the region and destroy the alien entity it had planted in their midst. It gave him its complete allegiance, which meant in practice that, for the time being, it opposed any resort to armed struggle for fear that this would provoke an Arab–Israeli war before its champion, and the regular Arab armies at his disposal, were ready for it.

THE 'BATTLE OF DESTINY' – AWAITING IT IN VAIN

Unfortunately, however, the battle never seemed to come. And, meanwhile, the pan-Arabism in whose name it was to be waged was suffering grievous setbacks, notably the collapse of the Syrian–Egyptian union, while the Israeli enemy was inexorably consolidating its grip on the usurped homeland. The first to put their faith in Nasser, the Palestinian masses became the first to nurture serious doubts about him. It was in this atmosphere that a rival to the ANM now arose, one that was to

shape the destinies of the Palestinian people for decades to come, as
well as to play a key role in the affairs of several Arab countries, but in
Lebanon's more dramatically, disruptively and enduringly than any
other. This was Yasser Arafat's Fatah. Self-reliance was its basic impulse.
The Palestinians should take their cause into their own hands. It was no
good relying on Arab governments, even Nasser's, which had
'contented themselves with hysterical or anaesthetizing broadcasts and
rousing speeches, stopped Palestinian mouths, tied their hands, turned
them into a theatrical claque which applauds this and reviles that'. All
that talk of revolutionary transformation, of Arab unity as the prerequisite for the recovery of Palestine, had become a mere pretext for
endless procrastination and delay. In emulation of their revered,
original 'martyr', Sheikh Izzedin Qassam, the Palestinians should set
up a guerilla force, and launch a 'popular liberation war' of their own.

Fatah's leaders were lower middle-class in origin; many of them were
educated at Cairo University, and, going on to well-paying jobs in the
Gulf, they had acquired a relatively privileged social status. But Fatah's
rank and file, its fighting men, were to come from the refugee camps.
Thanks to the humiliations and insults of their Arab exile, they were
the readiest of recruits to its go-it-alone credo, and to 'armed struggle'
as the quintessential expression of it. 'Life in the tent has become as
miserable as death', proclaimed the underground Fatah magazine,
Falastinuna ('Our Palestine'). 'We, the sons of the Catastrophe, are no
longer willing to live this dirty, despicable life which has ... destroyed
our human dignity.' Not that there wasn't an Arab dimension to their
struggle. But it was the Arab masses, not their governments, to whom
they would look. Operations conducted from bases inside and outside
occupied Palestine would win the backing of ordinary people
everywhere. A 'supporting Arab front' would automatically spring into
being. All patriots, including soldiers and government servants, would
join it, if need be in defiance of their rulers.[11]

FROM LEBANON — FATAH'S FIRST RAID INTO ISRAEL

By 1964 Arafat and his men had gathered about themselves the nucleus
of a guerilla organization. Syria's radical Baathist regime, mainly to

embarrass Nasser, had agreed to give Fatah a secure base, and, in a small way, the operational support it needed to get going. As disillusionment with Nasser grew, so did Fatah's determination to act, and, though still a puny thing, on New Year's Day, 1965, it did. According to Military Communiqué No. 1 of the General Command of *al-Asifa* ('Storm') Forces, 'detachments of our strike forces went into action performing all the tasks assigned to them in the occupied territories [i.e. pre-1967, original Israel] and returning safely to their bases.'[12] Hardly anyone noticed it at the time. And, indeed, it is not surprising that Fatah's inaugural exploit should have been shrouded in a certain romantic obscurity. For it appears that it never actually took place. Perhaps, in retrospect, the most significant thing about it was its intended country of origin. That was not Syria. The 'beating heart' of Arabism, and the most passionate for Palestine of all Arab countries, it might have been, but, in its relations with the Palestinians, it was from the very outset pragmatic, not to say cynical, too. There was a quid pro quo for its support, which was that they should launch their raids from other Arab territories than its own.[13] Nor was it Jordan or Egypt, traditional starting points for the 'infiltrations' of the fifties and the bloody 'border wars' to which they led. No, it was the one country, Lebanon, which had hitherto been spared them. The raid never actually took place because the Lebanese security services, ever vigilant, had arrested the would-be raiders before they even set out.

But for the refugees in their camp, the mere attempt[14] was an occasion for rejoicing. And for Fatah, it marked the start of the Revolution, which would only deem itself victorious upon the complete liberation of Palestine, one and whole. For Nasser and the nationalists, on the other hand, it was an embarrassment, so much so in fact that they instructed their mouthpieces in the Beirut press – of which, in those days, they had many – to denounce its perpetrators. These were cast as instruments of a 'conspiracy, hatched by imperialist, CENTO and Zionist quarters', whose purpose was to furnish Israel with a pretext to attack its Arab neighbours and foil their scheme for the counter-diversion of the River Jordan.[15] It only intensified the oppression of the Deuxième Bureau, which, having captured and tortured to death one *fedayi* upon his return from a raid, threw his body from a high building to make it look like suicide.[16] Thereafter, Fatah's exploits, and those of lesser rivals which sought to emulate it, remained modest. By the outbreak of the 1967 war, they had killed a total of eleven Israelis for the loss of seven of their own men, either inside Israel proper or in raids from Jordan and Lebanon.

FATAH COMES INTO ITS OWN

It was only after that most devastating of Arab defeats, and the terrible blow it dealt to Nasser and the pan-Arabism he incarnated, that Fatah truly came into its own. At a stroke it not only vindicated its insistence on go-it-alone 'armed struggle', it rendered it virtuous – indispensable even – in the eyes of the regimes which had formerly disdained or thwarted it.[17] It also vindicated what others had formerly reviled as its 'localism'.[18] During the era of nationalism, it had been a kind of heresy to suggest that individual Arab states – those creations of Sykes–Picot – had in effect become distinct and separate 'nations' in their own right, with an intrinsic legitimacy, at least equal to those of the larger entity of which they were a part. But now, with the manifest failure of the pan-Arab ideal, this heresy was well on the way to establishing itself not, perhaps, as the new ideal, but at least as the pragmatic reality in which the Arabs had little choice but to acquiesce. In fact, Arabic has two words for nationalism, or patriotism. One, *qaumiyah*, denotes nationalism in its one and only pan-Arab dimension. *Wataniyah* usually denotes it in those multiple, more local forms, generally speaking coterminous with the individual states. With their resort to 'armed struggle', the Palestinians, formerly destined to be the principal bene-ficiaries of *qaumiyah*, had become pioneers in the development and ascendancy of *wataniyah*.

Fatah, together with a host of rival organizations that already existed or now came into being, enjoyed a spectacular ascent, in intrinsic strength, political impact and both 'local' and pan-Arab appeal. The ascent was very evident in Lebanon, but in this honeymoon of the guerilla movement, the main arena was elsewhere, and first of all in historical Palestine itself.

In the newly conquered territories of the West Bank and Gaza, among their own people, they sought – in accordance with Mao Zedong's famous dictum – their revolutionary sea in which to swim. Yasser Arafat crossed and re-crossed the Jordan, and scurried about under the noses of Israeli soldiers, trying to ignite a 'popular liberation war'. On the face of it, judging by their communiqués, they were making an effective start.[19] Officially, it was only, or mainly, enemy soldiers that they targeted; and it was not unusual for Fatah to announce that, in a single operation, they had killed and wounded fifty, sixty or even seventy of them for the most paltry losses of their own. But – attacking civilians too – they would put bombs in a Jerusalem supermarket, or a bus station in Tel Aviv.

Jordan, with its Palestinian majority and its proximity to Israel, was the movement's next most natural – albeit external – base. They took control of its Ghor Valley. And from there, the lowest point on earth, they carried out raids and artillery bombardments across the Jordan river. The Israelis struck back fiercely. Out of such reprisals grew the legendary 'battle of Karameh' in which a guerilla force of some 400 lightly armed men decided to confront head-on an Israeli force of 15,000, which included helicopter-borne commandos and an armada of tanks. They suffered huge losses, but, politically, their 'martyrdom decision' succeeded beyond their wildest dreams. King Hussein had been doing his best to check the growth of guerilla power. He now gave up the idea; his subjects would not stand for it. Even one of his most faithful henchmen, Wasfi al-Tal, redoubtable scion of an influential Transjordanian family, urged him to turn his kingdom into a latter-day 'Carthage'. The whole country – said this non-Palestinian – should be fully mobilized behind the guerillas, who should step up their operations 'a hundred-fold' to become a real torment to the enemy.

Volunteers – Arabs as well as Palestinians – flocked to enrol; some reports had it that the fighting forces of Fatah – some 300 before Karameh – and lesser, left-wing organizations had swollen to as many as 30,000 or so two years later. By their own count, their operations – of all kinds – increased from twelve a month in 1967 to 279 by 1970.[20] Then the resistance movement seized control of the Palestine Liberation Organization (PLO), a docile body of well-behaved notables, which Nasser and other Arab regimes had originally set up precisely in order to control it themselves. Arafat duly became its chairman. It was all beginning to look as though Fatah theory really was working out in practice, as if the revolutionary 'vanguards', through a process of spontaneous combustion, really were rallying the Arab masses behind them, bringing into being that 'supporting Arab front' which would strike down any ruler who stood in their path.

But Fatah's rise was as flawed as it was outwardly meteoric. Indeed, at the height of its success it was already in decline.[21] There was to be no popular uprising in the newly occupied territories. Among other things, the inhabitants, West Bankers in particular, were not yet ready for great self-sacrifice in a cause whose success they doubted. The *fedayeen* were the product of a refugee society which had lost all. The West Bankers still had something to lose. They were therefore more immediately interested in the withdrawal of the occupier than in the liberation of the whole of Palestine, and they still hoped that, by political or military means, the Arabs would accomplish it for them. The guerillas found it hard to hide among the local population; Israel's efficiency, and the severity of its reprisals, did the rest. But Fatah also had itself to blame, with its typically hasty and slipshod methods of organization, undiscriminating recruitment, poor security and a propensity, which soon became counter-productive, for making grotesquely inflated claims about its military exploits. Within six months of the 1967 war, Arafat, making a daring escape in which he apparently disguised himself as a woman, fled back across the Jordan for the last time.

That was his movement's first great strategic setback. The loss of Jordan three years later was the second. For all their initial popularity, the guerillas began to forfeit it even in this, their most sympathetic, largely Palestinian environment. But it was the conservative, loyalist, Transjordanian section of the population whom they particularly antagonized, with their indiscipline, their arrogance and the openly proclaimed ambition of some of them to replace the Hashemite kingdom with their own revolutionary new order. In what was after-wards known as 'Black September' 1970, Hussein unleashed his impatient Bedouin troops, and, in ten days of fratricidal strife, he broke the back of guerilla power in Jordan. Within a year of this disaster, they were driven from the country altogether in a ruthless campaign conducted by the self-same Wasfi al-Tal, now prime minister, who had formerly urged the King to throw all his weight behind them.

THE PALESTINIAN RESISTANCE HAS NOWHERE TO GO BUT LEBANON

They now had nowhere else to go but the all too permeable state of Lebanon. Of the other 'front-line' countries, Egypt, with the whole of the Sinai desert separating its population centres from the Israeli border, was impractical, and wouldn't have had them anyway. Syria was their principal sponsor, but it didn't want them either; nor did they want *it*, knowing as they did that the greater their presence on its soil, the more hostage they would become to the impulse of its despotic Baathist regime to reduce them to a mere extension of itself. Of course the Revolution did not come to Lebanon because Lebanon offered better guerilla country than anywhere else, though, with its rugged hills and valleys, it actually did; nor did it come in response to official or popular invitation, or because Lebanon had the strongest belief in Arabism and its principal, Palestinian cause. It came, basically, because as a state it could not stop them coming, and, once they were there, it could not control and subjugate them. 'The Revolution landed in Lebanon', as Shafiq al-Hout, the first PLO representative to the country aptly put it, 'because it was a garden without a fence.'[22]

So it was that, in 1970 and 1971, the whole apparatus, or a very substantial segment of it, into which the resistance movement had already grown, appeared on the scene. That meant not just Fatah, the original and by far the largest organization, but at least a dozen others; some of them, like the radical, left-wing PFLP, formerly the ANM, were more or less authentically Palestinian in their leadership and policies; others, like Saiqa or the Arab Liberation Front, were basically instruments, in the Palestinian arena, of those two most mutually hostile of Arab regimes, the Baathists of Syria and the Baathists of Iraq. That 'official' institution, the Palestine Liberation Organization, formally separate from, but in practice heavily intertwined with, the guerilla movement, was also present, in the shape of Arafat himself, as its chairman, various civil departments, and units of the Palestine Liberation Army. When the influx was complete, the original refugee community, now swollen to some 240,000 by natural growth, numbered another 100,000 more.[23] Just how many fighting men the resistance boasted was perhaps a less important question than their quality, but high-end estimates – local 'irregulars' included – were not far short of the 20,000 men of the Lebanese army.[24] The Palestinian 'headquarters' took root, hard by the refugee camps of Sabra and Shatila, in a district of Beirut called Fakhani. With its quasi-governmental bureaucracies, welfare and medical organizations, social, cultural and educational institutions, research centres, and the economic planning or industrial development boards of what was fast becoming the wealthiest resistance movement in the world, it engaged in functions that ranged far beyond the requirements of 'armed struggle'. 'The Fakhani Republic' was one appellation to which Lebanon's twelve-year 'Palestinian era', now beginning, gave rise; another, more familiar in the outside world, was 'Fatahland', essentially denoting those areas of the country over which Arafat and his men came to hold exclusive, or at least pre-eminent, sway.

Of course, when Arafat came to Lebanon he was not starting from scratch: a rudimentary Palestinian 'infrastructure', an embryonic state-within-a-state, was already in place. For, in its initial, meteoric rise, the Palestinian resistance movement had had the same electrifying effect in Lebanon as it did elsewhere, if not more so. At first, miracle of miracles, here was a pan-Arab cause which, just as it had done in the days of the Mufti and the Great Rebellion, appeared to unite as much as it divided this congenitally fissiparous land. The press ran riot with accounts of young men determined to enlist – like nineteen-year-old Wahib Jawad, who, opposed by his family, held up a shop to raise money for his fare to Amman, taking only 25 Lebanese pounds out of a proffered 300. A month after Karameh, Lebanon suffered its first 'martyr'. Khalil al-Jamal had died on the Jordan front, and when the funeral cortège reached the village of Kahhaleh, a Maronite stronghold on the road from Damascus, its inhabitants insisted on carrying the coffin themselves as church bells tolled. Beirut newspapers called this

a 'plebiscite', the 'real face' of a Lebanon carrying no 'stain of confessional fanaticisms'.[25] The Lebanese army even offered military
training of sorts to dozens of Palestinian refugees, and the Deuxième
Bureau slightly eased its iron grip on the camps.[26]

The cross-confessional solidarity may have been outwardly
impressive. But it was misleading. To be sure, with the debacle of pan-
Arab nationalism, the Maronites no longer had much reason to fear
Nasser's will or ability to stir up pan-Arab, pan-Islamic emotions at
their expense. And they could not but welcome, as a matter of
principle, the 'localism', the '*wataniyah*', that was taking nationalism's
place. Was this not essentially the same thing as the 'pluralism', the
view of the Middle East as a collection of minorities, after which they
– and of course the Israelis too – had always hankered? Unfortunately
for them, however, the self-same Palestinians who were, in a sense, the
most militant expression of this trend, became a more potent and
disruptive force, on the battlefield of other people's wars that Lebanon
was becoming, than Nasser ever had been at the very height of his
power.

'TO LET DOWN THE PALESTINIANS WAS TANTAMOUNT TO LETTING DOWN THE LEBANESE MUSLIM CAUSE'

They were not merely outsiders, like Egypt or any other such larger
state in the region, with the will and ability to exert their influence
from without. They *were* outsiders, of course, but, unlike them, in
everything except possession of an official Lebanese identity, they were
insiders too. Thanks mainly to the cohesion and solidarity of the camp-
dwellers, they were in effect another local community, another political
actor on the domestic scene. They may, proportionally, have been one
of the smaller ones, but they had the potential, once enfranchised and
armed, to become the most powerful one of all. They depended for
their advancement, not on Lebanon or its government as a whole, but
on the special sympathy and support which they could all but
automatically garner in one or more communities, even if that meant,
as in fact it did, earning the equally automatic fear and hostility of
others. It was the country's Muslims, mainly Sunni but Shiite too, who

rallied instinctively to them. How could it be otherwise? Their hearts always lay with pan-Arabism, and the resistance had established itself – albeit in its post-Nasserist, 'localist' guise – as the pan-Arab cause *par excellence*. But they rallied to them with all the greater fervour because, in addition to the general sentiment common to Muslims and Arabs everywhere, they had their specifically Lebanese sectarian reasons for doing so. It was an elementary quid pro quo: the Palestinians promoted their cause through them, they promoted theirs through the Palestinians. Drawn together by the anti-Israeli struggle, the Palestinians were among the least sectarian-minded of Arab peoples; nonetheless, they were overwhelmingly Sunnis, and, not surprisingly, their Lebanese co-religionists looked upon them as a major possible reinforcement of their own numerical strength, as well as ally in their quest to achieve a fairer representation, and distribution of wealth and status, for their community, *vis à vis* the dominant Maronites, within the confessional polity. For 'the ordinary Muslim', wrote Lebanese historian Kamal Salibi, 'to let down the Palestinians was tantamount to letting down the Lebanese Muslim cause'.[27]

But there was more to it than the merely sectarian. The 1960s was the era of the Paris student 'uprising', of new, sometimes violent kinds of left-wing European radicalism, and of Che Guevara and Third World 'revolution'. Naturally enough, their Lebanese emulators had specifically Lebanese aims. Some wanted not merely to 're-adjust' the sectarian balance, but to abolish it altogether; others wanted fundamental reform of the whole gamut of social, economic and political afflictions which the sectarian system itself was deemed to engender and perpetuate. The entrenched, unchanging elite of traditional chieftains, urban notables, business tycoons, who represented and managed the system, derived their power more from the patronage and access to resources that they could furnish their respective communities, than on national strategies for the progress and welfare of all; they effectively connived, across the confessional divide, in a harsh form of *laissez-faire* capitalism. It was mercantile rather than productive, steeped in cronyism and corruption, and marked by great disparities of wealth, by a sybaritic luxury that flaunted itself side by side with the poverty and squalor of Beirut's spreading slums and shanties, by a massive brain drain, unemployment, exploitation, and a favouring of the capital at the expense of the provinces, especially the remote and mainly Shiite South.

Physically and militarily, the 1967 war might have passed Lebanon by, but it exacerbated these conditions, and its resultant discontents, and sharply intensified the radicalization of the Muslim intelligentsia, especially the students, and the urban and rural masses, mostly under left-wing banners but sometimes under newly emergent Islamist ones.[28] For all, there was an intrinsic link between Lebanon's domestic woes and the shattering Arab defeat; both were part and parcel of the same general backwardness and misrule. They naturally looked to the Palestinians, especially those left-wing organizations like the PFLP which, like them, believed that only through the transformation of the whole existing order could the Arabs recover their strength and dignity as a nation, along with their lost province of Palestine. They came to be known as Muslim/leftists – although the coalition of parties, known as the National Movement, to which they belonged, included many, mainly Greek Orthodox, Christians too. Since they were mainly Sunnis it would have been normal enough, in Lebanon's old/new political culture, for a traditional Sunni grandee to have assumed its leadership. But, instead, and more remarkably, that role fell to Kemal Jumblat, hereditary leader of the Druzes, the small but strategically located sect that, like their historic adversaries, the Maronites, considered themselves the most rooted, most authentically 'Lebanese' of Lebanese. A cultured, Sorbonne-educated intellectual and socialist, Jumblat was at the same time the most archetypally seigneurial of the country's politicians. Modernist, anti-sectarian in his nation-wide, reformist ambitions, he could not but look to his essentially pre-modern, sectarian sources of authority, the clan solidarities and martial prowess of his community, as the mainspring of his bid to achieve his goals. He held sway from his family seat, the almost fairyland castle of Moukhtara, in the ancestral Druze heartland of Mount Lebanon.

It was chiefly among the Maronites, with their ingrained fear and mistrust of the pan-Arab or pan-Islamic in any form, that the automatic hostility to the Palestinian resistance arose, and automatically intensified at the spectacle of their Muslim compatriots' adherence to it. For them it was the Trojan Horse through which 'Christian Lebanon' would come under generalized assault. Ultimately, they deemed their identity and survival as a community to be at stake.[29] There were many poor Maronites who suffered under essentially the same socio-economic hardships and disabilities as their Muslim counterparts, but, fearful about the repercussions of change of any kind, they liked the 'revolutionary' or leftist aspects of the Muslim–Palestinian convergence as little as they did the merely sectarian ones. There was no comparable complexity or contradiction about the persons – and party – in whom the Maronites found their principal answer to Jumblat and his disparate array of allies. It was after a visit to the Berlin Olympics, where he was impressed by the discipline and strong sense of national identity he discerned in Hitler's Germany, that Pierre Gemayel, scion of a family of notables from the village of Bikfaya, in the Maronite heartland of 'the Mountain', founded the Lebanese Phalange. Fervent Lebanese nationalists, the Phalangists began life agitating – in concert with similarly rebellious Sunnis – for a sovereign Lebanon freed from French Mandatory rule. But confessionally minded as they were, conservative and authoritarian, their nationalism became inextricably bound up with a conviction that the Maronites, in their deep mistrust of Arabism, were the only true embodiment of it and that their own salvation as a community lay in a strong Lebanese state and their institutionalized ascendancy within it that their opponents were now seeking to dismantle.

There could be no 'Black September' against the Palestinians in Lebanon, because there was no central authority cohesive or resolute enough to carry one out. But there could be civil war, and a splintering of the central authority itself. As civil wars are apt to do, Lebanon's crept up by stealth, in an incremental interplay of action and reaction among all the players, internal and external, involved. But, as was only to be expected of the small, sectarian state, it was to surpass all others in its complexity, qualifying, in the opinion of British journalist Jim Muir, one of its most seasoned chroniclers, as 'perhaps the most convoluted to have stricken any part of the world ever'.[30]

RAIDS AND REPRISALS: THE INFERNAL CYCLE BEGINS

In the immediate aftermath of 1967, Palestinians began filtering down
to those southern frontier regions from where, a generation before, the
Mufti's men had operated in support of the Great Rebellion. They
could do very little because, thanks to the vigilance of the Deuxième
Bureau, they simply did not have the manpower for the job, and
because the Lebanese army was still heavily present, and active in
combating them. But after the battle of Karameh, young men went from
the Lebanese camps to train in Jordan's Ghor Valley;[31] then, as intensified Israeli reprisals made things more difficult there, they came back
to Lebanon, where Fatah had decided to open up a whole new, second
front, in order to supplement the Jordanian one. And it was partly with
the help of the Muslim/leftist opposition, and the oppressed and
impoverished Shiite villagers of the south, that they established their
first bases – and a clinic for the local population – in the wild and
remote Arkoub region, high up on the flanks of Mount Hermon, and
then spread westward and downward, the whole length of the frontier,
towards the Mediterranean.[32] A few minor operations, a mine-laying
here, a mortar round there, were still all they could manage. They were
enough, however, for Israel to begin those cross-border reprisals which,
on and off, it has been visiting on the country till this day. In May 1968,
the Shiite border village of Houle became its first victim; an artillery
salvo killed one woman, injured another and a child. That was a paltry
toll compared with the eighty who, in that self-same village's last
experience of Israeli violence, had died there in one of the massacres
of 1948.[33] But it was also – little though they knew it at the time – the
harbinger of almost unimaginably worse to come.

   In fact, it was not in reprisal for one of these cross-border guerilla
incursions that Lebanon suffered its first great, post-1967 shock, the first
really incontrovertible, and spectacular, indication that it was liable to
be drawn into the cycle of raid and retaliation which it had been spared
in the first two decades of the Arab–Israeli struggle. It grew out of that
other form of warfare, international terrorism, which, in addition to
regular guerilla operations, the Palestinians were now embarking on.
Ironically, it was the particular speciality of organizations, notably

George Habash's PFLP, which, in their earlier, Nasserist phase, had disapproved of 'armed struggle' of any kind, but which, in their new, Marxist, 'revolutionary' one, adopted it in this extreme and deliberately shocking form. In December 1968, two members of the PFLP machine-gunned a Boeing 707 of the Israeli national carrier, El Al, at Athens airport, killing one Israeli aboard and wounding another. The two men hailed from refugee camps in Lebanon. Two days later, helicopter-borne Israeli commandos landed at Beirut airport and systematically blew up thirteen passenger jets – almost the entire fleet – of Lebanon's national carrier, Middle East Airlines. Three days after that, the PFLP fired Russian-made Katyusha missiles across Israel's northern frontier; they killed three persons in the northern town of Kiryat Shmona, another 'first' (like the Israeli attack on Beirut airport) – this one in the opposite direction – which would repeat itself endlessly, and in the end devastatingly, down the years.

For a moment, the whole of Lebanon was in a daze. Given the efficiency, and sheer surprise, of the airport attack, no one could have seriously expected the Lebanese army to have countered it. But hardly had the country recovered from the shock than the Muslim/leftists went on a violent propaganda offensive against this Maronite-led institution, charging it with gross neglect of its duty – which, they said, was to defend Lebanon, as an Arab country, against Israel, not to thwart the legitimate activities of the Palestinian guerillas on its soil. The so-called 'Student Revolution' organized a general strike, accompanied by demonstrations in Beirut and several other cities, against the whole, dysfunctional ruling system. The traditional Muslim oligarchs, though hardly less anxious than their Christian counterparts to preserve this system, could not but bend before the strength of Muslim/leftist opinion. It tied them in knots of verbal ingenuity. Even as, on the one hand, the prime minister of the time, Abdullah Yafi, was denying, 'for the hundredth time', the existence of guerila bases on Lebanese territory, on the other he was endorsing the guerillas' 'sacred right' to liberate their land from Lebanon. When Maronite leaders opined that Lebanon's best defence lay in its weakness, in curbing the guerillas and giving Israel no pretext to attack it, the Muslim oligarchs claimed that its best defence was to protect and support them, by introducing

national conscription and coordinating its defences with other Arab
countries.

COUNTDOWN TO CIVIL WAR

In these contradictory responses lay the countdown to civil war. The cycle
was inexorable. The guerillas steadily intensified their operations. These
would come in one or other of their two, by now well-established, forms:
direct incursions across the southern border against Israel proper, or acts
of terror, hijackings and the like, against Israeli or non-Israeli targets in the
world at large. In either case Israel would hold Lebanon responsible in its
capacity as the main, and before long the only, quasi-independent
sanctuary of the entire resistance movement. Its steadily intensifying
retaliatory actions might be chiefly directed at the Palestinians, but,
accidentally or intentionally, they took in strictly Lebanese targets,
military or civilian, too. As in the case of the 'border wars' against its other
neighbours in the 1950s, Israel's objective, at least primarily and
ostensibly, was to inflict sufficient pain to persuade the 'host' to turn
against the 'guest'. And if it couldn't manage that – supposing that, in
truth, it ever really wanted to – it wouldn't really matter very much, not
at least for interventionists of the Ben-Gurion school. For them it was
straightforward enough: the greater the chaos in their northern
neighbour the greater the opportunities it would offer them to carry out
some or all of the geopolitical grand designs which, under the general
heading of 'Christian Lebanon', they had so long harboured.

   The 'host' did attempt to discipline or destroy the 'guest'. But it
could never do so without risk of destroying itself. It was, of course,
the anti-guerilla components of the ruling system, especially the
Maronite-dominated army and security forces, which were to lead the
attempt, while its pro-guerilla components, led by Sunni Muslim prime
ministers, checked them. So guerilla activities continued, and so did
Israeli reprisals. And with state authority paralyzed, the rival camps
that it was supposed to collectively represent, and reciprocally
neutralize, increasingly took matters into their own hands – although
the Maronites, their superior status threatened and their atavistic
minority fears aroused, did so a good deal more quickly and far-

reachingly in opposition to the Palestinians than the Muslim/leftists did so on the Palestinians' behalf.

Both sides drew in their respective, regional backers. Broadly speaking, that meant that the Arab states aligned themselves with the Palestinians and Muslim/leftists, albeit with all the twists and turns, equivocations and outright perfidies which those two score entities habitually deploy at each other's expense, while the Israelis – and usually, in their guile, some, at least, of those self-same Arab states too – aligned themselves with the Maronites.

All the while, the rising violence and counter-violence across the frontiers caused ever-growing havoc and disruption in the lives of the southern inhabitants, some 80 per cent of whom were Shiites. Driven now by fear and insecurity, as well as by material want, they emigrated in ever larger numbers to Beirut. There they became by far the largest component – alongside Sunni Muslims, Palestinians and not a few Maronites as well – in the city's outlying 'belt of misery', and notably the subsequently famous *al-Dahiya al-Janubiya*, 'the southern suburb' (or simply *al-Dahiya*, 'the suburb', as it generally came to be known), the vast new slum that had arisen hard by the refugee camps of Sabra, Shatila and Bourj al-Brajneh. Naturally, too, they became a further source of sectarian friction and socio-economic radicalization.

So it was that, in January 1969, despite the airport raid, the Palestinians pressed ahead with the implantation of their officially 'non-existent' bases in the south. The army tried to stop them. In April, it besieged the southern town of Bint Jbeil, to which some *fedayeen* had just returned upon completion of a raid into Israel. The Shiite towns-people refused to hand them over. For they looked on the Lebanese army more like an army of occupation than their own. For them the Palestinians suffered a similar kind of statelessness or state indifference as themselves; for some, indeed, the Palestinians' dispossession could be seen as their 'Karbala', the passion of the iconic Shiite martyr, Hussein. Furthermore, as well as deserving support as patriots in their own right, the Palestinians offered an instrument through which the Shiites could challenge Lebanon's own negligent, corrupt – and confessionally hostile – regime.[34] But after a three-day siege and threat of bombardment, it was the guerillas themselves who surrendered to avoid bloodshed.

When news of their imprisonment reached the capital, the Muslim/ leftists and the Palestinians called for a mass demonstration. The government banned it. And when, on 23 April, they went ahead regardless, the riot police – or army disguised as such – fired into the unarmed crowds. Each time it did so, the throng would pause, as victims fell among them, regroup, and resume their march to shouts of '*Asifa, Asifa*' ('Storm' – the name of Fatah's military wing). The result was a two-hour confrontation in which twenty died and hundreds were injured.[35] The prime minister resigned, plunging the system into more or less perpetual constitutional crisis. Arab states, led by Egypt, intervened diplomatically on behalf of the guerillas, who resumed their build-up in the south.

In May, the army tried again. Clashes left seven guerillas and two soldiers dead. Arafat brought yet more reinforcements to the south, raising the total to some 600, and cross-border operations rose threefold in less than three months.

In September, Israel issued a stern warning: either Lebanon kept the peace along the frontier, or Israel would do it in its stead. This growing truculence was not lost on the authorities, already seeking to appease Israel by striking on a new front: the refugee camps. But these, though basically defenceless still, were now boiling with revolutionary fervour. When the police entered the northernmost camp of Nahr al-Barid and demanded the demolition of the local Fatah office, they got a rude shock: the inhabitants took *them* hostage instead.[36] That triggered the resistance movement's greatest breakthrough yet – the '*Intifada* of the camps'. There were seventeen such camps in Lebanon, and by October every one of them had thrown out police, army and the hated Deuxième Bureau in a spontaneous, largely bloodless uprising. In urban areas especially, such as Sabra and Shatila, the refugees were helped by a militant, local Lebanese populace closely intermingled with their own. Unarmed Lebanese demonstrators overran local police stations, seized their weapons, and donated them to the camps.[37] Everywhere, their 'liberation' barely accomplished and Palestinian flags raised, the camp-dwellers organized themselves as self-governing, extra-territorial entities, citadels of mass support for the Revolution and recruitment into its ranks as *fedayeen*; among the first of their more self-indulgent priorities was the enlargement of their squalid homes by means of the cement and solid materials so long forbidden them.

Still, the army would not give up. In October, with the guerillas' presence in the south continuing to expand, it cut their vital supply lines from Syria, and surrounded 150 of them near Bint Jbeil and, apparently in coordination with the Israeli army, killed sixteen in a six-day siege.[38] Again the Sunni Muslim premier resigned; again there was uproar and demonstrations. It was accompanied, this time, by outright insurrection among the Muslim masses over whom he, and traditional leaders like him, were gradually losing their grip. Leftist militias seized control of parts of the two, predominantly Sunni Muslim, coastal cities of Tripoli and Sidon. Arab capitals erupted in street protests on the guerillas' behalf. President Nasser proclaimed that, henceforth, any Arab government would be judged by its attitude towards them. However strictly it might control guerilla activities on its own territory, militantly leftist Baathist Syria, self-styled 'citadel of Arabism', had no qualms about condemning that practice in others, setting a pattern of behaviour that has persisted till this day. It closed its borders with Lebanon, attacked Lebanese military positions along them, and urged the Lebanese people to 'sweep away their treasonable [ruling] clique and assume their full role in the Arab battle'. Even conservative Arab regimes, fearful though they were of the explosive mix of Palestinian resistance and Arab radicalism, took the guerillas' side.

Besieged on all hands, President Charles Helou appealed for Nasser's mediation. Under the 'Cairo agreement' which that mediation yielded, the guerillas converted their *de facto*, but officially contested, presence in Lebanon into a *de jure* one. They acquired the right not merely to control the camps, but, most fatefully, to launch attacks on Israel through certain 'corridors' in the south; to launch them, moreover, with the assistance of, and in coordination with, the self-same Lebanese army which had been so desperately trying to prevent them doing just that. It was in effect, the charter of Fatahland, of the guerilla 'state-within-a-state', of the vital and – following his expulsion from Jordan nine months later – the one and only politico-military power base at Arafat's disposal for the conduct of the Palestinian struggle.

Another breakthrough, a triumph even, for the Palestinians and their Lebanese allies, it was, *ipso facto*, a very disturbing reverse for the other side: a betrayal of national sovereignty, a capitulation to the Arab and Muslim exterior, a body blow to Maronite domestic ascendancy, and a portent of more to come. It nurtured an already budding apprehension that, in the end, salvation might only come with the removal of the Palestinians, that this might only be attainable by force, and, if not the army's force, then that of the Maronite community itself. There began a process of non-state militarization. The Phalangists already boasted a militia, which they now strengthened, but others, such as followers of the former President Chamoun, or the northern Maronite 'strongman' and future president, Suleiman Frangieh, joined in.[39] And, naturally enough, those 'pro-Zionist' tendencies within the community, always latent but in retreat since at least the mini civil war of 1958, bestirred themselves again. An Israel at the height of its military pride and self-confidence could offer much to tempt them.[40] Most Maronite deputies reluctantly voted for the Cairo agreement whose text, a state secret, they had never actually read. The Lebanese state, said Pierre Gemayel, the Phalangist leader, was 'faced with two evils, a destructive civil war or this accord'.[41] Five years later, it was to get the war as well.

CHAPTER FIVE

Civil War in Lebanon

Proxy war for everyone else: 1975–1976

'SARAJEVO'

On the morning of Sunday, 13 April 1975, 'Sheikh Pierre' attended the consecration of a new church, in a street bearing his name, in Beirut's poor and populous Christian surburb of Ain al-Rummana. Four Phalangist militiamen, including one of his bodyguards, died in the scuffle that broke out between them and the armed, unidentified occupants of two passing cars. That same morning, Palestinian refugees had also been attending a ceremony of a very different kind: the first anniversary of an unusually successful guerilla raid on the northern Israeli town of Kiryat Shmona. A group of them were returning to the camp of Tal al-Za'atar, which lay on the eastern, Christian side of town. They had to pass through the Ain al-Rummana suburb to get there, and as they did so, Phalangist gunmen ambushed the bus in which they were travelling and shot dead twenty-seven unarmed passengers, including women and children.[1]

This was the 'Sarajevo of the Lebanese civil war',[2] though few people understood that at the time. For it looked like just another, albeit exceptionally serious, episode in that incremental interplay of developments – military, political or socio-economic, internal, external or the two combined – which, since the resistance movement descended on Lebanon, had been pushing it towards the brink, but never, so far, quite over it. These had been plentiful indeed, but a few random, if salient, examples suffice to give a sense of them:

- In March 1970 – and in the very same Maronite village of Kahhaleh which only two years before had so enthusiastically, so ecumenically mourned Palestine's first Lebanese 'martyr' – militiamen ambushed the funeral cortège of a Palestinian commander and shot ten guerillas dead. For several days thereafter Phalangists clashed with guerillas around the refugee camps, Tal al-Za'atar in particular; there were fears – even then – that Lebanese/Palestinian hostilities might broaden into intra-Lebanese, Christian/Muslim ones; they were only laid to rest with the help of Arab mediators.

- In May 1972 the PFLP, headquartered on a central Beirut thoroughfare, sponsored a massacre of tourists at Tel Aviv airport by kamikaze commandos of the Japanese Red Army. With Lebanon thereafter firmly established in its eyes as the 'host to murderers, to terrorists ... to all elements plotting against [it]',[3] Israel stepped up its border warfare from one of mere tit-for-tat reprisals, punishing though those already were, to the continuous 'hitting [of] terrorists wherever they are – and they are in Lebanon'.[4] In an echo of General Dayan's grandiose but never implemented project to 'create a Christian regime that [would] ally itself with Israel', Israel also began to talk of seizing and indefinitely holding Lebanese territory; indeed, in the deep South, a Christian officer, Major Saad Haddad, had already gone over to its side.[5] Throughout the year, Israel mounted air, artillery and gunboat attacks in which scores, even hundreds – Lebanese as well as Palestinians, civilians as well as soldiers and guerillas – were sometimes killed or wounded at a time. In the heaviest of these attacks, following the murder of Israeli athletes by Palestinian terrorists at the Olympic Games in Munich, nearly 200 travellers, mainly Lebanese or Syrian, died in the retaliatory strafing, on a public holiday, of the Beirut–Damascus highway.

- In April 1973, in a particularly audacious raid, Israeli commandos landed offshore from Beirut, drove into the heart of the city, killed (among others) three top Palestinian leaders, and made their getaway by the same means. If it even knew about it before it was over, the Lebanese army did nothing to stop them. The Sunni prime minister, Saeb Salam, demanded the dismissal of the army commander, but, spurned by the Maronite president, Suleiman Frangieh, he resigned himself. Denouncing 'collusion in theory and practice' between the Lebanese and Israeli governments, Druze leader Kemal Jumblat called Lebanon 'a state without honour'.[6] Then, in what amounted to a 'dress rehearsal' for civil war, some 150 Lebanese and Palestinians, soldiers, guerillas and civilians, died in the fighting – the heaviest yet – that erupted across the capital.[7] Mirage and Hawker Hunter fighters of the Lebanese air force, unused against any foreign foe, went into action for the first time: their targets – the refugee camps of Sabra, Shatila and Bourj al-Brajneh, or guerilla positions within them, already under tank and artillery fire. But operations ended in another humiliation for the army; and President Frangieh privately advised Maronite parties 'not to rely on the army after today, but on yourselves'.[8]

• In March 1974, with Shiite villagers now fleeing in greater numbers than ever for the capital's 'belt of misery', the *Dahiya* in particular, the up-and-coming, charismatic Iranian cleric of Lebanese descent, Musa Sadr, launched his so-called Movement of the Deprived at a huge rally in Baalbek. In his inaugural address, he described weapons as 'an ornament of man', and announced that he would open training camps for all Shiites who wished to defend their homes against Israeli aggression – if the Lebanese army would not do it on their behalf. He made it clear that, though he believed in the Palestinians' right to resistance, he was not very impressed by the way they went about it; they lacked the Shiites' 'sense of martyrdom'.[9] The training camps gave birth to Amal, a Shiite militia, which, clandestine at first, eventually evolved into the main political party of this 'crushed but awakened community' as a whole.[10] In further rallies, the largest and most fervent of their kind ever seen in Lebanon, he denounced the country's ruling elite as corrupt, monopolistic and socially insensitive, and threatened that his followers would attack and occupy the palaces and mansions of the rich and powerful if the plight of the poor and oppressed continued to go unheeded.[11] It 'sent shivers down oligarchic backs'.[12]

• In February 1975, Maarouf Saad, a popular Nasserist deputy in the
Sunni Muslim town of Sidon, was shot and mortally wounded when
the demonstration he was leading came face to face with army units
assigned to escort it. The demonstrators were protesting against the
concession awarded to an offshore fishing monopoly – headed by
none other than former president and Maronite grandee, Camille
Chamoun – which seemed to pose a grievous threat to the livelihood of thousands of traditional fishermen, in Sidon and pretty
much everywhere else. Palestinian guerillas from the nearby refugee
camp of Ain al-Hilweh, Lebanon's largest, joined their Muslim/
leftist allies in bloody clashes with the army. The incident
epitomized the intertwining of the socio-economic, the sectarian
and the Palestinian, those three characteristic ingredients of the
whole, ever more noxious brew. With the traditional Muslim
leadership openly endorsing *their* 'street's' clamour for dismantling
Maronite domination of the army, and the Christian leadership,
massively backed by theirs, insisting on its preservation, inter-
communal showdown loomed over the one institution whose
cohesion had saved the country in the mini civil war of 1958.

IT WAS A CIVIL WAR, BUT A REGIONAL ONE TOO: LEBANON THE BATTLEGROUND OF THE MIDDLE EAST

It was months before the full-scale civil war which actually *had* begun
that Sunday morning in that otherwise unremarkable Beirut slum was
generally understood to be one. It had started as a series of sporadic
skirmishes, or 'rounds' as they came, in their almost clockwork
regularity, to be known, shifting from place to place and steadily
escalating in scale and intensity. The skirmishes were punctuated by
formal or informal ceasefires, any one of which, it was fondly hoped at
the time, was going to end it. But, in the event, the ceasefires were to
run into the hundreds, lasting from a few hours to a few months or even
years, before the one – in October 1990 – that finally held. In the full
fifteen years that it ultimately endured this civil war would go through
several distinctive phases, and the most labyrinthine of geographic,
strategic and inter-communal permutations. But, very broadly speak-

ing, it fell into two main halves. The first, the 'Palestinian' one, ended with the departure of Yasser Arafat and the PLO in 1982; the principal feature of the second was the rise of the Iranian-backed, militantly Islamist, anti-Israeli guerilla movement, Hizbullah.

From the outset it was very much a *civil* war. It pitted Lebanese against Lebanese. And what they were fighting about, those questions of identity and belonging that had perplexed them ever since their country came into being, the dominion of the Maronites over the others, the reforms to correct this state of affairs for which those others clamoured – all that, and more, was strictly Lebanese too.

But, directly or by proxy, it was a *regional* war as well. To be sure, the Lebanese supplied its internal causes. But so intense, so congenital was the continuous interaction between their complicated country and the no less complicated region to which it belonged that – like binary chemicals which are only active when one element comes in contact with another – these would never actually have constituted cause at all without the input from outside. It was only the impact of regional factors – especially the coming of the Palestinians – on the pre-existing local ones that triggered the conflict, just as it was to be regional and international ones that would finally bring it to an end. Lebanon had always been other people's political or diplomatic battleground; now, 'war being' – in the Clausewitzian dictum – 'nothing but the continuation of politics with the admixture of other means', it was their full-blooded, their violent and military one too.

The conflict, then, was not just about the future of Lebanon, but of the whole Middle East, and, above all, about the place which Israel sought within it. For, thirty years after the Jewish state had come into being, just what kind of place that would be was still the region's central, unfinished business, still, as historian Albert Hourani had very early described it, 'the universal problem intruding into every political relationship in the Middle East'.[13] Ever since the Western sponsors of Israel had created this problem they had striven incessantly to solve it. But, by the mid-seventies, all that the so-called 'peace process' had come to signify was a great deal of 'process' – a great accumulation of wrangling, obduracy and delay – matched by very little tangible advance towards its well-nigh impossible goal – Israel's acceptance by an Arab world that viscerally rejected it. There was still no peace treaty, no formal recognition of one another's existence, between Israel and any of its neighbours; and it didn't look like there ever would be. There was only an ad hoc assembly of provisional arrangements – from the original armistice agreements to a host of supplementary ones that further hostilities had engendered – which 'contained' the problem, but did very little to settle it. It was all but inevitable that if the outside world could not accomplish that by peaceful means, Israel would sooner or later seek to do so by the violent ones on which the Zionist enterprise had always chiefly relied; if Arab acceptance could not be voluntarily conferred, it would have to be forcibly extracted. Lebanon was the arena in which the inevitable now came to pass.

THE PALESTINIANS TRIGGERED THE WAR, BUT ISRAEL TRULY WAGED IT

So not surprisingly, of all the external actors in the war, Israel was to be the chief by any measure, be it the scale of its ambition or the havoc that it wrought. While the Palestinians may have triggered it, it was Israel that would truly make it. For now, at last, its historic opportunity was at hand. Now it was going to implement that grand design, that 'fantastic' plan, of which its founder, Ben-Gurion, had always spoken, but never realized.[14] It was going to transform 'Christian Lebanon' into the 'natural' ally which Israel had always deemed it to be, and then – the 'periphery' acting on the 'centre' – to transform the whole region too, dismantling what was left of the Arab nationalists' Middle East, united in its hostility to the newcomer, and replacing it with the Zionists' one, a 'pluralist' Middle East, a 'mosaic' of minorities. And among these minorities, Israel was going to emerge so uniquely powerful that it would impose its quasi-imperial sway over all the rest. Now, at last, had come the great challenge, and, God willing, triumphant vindication, of Ben-Gurion's interventionist school of thought, of the use of force as the solution to every problem in which the interventionists put their faith. It was time for the 'war of choice', open and unashamed. Gone were the days when the Israel Defence Forces had at least presumed – myth though that had always largely been – to justify its name, when this people's army only mobilized and fought for the nation's very survival in wars of its enemies' choosing. Now defence had become outright offence, or, as Kirsten Schulze, chronicler of Israel's covert and not-so-covert doings in Lebanon, put it, 'war was no longer evil or immoral, but ... an instrument to achieve political goals'. These goals themselves should be 'determined' by one thing only: the 'military ability' to accomplish them. Since Israel 'had the power to dictate a military solution' (to the entire Arab–Israeli conflict), it 'should use it'. It should engage in nothing less than 'completely unprovoked, broad, active, military operations aimed at changing the geostrategic make-up of the Middle East'.[15]

The Israelis' principal adversaries were that other external actor on the Lebanese stage, the Palestinians. Initially, the Palestinian resistance had come to Lebanon to fight, and only to fight, the Israelis. And, officially, they were still wedded to 'complete liberation' and 'armed struggle' as their sole means of achieving it. In this, their continued militancy, they were still so to speak the progeny of the 1967 war, the debacle of Arabism which it consummated and the radicalism to which it gave rise. But in reality, while Israel had been growing more ambitious, belligerent and extreme, in relation to their original aims the Palestinians had been growing more moderate.

In the Fourth Arab–Israeli War – that of October 1973, and the only one, so far, which the Arabs, not Israel, incontestably began – Egypt and Syria had not emerged victorious. On the contrary, Syria had been clearly defeated, and Egypt very nearly so. But they did inflict a huge strategic and political shock on Israel, and, by extension, on the United States, its indefectible friend and protector. With this, the official Arab order – and especially the one-time 'revolutionary', nationalist parts of it – which had so discredited itself in 1967 achieved a partial recovery, as well as a very considerable shift in the Arabs' favour of the whole regional and international balance of power. So the Arab world decided to exploit the new balance not to pursue the conflict, but to end it. Or at least its 'great power', Egypt, so decided, and, 'radicals' or 'rejectionists' like Iraq and Libya aside, all the member-states of the Arab League collectively endorsed its decision. They threw themselves into the re-invigorated 'peace process' over which, in the person of

Dr Henry Kissinger, the US all but exclusively presided. The Palestinians now sought to insert themselves into the process too. Or, to be more precise, Arafat and the mainstream Fatah leadership sought to do so; for the Palestinians also had their 'radicals' and 'rejectionists', led by Habash's PFLP, who kicked and screamed against it.

FROM PROVISIONAL STATE-IN-EXILE TO PERMANENT ONE IN PALESTINE

What Arafat and his supporters wanted, first of all, was international recognition, for the PLO, as the 'sole, legitimate representative' of the Palestinian people. They already had it from all the Arab states, and some twenty others; and the PLO enjoyed observer status at the United Nations. But they wanted it too – and above all – from the US. For the US still refused to acknowledge that the Palestinian people *were* a people – as opposed to mere refugees – with a people's right to self-determination and statehood like any other, or even that they occupied a central place in the conflict. As for the PLO, American governments still regarded it not merely as an unrepresentative institution, but as a 'terrorist' one to boot; and in any case they were bound – by a secret promise Kissinger had made to Israel – never to enter into negotiations with it until it recognized Israel's 'right to exist'.[16]

Unfavourable though the prospects for diplomacy therefore looked at the time, it was nonetheless diplomacy, as an accessory to 'armed struggle', to which Arafat and his mainstream were now unquestionably turning as their means, and something less – much less – than 'complete liberation' to which they were turning as their aim. Under the 'provisional programme' which the Palestine National Council (PNC), or parliament-in-exile, had adopted in 1974, the Palestinians would now accept the establishment of a 'national authority' on any portion of Palestine which they, or the Arabs, managed to liberate by diplomatic or military means, without, however, forfeiting their 'historic right' to the whole of it. This was the beginning of the 'policy of moderation' which eventually led, via the PNC conference of 1988 and the Oslo accord of 1993, to that formula, the so-called 'two-state solution', which virtually the whole world now regards as the basis for a final settlement:

the Palestinians would confine themselves to a state established on the 22 per cent of historic Palestine comprised by the West Bank and Gaza, while relinquishing the remaining 78 per cent, once theirs too, comprised by the original Israel of 1948.

With diplomacy, the Palestinians certainly did not abandon their military option altogether. Ideologically, that would have been no less difficult, at this stage, than renouncing 'complete liberation' as their ultimate, if now theoretical, dream – pragmatically, too, given the ferocity with which Palestinian 'rejectionists' would have opposed it. But they could, and did, increasingly subordinate it to diplomacy. They still had *fedayeen* in plenty, and they still mounted attacks on Israel. But, as a matter of deliberate policy, these became rarer and rarer. And, as they did so, the more specific, if paradoxical, became the message which, in effect, they were intended to convey to Israel and the friends of Israel: 'If you would only deal with us diplomatically perhaps we wouldn't have to attack you at all.' Meanwhile, more and more of the *fedayeen* were simultaneously turning into conventional soldiers in a conventional army. And the bigger and stronger, on paper at least, that army became, with its artillery, its armoured cars and its ancient, Soviet-built T-34 tanks, the more manifestly defensive its function became as well. Even its growing abundance of Katyusha missiles – the emblematic weapon, *par excellence*, of Lebanese/Israeli cross-frontier warfare – was not offensive, but deterrent or retaliatory in purpose. What this army was defending was the Palestine state-in-exile, the 'Fakhani Republic', of which it was an intrinsic part. And the purpose of that provisional entity – embodiment of the Palestinians' national cause, expression of their independent will, and platform of their struggle – was to win the world's recognition and then to hold its own, come what may, until the world accorded them their permanent one: their Palestine state in Palestine itself.[7]

THE ARAB STATES WAGE REGIONAL WAR BY PROXY

Then, of course, there were the Arab states. 'Rejectionists' apart, they all wanted a settlement for the Palestinians; and each of the four 'front-line' states wanted one for itself as well. They were supposed to go about this collectively. But they soon fell into their habitual disarray, with none other than Egypt and Syria, allies in war, becoming the bitterest opponents in the quest for peace. President Sadat, stealing his way towards that separate Israeli–Egyptian peace agreement, ruinous for everyone else, which he had sworn he would never make, was chiefly responsible for that. Inevitably, it was in Lebanon that their dispute found its most virulent expression. In this post-Nasser, post-nationalist era of *wataniyah*, of 'every Arab state for itself', Syria had by now replaced Egypt as the principal Arab actor on the Lebanese stage. Indeed, Lebanon was now assuming that primordial importance for President Hafiz al-Asad and his Baathist regime which it has retained till this day: a strategic asset, and inestimable accretion of their own power, to the extent that they controlled or dominated it; a liability, and source of dangerous, even fatal, weakness, to the extent that they lost control of it to adversaries ever ready to prise it from them. President Asad now sought to construct a regional, a Greater-Syrian power base from which to conduct a rival peace-seeking strategy of his own. It was to be built round three countries, Jordan, Syria and Lebanon, and four peoples, with the PLO representing the Palestinians. What he sought in Lebanon was basically hegemony and control – over the Lebanese of course, but especially over the Palestinians – and the consequent ability to incite them against the kind of peace that he could not accept, or in favour of one he could. To this end he sometimes had to support the Palestinians and their Lebanese allies, sometimes to oppose them. President Sadat's only rule, in response, was to switch sides too, to be *for* whoever Asad at any one time was *against*. These were the two main antagonists in what amounted to an Arab regional war by proxy, but others – Iraq, Jordan, Libya or Saudi Arabia – were always in there too, often with high-minded, pan-Arab or anti-Israeli agendas that masked the most vicious and inextinguishable of inter-Arab feuds.

THE LEBANESE CONTENDERS: CONSERVATIVE MARONITES VERSUS REFORMIST MUSLIM/LEFTISTS

In the initial phase, 1975–6, it was the *civil* war that predominated. This did not mean that the regional one played no part in it, or even that the two key external actors in this phase, the Palestinians and the Syrians, were not decisive to its outcome. They very much were. After all, it had been a particularly savage Phalangist attack on the Palestinians, and the Palestinian response to it, out of which the whole conflict originally grew. It simply meant that the internal actors, the Lebanese themselves, led the way.

'Reform through arms' is what, for the National Movement, the coalition of Muslim/leftist parties, it all came down to. Resisting reform by the self-same means, initially and tactically at least, was what it meant for the Lebanese Front, the Phalangist-dominated coalition of right-wing Maronite parties. In its programme for the 'democratic reform' of Lebanon's 'backward, sectarian, semi-feudal political system', the National Movement called for the abolition of 'political sectarianism' in the legislature, the civil service, the judiciary and the army: the abolition, that is to say, of the entitlement of every sect to a parliamentary representation proportional to its share of the population, and the allocation of state employment on the same rigorous, if less formal, lines. Although the programme made no express reference to the Maronite ascendancy that the sectarian state enshrined, it was this ascendancy at which such reforms – hardly revolutionary in any other context but Lebanon – would have struck. For their part, the traditional Muslim elite were ready for reform of an altogether more modest kind, mere modifications, in their community's favour, of the existing system, rather than a root-and-branch assault on the system itself. In a formal dialogue, it proposed them to their Maronite counterparts.

But these would have neither. 'Consciously or unconsciously', said the Lebanese Front, 'the Muslim majority is oppressive, and a danger for the sheer existence of the Christians in all of Lebanon.' Reform, said Pierre Gemayal, was 'playing with fire'.[18] The Phalangists, said his son Amin, 'had recourse to violence ... to conserve the system ... to save the institutions from any change'.[19]

Thus, there was total deadlock on the political front; and once the fighting had started, total deadlock developed on the military one too. The Maronites wanted 'security' before 'reform'. And they wanted the army to provide it. Their desire was hardly surprising, given that, through the Maronite president, Frangieh, and the Maronite minister of the interior, Chamoun, that Maronite-dominated institution was already aiding and abetting the Maronite militias, one of which, the Tigers, just happened to be Chamoun's own.[20] What they really meant by 'security' was the suppression of Palestinian support for the Muslim/leftists as a prelude to suppressing the Muslim/leftists themselves.[21]

Naturally, the Muslim/leftists, being militarily weaker than the Maronites, put reform before security, with the Palestinians as *their* 'army' to help them achieve it. Arafat did not really want to play such a role – the PLO, he said, was 'not a sect or the adjunct of a sect – nor does it wish to be'[22] – but, by now, his movement was so entangled, in a reciprocal dependence, with its Lebanese allies that when things got serious he had little choice but to do so. George Habash and left-wing 'rejectionist' groups had no such qualms; for them, to support like-minded allies was to hasten the revolutionary transformation of which the whole Arab world, not just Lebanon, stood in crying need.[23]

FLYING ROADBLOCKS AND IDENTITY CARD KILLINGS

The fighting intensified, but the army still didn't go in; the Muslim premier, Rashid Karami, saw to that. And, with 'round' after escalating 'round', the fighting eventually slid into outright civil war, and into those characteristic forms of contemporary inter-communal combat of which Lebanon was a pioneer: the 'identity card killing', when militiamen of one community would seize any non-combatants on whom they chanced, check their papers to find out which 'side' they belonged to, and shoot them on the spot or kidnap them, if it was the wrong one; the dreaded 'flying roadblocks', suddenly sprung from nowhere, at which these kidnap/killings typically occurred; the snipers in one quarter who picked off anything that moved in the adjoining 'enemy' one; the massive, cross-city artillery bombardments whose first, and deadliest, salvos always took their victims totally unawares in the public places where they happened to be, out shopping, driving to work, reading a newspaper on a terrace, strolling on the sea-front Corniche, or reclining on a beach.

With 'Black Saturday', there came a fateful escalation in the intensifying cycle of tit-for-tat atrocities. These, though still driven by a vengeful momentum of their own, now fused with what was emerging as the higher strategic objective of both sides: the carving out of clear and uncontested control over territories which they considered to be essentially 'theirs': territories, that is to say, in which they, or the communities that made them up, had been historically and demographically dominant. For one side, the Maronites, the process carried more than a hint of eventual partition, and reversion of 'Christian Lebanon' to its reduced dimension of old, which was anathema to the other. The principal battleground was the capital.

After waking – that Saturday morning of 6 December 1975 – to the news that four of their commanders had been killed by unknown assailants during the night, Phalangist militiamen went on a mad, spontaneous rampage of summary, roadblock 'executions'. Right there, on the coastal highway, one of the city's busiest arteries, with the port on one side and the headquarters of Electricité du Liban on the other, just a minute's drive into the Christian half of town from the predominantly Muslim one – right there they shot every passing Muslim on whom they could lay hands; at least 200 died in the two-day pogrom that ensued. The Muslim/leftists responded with a major assault on the three great hotels, the St George, the Phoenicia and the Holiday Inn, in the fashionable, cosmopolitan heart of the city. They chose those targets mainly for strategic reasons: the hotels constituted the head of a Phalangist salient that projected deeply into Muslim West Beirut. In response to that, the Phalangists began the 'sectarian cleansing' of some 300,000 Muslims, mainly Shiite, and Palestinians who happened to have fetched up in a part of Beirut's 'poverty belt' which lay on the Christian side of town. They started with the smallest and easiest target, the Maslakh-Karantina coastal slum, overran it after a three-day battle, killed about a thousand of its 30,000 inhabitants and expelled the rest to West Beirut. With Palestinian help, the Muslim/ leftists then overran Damur, a small Maronite town that lay, in *their* domain, on the coastal road a few kilometres south of the capital, sacked it, killed some 150 of its inhabitants, and drove out the rest.

SYRIA STEPS INTO THE FRAY

Alarmed by these developments, that other external actor, Syria, now stepped firmly into the fray. At first, President Asad had thrown most of his weight, albeit cautiously, behind his natural allies, the Palestinians and Muslim/leftists, believing as he did that the Phalangists were on the offensive, and that their motives, secessionist and sectarian, ran counter to all that his pan-Arabist, Baathist regime officially stood for. He also believed that they were acting on America, Israel, and Egypt's behalf, and that these three powers sought not just to destroy – or in Egypt's case judiciously weaken – the Palestinian cause of which he deemed himself the foremost Arab sponsor, but to cut *him* down to size as well, break his opposition to President Sadat's go-it-alone, peace-seeking diplomacy and the latest, shameless, Israeli–Egyptian disengagement agreement, Sinai II, which Kissinger had just pulled off. Asad sponsored a charter of reform as the basis for a new political equilibrium of which he would henceforth be the guardian. The so-called 'constitutional document' provided for a modest adjustment of the National Pact in the Muslims' favour; among other things, they would now get half the seats in parliament instead of only a ratio of five to the Christians' six which had been their entitlement hitherto. But the document left Maronite ascendancy essentially intact. It won the acceptance of the embattled Maronite president. And it was good enough for the Muslim oligarchs.

But it angered the Muslim/leftists – as well as a disgruntled Sunni Muslim army officer. Constantly passed over for promotion by his Maronite superiors, Lieutenant Ahmad Khatib was apparently fired by personal pique as well as higher political principle when he proclaimed the formation of the breakaway Lebanese Arab Army (LAA), carried 2,000 Muslim soldiers with him, and took control of most barracks in the country. The national army was no more. The rebels threw in their lot with the Muslim/leftists, whose leader, Jumblat, in outright defiance of the Syrians, proclaimed that they would take over the whole country and 'change the system within the framework of a total revolution'. His 'joint forces' – the LAA, Muslim/leftists and the Palestinians – then launched big offensives in Beirut and in the mountains that overlooked the Maronite heartland. They quickly demolished the Phalangist salient in West Beirut, and, after advances in the mountains, were poised to push deep into the Maronite interior, where panic took hold and thousands prepared to flee by sea. Asad now rounded on his former allies, 'merchants of religion and revolution',[24] and sent in his army to save their enemies. Not merely was he afraid to lose the precious Palestinian 'card' in his diplomatic hand; even worse was the prospect that, together, Palestinians and Muslim/leftists might turn Lebanon, or their part of it, into a hotbed of revolutionary militancy, a 'Cuba' of the region, a platform for uncontrollable military escalation against Israel, and an avenue of subversion against himself. They would be doing this not just for themselves of course, but for all his Arab opponents, and chief among them Saddam Hussein and his hated Baathist rivals in Baghdad.[25] Another prospect, hardly less dire, was that the Maronites might be pushed into that open alliance with Israel of which its interventionists had always dreamed. Either eventuality would have dangerous, even regime-threatening repercussions inside Syria itself.

ASAD JOINS THE ENEMY CAMP

But it was an almost unthinkable volte-face. To send his army against the Palestinian guerillas, however imperfect an embodiment of the supreme Arab cause they might be, was as grave a heresy as any Syrian ruler could commit, and especially when, for all the pan-Arabist façade, that ruler belonged, as Asad did, to a small minority sect, the Alawites, and heavily, if surreptitiously, depended on it to preserve his autocratic regime in power. In Lebanon, openly and officially, sectarianism *was* the system; in Syria, though hidden and officially excoriated, it was, in a no less crucial if very different way, very much the system too. Perhaps the deepest, disreputable secret of Asad's rescue of the Maronites was the illicit sympathy it betrayed of one religious minority for another. No wonder the Americans and the Israelis found no objection to it, that in his memoirs Kissinger subsequently boasted of the 'astonishing reversal of fronts' he had helped to bring about, of an Israel 'serving as an arms supplier of the Christians even while Syria

was acting – temporarily at least – as their protector',[26] or that Israeli
Prime Minister Yitzhak Rabin once marvelled that 'forces operating
under Syrian control in Lebanon have killed more terrorists in the past
week than Israel has in the past two years'.[27]

In a three-stage offensive from April to October 1976, the Syrian
army steadily overwhelmed Syria's former allies, while, with Israeli-
supplied Sherman tanks and Syrian artillery support, its new-found
friends, the Maronite militias, laid siege to the last remaining
inhabitants of the Shiite slum of Naba'a, with a population of some
200,000, and the 30,000 Palestinians still left in their Tal al-Za'atar
camp. The defenders didn't really stand a chance. Tal al-Za'atar held
out for fifty-three days in appalling conditions of hunger and thirst,
untreated wounds, continuous shelling and tank-fire at almost point-
blank range; 3,500 died, between 1,000 and 2,000 of them after the camp
had fallen, crushed under bulldozers, shot and hacked to death, or
finished off by militiamen, or just ordinary folk on whom they chanced
in their desperate flight to the safety of Muslim West Beirut.[28]

AFTER 56 TRUCES, THE ARABS IMPOSE A LONGER ONE THAN USUAL

In the end, it was only the diplomatic intervention of the Arab world,
combined with the fierce resistance of the Palestinians, that checked
the Syrian advance. An Arab world which would not or could not move
to prevent the tragedy of Tal al-Za'atar, where only lives were at stake,
bestirred itself for things of greater moment: balances of power, spheres
of influence and the prestige of regimes. Syria was breaking all the rules
of *Realpolitik*, arrogating to itself, by brute force, a regional pre-
ponderance which its Arab 'sister-states' could not tolerate. So now,
when Arafat made his anguished appeal for an end to this 'massacre of
our people', the kings and presidents heeded him. It was time, they
decided, to stop this civil war that had expanded, both directly and by
proxy, into an inter-Arab regional one. An Arab summit conference
proclaimed a general ceasefire. Asad grudgingly rejoined the 'peace
process'; Sadat and the others grudgingly acknowledged Syria's pride
of place in the Arab Deterrent Force that would police the new status
quo in Lebanon. In that now broken and fragmented land, a single state

authority, manned by the old elite, remained at least symbolically, and, up to a point, functionally intact. But, in terms of real power and control, the Maronite militias, a shadow government in all but name,[29] presided over a fiefdom – popularly known as 'Marounistan' – incorporating most of the Mount Lebanon of yore. Arafat had preserved, even consolidated, his guerilla state-within-the-state, which held exclusive sway in southern areas, where Israel would not let the Syrians tread, and an uneasy joint one in the rest of the country where it did. But the ceasefire, the fifty-sixth since the war began, was no more than a truce, albeit a longer one than usual. No one was happy, not the Muslim/leftists, the main losers, whom the Syrians had robbed of all their reforms, not the Maronites, or at least those of them who wanted Greater Lebanon back, one and whole, with Palestinians, Syrians and other Arabs gone. In the next phase, however, it was, from the outset, the regional war that would shape and dominate the local one, and of the external actors engaging in it an interventionist Israel at the apogee of its power, arrogance and ambition would tower over all the rest.[30]

CHAPTER SIX

Imperial Hubris

Israel wages 'chosen war' in Lebanon: 1977–1982

THE FIFTH ARAB–ISRAELI WAR

On 6 June 1982, Israel went to war against its northern neighbour, killed some 20,000 people,[1] overwhelmingly civilians, in three months of land, sea and aerial assault; laid its first ever siege to an Arab capital, Beirut; drove out Yasser Arafat and the PLO leadership; destroyed the guerilla state-within-the-state; and presided over the Phalangists' massacre of Sabra and Shatila, by no means the largest such genocidal, or quasi-genocidal, slaughter of the twentieth century, but perhaps the most hideously ironic.

The Fifth Arab–Israeli War – or the First Lebanon War as, since July/August 2006, some Israelis now call it – had its roots in two historic developments, neither of which had anything particular to do with Lebanon. One was the coming to power of Menachem Begin, the leader of the right-wing Likud Party; the other was the Israel–Egypt peace treaty.

Begin's electoral triumph in May 1977 had been a political earthquake. As we have seen, the Labour Party, which had ruled Israel since its creation, practised what the Revisionist leader, Vladimir Jabotinsky, with his doctrine of the Iron Wall, had preached, even as it ostensibly disowned it. But here, coming into his own after twenty-nine years in the wilderness, was Jabotinsky's direct political heir, the embodiment, or not far from it, of what at the time was Zionism at its most chauvinist and extreme. Here was the man who, as chief of the Irgun terrorists, had, at Deir Yassin, perpetrated the atrocity which did more than any other to put the Palestinians to flight in 1948; the man of whom Ben-Gurion had said that, when listening to his speeches, he 'heard the voice and screeching of Hitler', and that – if he ever came to power – 'he [would] lead the State of Israel to its destruction'.[2] Two days after his election Begin chose the West Bank settlement of Kaddoum from which to proclaim that, as 'the property of the Jewish people', the 'liberated' territories of 'Judea and Samaria' would never be yielded up. That, at a stroke, made an utter nonsense of Arafat's diplomacy of 'moderation'. It was also a resounding snub to Jimmy Carter, the least anti-Palestinian American president since Eisenhower, who had formally acknowledged this moderation, led the Palestinians to believe that it would earn them the response it deserved, and dared to assert, to the consternation of Israel and the 'friends of Israel' in America, that a 'homeland' should be found for the refugees,'who have suffered for many, many years'.[3]

The Israeli–Egyptian peace treaty was the first between the Jewish state and any of its neighbours. Originating in President Sadat's historic pilgrimage to Jerusalem in October 1977 and concluded in March 1979, it wrought a fundamental change in the whole Middle East balance of power. Indeed, a great many Arabs perceived it at the time as an historic calamity, a lineal descendant of those earlier ones – the Sykes–Picot Agreement, the Balfour Declaration, the rise of Israel and the 1967 war – which had befallen them in the twentieth century. It put the very concept of an 'Arab nation' in jeopardy. For here was Egypt, its 'great power', seeming to opt out of it altogether, allying itself with the Zionist intruder and enormously enhancing Israel's ability to disrupt what was left of the existing Arab order. It should have been a step towards comprehensive peace; that was how Carter understood it. In fact it was Begin's and the interventionists' golden opportunity for war.[4]

It had been all but pre-ordained that Lebanon, other peoples' battle-ground, would pay the price of this double conjuncture. In the event, it took Begin five years to reach his openly proclaimed 'war of choice'. All the evidence suggests that he would have got there sooner or later anyway. But the Palestinians set him on his way – with a savage act that furnished the occasion for a larger one of his own.

'MODERATION' IN ATROCIOUS GUISE

In March 1978, Dalal Mugrabi, a young woman from Sabra refugee camp, and twelve male comrades mounted 'Operation Deir Yassin'. They sailed from Tyre for a Tel Aviv beach with orders to seize a seafront hotel, take its guests hostage and demand the freeing of Palestinian prisoners in exchange for their release. They ended up hijacking a bus instead; thirty-seven Israelis, together with Mugrabi and most of her companions, died in the shoot-out which ensued. In response to this came 'Operation Litani',[5] a first, full-scale Israeli invasion of Lebanon up to the river of that name.

The mayhem on the Haifa–Tel Aviv highway had not formed part of the traditional 'border wars', in whose tit-for-tat cycle the Palestinians usually attacked first and Israelis responded with disproportionate force. In that department, since the coming of Begin, the Israelis had already become much the more aggressive of the two. It was mainly they who initiated hostilities at times and places of their choosing. And it was mainly the Palestinians who responded, usually with cross-border artillery or rockets. It was an unequal combat. When, in July 1977, the Palestinians retaliated for the killing of three Lebanese fishermen in the coastal town of Tyre, and their rockets killed three civilians in the Israeli coastal town of Nahariya, Israel killed over a hundred, mainly Lebanese civilians, in *its* retaliation for that. Indeed, its aircraft virtually wiped out the entire hamlet of Azziya; but only three Palestinians were found among the sixty-plus bodies unearthed from the ruins, for this was a Shiite community that had tried to keep the guerillas out. As they rained down indiscriminate slaughter from the skies, the Israelis had also been pushing their recently formed surrogate force, the Maronite-dominated Army of Free Lebanon (AFL) led by Major Saad Haddad in the border enclave they had created, to engage in stepped-up proxy warfare against the Palestinians and their local Lebanese allies on the ground. In the course of this, a certain Eli Hobeika – whose greatest infamy, at Sabra and Shatila, was yet to come – and twenty other Phalangist militiamen had come down from Beirut, via Israel, to lead an AFL offensive against another border village, Yarin, that did harbour Palestinians; they had rounded up eighty people, mostly Lebanese, outside the local school and shot them all.[6]

Nor, paradoxical, specious or frankly preposterous though that might seem, was 'Operation Deir Yassin' a departure from Arafat's policy of diplomatic 'moderation'. It was – or it was supposed to be – one of those occasional, deliberate, spectacular exploits designed to reinforce it, or at least to prevent American-led international diplomacy from taking a particularly unfavourable turn at the Palestinians' expense. Which is precisely what, with Sadat on his way to a separate Israeli–Egyptian peace, it appeared to be doing. At first, the Carter Administration, striving for a 'comprehensive' Arab–Israeli settlement, had seemed embarrassed and nonplussed by Sadat's astonishing, go-it-alone gamble. But then it latched on to it with a vengeance. And if – as National Security Adviser Zbigniew Brzezinski none too subtly intimated – the PLO did not do likewise, then it would be 'bye-bye, PLO'.[7] So, 'by hitting at the heart of Israel,' said Abu Jihad, Fatah's second-in-command, 'we [wanted] to show that there will never be peace in the Middle East without the Palestinians'.[8]

Diplomatic message it might have been. It was also the deadliest, and most politically disturbing act of Palestinian terrorism that Israel had ever endured, and any new, Likud-style retaliation for it was going, quite simply *had*, to be more condign, more disproportionate than anything Labour had ever attempted. But, as in Labour's 'border wars' against Egypt, Jordan and Syria in the fifties, there was to be more to it than mere revenge and punishment; there was higher strategy too. Operation Litani's official objective was to 'liquidate the PLO'. But the 30,000 men, with tanks and artillery backed by massive air power, who executed it didn't do that at all; the guerillas had time in plenty to run for safety north of the river. What they did do was to kill between one and two thousand, mainly Shiite, Lebanese, turn 250,000 of them into refugees, destroy or damage some 6,000 of their homes – and leave behind unexploded cluster bombs that were still blowing people up by the time of the next, and very much greater invasion, which was to leave behind a great many more.

SAVING THE MARONITES

In fact, strategically speaking, it was things Lebanese, rather than Palestinian, to which the Israelis were now chiefly attending. And the clearest indication of that was the new politico-military order which – along with the cluster bombs – they also left behind. When, three months after the invasion, they withdrew their forces they should, in accordance with UN Security Council Resolution 425, have handed over the whole of the evacuated territory to the newly created peace-keeping force, UNIFIL; but, instead, they bestowed a large swathe of it, running the whole length of the frontier, on Major Haddad and his Army of Free Lebanon. Thus was born the so-called 'security zone', or 'Strip' as it was popularly known. For the next twenty-two years, this Strip, which varied in size according to circumstance, was to serve as a buffer between Israel and its enemies in Lebanon, who likewise varied in identity. But, at the time, it also looked very much like the first great practical step towards something very much grander: nothing less than the creation, at long last, of the 'Christian Lebanon', allied to Israel, of which Ben-Gurion and his generation of interventionists had dreamed. And it looked all the more like it because, ever since he came to power, Begin had been exhibiting a very special, perfervid concern for the well-being and safety of the Maronites, a concern which, by the time of the invasion, had turned into an exalted moral crusade. He whom Ben-Gurion had likened to Hitler habitually saw Arafat in that guise, with the Palestine National Charter as his *Mein Kampf.* In such a histrionic scheme of things, it was but a logical progression to cast the Maronites as potential victims of another holocaust, a progression which Begin duly made. 'Saving the Christians from genocide' – no less – became 'a responsibility of the Jewish people'.[9]

And the Maronites themselves were ready, in their fashion, to be 'saved'. Or at least their 'pro-Zionists' were. And that now mattered. For after the almost continuous, forty-year dominance of the 'Arabists', the 'pro-Zionists' were once more in the ascendant at last, and hardly more inhibited about it than their predecessors – the Eddés and the Aridas – had been in the thirties. They had not liked the political outcome of the 1975–6 campaign, even though, militarily speaking, they had been the principal beneficiary of the Syrian intervention which brought it about. Nor did they like the national reconciliation and reconstruction which the new, Syrian-favoured president, Elias Sarkis, was trying to achieve. His efforts would, in essence, have preserved the sectarian state, and – with some modification in the Muslims' favour – the Maronites' ascendancy within it. That was in line with what the Muslim oligarchs had originally proposed, and what, on the face of it at least, their Christian counterparts had accepted; for by this time the Muslim/leftists had virtually given up their ambitions for fully-fledged de-confessionalization, and – especially following Syria's assassination of their outstanding leader, Kemal Jumblat – they had fallen into demoralization and disarray. But with their 'pro-Zionists' in the saddle that was no longer good enough for the Maronites. Of course, all sides wanted reconciliation on their own terms; but theirs were the most exorbitant. In consequence, Sarkis was not getting very far with his reconstruction. It was a classic case of chicken and egg. The state institutions, army foremost among them, on which he depended for the furtherance of reconciliation could not be reconstructed without reconciliation – but reconciliation itself required the dismantling of those non-state institutions, each side's militias, which had taken the state institutions' place. For the Maronites, that meant that the 'Cairo agreement' of 1968 should be abrogated, and the Palestinian guerillas, whose presence it had legitimized, be disarmed. So should the Muslim/leftists. Until they were, the Maronites would not disarm themselves. There was no question of their doing so first, or even simultaneously. For, in their view, it was they who represented Lebanese 'legitimacy', while the others were 'rebels' against it. Arafat, though not in principle averse to national reconciliation, was not going to throw away his state-within-the-state for nothing in return. The deadlock was therefore complete.

BASHIR GEMAYEL, MARONITE CHRISTIAN PALADIN

The Maronites, or their 'pro-Zionists', now reckoned, however, that not merely could they break this deadlock, but that historic opportunity lay in the breaking. They were in exultant and defiant mood. In

1978 a militia spokesman claimed that for the first time since the four-
teenth century the Christian 'resistance' boasted a unified regular army
to protect and preserve its own.[10] They thought that, militarily at least,
they had won the last campaign, and that now, with the coming of
Begin, they would win the next, decisive one. Israeli help under Labour
had been discreet and indirect, designed only 'to help the Maronites
help themselves'.[11] They had very good reason to believe that, under
the Likud, it would become open, direct – and very large. Their leader
was Bashir Gemayel, the younger son of 'Sheikh Pierre'. He headed
the 'Lebanese Forces', as the Phalangist militia came to be known after
he had bloodily suppressed its rival, the Chamounist 'Tigers'.
Ambitious, ruthless, barely thirty, he was the first Maronite leader ever
to command such undisputed, autocratic sway over the whole community. For him, as for Begin and the interventionists, force was but an
instrument for the achievement of political goals.[12] He had been wooing
the temperamentally not dissimilar Israeli prime minister ever since
he came to power. With certain reservations, each had impressed the
other.[13] But nothing had impressed Bashir like Begin's first invasion. He
wanted another, and larger, one.[14] Thus it came about that, under this
youthful paladin, the community that had traditionally looked to the
Christian West for its protection or advancement, and had then briefly,
opportunistically – and with great distaste – turned to Arab/Muslim
Syria, sought ultimate deliverance at the hands of the Western-created
newcomer, now full-grown regional superpower, just next door.
Gemayel resolved that, with Israel's assistance, the Maronites would
regain the Greater Lebanon which they had lost; and if, perchance,
they did not manage that, they could always fall back on 'Marounistan'
– their tight little 'Christian Lebanon' of old – still securely in their
hands.[15]

BEGIN PUTS WAR ON THE AGENDA – WITH OFFERS OF PEACE

It was in the wake of the second historic development, the conclusion
of the Israeli–Egyptian peace treaty, that Begin first put full-scale war
in Lebanon on the agenda – albeit in the guise of peace. In May 1979,
he made the first of a series of theatrical 'peace offers', which came,

characteristically, in the wake of a bloody reprisal raid. Striking at what they may have thought were Palestinian military targets, Israeli warplanes had killed Lebanese civilians instead, among them the bride and four of her guests at a wedding. Israel, Begin pledged, would go on hitting these 'Palestinian murderers' by land, sea and air in order to 'destroy them completely'. Then, after the threat, the offer: 'I hereby invite President Sarkis to come' – like Sadat before him – 'to meet me here in Jerusalem.' He himself was 'ready to go in an aircraft to Beirut or any neutral place to meet President Sarkis ... and the only subject we would discuss would be the signing of a peace treaty between Israel and Lebanon'. Turning to the Syrians, he said that their 'army of occupation must leave at once'. It was 'destroying Lebanese villages and firing on innocent Christians'. As for the Palestinian refugees, they should all be resettled in Saudi Arabia, Syria, Iraq and Libya, 'very big countries rich in resources and petroleum, with millions of square kilometres of land'. Neither Lebanon nor Israel had any territorial claims on the other and a peace treaty could be worked out 'in two days or so of talks'. Jordan, he forecast, 'would also then make peace with us'. President Sarkis spurned the offer, while the prime minister, Salim al-Hoss, said that Israel, through 'blackmail, terrorism and brute force', was planning to tear Lebanon away from its Arab moorings. In the words of the Beirut newspaper *al-Safir*, it was intended to 'blow up Lebanon from within'. Bashir Gemayel, and the Maronite 'pro-Zionists', were the only ones to welcome it; naturally enough, considering that they were to be its indispensable instruments.[16]

SHARON PLOTS THE 'HOW' AND 'WHEN'

After this it was essentially a question of how and when Begin would make war. The 'how' went through various formulations, by various quarters; eventually, however, it was chiefly determined by General Sharon, whom Begin made his defence minister after his second electoral victory in the summer of 1981. Even he, superhawk though he was, had had the deepest misgivings about this choice, less because Sharon was – as Israelis put it – 'a war looking for a place to happen' than because he himself knew he was liable to be overborne and misled

– as indeed he ultimately was – by this notoriously most 'reckless, duplicitous, untrustworthy' of Israel's military heroes. The inevitable upshot of his and other appointments was that, in the Israeli decision-making process, the last restraints were swept away; and pure, unbridled extremism ruled.[17]

So when the war finally came, it was no surprise at all. Neither were its dimensions. The range of possible objectives had been endlessly rehearsed. The minimum aim was to enlarge the 'security zone', to a width of some forty kilometres, in order to protect northern towns and settlements against Palestinian rocket and artillery bombardment. A more ambitious, much-canvassed objective was, as its proponents usually and somewhat vaguely put it, to 'destroy the PLO infra-structure'. But more ambitious still, a throwback to Ben-Gurion's 'fantastic' geopolitical grand designs of the fifties, was the so-called Sharon Plan. There was more to this than the mere reconstitution of Lebanon as a Christian or Christian-dominated state that would make peace with Israel. That was just a start. In addition, the Palestinians should be driven out of the country to Jordan, and not just those who, in their tens of thousands, had descended on it with Arafat and the PLO, but all those 'legitimate' residents, the refugees who had fetched up there in the original, 1948 flight from Palestine. That the final solution to the 'Palestine problem' lay in Jordan had long been one of Sharon's *idées fixes*. Palestinians already made up more than half its population and all they had to do in order to satisfy their national aspirations was, with Israel's assistance, to replace the Hashemite kingdom, whose power base was essentially Transjordanian, with a Republic of Palestine. That, in turn, was intimately bound up with his plans for the occupied Palestinian territories. In the West Bank, he had recently introduced a new-fangled scheme to create a quisling leadership; known as the Village Leagues, many of its personnel, recruited and armed by Israel, were known criminals.[18] It was supposed to furnish the necessary Palestinian 'cover' for all his Greater-Israel, expansionist designs. Achieving this was 'the most important political battle Israel had fought since its creation'. But West Bankers and Gazans would have none of it; the only leadership they acknowledged was the PLO's. So destroying that organization in Lebanon became the prerequisite for destroying their resistance to the Village Leagues in Palestine. Once that was achieved, they could be induced to cross the Jordan to become citizens of their very own 'Palestine state' that awaited them on the other side.[19] As for Syria, if Sharon's Lebanese project meant full-scale war with it, that was no great tragedy; had he not, in any case, frequently advocated pre-emptive attack on the neighbour which Israel regarded as its most implacable foe?

'THE TOTAL DISINTEGRATION OF LEBANON IS THE PRECEDENT FOR THE ENTIRE ARAB WORLD'

Nor was the Sharon Plan even the most far-reaching of the geopolitical fantasies which, with the rise of the extreme right, were now entering mainstream Zionist thinking. The learned article entitled 'A Strategy for Israel in the Nineteen Eighties', which appeared in the World Zionist Organization's periodical *Kivunim* on the eve of the invasion, could not be dismissed as the ravings of a lunatic fringe. The author, Oded Yinon, was formerly a senior foreign ministry official.

> The total disintegration of Lebanon into five regional, localized governments is the precedent for the entire Arab world ... The dissolution of Syria, and later Iraq, into districts of ethnic and religious minorities following the example of Lebanon is Israel's main long-range objective on the Eastern front. The present military weakening of these states is the short-range objective. Syria will disintegrate into several states along the lines of its ethnic and sectarian structure ... As a result there will be a Shiite Alawi state, the district of Aleppo will be a Sunni state, and the district of Damascus another state which is hostile to the northern one. The Druze – even those of the Golan – should form a state in Hauran and in northern Jordan ... The oil-rich but very divided and internally strife-ridden Iraq is certainly a candidate to fit Israel's goals ... Every kind of inter-Arab confrontation ... will hasten the achievement of the supreme goal, namely breaking up Iraq into elements like Syria and Lebanon. There will be three states or more around the three major cities, Basra, Baghdad and Mosul, while Shiite areas in the south will separate from the Sunni

north, which is mostly Kurdish ... The entire Arabian Peninsula is a natural candidate for [dissolution] ... Israel's policy in war or peace should be to bring about the elimination of Jordan ...[20]

So much for the 'how'. As to the 'when', all but inevitable though this most overtly 'chosen' of wars might have been, Israel still had to await – even as it simultaneously sought to shape – at least a semblance of justification for waging it. Indeed, one thing might even have prevented it altogether. That was if President Sarkis had somehow managed to put Lebanon together again. The Israelis therefore made sure that he did not. The South was key. It was indispensable for national reconciliation and reconstruction that the central government regain sovereignty over it. Otherwise, it would remain 'like a gangrened limb' that 'spread its poison throughout the country'.[21]

Time and again, Sarkis tried to send the national army south. Thus it came about that, in April 1979, there happened exactly what had already happened on two occasions before. But this time, coming in the immediate aftermath of the Israeli–Egyptian peace treaty and Begin's menacing 'peace offer', it was more serious. Amid the enthusiasm of the southern population, showering them with rice and flowers, the soldiers did get a bit further than they ever had previously. But when the usual shooting started, and stopped them in their tracks, it did not just kill and injure Lebanese, it killed recently installed UNIFIL peacekeepers too. Private Jarle Warger became the first Norwegian to die at his post, struck down by the artillery round which exploded in the centre of the village of Ebl Saqi, his contingent's head-quarters. The 155-mm shells, American-made and supplied for 'self-defence' purposes only, had, as usual, been fired from Israel or the 'Strip', though Israel, as usual too, indignantly denied it. The PLO was responsible, said General Ben-Gal, the head of the Israeli Northern Command, both for this and for all the other ordnance that rained down on the UNIFIL headquarters at Naqura that day. But two American officers serving as UN observers were so incensed at this lie that, breaking the rules, they went to the press to denounce it. Like most international peacekeepers, the Norwegian general in charge had originally come to the Middle East with a prejudice in the Israelis' favour; but, like most too, he had quickly shed it:

We expected the Israelis to be honest types ... never in my wildest fantasy had I imagined we were confronting an organization [Israel] which considered itself served by fooling people, by telling stories which they insisted we should believe, or deny things we had seen with our own eyes.[22]

MURDERING IRISH PEACEKEEPERS

Actually, from time to time, Palestinians did kill UNIFIL peace-keepers, not just in battle but in cold blood. Usually, it was the 'rejectionists', who had never taken kindly to them, making some viciously explicit, intra-Palestinian point about 'surrender solutions' and their determination to prevent the all too 'moderate' Arafat's acquiescence in them. In 1979 the PFLP shot three Fijians in an ambush; in 1981 they kidnapped three more, and began 'executing' them, a bullet to the head, one by one; after abuse and torture, chance alone saved the life of the third.[23]

But it was not some renegade guerilla band which had murdered two Irish peacekeepers the year before. It was a UN member-state, the member-state that owed its very existence to the UN.[24] Once upon a time, in pre-state days, the Irgun underground over which Begin presided had hanged two British sergeants from a eucalyptus tree and booby-trapped their dangling corpses;[25] thirty years on, as Karsten Tveit recounts in his book *A Pattern for Defeat*,[26] the state of Israel over which he presided not merely connived in, it wilfully instigated similar villainies in the South Lebanese 'badlands' of its own creation.

No sooner had UNIFIL arrived than Israel wanted it out, portraying it as an incompetent, worthless accessory of an ill-intentioned Lebanese authority, if not an outright collaborator of the terrorists themselves.[27] One method which – it thought – might achieve this was to hound and harass one or other of its contingents beyond the political endurance of the nation that contributed it. It singled out the Irish. 'Get your troops out of South Lebanon,' the deputy defence minister, Ezer Weizmann, told the Irish ambassador, even as a certain Major Haim Misrah – one of Israel's two unofficial 'bosses' in the Strip – was organizing a violent confrontation, between a local mob and Irish troops, in which stone-throwing children were deployed as human shields in front of an advancing Army of Free Lebanon armoured car. Two UNIFIL soldiers were killed. But so were two children. Where-upon AFL commander Major Haddad personally radioed Irish headquarters with his ultimatum: 'the UN must pay 40,000 Lebanese lira [about $10,000] in reparations for the two children you have killed – or give me the bodies of two Irish soldiers'.[28] Thus was the time-honoured clan or family 'blood feud', the *lex talionis*, enlisted in the service of state policy. Major Misrah told Mahmoud Basi, brother of one of the dead 'children' – a sixteen-year-old aboard a tank which had fired on the Irish and on which the Irish had fired back – that he wanted him to 'take a UN soldier and kill him'.[29] Basi and his gang duly took three, and murdered two of them; the third, shot in the stomach, miraculously survived.[30]

Even the US, Israel's great benefactor, did not escape its homicidal attentions. Its ambassador to Beirut, John Gunther Dean, a German Jew who fled Nazi persecution as a child, had been trying his courageous best to carry out stated US policy in Lebanon, fundamental to which was the deployment of the Lebanese army in the South. Twice he found himself condemning Israeli actions which subverted that policy, a stand which first earned him a public disavowal from his own, 'Lobby'-shy masters in Washington, and then an unsuccessful attempt by the Israeli intelligence service, Mossad, to assassinate him. The anti-tank missiles fired at the convoy in which he and his family were travelling had been supplied to Israel by the US.[31]

THE SHIITES TURN AGAINST THE PALESTINIANS

Keeping the war option open, by keeping Lebanon in unreconstructed turmoil, meant keeping all those non-state actors that profited from it in business. And that, in turn, meant not just Israel's friends, 'Sheikh Bashir' and his Maronite warriors, but its enemies, Arafat and his Palestinian ones, too. That necessity did not bother Israel very much. On the contrary, it was in one important respect positively beneficial, if not – till 'D-day' came – its active desire. For the fact was that while the Muslim population might still have looked to the PLO as a bulwark against Maronite revanchism, it was steadily losing its popularity among them, and that was a process it was well worth Israel's while helping along – especially among the Shiites. The Shiites had never been as ideologically committed to pan-Arab causes as the Sunnis in the first place, and yet, by the late seventies, this poorest and most oppressed of Lebanon's communities had suffered vastly more in the name of Palestine than any other. They had first been driven, under Israeli retaliatory raids, from their homes in the South to Beirut's 'belt of misery', only to be driven in large numbers from there, by Israel's Phalangist protégés, in the ensuing civil war. From the South to Beirut and back – it was an infernal cycle that went on and on. And Israel deliberately exacerbated it.

The 'policy of pre-emption' which Defence Minister Weizmann announced in January 1979 required the bombardment of civilian neighbourhoods with the express intention of turning them against the Palestinians in their midst. Not surprisingly, the policy did not earn it any affection among its victims.[32] But it remorselessly achieved its purpose; the Palestinians were doubly blamed – for their own mis-demeanours, and for the Israeli ones they brought down on the Shiites' heads. 'Everyone', said a militia leader, 'knows Israel's game. But the Palestinians are the visible cause of their misfortunes.'[33]

Thus, what the Palestinian refugees once felt about the Lebanese army and police – that they, not the Israelis, were the direct oppressor – the Shiites now felt about these refugees-turned-guerillas. And the Palestinians had indeed done much to bring it on themselves. Their leadership itself admitted to the many, reprehensible 'excesses' of 'undisciplined elements' – elements which, however, it was seemingly unwilling or unable to discipline. Some of the 'excesses' came, so to speak, in the official line of duty. 'We know the Israelis usually start the shooting,' said a disillusioned Shiite sympathizer, 'but we don't see much point in Palestinian bombardments at all. It does Israel no real damage. If someone starts shooting from Nabatiyah [a market town which, by 1980, had been almost emptied of its inhabitants] Haddad will reply here in Tyre [where a third or more of them still hung on].'[34] He, like other Southerners, had by then concluded that the Pales-tinians, nursing a long-standing sense of betrayal by their fellow Arabs, were imbued with a kind of egoism that made them indifferent to the sufferings which the redressing of their own injustice inflicted on others. But for other 'excesses' – petty warlordism, theft, 'confiscation', the occupation of houses and land, 'protection money' and the levying of 'taxes' on local produce, the hamfisted exploitation of parish pump politics – there could be no such excuse or extenuating circumstance.

Like other communities, Maronites especially, the Shiites were also worried – or so they claimed – about *Tawteen*, 'implantation', and *al-Watan al-Badil*, the 'alternative homeland', which, the longer they stayed, the more the Palestinians would be tempted to establish in Lebanon instead of Palestine itself.

By 1980, the Shiite militia, Amal, which had come into being to defend Southern villages against Israel, was turning the arms with which the Palestinians had first supplied it against those self-same Palestinians instead. Not all its members were so inclined – a minority, precursors of a Hizbullah that was yet to be, definitely were not – but those that were took on the Palestinians wherever they found them, in the south of the country, or in Beirut's *Dahiya*.[35] It was – to take just one serious example – some rather trivial 'excess' that provoked the fighting in the southern village of Zifta that summer. The Palestinians, far better armed, subjected it to an artillery bombardment. The Shiite militiamen, having no means of reply, just waited till it was over. Then, as the Palestinians and their Muslim/leftist allies approached, presuming it was pacified, they shot twenty-six of them from close range.[36] Before long Amal was able to seal off substantial parts of the South to the Palestinians and Muslim/leftists, as well as – through its inroads into the *Dahiya* – to wrest control of parts of their urban heartland.[37] The Palestinians and Muslim/leftists were also losing sympathy and support, though to a lesser extent, in their natural, bedrock Sunni constituency. And there were growing tensions and disenchantment between these allies themselves.

BOMBING THE PALESTINIANS OUT OF THEIR 'MODERATION'

What did worry the Israelis was less the PLO's continued existence than its 'moderation'. The moderation became more pronounced, and therefore more exasperating, the more the Israelis tried to 'bomb' the Palestinians out of it, and especially after the so-called 'artillery war' of July 1981 in which – for once replying – the Palestinians bombed them back more effectively than they had ever done before. This 'artillery war' had grown out of a spiral of tit-for-tat exchanges which Israel had initiated and perpetuated, evidently with the original intention of expanding it into an invasion which would have been very big, yet – since superhawk Sharon had not yet joined the cabinet – not quite as big as it eventually turned out to be.[38]

In April, Israeli aircraft shot down two Syrian helicopters. These were supposedly on their way to 'kill Christians'. The truth was that, in a ground offensive devised and supervised by Mossad 'advisers' on the spot, Bashir Gemayel's Phalangists were mounting an intolerable challenge to Syria's control of the region, the Beqa'a Valley, over which the helicopters had been shot down.[39] In retaliation, Syria introduced surface-to-air (SAM) missiles into the Beqa'a, prompting Begin to declare that, as a threat to Israel's security, these could 'under no circumstances' be permitted to stay. Thanks largely to American pressure, however, stay they did. Then, in a diversion from the 'missile crisis', Begin made another incautious pledge: no more Palestinian rockets would fall on Kiryat Shmona. But they soon did – and with a vengeance.

The Israeli army had been making no secret about its intentions: 'We are the aggressors', proclaimed military spokesman Brigadier-General Yaakov Even, 'we push through the so-called border to the so-called sovereign state of Lebanon and we are going after them (the Palestinians) wherever they might hide.'[40] But this time it had pushed a bit too hard. It was not Arafat, but his commanders, who, fretful at his docility, ordered the gunners to fire. They did so for twelve days solid; 1,230 shells and rockets struck thirty-five settlements and seven army camps in northern Israel. The cost in reprisals was high, for when, in the course of it, the attacks killed three civilians in Nahariya, the Israelis struck back at Fakhani, the PLO's Beirut headquarters itself. Choosing the height of the Friday rush hour in which to do it, they killed 150 civilians, more Lebanese than Palestinian, and injured 600 in a single air raid; some thirty PLO personnel also died. And by the end of the 'artillery war' the casualty ratio stood, typically enough, at about forty to one: at least 2,500 Palestinian and Lebanese dead and injured against some 65 for the other side. Still, with tens of thousands fleeing Kiryat Shmona and the north, the Israelis had never experienced anything quite like this before. It shook and angered Begin – but, maddeningly for him, only strengthened Arafat in his moderation.[41]

There was both a fundamental strategic and tactical reason why the more extreme they grew themselves, the more Israeli leaders so detested the Palestinians' movement in the opposite direction. The strategic one grew out of the fact that while the PLO might have been weak and vulnerable militarily, it had in recent years been making steady headway diplomatically. Its spirit of compromise, its readiness to settle for half-a-loaf, half-Palestine – indeed less than a quarter of it – in a final settlement, won it international credit. The Soviet Union was soon to 'recognize' it; it looked as though Europe might one day do so too. It was President Reagan's special envoy, Philip Habib, who had negotiated an end to the 'artillery war'; and that – some mischievous people were saying – meant that, implicitly at least, the US, if not Israel itself, had thereby 'recognized' it as well. At the same time, Saudi Arabia's King Fahd, a close friend of Washington, was trying to interest it in a 'two-state' Middle East 'peace plan'. If things had gone on like this, Israel might have found itself dragged into peace talks to which the PLO would have been a party. Heaven forbid! So the more accommodating, the more 'civilized', this abhorrent organization became the more it alarmed the Greater-Israel expansionists who, in power at last, were bent on securing the whole of Palestine for themselves, and extinguishing any rival national claim to the territories on which the Palestinian nation-state would have arisen. And what, after the 'artillery war', now made matters even worse was the way the PLO was so scrupulously respecting the ceasefire. For the Israeli government, wrote Professor Yehoshua Porat, Arafat's ability to persuade his guerillas, even the most radical of them, thus to abide by it presaged a 'real catastrophe'. For it meant that they could eventually have approved a broader, longer-term agreement too, 'and if, in the future, we approach a period of negotiations between ourselves and certain Arab parties other than Egypt, will our government be able to claim that the PLO

is a gang of uncompromising assassins who are not legitimate inter-
locutors?' The government therefore wanted the PLO to 'return to its
earlier terrorist exploits, to plant bombs all over the world, to hijack
plenty of aeroplanes and to kill many Israelis'.[42] 'If' – concurred
another scholar – 'it were to "go political" and gradually renounce
military action and terrorism, it would increase the political menace of
a Palestinian state. *To escape this trap ... Israel could do only one thing – go
to war.*'[43]

'IT'S POSSIBLE I WILL BE IN BEIRUT TOMORROW.'

But even the most brazen of aggressors can hardly go to war without at
least the semblance of a pretext. Therein lay the Israelis' tactical
problem; for even the US was insisting that – while an invasion might
be inevitable – it must not take place without a 'recognizable provocation' that was 'understood internationally'.[44] And the PLO just would
not provide it. For over eight months following the ceasefire UNIFIL
forces reported not a single hostile act directed against Israel from
Lebanon. Nor could Israel prove any. So, as Begin and company
orchestrated a steady crescendo of threats to 'destroy', 'crush',
'annihilate' or 'finish off' what one of them called 'those bastards on
the other side of the northern frontier', they simultaneously cast about
for reasons for doing so.[45] When, in January 1982, five guerillas crossing
the Jordan planted mines in the West Bank, Israel denounced this as 'a
grave violation of the ceasefire'. The US disagreed: it wasn't 'reason
enough' for Israeli retaliation. According to Israeli newspapers, an
attack on Lebanon was called off at the last moment.[46] In April, the
second secretary of the Israeli embassy in Paris – actually a Mossad
agent – was assassinated by a group calling itself the Lebanese Armed
Revolutionary Factions. Israel promptly blamed the PLO; it was
therefore another ceasefire violation. Not so, said the State Department; and the Israeli opposition accused the government of a
'demagogy' that threatened to drag the country into a conflict for which
there was no 'national consensus'. But again the army mobilized for an
invasion which, it was forecast, might carry it to Beirut. Again, bowing
to the US pressure, Begin called it off.

It was the Israelis themselves who, in April, first violated the ceasefire with an air raid, killing twenty-five and wounding eighty, on a string of Palestinian positions between Sidon and Beirut. What, according to Chief of Staff Raful Eitan, had finally 'broken the camel's back' was the killing of an Israeli officer by a landmine in Major Haddad's border enclave. For Eitan, the question of what the officer was doing in Lebanese territory was beside the point. The Palestinians did not reply. And the Israelis blithely asserted that, so far as they were concerned, the ceasefire was still in effect. Three weeks later a boy and a girl were injured by a bomb blast in Jerusalem. This, too, was supposedly a south Lebanese ceasefire violation; so the planes struck again, killing eleven and wounding twenty-eight. This time the Palestinians did reply with rockets and artillery, but, since they deliberately avoided population centres, there were no casualties. The Israeli cabinet now decided, however, that all these Palestinian violations had rendered the ceasefire 'null and void'. Eitan could not hide his eagerness for the fray: 'Now that I've built a military machine which costs billions of dollars I have to use it. It's possible I will be in Beirut tomorrow.'[47]

Clearly the Israelis had just about dispensed with pretexts altogether. For form's sake, however, they did claim one for the launching of the Fifth Arab–Israeli War. The attempted assassination, on 3 June, of the Israeli ambassador in Britain, Shlomo Argov, was not the doing of the PLO, which promptly denounced it. It was another exploit of Arafat's arch-enemy, the notorious, Baghdad-based Fatah dissident Abu Nidal, who directed his particular brand of pure, unbridled terrorism more against the mainstream PLO leadership, particularly moderates within its ranks, than against the Israel enemy – for whom, it was said, he also later worked.[48] One of the assassins was actually a colonel in Iraqi intelligence; for reasons of their own the Iraqi Baathists were desperately anxious to provoke an Israeli onslaught on their Syrian rivals. The Israelis scorned such distinctions. Arabs had attacked a Jew. It didn't matter where. That, too, had become a ceasefire violation. This time Begin didn't hesitate. The assassination attempt, said his spokesman, had 'put an end to a long period of Israeli restraint. Those who believed that the ceasefire … on the Lebanese front meant that everywhere else Jewish blood could flow with impunity are mistaken.' He unleashed his air force on Sabra and Shatila. Sixty to a hundred people were killed, some 275 wounded. Palestinian artillery opened up on northern Israel. One person was killed and four wounded. The planes came back the next day: 130 died. Palestinian artillery killed three in northern Israel. An Israeli minister went to Galilee and told the inhabitants: 'Begin pledged that not a single rocket will fall on Kiryat Shmona. *Tsahal* [the Israeli army] will ensure that this pledge is respected.'[49]

ITS 'GREATEST FOLLY': THE ISRAELI ARMY ENTERS THE MORASS OF LEBANON

The next morning – fifteen years, almost to the day, after its greatest triumph, the Six-Day War – the Israeli army embarked on what its well-known historian, Martin van Creveld, called its 'greatest folly'.[50] It entered what was famously to become the 'morass', the 'quagmire' of Lebanon. It did so with an enormous force. Composed of up to 90,000 men, or six and a half divisions, plus one in reserve, with some 1,300 tanks and 1,500 armoured personnel carriers, it was twice the size of the one which, in 1973, had checked the entire Egyptian army. For the first time, they were pitted not against one or more regular Arab armies, of comparable size and comparably equipped, but against a hybrid, guerilla-cum-conventional force of some 10,000–15,000 men – perhaps only 4,000 of those real fighters – without any air or naval power, only recently and hastily thrown together, poorly coordinated, poorly armed, indifferently trained, and seriously lacking in popular support.[51]

Years in the making, this was also a war that had been planned and prepared down to the minutest detail.[52] So when, at 11 o'clock in the morning of Sunday, 6 June, Israeli ground forces – greeted with rice and rosewater by southern Maronites and even some Shiites too – crossed the frontier at three points and pushed, unresisted, through UNIFIL lines, while others made amphibious landings near Tyre and Sidon, they were very confident of swiftly and smoothly accomplishing what 'Operation Peace in Galilee' called upon them to do. That, according to the first communiqué, was to 'place the whole of the civilian population of Galilee out of range of the terrorists who have concentrated their base and their headquarters in Lebanon'. It was hardly a modest aim, involving as it did the seizure of a third of the country. But this was no more than the minimum objective of any invasion, the creation of the forty-kilometre-wide 'security belt', as both government and opposition had long anticipated it. Within twenty-four hours the invaders appeared well on the way to achieving it. 'Tyre, Beaufort [the celebrated, guerilla-held, medieval fortress that commands the central approaches to Galilee] Fall As Israel Defence Forces Operation Nears Completion', was the *Jerusalem Post*'s headline of Tuesday, 8 June. Evidently the newspaper really believed what Begin had promised the Knesset: that the campaign would be over within forty-eight hours.

AN AMERICAN 'HUNTING LICENCE' FOR SHARON

In officially confining itself to this objective, the government was only seeking to mollify the opposition and those among the public who, though very uneasy, were ready to support a military action that went no further than that. It was also seeking to reassure the US, confirming what Begin had privately assured Reagan: that Israel had no intention of going beyond that 40-km limit, still less of attacking the Syrians.[53] Not that, should it actually do so, the US was going to be very angry, or very surprised. If the coming to power of the Likud and the Israeli–Egyptian peace treaty had been the two most important factors behind the Fifth Arab–Israeli War, the advent of the Reagan Administration, in 1981, had undoubtedly constituted a third – if subsidiary – one. As Begin himself acknowledged, there had never been an administration as favourable to Israel as this one. It included many luminaries, largely Jewish, of the 'neoconservative' movement, now achieving real influence for the first time, and was impregnated with their 'good-versus-evil' view of the world, their crusading zeal against the Soviet Union, their strident advocacy of military power, and, above all, their devotion to Israel, especially the militant, expansionist, right-wing Israel of Begin and Sharon. For them American and Israeli interests were one and the same, and the PLO was an enemy of peace, a Soviet proxy, which, as Sharon said, had 'converted [Lebanon] into the world centre for terrorism operated by the Soviet Union'.

America's love affair with Israel was no longer an embarrassment, or liability, in its relations with the Arab world; Israel was now elevated, more clearly than ever before, to the status of 'strategic asset', and – in Reagan's words – the only ally on which, thanks to its 'democratic will, national cohesion, technological capacity and military fiber', the US could 'truly rely' for the prosecution of its policies in the region.[54] In General Alexander Haig, his secretary of state, the Israelis rejoiced to have a vintage Cold Warrior, who saw the Middle East from one, simplistic perspective only: as an arena of superpower conflict, with Israel as a vital Western bulwark against the Soviet bloc, global terror and Arab extremism. For all his admonitions about a 'recognizable pretext', and a 'proportionate response', Haig effectively gave Sharon a green light to proceed, or, as his assistant secretary for the Middle East, Nicolas Veliotes, later put it, he spoke to him in such a way that, 'however [he] intended it', a man like Sharon could only see it 'as a hunting licence'.[55]

But the real, larger ambition was already implicit in that first communiqué. Israel, it had said, would not attack the Syrians unless the Syrians attacked first. But no sooner had Sharon's troops reached the forty-kilometre line than they were heading down the coastal highway to the outskirts of Beirut and pushing through the thinly defended Shouf mountains where they were poised to cut the Beirut–Damascus highway and Syrian communications with the capital. It had actually been Sharon's intention to take on the Syrians and go to Beirut all along. But he had pretended otherwise. From the outset there had been two versions of his campaign. The so-called 'Big Pines' was the real one, and the one he did not reveal to his cabinet, the Americans, or even many of his army commanders. 'Little Pines' was – officially at least – the only one they knew about. But Little Pines was already accomplished. In other words, wrote Sharon's biographer, he, Begin and Chief of Staff Eitan had lied to just about everyone, joining forces in a 'national deception the likes of which had never been seen in the State of Israel'.[56] And they would effect the transition from Little Pines to Big Pines with innumerable further lies, with allegations that Syria had violated the latest ceasefire whereas in fact they had violated it themselves, and with excuses for further advances which supposedly unforeseeable, but in reality deliberately engineered, battlefield developments provided. However hard they tried to keep out of the way, the Syrians were drawn into unequal combat, in which they took heavy and humiliating losses: 1,200 men killed, 300 taken prisoner, over 300 tanks destroyed.[57] On 11 June, in a long promised, technological *tour de force*, the Israeli air force took out their SAM missiles in the Beqa'a Valley and shot down some eighty aircraft, about a quarter of the Syrian air force, for the loss of only one of their own. On 13 June Sharon, in full battle dress, exultant 'like a latterday Tamburlain',[58] led a column of tanks towards Lebanon's presidential palace, from which a hapless Elias Sarkis, overlooking a blitzed and burning Beirut, enjoyed sovereignty over about six square miles of his country. With the Beirut–Damascus highway now cut and the capital encircled, Sharon was linking up with Bashir Gemayel and his Phalangists. It was a military exploit whose political symbolism was also plain: henceforward Israel would shape its neighbour's destiny through the presidency itself – with Bashir as its next incumbent.

'UNDER THE PROTECTION OF ISRAELI BAYONETS'

This and related objectives of the Sharon Plan were now emerging as public policy. Ever since his 'peace offer' of three years before Begin had been uncharacteristically discreet about his heart's desire – a peace treaty with a second Arab country – but now, once again, he was ready to go to Beirut and sign one 'tomorrow'. The pro-government press began to talk about 'a new political order in Lebanon', and Likud deputies bluntly asserted that 'a Lebanese government must be formed under the protection of Israeli bayonets'. All the 'terrorist organizations', Begin went on, must leave the country with their Soviet, Syrian and Libyan weapons. And Palestinian civilians should go with them. The reason why the invading army set about demolishing refugee camps in South Lebanon with bulldozers and dynamite after it had bombarded them with artillery was not merely to finish off the 'terrorists' who continued to resist from bases there, it was to break up and scatter the whole community from which they sprang. 'Push them east to Syria,' said Yaacov Meridor, the minister responsible for refugee affairs, with an appropriate gesture. 'Let them go, and don't let them come back.'[59] According to a critical Israeli history of the war, Sharon envisaged 'the destruction of the refugee camps in Lebanon and the mass deportation of the 200,000 Palestinians from that country'.[60]

As for the Israelis, Begin and his officials never tired of repeating that they would leave as soon as the Syrians and the 'terrorists' did. For they did not covet an inch of Lebanese territory. Yet some Israelis clearly did. They included Yuval Ne'eman, leader of the neo-fascist Tehiya Party, who became a cabinet minister during the invasion. Israel should prepare for 'a long stay in Lebanon', he urged, and 'could possibly even reach an agreement on border rectification' in a region 'which geographically and historically is an integral part of *Eretz Israel*'.[61] The Gush Emunim, or Bloc of the Faithful, the fundamentalist settler movement beloved of Sharon, rushed in with biblico-strategic claims of its own. Had not the conquered territory once belonged to the tribes of Asher and Naftali? One of its spiritual mentors, Rabbi Israel Ariel, called for the annexation of most of Lebanon, including Beirut, which 'our leaders should have entered without hesitation' and 'killed every single one [of its inhabitants] … not a memory or trace should have remained'.[62]

Older conquests were not forgotten in the excitement of the new one. On the contrary Sharon vigorously enacted his conviction that the harder he hit the PLO the more readily the West Bankers and Gazans would acquiesce in the new order he had in store for them. 'We can do anything we want now in the territories', exulted a senior official, 'and no one will be able to stop us. If they didn't stop us from going to Beirut, then we will certainly be able to install an order favourable to us in Judea, Samaria and Gaza.'[63]

The attitude of the United States at first seemed to keep pace with the expanding objectives of its protégé. In contrast with former President Carter's disapproval of the much less ambitious, much less indefensible invasion of 1978, the Reagan Administration refused, again and again, to go along with Security Council draft resolutions calling for Israel's immediate withdrawal. Secretary of State Haig said that there should be an evacuation of 'all foreign forces', thereby putting the Israelis on the same footing as the Syrians and the Palestinians who, however unwelcome, were at least Arabs in an Arab country, with Arab and Lebanese sanction for their presence. Privately, he said that the only way to accomplish that was to have the PLO and the Syrians believe that 'if the Israelis were forced to, they were going to do what they had to do militarily: take Lebanon! Take West Beirut! And if necessary even go to Damascus.'[64]

THE 'KING OF ISRAEL' PROMISES FORTY YEARS OF PEACE

No wonder Begin exulted, and his supporters with him. The 'King of Israel' had made good his electoral promise. No more rockets on Kiryat Shmona, of course – but that, by now, was subsumed within the infinitely grander, demonstrated fact of Israel's power and impregnability 'There is no other country around us that is capable of attacking us,' he told the National Defence Council with a pride which, on this occasion, did not impair his objectivity. 'We have destroyed the best tanks and planes the Syrians had ... Jordan cannot attack us ... and the peace treaty [with Egypt] stood the test.' More than that, the King of Israel had acquired an empire that now reached beyond the bounds of *Eretz* Israel proper, or, at least, an ability to prosecute those quasi-imperial, hegemonic designs which, since Ben-Gurion's day, Lebanon had been destined to be the first of Israel's neighbours to experience. No, the 'terrorists' had not threatened Israel's existence, only the lives of its citizens. But there was no moral obligation to launch a war only when there was no choice. 'On the contrary, a free people ... which hates war, loves peace, but insists on its security must create conditions in which its war – though necessary – is not unchosen.' And he forecast forty years of peace – more or less.[65]

But that was just about the last time this most florid of orators was ever so plausibly to vouchsafe such florid pronouncements. For pride was soon to have its great, if long-drawn, fall: imperial hubris its steady, demoralizing nemesis. Unquestionably, the Israelis did quite quickly achieve one key objective. They did drive Arafat out of Beirut; they did destroy his state-within-a-state. But they only achieved that at the price of what amounted, in the long run, to a huge strategic setback of their own. For the first time in its history, their army, whose legendary prowess had held the entire Arab world in awe, found itself very seriously unequal to the waging of a war which should, in principle, have been its easiest ever. From the outset, wrote Palestinian scholar and on-the-spot observer Rashid Khalidi, it had been vital that, for the achievement of any of Sharon's aims – from the 'peace in Galilee' to the grandiose feats of geopolitical engineering that were supposed to come in its wake – it score 'a rapid, indisputable and psychologically over-whelming triumph. It was not enough simply to beat the PLO. It was essential that in virtually every battle, PLO forces [as well as the Lebanese Muslim/leftists and Syrian units in Lebanon] be routed, and their men killed, captured or sent streaming in flight, sowing panic before them.'[66]

It did at first look as though something like that might happen; as though, having reached the gates of the guerilla-held, predominantly Muslim, western half of Beirut, Sharon's troops would proceed to storm the city itself, and – as Philip Habib, Reagan's special envoy, put it – 'totally and visibly smash [the PLO] into oblivion', or – as a Lebanese politician put it – 'carry off Arafat like Adolph Eichmann in a cage'.[67] But whatever Sharon had originally intended or desired, those initial lightning advances had obscured a painful, unforeseen reality. Some of the guerillas may have been the cowards so many Israelis always said they were. Others were not. Surrounded in the camps of Tyre, Sidon and other southern strongholds, outnumbered and hugely outgunned, they fought till the end. One of their best commanders, Abdullah Siyam, died, along with dozens of his men, in a rearguard action which held up their enemy's progress at the vital Khalde junction outside Beirut by a full six days. The casualties the Israelis were suffering – 269 dead within three weeks – were a warning of what awaited them if they tried to take the capital itself, a sprawling high-rise jungle, a street-fighter's dream, on which the guerillas were falling back, organizing and fortifying it for their last stand.[68]

BEGIN AND SHARON BEGIN TO LOSE THEIR WAR

So the Israelis halted at the gates. It was not clear at the time, but this was actually the critical moment of hesitation, failure of nerve even, when Begin, Sharon and Chief of Staff Eitan began to lose their war, to lose the initiative that only complete and devastating success in its earliest phases could have assured them. On the one hand, they were flinching at applying that central tenet of their own, interventionist credo: that with force, and force alone, they would get their way. On the other, in the politico-diplomatic sphere that was increasingly impinging on the military one, they were ceding ground to others, and chief among them, of course, the US. Even Reagan's America, uniquely friendly though it was, realized that it could not go all the way with its unruly protégé without incurring grievous risk to its larger, Arab interests in the region. It was, at least in part, precisely because he thought it could that Haig was driven from office a mere three weeks after the war began; and when he was the reins of diplomacy fell mainly into the hands of special envoy Habib, an altogether less partisan personality, who not merely confronted Sharon, but came to hate him, 'with a deep, dark passion', for what he considered him to be: a 'killer' and 'the biggest liar this side of the Mediterranean'.[69]

From the very outset of the seven-week siege an unaccustomed Israeli confusion and uncertainty reigned. Eitan said that, though his men had not been given orders to enter it, they would 'encircle and completely destroy the terrorist nerve centre'. Their leaders had already fled, he claimed. But that was wish-fulfilment. For Arafat was very much in evidence. He popped up all over the place, touring his front-line positions, even playing chess with foreign correspondents. His men would never leave or, if they did, only for Palestine. He would sooner die at his post. That, however, was as rhetorical as the Israelis' threat to come and get him; at the same time, through negotiations via Lebanese intermediaries with Habib, he was seeking a diplomatic solution, one in which he preserved at least something, if only the shadow, of his state-within-a-state.

Sharon would not have it. The PLO must 'disappear', he told the Knesset. There must be no military presence – even just to protect the refugee camps of Sabra, Shatila and Bourj al-Brajneh – nor a political or symbolic one. As the wrangling dragged on, the Israelis, in their frustration, repeatedly threatened to storm the city. But that was rhetoric too. Indeed the siege degenerated into the very antithesis of the *Blitzkrieg* brilliance in which they, and no one more than the daredevil defence minister himself, had once taken such pride. Instead of those swift, clean victories in the uninhabited wastes of Sinai or the sparsely populated Golan, here they were, reduced to the same tactics that the Syrians had used before them: stationary wars of attrition, endless artillery duels which slaughtered civilians by the hundreds but achieved no military objectives. They also emulated, outdid them in fact, in other, decidedly non-military activities, such as the looting of private homes, stealing cars, telephones, video and telex machines, even wooden school benches. And they left their distinctive calling card all over the country: human excrement in drawers, on beds, in churches and mosques, on hospital floors – and in the cigar boxes of the opulent.[70] The only difference, militarily, was the sheer weight and sophistication of the firepower at their disposal; in addition to the conventional ordnance, delivered from 800 tanks and artillery pieces deployed around the city, from gunboats offshore and an air force in total command of the skies, they launched concussion, cluster and phosphorus bombs.[71] Their targets were not just, or even mainly, military, but every kind of civilian one: multi-storey apartment blocks demolished at a stroke, hospitals, hotels and embassies, schools and refugee camps. Sharon would usually unleash the air force – in raids that would kill one, two, or three hundred people at a time – not to reinforce Habib's diplomacy, but in annoyance at its achievements.[72]

There was more to this than hatred or vindictiveness: Sharon was afraid that diplomacy would forestall not only the total defeat of the PLO, but his larger geopolitical designs for installing Bashir Gemayel and the Maronite 'pro-Zionists' in power as well. But in the end the wantonness and brutality with which he conducted his campaign further undermined his ability to conduct it at all, by provoking unrest within his army – one distinguished commander and hero of an earlier war went into open rebellion against this one – unprecedented wartime protest at home, ministerial dissension, international outrage and, finally, the fury of President Reagan, who, after a particularly murderous air raid, told Begin that the onslaught must cease. To which Begin replied:

I feel as a Prime Minister empowered to instruct a valiant army facing 'Berlin' where, among innocent civilians, Hitler and his henchmen hide in a bunker deep beneath the surface. My generation, dear Ron, swore on the altar of God that whoever proclaims his intent to destroy the Jewish state or the Jewish people, or both, seals his fate, so that which happened once on instructions from Berlin – with or without inverted commas – will never happen again.[73]

But his confidence in Sharon had been shaken, and when, with the next great raid, the call that Reagan made to Jerusalem betrayed even greater fury still, he and his cabinet were moved to strip the defence minister of his powers to order ground or aerial bombardments at all, assuming them in his place.[74]

Occasionally, under cover of massive bombardment, ground troops did push forward into guerilla-held territory, but whether they held what little gains they made or were forced to relinquish them, they got more very unpleasant foretastes of what awaited them if they attempted to take the whole of it. Indeed, if anything it was the guerillas who, in their particular form of combat, were displaying the panache, daring and ingenuity that the Israelis used to display in theirs. 'We don't want to sound arrogant', said Abu Khalid, a front-line commander at the international airport, 'but it is we who are teaching the Israelis now, we who have mobility. They wait in their tanks with their electronically controlled machine-guns. They have become cowards, really. And they lie about their casualties.'[75]

'BEIRUT IS NOT OURS TO DESTROY.'

In time, however, Arafat and his guerilla leadership decided that they would have to withdraw, leaving no military and very little political or symbolic presence behind. Their enemy's firepower and overall strategic advantage were too great and it was apparently ready to use them to destroy the whole city over the heads of its inhabitants. The rank and file did not like this decision, and there were murmurings of 'treason' from some of Arafat's harsher critics. Had they not already held out, far longer than any Arab country in any former war, against all that the most powerful army in the Middle East – and the fourth most powerful in the world, according to Sharon[76] – could throw against them? Surely, if they held out longer still, the Israelis would be forced, under mounting international pressure, either to retreat or to take that decision they clearly dreaded: not just to go on bombing the city from afar, but to conquer it, street by blitzed, blood-drenched street, in an operation that might end up costing them hundreds, if not thousands, of soldiers' lives? It was probably Lebanese, American and Arab factors more than strictly Palestinian ones that swayed their leaders. In Lebanon, with Sharon's blitz and the outrage it caused, the Palestinians had actually won back a good deal of the sympathy and support, among their natural Muslim and leftist constituency, which their pre-war conduct had cost them. But they knew that, if they expected too much, they could easily lose it again. 'If this had been Jerusalem,' they said, 'we would have stayed to the end. But Beirut is not ours to destroy.'[77] Despite all the damage the Israelis had done themselves in American eyes, the PLO remained the *bête noire*, the bad guy, it always had been, its politically unconditional departure from Beirut almost as much an American as an Israeli demand.

But it was the Arabs who did most – or, to be more precise, least – to drive the Palestinians into their new, and far-flung, exile. Here, for the first time in the history of the Arab–Israeli struggle, was the hated 'Zionist enemy' besieging an Arab capital. Its arrogance and its savagery had surpassed all limits. Arafat was right: it would have been better for the Arab regimes if he *had* fled or his fighting forces had crumbled beneath the initial onslaught.[78] It would at least have spared them the ignominy and contempt they earned during the two and half months in which, as the Palestinians fought alone, they did nothing, by arms or diplomacy, to help them. The 'kings and presidents' could not even rise to that old stand-by, an emergency summit conference, let alone decide on a collective course of action. President Mubarak of Egypt denounced the invasion as 'illegal, inhumane and contrary to the spirit of the Camp David agreements', but he resisted all guerilla appeals to repudiate the agreements in retaliation. King Fahd said that Saudi Arabia was putting 'all its resources and potentials' at the disposal of the Palestinians but, as Israel rained down death and destruction with

American-supplied weapons, this champion of Pax Americana in the Middle East just as steadfastly rejected Palestinian appeals to use its oil and financial power against Israel's incorrigible superpower supporter. Syria, self-styled protector of Lebanon and the Palestinian resistance movement, did fight for a while. After its annihilation of Syria's missile defences and other deadly blows, Israel declared a unilateral ceasefire. The Baathist regime promptly accepted it – and staged victory celebrations in Damascus. For this, it said, was the first time in the history of the Arab–Israeli conflict that Israel rather than an Arab country had asked for a ceasefire. When Israel proceeded to break its own ceasefire, not once but a dozen times – for every ceasefire was a ruse – the Syrians, withdrawing from the fray themselves, told the Palestinians to stand, fight and turn Beirut into 'a cemetery for the invaders'. Any agreement achieved through Habib, they said, would be 'like Sadat and Camp David'. As for Colonel Gadafi of Libya, patriot of patriots, he only had advice to offer: the Palestinians should commit suicide rather than withdraw.

Withdraw – under the protection of a multi-national force of Americans, French and Italians – 11,500 Palestinians and 2,700 Syrians trapped with them finally did. But it was no wonder, as they did, that the guerillas reserved their bitterest curses not for Israel – whose villainies they took for granted – but for their Arab brethren, whose 'betrayal', in this latest instalment of what Arafat once called an 'Arab plot', had exceeded what even they had expected. 'Save your tears for the Arab rulers,' shouted one departing fighter to his weeping kinsfolk. 'Ask them, ask Gadafi', shouted another, 'where were their MiGs and Mirages.' At the port, within earshot of clean-faced young Marines come to protect the 'stability' of the Middle East, a third fighter, younger even than they but hardened beyond his years, swore that 'we are going to put Israel aside for five years and clean up the Arab world. All our rulers are traitors. There must be vengeance, assassinations.' He clearly planned to be among the assassins. Gentler comrades smiled but did not dissent.[79]

The Beirut siege was soon to pass into heroic legend. The PLO bravely called it a victory. Morally, and measured by the expectations of both sides, perhaps, on balance, it was. But historically, like 'Black

September' 1970, or the cruel blow that Syria dealt it in 1976, it was another political and military setback for Arafat and the Revolution he had founded, the greatest, in fact, that he had suffered so far. He lost his one and only politico-military powerbase; most of his fighters were exiled to no fewer than eight Arab countries, some of them – the two Yemens, Sudan, Tunisia, Algeria – a good thousand miles and more from the Palestine it was their mission to liberate. And he lost it for no political quid pro quo, no firm American or international promise, or even reasonable expectation, of that permanent state, in Palestine itself, for which he had aspired to trade in his provisional one in exile. Thereafter, his movement was to be racked by political dissension, and what was left of its forces in Syrian-controlled regions of Lebanon to be rent by a mini civil war. But first there was Sabra and Shatila, a tragedy for the Palestinians – but Israel's much greater disgrace, and downfall as a would-be imperial power.

CHAPTER SEVEN

The Massacre of Sabra and Shatila

Israel's imperial nemesis: 1982–1985

'A PEACE WITH LEBANON BEFORE THE END OF THE YEAR'

Driving out the Palestinians, however important in itself, had always been the minimum prerequisite for the larger, more creative elements of Sharon's geopolitical grand design. He was now free to concentrate on the first of these, the final consummation of that early Zionist dream of 'Christian Lebanon' as Israel's 'natural ally' in the Arab world. For him and Begin, establishing such a Lebanese 'new order' had been the real point of the war.[1] Without it their whole enterprise – not to mention the unexpectedly high price in blood and treasure it had already incurred – would lose its justification. And six weeks into the invasion, had not the 'King of Israel', his glory at its still untarnished height, assured a vast, adoring throng that 'before the end of the year we shall have signed a peace treaty with Lebanon'?[2]

On 23 August, even before the Palestinian exodus was complete, they accomplished another, vital step in that direction. On that day, Bashir Gemayel, the man in whom they had vested all their hopes, the only man, idol of his community, who could ever in fact have fulfilled them, was chosen as the next president. In Lebanon, it is parliament that does the choosing, and it is certainly the most democratic process of its kind in an otherwise very undemocratic Arab world. All the same, though members of parliament cast the actual votes, greater states, both near and far, exert an influence over the way they do. In 1976, it was largely in deference to Syria that they had plumped for Elias Sarkis, because

Syria was the master then. This time it was Israel's turn. Gemayel's elevation was accomplished in the Fiyadiya barracks, just outside Beirut, where Phalangist militiamen formed an inner cordon, with Israeli soldiers just behind them. It had not been an entirely foregone conclusion, and Sharon and company had been obliged to exert themselves on his behalf with pressure, threats, cash – and even the helicoptering of one elderly parliamentarian from an isolated village in the Beqa'a before the Syrians could get at him.[3]

Occasion for rejoicing though this was – and even Mossad agents joined the Phalangists in their celebratory gunfire – there were still good reasons for apprehension too.[4] The use of military power for the achievement of quasi-imperial, geopolitical goals had proved problematic enough in the siege of Beirut; it was threatening to prove even more so now.

'SHEIKH BASHIR' TURNS AGAINST HIS ISRAELI BENEFACTORS

It was, in fact, that old, old story – that abiding conflict within the Maronite psyche.[5] Here it was, re-emerging again, and at this, the most critical moment it ever could have – Maronite 'Arabism' staging its comeback even as Maronite 'pro-Zionism' stood on the cusp of final victory. And it was doing it, irony of ironies, in the breast of a single man, 'Sheikh Bashir' himself. To be sure, that young blood would never have got where he was without Israel and its interventionists, or without the hearty show of 'pro-Zionism', sincere or otherwise, through which he had encouraged them into intervening so spectacularly on his behalf in the first place. He knew that. But, president-to-be, he also knew that he had better respect, insofar as he could bring himself to do so, the inter-communal conventions and compromises of the sectarian state. Yes, the Maronites were still *primus inter pares*; he would brook no doubts about that. Nonetheless, the time had surely come to shed the image of the militant Christian warrior who would very likely lord it over the Muslims with the same violence and coercion, so far mainly directed against his own community, which had stained his rise to supreme office; to be a 'strongman' perhaps – for surely the unruly Lebanese could do with one of those – but a

strongman who could woo and conciliate too. Already he was having
some success in that regard. He also had to shed the image of Israeli
puppet pure and simple. That, indeed, was something he had already
begun to do – and just when Sharon could least afford it. He had
reneged on what the Israelis had, or claimed to have, expected of him:
that *his* men, not theirs, would take on the job of storming West Beirut.
Nor was that all: he had not even allowed Sharon to land his combat
troops at Junieh, 'Marounistan's' principal port. And after his election
he began to sound positively unfriendly, even hostile, towards his Israeli
benefactors, insisting that he would never make peace with Israel
without the consent of 'all' Lebanese.[6]

It disturbed the Israelis, and all the more so because the Americans
were actually encouraging him in this stand. The Reagan Administration had appreciated the expulsion of the PLO and the humbling of
Soviet-backed Syria; but it had also been disturbed at various Israeli
excesses, as well as at the sheer enormity of Sharon's geopolitical grand
design, not least his ambition to transform America's loyalest of allies,
Jordan, from Hashemite kingdom into Republic of Palestine. It thought
that they were pushing Gemayel too hard, that it was unreasonable of
them to expect him, hardly installed as president, to defy at least half
of his population, and most of the Arab world, for the sake of a 'separate
peace'.[7] A serious divergence was opening up between Israel and the
infinitely indulgent superpower. It found expression in the 'Reagan
peace plan', an initiative designed to restore at least some of the favour
which its indulgence had cost it in the eyes of its Arab friends. The plan
was far from prescribing what Arafat wanted, an independent Palestine
state in Palestine itself; in fact it seemed to herald a return of
Hashemite rule over the West Bank – with formerly Egyptian-ruled
Gaza thrown in – which Arafat had once regarded as little better than
the Israeli variety. But at least it was something. And it infuriated Begin,
putting paid as it did to expectations that, via Lebanon and the crushing
of the PLO, he could now proceed with the full-scale absorption of the
occupied territories into his Greater Israel in the making. It was, as
ever, in Lebanon that Israel once again made known its displeasure at
a diplomatic initiative it did not like. In blatant violation of the
evacuation agreement, its ground forces advanced 600 metres from

their existing positions on the outskirts of West Beirut to the very edge of Sabra and Shatila. And it peremptorily summoned Gemayel to a meeting in Nahariya with Begin and Sharon.

THE DOUGHTY CHRISTIAN WARRIOR CRIED: 'PUT THE HANDCUFFS ON; I AM YOUR VASSAL'

Both these men considered that the first instalment had now fallen due on the huge debt their newly elected protégé owed them. But what they got was further evidence of his evasiveness and ingratitude. They kept him waiting for two hours and then – the champagne and welcoming cordialities swiftly dispensed with – Begin told him, in his starchiest tone, that 'the first thing you must do as president is to visit Jerusalem or at least Tel Aviv'. When Gemayel demurred, Begin demanded that they set a date for signing a peace treaty; and before the inwardly seething young president-elect could even respond to that, Begin decreed that it should take place before the end of the year. Finally, when Begin suggested that Major Saad Haddad, the commander of the Army of Free Lebanon whom Gemayel despised and wanted to put on trial for desertion, be appointed chief of staff in his administration, a shouting match ensued. It was, however, Sharon who shouted loudest, pointing out that Israel had Lebanon in its grasp and that he would be well advised – like Haddad – to do what Israel expected of him. Whereupon, the doughty Christian warrior thrust out both his arms, crying: 'put the handcuffs on; I am your vassal'.[8] The meeting ended in acrimony and without an agreement of any kind. 'He treated me like a child,' Gemayel confided to his father on his return to Lebanon. And his indignation was of a piece with sentiments now seeping into his community's consciousness at large. After exposure to Israelis in large numbers, at close range and for a prolonged period, many a Maronite, especially if young and female, found little in them of the blue-eyed, fair-skinned 'Europeans' of their fond imagining. On the contrary, they seemed so scruffy, slovenly, so sour a lot and – a great many of them – so positively 'Arab' in appearance; and even worse, it soon became apparent that these 'Arabs' – for that, in origin, is what so many of them were – in turn looked down on them, the Christians they had been sent to save from 'genocide', as just another species of Arab themselves. And anyway, some now muttered out loud, who, if not the Israelis, had saddled their country with these wretched Palestinians, source of all its woes, in the first place?[9]

THE ASSASSINATION OF 'SHEIKH BASHIR'

If Bashir was already trouble enough in life, he became trouble writ large in death. His 'Arabist' attitudes had come too late to save him and, like King Abdullah of Jordan or President Sadat before him, he suffered the fate to which Arab leaders who went too far in the service of the enemy were inherently liable. On 14 September he and twenty-six others died when a remote-controlled bomb went off in the Phalange party headquarters where he was making his last, weekly address to the faithful before assuming the presidency.

It was a huge setback for Sharon; in fact, his whole political future now hung in the balance. The Lebanese 'new order' of which Gemayel in person was to have been the central pillar was collapsing like a house of cards before it had even been erected. Sharon panicked; drastic action was required. He decided that his army had to go into Muslim West Beirut – and the Phalangists with it. The first of his official reasons for doing what Israel had solemnly assured the Americans that it would never do was to protect the Palestinians, or Lebanese Muslims, from the likely vengeance of these self-same Phalangists. The first of his real reasons was to try to ensure that, whoever succeeded Gemayel, Israel would retain its ability to shape the 'new order'. The Phalangists had immediately to fill the political vacuum left by their leader's dis-appearance; otherwise, he melodramatically warned them, the Muslims, backed by residual Palestinian 'terrorists', might turn the tables on them, destroy the very basis of the sectarian state and seize the presidency, that sacrosanct Maronite preserve, for themselves.[10] Could ever a man have more knowingly engineered the very horror he ostensibly sought to prevent?

In the fifteen years that, by the standard reckoning, it was destined to endure, the Lebanese 'civil war' yielded a rich variety of atrocities, in the perpetrating of which no protagonist, Muslim, Christian,

Lebanese, Arab or Israeli, was innocent. But if any one of them stood out, qualifying as an atrocity in what is generally felt to be its gravest form, 'genocide', it was not the one – of Christians by Syrians or Palestinians – about which Begin had so loudly warned. *That* one never did come to pass. It was the one which his own side, Israelis and Maronite Christians – those 'two progressive peoples of the Middle East', as Weizmann once called them – now jointly perpetrated against the Palestinians. The UN General Assembly pronounced it an 'act of genocide' by a vote of 98 to 19, with 23, including all the Western democracies, abstaining. Its critics contended, with some justification, that, coming from such a body, this was less objective definition than automatic anti-Israeli attitudinizing. But it was harder to say that of other bodies – such as the international commission of inquiry into the massacre headed by Sean MacBride,[11] four of whose six members also deemed it 'a form of genocide' – or of individuals, especially Jews, around the world who saw it likewise.

It had in fact been inherently likely from the outset that the Israeli invasion would bring some such grisly climax as Sabra and Shatila. That was why, in the negotiations over the withdrawal of the PLO the thorniest issue had always been the guarantees which Arafat demanded for the safety of the Palestinian civilians the fighting men were to leave behind. To the end, he had been agonizingly aware of the inadequacy of those that he finally accepted. True, the US had given its 'word of honour' that the Israelis would never enter West Beirut, and special envoy Habib had written to the Lebanese prime minister, Shafiq Wazzan:

> The government of Lebanon and the United States will provide appropriate guarantees for the safety ... of law-abiding Palestinian non-combatants left in Beirut, including the families of those who have departed ... The United States will provide its guarantees on the basis of assurances received from the government of Israel and the leaders of certain Lebanese groups [i.e. the Phalangists] with which it has been in contact.[12]

The truth was, however, that for all the passion, and righteous indignation at their scepticism, which he used to persuade both

Lebanese and Palestinians, even Habib himself had 'minimal confidence' in the purely oral assurances from the parties in whose hands he had so imprudently placed his country's 'honour'.[13] Nor was he at all happy that the multi-national force that supervised the evacuation was mandated to stay for only a month – and even less happy, enraged in fact, when it actually departed a full two weeks before it need have. The US Secretary of Defense, Caspar Weinberger, fearful of casualties, had insisted on that, against the advice of the colonel in command of the US contingent. So it was that the Americans, last in, had been the first out, with a smiling Marine holding up for photographers a sign reading 'mission accomplished'.[14]

Just six days later, at 3.30 in the morning of Wednesday, 15 September, Chief of Staff Eitan and General Amir Drori, commander of Israel's northern region, met with Phalangist leaders at their military headquarters in East Beirut. Together with Fadi Frem, commander-in-chief of the 'Lebanese Forces', and Elias Hobeika, the head of intelligence already well known to them as the 'hero' of Yarin,[15] they drew up the plan for Phalangist participation in the seizure of West Beirut. It was decided that – in order to spare Israeli lives – the Phalangists would be exclusively entrusted with 'searching and mopping up' the refugee camps. That was necessary because of a second, official reason which the Israeli government now adduced for going into Beirut, namely the presence of some 2,000 terrorists, equipped with 'modern and heavy weapons', whom the departing PLO had deceitfully left behind. Not merely was this absurdly incompatible with the first reason – protecting the Palestinians from the Phalangists – it was also, if not a fabrication pure and simple, the most ludicrous of exaggerations; and nothing more eloquently illustrated that than the size of the force, a mere 150 to 200 men, which both Israelis and Phalangists deemed sufficient to deal with them.[16]

ISRAEL SENDS THE PHALANGISTS INTO SABRA AND SHATILA

At five o'clock that morning the Israelis began their entry. It was easy: the multi-nationals had conveniently removed mines and barricades and resistance from the Muslim/leftists was little more than symbolic.

In the entire operation the Israelis lost only seven killed and a hundred wounded.[17]

At nine o'clock, Begin, receiving Habib's deputy Morris Draper, told him that Israel's sole objective was 'to maintain order in the town. With the situation created by the assassination of Bashir Gemayel, there could be pogroms.'[18] What he did not tell Draper was that Israel itself was now about to send into Sabra and Shatila the very people it most expected to carry out such pogroms. 'If we *had* been told ... I would have let out a howl,' said Draper, already aghast at Israel's action, and what, to him, it signified: a flagrant breach of promise, an 'unheard-of, straight-out, 100 per cent, baldfaced lie' told 'by the prime minister of a friendly state ... to the United States government, his great friend'.[19] In fact, at that point, Begin didn't even know about the Phalangist involvement himself. Typically, neither his defence minister, nor Chief of Staff Eitan – though both in regular contact – had yet deigned to tell him.[20] And in any case it would not be till the evening of the following day, Thursday, 16 September, that Hobeika and his men finally did go in.

But if Begin *had* known, he would also have known perfectly well what the Phalangists were going to do when they got there. So would any reasonably observant Israeli who knew anything at all about them. And many Israelis knew them very well indeed. They had after all been training them in Israel since 1976. The military correspondent of *Yediot Aharonot* had called them 'an organized mob, with uniforms, vehicles, training camps, who have been guilty of abominable cruelties'.[21] It was common knowledge, too, just what special hatred they reserved for the Palestinians; that, indeed, was the foundation of Israel's alliance with them. For Gemayel there had been 'one people too many: the Palestinian people'.[22] In his dealings with the Israelis he had left no doubt that, when he came to power, he would 'eliminate the Palestinian problem' – even if that meant resorting to 'aberrant methods against the Palestinians in Lebanon'.[23] His militiamen had never concealed their murderous ambitions. When a group of Israeli parliamentarians visited the southern border Strip, one such militiaman told them: 'One dead Palestinian is a pollution, the death of all Palestinians, that is the solution.'[24] *Bamahane*, the army newspaper, wrote on 1 September, just two weeks before the massacre:

A senior Israeli officer heard the following from the lips of a
Phalangist: the question we are putting to ourselves is – how to
begin, by raping or killing? If the Palestinians had a bit of nous,
they would try to leave Beirut. You have no idea of the slaughter
that will befall the Palestinians, civilians or terrorists, who remain
in the city. Their efforts to mingle with the population will be
useless. The sword and the gun of the Christian fighters will
pursue them everywhere and exterminate them once and for all.[25]

Political objectives as well as mere bloodlust drove them. In their
meetings with Israeli representatives their leaders had confided that it
would be necessary to resort to violence in order to bring about a
Palestinian exodus from Lebanon.[26] 'We knew that they wanted to
destroy the camps', said General Amos Yaron, the commander of the
Beirut area.[27] In this they saw themselves as mere executants of
Sharon's scheme to overthrow King Hussein and dump all Lebanon's
Palestinians on Jordan.[28]

The Israeli army also knew, at the highest level, just what vengeful
feelings had indeed taken possession of the militiamen after the
assassination of their idol. Even after inflaming those feelings yet
further – by telling them that Palestinians were surely behind the
assassination and should be made to pay for it[29] – and arranging for
their entry into the camps, the chief of staff told a cabinet meeting that
Phalangist officers had 'just one thing left to do, and this is revenge;
and it will be terrible … it will be an eruption the like of which has
never been seen; I can already see in their eyes what they are waiting
for.'[30] They also knew, from his exploits in South Lebanon and before
that at the siege of Tal al-Za'atar in 1976, what free rein Hobeika would
be likely to give his men. After Sharon had decided to 'cleanse the
camps', someone proposed that an Israeli liaison officer be seconded
to the Phalangists. But a superior, aware of Hobeika's past, vetoed the
idea, arguing that the Israeli army should not get itself mixed up in
atrocities.[31]

After passing through the Israeli roadblocks set up at its entrance the
first unit of the 'Lebanese Forces' entered Shatila camp at sunset on
Thursday. Some carried knives and axes as well as firearms. The carnage

began immediately. It was to continue without interruption till Saturday noon. Night brought no respite; the Phalangist liaison officer asked for illumination and the Israelis duly obliged with flares, first from mortars and then from planes.[32] Anything that moved in the narrow alleyways the Phalangists shot. They broke into houses and killed their occupants who, not suspecting anything, were gathered for their evening meal, watching television or already in bed. Sometimes they tortured before they killed, gouging out eyes, skinning alive, disembowelling. Women and small girls were raped, sometimes half a dozen times, before, breasts severed, they were finished off with axes. Babies were torn limb from limb and their heads smashed against walls. Entering Akka hospital the assailants assassinated the patients in their beds. They decorated other victims with grenades, or tied them to vehicles and dragged them through the streets alive. They cut off hands to get at rings and bracelets. They killed Christians and Muslims, Lebanese and Syrians as well as Palestinians. They even killed nine Jewesses who, married to Palestinians, had been living in the camps since 1948. Bulldozers were brought in to bury their victims. These also demolished houses which Israeli aircraft had not yet destroyed; for then, roofless as well as terrorized, all the Palestinians would surely have to flee.[33]

What was happening in the camps could hardly escape the attention of the Israeli soldiers surrounding them. Their forward command post was a mere 200 metres from the main killing ground, and from the roof of this seven-storey building they had a direct line of sight into the heart of the camps. It was, said one officer, 'like the front row at the theatre'.[34] Hobeika spent Thursday night on the roof of the command post. At 8 p.m., within an hour of the Phalangists' entry, Lieutenant Elul, General Yaron's *chef de bureau*, overheard a radio conversation in which a Phalangist officer inside the camp asked Hobeika what he should do with a group of fifty women and children. 'This is the last time you're going to ask me a question like that', Hobeika replied, 'you know exactly what to do.' Raucous laughter broke out among the Phalangist personnel on the roof and Elul understood that the women and children were to be murdered. He rushed to tell Yaron – who, not for the first time, warned Hobeika against harming civilians.[35] Later, another Phalangist officer, Jesse Suker, liaison man to the Israelis, was asked what to do with forty-five captured men. 'Do God's will,' Israeli wireless monitors heard him reply. Then Suker turned up in person at the Israeli command post itself with the news that 'up to now 300 civilians and terrorists have been killed'. Then, a short while after that, Yaron's chief intelligence officer informed him that the Phalangists had actually found none of those '2,000 terrorists' in the camp at all; instead they were 'gathering up women, children and probably old people'. He said they 'don't know quite what to do with them ...', but that he didn't like the sound of Suker's 'do what your heart tells you because everything is from God.' However, Yaron cut him off, assuring him, on the strength of assurances he had just had from Suker himself, that no harm would come to them.[36]

As dawn broke on Friday, 17 September, Israeli officers and men atop the command post could see the bodies piling up. Later they were to see bulldozers, one or two of them Israeli-supplied, shovelling them into the ground. Soldiers from an armoured unit stationed a mere hundred metres from the camp recalled how visible the killing had been. Their report went to the higher authorities, who were receiving similar ones from other points around the camp.[37] Lieutenant Avi Grabowski, second-in-command of a tank company, said that he had seen Phalangists killing women and children, and when his men asked them why, one replied: 'women give birth to children, and children grow up into terrorists'. Israeli soldiers were instructed to do nothing. 'We don't like it,' an officer told his men, 'but I forbid any of you to intervene in what is happening in the camps.'[38] The soldiers blocked the camp entrances, several times turning back refugees frantic to get out, and on one occasion a tank pointed its cannon at a group of 500 who, white flags held aloft, tried to explain that the marauders were 'assassinating everybody'.[39]

At about 4 o'clock on Friday afternoon generals Eitan and Drori met Phalangist commanders, some of them fresh from the camps. Eitan congratulated them on their operation and the Phalangists, explaining that the Americans had called on them to stop, asked the Israelis for 'just a bit more time to clean the place up'.[40] It was agreed that all Phalangists would leave the camps by Saturday morning and that, meanwhile, no extra forces would be sent in. However, even as Eitan left Beirut airport for Tel Aviv, a new Phalangist unit of some 200 men set off for Shatila, mowed down a group of women and children as soon as they got there, massacred all the occupants of the first house they came across and demolished it with a bulldozer. They seemed even less concerned about concealing their deeds than the first unit. They paraded Palestinian women on trucks through the streets of East Beirut, 'gleefully introducing them to passers-by as brand-new Palestinian widows courtesy of Phalangist guns'.[41]

About the same time, Sharon and Foreign Minister Yitzhak Shamir were again meeting Habib's deputy Draper, who asked that the Israelis hand over their positions to the Lebanese army immediately. Sharon told him that nothing could be done because it was the Jewish New Year. Besides, his own army's presence was already 'preventing a massacre of the Palestinian population in the Western part of the city'.[42] Later that evening, after hearing stories of summary executions and other 'horrors' from Israeli officers, the military correspondent of Israeli television, Ben Yishai, telephoned the defence minister and told him that something had to be done immediately. 'In a few hours the press of the entire world will know about it, and then we'll be in a real mess.' Sharon listened attentively and asked if he had any more details. He supplied some. 'The minister did not react,' he was later to recall. 'He thanked me and wished me a happy New Year. My impression was that he knew what was going on in the camps.' He knew very well, and so did most of the high command, both in the field and back at head-quarters in Israel; but no one lifted a finger to stop it.[43]

The next day the world did indeed learn. Journalists descended on Sabra and Shatila to find the hundreds of bodies which the Phalangists had not had time to bury, the limbs which protruded from the hastily dug graves of those they had, the naked women with hands and feet tied behind their backs, the victims of car-dragging, one of them with his genitals cut off, piled in a garage, the baby whose limbs had been carefully laid out in a circle, head crowning the whole. They stumbled across evidence of resistance from those '2,000 heavily armed terrorists' – the sporting shotgun that lay by the body of a young boy.[44]

The Lebanese army, local and international relief and medical teams attempted to count the putrefying remains as they buried them. But these did not include the many bodies that lay undiscovered in the mass graves and the rubble of demolished homes. Nor did it include those of the missing – those who, during the massacre, had been taken away to an unknown destination. How many had died? A Phalangist commander was asked. 'You'll find out', he replied, 'if they ever build a subway in Beirut.'[45] But it could have been a good 3,000.[46]

THE GREATEST MISFORTUNE

It was as a supremely 'moral nation' that Israel had invaded Lebanon in the first place. That at least was what Begin had said, and perhaps sincerely believed. The Christian West had once abandoned the Jews to the tender mercies of Hitler and the Nazis; and if, similarly, it were now to do nothing for its co-religionists, the embattled Maronites, the Jews-as-Israelis would be different – and better.[47] It is from the Holocaust, perhaps above all, that Israel, as a haven for the Jews, has derived its moral *raison d'être*, its most passionately invoked, most unanswerable reason for being. It was, therefore, above all a moral crisis that Israel faced – the most grievous in its history – now that, far from saving the Maronites, it had joined with them in doing to others, on however reduced a scale, what the Holocaust had done to the Jews.

The dimensions of the crisis were measurable in the instantaneous and worldwide outrage. Inside Israel, the Peace Now movement, whose main role was to agitate against Israeli policies towards the Palestinians and the occupied territories, was first in the field with an immediate, thousand-strong demonstration outside the prime minister's residence. 'Begin terrorist, Begin assassin, Beirut–Deir Yassin 1982' were their slogans. Among them was an eighty-year-old Professor Epstein, who sobbed: 'after what happened in Beirut I'm ashamed to be an Israeli. It reminds me too much of the Nazis who brought Ukrainians into the ghetto to massacre the Jews. I don't understand how that could happen to us.'[48] 'War crime in Beirut,' headlined *Haaretz*, Israel's leading newspaper, above an article by its military correspondent Zeev Schiff, who wrote that, with the knowledge of the Israeli authorities, the Phalangists had done to death men, women and children 'in exactly the same way as the pogroms against the Jews'. 'This massacre', said *al-Hamishmar*, 'has made of the war in Lebanon the greatest misfortune to befall the Jewish people since the Holocaust.'[49] Under immense pressure from home and abroad, the Labour opposition, which had generally supported the invasion because of its popularity with most of the electorate, joined the hue and cry calling on the government to resign. 'The Jewish people', said Labour leader Shimon Peres, 'is face to face with its conscience ... The fate of Israel, David Ben-Gurion said, is dependent on its strength and righteousness. Righteousness, not just strength, has to guide our deeds.'[50]

In the US, a very angry President Reagan pointed out that Israel had justified its entry into West Beirut on the ground that it would thereby forestall just the kind of tragedy which had now taken place. Like Reagan, Israeli supporters everywhere felt a kind of betrayal. This was not the Israel they thought they knew. Nowhere was this more potentially dangerous than in the US – its Administration, Jewish community or the public at large. A New York woman, interviewed by National Public Radio, said that if Jews could not retain their ethically high standards, she no longer wanted to be one. A Jewish lawyer in Connecticut said he now believed that even Jews were capable of genocide.[51] The Washington correspondent of the *Jerusalem Post*, Wolf Blitzer, called the massacre 'a disaster for Israel in Washington – indeed throughout the US. It will take many years – if ever – to regain its once very high moral image in America.'[52] It did indeed look as though Israel had squandered much of the moral credit on which it had so often to draw in order to wrest political, military and economic support from a sometimes reluctant, if basically subservient, administration.

'GOYIM ARE KILLING GOYIM, AND THE WORLD IS TRYING TO HANG THE JEWS FOR THE CRIME'

The dimensions of the crisis were also measurable by the outrage against the outrage, the blatant falsehoods and preposterous exculpations, that issued from the Israeli government. Begin chaired an emergency cabinet meeting whose agenda was not the massacre itself, but 'the frontal assault against the State of Israel and its people'. '*Goyim* are killing *goyim*,' he raged, 'and the world is trying to hang the

Jews for the crime.'[53] At a cost of $54,000 his government took a full-page advertisement in the *New York Times* and the *Washington Post* to denounce the 'blood libel' and declare that 'any direct or implicit accusation that the Israel Defense Forces bear any blame whatsoever for this human tragedy is entirely baseless and without foundation. The people of Israel are proud of the IDF's ethics and respect for human life.' According to another official pronouncement, the survivors of Sabra and Shatila had 'thanked the Israeli army for coming so swiftly to [their] aid'.[54] In the US, Julius Berman, Chairman of the Conference of the Presidents of Major Jewish Organizations, contended that 'the injunctions of Jewish law are too powerful a force in Jewish consciousness to have permitted or even countenanced a Jewish role in this awful incident. Any suggestion that Israel took part in it or permitted it to occur must be categorically rejected.' If the apologists blamed anyone, it was the Israeli leaders only, guilty of an 'aberration' of which the state and society were innocent.[55]

When denial failed to still the fury, but merely exacerbated it, the government resorted to damage control, to the commission of inquiry for which Israelis – in a huge demonstration in Tel Aviv – and the world clamoured. Its partners-in-crime had already beaten it to it. Lebanon's official report was completed, signed, sealed and delivered within eleven days of the massacre. It was a total cover-up, part of the campaign on which the Phalangist leadership had immediately embarked to shift all blame to the Israelis – and thereby overcome any Muslim reservations about the choice of Amin Gemayel, brother of Bashir, as president in his place. The report was never published. Indeed, it was said to have 'disappeared' from the files of the Lebanese government, or of any person connected with it, including its author himself. However, it is known to have completely exonerated the 'Lebanese Forces', the inference therefore being that, unless ghosts had done the dreadful deed, it could only have been the Israelis themselves, or just possibly – as 'Sheikh Pierre', the Phalangists' grand old man, would privately concede to Muslim oligarchs ready, for the sake of inter-communal co-existence, to connive in such a fiction – those 'Israeli agents', those 'good many Judas Iscariots', whom Sharon had planted 'in our ranks'.[56]

Israel's own commission of inquiry replied in kind. Like the Lebanese one its report was a product of the ruling establishment, and in one respect its purpose, to assuage a grave internal crisis, was not dissimilar. But it also had another, closely related one: to secure, if not the total, then at least the maximum possible exoneration from a credulous US public.[57] It did tolerably well on the home front, where, symptomatic of a nation's conscience broadly speaking cleared, the *Jerusalem Post* waxed lyrical about this 'splendid example of Israeli – not to say Jewish – justice at work'.[58] It did even better in the US, where the *New York Times* announced the advent of a 'Jerusalem ethic', no less, and exclaimed: 'how rare the nation that seeks salvation by such means'.[59] The report certainly was not as shamelessly mendacious as its Lebanese counterpart. But it was a blatant whitewash all the same. It exemplified a propensity for moral and intellectual sophistry by which, since the earliest days, official keepers of the Zionist conscience sought to persuade themselves and the world that theirs has always been a humane and righteous creed.

The Kahan Commission – so called after its chairman, Itzhak Kahan, President of the Supreme Court – enunciated its own, judicially spurious and morally expedient doctrine of 'direct' and 'indirect responsibility'.[60] The Phalangists' responsibility turned out to be the direct, and therefore truly culpable, one, that of the Israeli authorities merely indirect. The latter's only fault lay in the fact that, although they sent the Phalangists into the camps for the legitimate reasons they said they did, their decision to do so was taken 'without consideration of the danger that the Phalangists would commit massacres and pogroms' when they got there, without 'proper heed' being paid to reports of killings as they came in or 'energetic and immediate action' being taken to stop them.[61]

Although the Commission was charged with examining 'all the facts and factors' connected with the massacre, it confined itself in practice to the narrowest of spheres, treating it as an isolated, exceptional event, unrelated to the whole conduct of the war, let alone the larger moral, ideological and historical context in which it took place. Nor did it examine all the clearly relevant 'facts and factors' themselves. Or if it did, it did not, by its own admission, disclose any of those that could be

injurious to Israel's 'national security' – among them, for example, the
fact that Phalangist commanders not only took orders from Israelis but
actually received salaries from them too.[62] The Kahan Report was also
notable for its errors, omissions and contradictions. Of the errors,
perhaps the most grievous and demonstrable was its assertion that 'it
was impossible to see what was happening within the alleys in the camp
from the roof of the [forward] command post'. This assertion was based
on the evidence of the soldiers concerned, who would have incrim-
inated themselves had they admitted it *was* possible. According to
other, independent witnesses, such as *Newsweek* correspondent Ray
Wilkinson, the seven-storey building (not five-storey as the
Commission had it), a mere 250 paces from the camps, provided a
direct, grandstand view that would have enabled anyone on it, with the
aid of binoculars, 'to see even the smallest details'.[63] The concept of
'indirect responsibility' would have been utterly unsustainable without
such errors or omissions. It was in any case hard enough to sustain in
the light of the 'facts and factors' which the Commission did expose,
and even harder still when these were placed in that larger context
which the report ignored.

'In all the testimony we have heard', it said, 'there has been unanimity
regarding the [fact] that the battle ethics of the Phalangists differ greatly
from those of the Israel Defence Force.' Higher standards were naturally
to be expected from a regular army than from a private militia, but after
that was taken into account, was there really any substantial difference?
Since when had 'purity of arms' become anything more than the
nostalgic memory of something that had never really existed in the first
place? Not for a very long time, according to General Mordecai Gur,
chief of staff during the previous, 1978, invasion of South Lebanon.
Asked whether, during Operation Litani, the Israeli army had
bombarded Lebanese civilians 'without discrimination', he replied:

> 'I've been in the army thirty years. Do you think I don't know what
> we've been doing all those years? What did we do the entire length
> of the Suez Canal? A million and a half refugees! Really, where do
> you live? Since when has the population of South Lebanon been so
> sacred? They know very well what the terrorists were doing. After

the massacre of Avivim, I had four villages in South Lebanon
bombarded without authorization.'

'Without discrimination?'

'What discrimination? What had the inhabitants of Irbid
[a non-Palestinian town in north Jordan] done to deserve
being bombarded by us?'

'But the military communiqués always spoke of returning
fire and counterstrikes against terrorist targets.'

'Be serious ... You don't know that the whole Jordan Valley
was evacuated during the War of Attrition?'

'You maintain that the civilian population should be punished?'

'And how! I am using Sabra language: and how! I never doubted
it, not for one moment. When I said ... bring in tanks as quickly as
possible and hit them from afar before the boys reach a face-to-
face battle, didn't I know what I was doing ... ?'[64]

Gur was a pillar of the 'moderate' Labour establishment. What was
to be expected of the Likud 'extremist' who succeeded him? There was
a difference, certainly, but it was one of degree, not kind, of posture
rather than conduct. Ethically speaking, what the army did under Eitan
represented an aggravation, no more, of what it had done under Gur.
It was Begin himself who, in the Knesset, deftly and deliberately
stressed the essential continuities of Israeli military practice. When,
sixty-eight days into the invasion, the Labour opposition was growing
restive at the brutalities of the campaign and the bad impression they
were making on the outside world, all that Begin had to do, in his own
defence, was to cite the text of that famous interview.

'PERSONALLY I WOULD LIKE TO SEE THEM ALL DEAD.'

If anything, then, Sabra and Shatila merely highlighted what Israelis
and Phalangists had in common, the main difference between them
being an essentially operational one, whereby, characteristically, the
high-tech Israelis killed civilians from afar, with aircraft or long-range
artillery, while the low-tech Phalangists did it 'face-to-face', and, as
Eitan so delicately put it, 'in conformity with their code of conduct in
warfare, if one can put it that way'.[65] And the two certainly had motives

and aims in common beyond the strictly military. In this larger sense, Sabra and Shatila was not an 'aberration'. On the contrary, it was a culmination – and a dreadful one – for a state, a society and the ideology which infused them.

> One does not [wrote Larry Davidson, an American commentator] enter upon the ruination of most of a neighbouring country, culminating in complicity in a genocidal act, and then turn round and excuse it simply as a deviation from one's normal way of doing things ... What happened in Lebanon was the consequence ... of a 34-year effort to create and preserve a racially-based state ... Israeli law has created first and second-class citizenship based on race and religion, which affects most areas in, and the right of immigration to, Israel. Over time large numbers of non-Jews have been pressured or evicted from land on which they had lived for generations. Not surprisingly, these efforts fostered an enemy which Zionists feel obliged to castigate. Therefore the Palestinians have been labeled terrorists and identified with the Nazis and anti-Semitism.[66]

That was putting it mildly. By the time of Sabra and Shatila that time-honoured Israeli reflex[67] – demonizing all enemies as terrorists and thereby legitimizing any means of combating them – had reached a new level of intensity; and it was all the more effective in that it coincided with the new American one, which the Israelis themselves had done much to foster, of portraying 'international terrorism' as the great new global menace, the 'vogue evil' that made of 'anti-terrorism ... the fashionable crusade'.[68] And the reflex came, in this Begin era, laced with a contemptuous, racist terminology, which was replete with genocidal overtones and tended to reduce the Palestinians to a 'subhuman' category. He himself called the Palestinian militants 'two-legged beasts'. And he never tired of his Nazi analogies; the alternative to the invasion of Beirut, he said, was Treblinka.[69] Shortly *before* the massacre, a group of Israeli 'doves' had discussed the pernicious influence of such expressions as 'nests of terrorists', their 'purification', and the 'extermination' of the 'two-legged beasts' who inhabited them. 'Every child now killed in the bombardment of Beirut', said one, 'is being murdered by an Israel journalist.' These journalists' 'original sin' was the very use of the word 'terrorist', first to denote 'all PLO fighters', then 'all PLO members – diplomats, officials, teachers, physicians, nurses in the Palestinian Red Crescent' – and finally 'the whole Palestinian people'.[70] An Israeli soldier did not conceal the effect which this insidious propaganda had had on him. 'Listen,' he said:

> I know you are tape-recording this, but personally I would like to
> see them all dead ... because they are a sickness wherever they go
> ... Seeing dead children and women here is not really nice, but
> everyone is involved in this kind of war, the women too, so we
> can't always punish exactly the right people because otherwise
> it would cost us a lot of deaths. And for us, I guess, I hope you
> understand this, the death of one Israeli soldier is more important
> than the death of even several hundred Palestinians.[71]

In short, concluded Davidson, 'once a nation starts down the road the Zionists have followed in order to build the Jewish state, one comes to Sabra and Shatila. There are no aberrations here.'[72] And no essential differences in the 'battle ethics' of Weizmann's 'two most progressive peoples in the Middle East'. The finding of 'indirect responsibility' was based on the single premise – and even that one was debatable[73] – that Israeli soldiers did not pull the triggers; they merely got their protégés to do so. 'If you invite the Yorkshire Ripper to spend a couple of nights in an orphanage for small girls,' said novelist Amos Oz, 'you can't, later on, just look over the piles of bodies and say you made an agreement with the Ripper – that he'd just wash the girls' hair.'[74]

For all its casuistry and emollience, the Kahan report produced demonstrations and counter-demonstrations in the streets and – with the grenade that killed a young soldier protesting the war from which he himself had just returned – the first political murder of its kind in the history of the state. A few hours after Emile Grunzweig's death, the Begin cabinet accepted the Commission's findings, as well as its indulgent recommendations, the most far-reaching of which was that Sharon, the chief culprit, should resign.

It was a specious acceptance. All that Begin did was to move Sharon from one cabinet seat to another – that of minister without portfolio. This hypocrisy cried out to heaven, commented the leading newspaper

Haaretz. It nonetheless accorded with the dominant mood of the country. According to the *Jerusalem Post*, the man in the street was largely indifferent to Grunzweig's death. 'You should put them all up against the wall and shoot them,' said a taxi-driver about the Peace Now movement.[75] Opinion polls showed that 51.7 per cent of the population thought the Commission had been too harsh. Only 31.4 per cent deemed it just, while a tiny minority, 2.17 per cent, deemed it too lenient.[76] The columnist Yoel Marcus concluded:

> In the matter of Sabra and Shatila, a large part of the community, perhaps the majority, is not at all troubled by the massacre itself. Killing of Arabs in general, and Palestinians in particular, is quite popular, or at least 'doesn't bother anyone', in the words of the youth these days. Ever since the massacre I have been surprised more than once to hear from educated, enlightened people, 'the conscience of Tel Aviv', the view that the massacre itself, as a step towards removing the remaining Palestinians from Lebanon, is not terrible. It is just too bad that we were in the neighbourhood.[77]

ISRAEL IN DECLINE ...

Sabra and Shatila, profoundly shocking and damaging in itself, was part and parcel of the much larger debacle – strategic, diplomatic and political as well as moral – which the Fifth Arab–Israeli War represented and which, in retrospect, was a turning-point in Israel's history. In its own eyes and those of much of the world, the Third Arab–Israeli War of 1967, the quintessential war of 'self-defence', had marked the high point of Zionism, the supremely just and well-nigh miraculous triumph of an historically persecuted race; but this war, the imperial 'war of choice', had the opposite significance. It marked the beginning of Israel's decline. The decline was in the first instance military. But, given the primordial importance which Israel, because of the nature of the struggle in which it was engaged, assigned to military power and performance, military questions almost by definition begged much larger, existential questions too.

For historian Martin van Creveld, writing many years later, Operation Peace in Galilee was perhaps the first great landmark in an unfolding tragedy that would reduce the Israeli army from the superb, completely trusted, fighting force of a 'small but brave people' it had been in its heroic, early days into a 'high-tech, but soft, bloated, strife-ridden, responsibility-shy and dishonest army', ever more mistrusted by the people.[78] It would take a decade or two for that degeneration really to make itself felt, but what did quickly become obvious, even as the invasion was still under way, was that Israel had thoroughly over-reached itself at last, that it lacked the intrinsic strength, the moral conviction and the will, the manpower and the economic resources, to sustain the adventure into which its generals, in their overweening pride and self-confidence, had dragged it.

Indeed, the whole enterprise soon proved itself to have been completely useless. By 1985, after sustaining greater losses, pro-portionally, than the Soviet Union in its disastrous Afghanistan war, Israel was back in the South Lebanese 'security zone' from which it had started out, subject, yet again, to those 'rockets on Kiryat Shmona' which Begin had sworn forever to eliminate. But it was altogether worse off than before. Among other things, Israel had suffered serious damage to its aura of invincibility, to that sacrosanct 'deterrent power' by which it presumed to keep its Arab enemies permanently in awe. Worse, perhaps, it had widened and deepened the circle of hatred and hostility that surrounded it, and created a new, principally Shiite enemy, from whose ranks had arisen an authentic grassroots resistance movement altogether more formidable than the Palestinian one it had largely defeated.

... AND THE MARONITES LOSE THEIR PRIMACY

As for the underlying assumption of the invasion – that the greater the force deployed the more far-reaching the political 'facts on the ground' it could create – that was shattered beyond repair. Little Lebanon alone, never mind the region as a whole which Sharon's larger purposes had also encompassed, utterly frustrated the interventionists. All hopes for the consummation of the 'minority alliance', for the fulfilment of the six-decade-old dream of a Maronite-run Lebanon finally and com-pletely throwing in its lot with Israel, evaporated almost overnight.

Indeed, it was actually in the wake of this intervention, designed to reinforce and perpetuate the primacy of the Maronites, that they most seriously began to lose it to the other communities, and, above all, to the Shiites, the underdogs of old now poised for an historic reversal of fortunes.

True, the Maronites retained their constitutionally prescribed pre-eminence within the sectarian state. But having come to power, like his late brother Bashir, at the point of Israeli bayonets, Amin Gemayel proceeded to abuse it. He 'Phalangized' his administration and used the army, in conjunction with the Phalangist militia, to intimidate, repress and lord it over the other communities[79] until eventually these rose up against him. In a blood-letting reminiscent of the massacres of 1860, the Druzes drove the Israeli-assisted invading militia, and virtually every Maronite, out of the Shouf highlands, where the two communities had lived cheek by jowl for centuries, and, in the 'uprising' of 4 February 1984, Nabih Berri's Shiite militia Amal, the Druzes and the Sunnis joined forces to seize control of the whole of West Beirut and strategic areas around it. Once again, though in very different circumstances from 1976, the national army disintegrated after Berri called on its Shiite members to defect. Once again a Maronite president's writ was reduced to little more than his palace. Once again – but more than ever – his whole community were plunged into collective fear and paranoia, with refugees fleeing in droves from the port of Junieh, 'capital' of 'Marounistan', that last remaining 20 per cent of the country which, thanks to the Phalangists rather than Gemayel himself, the Maronites could still call their own. But it was not Israel to whom they turned for salvation – though that is what diehard 'Bashirians' still wanted – because Israel, most of them now realized, had brought them only disaster the last time it presumed to save them. In the person of Gemayel, they turned once more to the Syrians. President Asad was ready to forgive him, and preserve him in the office from which his Lebanese adversaries had been bent on driving him – provided only that he repudiated Israel and all its works, and especially the infamous '17 May agreement'.

AN ISRAELI 'HOUSEWARMING PRESENT' TO THE MARINES

The debacle was such that the Israelis no longer had the slightest chance of securing the fully-fledged peace treaty on which they had set their sights; and the agreement which Lebanon and Israel concluded on 17 May 1983 was what the Americans negotiated in its stead. It had inevitably fallen to them to clear up the mess which the Israelis had left behind. This mess was not merely the one which confronted 1,500 US Marines, when, returning to Lebanon along with the rest of the 'multi-national' force, they took up position at Beirut international airport. Their first task there had been to remove the stinking mounds of excrement that, as in so many other places in the country, adorned just about everything, floors, elevators, chairs, desks and drawers. The Marines got the message. This, they quickly understood, was a 'house-warming present' from the Israeli soldiers whose place they were taking; it was their way of venting their spleen on those 'Arab-loving' American allies of theirs, who had bought all that Arab 'propaganda' about Sabra and Shatila, the Beirut blitz, and the iniquity of a nation that had done such things. Less disgusting, but decidedly more dangerous, was their other gift: the countless cluster bomblets, golfball-sized, which they had strewn the length and breadth of the airport buildings.[80]

Even so, the real, and greater mess was the strategic one. The role of America's 'strategic asset' in which, upon invading Lebanon, Israel had cast itself, and to which America, under Reagan, had for the first time wholeheartedly subscribed, had turned out to be way beyond its capacities to perform. Indeed, to any but the most ardent of the American 'friends of Israel', it had proved itself to be quite the opposite: a strategic liability, and menace to America's interests and reputation throughout the Middle East. It was as troubling to the so-called 'moderate' Arab regimes, such as Egypt, Saudi Arabia and Jordan, in which those interests were vested, as it was gratifying to their 'radical', pro-Soviet rivals, of which Syria was the chief.

To clear up this particular mess, the US now sought, on the surface at least, to distance itself from its troublesome protégé, to act as impartial arbiter, as 'honest broker' among all the parties, in the creation of a new Lebanese order. In accordance with the '17 May agreement', Syrians, Israelis and Palestinians would all, on the face of it, withdraw from the country. But, in practice, given its tolerance of Israeli overflights and military manoeuvres, its restrictions on Lebanese force deployments and the integration of Israeli-controlled proxy forces into a 'territorial brigade', the South would still, *de facto*, fall under Israeli control. These southern arrangements apart, the Lebanese state would in principle spread its exclusive authority over all the rest of its territory, and rebuild its governing institutions on pretty much the same old Maronite-dominated, multi-sectarian basis.[81] The trouble was, however, that if the Israelis did not like the agreement, the Syrians and their Lebanese allies liked it very much less; for them it had the makings of another 'Camp David', another Sadat-like treachery against the common Arab cause. And in its determination to push it through, America became anything but an impartial arbiter. Indeed, said a former Lebanese prime minister, it became 'just another sectarian militia'[82] – albeit a militia extraordinary, with carrier-borne ground-attack aircraft of the Sixth Fleet, assembled offshore, strafing Syrian positions in the mountains above Beirut, and its mightiest battleship, the *New Jersey*, hurling shells the size of a Volkswagen car at Druze militiamen storming Gemayel's loyalist troops engaged in their desperate, last-ditch defence of the Maronite heartland.

THE MARINES TAKE TO THE BOATS

But all this firepower was useless against the Muslim/Druze insurgency – and that deadly new weapon, the suicide bomber, which came with it. Two hundred and forty Marines died at a stroke in one of the earliest, and the most devastating truck-bombings of all times. The result was that, where America's first ever military intervention in the modern Middle East – Lebanon, 1958 – had been a relative success, this, its second, was a humiliating fiasco. After the Shiite-led 'uprising', the Marines, now completely encircled by hostile forces, took to the boats, the Syrians and their army triumphantly re-established themselves as the indisputably preponderant foreign power in Lebanon, and the hapless President Gemayel, repentant 'Arabist' once more, repudiated the '17 May agreement' – turning what was supposed to have been the first, indispensable building block of a wider Pax Americana in the region into its ruin for years to come.

Of all the diverse parties that inflicted these vicissitudes on the US, Israel and their Lebanese protégés, the most important and immediately effective was undoubtedly Syria. After the beating the Israelis gave him in 1982, the Reagan Administration had virtually written off President Asad as a major player in the region. It was a fundamental error. Thus scorned, this unforgiving, and most cunning of Arab leaders quietly plotted, and then exacted, his swift, spectacular revenge. But the most significant of them, in the longer run, were those new, militant, but still mysterious, Islamist forces of which Hizbullah would eventually emerge as the most potent and celebrated vanguard.

FIRST THE PALESTINIANS, NOW HIZBULLAH

In the first half of the Lebanese civil war the Palestinians had been the main source, and engine, of conflict, in its local, regional, and ultimately international dimensions. It was the Islamists who, after their expulsion in 1982, replaced them in the second half. These Lebanese militants were, of course, an intrinsic part of a much greater movement. By the 1980s, political, fundamentalist Islam had supplanted national-ism as the great new credo and popularly mobilizing force of the Middle East and beyond. Lebanon could not escape its consequences. Indeed, true to form, it found itself in their very cockpit. Unlike the Palestinians, Lebanon's warrior-Muslims were native and home-grown, and that was a source of strength the Palestinians never had; but, like the Palestinians, they also had an agenda, allegiances and support which transcended Lebanon altogether. Their patron and other great source of strength was the only – yet pivotally important – country in the Middle East where Islamists had recently achieved the great objective of all their kind: the taking of political power. During the second half of the war, which came to an end in 1990, the Islamic Republic of Iran and its protégé, Hizbullah, were to forge a relationship which not merely long outlived that war, but played a role in the region's affairs seemingly out of all proportion to the small and strife-ridden state on whose territory it was chiefly enacted.

CHAPTER EIGHT

Khomeini, Islamists and the Shiite Uprising
1979–1985

LEBANON AND THE ISLAMIC REVOLUTION

In February 1979 Ayatollah Ruhollah Khomeini overthrew the Shah of Iran, ending 2,500 years of Persian monarchy, and replacing it with the Islamic Republic, the first of its kind in history. It was a seminal event. Constitutionally, a modern, 'popular' concept – the sovereignty of the people over their own affairs – furnished one of two key pillars on which the new theocracy rested; but it was the other, the retrogressive, 'sacred' one – the people's subordination to the sovereignty of God – which chiefly defined it. Under the doctrine of *Wilayat al-Faqih*, or 'Guardianship of the Religious Jurisprudent', it was the Shiite clergy who, after centuries of quietist confinement to their mosques and seminaries, now assumed full temporal authority in addition to the spiritual one they already possessed. At the apex of the 'divine–political system' was the *Wali*, the 'honest, virtuous, well-informed, courageous, efficient administrator and religious jurist' upon whom fell the task of interpreting God's purpose on earth.

This first great triumph of Islamism – the toppling in its name, and by 'people power' virtually alone, of one of the world's most repressive, influential and American-favoured regimes – had a universal import. But, inevitably, it was among the Arabs that the import was most strongly felt, because of the proximity, strategic weight and prestige of the country, one of the world's oldest and most illustrious nation-states, in which it took place, as well as the centuries of intimate interaction

– religious, political, cultural, military – between Iranians and themselves. As the people who gave birth to Islam the Arabs were all but bound to be, if not the most susceptible to, at least the most fascinated by, the bold new political gospel that Khomeini preached. Bizarre, anachronistic, obscurantist it may have been, but it certainly offered a fundamental, comprehensive alternative to the Western-style secular nationalism in which, since the Arab Awakening, they had mainly put their faith – a faith which, given the manifest flaws, failings and catastrophic military defeats of the existing Arab order, now seemed to have been hopelessly betrayed.

Every Arab country felt the impact. Although the Islamic Republic claimed, strove – and to some extent actually managed – to be pan-Islamic in its appeal and transcend Islam's historic schism, it was in practice unavoidably sectarian too. Thus, it was the countries which counted Shiites among their populations in addition to orthodox Sunnis where the impact was greatest. That, first of all, meant Iraq. Large, powerful and materially blessed, Iraq was located right next door and was only one of two Arab countries (the other being the tiny island of Bahrain) whose Shiites, elsewhere minorities or non-existent, constituted the majority of the population. Its ruler, Saddam Hussein, the very epitome of the Sunni, pan-Arabist despot, had largely built his power on their subordination and persecution. In 1980, he had gone to war against the Islamic Republic, and, in response, Khomeini had resolved not merely to defeat him and his 'godless' Baath, but to replace them with the world's next Islamic Republic. But secondly the 'Shiite factor' meant Lebanon. After Iraq, Lebanon and Saudi Arabia were home to the two largest Shiite communities in the region. But whereas in Saudi Arabia they constituted a small minority, in Lebanon – where their numbers were inexorably rising, from 166,545 in 1932 to more than a million by the turn of the century – they constituted (after Iraq and Bahrain) the largest Shiite component of any one Arab country's population. More importantly, they were already undergoing a communal 'awakening' of their own, and, as a result of civil war and foreign invasion, they offered just the kind of 'revolutionary' potential which Iran was supremely tempted, and well-equipped, to exploit. In the event, therefore, it was Lebanon where the

Khomeini gospel was to have its earliest, most obvious and dramatic consequences.[1]

But there were other, special reasons for the Iranian interest in Lebanon. One of the most telling marks of its involuntary centrality in the region's affairs, usually as object but sometimes as agent too, was that Lebanon, or, to be more precise, people acting out of Lebanon, had made a greater contribution than any other Arab country to the Islamic Revolution itself. Relations between the two countries went back a long way. The southern hill regions of Jebel Amil[2] – remarkably, it might seem, for such a rustic backwater – had been for centuries a leading centre in that multipolar universe of Shiite faith and erudition whose heart had always lain in the holy cities of Najaf and Karbala in Iraq and, later, Qum in Iran. Its high point came at the beginning of the sixteenth century, when the first monarch of the Safavid dynasty resolved to make Shiism the official religion of the state, and invited scholars from the Arab world, but especially Jebel Amil, to oversee the conversion. In recent times, in addition to the multi-national, traditionally migratory mullahs, members of the modernizing, secular Iranian elite also came to Lebanon, drawn by very different things which it had to offer, such as high standards of Western education in a Middle Eastern environment. They would often delight in its cosmo-politan ambience, its intellectual vibrancy, and what, in its golden years at least, seemed to them to be religious tolerance and inter-communal harmony at its most exemplary.

In the 1960s and '70s, however, another kind of Iranian visitor, or exile, began to turn up, one who was much more inclined to find in Lebanon an exemplar of Western 'corruption', decadence, materialism and impiety, and to identify with his downtrodden Shiite co-religionists whom the Lebanese 'miracle' had largely passed by. Not unlike the Palestinian guerillas before them, these people came to the country because they saw it as an easily accessible haven and convenient base for their own subversive, national purposes. A typical example was Mustafa Shamran, an American-trained engineer who arrived in 1971. Deciding that Lebanon was the most 'Westoxicated' country in the Middle East, he immediately plunged into its politics. He became a right-hand man of his compatriot, the charismatic cleric Musa Sadr, in founding the Movement of the Deprived, and, in 1976, during the Phalangist siege of Tal al-Za'atar refugee camp, he organized the Amal militia's unsuccessful defence of the adjoining Shiite slum of Naba'a.[3] Subsequently Khomeini's defence minister, he was one of many persons who had once spent time in Lebanon to occupy powerful positions in the new-born Republic.[4]

Others, usually left-wingers – who subsequently fell out with Khomeini – or the more radical kind of Islamists – some of whom did so too – threw in their lot with the Palestinians rather than the Lebanese Shiites. Among the latter was Ahmad Montazeri – firebrand young cleric, and son of Ayatollah Hussein Ali Montazeri, Khomeini's first, officially designated heir apparent – who underwent military training in Fatah camps, and dreamt not merely of overthrowing the Shah, but of establishing a worldwide, Iranian-led 'Islamist International'.[5] Ali Akbar Mohtashemi, cleric and former pupil of Khomeini in Najaf, was both an energetic pro-Palestinian and a specifically Shiite militant too. Graduate of a Fatah camp, he also lived for a while in the remote Shiite village of Yammoune in the Beqa'a Valley, and was favourably impressed by its people. 'Their men', he wrote, 'are courageous and mostly armed ... They don't submit to government authority and don't pay for water and electricity. They have fought several times with neighbouring Christian villages and have won. They like the [Shiite] clergy.'[6]

At one point it looked as though Khomeini himself might move to Lebanon from his Najaf exile; that, at least, is what he publicly proclaimed he was going to do when, in the early seventies, Saddam Hussein began a policy of expelling Iranians and Iraqis of Iranian origin. And when, in 1978, Saddam finally expelled the Ayatollah himself, Yasser Arafat reportedly invited him to enjoy his hospitality and protection in that part of Lebanon, his 'Fakhani Republic', where he was in a position to offer it.[7]

In the event, however, it was not from the *Dahiya*, or some village in Jebel Amil, but from Neauphle-le-Château, France, that Khomeini plotted the last stages of his Islamic Revolution. However, revolution accomplished, Lebanon soon loomed large in the foreign policy priorities of his first, provisional government. Thus began that era, continuing till this day, in which Iran was to exert the dominant regional influence on Lebanon's affairs – and, as the fountainhead of Islamism, to be every bit as potent in that role as Nasser's Egypt, its only comparable predecessor, had been in the heyday of Arab nationalism. The most famous, effective and enduring progeny – and symbol – of this era was to be the anti-Israeli resistance movement, Hizbullah. Of the many Islamist organizations that have come and gone in recent times, none was destined to make so great an impact, in the Middle East and beyond, as it has. Various strands of Iranian thinking contributed to its birth.

FIGHTING THE CANCEROUS GOITRE OF ISRAEL UNTIL ITS OBLITERATION . . .

Like other revolutionaries before them, Iran's did not confine their ambitions to one country. The new-born republic was bound, by the terms of its constitution, to 'strive with other Islamic and popular movements to prepare the way for the formation of a single world *Umma* ('Muslim nation'); and its army and Revolutionary Guards were 'responsible not only for guarding and preserving the frontiers of the country, but also for fulfilling the ideological mission of *jihad* in God's way – that is, extending the sovereignty of God's word throughout the world . . .' In this scheme of things, Hizbullah was but an intrinsic part of the 'Islamic order' which the Republic was doctrinally required to establish wherever it could.[8] Naturally, it was the local Shiites to whom Khomeini delegated this task in Lebanon. But, at the same time, their intended role was directly and inextricably bound up with that of another people, the Palestinians, who had long preoccupied him, not just doctrinally, but, it seems, in an intensely personal way too. It was wholly symptomatic that Arafat should have been the first foreign 'head of state' whom he received after his triumphant homecoming, and that, by way of marking the immediate, total reversal of the pro-Israeli policies of the Shah, he had offered him, among other honours, the keys of the abandoned Israeli embassy in Tehran. For the Ayatollah considered that the existence of Israel, and its presence in the holy city of Jerusalem, were fundamentally, Islamically sinful; the Jewish state was a 'cancerous goitre that occupies the liver of the *Umma* – Palestine' – and should be fought by all Muslims 'until its obliteration'.[9] According to an Islamist publication which closely reflected Ali Akbar Mohtashemi's opinions, Khomeini 'told Palestinians to kill all the Jews in Israel and throw them out to the last person'.[10]

One of Khomeini's objectives here was to emphasize the ecumenical, pan-Islamic credentials of his revolution, by identifying it – and far more militantly than Arafat himself, let alone the vast majority of Arab governments – with this pan-Arab, and *ipso facto* Sunni, cause *par excellence*. By 1982, Iran had recovered all the territory it had lost in Saddam's initial *Blitzkrieg*, but the Ayatollah, determined to 'export' his Revolution, refused to end the war until he had overthrown those 'godless' Baath. But those 'godless' Baath frustratingly held on. And the longer, in consequence, he had to prolong the war, at ever mounting, horrendous cost, the more, in Arab eyes, it tended to look like a new phase of the age-old Arab–Persian, Sunni–Shiite rivalry, with himself and his ruling clerics as the 'turbaned Shahs' bent on imposing their hegemony over the Arabs in the guise of 'political' Islam.[11] What better way of allaying these Arab and Sunni suspicions and resentments than the sponsoring of a Shiite *jihad* against Israel – after 1982 the occupier of half of Lebanon – in place of Arafat and his now scattered *fedayeen*?

... AND RESISTING THE 'GREAT SATAN'

Khomeini's interest in Lebanon was strategic and pragmatic. The war with Iraq was his revolution's baptism of fire, its first great test, in which defeat might not have broken it, but victory would have mightily enhanced it, at home, in the region and the world. All its main adversaries, regional and international, perceived it that way too, and openly or surreptitiously threw their weight behind Saddam, now cast as the vital, eastern bulwark of the whole, decrepit, trembling, Sunni-dominated Arab order. But, with the Israeli invasion of 1982, some of these adversaries themselves became heavily engaged, militarily and politically, in the quagmire that was Lebanon. Chief among them was the United States – closely followed by France. At the head of the multi-national force in Lebanon, itself the intended launching-pad of a whole new Pax Americana in the region, the US was directly blocking the export of Khomeini's revolution – yet simultaneously furnishing it with unrivalled opportunities for deadly counter-attack. And Khomeini used them to the full, ensuring that American actions in one arena were severely punished in another. 'It is a truism', wrote Iranian scholar R. K. Ramazani, 'that all things in the Middle East are interconnected'.[12] Nowhere did this truism manifest itself like it did in Lebanon. With the coming of Iran, its role as the region's battleground now took on a whole new dimension which, if anything, only expanded and deepened with the passage of time.

IRAN AND SYRIA, MOST IMPROBABLE BUT ENDURING OF ALLIES, FIND COMMON CAUSE IN LEBANON

But Iran could never be alone in Lebanon. In particular, there was always Syria. Whoever ruled that country, Lebanon was always its special preserve. That was not because, like Egypt once and Iran now, it ever rose to be the foremost, proselytyzing power in the region as a whole. It was because, as a middle-sized fish in an Arab pond where Lebanon was a very alluring minnow, it was forever the overbearing 'sister-state' just next door. This was an immutable reality in which the Ayatollah had to acquiesce. 'Godless' in Iraq, the Baathists might have been. 'Godless' in Syria he could not admit them to be. Not that, from an Islamist point of view, there was any great difference between the two, or that President Asad treated his Islamists – Sunnis – all that much better than Saddam treated his – Shiites. On the contrary, the great siege and bloodbath of Hama, in April 1982, was an early example of the Arab establishment's relentless war on fundamentalism which, in its thoroughness and ferocity, no other regime would ever significantly outdo. It was just that Khomeini saw in Asad a partner with whom he could do serious business. And Asad, who had long and presciently divined his future potentialities, just as quickly saw the same in him.

What, above all, they had in common was their fear and enmity of Saddam Hussein. The great inter-Baathist feud, rooted in personal and factional animosities which few outside it wholly understood, was perhaps the most vicious and implacable in the Middle East. So when the Ayatollah came to power, Asad had even more compelling reasons than Arafat to befriend him, and collaborate with him against his brother-enemy in Baghdad. And when Saddam invaded Iran, in an act of aggression which the Islamic Republic, still racked by post-revolutionary turmoil, was at first unable to repulse, Asad rushed to his assistance. Thanks to him, Iran was able, in a single air-raid, to destroy a fifth of the Iraqi air force at a base close to the Syrian frontier.[13] Later, through a liaison unit permanently installed in the Iranian ministry of defence, Syria furnished continuous advice and intelligence on the conduct of the war.

It was Saddam, in his madness and megalomania, who spawned this alliance, but other elements of mutual interest contributed to it too. Yet, however compelling these might have been, from a pan-Arab nationalist point of view the relationship was always an extraordinary one. On the face of it, in fact, it was an even more flagrant case of *lèse-Arabism* than Asad's siding with the Maronites against the Palestinians had been in the early stages of the Lebanese civil war.[14] Many were the attempts by other Arab regimes, especially those the West dubbed 'moderate', to wean their aberrant 'sister-state' back into the collective Arab fold, and many the strains and stresses to which, under these and other pressures, the alliance was subjected. But, in the end, it always survived, both parties so highly valuing it that neither was ever ready to push its own selfish aims beyond the endurance of the other. Not that it didn't have its ups and downs, or that, at any given stage, one party was not inherently likely to stand in greater need of it than the other. At first, with the outbreak of the Gulf War, Syria was up, Iran down. Two years later, with the Israeli invasion of Lebanon and Syria's fortunes at their lowest ebb, it was the other way round.[15]

It was, in fact, in Lebanon that the alliance found, if not its most important, certainly its most fertile expression; there that the allies' respective interests most fruitfully converged — but not infrequently diverged as well. The convergence lay essentially in the combating of common enemies — the US, Israel and their protégés in Lebanon. The divergences came when one party sought to consolidate its presence, or promote its interests, in a way that impinged on the already established presence or interests of the other. Not surprisingly, the up-and-coming, ideologically driven and would-be regional hegemon, Iran, was the more prone to such transgressions. Characteristically, it would push for the full-scale 'Islamicization' of Lebanon or for all-out, visionary *jihad*, while Syria, its one-time revolutionary fervour long since supplanted by survivalist *Realpolitik*, simply wanted to keep its grip on Lebanon, sectarian system and all, as the most important single card in its strategic hand, and to press *jihad*, judiciously regulated, into the service of a peace-seeking diplomacy whose only, mundane objective was the recovery of the Golan Heights. But, generally speaking, whenever any divergence became so serious as to imperil the whole alliance, it was Iran that deferred to Syria. For Syria's fundamental interests were at stake in Lebanon in a way that Iran's were not. In his own backyard, Asad always had to have the last word. And Khomeini had to cede it to him. Otherwise he risked losing Lebanon altogether.

From the outset, therefore, Khomeini sought where possible to insert himself into Asad's purposes. And Asad's purposes, in the wake of the Israeli invasion, were to stage his comeback in Lebanon by a combination of 'shield and sword'. This was a simple strategy in which Syria's traditional superpower patron, the Soviet Union, and its new regional partner, Iran, both had their indispensable part to play. The shield came, with Soviet help, through the reconstruction of Syria's own military power to the point where, in defensive mode, it could hold its own against Americans, French or Israelis and whatever in the way of conventional warfare they might throw at it. The sword, with Iranian help, came through the mobilization of all those proxy forces, non-state actors, which would now wage offensive, unconventional, guerilla-cum-terrorist warfare against them.[16]

'A SCUFFLE OF CAMELS' IN THE DESERT

The chief and, in the end, virtually the only one of these proxy forces was Hizbullah. It had two progenitors. If Iran was one – with Syria, so to speak, as midwife – Israel was unquestionably the other. Iran furnished the model and the means, Syria the facilities, Israel – with its invasion – the provocation, the anger, the turmoil, or, as Israel's like-minded American friends, the neoconservatives, might have put it, the 'constructive chaos' out of which new orders grow. 'Had the enemy not taken this step,' said Hassan Nasrallah many years later, 'I don't know whether something called Hizbullah would have been born. I doubt it.'[17] The birth itself went virtually unnoticed amid all the tumults of Lebanon at the time. As one of Nasrallah's predecessors, Sheikh Subhi al-Tufayli, the organization's first secretary-general, rather picturesquely recalled it, Hizbullah came into the world in circumstances which, full of noise and dust, were like a 'scuffle of camels' in the desert.[18]

Other such groups had preceded it. They first made themselves formally known, as members of the Lebanese National Resistance Front, on that fateful day, 16 September 1982, when Israel invaded West Beirut, paving the way for Sabra and Shatila and all that flowed from it, locally, regionally and internationally. They were mainly members of the Muslim/leftist coalition, notably such strongly secular organizations as Lebanon's two rival communist parties or the National Syrian Socialist Party; the latter was a small, muscular, visionary organization, originally inspired by European fascism and mainly Greek Orthodox in membership, which believed that Lebanon should be subsumed, and its sectarian demons exorcized, within a 'Greater Syrian' national/territorial identity. Indeed, it was a young NSSP militant who, just two days before, had planted the remote-controlled bomb that killed Bashir Gemayel – the first, spectacular stroke of Syria's 'sword' in the making. Others, including remnants of the Palestinian guerilla movement about to be torn apart by a small-scale civil war, were tacitly associated with them. In due course, however, resistance became an overwhelmingly Shiite affair. This, especially in its anti-Israeli dimension, was largely spontaneous in origin, but insofar as it was organized, Amal, the main Shiite political party, profiting from its pre-invasion networks in the South, at first took charge. It was said to have as many as 30,000 armed men at its disposal.[19] The anti-Israel struggle became something of a national epic, and, politically, it was to Amal that the prestige of it chiefly redounded. Amal, and the Shiite-dominated 6th Brigade of the army which deserted to it, played the key role in the February 1984 'uprising' which, with the seizure of West Beirut, turned the tables on Gemayel's Maronite-supremacist regime, the Americans and the Israelis. Thus did Amal's dominance over the resistance lead to its dominance in the traditionally Sunni-dominated capital, and thence to a higher ranking for the historically under-privileged Shiites in a re-ordered sectarian state.

But Amal was not to the taste of the Islamic Republic and its local, Lebanese protégés. For them it was neither Islamist nor jihadist – and it was anti-Palestinian to boot. Its leader Nabih Berri – the successor to Musa Sadr, who had mysteriously disappeared, almost certainly murdered, on a visit to Colonel Gadafi's Libya – was a lawyer by training, middle-class in origin and outlook. Under him, Amal moved in a distinctly secular direction. Once a truly popular grassroots movement, embracing a wide range of political and social forces, it eventually became a vehicle for the advancement, less of the Shiite community as a whole, than of the new bourgeoisie within it; once contemptuous of sectarian politics, its clientelism and corruptions, it was already on its way, in the person of its new leader, to becoming a leading practitioner of them.[20] While it had formally condemned the Israeli invasion, it had also surreptitiously savoured the destruction of Palestinian power which it wrought, that being a prerequisite for its own ascent. Berri early on committed what, in Iranian and Islamist eyes, was the dreadful solecism of joining the National Salvation Committee – a multi-sectarian body that was to help negotiate the withdrawal of the Palestinians – of which the Israeli protégé, Bashir Gemayel himself, was a member. His party had at first been ready for a *modus vivendi* with the Israelis in the South; some local Amal leaders effectively col-laborated with them. Only after eight months, amid mounting popular pressure, did Amal take to resistance.[21] It had always been lukewarm about the Iranian Revolution, deeming that the Shiites' basic identity should be a national, Lebanese one, and not the supra-national religious one, promoted by the Ayatollah, that would inevitably collide with it. If Amal did have external allegiances they went far less to Iran than to its partner-cum-rival in Lebanon, Syria. Asad bent Amal to his hegemonic purposes, so much so, in fact, that whenever he needed his 'sword' for disciplining 'friends', like the self-willed Palestinians, as opposed to smiting enemies, like the Americans, he could count on Amal to wield it on his behalf. As a legacy of its broad-based origins,

Amal did have many Islamists in its ranks, and, through them, the Islamic Republic itself had at first attempted to shape it in its own image.[22] But it had little success. And in the wake of the Israeli invasion, it decided that the time had come to create a completely new, and rival, organization of its own.

IRAN MAKES SYRIA A VERY GENEROUS OFFER INDEED

The invasion itself put Iran in a strong position to do so. On 6 June 1982, the very day after Israel went into Lebanon, the Iranian minister of defence was in Damascus bearing a very generous offer indeed. Syria had greatly aided Iran to turn the tables on its Iraqi aggressor after 1980; Iran was now ready to return the favour with interest. It was ready, in fact, to join Syria in all-out war against the Israeli aggressor, and immediately to dispatch 40,000 regular troops, with heavy armour, plus 10,000 lightly armed Revolutionary Guards, for the purpose.[23] They could even get there, quickly, through the territory of the very state with which it was still at war. For at the time Saddam was in his very direst straits. Iran had just driven him out of his last major foothold on its soil, the port city of Khorramshahr, and, its martial ardour at its height, was preparing to carry the war into Iraq itself. In a desperate bid to ward this off Saddam had announced a unilateral ceasefire and his readiness to pull all his troops back to the international frontier. And when, as a new condition for accepting the ceasefire, Iran demanded passage for its forces on their way to Lebanon, he had instantly agreed.

SYRIA REJECTS IT, BUT LEBANON LIVES EVER AFTER WITH ITS LEGACY

These first few days of the Israeli onslaught were a pregnant moment in recent Middle Eastern history, a moment when it might easily have taken a very different course. It did not do so, in the first place, because Asad turned down that very generous offer. For one thing, his forces had been so swiftly and badly mauled that he did not believe the Iranians, even massively involved, could sway the outcome in his favour. On the contrary, he was afraid that if they tried Israel would respond with total war that would destroy the rest of his army – and probably his regime with it. For another, he feared that, if there were a ceasefire in the Gulf War, Saddam would in due course regain all his lost prowess, and then turn it, in unquenchable revenge, against himself. This was surely pan-Arabism, of which the two Baathist regimes deemed themselves to be the supreme upholders, at its very nadir. With Abu Nidal's attempted assassination of the Israeli ambassador in London, and the *casus belli* it created, Saddam had, actually or in effect, collaborated with Israel in a bid to secure the annihilation or abject humiliation of the Syrian army in Lebanon;[24] now, for Asad, Iran's curbing or destroying of an Arab foe was more desirable than its help in combating the historic Zionist one. His decision tipped the scales in favour of an even more important Iranian decision. For there were two schools of thought in Tehran. One argued that instead of pursuing costly and uncertain war against Iraq, Iran should instead invest military resources and martial ardour in the less risky but, for the winning of Arab/Muslim hearts and minds, vastly more promising option of war against Israel. The other, led by Khomeini himself, argued that the 'road to Jerusalem passed through Karbala',[25] and that stopping the Gulf War now 'would be like strangling the Revolution with our own hands'. Not surprisingly, after Asad's rejection, this school of thought emphatically prevailed.[26]

The historic moment passed. But it left a very considerable, and enduring, legacy. For even as the Iranian leadership was locked in fateful debate, several hundred of Iran's best and most experienced troops, some of them fresh from the blitzed and blood-drenched ruins of Khorramshahr, had already been airlifted to Damascus, and from there had proceeded to Lebanon. They had been warmly received by both Syrian officials and ordinary people, who noted that no Arab states, not even Syria's closest, 'radical' allies like Libya, Yemen or Algeria, were doing anything comparable to help, a shaming contrast which prompted one of Iran's top clerics, Ali Akbar Rafsanjani, to boast that 'according to Syrian and Lebanese assertions, the value of a few planeloads of Iranian combatants is far more than if ten divisions had come from Arab countries'.[27] Many of them were recalled to Tehran when it became clear that the Syrian leadership – which, in the person of Asad's brother Rifa'at, was very much less than welcoming[28] –

opposed a full-scale Iranian military intervention. But some of the Revolutionary Guards stayed on, later to be joined by others, and in due course there were a good 1,500 to 2,000 of them permanently stationed in Lebanon.[29] These were the shock troops of Khomeini's mission to 'export' the Revolution, either through outright military intervention, or covert political action. They came with their 'cultural units', responsible for 'eradicating falsehood in any land where falsehood exist[ed]'.[30] Their activities were overseen by the one-time, pre-revolutionary exile in Lebanon, Ali Akbar Mohtashemi, now ambassador to Damascus. It was a level of Iranian intervention in his own backyard which the ever suspicious Asad could live with and from which he was determined to profit, constituting as it did the nicely manageable marriage of his own 'shield' with the Iranian-sponsored 'sword'.[31]

HIZBULLAH IS BORN

It was out of this coming together of the Ayatollah's holy warriors and their counterparts in Lebanon that Hizbullah grew. The fusion first took place, physically and practically, in the Beqa'a Valley. Now Syrian-controlled, the Beqa'a was home to the only one of Lebanon's three main concentrations of Shiites – the others being Jebel Amil and Beirut's *Dahiya* – which lay effectively beyond the reach of the Gemayel government, the Israeli occupier, or any of the sectarian militias, including Amal, that might have stifled the new-born in embryo.

It had all begun when Amal leader Berri, already tarnished by his membership of the National Salvation Committee, formally accepted Philip Habib's plan for evacuating the Palestinians from Beirut. Islamists in his organization immediately rebelled. Encouraged by Mohtashemi, who of course fiercely opposed the plan, Hussein Musawi, Amal's military commander, absconded to his native Baalbek, proclaimed that only the Iranian leadership could define what was Islamic and what was not, and announced the formation of an 'Islamic Amal'.[32] His action triggered the 'scuffle of camels' of which Hizbullah's first secretary-general spoke, that 'extremely complex' imbroglio in which 'religion, politics and opportunism were mixed' and 'even some of the sheikhs were political traders' – but through which, in the end, they were safely guided by 'the instructions of the leader, Imam Khomeini … to create a movement that [sprang] from pure Islamic fundamentals, a movement that [shook] the current situation'.[33]

A host of disparate but like-minded groups and individuals rushed, like Musawi, to the Beqa'a. These included other, subsequently famous Amal defectors, such as the 22-year-old Hassan Nasrallah; embryonic resistance groupings headed by the Association of the Ulema of Jebel Amil;[34] members of 'committees for the support of the Islamic Revolution'; individual clerics with their own following; students; Islamists who had been active in Palestinian guerilla organizations and now had nowhere else to go,[35] or others who had spontaneously joined the Palestinians in defence of the *Dahiya*; and even a convert or two from communism.[36]

They came together burning with zeal to implement the new Khomeinist credo. This, as enunciated later in Hizbullah's inaugural manifesto, its grandiose 'Open Letter to the Oppressed in Lebanon and the World',[37] and sundry other texts and pronouncements, incorporated two main aims. One was to establish an 'Islamic order' in Lebanon modelled on the *Wilayat al-Faqih* in Iran. Such an order – an expression of God's just rule that would ultimately prevail over all mankind – was a doctrinal necessity. The party gave specific obedience to the *Wali* – Khomeini or his successor – in his capacity as supreme religious leader and head of the only true 'Islamic state', or approximation thereof, to which the *Umma* had so far given rise. The *Wilayat* was its 'spinal cord, the secret of [its] strength, growth, struggle and martyrdom'; without it, it would have been a 'dead body'.[38] To the *Wali*, it entrusted basic policy, and decision-making powers on such matters as the waging of war, the classification of friends and foes, or the attitude to be adopted towards other political systems.[39] As for the existing Lebanese state, it rejected it as an artificial, colonially created entity, 'a protégé of global arrogance' that had been severed from the rest of the *Umma*;[40] and its political system was rotten to the core. Together they were beyond reform, and should give way – by freely chosen and peaceful means – to an Islamic state.[41] The second aim, and similarly imperious necessity, was to initiate *jihad* against Israel. This aim flowed essentially from the first, but, in Hizbullah's operational priorities, actually took precedence over it.[42] In its very existence, Israel was an 'absolute evil', a negation of divine justice on earth, the 'central enemy' of the *Umma* engaged in perpetual aggression against it.[43] The only real *Umma* was not a community of passive believers – 'weak', 'useless', effectively 'dead' – that merely abided by the Koran and observed Islamic rituals, but 'Hizbullah's *Umma*' – currently Iran, Lebanese Shiites and some Palestinians – which fought in God's cause against Israel and the hegemonic West. *Jihad* was a *wajib sha'ri*, a 'religious duty', that would only end, not just with Israel's expulsion from Lebanese territory, but with its 'final obliteration'.[44]

Appropriately enough, Khomeini himself chose the name of a movement sworn to practice a brand of revolutionary Shiism that was, after all, almost exclusively his. Unable to agree on one themselves, its Lebanese founders had sent a delegation to Tehran to consult him. His choice, Hizbullah, or 'party of God', came from a verse in the Koran: 'Lo! The party of God, they are the victorious.' It was a name, he said, that should unite all Islamists. But it hardly did that even in Iran itself. On the contrary, there it was the name by which, in the power struggles of the Revolution's early years, the winning side, the extremists, the out-and-out Khomeinist zealots, distinguished themselves from the disgraced and defeated moderates.[45] Then, at the request of the Lebanese, he sent a representative to act as the arbiter of any differences among them. And he approved the formation of a five-man committee which gradually, secretly forged the new-born party's institutional structures and ideological tenets.

AN ISLAMIC REPUBLIC IN MINIATURE

The ardent young men, clerical and lay, who yearned to do battle with 'the enemies of Islam' immediately began training under the Revolutionary Guards. The town of Baalbek, site of magnificent Roman ruins, became their joint headquarters. There, in bygone years, Lebanon's social and cultural elite, and its large expatriate community, had gathered in the temples of Jupiter or Bacchus to hear world-famous virtuosi perform beneath the stars. Now, its new masters turned the town and its environs into an Islamic Republic in miniature where outsiders ventured at their peril. On completion of their training, Revolutionary Guards and the local militants jointly seized army bases and other remnants of Lebanese government authority. In the spring of 1983, the Guards permanently installed themselves in Baalbek's Sheikh Abdullah barracks. A cut above the average, predatory, Lebanese militia, they made themselves quite popular with the local people, by providing technical services and volunteer labour as well as sermons on revolutionary Islam.[46] The region's public *mores* took a sharply puritanical turn, its women disappeared beneath all-encompassing black *chadors*, its walls bore posters of the Ayatollah's stern, unsmiling countenance, black-framed epitaphs to recent 'martyrs' and the invocation: 'Israel must be wiped from the face of the earth.'[47] And from their Syrian- and Iranian-protected lair, the new warriors of Islam, like the Assassins of old, sallied forth to strike down Zionists, imperialists and local oppressors alike.

The outside world knew little of what was stirring in Baalbek. Western intelligence agencies which took an intense interest in the affairs of the Islamic Republic of Iran evidently did not devote any comparable attention to its diminutive clone in Lebanon. It was an oversight they were to regret. Partly, no doubt, it came about because if that 'scuffle of camels' was confusing to its participants, it was all the more so to watchers from afar. Besides, in this, its second, 'Islamist' half, Lebanon's civil war was growing even more complex than in its first, 'Palestinian' one. There were so many separate, yet interrelated, arenas of conflict, and so many militias engaged in them, that no one was going to attach any particular importance to the emergence of what at first sight was just another one.[48] Partly, too, it was because, though Hizbullah may already have been a going concern with a local habitation and a name, it did not, like other newcomers of the kind, go out of the way to advertise itself.

Some now argue that the period between 1982 and 1985, between Israel's invasion of Lebanon and its partial withdrawal from it, was an especially significant one in recent Middle Eastern history, that the regional and international dramas which it witnessed were a foreshadowing, a dress rehearsal, of very similar but even weightier ones that would unfold a quarter of a century later. The main actors – America and Israel, Iran, Syria and Hizbullah – would remain essentially the same. But whereas, today, Hizbullah is a household name, it was virtually unheard-of then. Just what connection it might have had with organizations such as Islamic Jihad, if indeed these organizations enjoyed any serious, autonomous existence at all, is still a matter of some controversy or deliberate mystification among those, the participants themselves or academic specialists, who concern themselves with such historical detail. Generally speaking, however, these were the organizations, or just the names, through which Hizbullah, or the Islamist milieu from which it grew, first made its mark on the world – and through which Syria and Iran, plotting spectacular exploits for it to perform, preferred for the time being to disguise it.[49]

'THE SWORD AND THE SHIELD'

Ever since the Israeli invasion, Syria had been busy digesting the generous amounts of new weaponry – tanks, artillery, and the very latest SAM-11 and SAM-14 anti-aircraft missiles – and their accompanying 'advisers' with which the Soviet Union had rushed to supply it. The humiliation of its protégé had been Russia's humiliation too; and now, on top of that, it saw its rival superpower seeking, via Lebanon, to establish a kind of 'NATO base' in the East Mediterranean.[50] Meanwhile, as Syria was furbishing its deterrent 'shield', Iran, with its help, was sharpening the 'sword'. This would be unsheathed against two distinct, if related, targets: 'the imperialists', mainly American and French, in and around Beirut, and 'the Zionists' in the South.

With the assistance of the Revolutionary Guards, the Islamist militants had so far secured only a tenuous foothold in the *Dahiya*, still Amal-dominated, from which they engaged in light and intermittent skirmishing with the 'multi-national' forces.[51] But they did have suicide bombers, whom Syrians and Iranians had helped them train. And on 18 April 1983, it was one of these who drove a battered old General Motors pick-up truck, laden with hundreds of pounds of explosives, into the covered forecourt of the US embassy on Beirut's sea-front Corniche. It was the first such deadly attack on a US diplomatic mission anywhere in the world. It killed sixty-three people, seventeen of them Americans, including nine CIA personnel who were holding a conference specially convened to discuss the very phenomenon, Shiite political activism, to which they themselves now fell victim. The wedding ring of Robert Ames, the CIA's chief intelligence officer for the Middle East and Secretary of State George Shultz's special adviser on the region, was found floating a mile offshore, still affixed to his severed hand.

Only the faceless Islamic Jihad staked a claim. But Hizbullah, upon announcing itself to the world, was later to praise it as America's 'first punishment'.[52] It was punishment, in the first place, for its outright backing of the 'oppressive, hypocritical, blasphemous' Gemayel regime and for supplying and equipping the Lebanese army. This was supposed to be an impartial, national institution, but, under Gemayel, it had once again become a more than ever 'confessional' one, which undertook systematic campaigns of repression against Muslim parties and militias in West Beirut, but did nothing about the openly flaunted, Israeli-supported Phalangist militia in East Beirut. Often in connivance with the Phalangists, it had terrorized and kidnapped hundreds of Muslims and Palestinians, some of whom, among the estimated 17,000 'disappeared' of the fifteen-year civil war, were never to be seen again.[53] From the precincts of the presidential palace itself, it had used its newly acquired 155-mm howitzers to shell the nearby *Dahiya* even more heavily than the Israelis had ever done, 'slaughtering its inhabitants' – the very moderate, very official Higher Shiite Islamic Council was finally moved to protest – 'as if they belonged to another country altogether'.[54]

Reagan vowed that this 'criminal attack' would not deter him from what 'we know to be right'. And three weeks later, in pursuit of that 'right', America presided over the signing of the '17 May agreement', anathema to its adversaries, under which Israel would withdraw its troops from Lebanon if Syria did so simultaneously. But Syria would not – a rebuff which the exasperated Administration now met with the threat, and increasing use, of force. This came less from the 1,200 Marines, serving with the 'multi-national' force onshore, than from the

Sixth Fleet, and some of the mightiest guns afloat, now assembling in growing strength offshore. But, as a military man, Marine commander Colonel Tim Geraghty was aghast at what the politicians in Washington demanded of him. 'Sir,' he protested down the telephone when ordered to open fire on Druze forces then close to overrunning the army and the Phalangists' last stronghold in the hills above Beirut, 'I cannot do that. This will cost us our neutrality. Do you realize if you do that, we'll get slaughtered down here? We're totally vulnerable. We're sitting ducks.'[55] But he was overruled. And sure enough, it wasn't long before Damascus and Tehran decided that a second and greater 'punishment' was now required. This time the target was to be French as well as American. Lebanon was the ideal place to punish *them*. But the punishment was less for what they were doing there than in the Gulf. Or, rather, what they were about to do, and that was to supply Saddam Hussein with five Super Etendard fighter-bombers, along with the very latest in anti-ship missiles, the Exocet, which the Argentinians had just been using to such deadly effect against the British in the Falklands War. Armed with these, a now almost desperate Saddam might even turn the tables on his enemy, by disrupting the oil exports on which it heavily depended for the prosecution of the war. Don't do it; don't commit this 'suicidal act', because, if you do, neither you or the US will know 'a minute's rest'. Mir-Hussein Mousavi, the Iranian prime minister, and other high officials, almost screamed this and other such warnings from the rooftops. Even the Americans counselled the French against it. But the French proceeded regardless.

'THE LARGEST NON-NUCLEAR EXPLOSION EVER DETONATED ON THE FACE OF THE EARTH'

In the final week of September 1983, US naval intelligence reportedly intercepted a message sent to the Iranian ambassador in Syria, Ali Akbar Mohtashemi, from Iran's ministry of intelligence directing him to contact Hussein Musawi, the head of Islamic Amal, and tell him that an attack on the 'multi-national' force in Lebanon should include a 'spectacular action' against the US Marines.[56] Musawi's men duly acquired a Mercedes truck, fitted it with explosives and painted it to resemble a yellow water delivery vehicle that regularly stopped near the Marine barracks. At dawn on Sunday 23 October 1983 they ambushed the real truck and sent its lookalike on its way. Lance-Corporal Eddie DiFranco, the only survivor who saw how it all happened, reported that the driver was smiling as he sped towards the compound, broke through the protective barrier of sandbags and concertina wire, and detonated his vehicle in the centre of the barracks at approximately 6.22 a.m. Because they got an extra half-hour abed on Sundays, most of the Marines were still asleep.[57] 'The resulting explosion' – the US District Court that later found Iran responsible for the bombing was told – 'was the largest non-nuclear explosion that had ever been detonated on the face of the earth.' With a force equal to 15,000 to 21,000 pounds of TNT, it ripped locked doors from their frames in the nearest building, 256 feet (78 m) away. At a distance of 370 feet (113 m), trees were shredded and completely exfoliated. A kilometre away, the control tower of Beirut International Airport had all its windows shattered. As for the four-storey Marine barracks, it was reduced to 15 feet (4.5 m) of rubble, its reinforced-concrete columns stretched 'like rubber bands'.[58] 241 Marines died – and so did 58 French soldiers when their barracks was struck by another suicide bomber twenty seconds later.

DEBACLE

While this 'second punishment', likewise claimed by Islamic Jihad, shook the Americans to the core, it also stirred them to yet greater shows of at least outward resolve. Vice President George Bush flew to Beirut and announced that the US was not going to bow to a group of 'insidious, cowardly terrorists', and Reagan wondered out loud whether the Soviet Union, acting through Syria, Iran and their 'international criminals and thugs', could be permitted to 'take over' the entire Middle East, including the oilfields of the Arabian Peninsula. But they were only digging themselves into an ever deeper hole. Overlooking everything that Israel had done to drag it into this quagmire in the first place, and paying heed only to the views of its own, pro-Israeli neo-conservative hawks, to the extreme pique of its thwarted Secretary of

State, and to the risk of incurring 'the Lobby's' wrath as presidential elections neared, the Reagan Administration now reverted to its all-out pro-Israeli self. It announced the first ever 'strategic cooperation agreement' with the pampered but unruly protégé whose value as a 'strategic asset' had just been so conclusively disproved. It also granted Israel the precious status of a 'non-NATO ally' and initiated 'the greatest transfer of money and technology ever freely surrendered by one country to another'.[59] The principal, immediate message this unprecedented partnership was supposed to convey was that, together, Israelis and Americans would now use their overwhelmingly superior force to bludgeon 'radical', 'Soviet-backed' Arab states into mending their errant ways; and that this was how they would get the most stubborn of them, Syria, out of Lebanon. As for the 'moderate', pro-American states, embarrassed and aghast at this 'reward for Israeli intransigence', this 'Christmas present to the Soviet Union', the Administration intimated that it 'couldn't care less' about them any more. Just what had they done, anyway, to help bring Syria into line? The exasperated George Shultz was overheard to say that he now had 'nothing but contempt' for the Arabs, and that included erstwhile friends like Saudi Arabia and Jordan as well as adversaries like Syria and Libya.[60]

The trouble was, however, that by now the Syrian 'shield' and the Iranian-sponsored 'sword' were working all too well. On 4 December 1983, ground-attack aircraft took off from the Sixth Fleet to attack Syrian positions in the hills above Beirut. But in this, America's first ever aerial combat action in the Middle East, Syria shot down two of them, killing one pilot and capturing another. They were the first such losses since Vietnam. So much for the 'shield'. As for the 'sword', eight Marines, cowering uselessly in the compound from which they never ventured out, died in a four-hour artillery barrage by Druze and Shiite militias. The more this war of attrition developed, the more obvious it became that the US could never win it – unless it was ready to turn it into a full-scale war, and send in tens of thousands of troops to fight it. But, haunted by Vietnam, it absolutely wasn't.

In fact the whole American design for Lebanon – the consolidation of the client regime, the implementation of the '17 May agreement', the withdrawal of all foreign forces from the country – was on the point of collapse. This duly materialized three months later in the Shiite-led 'uprising' that first drove the regime and its army out of West Beirut, and then – even as Reagan was swearing yet again that America would never 'cut and run' in the face of 'terror' – the Marines out of Lebanon. Although, among the strictly Lebanese, as opposed to Syrian and Iranian, architects of this 'imperialist' debacle, the basically moderate, secular, even pro-Western Amal had been the chief, it was actually Hizbullah and its suicide bombers which had dealt the most painful, preparatory blows. It was an impressive debut for this late-comer among Lebanese militias which would in due course surpass, and then long outlive, them all. Meanwhile, it had already been turning its attention to 'the Zionists' in the South.

'PRINCE OF MARTYRS'

In fact, it had begun there with its fearsome speciality, human bombs, well before it directed them at the French and Americans. Ahmad Qassir, thirteen years old at the time, had lost several members of his family during Israel's first invasion of Lebanon, Operation Litani of 1978. Four years later, on 11 November 1982, he drove a car, packed with explosives, into the Israeli military headquarters in Tyre. Denied passage at a checkpoint near the building, he put his white Peugeot into reverse, then lurched forward, furiously accelerating through both checkpoint and entrance gate, and blew himself up, taking with him the entire eight-storey apartment block and as many as 141 people inside it.[61] Most of the victims were Israelis, but they included a good many Lebanese and Palestinians, held prisoner there, too. That had been foreseen. Normally, Islam prohibits suicide; and the ultimate sanction for such 'martyrdom operations' came from Khomeini himself,[62] just as it did for those *Basiji* 'volunteers', some no older than nine or ten, who, in the Gulf War, cleared the way for Iranian infantry by riding Suzuki motorbikes through Iraqi minefields.[63] But operations such as this one required special Islamic dispensation, sought and secured by Hizbullah, permitting military actions considered likely to kill fellow Muslims as well as enemy soldiers.[64] The attack was so unexpected, and so embarrassing to the Israeli authorities that they at first made out that it had been caused by a 'gas leakage', and some Israeli newspapers even waxed indignant about the criminal negligence of a Lebanese government that had permitted the construction of buildings so flimsy that they could collapse from such a cause. This was a fiction in which Hizbullah uncharacteristically connived. It was later to exalt Qassir as the party's first and 'prince of martyrs'; it also named 11 November as 'Martyrs' Day', and it now ranks, together with 'Jerusalem Day', as one of its two most important commemorative occasions.[65] But at the time it had no official existence, its activities were subsumed within those of the Lebanese National Resistance, and, in any case, to protect his family the seventeen-year-old had asked that his identity be kept secret until the South for which he gave his life was liberated.[66]

FROM RICE AND FLOWERS TO GRENADES AND HOME-MADE BOMBS

Identified or not, the Israelis hardly needed to be told that they were facing an entirely new kind of enemy, a potentially far more frightening one than the Palestinians they had just driven out. But their problem was not just the small band of zealots that would subsequently emerge as Hizbullah. It was broader than that. In the perception of its founders, Hizbullah may have owed its very existence to the Israel invader. But the Shiite 'uprising' did not owe its existence to Hizbullah. More than the one against the Gemayel regime, it was popular, spontaneous and community-wide, even if Hizbullah, the fish in the proverbial revolutionary sea, became its principal, and in the end virtually its only beneficiary.

That came as a shock to the Israelis. They had quite reasonably expected that, after the Maronites, the Shiites would have been the readiest to welcome them, if not with flowers and rice, at least with tolerance and understanding. And thanks to their prior hostility to the Palestinians, most Shiites did at first manifest a kind of 'positive indifference' towards the Israelis.[67] That was partly why Amal was so slow to embrace the resistance. The Israelis had even gone into certain villages – especially those which had been at open war with Palestinians – and told them: 'you are good people. You can keep your arms.'[68] But this reception did not last very long. And the more exclusively Shiite the resistance became, the fiercer it also seemed to be. Before long it reached a level of intensity, both armed and unarmed, that no other Arab people confronting the Israeli army had ever before achieved. The Israeli pull-back, though much less abrupt and complete than America's, was ultimately more painful, and more pernicious in its implications for state and society as a whole.[69]

It was Israel itself that changed the Shiites, which turned rice and flowers into grenades and home-made bombs. Indeed, observers never ceased to marvel at just how thoroughly, unnecessarily and counter-productively it managed to achieve this.[70] At bottom their metamorphosis was a completely natural – if initially delayed – response to what Israel had done to them, beginning with the invasion itself. They had not been the specific target of that, but they had none-theless suffered more than any other community if only because, as inhabitants of the South, they stood directly in its path. Mainly theirs were the villages – nearly 80 per cent of them – that were damaged or destroyed, theirs the majority of the 20,000 killed. They formed the overwhelming bulk of yet another great exodus from the South, further swelling the capital's 'belt of misery', and contributing to the fact that, in the massacre of Sabra and Shatila, perhaps a quarter of the slain were actually Shiites, not Palestinians.[71]

After the conquest – the occupation. Another reason why the resistance was slow in coming was that the Shiites had at first tended to assume that, having disposed of the Palestinians, the Israelis would soon withdraw. But they did not; nor did they show much inclination to do so. On the contrary, they put it about that the Lebanese govern-ment was too weak to take over, conveniently forgetting just how much they themselves, before and after the invasion, had done to weaken it. Now, instead of re-establishing state authority in the South, they took it over themselves, installing their own 'governors' and 'pro-consuls' in official premises.[72] At the same time, they tried to get Shiite notables, mayors and Amal politicians to set up a network of collaborators and client militias like Sharon's Village Leagues in the occupied territories.

But, just like Sharon, they mainly ended up relying on local toughs, criminals and social misfits who had been terrorizing the South for years.[73] Then came the '17 May agreement', which, in Shiite eyes, seemed to mean that they had only been rid of one 'occupation', the Palestinian one, to get another, which would bring the South, and Shiites in general, permanently under the control of Israel and its client regime in Beirut.[74]

ABOVE AND APART FROM 'THE MUD OF ARAB POLITICS'

The resistance was mainly non-violent at first, and – where it was violent – small-scale and sporadic. It was also spontaneous, localized, individual, without any overall direction or control. But it was enough to disturb the Israelis, who now began to intimate that, while they would eventually withdraw, they would not do so under attack. And they grew more aggressive themselves. But instead of turning the population against the resistance, as it had when the resistance was Palestinian, this had the opposite effect now that the resistance was theirs. With their political 'awakening' of the fifties and sixties, ordinary Shiites, lacking an effective communal organization of their own, had looked to others – the Palestinians and their mainly Sunni Muslim- or Christian-dominated secular, nationalist, leftist allies – to advance their cause; during the early part of the civil war they fought and died for them in such disproportionate numbers that 'cannon fodder' was perhaps not too harsh a description of their role. But now that the Shiites were fending for themselves alone, they began to take a special pride not merely in their resistance, but in the fact that they seemed to be better at it, more courageous, militant and self-sacrificial, than anyone else, be it Palestinians or other Lebanese.

Shiism – the priesthood and the faith – had a lot to do with this. In the conservative rural society of Jebel Amil, clerics were very close to their flock. And many were militants in the Khomeinist mould. Prominent among them was Sheikh Raghib Harb, of the village of Jibsheet. During the invasion, he and a group of future Hizbullah leaders had been received by the Ayatollah, who urged them to mobilize the people and turn the mosques into bases for *jihad*.[75] When

Harb, a stirring orator, preached he was listened to by much of the
South. And what he preached was steeped in the cult and imagery of
suffering and martyrdom which lay at Shiism's heart. But this no longer
served – in the quietist tradition – as an argument for fatalism, and the
acceptance of oppression; it served as an argument for its opposite, for
self-assertion, and the confronting of it. Harb would dwell on the
passion of Shiism's original martyr, Hussein, grandson of the Prophet,
at the hands of the Caliph, and Sunni usurper, Yezid. This was a drama
which, in its Khomeinist interpretation, had furnished inspiration for
the Islamic Revolution, and now did so for the Lebanese Shiite uprising
against Yezid's contemporary manifestation, the Zionists. What more
dramatic example of self-sacrifice than the human bombs of Hizbullah
and the plenteous flow of eager martyrdom-seekers, who 'neither
preached liberation nor gave public speeches' but 'simply launched
operations under [the] banner of the *taklif*, or religious command, of
the *Wilayat*'.[76] For Hussein Fadlallah, Lebanon's foremost Shiite cleric,
it was this total, unassuming dedication that distinguished the 'Islamic
resistance' from an earlier, secular generation of freedom-fighters. It
set them above and apart from the 'mud of Arab politics' and enabled
them to 'defeat the Israeli occupation – for the first time – in an
effective way'.[77]

About the same time as the 'anti-imperialist' struggle was coming to
a climax in and around the capital the 'anti-Zionist' one really took off
in the South. In October 1983, the month of the Marine truck-bomb,
Israel committed one of those fatal, but typical, blunders to which
occupiers are inherently prone. As they always did during *Ashura*, the
commemoration of Hussein's martyrdom, the faithful had gathered in
their tens of thousands in the southern town of Nabatiyah, wailing and
beating themselves in this, the holiest annual rite of Shia Islam. An
Israeli lieutenant, who had been ordered to avoid the town, accidentally
took a wrong turning – and his convoy duly rolled into a seething
throng of worshippers just as their lamentations had reached the point
of ecstasy. Thus rudely interrupted, some of them surged menacingly
towards the intruders, some cursed them, some threw stones or
threatened them with their bloodied ritual swords, and – in the critical
episode – some overturned and set fire to a jeep. In a panic, its

occupants responded with rifle fire and grenades, killing one and wounding several.[78] It was not in itself a particularly lethal affair, but, followed by the assassination of Sheikh Harb a few months later, it was a great turning point, plunging the whole of the South into a state of ever-growing, insurrectional ferment.

From 25 a month in the first year of resistance, to 47 in the second, operations increased to 90 a month by autumn of 1984, rising even higher as Israel's expected withdrawal drew nearer. At first – apart from the suicide bombers – they had mainly consisted of individual attacks with mines, rocket-propelled grenades or dynamite; then they developed into large-scale engagements with telecommanded explosives, automatic fire, bazookas or Katyushas. Dozens of villages were attacked, and blockaded with barbed wire, in battles that went on for days. In the forefront were those – like Jibsheet, or Bazouriyah, where Nasrallah was born – which had formerly led the fighting against the PLO. 'The PLO used to call me an Israeli agent,' said Daoud Daoud, an Amal leader and a moderate, 'now the Israelis call me a Palestinian agent.'[79]

THE INEXPLICABLE SHIITES

By the autumn of 1984, the Israeli infantry no longer went into the major centres of resistance without large numbers of tanks and armoured cars in support. And when they did, they were met with burning tyres, stones, and screaming women and children who swept into the streets to stop them seizing their husbands, brothers or sons. For, once apprehended, most young men were led off, beaten, shackled and blindfolded. Those who tried to flee were shot. As in Palestine, the Israelis blew up houses belonging to 'suspected terrorists' or the families of 'terrorists'; they cut down orchards where 'terrorists' may have sheltered. And although the resistance was directed at military targets in Lebanon, not at civilians in Israel, 'terrorists' were what the Israelis automatically called all those engaged in it.[80] Indeed, or so it seemed to the Israeli media, a once relatively friendly society had turned into what, by comparison with the Palestinians, were veritable demons and crazed religious fanatics. So it was no longer Palestinians who were carried off en masse to the dreaded Ansar concentration camp, it was these inexplicable Shiites, some 15,000 of them by 1985.[81] The rampaging Israeli soldiery smashed up homes, furniture and television sets, mixed oil with flour and salt with spices, stole money, jewellery, radios – and never missed the cigarettes. And in a refinement they apparently deemed especially apt for a religiously motivated enemy, they went into the mosques with dogs, cursed the Prophet, urinated, trampled on Korans, and either broke the loudspeakers, or, inserting their own cassettes, had them blare out pop music to which they danced in the square outside.

THE 'IRON FIST' AND THE 'INFERNO'

But it did no good. Israeli casualties continued to mount. By the beginning of 1985, they had lost 600 men, 300 of them since the official end of Peace in Galilee. That meant that, in two and a half years, their dead already amounted, proportionately, to more than the 60,000 Americans killed in a decade of Vietnam; as for their wounded, proportionately they were already more numerous, at some 3,600, than the US suffered in that entire misadventure.[82] The occupation was costing $1.2 million a day. Public opinion was moving dramatically against it. In January, 22 per cent of the population were still ready to keep the army in Lebanon; by March the Shiite fury had reduced that figure to only 1.7 per cent. By this time too, and in order to reduce casualties, Israel had already begun a three-stage pull-back. But even as it did so it inaugurated an 'iron fist' policy designed to give a foretaste of the kind of 'inferno' – Defence Minister Yitzhak Rabin's word – that would be visited on the Shiites if, after it was completed, they launched any more of those attacks across their southern frontier which Peace in Galilee was supposed forever to have banished.[83] But the 'iron fist' only generated even greater resistance than before. The Israeli army was facing a situation unprecedented in its history. Its response was un-precedented too, as a punitive raid on the village of Sur al-Gharbiyah showed:

> Seven young men were killed, six of them between the ages of fifteen and twenty. According to townspeople, the seven were

pulled out of the round-up of all the village men. They were machine-gunned in the legs; two were bayoneted in the abdomen. People told me that seventeen-year-old Yusuf Muhammad Dira, who was bleeding profusely, asked for a drink of water. The Israelis picked him up and dunked him head first into a water catchment basin until he drowned. The other six were allowed to bleed to death on the ground in front of the villagers.[84]

A young French soldier with UNIFIL, witness to such scenes, told the Israelis they were behaving like the Gestapo. More seasoned ones conceded that the French army had done even 'worse things' in the Algerian war – but that it never behaved like the 'band of pirates' which the Israeli army had now become.[85] For the brutality was motivated less by any strategic purpose than by fear, frustration and the desire for vengeance. This was an army whose commander in the South, General Ori Orr, reviled its foes as 'vermin, snakes and scorpions',[86] a demoralized army, whose soldiers' main objective was to get through their tour of duty alive. In years gone by, when Israel's military pride was at its height, the standard jocular boast about Lebanon had been that, if ever it needed to conquer it, its army band would suffice. Now, upon returning from their service there, its soldiers threw themselves to the ground and kissed Israeli soil in gratitude for their survival, or, in the despised Lebanese and Palestinian manner, expressed their immense relief in celebratory salvos of automatic fire.[87]

'THE INVINCIBLE ISRAELI ARMY IS RUNNING AWAY'

On 6 June 1985, three years to the day after it had first gone in, Israel was finally out. 'The invincible Israeli army is running away,' said Dr Ali Jaber, an Amal leader from the militant village of Bourj al-Rahal, and the Southerners shared his opinion almost to man.[88] They were jubilant – and not a little proud. 'We have destroyed the myth that Israel is the world's fourth military power,' said one. 'We have done it ourselves, without being paid like the Palestinians ... In all the Arab world no one has resisted like us.'[89] And the pull-back did add up to the first such unconditional, humiliating retreat from Arab territory that the Israelis had ever made. But they didn't go all the way. They couldn't bring themselves to take the final step. They feared – in the words of Uri Lubrani, 'co-ordinator' of Israeli activities in Lebanon – that they would 'wake up one day with a mini-Iran on their doorstep', attacked by Shiite fanatics 'whose target [would] not just be the northern settlements, but Jerusalem itself'.[90] So they retained their 'security zone', or Strip. This was actually a somewhat larger one than before. More than just a ten-kilometre-wide 'defensive' buffer zone, stretching the length of the frontier, it included a salient, offensive in nature, running north to the Christian mountain resort of Jezzin. This brought Sidon and the nearby Palestinian refugee camp of Ain al-Hilweh, as well as Syrian forces in the Beqa'a, well within artillery range. Altogether, the expanded zone comprised a good 10 per cent of the country, with about 150 small towns and villages, and some 6 per cent of its people.[91] Its mix of religious communities was intricate, but overwhelmingly Shiite. The Israelis set up a new, 2,000-man 'South Lebanese Army', overwhelmingly Maronite-officered, under the command of another renegade officer, General Antoine Lahd. A host of Israeli 'advisers' remained in the Strip to oversee it.

Retaining a presence in the Strip was a fundamental error. 'We let the genie out of the bottle', Israel's most decorated soldier and future prime minister, Ehud Barak, once said of Hizbullah.[92] If so, with the retention of their 'security zone', they only helped the genie to grow and prosper too, by furnishing it with completely legitimate, national – as opposed to merely religious – grounds for continuing the *jihad* that was central to its *raison d'être*. True, in its early, severely puritanical days, Hizbullah had poured scorn on the very notion of a Lebanese nation, or even a Lebanese state; only Islam and the *Umma* had mattered. But the great majority of Lebanese, Shiites plentiful among them, did subscribe to such secular profanities. So Hizbullah would have been doing itself no harm at all if it allowed people to believe that a conventional national struggle, confined to Lebanese soil alone, was at least implicitly subsumed within its larger vision of universal *jihad*. And Hizbullah did allow that; the fact, it said, that the resistance was Islamic in inspiration, and that liberating Lebanon was but 'a prelude' to the higher, nobler aim – the 'liberation of venerable Jerusalem' and Israel's 'final obliteration from existence' – did not 'negate its [Lebanese] patriotism, but confirm[ed] it'.[93] Nor was it doing itself any harm in the eyes of an international community predisposed to be far less disapproving of a guerilla war against an illegitimate Israeli occupation than of one against the Jewish state itself.

Three years on, Israel had already paid a very high price for Peace in Galilee. But it was to be far from the full one; after the incomplete withdrawal, Hizbullah would quickly see to that. 'No more rockets on Kiryat Shmona', Begin had famously pledged on the eve of the Israeli army's 'greatest folly'. But Kiryat Shmona was already refurbishing its many public bomb shelters, and its schools resuming bombing drill for students.[94] On 10 June, a mere four days after the folly had supposedly drawn to its close, the first Katyushas were landing in northern Israel once again – the only, though far from insignificant, difference being that, for the most part at least, these were now Lebanese Katyushas instead of Palestinian ones, or, so to speak, Islamist instead of secular, pan-Arab nationalist ones.

CHAPTER NINE

The Civil War Closes

Hizbullah rises: 1985–1992

THE LAND OF HOBBESIAN CHAOS

Apart from its own behaviour, nothing more aided the growth of this genie of Israel's creation than the conditions which, with the failure of Pax Americana, Pax Israelica, or a condominium of the two, 'the Zionists' and 'the imperialists' had left behind in Lebanon itself. These were conditions of breakdown and fragmentation, yet more extreme, more indecipherably complex, than any which even that hapless land, during a full ten years of civil war, had ever experienced before.

For there was to be no Pax Syriana either. True, President Asad had prevailed against his main external rivals in this, his all-important, Lebanese backyard. True, too, his regional friend and ally, the Ayatollah's Iran, was in there at his side. But he was still unable to prevail over the Lebanese themselves. There was an almost unanimous, if in many quarters very grudging, Lebanese acceptance that only Syria could now put the sectarian state together again. Yet it turned out that Syria simply couldn't. Lebanon became Asad's maddening Rubik's cube; no matter how hard he tried, one last piece of the puzzle would always stubbornly refuse to fall into place, even when it seemed that success was finally within grasp.[1] It became the *reductio ad absurdum*, in violent and barbarous form, of that politics-by-religion of which it was the archetypal expression, a *bellum omnium contra omnes* that would have done justice to Thomas Hobbes himself. The 'every man against every man', in this unique, contemporary vindication of the philosopher's treatise on the 'natural' condition of mankind, were the militias, gangs and politico-military factions, perhaps as many as 150 in all, among which the residual state itself was now reduced to but one of them, and by no means the strongest. They were the ten mini-states, or 'cantons', confessionally homogeneous or mixed, into which a country of a mere 10,000 square kilometres now broke down, all served by their own illegal or semi-legal ports, some eighteen of them, which had sprung into being along a coastline of a mere 200 kilometres in length, all usurping tax-collecting and other functions of the state, all supposedly defending their own 'subjects' against the others, and all demanding tribute and protection money in return for that service.[2] And finally they were a traditionally anarchic, *laissez-faire* economy which warlords and their cronies had turned into an all-embracing criminal one, securing a controlling interest in already existing, *bona fide* businesses, state-owned or private, or in new ones which engaged in the systematic spoliation of the state, the smuggling of arms, drugs and contraband of every kind, and – one particular East Mediterranean speciality – highly organized piracy on the high seas.

The fighting went on and on. But less and less, now, did it serve any discernible military or strategic purpose; it was more and more the institutional, the pathological, activity of a self-perpetuating warrior caste divorced from the society, and its conflicting causes, which had spawned it. 'They shoot', said former prime minister Salim al-Hoss, 'to show that they are there.'[3] This fighting went on across the original, so-called 'traditional' demarcation lines, separating Christian East from Muslim West Beirut, which had barely changed since the war began. There were the massive artillery duels, fought with the ever bigger weapons – medium and heavy mortars, 155-mm field guns, Grad and Katyusha multiple rocket launchers, US-built Super Sherman tanks and their Soviet-built T-54 counterparts – which the rival militias had now acquired; and of course there were the car-bombs, always the car-bombs, which, deliberately targeting the most crowded places, brought sudden death in perhaps its most feared, most diabolical and cruelly random form. This was a kind of warfare which, it was mathematically calculated, required on average the firing of about 275 shells to kill just one person, and in which, out of every twenty it did kill, nineteen were civilians and only one a combatant; and that was not to mention the so-called 'macabre discoveries', the dead and decomposing bodies of previously missing persons, usually civilian too, which turned up almost every day in wells, waste ground or deserted alleyways across the land.

In the eighties a whole new, even crazier layer of subsidiary 'fronts' and 'axes' was added to already existing ones, especially, but by no means only, on the Muslim side, where former allies, Shiites, Sunnis, Druzes and Palestinians, now turned in varying combinations against each other. But even then the ultimate absurdity was yet to come. That was when the sects, or at least the dominant ones, having achieved self-rule inside their respective cantons, began to fight against themselves. These intra-sectarian battles – mainly Christians versus Christians, and Shiites versus Shiites – were some of the bloodiest of the whole war. On one level, they were just a struggle for supremacy between rival militias of the same community. But, on another, they were aided and abetted by Syria in its everlasting quest to bring the whole country under its thumb. And, in the case of the Shiites, Iran had a hand in them too, less as Syria's friend than its competitor, and champion of its own, and very different, vision of Lebanon's future.

THE GENERAL'S 'WAR OF LIBERATION'

The five-year period of Hobbesian chaos only came to an end, in the early nineties, with the end of the civil war itself. That historic development grew, like so many others before it, out of a combination of internal and external factors. Internally, the Maronites, who still boasted the strongest of the country's quasi-independent 'cantons', were key. Fifteen years of bloodshed had done nothing to alleviate the country's sectarian animosities; in fact, it had only made them worse. But, by now, one thing every community did have in common was a popular distaste for militias, its own as well as everyone else's. The Maronites had spawned the first, and most militantly sectarian; they now inflicted on themselves the most calamitous consequences of this, their own creation. In 1988, when President Amin Gemayel's six-year term expired, the Lebanese parliament – or its seventy-three surviving members, out of an original ninety-nine – and the outside powers which traditionally influenced its choice, could not agree on his successor. The official state authority – or what was left of it – fell literally apart. For the first time since the war began, there were now two governments, two rival claimants to 'legitimacy'. The army commander, General Michel Aoun, appointed by the outgoing president as 'prime minister' of a provisional military council, moved into the presidential palace at Baabda, in Christian East Beirut. He was not, of course, the president, but, in the eyes of a large and fervent following, overwhelmingly Christian but including a fair number of Muslims too, he effectively had the popular mandate to be one; and he withheld recognition from the two candidates – the first having been promptly assassinated – whom parliament eventually did elect. In Muslim West Beirut, a rival administration, headed by the existing prime minister, Salim al-Hoss, continued to function, and appointed a rival army commander.

THE MARONITE COMMUNITY BLOWS ITSELF APART IN STYLE

Practically speaking, Aoun's writ did not run very far – not even, in fact, inside that 20 per cent of Lebanese territory that fell within the 'mini-state' of Marounistan. There the 'Lebanese Forces' militia, commanded by Bashir Gemayel's successor, Samir Geagea, held pre-eminent sway. It led an uneasy co-existence with the army, or that very substantial, Marounistan-based part of it which Aoun controlled. They did manage actively to combine when, from time to time, the Maronite heartland came under Syrian attack. But their aims and outlook were different. Geagea and his militia were narrowly sectarian, and looked on Marounistan, essentially their creation, as a would-be definitive political entity. Aoun – a staunch Maronite no doubt, but a supra-sectarian Lebanese nationalist too – wanted to use the army, the country's only 'legitimate' military institution and, compared with the militias, a respected one, to establish Greater Lebanon, sovereign and independent, once again. For that the Syrians – and the Israelis – had to go; and in 1989 he began a 'war of liberation' against the former, the more immediately oppressive of the two. It was a forlorn enterprise, whose principal feature was six more months of cross-city artillery duels, perhaps the heaviest Beirut had ever experienced. It did him little good with the Muslims he wanted to 'liberate'. But – as if that were not enough – it was interspersed with the far bloodier, full-scale war he also had to wage to wrest control of Marounistan from the 'Lebanese Forces'. About 20 per cent of his troops were Muslim, but essentially this was an intra-Christian contest, Maronite versus Maronite. It was the civil war's last great paroxysm of futile, demented, self-destroying violence. Its protagonists were the two most powerful military institutions in the country; some 16,000 men of 'Aoun's army', with most of the tanks and heavy artillery America had supplied during its brief, disastrous presence in the country, were pitted against the 10,000 men of the oldest, largest, best organized, Israeli-assisted militia, with an artillery strength not significantly inferior to its adversary's.[4] In addition, thanks to Iraqi supplies to both sides, supposed to have been used against Syria not each other, Marounistan's weapons stocks were at an all-time high. 'The Maronite community', wrote Lebanon scholar William Harris, 'could thus blow itself apart in style'.[5] And so it proceeded to do, the brother-enemies bludgeoning each other into profitless stalemate within the narrow, built-up confines of East Beirut and the densely populated hills to the north and east of it. The price, in casualties, physical destruction, economic loss and the large-scale emigration of a disgusted populace was very high. It was also psychologically devastating, bending this most stiff-necked of communities into benumbed acceptance of the settlement which greater states of the region – and beyond – at last had in store for their small, sectarian, and infinitely troublesome 'sister-state' of Lebanon.

THE 'POISONED CHALICE' OF A CEASEFIRE

The first of those external developments destined to impinge on the country at this time was the end of the Iraq–Iran War. In July 1988 a mournful, almost broken Khomeini announced that he had drunk from the 'poisoned chalice' of a ceasefire. In the six years since they had driven the Iraqi army from Iranian soil, his 'combatants of Islam' had been hurling themselves, at dreadful cost, in wave after human wave against Iraq's steadily improving defences. But all in vain. And now, suffering serious military reverses, the Islamic Republic no longer had the will and resources to go on. The 'godless' Baath had survived; no second Islamic Republic would arise in their place. This, and the demise of the Ayatollah himself a year later, dealt a heavy blow to the puritanical passion and expansionist fervour of the Revolution. It brought changes in Tehran. However, even though Ali Akbar Mohtashemi, the patron of Hizbullah, soon lost his job as interior minister, these changes did not break the power and influence of the Khomeinist zealots. They merely weakened them, reducing them, by and large, to the status of a competing wing, or tendency, within the system as a whole. They became more or less endemically at odds with its other wing, their newly emergent, relatively moderate – albeit still devoutly Islamist – rivals, subsequently to be broadly speaking identified as 'reformists'. They coalesced around the first post-Khomeini president, the powerful cleric Ali Akbar Rafsanjani, who, though a founding father of the Revolution, now wanted to improve relations with the outside world, and to concentrate on post-war reconstruction and economic development.

THE 'SECOND REPUBLIC' OF LEBANON

Then there came the 'Taif Agreement'. That was the name given to the document on whose basis the post-war, 'second Republic' of Lebanon was to arise. In October 1989, with the blessing of the US, and chiefly inspired by Saudi Arabia, the Arab League managed to assemble fifty-eight of the country's deputies in Taif, a Saudi mountain resort, where, after three weeks of munificent hospitality and vigorous arm-twisting, they approved a Charter of National Reconciliation. This was the final version of a long line of earlier, abortive proposals for amending those two founding texts of the sectarian state, the unwritten National Pact and the original, 1926 constitution itself. Like all of them it aimed at a fairer balance of power between the communities, premised mainly on a reduction in the Maronites' paramountcy vis à vis all the others. On the question of Lebanon's basic identity, it anchored the country more firmly in its Arab environment, with the formulation 'Arab in belonging' replacing the 'Arab in character' of the National Pact; but at the same time, chiefly in deference to the Maronites, it stressed that Lebanon was the 'final homeland for all its citizens' – implying that it would never be subject to amalgamation into some larger Arab entity. Like the original constitution, it did postulate the abolition of political sectarianism as a final goal, but in the meantime, with its formal endorsement of modifications in existing practice, it effectively re-inforced it for the foreseeable future. Under these modifications, the presidency continued to be reserved for a Maronite, the premiership for a Sunni and the speakership of parliament for a Shiite. But the powers of the first were curtailed in favour of the prime minister and his cabinet, the speaker and his assembly. And in place of the existing six-to-five ratio in favour of the Christians, parliamentary seats were to be shared equally between them and the Muslims (and Druzes). Among its immediate, operational provisions, Taif also called for the 'dissolution of all Lebanese and non-Lebanese militias'.

The agreement required outside persuasion or coercion for its implementation. That, too, was now more realistically available than it had ever been before. On the eve of the Soviet Union's final collapse, President Asad had become acutely aware that his traditional superpower patron was neither willing nor able to furnish the kind of diplomatic support and military hardware on which he had formerly counted. He began adjusting himself to the realities of a Middle East that would soon fall under the more or less exclusive sway of the world's one and only superpower.[6] The heresy of the Camp David 'separate peace' forgotten, he restored relations with Egypt, chief bulwark of Pax Americana in the region. And the US reciprocated in the one arena, Lebanon, where Asad chiefly desired it.

In 1976, at the outset of the civil war, it had given the green light for Syria's original military foray into Lebanon, at the Palestinians' expense; in 1983, deeming it a Soviet-backed, 'radical' Arab state, it had sought to expel it; now, in another volte-face, it saw it once again as the convenient, local stabilizer of its turbulent, diminutive neighbour. Lebanon was a never-ending nuisance, Aoun an irresponsible trouble-maker; furthermore, despite his dalliance with them, Asad could perhaps be trusted to rein in the new, Islamist forms of 'radicalism' of which it had become a hotbed. After Aoun, therefore, Hizbullah was the US's main target.[7] Thanks to strong American pressures on its behalf, Syria was the great beneficiary of Taif, which decreed that its 'forces – be they thanked – shall assist' the new Republic to 'spread [its] sovereignty' over the whole country.

THE MANIACAL FOLLY OF SADDAM HUSSEIN

Only General Aoun now stood in Asad's path. With the mountainous terrain as his ally, his defences were formidable; and vast throngs of supporters formed a protective ring around his palace. There could have been a frightful massacre had Asad gone in straight away. The Americans would not give him the 'cover' he needed. And they still withheld it even after the self-inflicted calamity of intra-Maronite civil war. In the end it was the maniacal ambition of his arch-enemy in Baghdad, who, having plotted, via Lebanon, to bring Asad down, now furnished him with the undreamt-of opportunity to consummate his triumph there.[8] Saddam's invasion of Kuwait, on 3 August 1990, transformed the Middle East. Suddenly the object of the most flattering Western attentions, Asad offered himself as a symbolically invaluable – because formerly anti-American, pan-Arab nationalist – partner in the American-led, Western–Arab coalition to liberate Kuwait. Could revenge come gratifyingly sweeter than this – to help defeat or unseat the other Baathist idol, who, with his reckless folly, had briefly established himself as the great new pan-Arab champion, heir to Nasser and potential latter-day Saladin, in the eyes of his most gullible, notably Palestinian, admirers? In return, Asad won *carte blanche* to clinch matters in Lebanon as he saw fit. At dawn on 13 October Syrian bombers struck the presidential palace; the Americans had secured a waiver of the Israelis' prohibition on any Syrian intrusion into Lebanese airspace – a 'right' which, since 1976, they had reserved exclusively for themselves. Syrian armour and infantry then invaded the Maronite heartland, with the 'Lebanese Forces', Aoun's one-time, if reluctant, partners in the 'war of liberation', giving them artillery support.[9] On the key, Souq al-Gharb front, the army, much weakened though it now was, killed about 400 Syrian soldiers before being overrun. Realizing that further resistance was hopeless, Aoun ordered his men to cease fire and took refuge in the French embassy. Surviving Syrian soldiers took murderous revenge on a lot of people and looted the presidential palace of the 'sister-state' that Asad was poised, at last, to bring entirely within his grasp.[10]

PAX SYRIANA AT LAST

He lost no time in doing so. And by now, in their profound war-weariness, the Lebanese yielded with little ado to the only external power that could end a nightmare they were seemingly incapable of ending themselves. But if Syria was indispensable it quickly made itself bitterly resented too. Asad barely found it necessary to observe even the outward forms of a sovereign Lebanon which, in substance, he subverted utterly. Of the thirty ministers in the first, post-war government, a good twenty-seven qualified as 'pro-Syrian'; the Maronites, one-time masters, were especially reduced and humiliated. Among the seven former warlords in its ranks was the renegade of renegades himself, none other than Eli Hobeika, the one-time Israeli agent – and 'hero' of Sabra and Shatila – now well on the way to becoming an all-out Syrian one. A year later, the Syrians and their local henchmen so blatantly rigged the first post-war general election, turning an already very pliant parliament into an ostensibly freely chosen and therefore fully 'legitimate' one, that the great majority of Christians decided to boycott them altogether. And they were not alone in 'mourning the death' of that virtue, democracy, in the practice of which, however inadequately, the sectarian state embodied a signal contrast with almost all its neighbours.[11]

But Asad went much further than that. With a Treaty of Brotherhood, Co-operation and Co-ordination, and the 'unity of destiny' which it prescribed, he spread his tentacles deep into the fabric of authority and decision-making in the 'second Republic'. His basic interests were strategic and diplomatic, and he turned Lebanon's foreign policy into an integral extension of his own. But, as if to ensure that his turbulent new dependency would never again slip from his grasp, he brought to it the methods of repression and control tried and tested in Syria itself. He created a 'joint security regime', eventually headed, on the Lebanese side, by one Jamil Sayyid whom the Syrian 'pro-consul' in the country, General Ghazi Kenaan, called 'my eye and my ear'.[12] In fact, Syria's dominion was in its way so successful, so pervasive, and – through corruption – so profitable for members of the Baathist elite that ministers would travel to Damascus to seek guidance not only on such matters as the appointment of some high-ranking civil servant, but on parcelling out the market for, say, that latest milch cow of Middle Eastern crony capitalism, franchises for mobile telephones.

With the help, and sometimes under the control, of the Syrian army, the new regime proceeded with its first main task: the dissolution of the militias. One by one, the three main Lebanese ones – Maronite, Druze and the Shiites' Amal – and a host of lesser ones publicly yielded up some, at least, of their heavier weapons, and closed down their head-quarters, barracks and training camps. Only the non-Lebanese offered any violence; sixty people, mainly Palestinian, died when the army took on Arafat's last great autonomous military stronghold in the country, centred around the Ain al-Hilweh refugee camp in Sidon. There was, however, one key militia which, in theory, the government was supposed to deal with at the end of the process, but which, in practice, it was probably never really intended, mainly for Syrian and Iranian reasons, that it ever would – Hizbullah.

THE END OF THE WAR AND THE DISSOLUTION OF THE MILITIAS – EXCEPT FOR HIZBULLAH

With Taif and Pax Syriana, it became steadily clearer that, of all the non-state actors on the Lebanese stage, the one which hardly even existed till at least half-way through the war had, by the end of it, established itself as the most formidable of them – and in a class quite its own. In his study of Hizbullah, Ahmad Nizar Hamzeh contended that it was not very useful to speculate whether it was an inherently extremist and primarily military organization, or a moderate and primarily political one, or about its possible, eventual gravitation from the first condition to the second. As a jihadist movement, it was con-stitutionally bound to strive for the establishment of an 'Islamic order'

and for the 'liberation of Jerusalem'. It was more persuasive to argue
that in pursuit of these unchanging goals it would always navigate
between two modes of action: 'militancy and armed *jihad*' on the one
hand and 'gradualist-pragmatic and unarmed means ... within the
confines of legality' on the other. The more favourable the
circumstances, the more likely it was to adopt the first course, the less
favourable the second.[13] It hardly needs to be said that they could never
have been more favourable than they were during Lebanon's period of
Hobbesian chaos, along with the general rise of Islamism and the all-
out support – ideological, political, technical and financial – of the
world's only Islamist power, Iran, that came with it. The 'militancy and
armed *jihad*' expressed itself in four main fields – the 'Islamic
resistance' to the Israeli occupier of Lebanon, hostage-taking directed
at 'global arrogance' or the 'imperialist' West, the consolidation,
involving much violence, of its own power, and the construction of an
embryonic 'Islamic order'.

THE ISLAMIC RESISTANCE

Hizbullah's rival, Amal, was still Israel's main tormentor in the South
when, in 1984, it established an 'Islamic resistance' entirely separate
from the 'national resistance' to which most other groups, secular or
sectarian, had hitherto belonged. Organizationally, as well as ideologically, it was dedicated to armed struggle above all else. 'We don't
have a military agency separate from the other parts of our body,' its
Open Letter explained, 'and each of us is a combat soldier when the call
of *jihad* requires it.' The fighting apparatus was the core; other
institutions, political and social, that developed later were integral, but
subsidiary, to it. Fighting the Zionists, Hizbullah's initial *raison d'être*,
would always constitute its 'priority of priorities'. Or, as Amal Saad-
Ghorayeb puts it in her exhaustive study of the organization's political
outlook and ideas, it would be 'the very backbone of its intellectual
structure, the one pillar of [its] political thought that [was] not
amenable to any form of temporization or accommodation to reality,
not only on account of the party's inbred abomination of Zionism, but
also by virtue of the pure logic of armed resistance, as opposed to non-

violent means of confrontation'.[14] Armed struggle was the only way to deal with Israel. All forms of accommodation with it – negotiation or mediation, ceasefires or truces, let alone fully-fledged peace treaties – were 'treason against Islam, Muslims and the Arabs'.[15] In any case, what had Arab diplomacy ever achieved? 'Even in the heyday of Arab unity' it had not liberated 'a single inch of Palestinian land by means of negotiation'.[16] For Hizbullah, as for Khomeini, there was nothing like the anti-Zionist resistance, or the so-called 'Jerusalem liberation culture', to unite all Muslims in a common cause. 'Jerusalem day' – a Khomeinist innovation – commanded an emotional appeal among Sunni movements that otherwise took no interest in Shiism.[17]

On the day that, evacuating Sidon in February 1985, Israel began its three-phase pull-back to the south, Hizbullah made its very public debut. Parading through the city in hundreds of trucks and buses, young men in jeans and fatigues, chanting 'God is Great' and raising rifles rhythmically aloft, took temporary control of this predominantly Sunni city.[18] While the 'national resistance' favoured a respite, arguing that if the Israelis were not attacked in their newly created 'security zone', the newly liberated areas would not be subjected to air and artillery bombardment in retaliation, the Hizbullahis craved action, with some of them immediately seeking ways to infiltrate across the Litani river.[19]

'THEY JUST WALKED INTO THE LINE OF FIRE AND WERE CUT DOWN VERY BADLY'

To begin with they were much less proficient in their general guerilla activities than they were in their still continuing, occasional suicide operations. They engaged in the usual gamut of smaller-scale operations inherited from the Shiite uprising. But, already, they were also achieving some more audacious successes; an early one – and portent of things to come – was the abduction of two Israeli soldiers. And already they were inflicting a small but steady toll of casualties – one or two fatalities a month – on the Israelis, and a much greater one on the SLA who, as 'sandbags' for their patrons, were more exposed. Sometimes they would attempt larger, altogether more sophisticated exploits. Within a year of the pull-back came first reports of surprise attacks on SLA positions employing scores of men who advanced under covering mortar fire.[20] But at this stage the self-sacrificial ardour still outstripped the military skills and wisdom. 'They just walked into the line of fire and were cut down very badly', said Timur Goksel, or 'Mr UNIFIL', as the peacekeepers' long-serving official spokesman came to be known; it was 'just like watching Iranian assaults against the Iraqis'.[21] Once they lost twenty-four men in a single operation. They were also forfeiting popular support through ill-considered acts which, as in the bad old Palestinian days, brought down Israeli reprisals on the heads of the local population. From time to time, they even fell into that other Palestinian habit of grossly exaggerating their achievements, such as 'forty or fifty Israelis killed' in a single operation near Merjayoun. On one occasion, they blamed 'spies' in UNIFIL for very heavy losses that were really of their own, reckless making.[22] Nor did they balk at unprovoked aggression against the peacekeepers. If they singled out France's UNIFIL contingent – three of whose men were blown up while out jogging in the peaceable village of Jouwayya – that was in part because of French support for Iraq in a Gulf war now going less and less well for Iran. But it was also because, in the élan, exaltation and intense xenophobia of Hizbullah's early years, they were already – in their own minds at least – on their way to the 'liberation' of Jerusalem. And since the peacekeepers were but an instrument of 'global arrogance' for the protection of Israel, they deemed themselves entitled to 'deal with them exactly as we deal with the Zionist invasion forces'.[23]

Back came the dismal cycle, the bloody tit-for-tat, of the 'border wars' of yesteryear. Hizbullah only went after military targets, and inside Lebanese territory at that. But for the Israelis, this, as ever, was 'terrorism'. So back came the fulminations of the interventionists. Uri Lubrani, 'co-ordinator' of Israeli activities in Lebanon, brandished his 'iron fist' once more, even as Yitzhak Rabin, the defence minister, declared that, in order to 'completely break' this maddeningly resurgent resistance, still relatively ineffectual though it was, 'we feel free to use every means, attack helicopters, aviation, artillery and tanks'.[24] And they did, along with occasional ground incursions to boot.

Not surprisingly it was mainly Shiite villagers who died. And as a result of that, back too came the Katyushas. They were the only means by which Hizbullah could deliver an important message: if Lebanese civilians were targeted, Israeli ones, inside Israel proper, would be as well. In this domain, as in the strictly military one, it was a very uneven score. Once, in a 'lucky' shot, a single Katyusha did lightly wound ten people, but, in the first two years after the pull-back, not a single person died inside Israel.[25] It was, however, an imbalance that Hizbullah would in the fullness of time dramatically redress.

Steadily, the 'Islamic resistance' was emerging as the only really serious one. Not that, in these free-for-all, Hobbesian days, there weren't others still in the field. Indeed, of all the 'martyrdom operations' carried out against the Israelis in the South, it accounted for only about a third, clearly demonstrating that nationalist or patriotic, as opposed to purely religious, exaltation had the power to inspire them too.[26] Three such non-Hizbullah 'martyrs' were women. The youth and beauty of one of them, a seventeen-year-old Sunni girl, Sanaa Muhaidily, of the very secular National Syrian Socialist Party, poignantly impressed itself on the whole Arab world. In the traditional video-taped farewell which she had recorded before killing herself and two Israeli soldiers, she asked her mother to treat her death as if it were her wedding day, to remember her as the Bride of the South, and to share in her own inexpressible joy, now planted as she was 'in the earth of the South and irrigating and quenching her with my blood and love for her'.[27] Apart from Amal, still active from time to time, there were the Lebanese communists, small and mainly confined to the rugged foothills of Mount Hermon, as well as pro-Syrian organizations, like the NSSP or the Lebanese Baath party. Although the 'martyrdom operations' by member-organizations of the 'national resistance' were more numerous, they were less effective than those of its Islamic rival. A young communist blew himself up – but nobody else – on a donkey, after which the Israeli occupiers forbade farmers to ride to their fields on beasts of burden without express authorization from themselves.[28]

A PALESTINIAN COMEBACK

Then there were the Palestinians. In the south, in that strategic no-man's land between Israel's military deployment and Syria's, they had made a remarkable comeback. According to Rabin, by 1987 they boasted a full 10,000 guerillas; and that meant, he said, that, with Hizbullah thrown in, there were now 'more terrorists' in the country than there had been, before Israel's 1982 invasion, in the first place.[29] And they were actually carrying out far more operations – forays into the Strip and sometimes into Israel itself – than they ever had in the last days of the 'Fakhani Republic'. The Israelis intercepted and killed no fewer than thirty such cross-border raiders in the first eight weeks of 1989.[30] Particularly disturbing for Rabin was 'the growing cooperation between the PLO and the Hizbullah forces'.[31] Deeply mistrustful, even paranoid, though Hizbullah was about others, and not least Palestinians, there was one organization – Ahmad Jibril's Popular Front for the Liberation of Palestine – General Command (PFLP–GC) – with which, despite its strongly secular bent, it did appear to have a special relationship. In part, no doubt, that was because the Front had always been a protégé of Syria, and now, by extension, of Iran too. It was among the more active in the South; its most successful, and original, operation was the killing of six Israeli soldiers in a quasi-suicidal hang-glider attack on a barracks in Kiryat Shmona. Throughout this period there was no abatement in Israeli air-raids. Indeed, between 1985 and the end of the civil war, there were a good hundred of them or more, by helicopter or fighter-bomber; and, in spite of the growing menace of Hizbullah, they were mainly directed at the Palestinians, many hundreds of whom, largely refugees in their camps, were killed and wounded.

Most of the Palestinians operating out of Lebanon belonged, of course, to the old, secular-nationalist tradition. And while their revival was gratifying to Iran and its Lebanese protégé, far more so was what now came to pass in Palestine itself. For the Iranian leadership, it was a vindication of the central importance they gave to the Palestinian cause, and its potential for unifying Muslims everywhere. On 8 December 1987, an Israeli truck ran into, and killed, four day-labourers queuing at a road-block on their way home to Gaza from Israel. It was the spark that triggered the Palestinians' first *Intifada*, the spontaneous, mass uprising of an oppressed and colonized people. The 'uprising of stones', as it was called, was essentially non-violent, or at least unarmed. But it was met by a surfeit of arms and by Rabin's policy of 'force, might and beatings', a policy that led, and was intended to lead, to breaking the bones, deliberately and systematically, of bound and shackled men.[32]

IRAN, HIZBULLAH — AND THE FIRST PALESTINIAN INTIFADA

This was a 'gift from heaven' for Palestinian Islamists, and, more specifically, for the Palestinian branch of the region-wide Muslim Brotherhood movement.[33] Like their counterparts everywhere, they had long presented themselves as a new, clean, dynamic force for political and social change. But, in their case, there was an additional dimension: the harnessing of religion, as an ideology and a frame for action, to the national struggle. With an underground organization already in place and the PLO increasingly discredited, they were ideally placed to propel the *Intifada* into the more violent courses it eventually took. Under their leader Sheikh Ahmad Yassin, wheelchair-bound, half blind and deaf, they formed a militant, initially clandestine, sub-group called Hamas, acronym for Islamic Resistance Movement, whose meaning in Arabic is 'Zeal'. In its founding charter, they called — as Arafat once had — for the liberation of the whole of Palestine, because Palestine was 'an Islamic *waqf* ['endowment'] property consecrated to the generations of Muslims till the Day of Judgement'. Though Sunnis, they obviously had much in common with Khomeini's Shiite brand of revolutionary Islam. Indeed, both the 1979 Revolution and the rise of Hizbullah had done much to inspire them. One small, extremist offshoot of the Muslim Brothers, Islamic Jihad, which was particularly drawn to Khomeinism, had already resorted to 'armed struggle' and earned instant popularity for doing so. When, in 1988, its leader, Fathi Shiqaqi, was deported to Lebanon, Iran established contact with him and his followers both directly and — of course — via Hizbullah.

As soon as the fully-fledged *Intifada*, a surprise to almost everyone, finally did break out, Iran rallied strongly to it. It convened a series of conferences and 'seminars' to discuss ways and means of strengthening this 'Islamic revolution' in Palestine, even at one of them proposing the creation of a 'Muslim army' to intervene on its behalf.[34] It regarded support for the Palestinians as a natural extension of its support for Hizbullah, as an even better opportunity to pose, in an ecumenical, pan-Islamic spirit, as the champion of a cause that was not a 'monopoly of the Arabs and Palestinians'.[35] It ostentatiously joined forces with Palestinian Islamists in order to subvert the 'peace process', which, via the Madrid peace conference, the US was now promoting with fresh vigour. Obviously, that also meant fierce opposition to Arafat's efforts to insert himself into these 'evil schemes'.[36] So it was that the PLO leader, who had once moved heaven and earth to be the first world leader to congratulate Khomeini on his Islamic Revolution, now became one of its bitterest foes. In October 1992, a Hamas delegation arrived in Iran and held lengthy meetings with its senior leadership. The reported outcome was Tehran's promise of $30 million in annual aid and sponsorship of military training for Hamas militants both in Iran itself and in Hizbullah and PFLP–GC camps in Lebanon. Hamas was invited to open an office in Tehran that both parties subsequently referred to as an 'embassy'. It was even said that Iran was going to 'recognize' Hamas as 'the sole representative of the Palestinian people'. Though denied by Hamas, that, and much else besides, was already more than enough for Arafat, who, deeply troubled by the Islamists' inroads into the PLO's standing in the occupied territories, vehemently denounced Iran's 'open interference in Palestinian internal affairs'.[37]

Naturally, both Iran and Hizbullah were deeply worried about Taif; the renascent Middle East peace process; America's growing ascendancy in the region; Syria's active participation, or connivance, in all these developments and the favour these earned it in American eyes. Hizbullah called Taif 'an American plot', and Iran – or its weakened, but still far from defeated, Khomeinist zealots – saw it as a fundamental challenge to their whole investment in Lebanon, the only place in the whole Middle East where, after Saddam's survival in the Gulf War, they could be said to have secured a solid, 'revolutionary' foothold. They liked almost nothing about Taif, but least of all its provision for the dissolution of the militias. If that were to apply to Hizbullah, and in principle it was clearly intended to do so, it would put an end to its 'Islamic resistance' at the very moment when a very similar one was emerging in Palestine itself. Taif placed a huge strain on Iran's strategic partnership with Syria, so much so, in fact, that for a while the Iranian foreign minister made the Iranian embassy in Damascus his headquarters in a campaign to oppose it, while Ali Akbar Mohtashemi went to Lebanon to fortify the organization he had helped to found against any compromise with 'global arrogance' and its local allies.

HIZBULLAH WAGES SYRIA'S PROXY WAR

But, in one key respect, Hizbullah was to be spared the effects of Taif. Its militia would not merely be preserved, but go from strength to strength. In the end, it was not just pressure on Syria, but Syria of its own volition, that ensured an outcome quite at odds with what, in support of Lebanese sovereignty, it had pledged to do under Taif. Though wedded to a peaceful settlement, President Asad had simply had too much experience of America's wayward, Israeli-influenced ways, too little confidence in its will or ability to secure the Golan's return. So whatever might have been his original intention, and however much he disliked Hizbullah, he was not going to yield up for nothing in return the services which, even as it pursued its own, high-minded jihadist struggle, Hizbullah could render Syria in the process. He had lost so many important cards in his steadily eroding strategic hand that his great new windfall – internationally accepted suzerainty over Lebanon and the formidable, freelance fighting force which came with it – amounted to the most timely and felicitous of trumps.

Together the Lebanese state and Hizbullah, the non-state actor with which it was frequently at odds, willy-nilly became integral parts of Syria's 'two-track' peace-seeking diplomacy. Thanks to its control of its neighbour's foreign policy, formalized as 'total coordination' in 1993,[38] it made sure that Lebanon never entered into a separate peace with Israel – as Egypt had done in 1979 and Jordan would soon be doing too – despite all the hankerings Lebanon actually harboured in that regard. Ever since the Syrian–Israeli 'disengagement' agreement negotiated by Henry Kissinger in the wake of the 1973 Arab–Israeli war, the Golan

Heights had been among the quietest of Arab–Israeli frontiers. One thing the Baathists would very rarely permit their army, let alone any would-be, home-grown, Syrian version of Hizbullah, to do was risk a fight, or just a skirmish, with the Jewish state – of which, nonetheless, they proclaimed themselves to be the last, serious and truly steadfast adversary. By contrast, they very deliberately kept the Lebanese–Israeli frontier, long the only militarily active one, in a state of continuous effervescence. Israel had always thwarted the Lebanese army's advance to the South. Although, under Taif, Syria was supposed in theory to help it get there now, in practice it connived with Israel in continuing to keep it out. That left the South, where all Lebanon's troubles had begun, as the last preserve of externally supported militias – Hizbullah on the one hand, the South Lebanese Army on the other – and, in consequence, as the very place from which those troubles were liable to erupt again. And so, indeed, they were to do.

As long as Israel stayed in the Golan, it could expect to enjoy no peace or security in Lebanon. And it did not. For Asad, it was a very convenient, low-cost 'proxy war'. Whenever, in response to the constant, low-level violence against it, Israel raised the stakes with periodic bouts of massive retaliation, it was sister-Lebanon, not Syria, that paid the price. In pursuit of this self-serving policy, Asad was ready to accept, and in the end actually to promote, the complete 'Islamicization' of what had formerly been the multi-party, largely secular resistance. He actively thwarted guerilla operations by organizations, such as the communists, to which in principle his ruling Baathists were historically and ideologically closest; and in due course even their most loyal accomplices, such as the Lebanese Baath or the National Syrian Socialist Party, all but left the field to Hizbullah. Thus was an overtly secular-modernist, but decadent and cynically pragmatic, regime cashing in on a non-state actor's operational efficiency, born of a high religious zeal which few, and certainly not itself, could match. At the same time it was throwing a well-rewarded sop to the strategic partner, Iran, with which, at bottom, it had little more in common than it did with Hizbullah itself. The upshot of all this was that if, with the coming of Taif, Hizbullah was obliged, in certain fields, to go into what Ahmad Hamzeh called its 'pragmatic-gradualist mode', resistance was not one of them. And resistance, of course, was Hizbullah's very *raison d'être*.

THE HUNT FOR WESTERNERS

In the mid-eighties Lebanon became notorious for the kidnapping of foreigners. Nothing could have more starkly illustrated the xenophobic travesty of itself into which the one-time 'jewel of the Levant', renowned for its cosmopolitanism and conviviality, had fallen. Hizbullah was perhaps not the only or even primary culprit, but whatever part it did play in it, hostage-taking represented – in Ahmad Hamzeh's formula – the second main field in which, profiting from favourable circumstances, it had gone into 'militant and armed jihadist' mode. Emotionally, the phenomenon grew out of the Shiite militants' anger towards the West, America in particular; practically, it was an extreme, and cruel, application of Hizbullah's declared ambition to expunge America from Lebanon. It had already been working on that militarily, politically, culturally; now it was going after its enemy's very citizens too. On the one hand, kidnapping foreigners was very local and obscure. On the other, its repercussions, regional and international, were extraordinary. In 1986, it yielded 'Irangate', that great scandal of the Reagan Administration, involving the biggest single (if short-lived) drop in the approval ratings of any president in history, the trial and conviction (subsequently overturned on technical grounds) of two top officials on multiple felony charges and the indictment, for lesser offences, of six others (subsequently pardoned). In 1989, when a lone American citizen came under threat of imminent 'execution', Reagan's successor, George Bush senior, ordered the Sixth Fleet to battle stations in the East Mediterranean.

The taking of hostages, Lebanese by Lebanese, had been common practice since the beginning of the civil war. But the first *foreign* hostages were Iranian. When, in the immediate aftermath of the 1982 Israeli invasion, Ahmad Motevasselian, commander of the advance guard that Iran had already dispatched to Syria and Lebanon, learned that President Asad did not want the further 40,000 troops that it also offered him, he volunteered for another mission instead: to go to Beirut under diplomatic cover to destroy sensitive documents in the Iranian embassy, then surrounded by Israelis and Phalangists. But the hero of Khorramshahr and his three companions were kidnapped by Christian militiamen on the way. Their fate was never determined; but they were probably killed on the orders of Phalangist intelligence chief Eli Hobeika.[39] Two weeks later, in obvious retaliation, David Dodge, acting president of the American University of Beirut, was seized on campus, eventually fetching up in Tehran's notorious Evin gaol, where his interrogators never ceased to ask him about them.[40] President Asad, furious at his ally for having smuggled Dodge through his territory, personally secured his discreet release.

Hizbullah has always vehemently denied involvement in hostage-taking. 'There was an organization other than Hizbullah called Islamic Jihad', said Hassan Nasrallah, 'they carried out the operations against the US Marines and the French, and kidnapped the Western hostages. It [was] independent from the party. It is absolutely incorrect that the Islamic Jihad [was] a cover name for Hizbullah.'[41] Whether a real, autonomous body or little more than a name, Islamic Jihad was undoubtedly the backbone of the whole campaign. It was closely associated with Imad Mughniyah, the man who in most accounts emerges as the single, outstanding mastermind behind this anti-Western 'reign of terror' in all its characteristic aspects, the suicidal car- or truck-bombing, the aerial hijack or the more professionally executed type of individual kidnapping. Once a member of Fatah's elite security apparatus, Force 17, he then moved in a similar capacity to Hizbullah, but is believed, in his major operations, to have worked very closely with Iran and the Revolutionary Guards. In fact, for Ghazi Kenaan, Syria's military intelligence chief in Lebanon, he was nothing but one of Iran's 'hunting dogs'.[42] On paper at least, there was a plethora of secondary kidnapping organizations, seventeen at least if one includes those which surfaced for a single operation never to be heard of again. Judging by their high-sounding religious names, the majority fell within the Iranian-inspired, Islamist trend. But in due course it became clear, not least from the experiences of the hostages themselves, that these were little more than fictional adjuncts of Islamic Jihad. A minority were more secular-nationalist than religious; if they owed allegiance to any anyone it was to Colonel Gadafi's Libya, then as fiercely at odds in its own way with America as the Khomeinists were in theirs. Some, often without a name at all, were just criminal gangs, making a business of grabbing Westerners and 'selling' them to the highest bidder among politically motivated 'buyers', religious, nationalist – or, not infrequently, that most notorious impresario of Palestinian terror, Abu Nidal.

The hunt for Westerners began in earnest in 1984. In all, over a seven-year period, eighty-seven were taken. Most – seventeen Americans, fifteen French and fourteen British – came from the three states which, with their continuing history of political interference in the Middle East, were deemed most representative of 'global arrogance'. Though there were kidnappees from a dozen other states, these were the highest-value merchandise in the hostage bazaar. A few of them were, or were considered by their captors to be, military or intelligence personnel; and so, easily branded as 'agents' and 'spies', they ended up being killed as well as kidnapped. The vast majority, however, were ordinary citizens doing more or less ordinary jobs. Of these, some had spent much of their lives in Lebanon and developed a deep attachment to the country; some were married to Lebanese; some were overtly sympathetic to the Arab, and more particularly the Palestinian, cause and actively expounded it to a Western world still mainly, if decreasingly, sympathetic to Israel's.

'THAT RAG IN BEIRUT'

Little did their 'innocence' avail them. In their captivity, lasting anything up to seven years, they were held in variable but often appalling conditions; shackled, blindfolded; moved around in the boots of cars, or boxes strapped beneath lorries; tortured, beaten and humiliated. But most, in the end, were released, that being the intended consummation of the purpose – to serve as bargaining counters – for which they had been abducted in the first place. Initially, the kidnappers may have acted mainly on their own initiative. Their principal demand was the release of seventeen Shiite militants, a few of them Lebanese, under sentence of death in Kuwait for their part in the bombings which, back in 1983, had struck the American and French embassies soon after those far deadlier ones against American and French barracks in Beirut. But, with the involvement of Iran, their activities took on an entirely new dimension, with 'Irangate' as the climax.

In that extraordinary affair, the US sent Iran five or six deliveries of over-priced, black-market arms – including thousands of TOW anti-tank missiles and spare parts for Iran's Hawk anti-aircraft missile batteries – in return for the phased release of three American hostages in Beirut.[43] The proceeds helped finance the Reagan Administration's secret and illegal sponsorship of the right-wing Contra insurgency against the elected government of Nicaragua.

The scandal was first broken by an obscure, Syrian-backed Lebanese weekly called *al-Shira'a*. It disclosed that, in the most picaresque twist of a picaresque tale, Robert McFarlane, Reagan's former National Security Adviser, and three other high officials had secretly flown to Iran with another consignment of arms aboard their plane. Reagan promptly denounced 'that rag in Beirut'. But a few days later Ali Akbar Rafsanjani, then speaker of the Iranian parliament, confirmed everything it had said – and added some piquant details of his own, such as the fact that, as well as weapons, Reagan's cloak-and-dagger emissaries had brought a bible inscribed by the president himself, two Colt pistols and a cake in the shape of a key.

So here, after telling everyone else not to do business with 'terrorist-sponsoring' states – here was the United States itself doing precisely that, and doing it, moreover, with what, in its own book, was the very worst of them. Here it was, a supporter of, and purveyor of intelligence and technical assistance to, Iraq in the Gulf War, supplying badly needed weaponry to the other side. For the so-called 'moderate,' pro-Western Arab states, Iran, in its ambition to establish the 'Islamic Republic of Iraq', had become no less a peril than Israel itself, a threat to the whole existing Arab order in fact. Yet even as America did nothing to help them vis à vis the old adversary – for how, it asked, could they expect Israel to enter into negotiations with a 'terrorist' organization like the PLO? – here it now was, helping the new one to bring about the very catastrophe they feared. Furthermore, America's 'folly and duplicity'[44] – as they called it – did not even work. For even as the arms were being delivered, and the hostages released, Islamic Jihad set about kidnapping three more Americans to take their place.

Of at least ten Westerners who died in captivity, four were 'executed', and three plain murdered. The first victim, William Buckley, was the CIA station chief in Beirut, who, taking no special precautions, was abducted as he walked from home to the US embassy. Evidently, Islamic Jihad knew exactly who he was; that was a secret gleaned from that seminal hostage drama, when, in 1979, Khomeinist students stormed the US embassy in Tehran, held fifty-two diplomats for 444 days – and, with infinite patience, pieced together all the documents which they had managed to shred before the takeover. Islamic Jihad apparently also believed that he was the effective controller of Gemayel's Phalangist-dominated regime.[45] He died after being severely tortured; his kidnappers announced that he had been 'executed'.[46] Another who perished similarly – after once having been bizarrely permitted to visit his Syrian wife – was the French orientalist Michel Seurat. An Islamic Jihad sub-group, called the Organization of the Oppressed of the Earth, abducted Colonel William Higgins, the American deputy commander of the UN Truce Supervision Organization in south Lebanon, and a year later 'executed' him, apparently by hanging, in reprisal for Israel's helicopter-borne kidnapping of Sheikh Abdul Karim Obeid, the Hizbullah chief in the South. Two British academics, Leigh Douglas and Philip Padfield, and an American librarian, Peter Kilburn, were dispatched, a bullet to the head, by the Arab Revolutionary Cells, in straightforward revenge for America's 'anti-terrorist' air-raid, launched from bases in Britain, on Libya in 1986. The Revolutionary Organization of Socialist Muslims, probably an Abu Nidal front, said it had hanged British journalist Alec Collett for the same reason.[47]

'EXECUTING' THE JEWS

Perhaps the most poignant victims of the anti-Western terror were not Westerners at all, even if, in the minds of their tormentors, they were closely associated with them. They were Lebanese Jews. A community of something like 10,000 in 1948, at the time of Israel's creation, they had, like the rest of Arab Jewry, emigrated in large numbers since. The process had accelerated with the outbreak of the civil war, so that by the mid-eighties those, by now reduced to a few score, who chose to remain were taking as great a risk as any Westerner, as well as displaying a greater – because far more perilous – loyalty to their native Lebanon than its Muslims or Christians. Clearly, there were divisions of labour within the kidnapping fraternity, and to the Organization of the Oppressed of the Earth fell responsibility for dealing with the Jews. It acquired a stock of them over time, eleven in all. One of its 'policies' was that whenever Shiite civilians died at Israeli hands in the South, a Jewish hostage would die too. And so, one by one, they did, including Isaac Sassoon, the head of the Jewish Council whom the Oppressed of the Earth described as the 'chief Mossad agent' in Lebanon.[48] Another was Elie Hallak, known as the 'doctor of the poor' for the way he ministered to the homeless squatters, mainly Shiites, who had settled in and around Beirut's old, now desolate and war-ravaged Jewish quarter of Wadi Abu Jamil. His kidnappers even used him to treat Michel Seurat. As Hallak told the dying Frenchman and his three compatriots, he knew that he himself was doomed, because, unlike them, he was never blindfolded in his captors' presence. Sure enough, shortly after Seurat's death, his possessions were brought to the surviving hostages' cell. And two months after that they heard on the radio what they had already surmised: that the Oppressed of the Earth had 'executed' him too.[49]

Few of those best placed to know could take Hizbullah's claims to non-involvement seriously, certainly not Giandomenico Picco, the UN emissary who took on the dangerous task of negotiating the hostages' release. Hizbullah was the 'political force behind the whole crisis': there was 'no doubt in [his] mind' about that.[50] The kidnappers mouthed essentially the same ideology as Hizbullah.[51] They came from Hizbullah's social and cultural milieu, and operated in its geopolitical space, mainly the *Dahiya* and the Beqa'a Valley; if it had really disapproved of them, it had every means of stopping them. But it did not; on the contrary, it provided them with cover and protection.[52] Even if the party condemned hostage-taking in principle, it was not prepared to do so in practice.[53] Even if the *mujahideen* were misguided in method, it said, they were 'honest' in purpose.[54] There were 'extenuating' circumstances; and when those – above all the overwhelming Western/ Israeli onslaught against the Shiite community – were taken into account, hostage-taking could be seen as a form of 'self-defence', which Hizbullah fully 'understood'. Besides, why should it 'serve [America] politically' by condemning kidnapping when Americans themselves 'don't condemn Israel's acts against our people'.[55] In 2008, Hizbullah adopted Imad Mughniyah, blown up by a car-bomb in the heart of Damascus, as the latest and perhaps most illustrious of its 'martyrs'. For twenty years mystery had surrounded the role and whereabouts of this legendary, central figure of the hostage-taking era. And his beatification was all the more remarkable – and telling – in that this murkier aspect of its early life was one which, in its maturity, Hizbullah had become distinctly keen to put behind it, with party officials going so far as to flatly deny that he had ever held a position in the party, or that they had ever even known anyone by that name.[56]

'CLOSING THE HOSTAGE FILE'

Perhaps the single most convincing argument Hizbullah might have adduced in its own defence was precisely the one it never did – or very likely never could, so little short of blasphemous, even if true, it would have seemed. This was that the Islamic Republic had always been the real instigator, and beneficiary, of the whole unsavoury business. If that hadn't been clear at its outset, it became abundantly so in its denouement. For, patently, it only came to an end when Iran decided that it should. The first post-Khomeini president, Ali Akbar Rafsanjani, immediately signalled that his government would use its 'influence' to secure the hostages' freedom. And it did – though not without a rearguard action from the unregenerate Khomeinist zealots. Thus it was that Lebanon, normally the battleground for conflicts *between* states, now became so for one *within* a single state. For no sooner did Rafsanjani and the 'reformists' let it be known that their patient efforts 'to close the hostage file' were about to bear fruit than the zealots cried havoc at their would-be sell-out to 'global arrogance'; Ali Akbar

Mohtashemi (though he was later to join the 'reformist' camp himself) likened the release of such 'spies and agents' to the release of 'hungry wolves', and proclaimed, from Khomeini's graveside, that 'our dearly beloved Imam', to whose 'sacred breath' Hizbullah owed its very existence, would never have countenanced such a disgrace.[57] The zealots lost this particular contest; Picco escorted the last two hostages to freedom in June 1992. But that did not seriously undermine Iranian support for their protégé, which mainly came, in any case, from a quarter which generally favoured the zealots over the 'reformists'; that is to say, from the largely unelected, unaccountable, arch-conservative clerics, from the 'sacred', as opposed to the 'popular', institutions of the 'divine–political' system and their loyalist instruments, the Revolutionary Guards and the intelligence.[58] And it did not undermine Hizbullah itself, whose 'militant and armed jihadist mode' had fared rather better in its third, and more important, domain: the forceful seizure of power.

SHIITE VERSUS SHIITE

In the era of cantons and sectarian militias, every non-state actor sought maximum sway for itself at the expense of every other. Hizbullah came into being principally to confront external adversaries. But, unable to do that without a local power base of its own, it inevitably found itself in confrontation with internal ones too. The external struggle, against the 'Zionists' and 'imperialists', was *jihad*, the internal one, against other Lebanese, was the outcome of *fitna*, variously rendered into English as strife, sedition or riot.[59] It proved as adept and resolute in the second as it already was in the first.

During its extraordinary ascension, from the next-to-nothing it had been before the 'scuffle of camels' to the country's most formidable and only surviving militia, Hizbullah clashed with various quarters, be it what it called its 'basic enemies' and instruments of 'global arrogance', such as the Phalange or Amin Gemayel's Phalangist-dominated regime, or what it sometimes called its 'friends',[60] anti-Zionist, anti-imperialist, yet secular, nationalist rivals such as the communists or the National Syrian Socialist Party. But, ironically, those with whom it had to do really serious and prolonged battle in order to survive and prosper, were those to whom it was closest.

Internally, that meant other Shiites, in the shape of the rival militia, Amal, from which Hizbullah originally stemmed. The fratricidal conflict to which this led had its parallel in the roughly simultaneous intra-Maronite one, and, if rather different in technique, it was no less murderous in effect. Thousands died. In 1984, Amal had reigned supreme; by the end of the intra-Shiite war, coterminous with the end of the fifteen-year civil war as a whole, Hizbullah had supplanted it as the dominant Shiite power.

Externally, Hizbullah's chief adversary was Syria. In his unremitting struggle to impose his Pax Syriana, President Asad where possible evaded direct, physical force in favour of remote control through local surrogates. After the Israeli invasion, and the upsurge of the Shiites, Amal became the most important of these. While Asad much appreciated Hizbullah's external *jihad*, he had a very different view of its internal empowerment, not only because this new actor on the Lebanese stage posed a direct challenge to Amal, but also because it displayed an alarming ability to win hearts and minds in a way that his chosen vessel did not, it had a vision of Lebanon's destiny utterly at odds with his own, and it drew enormous sustenance from Iran, which, though Syria's ally, was increasingly its bitter rival too. For after 1985, by which time the two had basically achieved the initial, joint goals of their alliance – the defeat and humbling of Israel and America in Lebanon – all their latent divergences came to the fore. And it was this struggle between their respective Shiite protégés that put their own relationship to its greatest test.

THE WAR OF THE CAMPS

The struggle arose gradually, a consequence, to begin with, of one of those innumerable 'side-wars' that the Hobbesian chaos threw up. A particularly serious one, however, it pitted Amal against the Palestinians in the Beirut refugee camps of Sabra, Shatila and Bourj al-Brajneh. For both Amal and its Syrian patron the greatest threat to their grip on Muslim West Beirut was the comeback that Arafat was staging there. By 1985, several hundred of his guerillas had re-infiltrated the camps. His purpose was much less to fight Israel than it was to re-establish himself as a political force in the domestic Lebanese arena. Amal sought to subjugate the camps, even remove them, once and for all.[61] It thought this would be a walk-over, but it turned into a grim, two-year struggle, replete with Lebanon's familiar brutalities. Amal used its Syrian-supplied T-54 tanks to fire at almost point-blank range into the densely packed dwellings.[62] In a third and final, five-month siege, it brought the inhabitants to the brink of famine, amid rumours of a resort to cannibalism in Bourj al-Brajneh.

Though the so-called 'war of the camps' was humanly terrible for the Palestinians, it was disastrous for Amal. It failed militarily, sustained very heavy casualties, and generally demonstrated a shambolic incompetence. It also earned itself huge opprobrium in Lebanon and the Arab world at large, seen as it was to be trying to 'finish off', in implicit collaboration with both Israel and Syria, what in earlier such sieges – Tal al-Za'atar 1976, Sabra and Shatila 1982 – the Phalangists, with similar complicities, had begun.

Contributing to its failure was the opposition of other militias, its former Sunni, Druze and leftist allies, and even the Phalangists, who, in a bizarre volte-face wholly characteristic of Lebanese sects and tribes at war, now helped the Palestinians return to Beirut through the illegal Maronite port of Junieh.[63] Most serious, however, was the outright hostility of Iran and its Hizbullah protégé, likewise assisted by the Phalangists. Iran denounced these Syrian and Shiite 'traitors to Islam' who thus served 'imperialist-Zionist' aspirations to 'annihilate' the Palestinians.[64] Hizbullah smuggled in food and arms to the camps.[65] Many Amal fighters deserted to its ranks.

The 'war of the camps' came to an end in early 1987 when Asad, almost at his wits' end, sent 7,000 troops back into West Beirut to save his Amal protégé from total collapse.[66] But, in the process, what had been merely a proxy conflict between Hizbullah on the one hand, Amal and himself on the other, now turned into a direct one. The Syrian army shot or stabbed to death twenty-three bound and defenceless young Hizbullahis, including five women, who had peaceably surrendered in a West Beirut barracks; it then went around tearing down portraits of

Khomeini. 'Hideous and inexcusable crime,' screamed Tehran, and warned that it could make Syria's position untenable in West Beirut – a threat which prompted Asad to assure his ally that he had no intention of invading the *Dahiya*, by now a well-established Hizbullah redoubt.[67]

HIZBULLAH VERSUS AMAL

It was only a matter of time before the *fitna* erupted into full-scale war. The almost certainly Iranian-inspired kidnapping of Colonel Higgins, a dire provocation to both Amal and Syria, set it off. In the decisive battles of April and May 1988, Amal first attacked Hizbullah in the Nabatiyah and Jezzin areas; after three days of fighting in which fifty died, it captured Siddiqin, Hizbullah's last stronghold in the South, and drove out the Revolutionary Guards from their positions in Jibsheet and Sharqiyah.[68] Next, the Israelis launched an unusually bold ground offensive against the village of Meidoun, a Hizbullah stronghold, in the southern Beqa'a, slaying forty.[69] For the embattled and increasingly paranoid jihadists this meant that the Israelis were in on the *fitna*. Then, three days after that, Amal launched an all-out assault on the *Dahiya*, Hizbullah's last real autonomous bastion. Amal, and Syria behind it, calculated that, demoralized and reeling from earlier blows, it would easily succumb. But they were as wrong as they had been about the Palestinians. Realizing all too well that its survival was at stake,[70] Hizbullah rallied *in extremis* and entirely turned the tables on its adversaries. It brought in reinforcements from the Beqa'a; these included a large contingent of Revolutionary Guards. Together they slipped into the capital courtesy of the Druzes and their illegal port of Khalde, which, in the crazy, microscopic geopolitics of the times, lay cheek by jowl with the illegal, Amal-controlled Shiite port of Ouzai.[71] It mounted a well-planned counter-offensive, driving Amal's ill-disciplined troops out of 80 per cent of the *Dahiya* in six days. It then rejected the ceasefire upon ceasefire which Syria and Iran, collaborating even as they quarrelled, sought to install. It would not even consider one without the right to return to the South, which Amal's top Southern leader, Daoud Daoud, had vowed to retain as its exclusive preserve even 'at the price of a thousand martyrs'.[72]

After three weeks of some of the bloodiest fighting of the civil war, with 300 dead, over 1,000 wounded and 400,000 fleeing the suburbs, Hizbullah was on the point of inflicting complete defeat on Amal. Asad stepped in, a second time, to avert that. Even as Amal leader Nabih Berri[73] rushed to Damascus to beg Asad for full-scale Syrian intervention to crush Hizbullah – a course which he was evidently seriously contemplating – Asad himself invited Hizbullah's leaders to his summer palace in Latakia for a first ever meeting between them. There it was agreed that while 3,500 Syrian troops would enter the *Dahiya*, Hizbullah would retain all its military gains there intact. It was also agreed, implicitly, that it could resume its *jihad* in the South.[74] Asad praised the organization as the 'true Islam' in Lebanon.[75] Berri announced the dissolution of his militia in Beirut.

It was a basic turning point, whose consequences persist to this day. Making a virtue of necessity, Asad had decided that, instead of breaking Hizbullah, he would turn it into an instrument for his own ends, externally vis à vis Israel, America and the pro-Western 'moderate' Arab regimes, internally as another surrogate, supplementary to Amal itself, which he could co-opt in his everlasting, divide-and-rule manipulation of the uncontrollable Lebanese.[76] It was consolidated six months later by the 'Damascus agreement', Iranian-brokered, under which the warring militias were to set up a joint 'operations room' for resistance activities against the common Israeli enemy.[77] However, this formula, essentially a face-saving one for Amal, was not good enough for Hizbullah. So the intra-Shiite war continued; moving relentlessly from neighbourhood to neighbourhood, it eventually inflicted more casualties – if less destruction – than the Israelis had themselves. From the hills above Sidon to the villages around Nabatiyah, from clash to truce to further clash, Hizbullah remorselessly eroded Amal's sphere of influence in the South. In November 1990, yet another, and final, ceasefire consecrated the permanent, post-civil war supremacy of the Islamists both there and in Beirut.[78]

The Amal–Hizbullah settlement was also, in effect, a settlement between their respective sponsors. Often enough, their improbable alliance had seemed about to collapse.[79] Yet, clearly resolved that it should not, neither Iran nor Syria had ever despaired of finding a median way. In the end, far from weakening it, the supreme test actually tempered, refined and consolidated it into one of the strongest of Middle East axes which, try as they might, its adversaries were never able to prise apart.[80] Asad impressed on the mullahs that, in his Lebanese backyard, his interests must always take precedence over theirs, but, once that was understood, he greatly valued their support, both inside Lebanon and outside it, and not least against Saddam Hussein, the original begetter of their alliance, who, in the hubris of 'victory' in the Gulf War, now posed a greater threat than ever.[81] For their part, the mullahs, acknowledging that without him they would never have made the important inroads into Lebanon they already had, were ready to set limits on their 'revolutionary' ambitions there. The settlement left Hizbullah free to pursue the first of those two basic purposes for which it had come into being, the 'Islamic resistance' – albeit at the price, not of altogether forsaking the second, the building of an 'Islamic order', but of at least deferring it to another day.

ISLAMIC STATE WITHIN THE STATE

For Hizbullah, an 'Islamic order' meant an 'Islamic state', 'the only right system for mankind'[82] which it was a religious duty to establish wherever the possibility to do so arose, and, in its own and its Iranian patron's judgement, it arose in that primordial chaos for which Lebanon was now an international byword. In its Open Letter[83] it called on all citizens, of all faiths, to work for a society 'ruled by Islam and its just leadership'. The Christians should 'join Islam' because in it lay their 'salvation ... in this world and the next'. As for those who already belonged to it 'denominationally', they should start to observe it 'practically'; although their misguided, secular 'ideas' did not 'stem from Islam', their 'motives' were 'fundamentally Islamic' in that they were inspired by 'opposition to tyranny and oppression', and they would 'inevitably revert to their essence' once it became clear that 'revolutionary Islam [was] the force leading the struggle'.[84] In Tehran, the Khomeinist leadership wanted to cash in on the large investment it had already made in Lebanon, to profit from the vacuum left by America and Israel's retreat and the impotence of their surviving client regime; its continuing failure to install an 'Islamic Republic of Iraq' seemed only to increase its determination to install one in Lebanon instead.[85] In early 1986, at a conclave in Tehran, Lebanese clerics, in consultation with their Iranian counterparts, were reported to have secretly drawn up the constitution of an 'Islamic state' in which they would enjoy a paramount authority limited only by local autonomy for 'minorities'.[86] No other militia, not even the Maronite 'Lebanese Forces', envisaged a Lebanon-to-be so radically different from the old. Like others, Hizbullah carved out 'cantons' in its own areas – Baalbek, the *Dahiya* and a part of the South – but when it encroached on what was left of state authority it did not, like others, do so merely, or ostensibly, as a temporary necessity until the state returned, but as a preparation for God's 'just rule'. The basic functions it appropriated were destined, in principle, to become permanent.

THE CIA'S REVENGE

In this spirit, it imposed its version of the *Shari'a*, or Islamic law, and entrusted its application to a judiciary whose members, from a high court down, were appointed, or advised, by itself. The high court had jurisdiction over espionage, treason and crimes against the party and its members. Its most important and – in this history – its most pertinent case arose out of the car-bomb which, in March 1985, had exploded outside the home of Sayyed Hussein Fadlallah. This act of large-scale terror was apparently the CIA's revenge for the truck-bombings of the American and French barracks three years before. The choice of target was inspired by the belief – a then prevalent but apparently never very accurate one – that Fadlallah was Hizbullah's 'spiritual guide', had an operational role in its leadership, or had even blessed the two suicide bombers who had carried them out.[87] It was the handiwork of Lebanese proxies, reportedly in collaboration with Saudi Arabia, whose ambassador to Washington, Prince Bandar bin Sultan, paid CIA Director George Casey in person a top-secret $3,000,000 for his services.[88] Fadlallah himself escaped unscathed, but eighty-five others, including children and pregnant women, were killed and nearly two hundred wounded. After investigations by Hizbullah's security apparatus, eleven people confessed that they had done it on the CIA's behalf. The high court sentenced them to death. One of them was the daughter of an acquaintance of Fadlallah. The girl's father reportedly pleaded with him to spare her life and accept 'blood money' instead. Fadlallah, however, would not or could not prevent the *hukm Allah* – the verdict of God – which, once pronounced, was final.[89]

With the laws of the Islamic Republic came its *mores* too, fanning out from Baalbek, cradle of Hizbullah, to embrace the whole of its expanding demesne. In the newly liberated South, there was no more card-playing and beer in sea-front cafés – a favourite local pastime – and no more female swimmers on the long sandy beaches. Even the men now had to wear shorts that reached down past their knees.[90] In Beirut, the *Kulturkampf* spilled out of the *Dahiya* into the city's traditionally liberal, multi-sectarian heart, where Western 'decadence' still persisted, with the harassment of insufficiently covered women or the intimidation of shops and restaurants where alcohol was served. The targeting of Western seats of learning such as the American University, ten of whose Western staff and students were kidnapped, was of a piece with this campaign.[91]

WELFARE AND SOCIAL JUSTICE

In another key arena, the socio-economic one, Hizbullah quickly developed a quasi-statist role. Most of the country's leading parties and militias went in for community services, but Hizbullah's surpassed them all in their efficiency, scope and continuous expansion. Welfare and social justice, in the face of the corrupt and negligent state, has been a preoccupation of Islamists in whatever country they arose. But in Hizbullah's case, they grew out of, and were reinforced by, its primary, jihadist role, and the need it engendered to provide assistance for the families of *mujahideen* and 'martyrs'. It had one great advantage over everyone else. Whereas others had to raise money from mainly domestic sources, and incurred much resentment in doing so, Hizbullah enjoyed regular, guaranteed subventions from an external patron, Iran. One informed estimate put them at about $140 million a year,[92] a very useful sum at a time when the national currency, which once stood at some two lira to the dollar, had gone into free fall, fetching up, at one point, as low as 2,500 to the dollar, with disastrous effects on the living standards of the already poor, Shiites in particular. Amal, in its jealousy, called its rival the 'petro-party'. But the taunt, while perhaps true in a narrow sense, was specious in a larger one. For Hizbullah had another, altogether more meritorious advantage. While other parties and militias were often taxed with corruption, racketeering and self-enrichment, Hizbullah never was. On the contrary, its discipline, integrity and dedication 'generated feelings akin to awe among many Lebanese, Christians and Muslims alike'.[93] It set up the Mu'assasah Jihad al-Bina, or Jihad for Construction Foundation, inspired by an Iranian organization of the same name, and together with other institutions, such as the Martyrs' Foundation, virtually an arm of Iran too,[94] it engaged in a vast range of public services and infrastructural projects – from which Christians and Sunnis, not just Shiites, often benefited – such as hospitals and schools, cut-price supermarkets and pharmacies, low-cost housing, land reclamation and irrigation. It even opened Lebanon's first employment bureau.[95] In the *Dahiya*, where the absence of the state was at its most flagrant, Jihad al-Bina assumed responsibility for most of the water supply, electricity, refuse collection, sewage disposal and general maintenance – services that were so long prolonged into the post-war period that Hizbullah was widely credited with helping the Lebanese state avert a 'social catastrophe' there. All these activities were held to be an Islamic imperative and Hizbullah would have gone ahead with them 'whether Lebanon [was] an Islamic state or not'; but at the same time it was well aware that the better it performed them the more public favour the idea of Islamic statehood would garner.[96]

THE 'LEBANONIZATION' OF HIZBULLAH

Statehood, however, was not to be. Hizbullah in due course acknowledged its sheer impracticality in any foreseeable circumstances. That was a deferment of ideals which it did not accomplish without resistance from the usual, hard-line quarters. In 1989, as Taif and a general Lebanese settlement loomed, a conference in Tehran defiantly asserted that 'Muslim warriors and patriotic forces in Lebanon did not shed their blood to see confirmed again the old, unjust rule of one sect over the others.' Then, at a Hizbullah conclave, likewise in Tehran, Sheikh Subhi al-Tufayli, its secretary-general, insisted on perpetual *jihad* against all who stood in the 'Islamic order's' path. But he was opposed by a majority of the party cadres, who argued that while the goal of a *Shari'a*-based society remained immutably the same, the means of achieving it should be flexible; the time had come to supplement the militant mode with the 'gradualist-pragmatic' one.[97] After all, as the Koran had famously laid down and even Hizbullah's own Open Letter had – *sotto voce* – conceded, 'there is no compulsion in religion'. And there would have to have been an awful lot of that in a country where Christians, Druzes or Sunni Muslims combined still far outnumbered the Shiites, rapidly multiplying though they might be, and where, according to one survey, only 13 per cent of these themselves were in favour of it.[98] An Islamic state established by force would not merely have been inherently unjust, it would no longer have been Islamic.[99]

Indeed, any attempt, in such conditions, to establish one would have led to the Islamically abhorrent condition of *fawda*, anarchy; it would also have deeply antagonized Syria. And those two circumstances would in turn have collided with Hizbullah's other main purpose – *jihad* and the 'liberation of Jerusalem'. In any case, in Hizbullah's view, Zionism represented a far greater 'injustice' than a Lebanon still perversely wedded to its secularism.[100] On both ideological and pragmatic grounds, therefore, the struggle for an 'Islamic order' had to give way to 'Islamic resistance'.

So, instead of seeking to overthrow the system, however rotten it might be, Hizbullah resolved to work and advance its cause within it. This did not mean that, doctrinally, it approved of it, of its institutionalized sectarianism, or the Western-style democracy on which it was modelled. It simply meant that, for the foreseeable future, it would seek the 'possible justice' that was attainable through it, rather than the 'absolute justice' of an 'Islamic state' that was not.[101] It also, as earlier noted, hoped to win the support of the majority of the Lebanese people for its *jihad* on what amounted to nationalist, or patriotic, as

well as Islamic grounds.[102] Since to join or not to join the system divided
Hizbullah itself, and since this fundamental question required one of
those strategic decisions which only the *Wali* himself could take, it was
Khomeini's successor, Ali Khamenei, who finally clinched the matter.
Asked whether Hizbullah should participate in the first, post-war
parliamentary elections in 1992, he decreed that it should; it would
thereby 'combine *jihad* with political activities'.[103] Although, with this
critical step, perhaps even watershed, in its history, Hizbullah became
a conventional political party, with a conventional domestic agenda, it
remained the militia, with an external, visionary, Islamist agenda, that
it already was. And although, as it was said at the time, it had thus
'Lebanonized' itself, in its wider, trans-national allegiances it remained
in a very real sense Iranian and even Syrian too. Thus were born
ambiguities, and potentially explosive contradictions, that would never
go away.

CHAPTER TEN

Triumph of the Warrior-Priest

Hassan Nasrallah humbles Zion: 1992–2000

'A MESSAGE TO TERRORISTS EVERYWHERE'

On 16 February 1992, Israel assassinated Sheikh Abbas Musawi, Hizbullah's second, recently elected secretary-general. Hovering high above the militant southern village of Jibsheet, a pilotless drone had kept watch as he departed for Beirut, relaying a real-time, high-precision picture of his progress to two Apache helicopters, against whose Hellfire missiles his armour-plated Mercedes did not stand a chance. Thus did Israel make its sensational debut in the state-of-the-art, spy-in-the-sky technology which the Americans had used to deadly effect against Iraq in Desert Storm the year before. Long and meticulously planned, this very public, provocative killing of one of Lebanon's most powerful and popular leaders came quite out of the blue, with no serious claim to constitute revenge or punishment for any such act of violence that Hizbullah itself had perpetrated. 'It was a message', said Israeli Defence Minister Moshe Arens, 'to terrorist organizations everywhere.' This 'message' also incinerated Musawi's wife and six-year-old son, whose remains were likened to 'a charred log'; at least half a dozen of his escort, in Range Rovers fore and aft, also died.[1]

A NEW LEADER FOR HIZBULLAH

Two days later, at an emergency assembly in Baalbek, Hizbullah unanimously elected Sheikh Hassan Nasrallah in Musawi's place. His first message to those who had killed the man he called 'friend, brother, mentor and companion'[2] came swift and uncompromising. 'We say to the Jews: the language of force is the only one between us. Leave our soil.' A mere 32-year-old, he had, it seems, been his colleagues' obvious, indeed only possible choice.

Born and raised in those conditions of poverty, social upheaval, war, violence and displacement that were the common lot of countless Shiites at the time, he gave early sign of very uncommon personal qualities. Eldest of the nine children of a fruit and vegetable seller in Maslakh-Karantina, the small, sea-front, mainly Shiite slum in East Beirut, he quickly developed a passion for learning and religion; while his younger brothers helped their father in his stall, he would walk to the city centre in search of second-hand books, or read and pray in such mosques as he could get to from this Christian side of town. When Maslakh-Karantina was overrun by the Phalangists in the first major massacre of the civil war,[3] the Nasrallahs relocated in Bazourieh, the family village in the South. There, continuing his education at a state school in Tyre, he was drawn into politics, and, precocious youth that he was, quickly found himself head of the local Amal branch at a mere fifteen years of age. A year later he arrived, penniless, in the holy city of Najaf, Iraq. Taken in hand by a fellow student, none other than Abbas Musawi himself, who had preceded him there, he was admitted to the seminary of the illustrious theologian Ayatollah Baqr Sadr, who, upon deeper acquaintance with his brilliant new pupil, discerned future 'greatness' in him, saying: 'I scent in you the aroma of leadership; you are one of the *Ansar* [followers] of the Mahdi ...'[4] Under the guidance of Sadr, himself a pioneering theorist of 'Islamic government', Nasrallah was profoundly influenced by the very similar teachings of Khomeini, whom he later described as 'the greatest, most dignified and undisputed personality of the twentieth century'. In 1978, Saddam began a ferocious campaign of repression against Shiite Islamists, in the course of which Sadr, who had declared himself a supporter of the Islamic Revolution, was hanged, after being forced to witness the rape and murder of his sister Bint Huda. Dozens of Lebanese seminarists were expelled from Iraq; Nasrallah also returned home, resuming his religious studies and his political activities with Amal. After his 1982 defection to the nascent Hizbullah, he rapidly ascended its hierarchy, impressing all with his personality, intelligence and organizational skills. And now, installed at the head of it, he set about turning the party from a small, secretive band of zealots, principally known for the kidnapping of foreigners and the suicide bombings of Western and Israeli targets, into the doubly effective powerhouse it is today – both the most influential political player in Lebanon and probably the most proficient guerilla organization in the world.[5]

Among the first, outward signs of a new, more tolerant Hizbullah that Nasrallah brought with him was an easing of those fiercely puritanical social and cultural observances which, in the early years, had alienated many who, while otherwise well disposed towards the organization, had no desire to live under a Khomeini-style Islamic government. Nasrallah was also the moving spirit behind the *Infitah*, or 'opening up',[6] to the Lebanese political system and society at large, and the 'dialogue' with others, which now began in earnest, softening the party's menacing image and persuading many that only where Israel was concerned was it truly radical or extreme.[7] 'We fight on mountain-tops and in the valleys', he said, ' but live in this community and are part of it'; the party's jihadist mission embraced 'a civilized social pro-gramme that [went] beyond the mere carrying of a gun'.[8] With some 200,000 members, it became the country's largest political organization, combining the features of both a 'mass party' and a party of elite, highly disciplined 'cadres'.[9] In the first post-war elections, it won eight seats and, with the cooperation of four Islamist allies, headed the largest single bloc in parliament; it would have fared even better in this and subsequent polls had it not been for Syria's determination that it should not eclipse its principal Shiite ally, Amal, and Syria's insistence that it run on joint electoral lists with it.[10] Municipal elections were a truer test of popularity, and in 1998, in the first of these to be held for thirty-five years, it won overwhelming victories in the *Dahiya* and other important areas of the country, not to mention very significant ones elsewhere.[11]

Although Hizbullah was a prime beneficiary of Syrian hegemony, its deputies represented, in their domestic socio-economic agenda at least, what amounted to the 'only opposition' in parliament.[12] Politicians across the confessional spectrum gave them high marks for seriousness, professionalism and flexibility.[13] They inveighed against clientelism and corruption, withheld votes of confidence from successive governments, rejected budgets and, in the words of a former – and, of course, Sunni – prime minister, conducted themselves in a 'morally upright' manner that 'distinguished [Hizbullah] from other parties'.[14] All the while, however, it shunned a deeper political engagement – such as taking ministerial positions – in order to avoid the 'bazaar' of compromises and quid pro quos to which that would risk exposing it.[15]

'BETWEEN HONG KONG AND HANOI'

All Hizbullah's domestic strategies, however important or creditable in themselves, were subordinate to one overriding purpose: to ensure as much official and popular support as possible for the prosecution of the war on Israel.[16] Inevitably, this entailed a conflict of interest between the post-war state and much of society at large on the one hand and the resistance on the other, or – as Walid Jumblat, the Druze leader and sharpest-tongued of Lebanese politicians, once put it – between 'Hong Kong and Hanoi'.[17]

Rafiq Hariri was the personification of Hong Kong. The ambitious youth of humble Sidon origins, whose spectacular career as a contractor in the Saudi Arabia of the great oil boom years had made of him one of the world's wealthiest men, became prime minister in 1992; and, in or out of office, he dominated the country's political and economic life thereafter. Architect of Lebanon's post-war reconstruction, he dreamt of the special place, reminiscent of its pre-war glory, which the country would regain in the much-touted 'new Middle East' of peace, prosperity and economic integration now widely deemed – with the Madrid peace conference, Oslo, and the Israeli–Jordanian peace treaty – to be all but inevitably at hand.

Unfortunately, however, continuing hostilities across the last militarily active frontier of the Arab–Israeli conflict, undermining business confidence and deterring investment, disturbed this alluring prospect. In 1993, tensions between the contradictory visions of Lebanon's future grew so sharp that, even as Hizbullah was displaying formidable new prowess on the battlefield, the army was opening fire on pro-resistance demonstrators protesting the 'treachery' of Oslo[18] in much the same way that it had done a quarter of a century before when the resistance was Palestinian, not Lebanese Shiite. On one occasion the army killed nine demonstrators, and earned Hariri's defence minister that gravest of insults, to be denounced as Lebanon's 'Ariel Sharon'.[19]

In the event, 'Hanoi' never buried 'Hong Kong', but, in the uneasy co-existence between them, it generally secured the upper hand. Syria, with its dominion over official Lebanon, was a major reason for that. But Hizbullah's own persuasions were very much part of it too. Within a month of Nasrallah's assumption of the leadership, parliament was urging that the national territory be liberated 'by all means'.[20] According to an opinion poll conducted before the first post-war elections, 62 per cent of the people, Christians and Muslims, said they were ready to cast their vote for representatives of the resistance, clearly distinguishing them – and their cause – from the wartime militias of recent evil memory. In later years Hizbullah's armed struggle won it more parliamentary support than any of its rivals even among those whom that struggle most imperilled.[21] In the circumstances the Lebanese state, in the person of Hariri, had little choice but to endorse the 'legitimacy' of the resistance, which, he said, could – and would – only come to an end with the end of the Israeli occupation itself.

BLEEDING THE ENEMY SLOWLY

'Some people think', said Timur Goksel, 'that Nasrallah was really meant to have been a general, not an ayatollah.'[22] Certain it is that, under this warrior-priest, Hizbullah developed military capabilities of a high order, severely exposing the vulnerabilities of a state which, unlike any other in the modern world, owed its very existence and survival to military force and its almost legendarily effective use of it. It embarrassed virtually all regular Arab armies and undermined the notion, deeply embedded in the Israeli psyche, that Arabs are inherently inferior in the arts of war. For the first time in their history Israelis faced a true guerilla enemy – an enemy, nonetheless, who in this period probably never numbered more than 1,500 fighters, of whom perhaps only 500 were full-time professionals.[23] The *mujahideen* still retained that religious fervour and self-sacrificing zeal which were the mainspring of their prowess. But the leadership now all but outlawed 'martyrdom operations' and gratuitously wasteful, Iranian-style 'human wave' assaults against well-defended positions. Instead, it married the undimmed martial ardour with greater military skills – with advanced weapons training, ingenious battlefield tactics, elaborate reconnaissance, staff work, the ability to innovate and learn from mistakes. In the old days, field security had been minimal, and every sheikh would involve himself in military affairs. Now Nasrallah ensured that they knew nothing of operations in advance. He also set up an autonomous military headquarters in the South. Accustomed to Palestinians whose security was so lax that – in Goksel's sardonic judgement – 'the only thing they didn't do was put a big neon sign saying "here are our guns and ammunition"',[24] the Israelis now faced a highly compact, invisible enemy force that was virtually impossible to penetrate.

Hizbullah's objective was the classic guerilla one, to make the enemy 'bleed slowly'.[25] And bleed, increasingly, it did. Operations steadily increased in number – from a mere 19 in 1990 to 187 in 1994 – as well as sophistication.[26] 'Terrorists', in earlier days and other arenas, they might have been, but in the Strip they fought clean – cleaner, at least, than their enemy. That looked better morally, of course; but it was in their political and diplomatic interest as well. They confined themselves to strictly 'legitimate', military targets – Israeli soldiers and their South Lebanese Army accessories – in occupied territory. Nasrallah spelled it out from the outset: if Israel hit civilian targets in Lebanon, Hizbullah would seek to hit them in Israel, with the Katyushas that were its only means of doing so.[27]

THE RULES OF THE GAME

Such became the 'rules of the game' in warfare South Lebanese style. The Israelis themselves were the first to call them that – and yet the first, almost always, to break them.[28] When, in retaliation for the small but steady toll of military lives, they attacked what they called 'Hizbullah targets' north of the 'security zone' they were actually attacking civilians in their villages, usually with bombing and shelling, occasionally in ground incursions.[29] Their purpose, said Israeli military commentators, was 'educational' – teaching the Lebanese about the worse-to-come if they did not get the 'terrorists' in their midst to desist.[30]

ACCOUNTABILITY, 1993

But Hizbullah did not desist, and that worse-to-come eventually materialized in the shape of two onslaughts which, the Israelis hoped, were to finish it off altogether. Despite all the furore on the subject, Operation Accountability – July 1993 – and Operation Grapes of Wrath – April 1996 – did not come about because of Hizbullah's Katyushas, and the pain they inflicted on Israeli civilians. For these obsolete and inaccurate projectiles rarely killed anyone; and the casualty ratio in this field remained pretty much what it always had been – about thirty dead Lebanese to one dead Israeli a year.[31] They came about because Hizbullah simply got too good at what it was doing *within* the 'rules' – that is to say, as Goksel put it, 'killing too many Israeli soldiers in too short a space of time'.[32] The onslaughts did not take the form of large-scale ground invasions, as they had of old; instead, they were so-called 'stand-off' operations, a merciless pounding from afar. Their purpose was two-fold: militarily to smash the guerillas themselves, their bases and their personnel; politically to persuade the Lebanese state and people, by punishing them too, to turn against Hizbullah, and then to make a final peace with Israel independently of Syria. They were the characteristic recourse of a highly developed military machine which, to minimize casualties, had wherever possible abandoned the face-to-face combat of its highly motivated early years – a machine which, perhaps largely unbeknown to itself, had also undergone a steady erosion of real battlefield valour and competence. For, increasingly, the only form of warfare that it ever engaged in was the colonial-style repression and brutalization of a subject people, and this had been reducing its average conscript soldier 'from a crack fighter to a flak-jacketed bully with few military skills beyond the stamina to chase Palestinian children down alleyways'.[33]

On the face of it, it might not have looked like that. Indeed, said military historian Martin van Creveld, 'to the initiate, it was nothing short of awe-inspiring'. On the ground, artillery radar and laser range-finders fed coordinates to the computers that now equipped every big gun, theoretically enabling them to locate Katyusha sites even as the rockets they had fired were still in the air and to shift from one target to the next in seconds. At sea, missile boats shelled the coastal highway. Overhead were the all-seeing drones, and helicopters that could, at will, direct their missiles through a particular window of a particular high-rise apartment of a densely populated city. All told, it was more stunningly sophisticated even than the Desert Storm on which it had been modelled, and especially, perhaps, because it went on, uninterrupted, twenty-four hours on twenty-four.[34] But, in practical terms, it achieved virtually nothing.

With the launch of Operation Accountability Prime Minister Yitzhak Rabin denied that he was making war on Lebanon. He was only trying to 'push [its] inhabitants' to act against the Hizbullah in their midst, to 'force' the Shiites to 'flee northwards', thereby inducing them to 'pressure [their] government to extirpate [it] from their villages'.[35] But what kind of non-war could this have been in which an army command looked forward to 'transforming fifty-four villages on the edge of the security zone into a field of ruins'[36] or in which, half-way through it, an artillery officer announced that 'we have now reached the stage of bombarding the internal fabric of villages, wrecking their infrastructure, destroying them and the homes of the activists'?[37] In the seven-day campaign, some seventy villages were indeed destroyed or severely damaged, not to mention the roads, bridges, water systems and electricity networks that served them.[38] One hundred and forty Lebanese civilians died – compared with two Israelis – and more than 350,000 fled to Beirut.[39] On the other hand, only nine Hizbullahis were killed – and their Katyushas kept coming till the end.[40]

If turning government and people against the 'terrorists' had worked in Palestinian times, it did not do so now. There was some grumbling, even a small demonstration or two, about the firing of Katyushas from the vicinity of villages. And a few politicians did call for Hizbullah's disarming. By and large, however, the Israeli blitz, and Hizbullah's response to it, generated patriotic feelings and a level of national unity spanning the confessional divide unseen since at least before the civil war. As for the government, it said it 'couldn't stop legitimate acts of national resistance from Lebanese soil'; nor was it the Lebanese army's job to 'guard Israel's frontiers'.[41]

Far from breaking Hizbullah, then, the Israelis fetched up reinforcing it, militarily, politically and diplomatically. At first, with characteristic partisanship, President Clinton's administration blamed it for the violence, and barely disguised its approval of what, in its book, was Israel's legitimate response. But before very long, with its protégé manifestly floundering, it had to change its tune entirely, seek a ceasefire and go cap in hand to Damascus to get it. And the ceasefire agreement itself was just about everything that Hizbullah could have wished for, corroborating as it did the existing 'rules of the game' that outlawed all attacks on civilians. Though unwritten and unsigned, it meant, in effect, that Israel and America had now implicitly acquiesced in Hizbullah's right to go on attacking Israeli soldiers in the Strip.[42] And within three weeks of the ceasefire it killed nine of them in a single day – two more than had provoked the whole operation in the first place.[43]

GRAPES OF WRATH, 1996

With Grapes of Wrath, Israel tried again. In the three intervening years it had attacked civilians 231 times, killing some forty-five of them, and Hizbullah had retaliated with Katyushas into northern Israel thirteen times, killing three.[44] But as for the real war, the one against the Israeli military in the Strip, Hizbullah's operations had continued to grow in frequency, scale, daring, ingenuity – and in the use of what had become one of its most important weapons, the video camera.

Perched on a gaunt, treeless height, the Israeli position at Dabshe had long tormented the citizens of Nabatiyah and nearby villages. One day in October 1994, for reasons locals could only guess at, it opened up with tank fire on a Nabatiyah suburb. When eight terrified members of the Atwa and Basal families gathered together under a single roof, it first struck with four conventional shells. But it was the fifth that took the toll. This was filled with a thousand 'nails', straight ones that penetrated deep into concrete walls and bent ones that bounced off them. 'Look,' said Ali Basal, pointing to a funerary photo-montage, 'this was my brother, this my brother-in-law, this my cousin, and this my fourteen-year-old son.'[45] Before dawn, a week later, some twenty *mujahideen* with rifles, machine guns, rocket-launchers – and a video – crept up Dabshe's perilously exposed western slope and, at 8.30 am, in broad daylight, they assaulted the fortress on top, manned by a unit of the elite Givati Regiment and equipped with Merkava tanks, armoured cars and sophisticated automatic firing devices. Of the four soldiers on west-side sentry duty, three fled or cowered beneath the ramparts and a fourth, under sniper fire, could do nothing. The other seventy just sat in their bunkers. The assailants walked to the post, hurled grenades into it and hoisted the Hizbullah flag above it.

The extraordinary exploit which the video recorded became a sensation on television, Israeli and Arab, throughout the region. By sheer luck, only one Israeli was killed. As for the Hizbullahis, they simply withdrew at will, without a single casualty. An Israeli soldier confessed what an eerie experience it had been for him. 'We had always said, "let them come."[46] And we never thought they would dare. But there was the flag.' That was the Israeli version. According to Sheikh Nabil Kaouk, Hizbullah chief for the South, the true one was even more shocking. 'Our men', he said, 'saw tens of soldiers fleeing into the woods on the other side, and we destroyed at least one Merkava tank.'[47] It shook the whole of Israel. What the video really exposed, said Yoav Gilber, a historian, was that the spirit of sacrifice which had carried Israel through five wars was crumbling, that 'a system of norms' had taken over 'where it's every man for himself – and don't worry about the masses and don't be a sucker'.[48] The *Jerusalem Post* called the Hizbullahis' video 'the most effective recruiting film they could ever dream of'. 'Yes,' said Sheikh Kaouk, 'we always get volunteers after successful operations, but we can hardly count them this time.'[49]

Hizbullah's camouflaged cameramen accompanied the *mujahideen* on even the most audacious of operations, and, wherever possible, got their electrifying, on-site footage back to Beirut, often across miles of 'enemy' territory, in time for peak-hour news bulletins on Hizbullah television station. Al-Manar, 'the Lighthouse', soon became one of the most popular in an Arab world that was thrilled and astonished at the spectacle of a little band of freelance fighters inflicting such pain on an Israeli army at whose hands its regular Arab counterparts had suffered little but serial defeat and humiliation. For the opposite reason, Israelis became compulsive watchers too; as their toll of dead and injured steadily mounted al-Manar sought to taunt and demoralize them with its famous Hebrew- and Arabic-language programme, 'Who's Next?', a continuously updated photo gallery of the latest Israeli casualties which always ended with a blank space and a large question mark over an anonymous silhouette.[50]

THE SHADOW OF IRAN

Once again, it was military exploits like these, not the Katyushas, which were to provoke the new onslaught – these, plus the larger regional and international forces of which South Lebanon was, once more, the hottest, 'proxy' point of collision. For the shadow of Iran fell more darkly over Grapes of Wrath than it already had over Accountability, or at least it did in the minds of Israelis and Americans. That was because, between the two operations, a fundamental change in Israeli foreign policy, already in the making, had come to full fruition – and, given its deference to all things Israeli, in America's foreign policy too.

For decades Iran had been the mainstay of the 'alliance of the periphery', the Israeli strategy of seeking to corral a hostile Arab 'centre' inside a ring of Israel-friendly, non-Arab states on its fringes.[51] The strategy suffered a grievous blow with the advent of the Islamic Revolution, and its espousal of ferocious anti-Zionism as a basic tenet of its foreign policy. But for all the animosity, the vehement rhetoric and the maxim, inculcated into schoolchildren and endorsed by a majority vote in parliament, that Israel should be 'erased' from existence[52] – for all that, the Israelis stubbornly persuaded themselves that Iran under the mullahs still set store by the utilitarian relationship inherited from the Shah which, publicly, it indignantly disowned. And anyway, even if it did not, this extreme Islamist theocracy to which its former ally had fallen prey was surely a temporary aberration; ancient nation-state that it was, it would surely rediscover where its real, and perennial, geopolitical self-interest lay. So tenaciously did Israelis cling to the 'periphery' doctrine that they – and their neoconservative friends in the US – actually lobbied successive US administrations *not* to pay attention to the annihilationist rhetoric which, of all things, seemed most poisonously to discredit it.[53] It was out of this diehard mind-set that the 'arms-for-hostages' scandal had grown. The first of the secret weapons deliveries had come from Israel itself. But in persuading the Americans to join in, its objective had not been to win freedom for American hostages; it had been to lure the aberrant Iran back into the strategic partnership of old.[54] For Defence Minister Yitzhak Rabin, Iran was still Israel's 'natural ally', even its 'best friend', towards which it '[didn't] intend to change [its] position … because Khomeini's regime [wouldn't] last for ever'.[55]

But last it did. And by the early 1990s, it seemed to dawn on Israeli leaders that the 'periphery' – in its Iranian, Shiite guise – now posed a greater threat than the Arab, predominantly Sunni 'centre'. The periphery was militant, purposeful and increasingly powerful, the centre was weak, decadent, divided, and, with a realism born of exhaustion and defeat, some of its key components – Egypt, Jordan, the PLO – had already made formal peace with Israel, or were striving to do so. Then, with two great events – the collapse of the Soviet Union and the rout of Iraq by the American-led Western/Arab coalition in the war to liberate Kuwait – the common threats which had once obliged Iran and Israel to collaborate all of a sudden ceased to exist. With Russia as a new friend, with Iraq virtually *hors de combat*, Iran was free to develop a regional role commensurate with its natural weight, and to do so at Israel's expense. So it was that these former partners, the two most powerful states in the region, found themselves locked into a vicious struggle for strategic dominance over it.[56] In Israel, Rabin and Shimon Peres, once the most fervent advocates of the 'periphery alliance', were now the most fiercely opposed to it. They took to demonizing Iran and Islamism as the great new peril with an even greater passion than once they had the Soviet Union and communism.[57] Iran, said Rabin, wanted to become 'the leading power in the region'. Although that was precisely what Israel itself had been striving for ever since it came into being, such ambitions, when harboured by Iran, were the 'megalomaniac tendencies' of an 'insane' regime. Technological progress, in the form of long-range missiles, conferred on Iran an 'over-the-horizon' military capability which dealt a further, radical blow to the 'periphery' doctrine. Worse still, Iran was trying to do what Israel had long since done itself – develop nuclear weapons that would make it, said Peres, 'more dangerous than Nazism, because Hitler did not possess [them]'.[58]

But perhaps what worried Israel most of all was the possibility that, in this new, unipolar, post-Soviet world, it would lose its strategic utility in America's eyes, that even the Islamic Republic itself might gain favour at its expense. Rafsanjani and the moderate 'reformists' were making every effort to interest the Americans in an historic reconciliation, repeatedly signalling that in return for US acceptance of the Islamic Republic, of its legitimacy and its inherent right to play a major role in the region's affairs, it would renounce or seriously modify the anti-American, anti-Zionist rhetoric and behaviour of its earlier, full-blooded 'revolutionary' years. Small wonder, then, that Israel strenuously opposed a US–Iranian 'dialogue' of any kind – because, as Ephraim Sneh, a Labour Party hawk, bluntly put it, 'the interests of the US did not coincide with ours',[59] and that the 'friends of Israel' in the US strove to sabotage one.

And they succeeded. 'It is scarcely possible', James Schlesinger, who had held cabinet-level positions in a number of US administrations, wrote at the time, 'to overstate the influence of Israel's supporters on our policies in the Middle East.' And it was with perfect objectivity that an exultant Steve Grossman, the chairman of AIPAC (the powerful American Israel Public Affairs Committee), described President Clinton's as 'the most pro-Israeli in the history of this country'.[60] Far from responding to the Iranian reformists' overtures, even though Clinton himself was deeply interested in them, it adopted just about everything that Israel, the Lobby, the neoconservatives and Congress prescribed for it. No matter that the so-called 'dual containment' policy, designed to produce 'dramatic changes in Iran's behaviour', was in origin an Israeli proposal pure and simple, no matter that many officials privately conceded that it was a thoroughly 'nutty idea', Martin

Indyk, the former pro-Israeli lobbyist, now Special Assistant for Near East and South Asian affairs on the National Security Council, solemnly promulgated it in an address to the Washington Institute for Near East Policy, the leading pro-Israeli think tank which he himself had helped found. Then there was the Iran–Libya Sanctions Act, passed by a House vote of 415–0, which Clinton signed into law, even though for 'much of the executive branch "hatred" was too mild a word' to describe what they thought about it.[61] For the Administration, Iran was an 'outlaw state', 'public enemy number one'; for congressmen such as Newt Gingrich it was nothing less than 'a permanent, long-term threat to civilized life on this planet, a terrorist state, committed to defeating the West anyway it [could]'.[62]

Such boundless hostility produced quite the opposite effect from what, ostensibly at least, was intended; it shackled the Iranian 'reformists', and freed their militant rivals to seek punishment and revenge on America in the arena – the Middle East 'peace process' – where they were best placed to do so. That in turn generated yet more hostility from the United States, whose secretary of state, Warren Christopher, was moved to declare that 'wherever you look, you find the evil hand of Iran . . . projecting terror and extremism across the Middle East and beyond', sponsoring 'subversive' organizations like Hizbullah, Hamas and Islamic Jihad – and, according to him, promoting the series of Palestinian suicide bombings which, more than anything else, had led to Operation Grapes of Wrath.

A PUBLIC THIRSTING FOR VENGEANCE OF ANY KIND

In point of historical fact, it had actually been neither Hamas, nor Iran behind it, which spawned the first great suicide exploit of the Israeli–Palestinian conflict. In 1994, by way of protest against the Oslo accord, Dr Baruch Goldstein, an émigré from Brooklyn, had machine-gunned to death twenty-nine Muslim worshippers in the Ibrahimi Mosque, Hebron, before being shot himself. Moreover, in contrast with the outrage which such atrocities aroused when Israelis were their victims, he had earned either the open praise or not-so-surreptitious sympathy of a good half of the Israeli public for a 'heroism so lofty' –

as one Lubavitcher rabbi put it – that it should inspire the Jews 'to possess the entire Land of Israel'.[63] His tomb in due course turned into a large and sumptuous memorial, and place of pilgrimage for Jews from all over Israel, Europe and the United States, who lit candles and sought the intercession of the 'holy saint and martyr'.[64]

Hamas had responded with a vengeance. Then, in early 1996, after the assassination of its 'master-bomber', it had gone on a second rampage, with four suicide operations killing sixty people in the space of a week. Things had got so bad that President Clinton, and leaders from twenty-seven, mainly Arab countries had come together at a so-called 'peace-makers' conference' in Sharm al-Sheikh. It amounted to a demonstration of solidarity with Israel in its 'war on terror'. Unable to strike too hard against the Palestinians for fear of totally disrupting the 'peace process', the prime minister, Shimon Peres, interpreted Sharm al-Sheikh as a green light to go after Hizbullah as a surrogate in their stead.[65] And no sooner had Hizbullah furnished a pretext of its own – with the killing of six soldiers in an escalation that ended up, once more, with the familiar 'rockets on Kiryat Shmona'[66] – than he duly did so, with across-the-board support from an Israeli public craving retribution of any kind.

A GRISLIER FIASCO THAN 'ACCOUNTABILITY'

It was another, grislier fiasco than Accountability, another attempt at 'linkage politics of the cruellest kind'[67] – the object, this time, being to get the southerners to pressure their own government to pressure Syria's, which would then pressure Hizbullah to submit to the entirely new 'rules of the game' which Israel intended to impose, effectively neutralizing it. In other words, after having pulverized Hizbullah itself, it was expecting its foremost Arab adversary – and Iran's ally – to finish the job, subduing what might be left of the organization on its behalf. This time, the villagers were given two hours' notice to flee for their lives; 'he who forewarns is excused', said the SLA, meaning that neither Israel nor itself could be held responsible for what befell them should they stay put. Within minutes the first of some 500,000 refugees[67] were jamming the coastal road to Beirut, in a state of shock and disbelief at this, their fourth such mass evacuation since 1978.[69] But this time it was not only Shiites the Israelis targeted. Just four months after the Lebanese government, at a cost of a billion dollars, had completed the post-war reconstruction of the country's electricity grid they were trying to knock it out again with the bombing of Beirut's three power stations. That amounted to punishment of the whole population.

Once again, militarily speaking, the onslaught achieved virtually nothing. 'We shall hit Hizbullah until it is broken,'[70] Israel's chief of military intelligence had proclaimed at the outset; but sixteen days, 25,132 artillery rounds and 2,350 air sorties later, they had killed only thirteen of its men and destroyed not one of its Katyushas. Hizbullah fired some 700 of them altogether – and, by the end of the campaign, they were impacting northern Israel at a faster rate than they had been at the beginning.[71]

MASSACRE AT QANA

Once again – and overwhelmingly – it was Lebanese civilians who bore the brunt; 165 died, compared with not one Israeli, military or civilian.[72] Two-thirds of them fell victim to the great atrocity, amply preceded by lesser ones, that forced Grapes of Wrath to a close. That was the carnage in the village of Qana – the self-same biblical Qana where, it is said, Christ performed the first of his miracles, the conversion of water into wine. On the campaign's eighth day, thirteen 155-mm, anti-personnel howitzer shells struck the local UNIFIL compound, manned by a battalion of Fijians, killing 102 people, half of them children, who were buried in only eighty-three coffins, because nineteen of them had been blown into so many pieces that they could not be put together again.[73] The gunners knew precisely what they were hitting, and they knew, too, that several hundred Lebanese civilians had taken refuge there. They knew because UNIFIL had told them so, and because of the drone which was directly overhead at the time. This was a fact which they had at first denied – claiming that the drone had been on 'another mission' altogether – but then admitted when confronted with the incontrovertible, photographic evidence that it had not.[74] That they not only knew what they were hitting, but that they hit it on purpose, was the verdict of Amnesty International,[75] of UN observers on the spot,[76] and – as near as dammit – of the special inquiry, conducted by Dutch general Frank Van Kappen, military adviser to UN Secretary-General Boutros Ghali, who concluded that 'while the possibility cannot be ruled out completely, it is unlikely that the shelling of the UN was the result of gross technical and/or procedural errors'.[77]

Once again, the reprisals thus deliberately inflicted on them failed to turn the people against the 'terrorists' in their midst. On the contrary, Qana, two-thirds Muslim, one-third Christian, became the tragic symbol of 'national unity' restored. Most Lebanese now supported the 'Islamic resistance' as never before. Christians as well as Muslims inundated the country's numerous 24-hour chat shows with enquiries about the location of Hizbullah's recruitment centres – or how many Katyushas it had fired at Israel that day, and where they could send money to buy more of them. A wealthy Christian woman who had donated $15,000 for the purpose went on air to say that she had only done so on condition that *her* Katyushas be expressly directed at Israeli civilians – to let them know that 'our people in the South' had as much right to a safe life as they. Once, two of Hizbullah's top press officials were visiting a media centre in Ashrafiyah, the heart of Christian Beirut, and, as they got out of their car, an old man, spotting them from across the street, began shouting:

> 'Hizbullah, Hizbullah, we are all Hizbullah. We are all behind you. God be with you, you have made us proud.'
> 'Part of me [confided one of them later] initially panicked at his public shouts of the word Hizbullah in the middle of this Christian quarter [but] another part was filled with emotion when I saw the other pedestrians and shoppers look at us with smiles of acknowledgement and acceptance. I knew then that we had come a long way as a group, and, more importantly, as a people; so I waved back to the old man and carried on with my journey.'[78]

There was also a very much stronger reaction from the Arab world which, predominantly orthodox Sunni though it was, took pride in the anti-Israeli exploits of the Iranian-backed, Shiite militia. But where, oh where, *were* these Arabs, lamented the Lebanese, especially their

Shiites? – just like the Palestinians before them. For once again here was little Lebanon, eternal battleground, eternal victim, fighting and suffering in their stead. In fact, the Arab 'street' was boiling; and Arab governments, especially those so-called 'moderate', pro-Western ones, were deeply embarrassed at their own impotence, as well as their identification, in the popular mind, with Israel's incorrigible US patron. If Israelis thought that Iran and its protégés were 'mad', nothing since Sabra and Shatila had done more than Qana to persuade the Arabs that Zionism was 'evil incarnate'.[79] How long could it be before the 'street', here, there – or even everywhere – finally erupted, either exacting action from Arab governments, or bringing about their downfall? That was the question asked – at least implicitly – by no less a personage than Sheikh Salim bin Hamid, imam of the Grand Mosque of Mecca and member of Saudi Arabia's Consultative Council, and on no less solemn an occasion than his address to the multitudes assembled for the *Haj*, or annual pilgrimage. 'How long the silence of the people, how long the subjugation of the oppressed?' The words could almost have come from Khomeini himself, rather than this arch-conservative primate of the Sunni Arab establishment.[80]

Once again, America lent Israel its full and automatic support. Hizbullah, it asserted, had started it, and Israel had been 'compelled to respond'. And when that response got going, it sought to ensure it all the 'running time' it needed to finish what it had begun.[81] It almost went without saying that even Qana was entirely Hizbullah's doing too. Israel claimed that the organization had been using civilians as a cover for military activities, or, worse still, 'hiding in the middle of the population, hoping that we will hit them',[82] and the US – 'having no reason to believe that Israel [was] not telling the truth' – effectively endorsed the claim. It was 'a despicable, an evil thing' that Hizbullah had done, opined Nicholas Burns, State Department spokesman. Madeleine Albright, US ambassador to the UN, said that the 'measures' that Israel had taken at Qana were a 'direct consequence' of Hizbullah's actions. As for President Clinton, he was categoric: 'make no mistake about it', he told a wildly applauding audience at the annual conference of AIPAC, flagship of the Lobby, the 'deliberate tactic of Hizbullah' was indeed responsible for Israel's 'tragic misfiring, in the legitimate

exercise of its right to self-defence'.[83] Both countries gave short shrift
to the UN report. 'One can have no confidence in the UN', said Peres;
anyway, he added, 'what the *goyim* say doesn't matter, it only matters
what the Jews do.'[84] Both exerted extreme pressure on the Secretary-
General – an Egyptian – not to publish the report, and when he did the
State Department accused him of manipulating its conclusions to win
Arab support in his bid for re-election for a second term.[85] No
American newspaper saw fit to mention the interview which the radical
Jerusalem weekly *Kol Ha'ir* conducted with the gunners who had fired
the fatal shells:

> The commander ... told us that we were firing well and we should
> keep it up, and that Arabs, you know ... there are millions of them
> ... Even 'S' said they were just a bunch of *Arabushim* [derogatory
> Hebrew word for Arabs]. How many Arabs are there, and how
> many Jews? A few *Arabushim* die – there's no harm in that.[86]

Once again, the US had to come to Israel's rescue. It is true that
when, in the build-up to Grapes of Wrath, it had told Israel to 'go
ahead in Lebanon', it had also advised it that 'if things go wrong don't
come running to us'.[87] But that caveat went out of the window as soon
as things actually, and so very foreseeably, did. This was a presidential
election year, and the Clinton camp was worried about the
punishment which the 'friends of Israel' could have inflicted on it at
the polls. So it was not just the protégé that 'came running' to the
patron, the patron itself went running on its protégé's behalf. The
place to which it ran was the same as before – Damascus – but the
humiliation was greater.

CONVERSION ON THE ROAD TO DAMASCUS

Only after Qana and the outrage it caused did the US have to terminate
its diplomatic shilly-shallying on Israel's behalf. Clinton called for a
ceasefire; and his Secretary of State, Warren Christopher, at last headed
for the region to arrange it. Yet even then it was to be a ceasefire
entirely on America and Israel's terms – Hizbullah should disarm, and
if, after that, it launched no attacks over a six- to nine-month period,

Israel would engage in 'discussions' about a full-scale withdrawal. Syria, Lebanon and, of course, Hizbullah dismissed it out of hand. At this point Christopher apparently concluded that he had only one realistic course left, which was to seek the assistance of President Asad in Damascus. For he whom the whole, American-approved Israeli mis-adventure had been designed to bring low had actually been elevated, once more, into the only person who could now help bring it as face-savingly as possible to an end. After six days of shuttling around the region, during which he had to cool his heels – twice for hours and once for a whole night – as President Asad bestowed his pleasure on the emissaries of a host of lesser powers, Christopher finally capitulated. The new 'understandings' in which he acquiesced were barely American-made at all. The French foreign minister, Hervé de Charette, quite reasonably claimed that they were '80 per cent French'; for France, more than any other European power, had stepped in to administer an indispensable corrective to what, in its partisanship, would otherwise have been the utterly profitless diplomacy of the Americans.

With their more rigorous prohibition of Israeli attacks on 'civilians and civilian targets' in Lebanon, the 'understandings' added up to quite the opposite of what America and Israel had originally intended: written but unsigned, where the old ones had been merely oral, they further consolidated the 'rules of the game' in Hizbullah's favour, and established an international Monitoring Group to police them. In 1995 the Clinton Administration had, by Executive Order, designated Hizbullah an enemy of the peace process; but now, here it was, effectively recognizing its right to pursue its war against the Israeli party to that process. For Nasrallah, it was a 'wonderful victory ... for Lebanon, Syria, the Arabs, and Muslims ... a lesson and example to all those at the receiving end of Israel and America's belligerence'.[88] His elation was justified. But the warrior-priest and his devoted followers were not planning to rest on their laurels, or retreat from their determination to drive the Israelis out of Lebanon unconditionally and by force of arms alone – a feat, first of its kind in the history of the Arab–Israeli conflict, which, four years later, they duly accomplished.

JUMPING CLAYMORES, ROCK BOMBS AND OTHER EXPLOSIVE DEVICES

Just as they had after Accountability, Hizbullah wasted no time in killing more Israeli soldiers – nine, in fact – within the refined and re-imposed 'rules' that had provoked the whole operation in the first place.[89] And from then on it went from strength to strength, soon tripling the number of its operations, from an average of about 200 a year before 1996 to 1,000 a year thereafter, peaking at 1,500 in 1999–2000.[90] Perhaps more telling still was the dramatic decline of Hizbullah's casualties in relation to those of its enemy. According to its own calculations, it lost 1,248 men in action against Israel and the SLA between the 1982 invasion and 1999.[91] The Israelis put their own losses, for the period between their 1985 pull-back and mid-1999, at 332 (though that figure included 70 in a single helicopter crash).[92] However, the SLA's losses, at an estimated 1,050 for 1982–2000, were much higher than the Israelis'. So when these were taken into account the total for both sides was not that far apart. Had it gone on, the Israel/SLA toll would certainly have overtaken Hizbullah's. For, by 1997, in place of the five- or even ten-to-one casualty rate of earlier years, it had almost achieved parity; it lost 60 men in combat, compared with 39 Israelis – the highest figure ever – and 25 SLA.[93] The following year, it killed more of its enemies – 24 Israelis, 33 SLA – than the 38 of its own it lost.[94]

Hizbullah also continued to grow in organizational and technical prowess, outsmarting its enemies' defensive innovations with ingenious, offensive ones of its own. Thus, though its simplest weapon, the road-side 'improvised explosive device', remained the most consistently effective, it only did so because of its ability to develop new ways of using it, such as the Claymore disguised as a rock. The Claymore was a jumping mine of American origin. In the 'improved' Hizbullah version, it catapulted an exploding capsule of ball-bearings lethal within a range of fifty metres. The 'rock' was a fibreglass imitation costing fifteen dollars in any Beirut garden centre. Hizbullah guerillas would also put explosives amid the branches of trees instead of on the ground where their targets normally looked for them; or place an ancient T-55 tank in a cave, and fire it from time to time without risk of detection because it did not show up on Israeli heat sensors; or use shepherds and their flocks in sophisticated diversionary manoeuvres.[95] But after Grapes of Wrath Iran supplied them with a whole new category of advanced weaponry, wire-guided anti-tank missiles, first the Russian-made Saggers and then the even better American TOWs; the latter came from stocks which Israel itself had supplied to Iran during the Iran-Contra affair. Faced with this new threat, the Israelis withdrew their inadequately armoured Centurions and M60s – only to learn, with the death of seven soldiers in quick succession in November 1998, that even their very own, ultra-modern Merkava, pride of their military industries, was by no means invulnerable either.[96]

'THIS MOLOCH, THIS CURSED PLACE'

There was only one way the 'slow bleeding' that Nasrallah had promised could be staunched, and that was to get out, once and for all, from 'Israel's Vietnam' – as the columnists had long been calling it – from 'this cursed place', this 'Moloch' devouring its young manhood. That was becoming clearer and clearer to everyone; so clear, in fact, that the 'Four Mothers' campaign, founded in 1997 with the object of bringing it about, rapidly developed into the most influential protest movement in Israel's history. The country's political and military leaders started to think about the hitherto unthinkable, not just about a withdrawal, but about a unilateral one incorporating none of the conditions – the disarming of Hizbullah, the deployment of the Lebanese army along the frontier, the integration into its ranks of SLA personnel – on which they had always insisted. Victorious in the parliamentary elections of May 1999, the new Labour leader, Ehud Barak, now reiterated the pledge he had earlier made that the army would be out of Lebanon within a year. He still wanted withdrawal by agreement. For that he needed another, and complementary, agreement – with Lebanon's overlord, Syria – for an Israeli withdrawal from the Golan Heights. But the resounding failure, in March 2000, of a make-or-break summit in Geneva between Asad and Clinton put paid to any prospect of that. The exit now had to be unilateral – or not at all.

As the self-imposed deadline drew closer, Israel grew more bellicose, more contemptuous of the 'rules of the game'. Indeed, it repudiated them altogether. Partly it was a quest for vengeance that was openly, officially proclaimed, most famously – or infamously – by Foreign Minister David Levy, who told the Knesset that the 'killing of Jews' might be 'the declared goal' of that 'insane organization' Hizbullah, but the Lebanese should know that if Kiryat Shmona burned, Lebanon would too. 'One thing will bring the other. Blood for blood, soul for soul, child for child.'[97]

Partly, it was the sabre-rattling which, in the thinking of its leaders, Israel's unfamiliar plight required. For here it was, about to do what it had never done before – relinquish Arab territory it had conquered and occupied for nothing in return. It was the doctrine of interventionism, of military force for political ends, finally brought to nought in the place where twenty years before, with Begin, Sharon and Peace in Galilee, it had been supposed to achieve its apotheosis. 'I don't', said Barak, 'advise anyone to test us when we draw back and are sitting on the border.'[98] But how could he be sure that the Lebanese, in their exhilaration, would heed that advice? Clearly, *before* it left, Israel had to give them a very practical demonstration of what it would do to them if, *after* it had, 'peace in Galilee' still did not prevail, or 'rockets on Kiryat Shmona' cease.

Such were the motives behind the assault on civilian, 'infrastructural' targets, outlawed by the 1996 'understandings', which Israel now resumed. Naturally, there was an official – and more respectable – pretext too, namely that, in violation of the 'rules', Hizbullah's attacks on Israel's soldiers in the Strip had originated in 'populated' areas. But even though Israel's leading military correspondent, Zeev Schiff, not to mention UNIFIL, pronounced this completely unfounded, the US lent it credence. All that the Israelis were doing, said Madeleine Albright, now Secretary of State, was sending 'a very strong signal about the fact that they [didn't] want this escalation' that Hizbullah was so 'egregiously' forcing on them.[99] In the first of three such 'signals' – another blitz on a key Beirut power station and sundry other targets – Israeli planes killed twice as many Lebanese civilians, half of them fire-fighters, as Hizbullah had killed Israeli soldiers to provoke it; they also did tens of millions of dollars' worth of damage, and plunged the capital back into the semi-darkness of the civil war. But this, and the two more that followed, did nothing to deter a Hizbullah now more than ever determined that, if Israel was going to withdraw, then it should do so 'in catastrophic conditions, under fire ... unconditionally, defeated and humiliated'.[100] Towards the end, Hizbullah stopped retaliating against civilians altogether, leaving such repugnant practices to the Israelis alone. Instead of 'more Katyushas on Kiryat Shmona', it killed more soldiers in the Strip, including an Israeli general and the second-in-command of the SLA. It was this ability of the 'terrorists' to strike so painfully within the 'rules' – to be the 'good guy' where they were manifestly the bad one – which seemed to infuriate Israeli leaders above all.[101] It was this that prompted Deputy Defence Minister Moshe Sneh to exclaim: 'they have killed Israeli soldiers, and therefore *they* must be killed ... the rules have changed'.[102] This that drove Foreign Minister Levy to that intemperate and sanguinary outburst that even Mrs Albright saw fit to reprove.

AN IGNOMINIOUS SCUTTLE

The withdrawal, when it came, was an ignominious scuttle, sudden, furtive and unannounced, and, in almost every way, a triumph for Hizbullah. It was under cover of night, in the early hours of 23 May 2000, that the last Israeli forces in the Strip stole out of their bunkers, and made their dash to the frontier. In their selfish haste and secrecy, they forsook their Lebanese allies. They took only a few of the SLA's top commanders, its secret policemen and interrogators with them. The rank and file they simply left to their own devices. Some 1,250 of these, and their families, managed to flee across the frontier with them; but others had no choice but to risk surrender to Hizbullah. Meanwhile, no sooner were the occupiers and their collaborators on their way out than tens of thousands of long-exiled Southerners were streaming in, in cars, on donkeys or on foot. All along the route, they were greeted by jubilant throngs, pelted with rose water, flowers and ferns. A few flew communist, or Amal, flags, but for the overwhelming majority the only possible one was the clenched fist and Kalashnikov of Hizbullah.

And of course Hizbullah came with them. Within forty-eight hours the entire Strip was in their hands. Its take-over had been about as smooth as could be; only minor incidents had marred it. And that – within the larger triumph – had been a remarkable achievement in itself. The South, after all, was the soil out of which, more than thirty years before, the civil war had originally grown; now it was the soil in which, ten years after Taif and its 'official' ending, it was finally laid to rest – and without bloodshed of any kind. Throughout that war, major geostrategic turning points such as this had usually been stained by inter-communal killings and atrocities. Fears had been expressed that this would happen once more, that Hizbullah and its followers would 'slaughter Israeli agents' – chiefly Maronite ones, of course – 'in their beds'.[103] But it did not happen. All the SLA personnel Hizbullah captured it handed over, unharmed, to the state for the trial – and rather lenient punishment – that ensued. It then imposed on the newly liberated territory an order and a security which it had barely known since Arafat's *fedayeen* had begun to filter down there in the late 1960s. It was so remarkable that those whom much of the world still looked upon as 'terrorists', or wild-eyed religious fanatics, now earned a grudging respect in unfamiliar quarters, including European officialdom[104] – and even an unprecedented accolade from the UN Secretary-General. After a tête-à-tête with Nasrallah, Kofi Annan praised Hizbullah's restraint and its promise of cooperation with the international body whose peacekeepers it had once branded – and killed – as tools of the Great Satan and 'global arrogance'.

AN ALMOST IMPOSSIBLE CHOICE

This was a triumph indeed – but a fundamental, indeed an existential, dilemma too. For Hizbullah's very success brought it face to face with what had so long lain in wait for it – the need to make a decisive choice between the two identities which, over time, it had taken on, between its 'Lebanonization' and its wider, trans-national allegiances, between ordinary political party with a national agenda and militia with a universal, jihadist one. The choice pressed. For here, after an eighteen-year struggle, its fighters now were, entrenched along the entire,

140-kilometre frontier, from the mist-shrouded foothills of Mount Hermon to the lush Mediterranean littoral, eyeball to eyeball with Israeli soldiers on the other side of it. They had northern settlements within rifle range, and a direct line of fire down to Kiryat Shmona on which they, like the Palestinians before them, had for so long lobbed their Katyushas, but rarely actually seen. For them, it was a dream come true. For Israel, it was closer to a nightmare, precisely the kind of outcome to its Lebanese misadventure which it had been vainly striving to forestall – the presence, on its most exposed and difficult border, of what, in its way, had proved to be the most implacable and formidable adversary it had ever known. It was a strategic setback, a major dent in the military superiority and deterrent power of a state which so heavily depended on them for its well-being, security, and ultimately its survival.

Hizbullah had long foreseen, maybe even dreaded, this moment. Whenever it had been asked whether, after liberation, its armed struggle against Israel would or would not continue, its leaders had unfailingly taken refuge in the equivocal and the oracular. 'The enemy is deeply confused about that,' said its military commander in the South, Sheikh Nabil Kaouk, 'and long may it remain so.'[105] And so long as it was fighting on Lebanese soil alone, the ambiguity was not too difficult to sustain, the national and the jihadist being inextricably intertwined. But, after liberation, everything would become inescapably clear-cut: the very first shot that Hizbullah fired across the frontier would be the very first shot in *jihad*, and *jihad* alone, in the 'liberation of Jerusalem' and that 'obliteration' of the Jewish state towards which its expulsion from Lebanon had only been an indispensable first step.

The choice, indeed, was a well-nigh impossible one. Not to continue the struggle was to negate Hizbullah's *raison d'être*, to throw away, at the very moment of triumph, the military machine that had achieved it. To continue it, in the conditions that now prevailed, was unrealistic to the point of folly. It was to give Israel *no* choice – no choice but to make good the threats in which it had wrapped its humiliation and defeat, to 'flatten' Lebanon and 'hit it harder than it had ever been hit before'.[106] That was something which, after all that they had already endured, very few Shiites, let alone Lebanese at large, would have voluntarily accepted; and they would not have looked kindly on the leader, however revered, who brought it on them. Nasrallah might have been a religious visionary; he might really have believed – as he put it in his victory address to the liberated southern town of Bint Jbeil – that Hizbullah's triumph was a 'gift from God Almighty', or even that 'He [it was] who threw the stone and hit the target, destroyed enemy bunkers and fortified positions, and killed the mighty ...'[107] But the warrior-priest was a realist, a strategist and a politician too. He was not prepared to renounce *jihad*. But he *was* prepared to modify it. He had, after all, done that once before. In the early nineties, with the end of the civil war, he had taken Hizbullah into 'pragmatic-gradualist' mode with respect to one of *jihad*'s two basic goals – the building of an 'Islamic order' – the better to pursue the second – 'Islamic resistance'. Now the time had come to do the same with respect to 'Islamic resistance' itself.

BLACKSMITH WITH A HAMMER BUT NO ANVIL

The solution which he came up with was, in effect, *not* to make a choice. And he did that by the simple, if patently contrived, device of contending that, territorially and in other ways – notably the nineteen Lebanese prisoners[108] still in Israeli gaols – the strictly Lebanese, or national, struggle was not yet complete. The strategem was all the more felicitous in that it furnished Hizbullah's regional backer, Syria, with the *deus ex machina* which, albeit for very different reasons, it badly needed too. For when it had finally dawned on President Asad and his foreign-policy chiefs that Barak's pledge to withdraw was not just a threat but a very serious intent, they had all but panicked.[109] Suddenly, they were to be robbed of the most powerful bargaining counter they possessed, their proxy war as diplomacy by other means; suddenly, they were to be a blacksmith with a hammer – Hizbullah – but no anvil – Israeli soldiers in the South – on which to strike it. 'If they stay in a piece of land that we consider to be Lebanese', said Nasrallah, 'we will persist in our resistance until it is freed.'[110] And, hardly had he said it than, lo and behold, there was such a piece. There were the 'Sheba'a Farms' – all twenty-five square kilometres of them – of which, till then, very few Lebanese had ever even heard. Adjacent to the Golan Heights, Israel had conquered them in the 1967 war. The nine plots of which they were composed had been Lebanese-owned, but, in terms of national sovereignty, they were Syrian. All the maps – the UN's, Syria's, even Lebanon's too – corroborated it. Or they did, at least, until, with Israeli withdrawal only weeks away, Nabih Berri, speaker of parliament and Syria's 'man' within the political establishment, came along and staked a formal claim to them on Lebanon's behalf, a claim which Syria itself graciously proceeded to acknowledge.[111]

As for the other, involuntary party to this subterfuge, the hapless Lebanese government, it duly forsook the position which Hariri had so long and repeatedly proclaimed, namely, that once Israel withdrew, 'resistance' would lose its *raison d'être*, Hizbullah would disband, and – in accordance with Security Council Resolution 425 of 1978 – the state would re-establish its long-lost authority in the South. It now asserted that it would not serve as Israel's 'guardian' by sending the army south – not so long as a particle of Lebanese soil remained in Israel's hands. Nor would there be any Lebanese–Israeli peace agreement before the Palestinian refugees – those ever-present, potential disrupters of the country's internal sectarian balance – had exercised their 'right of return', and Israel had withdrawn from the Golan as well. Meanwhile – it furthermore at least implicitly acknowledged – Hizbullah's non-state irregulars would make better defenders of the state and nation than the regular army itself.[112] Thus to Hizbullah went the mandate to fill the unexpected vacuum in the South. It duly did so, with, on the one hand, the kind of services that states normally provide[113] – public works and reconstruction, health care and agricultural assistance pro-grammes – and, on the other, with a full-scale military capability, with tunnels and bunkers, the stockpiling of weapons, observation posts and the monitoring of enemy activities, training and the drawing up of battle-plans. Before long it had assembled, ready for instant use, a massive arsenal of Katyushas and other missiles. According to the Israelis, there were a good 10,000 of them. They included updated and longer-range models which, from these new forward positions, need no longer be trained on Kiryat Shmona as their only decent urban target; now they could reach Safad, Tiberias, Nahariya or even Haifa too.

WEAKER THAN A SPIDER'S WEB

With this legitimacy, this popularity, freedom of action and weaponry, Hizbullah resumed its 'resistance'. It was strictly national, strictly Lebanese in official purpose, presented as a tending of the country's still 'bleeding wounds' – the continued occupation of a small piece of the country's territory, the detention of its citizens and the ongoing violations of its sovereignty. What Hizbullah sometimes called its 'reminder operations' were relatively few and far between, and very carefully calculated in scale, timing and likely political impact. In the six years that followed the withdrawal, only nine Israeli soldiers died in premeditated attacks on Sheba'a, and only eight more in clashes that spread, for one reason or another, to the rest of the frontier.[114] Nonetheless, in spite of the great reduction in its activities, Hizbullah was actually, in a way, achieving quite as much, militarily and strategically, as it had been doing before. It did not want to push the Israelis too far, thereby igniting that massive retaliation against civilians that would in turn redound against itself. On the other hand, the Israelis themselves were well aware that if they did respond too forcefully to Hizbullah's occasional, but deadly, assaults, they risked Katyusha barrages of an intensity they had never before experienced. Thus it came about that an irregular, part-time force of a few hundred highly trained, highly motivated guerillas succeeded in establishing a 'balance of terror' with the Middle East's military superpower, keeping it in a permanent state of uncertainty, apprehension and frustration. This semi-official, 'quasi-Lebanonization' of the resistance corresponded with a deepening of Hizbullah's role in domestic politics. It performed handsomely in the first parliamentary elections to follow the withdrawal, and even better in subsequent municipal ones.

Yet, however 'Lebanonized' the resistance became, it remained inescapably jihadist on Palestine's behalf, too. There was an inevitable confusion between the two. But though the rhetoric on the subject may have been deliberately vague and allusive, its import was unmistakable.[115] It was not that Hizbullah presumed to take on the Palestinians' struggle in their place. Rather, as Nasrallah put it in his victory speech:

We offer this lofty, Lebanese example to our people in Palestine. You don't need tanks, strategic balance, rockets or cannons to liberate your land; all you need are the martyrs who shook and scared this angry Zionist entity. You can regain your land, you oppressed, helpless and besieged people of Palestine; you can force the invading Zionists to return whence they came; let the Falasha go back to Ethiopia and the Russian Jews to Russia. The choice is yours and the example is clear before your eyes. I tell you: the Israel that owns nuclear weapons and has the strongest air force in the region is weaker than a spider's web.[116]

In the occupied territories, Hizbullah's flags flew in refugee camps;[117] in Israel itself, the Arab minority staged rallies in celebration of its 'victory over Israel'.[118] And it was not just the failure of the Camp David summit conference between Clinton, Barak and Arafat, or the calculated incitements of General Sharon,[119] which provoked the second, more violent *Intifada* that erupted in September 2000, it was a combination of Palestinian despair and the climate of defiance which, by its example, Hizbullah had helped to inspire.[120]

Hizbullah immediately sought to link itself with this renewed Palestinian struggle. Supporting it was a 'religious and Islamic duty'.[121] Naturally, its first operation in the 'Sheba'a Farms' – the abduction of three Israeli soldiers as bargaining counters for the release of Israeli-held prisoners – had its official, its strictly Lebanese purpose, but more important, really, was its unofficial, jihadist, one: which was to coincide with, and add encouragement to, the *Intifada*.[122] When, in 2002, Sharon, now prime minister, launched Operation Shield, his re-invasion of the West Bank, Hizbullah unleashed a two-week barrage of very professional mortar, anti-tank and rocket fire on Israeli positions in the 'Sheba'a Farms.' In prisoner exchanges it demanded freedom for Palestinians as well as Lebanese, and secured the release of 400 of them in one such deal in 2004.[123]

It also furnished the *Intifada*, where possible, with direct if clandestine assistance: funding, training, technical expertise and the smuggling of weapons into the occupied territories. It apparently played an important role in the '*Karine-A* affair'. In January 2002 the Israelis intercepted a ship of that name which, they said, was bound for Gaza with fifty tons of brand-new, mostly Iranian-manufactured weapons – Katyushas, mortars, rifles, machine guns, anti-tank mines and other explosives – on board. What really disturbed them, and caused them to raise an international hue and cry, was the fact that, according to them, the weapons were not just destined for like-minded Islamist organizations, Hamas or Islamic Jihad, but for the Arafat-led resistance as a whole.[124]

Then there was the publicity, the endless, highly empathetic publicity, on Palestine's behalf. In addition to its raw coverage of the *Intifada*, using Palestinian correspondents and cameramen on the spot,[125] Hizbullah's al-Manar television station offered a kind of 'how to' campaign designed to instruct as well as inspire.[126] South Lebanon, Palestine – they were one and the same. Thus, during Operation Shield, shots of Palestinian youths resisting Israeli advances into Ramallah were interspersed with those of Hizbullah fighters simultaneously storming an Israeli position in the Sheba'a Farms from which the defenders had been driven out, and planting their flag on top of it. Around the clock the names of the latest Palestinian 'martyrs' flashed across the bottom of the screen. At a conference in Beirut, Hizbullah brought together Sunni and Shiite *ulema*, with Ali Akbar Mohtashemi, the firebrand Iranian cleric who had presided over Hizbullah's creation, hobnobbing with the likes of Sheikh Yusif al-Qardawi, the stately, erudite Egyptian television preacher, who declared that 'Arabs and non-Arabs, Sunnis and Shiites, are forbidden to give up an inch of Jerusalem, and we are ready to fight until the last breath in us.'[127] Hizbullah was not only making itself a bridge between Shiism and Sunnism, Iran and the Arabs, but, as the only external force engaged in active combat on the Palestinians' behalf, projecting itself as the spearhead of the whole Arab/Muslim struggle against the historic Zionist foe.[128]

GOOD – BUT NOT GOOD ENOUGH

And there was little doubt about it: Hizbullah really was a more inspiring example of its kind than any that Arabs and Muslims had known in recent times. Not since Nasser – and Suez – had an Arab leader acquired the lofty stature of Nasrallah, all the more deserved because, in the strictly military as opposed to the political field, his achievement was pure gold to Nasser's dross. Naturally, from Hizbullah's point of view, it was very good to have set such an example, to have demonstrated that Israel could be defeated in a battle, and, ultimately, it believed, in an all-out war. In other words, the liberation of Palestine – the only possible, final goal of *jihad* – really was attainable; for many Arabs, secular as well as Islamist, Hizbullah had proved it.[129]

For Nasrallah it was good – but it was not good enough. Arabs and Muslims had to do more than merely admire Hizbullah, they had to emulate it. Its leadership knew very well that neither it – nor it, Hamas and Islamic Jihad combined – could get back Palestine on their own. It knew that for the foreseeable future the whole existing balance of power was weighted overwhelmingly against it, and that the only way to shift it in its favour was to spread the circle of resistance all around the enemy's frontiers. Other 'front-line' peoples, Egyptians, Jordanians, Syrians, had to make their contribution too, either by throwing up non-state actors, other Hizbullahs, of their own, forcing their governments to join the fray, or replacing them with new ones if they would not. In the end, everything hinged on this. It was, in effect, the Islamist version of that 'supporting Arab front' which, forty years before, Yasser Arafat and his Fatah comrades had so fondly, but fancifully, expected to spring spontaneously into being once they launched their 'popular liberation war'.[130] Meanwhile, the most that Hizbullah could realistically do was to go on waging *jihad* in the 'gradualist-pragmatic', essentially symbolic, mode it already was. For who could tell how long it might be before the *Umma* actually followed this example, summoned up the will and means to join it in the general, all-out 'militant and armed *jihad*' which alone could bring final victory?[131] As things stood, that was unthinkable. For the regimes would strain every nerve to stop it. They were more afraid of Hizbullah, and its potentially explosive impact on their 'street', than they were of Israel itself. That was certainly true of the so-called 'moderate', pro-Western regimes such as Jordan's, Egypt's or Saudi Arabia's. But it was little less so, probably, of 'radical', Hizbullah-supporting Syria; since its patriotic pretensions were much greater than theirs, so, in the eyes of its people, was the gap between pretensions and actual performance.

Not surprisingly, the only regime which looked with unmixed satisfaction on Hizbullah's triumph was the one – non-Arab Iran's – which had nurtured Hizbullah in the first place. For Ayatollah Khamenei, to whom Nasrallah once more proclaimed his absolute allegiance, Hizbullah had now positioned itself 'in the front line of the Islamic world in its fight with the Zionist enemy'; what had happened in Lebanon could happen in 'occupied Palestine'; 'sections' of it and 'ultimately the whole of it could be returned to the Palestinian people'.[132] Eight years before, Khamenei had authorized Hizbullah to 'Lebanonize' itself and join the domestic 'political' process without, however, renouncing the 'resistance' which at the time was still amply justifiable in national, Lebanese terms. Now, with those justifications all but gone, it was he who decreed that 'resistance' should continue all the same. And, in response, Nasrallah pledged that, 'as you are the *Wali* of the Muslims', it would do so 'until the liberation of all the occupied [Palestinian] land'.[133]

9/11 AND THE GREAT UNRAVELLING

Obviously, given the circumstances in which it was made, that pledge was more rhetorical flourish, lip-service to an ultimate ideal, than statement of immediate, practical intent. For otherwise it would have meant war. And, as we have seen, Nasrallah did not *want* war,[134] not one, at least, which his own people, never mind the rest of the world, would have blamed him for starting. All he wanted, for the foreseeable future, was *jihad* within those new, expressly ambivalent 'rules' of his own creation, in the hope – and not unreasonable expectation – that Israel, not wanting war either, would confine itself to them too. Yet he was running the ever-present risk of getting one. His own actions – however judicious, however finely calibrated they might be – were reason enough for that. But the actions of his enemies were, or would soon become, much greater reason still: if Hizbullah did not bring war to them, they assuredly would to it. For one thing, the ignominious withdrawal itself, and the second *Intifada* which it had helped inspire, bred in Israel the desire for an eventual settling of scores; fortress state that it was, this was also a question of strategic necessity. Then – for another, infinitely greater thing – came 9/11. With that, the epic, masterly, defining atrocity of our times, Osama bin Laden and his al-Qaeda global terror network excited in Bush's America emotions and ambitions which dovetailed almost perfectly with those of Israel. But, of course, the US being the world's only superpower, they far surpassed them in their consequences. Indeed, they brought to full fruition a determination, long in gestation, to tackle the whole Arab/Muslim milieu from which the diabolic deed had sprung: to invade, subdue, shape, and utterly transform it. As a result, the Middle East and beyond entered an era of turbulence and upheaval the like of which it had not witnessed since the fall of the Ottoman Empire, Sykes–Picot, Balfour, the Versailles peace conference and the whole new order which it had brought into being. If this order could be said to have taken on any formal, constitutional expression, it was what the Arabs had in due course come to call *al-Nitham al-Arabi*, or 'the Arab system', with the 22-member League of Arab States, originally a British-encouraged creation, as its central institution. Already in advanced decline, the 'system' now began, quite manifestly, to fall apart, in a process which the noted Palestinian columnist, Rami Khouri, dubbed the 'Great Arab Unravelling'.[135] Eventually, no doubt, it would throw up a new system in its turn. What shape that might take was, at this early stage, very difficult to foresee. For in its torment the Middle East had not only established itself as the most pivotal, and globally contentious, region on earth, it was also, in and of itself, about the most complex too; and that meant that, in addition to the foreign actors, its vast profusion of domestic ones – dynastic and tribal, ethnic and sectarian, religious, secular and ideological – were going to involve themselves in the 'Great Unravelling'.

It made for an almost unfathomable maelstrom. Nonetheless, for the foreseeable future, it could be said that, at its simplest, this would break down into two broad, opposing camps. In one stood the region's Islamists, or Islamo-nationalists. These were composed, essentially, of Iran and Syria, non-state forces such as Hizbullah, Hamas and Islamic

Jihad, and, very loosely speaking, a range of movements and parties such as the multi-national branches of the Muslim Brotherhood. This all added up, of course, to a very motley crew; its chief anomaly was the stoutly secular Syrian Baath, which, ideologically, did not really belong to it at all, but which, in terms of actual policies and alliances, was central to it. By contrast, although al-Qaeda seemed supremely qualified ideologically, in practice, being almost a law unto itself, it had no role in it at all, or, at most, a very occasional and furtive one. The rival camp was even less coherent, an agglomeration of forces so diverse, and often so frankly hostile to one another, that it was really only in opposition to the Islamist camp that they qualified as any kind of coalition at all. It was composed, essentially, of the United States, Israel, 'moderate' Arab states such as Egypt, Jordan and (the highly Islamic) Saudi Arabia, and, very loosely speaking, the non-state secular, liberal, or democratic forces of the region. Its greatest single contradiction lay in the fact that, for the most part, its Arabs and Muslims – though people much more than regimes – disliked or feared its Americans and its Israelis quite as much as the Islamists or Islamonationalists did themselves. And what made this contradiction all the more peculiar was that, out of the Great Unravelling, 'neo-imperial' America was striving to shape a new order which, if it ever came to pass, would be no less unpalatable to the inhabitants of the region than the one which once-colonial Europe built before it; indeed, in one central respect – the pride of place it assigned to their historic Zionist foe – it would be even more so.

As for Lebanon, its role and destiny in the Great Unravelling were likewise hard to foresee. Certainly, however, it already was, and would remain, in the thick of it – all the more certainly, indeed, in that it was no longer quite the 'small state', object rather than agent, in the sense that Mikhail Bakunin meant. Its aggrandizement was Hizbullah's doing, thanks to the unique standing which it had acquired, not only in Lebanon itself, but in the region at large. From Kurdistan to Palestine, Iraq to Lebanon, an obvious feature of the Great Unravelling was the emergence of non-state actors assuming functions, most crucially military and coercive ones, that are normally the exclusive preserve of states. Typically, these actors were nationalist, or ethnic, in identity –

as in the case of the quasi-secessionist Kurds of Iraq – sectarian – as in the case of its Sunni or Shiite Arabs – or both sectarian and Islamist at once. Uniquely, thanks to its exemplary struggle against Israel, Hizbullah commanded authority and prestige on all three grounds, the pan-Arab nationalist as well as – and in spite of – the sectarian and Islamist. Another thing was certain too: in the Great Unravelling, those other peoples' wars and conflicts of which Lebanon seemed forever doomed to be a battleground would at least equal, or outdo, any of their predecessors in their scope, means, and import for the region and the world.

CHAPTER ELEVEN

Redrawing the Map of the Middle East

2001–2006

CLEAN BREAK

In the summer of 1996, thanks largely to the failure of Operation Grapes of Wrath over which he had presided, Shimon Peres and his Labour Party were defeated in general elections by Binyamin Netanyahu and his right-wing Likud. Before the new prime minister took office, a group of American neoconservatives, some of them, such as Richard Perle, former and future government officials, took it upon themselves to advise him what to do when he did. In a paper entitled *Clean Break: A New Strategy for Securing the Realm*, they outlined the means by which Israel – 'proud, wealthy, solid and strong' – should make itself the cornerstone of 'a truly new and peaceful Middle East', one in which it would no longer simply 'contain' its foes, but 'transcend' them. First it should replace 'land for peace', the core principle of the American-supported Oslo peace process, with 'peace through strength', and secure the Arabs' 'unconditional acceptance' of its rights, especially its 'territorial' (that is expansionist) ones. Then, in 'partnership' with the US, it should embark on a grandiose scheme of geopolitical engineering for the whole region. It would start by 'removing Saddam Hussein from power', and supporting King Hussein of Jordan in his 'redefining' of Iraq through the restoration of a fellow Hashemite dynasty there. The 'natural axis' – composed of Israel, Turkey, Jordan and 'central' Iraq – would join forces in 'weakening, containing or even rolling back Syria', seeking to 'detach it from the Saudi Peninsula', and 'threaten[ing] its territorial integrity' as a prelude to a 'redrawing of the map of the Middle East'. Since Lebanon's Syrian-controlled Beqa'a Valley had 'become for terror what the Silicon Valley has become for computers', Israel should 'seize the strategic initiative along its northern borders by engaging Hizbullah, Syria, and Iran, as the principal agents of aggression in Lebanon'. It should hit Syrian military targets there, or 'select' ones in Syria itself. Syria might also come under assault from 'Israeli proxy forces' operating out of Lebanon.[1]

Clean Break was a seminal document, an early authoritative expression of ideas and prescriptions – extreme, violent, simplistic and utterly partisan – originally intended for the Israeli leadership but eventually emerging as 'a kind of US–Israeli neoconservative manifesto'.[2] At the time, the neoconservatives were out of office. Not since President Reagan, and their enthusiastic backing for Israel's 1982 invasion of Lebanon, had they commanded serious influence from within the corridors of power. Ultimately disappointed by him, whom they considered too moderate, as well as by his two successors, they now constituted a very influential, ambitious, militant pressure group,[3] mostly denizens of a plethora of interlocking, pro-Israeli Washington think tanks, impatiently awaiting the champion through whom they could put such ideas into effect. They found him in President George Bush; they entered his Administration *en masse*, some of them in positions of great power. But it was only when bin Laden's nineteen kamikazes steered three of their hijacked aircraft into the Twin Towers and the Pentagon that they truly came into their own; only then that Bush, who, in his electoral campaign, had pledged himself to a 'humble' foreign policy imbued with the 'modesty of true strength', became a convert to their millenarian vision, and the belligerence that came with it. In their speedy and well-orchestrated reaction to what they saw as the most providential of national emergencies,[4] the neoconservatives succeeded in 'hijacking' the foreign policy of the world's only superpower; in persuading its leader to endorse a pre-existing plan of action which had little to do with the nature of the emergency itself, with bin Laden and al-Qaeda, but everything to do with their extravagant project for a future Middle East.[5] It was quite as much an Israeli as an American one. The *Jerusalem Post* described its authors as 'Arik's

[Sharon] American front',[6] and a high American official told the *Washington Post* that the '*Likudniks* are really in charge now'.[7] Bush himself was said to be 'mesmerized' by Sharon.[8] As for the degree of influence, steadily rising from administration to administration, which the Israeli protégé had now attained over its American patron, this – wrote scholar Anatole Lieven – was no longer 'a case of the tail wagging the dog', but of 'the tail wagging the unfortunate dog around the room and banging its head against the ceiling'.[9]

What the Americans and Israelis envisaged was a transformation – strategic, political, economic, religious, cultural – of the entire Middle East. In place of tyranny, extremism, social oppression, corruption and economic stagnation – basic maladies which, in their view, had thrown up 9/11 and turned the region into a menace both to itself and the world – would come freedom and democracy, human rights, the rule of law, pluralism and market capitalism. Of key importance was the notion that since – or so they argued – democracies tend by nature to be more peace-loving and good-neighbourly than despotisms, democratization would contribute mightily to that abiding American quest in the region, an Arab–Israeli peace settlement.[10]

'A FUSION OF BREATHTAKING UTOPIANISM WITH BARELY DISGUISED MACHTPOLITIK'

These blessings of Western civilization were, however, to be delivered to the people of the region by force. In a departure from the principles of 'containment' and 'deterrence' which, officially at least, had guided US defence and security policies for the past half-century, the neo-conservatives adopted 'pre-emption' instead. Andrew Bacevitch, a professor of international relations, described the National Security Strategy of 2002, in which these principles were formally enshrined, as a 'fusion of breathtaking utopianism with barely disguised *Machtpolitik*. ... the product of an unlikely collaboration between Woodrow Wilson and the elder Field Marshal von Moltke'.[11] Armed with their radical new doctrine, they would forestall any emergent, potential, or merely hypothetical threat to the US or its allies long before it had a chance to become a real and imminent one; they would bring about 'regime

change' in the Middle Eastern 'rogue states' which, in America's judgement, posed such threats to Israel or itself. It all bore an obvious
resemblance, writ large, to the long-established Israeli theory – and
practice – of the 'chosen war', of military force in the service of
strategic and political goals. And it was clear: the chief of these goals,
that elusive Arab–Israeli settlement, was to be achieved less through
democracy – that was just an idealistic, one might almost say
'missionary', window-dressing – than through a far greater level of
external coercion than had ever been brought to bear before.
Essentially the *Likudnik* version of a Middle Eastern 'peace', it would
constitute a drastic regression from the two-state solution which,
during decades of international diplomacy, the world, the US included,
had come to regard as a reasonable and practicable one.

As *Clean Break* intimated, the great transformation was to begin with
'regime change' in Baghdad. Within hours of 9/11 Secretary of Defense
Donald Rumsfeld – though not himself a neoconservative – was
ordering his staff to look for 'things related and not' that could furnish
'good enough' reasons to 'hit S.H. [Saddam Hussein] at the same time
[as] UBL [Osama bin Laden]'.[12] His deputy, Paul Wolfowitz – who *was*
a neoconservative – went so far as to suggest that America should first
attack Iraq, not Afghanistan, bin Laden's sanctuary, because Iraq was
'doable' where Afghanistan was 'uncertain'.[13] Richard Clarke, the
official in charge of counter-terrorism, protested that 'for us to go
bombing Iraq in response would be like invading Mexico after the
Japanese attacked us at Pearl Harbor'.[14]

RIDDING THE WORLD OF EVIL[15]

In the event, the US did first attack Afghanistan, overthrowing the
Taliban, but failing to capture bin Laden. However, its attention
quickly reverted to Saddam Hussein. And the neoconservatives lost no
time in developing a rationale for attacking their principal villain. This
grew out of the deliberate elasticity of the global 'war on terror' which
Bush now launched. Terrorism was the new form of 'evil'. America had
the 'responsibility to rid the world of evil'. Iraq was a member of the
'axis of evil', along with Iran, North Korea and 'other states like these

and their terrorist allies'. It was 'evil' that linked Saddam to al-Qaeda and the whole shadowy realm of 'Islamic terror'. More particularly, the neoconservatives injected into Bush's discourse a commitment to target not just the terrorists but 'those who harbour[ed] them'. Saddam – most brutal of Arab despots and arch-practitioner of terrorism though he was – actually had nothing to do with al-Qaeda and 9/11. But the neoconservatives were extraordinarily successful in persuading the American public that he did, and that, in consequence, 'war on terror' and war on Iraq were joined at the hip. They set up their own ad hoc secret agencies, within the Administration, whose business was to prove by any means possible this Iraq/al-Qaeda connection which the regular intelligence community could not, as well as to conjure up that other non-existent *casus belli*, the weapons of mass destruction capable of inflicting 'massive and sudden horror' on the US, which Saddam was supposedly still developing. In Israel, Sharon set up a similar unit that fed fake intelligence to the American ones.[16] Indeed, say professors John Mearsheimer and Stephen Walt in their ground-breaking study of 'the Lobby', were it not for Israel and the 'friends of Israel' in the US there would probably have been no invasion of Iraq at all. The vigorous fashion in which these confederates agitated for it was, however, a taboo subject in US political discourse, 'the proverbial elephant in the room' which 'everybody sees', but – for fear of being branded anti-Semitic – 'no one mentions'.[17]

On 17 March 2003 US and British forces invaded Iraq. It was not far from the 'cakewalk' that leading neoconservative and Pentagon insider, Kenneth Adelman, had famously predicted.[18] Within three weeks the Americans were in Baghdad; on 9 April, with help from the Marines, an exultant throng toppled the statue of Saddam Hussein in Ferdus Square; the Baathist tyranny was no more. But for the neoconservatives this was only the first, albeit 'seismic,' step[19] in the 'reshaping' of the whole region. For the ultimate possible dimensions of their grand design were truly extraordinary. They were all set forth, in their most comprehensive, well-nigh megalomaniac form, by Norman Podhoretz, the movement's veteran intellectual luminary, in the September 2002 issue of his magazine *Commentary*. Changes of regime, he proclaimed, were 'the *sine qua non* throughout the region'. And those that 'richly

deserve[d] to be overthrown and replaced [were] not confined' to the
two officially designated members of the 'axis of evil'. 'At a minimum
the axis should extend to Syria and Lebanon and Libya, as well as
"friends" of America like the Saudi royal family and Egypt's Husni
Mubarak, along with the Palestinian Authority, whether headed by
Arafat or one of his henchmen.' Such an all-encompassing purge might
'clear a path to the long-overdue reform and modernization of Islam'.
It was a formidable task, he conceded, but an achievable one, 'provided
that America has the will to fight World War IV – the war against
militant Islam – to a successful conclusion, and provided that we then
have the stomach to impose a new political culture on the defeated
parties'.

'OUR ENEMIES, THE SAUDIS'

The most important of these official US 'friends' did indeed have
grounds for worry. It was, after all, from Saudi Arabia that bin Laden
and most of his kamikazes hailed, its fiercely puritanical Wahhabite
version of Islam in which they were nurtured. And, a few months after
9/11, Saudi Arabia was the subject of a 'briefing' given by Laurent
Murawiec, a Rand Corporation analyst, to the Pentagon's Defense
Policy Board, which, headed by Richard Perle, was an influential neoconservative stronghold. Describing the kingdom as 'the kernel of evil'
in the Middle East, Murawiec urged the US to deliver it an ultimatum:
cease its backing for terrorism – as well as, *inter alia*, its hostile attitude
towards Israel – or face the 'targeting' of its oil fields and its financial
assets in the US. When news of this sensational advice leaked out, the
Administration rushed to disassociate itself from it. But, in fact, it
reflected a growing body of official opinion about what a leading neoconservative pundit called 'our enemies, the Saudis'.[20] Among other
so-called 'moderate', pro-Western Arab countries, President Mubarak's
Egypt was strongly criticized for its policy of 'deflecting frustration
with the lack of political freedom' by 'encouraging state-controlled
clerics and media to promote the anti-Western, anti-modern and anti-
Jewish propaganda of the Islamic extremists'.[21]

'OUR BIN LADEN'

Yasser Arafat and his Palestinian Authority (PA) fell into a category of their own. The PLO leader – mainstay of the American-led 'peace process', principal architect of the Oslo accord, Nobel prize winner, *habitué* of the White House, harsh critic of Iran and chastiser of its Hamas protégé – had long been an official, if never very trusted, 'friend'. But with the collapse of the 2000 Camp David summit, which America and Israel blamed entirely on him, and the outbreak of the second *Intifada*, described as his handiwork too,[22] the tide was turning strongly against him. And 9/11 was Sharon's God-given chance to portray his brutal pacification of a subject people as an integral part of America's global 'war on terror', with Arafat as 'our bin Laden'.[23] Secretary of State Colin Powell and the more balanced and reasonable, but weaker, wing of the Administration now and then balked at this highly tendentious definition of a popular uprising and the excesses of repression which it justified. Morality aside, the Arab indignation that Israeli actions engendered were obstructing Bush's already uphill struggle to build an Arab coalition in favour of war on Iraq. But then came the '*Karine-A* affair', the alleged, Hizbullah-assisted shipment of arms to Arafat and his Palestinian Authority. Many, even in the Administration itself, suspected that it was all a very timely Israeli hoax.[24] Nevertheless, on the strength of it, Bush now anathematized Arafat in person; his 'ordering weapons that were intercepted on a boat [was] not part of fighting terror; it [was] enhancing terror'.[25] Thereafter, every time Powell and his 'moderates' sought to curb Sharon's excesses they came under concerted public attack from Israel, the neo-conservatives, 'the Lobby' and its new-found friends – till recently condemned as anti-Semites – of the Evangelical Christian 'right';[26] always they – and on one occasion Bush himself – had to beat a humiliating retreat.

AFTER IRAQ, IRAN – THEN SYRIA TOO

But it was its well-established, official villains in the radical, Islamist or Islamo-nationalist camp – both states and non-state actors – on which, in lockstep with its Israeli ally, the US now most systematically set its sights. Delighted though Israel was that the US was taking on Saddam, it had long since regarded that other member of the 'axis of evil', Iran, as much the greater threat, especially since, with its apparent quest for nuclear weapons, it had begun its challenge to Israel's jealously guarded monopoly in this field. So, as one war drew nigh, another already seemed to be in the making; 'the day after' Iraq, said Sharon in Jerusalem, the US should turn its attention to Iran.[27] 'Everyone wants to go to Baghdad,' came the neoconservatives' echoing refrain in Washington, 'but real men want to go to Teheran.'[28]

On this, as so much else, Colin Powell and the State Department favoured a much less belligerent approach; they drew up a plan under which, in return for ending its support for Hizbullah, Hamas and Islamic Jihad, the US would offer Iran a new, constructive and long-term strategic relationship. The weaker, 'reformist' wing of the Islamic regime, centred round President Khatami, was more than interested and, with the crucial backing of the *Wali*, Ayatollah Khamenei, Iranian diplomacy offered, and handsomely delivered, what the Americans themselves acknowledged to have been indispensable assistance in the establishing of the post-Taliban new order in Afghanistan.

'WE DON'T SPEAK TO EVIL'

But the Israelis were so incensed at these efforts to win Iranian co-operation that one of their leading strategists, Moshe Sneh, said that by 'courting the terrorists in Tehran' the US and Britain were 'stabbing Israel in the back',[29] while in Washington forty-one leading neoconservatives, including Pentagon insider Richard Perle, delivered a virtual ultimatum to President Bush: target Hizbullah as well as al-Qaeda, summon Iran and Syria to 'immediately cease all military, financial and political support' for the organization, and, if they demur, 'consider appropriate measures of retaliation' against them.[30] Thereafter the neoconservatives sabotaged every attempt at American–Iranian détente. Repeatedly snubbed, the 'reformist' camp repeatedly tried again, till finally, after the fall of Iraq, they came forward with an 'offer that America couldn't refuse', but, to disbelief in the Powell camp, peremptorily did. It had been fear that induced Khamenei and his clerical hierarchy to go along with this 'stunning' initiative, fear of the strategic encirclement which, with American forces already installed in the Gulf, Afghanistan and Central Asia, the establishment of an American client regime in Baghdad would complete.[31] The offer put just about everything on the table, including the disarming of Hizbullah and its transformation into a purely political party, an end to Iran's support for Hamas and Islamic Jihad and its opposition to the Middle East 'peace process', and the opening up of its nuclear programme to intrusive international inspection. Unfortunately for the mullahs, however, their moment of grave existential anxiety coincided with the Bush Administration's moment of glory, and – for the president – of such personal hubris that he staged a triumphal landing, all got up in fighter-pilot gear, aboard the aircraft-carrier *Abraham Lincoln* in order to proclaim 'Mission Accomplished' and the end of 'major combat operations' in Iraq. It was not surprising that in such an atmosphere the neoconservatives, interpreting the offer as a mark of desperation, opposed any deal, however advantageous, on the ground that the US could eventually get everything it wanted by engineering 'regime change' in Tehran – military planning for which was already under way. Vice President Cheney and Defense Secretary Rumsfeld's words on the subject were final: 'We don't speak to evil.'[32]

It was a similar story with Syria. In the immediate aftermath of 9/11, it had, like Iran, been very helpful to the US, furnishing valuable intelligence about al-Qaeda. Powell and the State Department, even Bush himself, had openly appreciated it.[33] But not the neoconservatives. For them, Syria had always been the most intransigent and extreme of Israel's neighbours, its Baathist regime a last bastion of diehard, secular Arab nationalism that was, in its way, as inimical to Zionism as Iran and the new-wave Islamists were in theirs. Syria had been manifestly shaken by the swift collapse of its Baathist counterpart in Iraq, and neither the neoconservatives nor their Israeli confederates disguised their hopes and expectations of achieving a similar outcome in Damascus. 'War on Iraq', said the Israeli ambassador to the US, was 'not enough'; 'regime change' in Syria and Iran must come next. The US, said Sharon, should 'disarm' Syria, or Israel would 'deal with' this matter itself.[34] In Washington, the leading neoconservative Frank

Gaffney wrote in the *Washington Times* that the US 'should use what-ever techniques are necessary – including military force – to effect behavior modification and/or regime change in Damascus'.[35] In October 2003, Sharon ordered the first Israeli air-raid on Syrian territory in nearly thirty years, hitting a deserted Palestinian training camp, ostensibly in retaliation for a suicide bombing in Israel and what he claimed was Syria's role in sponsoring it. Bush called this gross provocation an act of 'self-defence'. Two months later it was reported – shades of *Clean Break* – that Rumsfeld was considering an attack, with air strikes and 'special forces snatch squads', on Hizbullah targets in the Beqa'a Valley, with the object of drawing Syria into a conflict that would lead to the downfall of the Asad regime.[36]

It very much looked, therefore, as if, instead of just waiting for the other dominos to fall of their own accord, the US and Israel were going to expedite the process by force. If they actually had done that, it would, to begin with at least, have been largely hubris that inspired it. But before very long the motivation would have been heavily inter-fused with something quite otherwise: the incipient fear of failure. Everything is interconnected in the Middle East. So the moment the US began to falter in Iraq, intended fulcrum of the neoconservative grand design, would have been the moment it began to falter in the region as a whole – and the region itself to strike back, inside Iraq, against its neo-imperial tormentor.

Sure enough, within a few short months America *was* thus faltering; the proud practitioners of 'shock and awe' – of *Blitzkrieg* in its ultra-modern form – simply could not master the more prosaic business of occupying, controlling, administering and reconstructing this very important Arab country, this latest addition to the American *imperium* that was also supposed to serve as a model of American 'values', of freedom and democracy, for all its brethren. For this there were local reasons – the Iraqis' resistance, their often atrocious violence, the Americans' arrogance and ineptitude – in plenty. But external actors could intensify it. Iran and Syria, threatened with the full-scale Iraqi treatment themselves, were naturally, if discreetly, the readiest to do so. At various stages, Syria openly helped, encouraged, turned a blind eye to, or simply could not stop, the volunteers who crossed its territory in search of *jihad* and martyrdom against the infidel invader, making Iraq, which was supposed to have become the bane of Islamist terror, into an ideal new front for the practice of it. 'The body count of US soldiers', said a Western diplomat in Damascus, '[became] the most accurate barometer of Syria's morale.'[37]

In Iran, the arch-conservative zealots, profiting from America's contemptuous spurning of their 'reformist' rivals, could only rejoice. Their idol, Khomeini, had fought, and lost, a gruelling, eight-year war to turn Saddam's Iraq into the world's second Islamic republic. Now – with the destruction of its Sunni minority rule and the political emancipation of the long-oppressed Shiite majority – the Great Satan itself had furnished Khomeini's heirs with a unique opportunity to try again, or at least to secure for themselves that ascendancy in Iraq, stepping stone to vastly increased influence in the region as a whole, which the US, Israel and 'moderate' pro-Western, Sunni Arab states were so very anxious to deny it. To be sure, the Islamic Republic still worried about American strategic encirclement. But it was emboldened by it too. For even if it *was* more vulnerable, so – over-extended and already floundering – was the invader. 'US forces [in Iraq]', exulted Revolutionary Guards commander Ali Shamkani, 'won't be an element of strength, but our hostage.' In the event, the US and Israel blustered, threatened, or sought to undermine from within, but they neither would, could nor dared to attack head-on. There was, however, to be a war – the war which, in July and August 2006, pitted Israel against Hizbullah. Although Hizbullah was a formidable adversary in its own right, this was to be very much a proxy war as well; for rather than Iran or Syria, state components of the Islamo-nationalist camp, Americans and Israelis decided to take on – and destroy – a lesser target, its principal non-state actor, instead. In fact, it was to be the first such large-scale military encounter since Israel had come into being in which no Arab state took part. But it became such a very considerable, and deeply significant, affray that the Arabs were quickly to dub it the Sixth (Arab–Israeli) War.

'THE MOST VICIOUS AND EFFECTIVE TERRORIST ORGANIZATION IN THE WORLD'

'Our war on terror begins with al-Qaeda', said President Bush in the wake of 9/11, 'but it does not end there. It will not end till every terrorist group with global reach has been found, stopped and defeated.' And states around the world could not be neutral; they were either 'with us or against us', depending on what they did, or did not do, to hunt down and punish the 'evil-doers' on their soil. Hizbullah had long been on America's list of terrorist organizations. But Bush's Administration did not at first single it out as a key, immediate target. That was essentially for the same reason that, in these early days, it didn't turn full force against Hizbullah's two state sponsors, Syria and Iran, either: Colin Powell and the State Department needed – and secured – their assistance in the campaign against al-Qaeda and the Taliban. The American ambassador to Beirut even assured Lebanese officials that Hizbullah had nothing to do with the kind of terror the US was after.[38] But that soon changed. By the time of Bush's famous 'Axis of Evil' speech, Hizbullah had become an integral part of a 'terrorist underworld' that 'operate[d] in remote jungles and deserts and [hid] in the centres of large cities'; 'winning the war on terror' meant 'getting rid of groups like [it]'.[39] According to Senator Bob Graham, former head of the Senate Intelligence Committee, this 'most vicious and effective terrorist organization in the world' already boasted 'combat-ready cells' in the US.[40] For Assistant Secretary of State Richard Armitage, Hizbullah was even worse than bin Laden's organization itself – 'the A-team of terrorism', while al-Qaeda was perhaps only 'the B-team'.[41]

Of course, the US had its own motives for turning on Hizbullah, including the 1983 truck-bombing that killed 241 Marines at Beirut airport.[42] Imad Mughniyah, its presumed organizer, was one of three Hizbullah members who now figured prominently on America's refurbished list of 'most wanted' men. Yet some Americans were prepared to argue that this butchery of sleeping men, and the bombing of the US embassy that preceded it, had been more Iranian than Hizbullahi; that, atrocious though such exploits were, they had been, if not legitimate, at least predictable responses to the Israeli/US invasion of Lebanon; or even that, with the CIA-ordered car-bombing which killed eighty-five Lebanese civilians in the *Dahiya* two years later, the US could be said to have already exacted more than adequate retribution.[43] To be sure, the hijacking to Beirut of a TWA airliner in 1985 – though itself, at least in part, retaliation for the CIA atrocity – and the murder of an American navy diver on board did constitute anti-American terrorism by any standard, as did the subsequent seizure and occasional killing of American hostages.

However justified they might or might not have been, such historical grievances now found a new lease of life. Yet they were not, in the final analysis, the real reason why the US decided to put Hizbullah so high on, if not at the very top of, its latest, expanded list of foreign terrorist organizations. The real reason lay in the same mind-set and agenda that took the American army so ill-fatedly into Iraq. 'It [was] a political issue here [in Washington]', said Robert Baer, the former CIA agent who, according to his own account, once came very close to arranging the assassination of Mughniyah, 'because the Israelis want[ed] the Americans to go after Hizbullah.'[44] And what the Israelis wanted, their neoconservative allies in the Administration automatically wanted too. It was 'a big fight',[45] apparently, which pitted them against Colin Powell's State Department. Nonetheless, as usual, they won it. Appropriately enough, it was after a meeting with Shimon Peres, the Israeli foreign minister, that Bush for the first time ascribed to Hizbullah a 'global reach', the characteristic that in America's post-9/11 lexicon put it in the same, heinous league as al-Qaeda; this was a new position – 'clearly show[ing] that there [was] no distinction between terrorism against Americans and terrorism against Israelis'[46] – on which 'the Lobby', also very active in these persuasions, heartily congratulated him.

Thereafter, just as they did in the case of Iraq, the Israelis diligently supplied Washington with such intelligence about Hizbullah as suited their purposes. Some of it was accurate enough, if already well-known, like the fact that Hizbullah aided and abetted fellow Islamists in Palestine, Hamas and Islamic Jihad, which were somehow deemed to have 'global reach' too. But much of it, designed to stress the danger that Hizbullah posed not just to Israel but to the world, was not. The most persistent contention in this respect was that Hizbullah – like

Saddam – had joined forces with al-Qaeda, and that – after his fall – it trained 'foreign fighters' who went to Iraq 'to kill American troops'; or that it was sending its own people there as well.[47] This improbable notion that the militant Shiites of Hizbullah would actively assist the Wahhabite extremists of al-Qaeda, who looked on Shiites as heretics, was readily taken up in Washington. And, in any case, said White House spokesman Ari Fleischer, 'you can't on the one hand denounce al-Qaeda and then go and join Hizbullah or Hamas'.

Hizbullah had been quick to realize that 9/11 would automatically intensify Western antipathy for any form of Islamic politics, not least its own.[48] And it took care to condemn it – without, however, forgetting to observe that 'repeated Zionist massacres' of the Lebanese had earned no such condemnation from the US.[49] It strove to differentiate itself, ideologically and politically, from al-Qaeda. It rejected the kind of mass, indiscriminate, international terror it practised, so much so, indeed, that it earned the reproaches of extremist Sunnis around the region.[50] Nasrallah denied that Hizbullah commanded any 'global reach'. There had long been strong suspicions that, in collaboration with Iran and as retaliation for Israel's 1992 assassination of its secretary-general, Abbas Musawi, Hizbullah had been behind the bombings, with heavy loss of life, of the Israeli embassy and a Jewish community centre in Buenos Aires; and Argentina had issued an international arrest warrant against Imad Mughniyah in this connection. But Nasrallah insisted: 'We haven't carried out operations anywhere in the world.' Calling on the US to prove that it had,[51] he also made it clear that he sought no confrontation with it. Furthermore, although the party considered itself to be in the forefront of the anti-imperial, anti-Zionist struggle, its hatred of Saddam Hussein and his ferocious persecution of its Shiite co-religionists caused it to take a distinctly ambiguous position towards the invasion of Iraq, and it never called for *jihad* against the Americans there.[52] However, it did, as we have seen, see fit to continue its military operations against the Israeli-occupied Sheba'a Farms. And in fact it was those, as well as its aggressive identification with and surreptitious assistance to the increasingly violent Palestinian *Intifada*, that so aroused US ire against it. In effect, for America, 'global reach' had come to include any form of attack on

Israel.[53] Hizbullah's disarming, rather than its disappearance as a political organization, was what it chiefly wanted; but for Nasrallah, that – except in the all but unforeseeable circumstances of an Arab–Israeli settlement that he himself could accept – was out of the question. And he repeatedly warned that if the US did make any attempt to achieve it by force his organization would strike at US interests wherever it could.[54] He also defiantly endorsed the right of Palestinians to carry out suicide bombings as 'the only way to defeat the Zionists' who, civilians or military, were 'all occupiers and invaders, partners in crimes and massacres'.[55]

'TURNING LEBANON BACK TO THE STONE AGE?'

For a while, in the immediate aftermath of America's feat of arms in Iraq, the only question – excitedly raised by neoconservatives and Israelis alike, in a rather different spirit by the potential victims – seemed to be: who next? Would it be Iran, or Syria – or Hizbullah? If it were to be the last, it was held likely that Israel would do the job on its own. Even before the Iraqi invasion dire threats had been emanating from the self-same Sharon who, as defence minister in 1982, had conceived and executed his country's greatest, and most catastrophic, foray into Lebanon. According to one of his 'senior officials', he was planning to 'wipe out' Hizbullah 'once and for all' in an operation that would '[turn] Lebanon back to the Stone Age'.[56] That was not to be, however – not during his tenure at least. For perhaps, after all, it was true – as some were saying at the time – that, given his earlier misadventures there, even this most reckless and ambitious of Israeli interventionists had developed a 'complex' of timidity about Lebanon. So for the time being the US pursued its own – and Israel's – purposes in the country by means that fell short of further war.

In accordance with the new, 'with-us-or-against-us' doctrines, these had begun with vigorous approaches to the Lebanese government. The US ambassador told it that it must 'seize terrorists, prosecute them and hand over, or expel, those who are wanted'. Then, unimpressed by its response, he publicly accused it of hosting 'terrorist organizations'.[57] Then he called on the Lebanese Central Bank to impose financial sanctions on Hizbullah, as the US itself was doing. The tone grew menacing. National Security Adviser Condoleezza Rice, well aware of the importance – and fragility – of Prime Minister Rafiq Hariri's great post-war reconstruction drive, warned the country that to 'survive economically' it 'needed to reintegrate into the international community'; its 'very existence' now depended on its 'compliance' with American demands.[58] Lebanese officialdom, however, thought rather strongly otherwise.

Their defiance was entirely in line with the public position adopted by virtually all Arab and Muslim states, including the US's closest 'friends'. This, in effect, was that for America to condemn Arab 'terrorism' against Israel, while failing to condemn the 'state terrorism' Israel habitually practised against the Arabs, was only the latest manifestation of Western 'double standards' that had bedevilled the Arab–Israeli conflict for decades. It was most authoritatively embodied in an official pronouncement of the Organization of Islamic Countries, which, while deploring what al-Qaeda had done, 'totally [rejected] ... any confusing of terrorism with the rights of people – notably the Palestinians and the Lebanese – to legitimate defence and resistance against Israeli occupation'. 'Hong Kong' to Hizbullah's 'Hanoi' the billionaire prime minister might have been, but he sprang valiantly to the organization's defence now. This whole, hugely emotive issue of what constituted terrorism and what did not, he said, was simply a product of the US's 'blind bias' in Israel's favour; and 'let no one think' that he would 'stand hand-cuffed in face of the demand for liquidating the resistance'.[59] He instructed the Central Bank not to freeze any Hizbullah assets. The clergy, both Christian and Muslim, rallied no less earnestly behind Hizbullah. Especially noteworthy was the forthrightness of the Maronite patriarch, traditionally most Westward-looking of churchmen, who, in the person of Cardinal Butros Sfeir, told an ecumenical conference in Rome that far from being terrorists Hizbullah fighters were 'Lebanese citizens trying to free their country ... and we all thank them for their effort'.[60] Though Hizbullah did indeed command a large measure of public, multi-confessional support there was a good deal of attitudinizing about the politicians and the prelates' anti-American defiance on its behalf. For they knew that, whatever their actual opinion of the organization, they could not realistically have taken any other position. Not only did the inter-communal consensus-seeking of the sectarian polity require it; the fact was that Hizbullah, an armed 'state within a state', was stronger, politically and militarily, than the state itself, and that to seek to dismantle and disarm it now would have been to provoke another civil war. They also knew that 'sister-Syria' would not stand for it.

So did the Americans – which was why, despite the initial harshness, the pressures they brought to bear on a congenitally weak and fissiparous Lebanese government to get it to pressure Hizbullah in its turn were in the end rather half-hearted. The Israelis had tried this stratagem again and again, far more violently, and it had never worked. So US leaders now identified Syria, not Lebanon, as the central problem – *and* the solution. By 'dealing with' the Syrian patron they would automatically be 'dealing with' the Hizbullahi protégé. Hitherto, in its periods of relative pragmatism, the US had managed to look on a Syrian role in Lebanon as an almost positive thing; but in the neo-conservative era the very idea was anathema. *Clean Break*, it will be recalled, had identified Saddam's Iraq as the first target in the grand design to re-order the entire Middle East, but only as a prelude to the more important goal of 'rolling back' Syria – Syria, the emotional heart of the Arab world, linchpin of its power system, and, as such, possessed of a special disposition and ability to involve itself in the region's trouble spots, Israel/Palestine chief among them. Lebanon, and its hegemony over it, was the most important component of Syria's regional power and prestige. So getting Syria out of Lebanon was not just a matter of 'getting' Hizbullah too.

In 1958, it had been in Lebanon that the Arab world's new, 'revolutionary', Soviet-supported republics, led by Nasser's Egypt – then in organic union with Syria – reached the high-water mark of their struggle against its 'reactionary', Western-backed monarchies.[61] In the 1980s, it had been the key arena where the US, Israel and 'moderate' Arab states engaged in, and lost, their military and/or political contest with a Syria backed by both the Soviet Union and its ideological antithesis, the new-born Islamic Republic of Iran. Now it became – and ever more intensely remained – a battleground in the latest, and perhaps most fateful, of these regional and international confrontations of modern times, between the Iranian-dominated, Islamo-nationalist camp and that same collection of improbable bedfellows in the opposing one.

CHAPTER TWELVE

Getting Syria Out of Lebanon

2004–2006

THE 'NEO-IMPERIAL' AND THE 'MISSIONARY'

Getting Syria out of Lebanon fell into the main, pro-Israeli, 'neo-imperial' side of America's post-9/11 grand design. But here was a case where the 'neo-imperial' stood particularly to benefit from its other, 'missionary' side – the promotion of 'freedom and democracy'. This had come increasingly to the fore as the original, official reasons for invading Iraq – weapons of mass destruction and the al-Qaeda connection – had been exposed for the inventions they were. For, in a region where hereditary monarchies or one-party republics were the norm, Lebanon had a resilient democratic tradition which, however flawed, set it apart from everywhere else. It was a tradition which the Syrian Baathists, after Saddam perhaps the most repressive of Arab dictatorships, had inevitably sought to smother. But, submerged though it had been, it now welled up again, underpinning the growing, nation-wide rebelliousness against the Syrians.

The apparatus of control which, in collaboration with their Lebanese henchmen, they had installed in the aftermath of the civil war reached its malignant height under Emile Lahoud, the former army commander who became president in 1998. The Syrian–Lebanese 'security regime' of which he was the titular head fell under the sway of a new and younger generation of Syrian officials generally identified with Bashar al-Asad, who succeeded his father, Hafiz, on his death in 2000. Cruder than their elders, they not only tightened Syria's political grip, the maintenance of which was one part of their functions, but also augmented the already immense corruption that was the other, and

more scandalous, one. They turned Syria's 'sister-state' and protect-
orate into such a cornucopia of extortion, racketeering and diversion of
public funds that the distribution of the spoils – authoritatively
estimated to be a good two billion dollars a year[1] – was said to be a
factor in the stability of their regime. Lebanese state and society still of
course defined itself by its multifarious sectarian loyalties, but, with
the Syrian overlordship, one great fault-line had come to dominate,
and blur, all others. That was the one that separated those who – by
nature, interest or opportunism – were *pro*-Syrian from those who were
anti-, the 'loyalists' from the 'opposition'.

Opposition to any kind of Arab encroachment on Lebanon had
always come from some communities, above all the Maronites, more
than others. So when, in 2000, after Hizbullah had driven the Israelis
from the South, agitation against the continuing presence of that other
intruder, Syria, began to make itself felt, the Maronites led it. Their
patriarch, Archbishop Nasrallah Sfeir, called on Syria to fulfil its long
overdue obligation, under the Taif accord, to pull back its troops to the
Beqa'a Valley; then, more boldly, a conclave of Maronite bishops
lamented Lebanon's 'loss of sovereignty' and the 'hegemony imposed
on all its institutions'.[2] However, the Maronites, the main losers in the
post-war settlement, no longer commanded the pre-eminence they
used to. More significant was the very similar position taken by Druze
chieftain Walid Jumblat, an official 'ally' of Syria, who in due course
emerged as the opposition's effective leader. Even more remarkable
still than this coming together of the two oldest and most rooted, but
historically perhaps most reciprocally hostile, of Lebanese communities, were the Muslim voices, mainly Sunni, now being raised in
favour of a more balanced and equitable relationship with Syria.
Stout defenders of Lebanon's Arab identity, the Sunnis had since
independence been Syria's most ardent friends. It was peculiarly
ironic, therefore, that their outstanding leader, Rafiq Hariri – or 'Mr
Lebanon' as he came to be known in his capacity as the country's
larger-than-life, dynamic and internationally influential prime
minister – was to become the focal point of Lebanon's struggle to
extricate itself from Syria's oppressive tutelage, and chief target of its
retaliatory wrath.

Hariri was far from anti-Syrian, partly because he considered himself to be an Arab nationalist and partly because, a pragmatist, he
realized that, for the small state of Lebanon, preserving the goodwill of
its greater neighbour was an imperious, unalterable necessity. He was
also said to be heavily involved in regaling the kleptomaniac appetites
of its rulers. He bent every effort to accommodate them, and so
assiduously used his international standing to promote Syria's interests,
besides Lebanon's own, that Jumblat called him 'Syria's unofficial
foreign minister, much more important than the real [one]'.[3] Hariri's
main problem and personal nemesis was Lahoud – he and the joint
'security regime'. In their obsession with control, they made it virtually
impossible for him to govern, let alone pursue his dream of Lebanon's
high capitalist renaissance; they thwarted him at every turn, to the
point where ministers would be handed instructions in sealed
envelopes before cabinet meetings telling them which way to vote on
every proposal tabled.[4]

It was in the wake of the Iraqi invasion that the US began seriously
to impinge on this Lebanese–Syrian imbroglio. Congress led the way,
with the re-introduction of the 'Syria Accountability and Lebanese
Sovereignty Act', which it had agreed to shelve the previous year in
deference to Bush's plea that he might otherwise forfeit the useful
intelligence Syria had been supplying about al-Qaeda.[5] Framed by
some of Israel's friends in the House and Senate, it was the fruit of
collaboration between them and the US Committee for a Free
Lebanon. Led by Ziad Abdul-Nour, a Lebanese-American business-
man, the committee was a close cousin of 'the Lobby'; it boasted an
impressive array of neoconservatives in its ranks, including Elliot
Abrams, so staunch a Zionist that some Israelis welcomed his appointment to the National Security Council as a 'gift from heaven'.[6] They
adopted the Lebanese opposition's cause in much the same spirit as
they had formerly adopted the Iraqi one, in the person of Ahmad
Chalabi.

On the face of it, Lebanon was the main beneficiary of the
legislation, but actually it was far less attentive to Lebanon's interests
than Israel's. In its charge sheet of Syria's misdemeanours, it portrayed
it as a fitting member of the 'axis of evil' – to which, indeed, 'the Lobby'

was working to have it formally assigned. It demanded that Syria stop 'undermining international peace and security', supporting 'international terrorism', hosting '[Palestinian] terrorist groups in Damascus', 'developing and deploying' weapons of mass destruction and the missiles to deliver them. Where Lebanon was concerned, Syria was to end its 'occupation', enable it to achieve 'full restoration of its sovereignty, political independence and territorial integrity', deploy its army in the South, and evict all 'terrorist and foreign forces, including Hizbullah and the Iranian Revolutionary Guards'. Thereafter both Lebanon and Syria were to enter into 'serious' and 'unconditional' bilateral peace talks with Israel; that meant, in effect, that Syria was now being expected to renounce all the gains which it had made in earlier, if ultimately abortive, US-sponsored negotiations. In December 2003 House and Senate passed the bill by overwhelming majorities. After his initial, tactical reservations Bush signed it into law, and in May 2004 he slapped on Syria a raft of not particularly debilitating sanctions. Hizbullah, his Administration endlessly insisted, should be dismantled in a Lebanon self-ruled and free of 'all' foreign forces.

'FINISHING OFF WHAT LITTLE OF THE DEMOCRACY WE HAVE TO BOAST ABOUT'

But the greater the pressure the US exerted on him, the harder President Asad struck back. Denouncing the Bush Administration as 'extremists' with a 'barbaric attitude to human society',[7] he resolved to impose his grip on Lebanon more firmly than ever. He ventured on the very provocative course of adding a three-year extension to the single, constitutionally permitted six-year term of the unpopular President Lahoud. No sooner had the merest hint of this intention emerged than Archbishop Sfeir said that it would 'finish off, once and for all, what little is left of the democracy we boast about'. Muslim clerics agreed.[8]

So did Hariri. But he did not advertise the fact, hoping, still, for reconciliation with Damascus. His position was critical. It was above all he and his parliamentary bloc who could make or break Asad's decision, by ceding or withholding the constitutional amendment and the two-thirds majority vote in favour of the extension required to get it through parliament.⁹ This was the issue on which the Syrian leadership went to war against him. Their mistrust grew, nourished by the malicious rumours, fed to them by Lahoud and his 'loyalists', to the effect that Hariri was an American agent and a 'traitor' who would disarm Hizbullah. At the end of 2003, he was summoned to Damascus; there, in a violent, 45-minute tirade, Asad and three intelligence chiefs accused him of plotting against Syria with both French and Americans.¹⁰ France's inclusion in this arraignment was no accident. For Asad had by now achieved the near-miracle of uniting against himself the two Western powers which had only recently diverged so bitterly over Iraq. Partly, no doubt, at the urgings of his good friend Hariri, President Chirac, alone among Western leaders, had tried to help the inexperienced new Syrian leader make his way in the world. Chirac had expected at least some recompense for his manifold favours, not least an easing of the Syrian grip on the country, Lebanon, which had so long occupied a special place in France's affections. But he had got worse than nothing – just snubs and discourtesy – in return.¹¹

'I WILL BREAK LEBANON OVER YOUR HEAD AND WALID JUMBLAT'S'

Eight months later, in August 2004, defying French and American appeals for the election of a new president by due constitutional process, Asad again summoned Hariri to Damascus and, in an even brusquer fifteen-minute encounter, flatly instructed him to change the constitution on Lahoud's behalf. There were varying, but essentially consonant, versions of the brutal, contemptuous language he employed to do this, but perhaps the most shocking was the one recalled by Hariri's son, Saad:

> This is what I want. If you think that President Chirac and you are going to run Lebanon, you are mistaken. It is not going to happen. President Lahoud is me. Whatever I tell him, he follows suit. This extension is to happen or else I will break Lebanon over your head and Walid Jumblat's … So, you either do as you are told or we will get you and your family wherever you are.¹²

'To them', said 'Mr Lebanon' that evening upon his arrival, shaken, humiliated and dejected, at his retreat in the mountain resort of Fakra, 'we are all ants.'[13]

Hariri had few illusions about the lengths to which the Baathists would go if he blocked the Lahoud extension. He had reason to believe that a score of car-bombs, already prepared, would go off around the city. And he had even larger fears. 'Do you think', he asked an aide, 'they could mobilize 100,000 Hizbullahi people to march on central Beirut?' 'Of course,' the aide replied. 'What do you think would happen if someone fired into that crowd?' 'Hizbullah would burn the city.'[14] Thus personally threatened, and afraid of plunging the country into bloodshed of a kind not seen since the civil war, Hariri presided over the ten-minute cabinet meeting which agreed to put the constitutional amendment to parliament.[15]

The Syrian *diktat* was a crude one; but justifiably perhaps, in the light of past experience, Asad and his henchmen thought that they would get away with it. But this time they were mistaken. Indeed, what they had actually done was to set in motion a chain of events that, within nine months, would all but prise Lebanon from their grasp. More than merely provoking general outrage among the Lebanese, they furnished America and France with the opportunity they needed. With unusual alacrity, their diplomats at the UN drew up and secured the passage of Security Council Resolution 1559. A characteristic mix, under neo-conservative/Israeli influence, of the 'neo-imperial' and the 'missionary', though with pride of place now assigned to the latter, it called for a new president to be chosen in a 'free and fair electoral process ... without foreign [i.e. Syrian] interference or influence', for 'all remaining foreign [i.e. Syrian] forces to withdraw from Lebanon' and for the 'disarmament of all Lebanese [i.e. Hizbullah] and non-Lebanese [i.e. Palestinian] militias'.

The resolution came as a genuine shock to Syria and its Lebanese allies, who denounced it as a flagrant interference in the internal affairs of a UN member-state. It certainly did imply a great deal of hypocrisy on the part of its principal sponsor. For here was the US harrying Syria into compliance with a resolution designed to end what it had taken to calling its 'occupation' of another country. However justified in itself, this was conduct that stood in blatant contrast with its infinite tolerance, encapsulated in countless Security Council vetoes, of a much older, and no less reprehensible occupation – by Israel of those remaining areas of Palestine which it had not already conquered and called its own and whose inhabitants it had not driven out.[16] While welcoming the primary thrust of the resolution, the anti-Syrian opposition could have done without the 'neo-imperial' part of it, particularly the demand for Hizbullah's disarmament. Hariri himself assured the organization that its weapons were a strictly Lebanese issue to be settled through internal dialogue, not external interference, and that he would persuade the international community of that. He would never, he said, permit 'an Algeria in Lebanon'.[17]

Barely twenty-four hours after the resolution, the Lebanese parliament was induced to cast its vote in defiance of it. The 128-member chamber had been well packed with Syrian allies and clients, but not well enough, on their own, to guarantee the necessary two-thirds majority. Intimidation and death threats made the difference, reducing the number of opponents from fifty to twenty-nine, and thereby ensuring Lahoud his extra three years.[18]

The Baathist security chiefs had apparently got their way. The trouble, however, was that, in their neurotic fear of Lebanese self-assertion, even this bold coup was not enough for them. In breach of their foregoing promises to Hariri that, as a reward for his compliance, he would not be required to fill his next cabinet with Syrian appointees, that was precisely what they now expected of him.[19] Then, a month later, Marwan Hamade, minister of economy and intimate of opposition leader Walid Jumblat, narrowly escaped assassination by car-bomb, an ominous revival of the methods beloved of Syrians, Israelis and others during the civil war. Like almost all such crimes, this one went unsolved – because never seriously investigated – by the joint 'security regime'.[20] But the political message was clear – a reprisal against Jumblat for his Druze-led parliamentary bloc's vote against the Lahoud extension and a warning to him and Hariri to be on better behaviour in future.

Then, sensing a diminution of UN pressure, Damascus decided that it could dispense with Hariri's services altogether. He was told to step

down as prime minister. And he did. But it was a cathartic moment for
him. He might have been forced out of office – but it was only to gird
himself, with greater determination, for another, spectacular, comeback. He believed that if, in the upcoming 2005 parliamentary
elections, he and his trans-sectarian allies could score an even greater
victory than their landslide of five years before, the Syrians would have
no choice but to deal with him as a valued equal rather than despised
minion.[21]

'YOU KNOW, IT COULD BE ME OR YOU IN THE NEXT TWO WEEKS'

Even now, however, he sought to avoid a full-scale showdown with
them. He tried not to publicly identify himself with other opposition
groups, principally Christian, whom he considered too hostile to Syria
and too sympathetic to 1559's call for Hizbullah's disarming.[22] But,
despite himself, he was inexorably becoming the opposition's central
figure, alongside an altogether more visible and flamboyant Jumblat
now growing ever bolder in his imprecations against 'the Syrian–
Lebanese mafia' and his demands that it be 'broken up ... for good'.[23] All
the signs were that Hariri's electoral juggernaut would transform the
Lebanese political landscape, and that he would triumph in the mainly
Sunni, Druze and Christian areas of the country, leaving only the
mainly Shiite south and the Beqa'a Valley in the hands of the pro-
Syrian Hizbullah/Amal alliance.[24] And when, for the first time, the
mainstream Christian/Druze opposition called for the full-scale withdrawal of Syrian troops, as opposed to their mere 're-deployment' to
the Beqa'a, the loyalists responded with vituperations of unprecedented
ferocity. Hariri was 'the snake of Koreitem' (the Beirut neighbourhood
where he lived) cunningly guiding the opposition from behind the
scenes. Jumblat was a 'foreign spy' who would be 'crucified on the
garbage dump of history'.[25] Hariri had received warnings from several
quarters, including Chirac, about the threat to his life. But he tended
to assume that, in the Syrians' estimation, he was 'simply too big',
internationally, to be dispatched without risk of major repercussion in
the outside world.[26] Amidst this crescendo of abuse and vilification,
however, his feeling of invulnerability was waning, and in early

February he pulled Jumblat aside and told him: 'You know, it could be me or you in the next two weeks. If they want to create trouble, they will kill either you or me.'[27]

THE MURDER OF 'MR LEBANON'

It was to be Hariri. At 12.56 p.m. on 14 February 2005, as the reverberations of a huge detonation echoed around their city and up into the surrounding hills, most Beirutis thought they came from the sonic boom of an Israeli warplane cavorting in the skies above. But, for those closest to it, that great, rending, unearthly crunch had to be something far more unusual, and deadly, than that. It was, in fact, a mixture of TNT and plastic, all 1,200 kilos of it, gouging a hole in the road three metres deep and ten broad, tossing vehicles into the air, hurling bodies and body parts far and wide, generating such a blast that it went round corners to splinter window frames hundreds of metres away and shatter panes many hundreds more distant still. Hariri had been returning home from parliament. Three possible routes had been available to him. But the bomber in a Mitsubishi van had so positioned himself that, on a word from a spotter outside parliament, he could move to intercept him on whichever one he actually took. He struck the motorcade, five armour-plated Mercedes and an ambulance, just outside the St George, the fine old sea-front hotel which still stood largely derelict ever since it had been gutted in the early days of the civil war, but which had no doubt been destined, in Hariri's dreams, to become a foremost symbol of Beirut's renaissance. Instead, Hariri perished in the inferno of burning, mangled vehicles beneath its once more ravaged façade. Twenty-two others, many of them more horribly charred and dismembered than himself, died with him: Basil Fleihan, the friend and adviser at his side, seven bodyguards, and fourteen ill-starred passers-by. It had been a very complex and technically proficient operation requiring *inter alia* the expertise to disable the state-of-the-art, anti-bomb electronic jammers installed in three of the convoy's cars. It was hard to believe that it could have been carried out without the knowledge of the Syrian and Lebanese intelligence services, or indeed, given their subsequent, ill-disguised attempt at a cover-up, that they had not done it themselves. That, indeed, was the supposition of the first, interim report of the UN Commission that was set up to investigate the killing. As for the Lebanese themselves, from the very first moment few in the opposition camp had any doubts about the identity of the principal culprit.[28]

'Look into your hearts', yelled a young man in the angry, grieving throng that had assembled outside Hariri's Beirut mansion, 'We know who did this! Syria!' It was a pivotal moment, the shattering of fifteen years of sullen Sunni acquiescence in Syrian rule. 'Like an aircraft carrier altering course in the ocean', wrote Nicholas Blanford in his book *The Killing of Mr Lebanon*, 'the Sunni community was turning with an inexorable momentum into outright opposition.' For the first time, under the aegis of his son and political heir, Saad, the movement Hariri had founded now openly joined forces with the others, Christian and Druze, who had preceded it down the anti-Syrian path. Together, they issued a declaration holding 'the Lebanese ... and Syrian authority responsible for this and other similar crimes', and demanded the formation of a provisional government and the withdrawal of Syrian forces before the upcoming parliamentary elections. The crowd outside shouted 'Syria out, Syria out.' It was the first time in history, said the newspaper *al-Nahar*, that Sunnis had given voice to such hostile sentiments 'against the country which they have always viewed as a strategic depth and support, if not a safe haven for them'.[29]

It marked the beginning of what came to be known as the 'Independence *Intifada*', a manifestation of 'people power' soon being likened to the 'Rose Revolution' that had recently swept Georgia or the 'Orange' one of Ukraine. 'Independence, Liberation, Sovereignty' became its principal slogans and establishing 'the Truth' – about who had killed Hariri – deemed vital for its ultimate success. The possible repercussions of a popular upheaval unique in modern Arab history were deemed to be great, for the region as well as for Lebanon itself. Samir Kassir, a Lebanese journalist of Palestinian origin, wrote in *al-Nahar*: 'The Arab nationalist cause has shrunk into the single aim of getting rid of the regimes of terrorism and coups, and regaining the people's freedom as a prelude to the new Arab renaissance. It buries the lie that despotic systems can be the shield of nationalism. Beirut has become the "beating heart" of a new Arab nationalism.'[30] And surely nowhere were the repercussions liable to be more intensely felt than in Syria – Arabism's original 'beating heart' – whose people, the more discerning of them at least, could hardly fail to grasp that what the Lebanese were really rebelling against was less Syria as such than the extension on Lebanese soil of what they themselves more drastically endured at home. That is to say the oppression of a once revolutionary new order which – like the now defunct, Soviet-style, single-party 'people's republics' on which it was largely modelled – had lost all true legitimacy.

THE CEDAR REVOLUTION

The *Intifada* was an essentially spontaneous, indigenous affair; and – regionally – a strictly Arab, or inter-Arab, one too. But the Bush Administration quickly got into the act. It dubbed it the Cedar Revolution – *Intifada* being too suggestive of Palestinian suicide bombers blowing up Israelis.[31] It could not but rejoice at a development easily spun as a major success in its Middle East crusade for 'freedom and democracy'. Addressing 'the people of Lebanon', Bush told them that 'the American people, millions across the earth, are on your side'. And he prophesied that once democracy had taken root in their country, it would 'ring the doors of every Arab regime'. But these Intifadists could hardly be principally defined as 'pro-American' – and many of them certainly did not want that discrediting label themselves – even if they did attract and accept American and European support. They were above all anti-Syrian, or, perhaps more precisely, anti-Baathist. It was that, rather than their love of democracy, which in Bush's book really put them on the side of the angels. No wonder that, as he stepped up his calls for a complete and immediate Syrian withdrawal, the neoconservatives were salivating over what they called this 'low-hanging fruit'[32] ripe for plucking without the resort to force that had been needed for the Baathists of Baghdad.

In its vast, initial ardour, the *Intifada* took the form of an escalating series of popular demonstrations. Yet there were soon to be counter-demonstrations too. For, authentic and unprecedented though it was, it could never claim to be nation-wide. It was true, perhaps, that the

combined numerical weight of these three key components of the
sectarian state, Sunnis, Christians and Druzes, was less important than
the manner in which, often such bitter adversaries in the past, they were
now coming together in an overriding common cause. Unfortunately
for them, however, the fourth main component did not join them. At
least 1,300,000 in number, and in their way perhaps the most dynamic
and upwardly mobile of communities, the Shiites, a mere 16 per cent of
the population in 1932, had by now risen to a full 35 per cent of it.[33] To
be sure, many Shiites, cleric and lay, grieved for Hariri, and took part
in his funeral. That was a multi-confessional event the like of which
Lebanon had never seen before. He was laid to rest in the vast new
Muhammad al-Amin mosque, largely his own creation, in Martyrs'
Square, the mid-town area where in pre-war years all confessions had
uniquely and ecumenically mingled. But the Shiites hardly compared
in numbers with the Sunnis and Druzes as, amid a cacophony of
muezzins' calls, they flocked to his burial-place from Muslim West
Beirut, or with the Christians who, church bells everywhere tolling,
converged with them from the East.

The funeral had of course been primarily a religious occasion. But
the Shiites, as a community, were notably absent from the entirely
political demonstrations that followed. Privately, many of them shared
the wider antipathy to Syrian domination, resenting among other
things the unfair competition which cheap Syrian labour, entering the
country *en masse*, posed to their own people, as well as the way in which
Syria waged its 'proxy war' against Israel without ever, like them,
having to pay the price in Israeli retaliation. But at the same time they
saw in Syria a natural external guardian of their interests; for it was,
after all, during its hegemony that their once impoverished, backward
and marginalized community had come in from the periphery of
Lebanon's sectarian politics to the central place it occupied now.[34] A
startling measure of the difference between Shiites and the rest came
in the form of an opinion poll about who they thought had killed
Hariri. Whereas the overwhelming majority of Christians, Sunnis and
Druzes said that Syria had, a mere 9.4 per cent of Shiites did so. In that
they were probably motivated more by political correctness than
sincere belief.[35] For they had a greater deference for their most

representative political organization – Hizbullah – than any other community had for theirs, given all that, in war and peace, it had achieved on their behalf; as a generally conservative, devout society in an era of revivalism there was also a religious dimension to their reverence for Sheikh Nasrallah. They therefore faithfully reflected Hizbullah's hopes and fears. And what Hizbullah feared was that, with Syria gone, there would come greatly intensified pressure on it to disarm, depriving it both of its basic vocation, *jihad*, and of the surreptitious leverage its weapons gave the Shiites, fearful of being brought low again, vis à vis everyone else.[36] It had little reason to love or trust the Baathists, with whom it had once come to blows, but, realistically, it could not turn against them now.

8 MARCH, 14 MARCH

On 8 March 2005, after a series of ever larger opposition demonstrations, Nasrallah stepped in with one of his own. Apologizing for the 'insults' which some of his compatriots had heaped on Syria, he swore that Lebanon would remain the country of 'Arabism, nationalism and resistance'.[37] With perhaps half a million attending, this was the largest yet. But it was a single-sect affair, and, with the party mobilizing its followers everywhere, a significantly regimented one too.

Undismayed by this impressive show of force, the opposition called for a yet greater one. And its followers rose to the occasion. This time, fully a million people converged on Martyrs' Square. That represented something between a quarter and a third of the entire population, 'equivalent', remarked Nadim Shehadi, a Lebanese scholar at Chatham House, 'to twenty million British demonstrators showing up at Trafalgar Square'.[38] The day on which this took place, 14 March, became the name of the political coalition to which the *Intifada* gave birth, just as '8 March' furnished the label by which Hizbullah and its friends identified themselves.

APRÈS MOI LE DÉLUGE

Thereafter it looked, for a while, as though the *Intifada*'s goals were being reached one by one. In March, the loyalist prime minister, Omar

Karami, was forced to resign. In April the Security Council called for an international investigation into Hariri's murder and, in a swift and humiliating withdrawal, the Syrian army ended its thirty-year sojourn in the country; officially, at least, Syrian intelligence bureaux went with it. In May and June, the anti-Syrian opposition, centred around the '14 March' coalition, won the four-stage parliamentary elections; it was not the landslide the late Hariri had hoped for, but, with 72 seats out of 128, they secured a majority in what was the most representative parliament since the end of the civil war, turning the pro-Syrian 'loyalists' into the new 'opposition'.[39] In September, at the behest of UN investigators, Lebanese police arrested the all-powerful Jamil Sayyid and three other barons of the joint 'security regime' as suspects in the Hariri killing. Their downfall electrified the Lebanese, and Arab commentators described it as 'an earthquake for the whole Arab region', one that could have 'the same impact [there] as the birth of the Solidarity trade union movement had had in eastern Europe twenty-five years ago, resulting in the collapse of the communist police state system'.[40] In October, the chief UN investigator Detlev Mehlis issued a first, interim report, which found 'probable cause to believe that the decision to assassinate ... Hariri could not have been taken without the approval of top-ranking Syria security officials'.[41] And the Security Council demanded, and in due course partially secured, the questioning of several heavyweights of the Baathist regime, including such relatives or intimates of Asad as his brother-in-law, Asef Shawkat, chief of military intelligence.

Then, for the first time since the Baathists seized power in 1963, a comprehensive array of Syrian opposition groups – secularists, Islamists, Kurds and prominent personalities – joined forces to issue their 'Damascus declaration', effectively offering themselves as an alternative to the regime. The US announced the establishment of a fund to 'accelerate the work of reformers' in Syria. A high-profile defector, former Vice President Abdul Halim Khaddam, forecast that the regime, already crumbling, would fall within a year.[42] Rumours swirled around Arab and Western capitals to the effect that Asad, in desperation, was preparing to play his last card – the prospect of his own collapse and Syria's consequent descent, Iraqi-fashion, into chaos, civil war, terror and Islamist fanaticism. That was a prospect, it was said, which should surely alarm the Americans almost as much as it was already alarming the Syrians themselves, and interest them in the grand bargain, emulating a precedent set by Colonel Gadafi of Libya, that Asad would offer them. He would yield up all his regional assets – control of Lebanon, Hizbullah, Palestinian militants, and the flow of jihadists into Iraq – in exchange for US guarantees of his continued mastery in his own house. Otherwise it would be *'après moi le déluge'*.[43]

SYRIA TURNS THE TIDE

But that was as far as it went. The low-hanging fruit fell not of its own accord, neither was it plucked. The Baathists weathered the storm. Regaining confidence at home, they counter-attacked in Lebanon. With their army's departure, their official public presence might have come to an end; but in other, surreptitious, and no less effective ways, they came back – if they had ever truly left in the first place. And nothing came, either, of what was to have been the automatic corollary of Syria's chastening: Hizbullah's too. On the contrary, the organization grew in defiance of all who sought to reduce it.

Lebanon's real emancipation from Syria, and its assimilation, in some way or other, of Hizbullah, might have come to pass had the *Intifada*, and what it stood for, truly imposed itself. The question of what it actually did stand for would have elicited different answers from different people. Suffice it to say, however, that for a great many, especially the younger, more educated or idealistic, their peaceful uprising meant more than merely ejecting the Syrians. It meant re-building Lebanon, state, institutions, society, on new and sounder foundations: thorough-going reform and modernization. Of central importance would have been a serious attempt, at long last, to address what had been an official objective ever since its enshrinement in the country's first, 1926 constitution – the phasing out of 'political sectarianism.' But to impose itself the *Intifada* needed to secure two main things: decisive mastery over the existing apparatus of power and the embrace of all the communities of which the sectarian state was composed. But it secured neither. Its potential may have been great, but, as a result of this failure, so were the countervailing forces that brought it to grief. Enough of the old, Syrian-backed order – embodied in President Lahoud and a residue of the joint 'security regime' – survived to thwart the rise of the new one. And the Shiites, as a community, stood outside it. In fact, far from overcoming the inherent divisions of Lebanese society, the *Intifada* only, in the end, led to their deepening, and to a crisis of national identity as profound as any the country had ever experienced. And, far from easing the inevitable consequence of internal rivalries – the interference of external ones – it intensified that too, with the Iranian-led, Islamo-nationalist camp backing the former, '8 March' order, and, in very diverse ways, Americans, Israelis and 'moderate' Arabs favouring the '14 March' new one. There were even fears of a new civil war.

To be sure, with the Syrian withdrawal, the balance of power had changed, and the '14 March majority', having won the elections, formed a new government under the premiership of Fuad Siniora, close friend and aide of the late Hariri. But even as the Syrians and their Lebanese friends seemed to be retreating, it was really a case of *reculer pour mieux sauter*.

'THE DIZZYING DUPLICITY OF LEBANON'S POLITICS'

The rot started with those parliamentary elections themselves. It was there that, to the disgust of many an Intifadist, the 'old politics' asserted themselves once more, there that 'people power' delivered the people back into the arms of the self-same elite of sectarian 'strongmen' that the system had always favoured.[44] Typically, rather than offering national agendas of a political or socio-economic kind, candidates in Lebanese elections make back-stage deals and alliances with the other candidates, be it of their own or another sect, who in their estimation can deliver them the most votes. What the Lebanese commentator Michael Young memorably and despairingly called the 'dizzying duplicity of Lebanese politics' could yield the bizarrest of bedfellows, and it did not fail to do so now.[45]

Thus it was that the most outspoken leader of the anti-Syrian camp, Jumblat, allied himself and his Druzes with those who were soon to become his polar opposite, Hizbullah and its Shiites. He did so at the expense of the man who would have been his most natural ally among the Maronites, General Michel Aoun, hero of the 1989 anti-Syrian 'liberation war' who had just returned, in the *Intifada*'s wake, from a fifteen-year exile in France. As for Aoun himself, while still insisting that Hizbullah should be disarmed, he did not hesitate, popular though he was in his own right, to ally himself with traditionally pro-Syrian Maronite personalities, such as Suleiman Frangieh, who boasted useful electoral machines.[46]

When it came to the formation of cabinets, the confessional system had its rules. And the chief one was that all the major sects be represented, and, however divergent the political tendencies which that brought together, all decisions had to be taken by consensus, or, failing that by a two-thirds majority vote which, in practice, was almost never achieved. Effectively, everyone had a veto over everything they didn't like. Although the new '14 March' parliamentary majority dominated the cabinet, what had become the new minority was represented there in the shape, most notably, of five ministers owing allegiance to Hizbullah and its ally Amal.

AN UNNATURAL MARRIAGE

With this, the latest stage of its 'Lebanonization', the puritanical Hizbullah was for the first time deigning to sully itself with the business of government.[47] Ironically, that meant joining an administration whose latent disposition was to oppose all it stood for. But that was precisely why it joined it. For, with Syria gone, it felt the need, in compensation, to insert itself more strongly into the Lebanese power structure. Syria's withdrawal, said deputy secretary-general Naim Qasim, 'made us directly responsible for providing the domestic protection in a better way than before'.[48] It was, however, an unnatural marriage from the outset, and before very long it led to tantrums, and then to virtual divorce.

At first the new government trod gingerly; in its opening policy statement, it praised the 'resistance' as 'a natural, honest expression of the Lebanese people's national right to liberate their land'.[49] A great many Lebanese still did not like that 'neo-imperial', pro-Israeli, anti-Hizbullah portion of 1559. In an opinion poll, 74 per cent of them said they supported the organization, and a large majority of all communities – especially Shiites, but Maronites too – opposed any idea of disarming it by force. Of the '14 March majority' leaders, Jumblat himself was the least responsive to America's clamour to bring the organization to heel, the least impressed by its consternation that a 'terrorist organization' should have been admitted to the government in the first place. International insistence on 1559, he said, threatened to bring Lebanon 'under foreign tutelage' and 'detach [it] from its Arab and Islamic belonging'.[50]

But as relations deteriorated between the new 'loyalists' on the one hand, and the '8 March' opposition and Syria on the other, the five Shiite ministers, protesting a violation of the consensus rule, staged a walk-out from the cabinet. Among the '14 March majority' it was Jumblat, the great 'prestidigitator'[51] of Lebanese politics, who now turned most strongly against the organization he had hitherto sought to accommodate. The 'war of liberation' was over, he said, Nasrallah should turn in his weapons and dismantle his 'state-within-a-state', for 'no country in the world allows an irregular militia to take law and order duties along with its regular forces'.[52] But Hizbullah would have none of it. Had not Nasrallah, in a rousing speech with this self-same Jumblat at his side, already warned: 'If anyone tries to disarm the resistance, we will fight him the way the martyrs fought in Karbala' and 'consider any hand that tries to seize our weapons an Israeli hand, and cut it off'?[53]

Hizbullah's fundamental reasons were its least admissible ones: its inability, on ideological grounds, to give up *jihad*, even if for the foreseeable future it was only able to practise it in symbolic 'gradualist-pragmatic' mode, and, intrinsically linked to that, its dependence on an Iran and Syria for which, were it bereft of its weapons, it would have lost almost all its utility. Publicly, therefore, it confined itself to 'Lebanese' arguments for its own indispensability. To those who said that it was wrong, unfair and ultimately dangerous for one community to retain the right to a militia when those of all the others had been disbanded, it retorted that it was not a militia but a resistance movement. This had been repeatedly, officially and, as it were, constitutionally acknowledged, most recently with the government's very own policy statement; furthermore, its weapons were 'national ones', never to be used against other Lebanese in order to 'defend or protect the Shiite community'.[54] That of course was only a promise, not a guarantee – all the less convincing at a time when, following the Syrian withdrawal, Hizbullah was increasingly turning back to sectarian loyalties as the basis of its public support, as well as closing ranks with its rival, Amal, in a manner liable to cause any move against itself to be interpreted as one against the Shiites as a whole.[55] To those who said that the 'resistance' had completed its mission, it retorted that it had not – there still remained the Sheba'a Farms.

And if, for many Lebanese, that was not a persuasive argument, it now trumped it with a grander one altogether. During a so-called 'national dialogue' between the country's major leaders, about a 'national defence' strategy and other contentious issues that were threatening to tear the country apart, it argued that Hizbullah itself, not the national army, should assume the principal burden of defence, since it, and it alone, had the capacity to 'deter' Israeli aggression. The 12,000 missiles of which Nasrallah now openly boasted would be the backbone of it. 'Today', he said, 'the whole of occupied northern Palestine [i.e. Israel] … its ports, its [military] bases, its factories, everything', lay within their range. There was no need, he added cryptically, 'for us to say whether they can reach beyond the north'.[56] To those who said that, instead of competing with the army, Hizbullah should become an effective part of it, it retorted that it could not, among other things because that would make it an easier target for the Israelis;[57] the most it could do, while retaining its organizational autonomy and freedom of action, was to 'co-ordinate' with the army. Finally, to the charge that, as a non-state actor, it was usurping functions that only belonged to a state, it retorted that 'when the state fails in carrying out some of its functions, society must help the state in carrying them out – even if the state doesn't ask'.[58]

JUST WHAT KIND OF A STATE WAS LEBANON?

And just what kind of state was Lebanon anyway? Or, rather, what kind of people were the '14 March majority' now heading it? This was the nub. It was not simply for operational reasons that Nasrallah refused to merge his *mujahideen* with the military; there were powerful political ones too. For he had no confidence at all in the government of which his organization was nonetheless a part. In any case, he contended that the 'majority' they claimed to represent was an 'illusory' one; Hizbullah itself stood for the real, the 'silent' majority, the majority of 'the true people'. Moreover, he pointed out, they were members of Lebanon's 'political elite', and, as such, much resented by the ordinary folk of every community for their endemic corruption, their intrigues and their egoism. In other words, who was really more representative of the nation's will, a Hizbullah whose leadership's probity and austerity not even its enemies impugned, or 'these giants' who thought only of their 'villas, wealth and bank accounts' as they 'made their empty speeches from behind their desks in their air-conditioned offices'?[59] Worst of all, it was their international allegiances that were suspect. 'What they had to do', said Nasrallah, 'was assure us that their decisions and positions are not dictated by Washington.'[60] For, as far as he was concerned, they were increasingly demonstrating the opposite.

It certainly did appear that the major Western powers were on their way back into Lebanon's internal affairs, not with their armies as in 1958 and 1982, but with their potent diplomacy. They conducted it largely via the United Nations. A string of Security Council resolutions reinforced and expanded the scope of 1559; a stream of rapporteurs and investigators were sent to monitor and enforce them. Had the UN, asked Nasrallah, ever appointed a single official to follow up, and make regular reports, on the progress of the countless resolutions which Israel had flouted down the decades? Of course not. But 'total international tutelage' was now 'being imposed on Lebanon and [Terj Roed-] Larsen [foremost of the UN officials dealing with Lebanon]' was 'the new high commissioner carrying the 1559 sword and using it to chase after the Lebanese, Palestinian and Syrian authorities'. Through this tutelage, he said, the so-called 'international community

... imposes its will, classifies people, passes judgement, differentiates, decides on the details and follows up on the smallest Lebanese issues'.[61]

'THEY NEVER LEFT IN TERMS OF THEIR CRIMINAL DEEDS'

If, for Hizbullah, the 14 March 'loyalists' were betraying Lebanon's Arab and Islamic identity by turning to the US, they, for their part, levelled a countervailing charge: the 8 March 'opposition' were instruments of foreign quarters too, in the shape of Syria and Iran. It appears, in fact, that it was less the matter of Hizbullah's weapons that really turned Jumblat against it than the way it behaved, within the government, as a fifth column on Syria's behalf. Nasrallah had considered Hariri to be his friend, called him a martyr, and agreed that establishing the 'truth' about the identity of his killers was a necessary and laudable task. But he strongly opposed the UN commission of investigation set up to carry it out. Like Syria itself, he said that the great powers were 'politicizing' it, and exploiting it as an instrument in their campaign against Syria, Hizbullah and an 'Arab' Lebanon. When the Lebanese cabinet decided – and by a majority, not a consensual, vote – to ask the UN to set up a mixed Lebanese–international tribunal to try any suspects the UN commission named, the cabinet's Shiite members 'suspended' their participation in the government. For Jumblat, Nasrallah was now no more than 'a tool in the hands of the Syrian regime', of the 'terrorist tyrant' Bashar al-Asad. Indeed, Hizbullah and its Amal allies did systematically seek to shield Syria and defend its interests in Lebanon. In early 2006, determined to secure full control of all the offices of state, the '14 March' coalition launched a campaign to impeach President Lahoud, held to be Syria's 'chief agent' and 'partner' in the murder of Hariri.[62] It was Hizbullah and Amal who chiefly foiled them – together with a surprise new recruit to the '8 March' opposition alliance, the once ferociously anti-Syrian general, Michel Aoun. Aoun was apparently determined that Lahoud should stay in place until it was sure that, with the Shiite vote behind him, he himself would be his successor.

Very useful to Syria though Hizbullah and Amal were, their exertions on its behalf only supplemented its own. 'The power and role of Syria in Lebanon are not dependent on the presence of Syrian forces there,' said Asad.[63] And so it amply proved. Conventional wisdom had it that he was ready, if need be, to turn Lebanon into 'another Iraq', so that he could then say to the world, as Jumblat put it, 'Look, the Lebanese are unable to rule themselves. We are the only people who can guarantee stability ... They never left in terms of their criminal deeds.'[64]

Sure enough, within weeks of Hariri's assassination, small bombs, gradually increasing in size, began to go off in public places. Then came the assassination of a string of anti-Syrian politicians and personalities. The first to die, in June 2005, was Samir Kassir, one of two journalists for whom Syrian intelligence apparently harboured a particular dislike;[65] a bomb, placed under the seat of his car, went off when he turned on the ignition. The other, Jibran Tweini, editor of *al-Nahar* and perhaps Syria's most fearlessly outspoken critic, died five months later. Within a day of his return from Paris, where he had taken refuge in the conviction that his name was at the top of Syria's 'hit-list', he was torn to shreds in the biggest and most sophisticated operation since the Hariri killing: a shaped-charge bomb struck his armour-plated four-wheel drive on a mountain road above Beirut.[66] Two months before, May Chidiac, a television talk-show host, had survived the loss of an arm and leg in another under-the-seat car-bomb. There was no such miraculous escape for George Hawi, a former communist party chief, and the first of the politicians to be so targeted.

If Syria, as most Lebanese believed, was indeed behind these seemingly effortless, ruthlessly efficient and always unsolved murders it had no shortage of willing perpetrators among the subversive networks its intelligence had left behind.[67] These suspicions found corroboration in a second, interim report from UN investigator Mehlis, who charged that, 'in order to create public disorder in response to any accusations of Syrian involvement' in the Hariri murder, Syria had supplied arms and ammunition for some of the bombings.[68] Top Syrian intelligence officials who had formerly been in charge of Lebanon were again sighted in various parts of the country, holding secret meetings to forge electoral alliances among their old Lebanese friends.[69] Pro-Syrian Palestinian guerilla organizations were reportedly smuggling in weapons on Syria's behalf.[70] Retaliation of another open and official kind came with Syria's resort to its time-honoured practice of closing Lebanon's only land frontiers to commercial traffic, costing it $300,000 a day. And when Mehlis pointed his finger of suspicion at Syria, it was against Lebanon that Asad poured out all his fury; it was, he said, 'a route, a manufacturer and financier ... for conspiracies', and Siniora was a 'slave' of the Americans.[71]

This vehemence and incitement of anti-Lebanese sentiment was part of a full-blooded counter-offensive which Asad now launched. In a keynote speech he told the Syrians that they were facing an American assault on their 'national identity and values' as an Arab people, that America wanted to destroy them, just as it had Iraq's. They had a choice, he said, between resistance and chaos. Palestine, and defiance of Western/Israeli schemes for it and the region, lay at the heart of it. It was a ringing, demagogic appeal to that pan-Arab nationalism – with its admixture of a specifically Syrian one – to which they, more than any other Arabs, remained deeply wedded. And the rallying-cry did rally. To be sure, the Syrians had little love for their ossified, decadent, corrupt and despotic regime, but much as they might yearn for change, they did not want America – champion of Zion, enemy of Arabism – to bring it. Even some of the small, liberal, secular opposition, soon to come under renewed oppression, went out of their way to show that the democratization they sought had nothing to do with the fact that America, in its 'missionary' self, apparently wanted it too. A great many Syrians did buy the official line that the Mehlis inquiry was biassed at their country's expense. And Baathist officials were probably right when they said that if Asad were to have made a spectacular, humiliating foreign policy volte-face, Gadafi-style, he would have 'lost his legitimacy and be laughed at by the people'.[72]

THE SHIITE CRESCENT

Then there was Iran. With 1559 and the expulsion of the Syrians, America had not merely planned to weaken or undermine the Baathist regime, but Iran too, and the whole Islamo-nationalist camp which it headed. That meant strengthening their own side – the so-called 'moderate' Arabs – in the perennially polarized Middle East. In its current form, the fault line went back to the 1979 Khomeini revolution. It had always had a sectarian hue to it; and it was this which, Shiite versus Sunni, now took on a new, virulent, region-wide and strategically unsettling intensity. The rise of Hizbullah in Lebanon was an already long-established manifestation of it. But the real turning point came after the invasion of Iraq – when what was supposed to have been the great 'transformational' moment of modern Middle Eastern history became pretty much the opposite of all that was expected of it.

Historically, Iraq was where the great schism of Islam had begun. Now, with the emancipation of its long-oppressed Shiite majority, it was erupting there anew. With the elections of January 2005, Shiites became the rulers – or at least the politically dominant community – of an Arab country for the first time in centuries, and a pivotal country at that. From now on, forecast Iranian scholar Vali Nasr, 'Shiites and Sunnis will compete over power, first in Iraq, but ultimately across the entire region.'[73] Sure enough, this electorally established ascendancy of the Iraqi Shiites deeply troubled the Sunni Arab establishment. For Jordan's King Abdullah, the great peril came from Iran, whose 'vested interest' was 'to have an Islamic republic of Iraq'. And he warned of a 'crescent' of Shiite movements stretching from the shores of the Gulf, via Iraq and Syria, to a Hizbullah-dominated Lebanon. 'This is the first time', said Lebanese commentator Joseph Samaha, 'that an Arab official has used such crude, direct and dangerous language to publicly incite against a particular confession and warn that it may turn into a fifth column to be used against the majority.'[74] President Mubarak of Egypt, however, outdid the King with his observation that 'most Shiites are loyal to Iran, not to the countries they live in'.

Iraq's Sunni minority resented their sudden, drastic loss of power, and the country steadily slipped towards an inter-communal civil war replete with atrocities that were if anything even more horrible than those of its Lebanese predecessor, and which only the Americans, themselves frequently under attack from both sides, could hold in check. As Iraq's troubles worsened, the alarm of other Arab countries grew, especially those in the Gulf that had substantial Shiite communities of their own, all of them nursing historical grievances against their

Sunni rulers. The Shiites were perhaps worst off in Saudi Arabia, where, constituting little more than 10 per cent of the total population but a majority in the oil-rich Eastern Province, they were still regarded as heretics by fiercely orthodox Wahhabite clerics. The Saudi foreign minister warned American policy-makers that full-scale civil war would not only 'dismember' Iraq for good, it would 'bring the whole region into a turmoil that would be hard to resolve'.[75] The Americans were later to discover that well over half the monthly flow of volunteer, Shia-hating Sunni jihadists infiltrating into Iraq came not from hostile countries such as Syria, but from its most important Arab ally, Saudi Arabia itself.

The 'Shiite crescent' was a misnomer, in that at least two of its supposed members, Syria and Hamas, did not, in their sectarian composition, properly belong to it at all. There were very few Shiites in Syria; if the Alawite minority which furnished the backbone of Baathist power could be described as Shiite at all it was at most a theologically esoteric, dissident sub-sect of the creed. As for its non-state members, only Hizbullah qualified by this criterion; Hamas (not to mention its lesser rival, Islamic Jihad) was entirely Sunni – and, as such, evidence, for Iran and Hizbullah, that their cause was not sectarian at all, but the truly pan-Islamic one they always claimed it to be. However, tensions *were* on the rise between the two great branches of Islam. Lebanon now had ample domestic reasons for its portion of them, but, inevitably, they both nourished and were nourished by the larger regional ones. If the worst came to the worst and another civil war broke out, it would differ, in its principal protagonists, from earlier ones; no longer would it mainly pit Christians against Muslims, it would be a mainly intra-Muslim, Shiite versus Sunni, affair. The physical flashpoints, the locations where scuffles and occasional shoot-outs were already occasionally breaking out, were no longer those – the Burj (or Martyrs' Square), the old Damascus Road, the 'Museum crossing' – that separated Christian East Beirut from its mainly Muslim West, they were all – Corniche Mazra'a, Tarik Jadide, Basta – neighbourhoods within the West where Shiite immigrants, spilling out from the *Dahiya*, lived cheek by jowl with the indigenous Sunnis. When skirmishes did erupt, they were as likely to be the product of regional tensions – between Saudi Arabia, say, and Iran, or Saudi Arabia and Syria – as they were of some strictly local quarrel. Lebanon, it seemed, had only thrown off Syrian overlordship to become, once more, the prize in a struggle for dominance over the whole Middle East. Its fortunes would mirror those of this larger contest. With the '14 March' Intifadists in disarray, Syria making its comeback, and Hizbullah more than holding its own, there could not be much doubt which side was by now in the greater trouble.

IRAN, VICTOR OF AMERICA'S WAR

By early 2006, virtually nothing of the neoconservative/Israeli grand design, be it the neo-imperial or the 'missionary', had been achieved, with regime change occurring in only one of the full seven or eight places where it had originally been hoped that it would. And that one, Iraq, was bidding fair, in the words of a retired American general, to become 'the greatest strategic disaster in US history'.[76] There, 'the cakewalk' was now 'the quagmire'. The Islamic Republic had always been seen as the greatest adversary, whose defeat would yield the commensurately greatest region-wide reward. But now, here it was, the only true victor of America's war. Now, more than ever, the Middle East could be defined, strategically, as the arena of a bipolar struggle between Iran on the one hand, America and Israel on the other. For its new, backwoods, millenarian president, Mahmoud Ahmadinejad, only America stood in the way of the regional supremacy that was Iran's 'incontestable right', an America, which, 'defeated' in Iraq, was but a 'sunset power' in its 'last throes' before the 'sunrise' of the Islamic Republic.[77] Like George Bush, he believed he was doing God's will. His government was paving the way for the 'return' of the Mahdi, or Hidden Imam, an event – associated in Shiite eschatology with 'chaos' and 'the end of days' – which he held to be imminent. Along with America's undoing, it would be preceded by the destruction of the Jewish state.[78] Unlike some others – including Ali Khamenei, the *Wali* himself – Ahmadinejad did not state that Israel must be 'wiped out' with quite the explicitness that most Western news agencies reported him as doing. He merely quoted 'our dear Imam', Khomeini, to the effect that 'this Jerusalem-occupying regime must disappear from the pages of time'.[79] Slightly milder this formulation might have been, but, constantly reiterated, it was hardly reassuring, especially given other outrages he perpetrated, such as his theatrical espousal of Holocaust-denial or his proposal that, if there really had been such a genocide, then Europe should make amends for it by relieving the Palestinians of the Jewish state themselves. But the main reason it agitated Israeli leaders and caused them to take such furious note of an annihilationist discourse they had formerly belittled[80] was the vigour which the new president imparted to Iran's nuclear programme – a programme, he intimated, the Mahdi himself was in charge of and would additionally speed his 'return'.[81]

In April 2006, Iran mastered the fuel cycle, enriching uranium to a level of 3.5 per cent, enough to power a reactor though not to produce a bomb. With this, said an exultant Ahmadinejad, his country had now entered 'the nuclear club of nations', thereby 'turning [it] into the biggest power in the Middle East and [changing] all the power equations in the region and beyond'.[82] For the Israelis and 'the Lobby' this was nothing less than the rise of Hitler all over again; the 'parallels' were 'stunning in their likeness, eerie in their implications'.[83] America's friends in the Sunni Arab establishment were not happy either, with some of them, especially in the Gulf, deeming a potentially nuclear Iran to be an even more threatening prospect than the already existing Israeli nuclear capability.[84] But they spurned America's call to 'stand firm' against it, largely because they knew that, for their people and especially their Islamists, the real enemy was still Israel, not Iran. And with America, its popularity in the region at an all-time low, backing its detested protégé more unashamedly than ever, their people could not but marvel at a jumped-up country bumpkin who was doing what none of them would ever have dared to do themselves. For Ahmadinejad exhibited nothing but contempt for the hypocrisy embedded in the West's insistence that Israel's monopoly on nuclear weapons was a *fait accompli* that no regional power should challenge, and its implicit presumption that an Iran in the possession of nuclear weapons would be any greater menace to the Middle East and the world than Israel itself.

SUPPORTING DEMOCRACY — BUT NOT DEMOCRATICALLY
ELECTED GOVERNMENTS

The 'missionary' side only made matters worse. Wherever there were elections, which America claimed some credit for promoting, the wrong kind of people — 'radical', Islamist, nationalist and anti-American – kept winning them, or, at least, faring much better than the right, 'moderate' and peace-loving kind, whom democracy was supposed to have encouraged and empowered. True, in Lebanon, the 'Cedar revolutionaries' had won in their elections; but Hizbullah had done very well too, as had the single most popular Maronite leader, General Aoun, who then proceeded – shortly after being received by neoconservatives in Washington – to enter into a formal alliance with it. In Iraq, it was Islamists, notably Iran-friendly Shiite ones, who came out on top, not the secular modernists the Americans had been counting on. In Egypt, the Muslim Brotherhood achieved remarkable gains in the face of severe obstructionism. But the most spectacular upset was the Hamas victory in the West Bank and Gaza. Although this actually constituted the most exemplary, authentic and peaceable rotation of power in recent Arab history, Bush was aghast. 'We support democracy', he said, 'but that doesn't mean we have to support governments elected as a result of democracy'; and his Administration set in motion nefarious and decidedly undemocratic schemes to achieve 'regime change' in reverse. America's adversaries, Iran and Syria, were no great democrats themselves, but, ironically, it was they that the Hamas triumph strengthened, America's 'moderate' friends that it weakened. Calling it 'proof that God's promises come true', Iran once more cast itself as the stoutest champion of the Arabs' most sacred cause.[85] For Israel, on the other hand, Iran and Syria, Hizbullah and Hamas, were now forging a 'new terror axis' that could trigger 'the first world war of the twenty-first century'.[86]

What was to be done? Nothing – neither carrots nor sticks – worked with Iran, and nothing probably ever would, short of a 'grand bargain' involving American acceptance of the legitimacy of the Islamic Republic. The mullahs seemed to be ready for one, but the Bush Administration clearly was not. So was it not time to resort to military means, to the 'pre-emptive' force ever central to neoconservative/ Israeli doctrine? By the spring of 2006, it looked as though it was. Fears of an imminent US strike were at their height. The British government, America's partner in Iraq, was said to believe that war was now 'inevitable'.[87] Some even said that, with US 'special forces' active inside the country, war had already begun. Pundits debated what form the full-blown assault would take. Would it be limited to hits on nuclear-related sites, or a sustained assault against a much wider range of political and military targets, Revolutionary Guards, intelligence departments or even leaders of the regime itself? Another burning question: might 'bunker-busting' tactical nukes have to be used against installations that were dispersed around the country and buried up to twenty-five metres deep, beneath reinforced concrete and earth?[88]

Had it actually come to war, said Scott Ritter, the former UN arms inspector, it would have been 'a war ... made in Israel and nowhere else', even more flagrantly than it had been in the case of Iraq.[89] And the plain fact was that Israel, and the 'friends of Israel' in the US, were now putting immense pressure on the Administration to take immediate action, and intimating, with more than a hint of blackmail, that if the US did not do the job, Israel might take it on itself – come what may for both.

But war did not come. In fact, even as they mounted, these expectations of an attack generated a counter-current of profound scepticism. Was it really possible that, after the fiasco of Iraq, President Bush would, as many put it, be 'mad enough' to risk another one by attacking the infinitely more formidable Iran? Would the US Army, already restive, or the general public stand for it?[90] Experts like retired Air Force colonel Sam Gardiner were unequivocal. War games he had conducted left him with 'two simple sentences for policymakers: You have no military solution for the issues of Iran. And you have to make diplomacy work.'[91] Other such exercises similarly concluded that Iranian retaliation could indeed be quite as 'devastating' as its leaders repeatedly threatened that it would be. With their Russian-built, 'Sunburn' anti-ship cruise missile, by far the world's most advanced weapon of the kind, they could turn the Persian Gulf into a death trap for the US fleet, causing its confined, shallow, manoeuvre-impeding

1 2

waters to 'run red with American blood'.[92] They could launch missile barrages against US forces in Iraq, then engage them on the ground, through Iranian para-military forces infiltrated into the country or, irony of ironies, through the pro-Iranian Iraqi militias patronized by the American-backed, Shiite-dominated Iraqi government itself. They could close the Straits of Hormuz, depriving the world of two-fifths of its oil supplies, and push the price of crude to stratospheric heights. And, of course, they could get Hizbullah to unleash its arsenal of missiles on Israel.

Sure enough, the US did, all of a sudden, revert to diplomacy – relatively conciliatory diplomacy at that – joining Russia, China, Britain, Germany and France in new, collective proposals for a negotiated solution to the dispute. But by this time it had also given its blessing for a war against someone else. It cannot be said that Bush decided to let Israel attack Hizbullah for the sole, simple reason that, for the time being at least, he himself had developed cold feet about attacking Iran. But it would have been quite logical if he had; if, in other words, instead of the US going after the main enemy, it delegated its protégé to go after the subsidiary one. After all, those missiles poised to rain down on Israel which Nasrallah called Lebanon's 'deterrent' were effectively Iran's too. Mindful of domestic Lebanese sensibilities, Hizbullah pooh-poohed the idea that, if Iran *were* attacked, it would react on its behalf,[93] but it was pretty clear to everyone that it very well might. For Israel, therefore, destroying Hizbullah would not only be an inestimable gain in itself, but a great strategic and psychological blow to its patron, rendering an eventual assault on it significantly less hazardous than it would otherwise have been. Nor could it be said – from the evidence so far available – that Israel, with US connivance, was actively conspiring to provoke this war, not, at least, to the extent that it had the last one, the Fifth Arab–Israeli War of 1982.[94]

A WAR WAITING TO HAPPEN

What can be said, however, is that this, the Sixth in the series, was a war waiting to happen, or, as British scholar Fred Halliday put it, a 'regional conflict long planned, if suddenly, almost casually, detonated'.[95] 'Of all

Israel's wars since 1948', said Gerald Steinberg of Israel's Bar-Ilan University, 'this was the one for which Israel was most prepared. In a sense, the preparation began in May 2000, immediately after the Israeli withdrawal ...'[96] The US knew of Israel's plans at least a year beforehand; in Powerpoint presentations to diplomats, journalists and think tanks, a senior Israeli officer had been laying them out in 'revealing detail'.[97] In the summer of 2006 several Israeli officials went to Washington to get 'a green light' for 'a bombing operation' and, with the help of two high-powered neoconservatives in the White House, they soon secured it from Bush himself.[98] In fact, the Administration had already been 'agitating for some time ... for a preemptive blow against Hizbollah', realizing, however, that Israel would have to be the one to administer it. According to Seymour Hersh, the renowned investigative reporter, the Bush Administration was chiefly interested in an Israeli attack as the prelude to an American strike on Iran; the way Israel 'hunt[ed] down and bomb[ed] missiles, tunnels and bunkers from the air ... would be a demo for Iran'. Bush had another objective too. Lebanon's Western-backed government had failed to dismantle Hizbullah by persuasion. Getting that done by force should enable it to assert its authority over the whole country, then turn it into a model of 'freedom and democracy' in the Middle East.[99] In this connection, Secretary of State Condoleezza Rice, not Israeli Prime Minister Olmert, was said to be the 'the leading figure' in 'the strategy of changing the situation in Lebanon'.[100] Furthermore, the Administration was in a hurry for the Israelis to act. 'Look,' they were told, 'if you guys have to go, we're behind you all the way. But we think it should be sooner rather than later – the longer you wait, the less time we have to evaluate and plan for Iran before Bush leaves office."[101] Having already decided that he would respond to any kidnapping of Israeli soldiers with 'a broad military operation',[102] all that Olmert needed was a pretext. And on 12 July 2006 Hizbullah furnished it. 'The War with Iran has Begun', ran the next morning's headline in one of New York's more extravagantly pro-Israel newspapers.[103]

CHAPTER THIRTEEN

The Sixth War

2006

OPERATION TRUE PROMISE

About 8.45 a.m., that fateful July day, seven men of the 91st Division, responsible for guarding Israel's frontier with Lebanon, set out in two armoured Humvees on their daily patrol along the central sector. It was their last day in three and a half weeks of reserve duty, and they all had the happy 'end-of-term' feeling which the prospect of getting home again that evening induced. But it was not to be. Just after nine o'clock, when they reached a particularly exposed spot, Hizbullah special forces, lying in wait on the other side of the border, opened up with heavy machine-gun and anti-tank fire on the second of the vehicles, so as to prevent it from coming to the rescue of the first, about a hundred metres ahead of it. They killed its three occupants. Simultaneously, another Hizbullah party, who had cut their way through the barbed-wire security fence during the night, fired two rocket-propelled grenades into the first Humvee. They wounded two soldiers, who managed to hide in nearby bushes, and pulled out two others, also wounded. As Hizbullah positions unleashed a barrage of diversionary shelling, the raiders slipped unseen back across the frontier, taking their hostages, sergeants Udi Goldwasser and Eldad Regev, with them. It took the 91st Division, confused, clumsy and locally under-manned, nearly two hours to mount the mere semblance of a pursuit. But hardly had the single tank engaged in it crossed the border than it ran over a Hizbullah-laid mine; its four-man crew were killed outright. Yet another soldier – the eighth of the day – died in a hail of Hizbullah mortar fire.[1]

Operation True Promise – as Hizbullah called it – came as no surprise. There had been a number of such attempts before, and the 'promise' it referred to was the one which Nasrallah had repeatedly, publicly made: that Hizbullah would not rest until it had secured the freedom of Samir Quntar, the longest-serving of Lebanese prisoners in Israel, and three others. Quntar was a Druze, not a Shiite, and the terror exploit for which he was convicted took place, in the service of a minor Palestinian guerilla organization, long before Hizbullah had even come into being. In a recent speech, Nasrallah had assured him that the hopes of freedom he had placed in the resistance were 'sound' and that 'the coming days and the spilled blood' would 'prove me right'.[2]

Immediately after the hostage-taking, Nasrallah told a press conference that Goldwasser and Regev would only be released, through indirect negotiations, in exchange for Lebanese and Palestinian prisoners. And he made it clear that, as far as he was concerned, Hizbullah's *coup de force* fell within the strictly national, Lebanese objectives of its struggle; it therefore did not justify any Israeli response outside the post-withdrawal 'rules of the game.' The most he seems to have been expecting was that Israel would 'just retaliate a bit, bomb a couple of targets and that would be the end of it'.[3] What he actually got was – according to him – beyond his wildest imagining. Neither he nor any of his fifteen-man leadership had rated at higher than one per cent the chances that Israel would resort to violence on the scale it did. If it had been otherwise, he said, he would not have agreed to the operation, 'nor would Hizbullah, the prisoners in Israel gaols or the families of the prisoners ... absolutely not, for humanitarian, moral, social, security, military and political reasons'.[4] Certainly, all prior evidence did suggest that Nasrallah never wanted a full-scale war, and, to his listeners, these post-war revelations sounded very much like his *mea culpa* for bringing one about.

If error it truly was then it was an extraordinary one, especially on the part of a leader who made such a point of 'knowing' his enemy. The passivity with which the Israelis had tended to respond to all

Hizbullah's border operations in the six years since they withdrew had apparently bred in him and his colleagues an *idée fixe*, comparable to the conviction – held by Israeli generals before the 1973 Arab–Israeli War – that Egypt would never even dare to send its army across the Suez Canal.

'WHAT HAVE YOU DONE?'

The Lebanese prime minister, for one, didn't agree with it at all. 'What *have* you done'? Fuad Siniora asked Hussein Khalil, an aide to Nasrallah whom he had called to his office. When Khalil assured him that 'it will calm down in twenty-four to forty-eight hours', Siniora pointed to the Gaza Strip, and what the Israelis had wrought there since Palestinian militants had abducted a soldier three weeks before. 'Lebanon is not Gaza,' Khalil calmly replied.[5]

But Lebanon *was* Gaza – and with a vengeance. Olmert may only have been waiting for a pretext to clobber Hizbullah, but the abduction was already provocation enough in its own right. Nothing exasperated the Israelis like the capture of their soldiers. Not only did this second one come hard on the heels of the first, the two, though carried out by different organizations on different fronts, were also clearly linked, politically, emotionally, and possibly even operationally. If the first already constituted a blow to Israel's 'deterrent power', the second multiplied it greatly. In Lebanon, therefore, Israel would surely have to out-Gaza Gaza.

And Gaza was already quite something. The abduction, there, of Corporal Gilad Shalit had been an almost perfectly executed commando raid against a strictly military target. One of Israel's more sober commentators called it 'almost legitimate'.[6] In their attack on an Israeli border position, a combined force of Hamas and other groups had killed two soldiers and spirited Shalit back to Gaza through the tunnel they had dug under the frontier for the purpose. This had come in the course of, and as express retaliation for, an Israeli military campaign in which some seventy-five Palestinians had already died, as compared with not one Israeli, be it among soldiers in combat or civilians exposed to the primitive, home-made Qassam rockets which the Palestinians had been firing into the border town of Sderot. Among its more recent victims had been the eight people – including three children – killed, and thirty-two wounded, in an artillery barrage that caught them picnicking on the beach.[7]

In response, Israel effectively re-invaded the Gaza from which it had 'disengaged', settlers and all, the year before. Its official aim – in Operation Summer Rains – was to secure Shalit's unconditional release. But its real reasons were two-fold. The first was to restore its 'deterrent power', its dented aura of invincibility, ideally by a brilliant rescue of the hostage himself. The other was to use its overwhelming military superiority to engineer a wholesale change in its wider political and strategic environment – in this instance to overthrow, or thoroughly emasculate, the democratically installed, Hamas-controlled government of Gaza. Thus, regardless of the risk that Shalit's captors might kill him in retaliation, it stepped up its already harsh military campaign, killing a further 300 Palestinians, many of them civilians, before it was over, arresting eight Hamas cabinet ministers and twenty newly elected parliamentarians, bombarding ministries, a university and the central power station, and turning what was already an internationally acknowledged 'humanitarian crisis' into something more like a 'humanitarian catastrophe'.

Lebanon was also Gaza because Hizbullah itself had made it so. True, in keeping with his 'national' rationale for taking Israeli hostages, Nasrallah denied that the exploit had anything to do with the punishment Israel was visiting on the Palestinians. But that was a pro forma denial that few took seriously. 'When the whole world does not react to Israel's attacks', asked Abd al-Wahhab al-Badrakhan in the pan-Arab newspaper *al-Hayat*, 'how do you expect resistance groups such as Hizbullah … to react?'[8] Solidarity with the Palestinian struggle had always constituted the main, practical expression of its universalist *jihad*. And if it had not done at least *something* to manifest that now it would have disappointed both itself and its army of admirers, Islamist or secular, everywhere. It would have begun to look not so very different from the Arab regimes it so despised. And *they* were doing almost nothing at all. Perhaps – as Talal Salman, the editor of the Beirut newspaper *al-Safir*, sardonically surmised – the kings and presidents were too busy watching the World Cup.[9] At any rate, insofar as they did bestir themselves it was virtually to take Israel's side. While failing to raise a whimper about the 10,000 prisoners in Israeli gaols, they were competing, through pressure on the Palestinians, to secure the release of the one and only Israeli one.

THE RETURN TO UNIVERSAL JIHAD

So when, to the consternation of the 'moderate' Arabs and the fury of the Israelis, Hizbullah proceeded to capture two more soldiers, it was, in effect, re-dedicating itself to the jihadist mission which, in its strictly Lebanese self, it had ostensibly renounced. And it was doing so, of course, as a spearhead of the Iranian-led, Islamo-nationalist camp to which, in its non-Lebanese self, it belonged. For the Israelis, this was the Middle East's 'new terror axis' in action. Indeed, it was the very thing they had been expecting; in the early stages of their Gaza onslaught, their army had raised its level of alert on the Lebanese frontier from two to four on a scale of five. And it was specific information, not just strategic prognosis, that prompted this precaution. Signals intelligence had picked up conversations between Khalid al-Mesha'al, the Hamas leader in Damascus, his counterparts in Gaza and Hizbullah in Lebanon. What they apparently revealed was that, even as Hamas was plotting its hostage-taking in the south, Hizbullah was preparing to 'warm things up' in the north.[10]

When Israel went to war on Lebanon its main, official objective was the rescue of its abducted soldiers. But, even more emphatically than in the case of Gaza, it was not the real one. That was not simply because, within a couple of hours, Israel knew that rescue would be all but impossible, or because, within a couple of days, it was pretty sure that both were already dead anyway, killed during the abduction or succumbing to their wounds soon after.[11] Israel, said Olmert, was now engaged in a two-front struggle whose objective was to create two 'new orders' on Israel's borders, one in a Gaza without Hamas and the other in a Lebanon without Hizbullah.[12] It was the second of these tasks on which, with Operation Just Reward, it now impetuously embarked.

'NASRALLAH MUST DIE'

Israel's strategy for the destruction of Hizbullah came in two parts.[13] One, exclusively military, was to take it on directly. The other – military in method but essentially political in purpose – was to inflict escalating pain and punishment on the Lebanese state and people until, turning against the delinquent in their midst, they disarmed it as Security Council Resolution 1559 required them to do. It was, in other words, the same strategy Israel had repeatedly used in Lebanon before, first against the Palestinians, and then against Hizbullah; it was those dress rehearsals – Operations Accountability, 1993, and Grapes of Wrath, 1996 – writ large.

'We expected Hizbullah to break the rules,' said Amir Peretz, the Israeli defence minister, 'so now we will break *it*.'[14] Israeli columnists, usually close reflectors, in military matters, of the mood and purpose on high, waxed bellicose about the fate awaiting the organization and its leader, who had by now achieved very special, demonic status in their nation's always well-stocked pantheon of foreign villains. 'Hizbullah', Ben Kaspit, of *Maariv* newspaper, typically wrote, 'must come out of this beaten, bruised, crawling, bleeding and screaming. It cannot be allowed to approach the border fence again. Its rocket storage facilities must be eliminated. The threat must be ended. Nasrallah must die.' For was he not the father of the 'spider's web theory', the one that said that 'Israeli society was weakening, softening, about to collapse in the face of the great Islamic resistance ... The event through which [Israel was] now passing [would] determine its fate for years to come, maybe beyond ... Not for nothing [were] comparisons being made with ... World War II, and the British resilience against Hitler's blitz. Because Messrs Ahmadinejad, Nasrallah and Mesha'al [were] as dangerous as Hitler, maybe even more so.'[15]

This was a test in which Israel would be under scrutiny by 'the entire Middle East'. Hence it was to the whole region, Iran and Syria in particular, that Israel had to send its reply: a display of 'overwhelming military might' telling it, in effect, that its 'proxy wars against Israel [would] no longer be tolerated'.[16]

As for the other, 'Lebanese' part of its strategy, Israel had a simple rationale for that. What Hizbullah had done, it said, was not merely 'a terrorist attack'; since Hizbullah was a part of the Lebanese government it was also an 'act of war' by one sovereign state against another. So Lebanon had to 'bear the consequences of its action'. And these, said Olmert, would be 'very, very, very painful'. One of his generals, Uzi Adam, commander of the northern front, said that 'everything, not just the line of Hizbullah positions', was now a 'legitimate' target. If the hostages were not returned, said Chief of Staff Dan Halutz, Israel would turn back 'Lebanon's clock by twenty years'. It would do this by hitting civilian, or 'infrastructural', targets. He did not explicitly spell that out at the time, though that is what he meant. His strong opinions were well known, and in the Israeli cabinet debate about whether – or rather to what extent – the army should go down that route, he was a constant advocate of its doing so.[17] But spelling it out at such a time would have been impolitic; after all, he was the head of an institution which still styled itself 'the most moral army in the world'.[18] And more importantly, the Israelis knew from past experience that America's tolerance of its excesses in Lebanon, though great, was not inexhaustible, that however much support they unfailingly secured from their superpower patron at the outset of their repeated military campaigns there, the more the civilian casualties they inflicted during them the more they risked eroding it in the end. In 1982, it had been General Sharon's indiscriminate air, land and sea bombardment of Beirut which finally moved a very indulgent President Reagan to angry demands for a halt. And they certainly did not need another Qana, that massacre of more recent memory which, more than anything else, had brought Operation Grapes of Wrath to its wholly unsuccessful close.

'A WAR OF CHOICE WHICH WE STARTED'

Israel was a warrior-state. From Ben-Gurion, the 'founder', to Sharon, last of the founders' generation, its most famous leaders had mostly been military, or quasi-military, men. Neither Olmert nor his defence minister fitted into this mould. Yet no one had ever taken Israel into any of its wars so swiftly, decisively and with such apparent nonchalance as they did now. It was almost as if, said a *Haaretz* columnist, they 'wanted to show that they were smarter, braver and more combative' than the legendary 'Arab-fighter', felled by a stroke, into whose shoes Olmert had so accidentally stepped.[19] In his last years, Sharon, mindful of his earlier, monumental misadventures there, had indeed been circumspect about Lebanon, resisting all temptation to go back in. How ironic, then, that his rookie of a successor was now, with Sharon-like boldness, doing precisely that.

However, neither Olmert – nor 'a defence minister who didn't have a clue about defence'[20]– derived their bravura entirely from themselves. They were heavily dependent for professional advice on the man who officially represented the military in their counsels. This was the chief of staff. And not only was Dan Halutz as eager for action as they were, as the first air force commander to hold that post he was the bearer of a particularly appealing message: that Israel could break Hizbullah with air power alone, and that a ground operation might not be needed at all.

With such authority behind them, they could not but be further emboldened down the headlong path on which they were already set. Not surprisingly, then, they devoted very little of a critical, three-hour, eve-of-war emergency cabinet meeting to the consideration of alternatives – diplomacy, negotiation, a limited local retaliation, or just a cool reflection on the situation. 'We're skipping the stage of threats', said Peretz afterwards, 'and going straight to action.'[21] They did not actually say that this action would amount to war; it would only – they implied – be some very much larger, more aggressive kind of retaliatory operation than usual; 'thundering' was the epithet Olmert favoured.[22] But war was what it would very quickly, and inevitably, prove to be. Not a 'defensive' war, still less a 'war of survival', though some politicians and pundits tried to suggest that it was, particularly in the context of Iran's ambitions to 'wipe Israel out'. No, basically, it was yet another of those 'initiated' wars in which Israel used 'military force to achieve political goals'. That was how an official inquiry, the 'Winograd commission', subsequently described it. Or it was another 'war of choice' which 'we started' – in the words of an officer who fought in it.[23]

IT WAS GOING TO BE QUICK AND EASY

It was going to be cheap and easy. So at least the ministers believed –
though they did have different ideas about just how long it might take.
Peretz thought it would be ten to fourteen days, Olmert that 'Lebanon
would be pounded from the air for a few days, during which time Israel
would weather Katyusha fire until Hizbullah sued for a ceasefire.'
Foreign Minister Tzipi Livni somehow persuaded herself that it would
be all over by the following day.[24] But, whatever its length, it was going
to be devastating – vintage 'shock and awe' – for the enemy. According
to *Maariv*'s Amir Rapaport, that 'well-oiled machine', the Israeli
Defence Force, was 'going to run amok ... in a very calculated manner.
The brakes [were] off and soon it would be difficult to find any trace of
Hizbullah conference halls in the heart of the "southern suburbs"
where Nasrallah put on his arrogant performances.'[25] Alex Fishman, of
Yediot Aharonot, forecast 'a few days of firestorm, particularly from the
sky, which [wouldn't] leave a single Hizbullah installation standing.
Every corner that [carried] the stamp of Hizbullah – command centres,
camps, forts, convoys, warehouses, and offices – [would] be hit.' The
air force would also go after other 'legitimate' targets, 'the interests of
the Shiite community' as well as [non-Shiite] 'power centres' which
'don't really care if an Israel soldier is kidnapped as long as they themselves aren't harmed'.[26]

In the eyes of its begetters, Just Reward began very well indeed. In
the first few days, the F-16 fighter-bombers and the Apache helicopter
gunships struck at a plethora of targets. Some were pre-eminently
civilian and 'Lebanese'; some were military/strategic/logistical and
'Hizbullahi'. Some, in varying proportions, were both. A few seemed to
make no sense at all. First among the high-profile, 'infrastructural'
installations to be hit was Beirut's brand-new international airport, its
runways disabled in a dawn raid. Then came roads and bridges whose
destruction was meant to impede Hizbullah's movement of weapons
and materiel. By day two, it was the turn of the *Dahiya*, headquarters
of Hizbullah, but also home to hundreds of thousands of ordinary
Shiites. The warplanes were trying to kill Nasrallah and his leadership
in what they supposed to be his subterranean bunker; they unleashed

twenty-three tons of high explosives on it in a single raid. In the process, they reduced street upon street of apartment blocks – whose residents Hizbullah had already advised to leave – to a smoking rubble, a 'ground zero, New York, writ large'.[27] Fifty-five people, overwhelmingly civilians, died in the first full day of fighting; more than 300 within a week. Sixteen perished in a single air strike on a convoy leaving the southern village of Marwaheen after Israeli leaflets had warned its inhabitants to get out while they could;[28] they were just a few of the unlucky ones among hundreds of thousands now fleeing northwards in this, the fifth such exodus since 1978. Twenty soldiers died in attacks on army barracks. Moving lorries became fair game; but those that paid the price were not transporting Hizbullah weaponry, only emergency supplies, such as medical equipment from the United Arab Emirates. It was a total land, sea and air blockade, and ports and jetties up and down the coast were targeted to enforce it. So were power plants, fuel depots, petrol stations, television masts, radar stations and a brand-new lighthouse off Beirut's famous Corniche; three people, two of them Belgian technicians, died in the bombing of 'Liban Lait', a dairy factory in Baalbek.

'WE'VE WON THE WAR'

The attackers' one, indisputable achievement was perhaps their nearest thing – for all the 'collateral damage' – to a truly military one. It came in their very first operation. In the thirty-four minutes which – according to the Israeli account – this took, they destroyed fifty-nine stationary rocket launchers, as well as half to two-thirds of Hizbullah's stock of medium-range rockets – mainly Iranian-built Fajrs – concealed in the homes of Hizbullah activists in south Lebanon.[29] As first reports of the raid came in, soon after midnight on 12/13 July, Halutz telephoned the prime minister and proudly informed him of the results. Then, after a short pause, he added: 'We've won the war.'[30] It must have been a major setback for Hizbullah. But whatever the demoralizing effect it might have had on it, this was hardly commensurate with the tonic it was for Olmert and Peretz. They were literally enchanted, and even likened it to that epic in the annals of

modern warfare, the pre-emptive strike that all but completely
destroyed the Arab air forces in the first few hours of the Six-Day War.
They also deemed it incontestable proof of their own boldness, savvy
and stern resolve. Olmert delivered a 'Churchillian' speech. When
some people, sensing that it might not have been quite the decisive
blow he thought, urged him to look for ways of ending hostilities before
the tide of conflict turned to Israel's disadvantage, he and his ministers
were scornful. They were too caught up in the 'euphoria of a mighty
Israel exacting revenge on its enemies' to listen to such advice.[31] And
who – asked a leading commentator – was this Nasrallah anyway? Who,
indeed, but 'a little man, frightened, fanatic, misleading and misled?
Sometimes he's a liar, usually a braggart. The mouse that roared. People
are in hiding, his chain of command is paralyzed, and the world is
against him.' And his organization? 'Not an army, not half, or quarter,
of an army. Not even a brave guerilla group … most of its efforts have
been devoted to putting on marches in the streets of Beirut.'[32]

'A SECOND WAR OF INDEPENDENCE'

If the war itself was going in Israel's favour, so, at first, were most of
the circumstances that surrounded it. Many Israelis had come to see
their country's earlier interventions in Lebanon as something like
'their Vietnam'. But, according to the opinion polls, a good 95 per cent
of the public, outraged by Hizbullah's action, stood four-square
behind this one, and most thought it should go on till Hizbullah had
been wiped out.[33] Some persuaded themselves that it was tantamount
to a 'second war of independence'. The activist 'peace camp' was
divided, with only a small minority coming out against it. Even after
hundreds of Lebanese civilians had been killed, one of the movement's
intellectual luminaries, the novelist Amos Oz, wrote that 'there could
be no moral equation between Hizbullah and Israel', because
'Hizbullah [was] targeting Israeli civilians wherever they [were], while
Israel [was] targeting mainly Hizbullah.'[34] The day after the war's only
conscientious objector went to prison, the leader of Peace Now, Yariv
Oppenheimer, told *Haaretz* newspaper that he felt like strangling
him.[35]

OUTRAGE IN LEBANON

Nor was it any secret that much of Lebanese public opinion was almost as outraged, from its perspective, as the Israelis were from theirs. The '14 March majority' politicians and press were almost unanimous. They had long charged that of all the rights of a sovereign state which Hizbullah had effectively usurped the most fundamental, and dangerous, was the right to decide on matters of war and peace. And now here it was, acting on that 'right' without consulting anyone, including the government of which it was formally a part. In addition to the unilateral arrogance and irresponsibility of Hizbullah itself, they saw the malign hand of its regional supporters. This, said Jumblat, was both Ahmadinejad pursuing Iran's nuclear trial of strength with Israel and the West, and Asad trying at any price to re-establish Syrian control of Lebanon and prevent the establishment of an international tribunal to try the killers of Rafiq Hariri. And why, asked Hariri's son, Saad, should Lebanon always be 'the front through which others seek to fight Israel' when 'their own fronts' – by which he meant Syria's Golan – had been absolutely quiet these thirty years?[36] The spurned and unconsulted government formally disassociated itself from the Israeli soldiers' abduction. But privately – or so at least the Israelis believed – the '14 March' camp actually went much further than that; it was 'downright happy' to see Israel attacking Hizbullah, and hoped that it would destroy it.[37]

'BREAK HIZBULLAH'S SPINE'

The larger Arab stance was no less gratifying to Israel. The day after the abduction Saudi Arabia announced that a distinction had to be made between 'legitimate resistance' and 'uncalculated adventures' undertaken by 'elements inside Lebanon and those behind them'. These 'elements' were exposing Arab nations 'to grave dangers'; it was up to them, and them alone, to 'end the crisis which they [had] created'. The two other leading 'moderate' states, Egypt and Jordan, quickly followed suit. This was something quite unprecedented in the history of Arab–Israeli conflict: the first time that one group of Arabs, and a very significant one at that, was aligning itself more closely with 'the Zionist foe' than with other Arabs doing battle against it. Their concern was with Iran as much as it was with its Lebanese protégé. In Cairo, the editor of the government daily *al-Gumhuriyah* discerned nothing less than 'an Iranian plan ... to destroy the Arab states from within ... and turn the entire Arab world into armed militias like Hizbullah'.[38] Sectarian incitement took an exceptionally virulent turn. In Saudi Arabia, bastion of extreme Sunni orthodoxy, leading *ulema* issued *fatwas* against Hizbullah and Shiite 'apostates' who stood with the enemies of Islam. Hizbullah was not 'the party of God', said one, but 'the party of Satan'.[39] According to an Israeli account of the war, 'moderate' Arab ambassadors at the UN begged Israel to 'break Hizbullah's spine'.[40]

'THIS IS OUR WAR TOO'

Internationally, Israel was suddenly faring pretty well too. Not in forty years, it was said, had it received such consideration in quarters it regarded as endemically unfriendly – proof, said one commentator, that 'the world is not always against us, that when Israel behaves with common sense, one can find common sense among the *goyim* and the "anti-Semites" too'.[41] It found its most gratifying expression in St Petersburg, where, assembled for their annual summit, the G8 leaders blamed 'extremist forces' – Hizbullah and Hamas – for both Lebanese and Gazan crises, and acknowledged Israel's 'right to self-defence'.

As usual, however, no one took Israel's part like the US. The war-plan for which it had already won the Administration's blessing must have had something to do with that,[42] but so too did a pro-Israel militancy in high places that passed all previous bounds. The neo-conservatives led the field. 'This is our war too', proclaimed William Kristol, of the influential *Weekly Standard*, and he urged the Pentagon to counter 'this act of Iranian aggression' with an immediate military strike on its nuclear installations.[43] Another leading neoconservative, Michael Ledeen, said America should 'go after' Bashar al-Asad too.[44] For Newt Gingrich, a former Speaker of the House much given to hyperbole, the time had come to fight a 'Third World War' in 'defense of civilization and America'.[45]

The Administration did not follow this extreme advice. But, with powerful neoconservatives still entrenched within it, it did just about everything else it could on its protégé's behalf. It saw the war as a watershed moment, a new and critical point of collision between all that America was striving to achieve in the region and its enemies to forestall. 'Tragic situations', said Bush, sometimes bring 'clarity', and what this one made clear beyond all doubt was that 'the root cause' of the region's woes was Hizbullah, and the 'terrorism' which it and the 'nation-states' behind it were practising against our 'democratic friends and allies'. 'Running through Damascus and the "southern suburbs" of Beirut to the Palestinians [of] Hamas', said one of his officials, was 'a hegemonic Persian threat' that sought to 'change the strategic playing field in the Middle East.' However, with Hizbullah's action, the threat had turned into a 'unique moment' of opportunity to strike back amid a 'convergence of interests' between Israel and the 'moderate' Arab states.[46] For Washington, Israel's first task was to 'break Hizbullah's bones'.[47] But Bush also wanted it to do by proxy what some of the neo-conservatives would have had him do himself, and take on the 'real' enemies behind Hizbullah. If Iran was perhaps too distant and formidable a target, its Syrian ally was 'weak and next door' – and, in Bush's mind, best able to 'get Hizbullah to stop doing this shit'.[48]

Unwilling to involve itself militarily, the US strove to furnish Israel with the diplomatic protection it needed to do so in it its stead. And before very long it was going to need a lot. For the sympathy the international community had exhibited at the beginning of the war was quickly dissipating as it saw how Israel waged it. Hizbullah's hostage-taking may have been illegal, but it was not entirely unprovoked; moreover its targets were military only. But most of the G8 powers, and especially France, did not take kindly to the way in which Israel – with its 'disproportionate' attacks on civilians and civilian infrastructure – interpreted its internationally acknowledged 'right to self-defence'. So the UN, Europe, Russia, China and the Third World were soon pressing for a ceasefire. Only the Bush Administration, with the faithful Tony Blair in tow, stood resolutely against one. The casualties, said Secretary of State Condoleezza Rice, were 'a terrible thing for the Lebanese people'; but – she daily, stubbornly reiterated – there was simply no point in a ceasefire that was 'unsustainable', or failed to tackle 'root causes'. 'What the world [was] witnessing' was 'the birth pangs of a new Middle East'. And it was time to show 'those who [didn't] want [one] .... that *we* will prevail – *they* will not'.[49]

Flagrant double standards had always informed American responses to military encounters between Israel and Hizbullah.[50] But this time they were all but elevated into official policy. John Bolton, America's ambassador to the UN and a devout neoconservative, was the first to spell it out. By the time some 200 Lebanese, overwhelmingly civilian, had died as compared with twelve Israelis, and Louise Arbour, the UN high commissioner for human rights, had already suggested that Israeli leaders could be charged with 'war crimes' – by that time he was still rejecting any idea of 'moral equivalence' between the protagonists, between casualties incurred as the 'unfortunate consequences of self-defence' and those which 'terrorists', targeting 'innocent civilians', actively 'desire[d]'.[51] Meanwhile, AIPAC, redoubtable arm of 'the Lobby', had drawn up a resolution which it wanted the House of Representatives to pass. In violation of the UN Charter and international legal norms, this effectively justified Israel's attacks on civilian targets even as it praised it for 'minimizing civilian casualties'.[52] Although a small group of congressmen sought inclusion of a clause urging '*all* sides to protect civilian life and infrastructure', AIPAC wouldn't have it, and 'our Knesset' – as maverick Republican Patrick Buchanan called it – duly ratified the original draft, word for word, 418 to 8.[53]

As for America's fourth estate, its mainstream media at least did little but echo and embellish the standpoint of authority – though possibly a columnist such as Richard Cohen, of the *Washington Post*, did so more intemperately than most. It was Israel's lot, he wrote, to be 'unfortunately located', to 'gentrify ... a pretty bad neighbourhood':

> [... its] only way to ensure that babies don't die in their cribs and old people in the streets is to make the Lebanese ... understand that if they, no matter how reluctantly, host those rockets, they will pay a very, very steep price ... These calls for proportionality rankle. They fall on my ears ... as ugly sentiments pregnant with antipathy toward the only democratic state in the Middle East.[54]

Not *much* more intemperately, though, judging by the verdict of Britain's *Independent* newspaper:

There are two sides to every conflict [observed its correspondent in the US] unless you rely on the US media for information about the battle in Lebanon. Viewers have been fed a diet of partisan coverage which treats Israel as the good guys and their Hizbullah enemy as the incarnation of evil. Not only is there next to no debate but debate itself is considered unnecessary and suspect.[55]

WAS ISRAEL JUST THE SPIDER'S WEB NASRALLAH SAID IT WAS?

Israel's war did not go very well for long. And in the end it actually lost it, making this, the Sixth Arab–Israeli War, the first which, on points at least, the Arab side won. Its victory, said Alistair Crooke and Mark Perry in one of the first serious assessments of it, was 'complete and decisive'.[56] Measured by the initial expectations of the protagonists, it certainly was. The Israelis failed utterly in their ambition to destroy Hizbullah and kill its leader. As for Hizbullah, it only had to survive in order to win, but, more than merely doing that, it emerged stronger from the contest than it went into it. What the victory would actually mean, for the region and the world, only time would tell. In its immediate aftermath, however, if there was one, dominant, and very widely shared, emotion, it surely had to be astonishment. How was it possible, asked friend, foe, and uninvolved observer alike? How was it possible that a clutch of clerics and a few 'combatants of Islam' had prevailed against one of the most powerful and best-equipped armies in the world?

Could it really mean that Israel was just the 'spider's web' that Nasrallah said it was, its military prowess and 'invincibility' a myth only awaiting the man of destiny who would expose and puncture it? Hardly. But one thing, at least, was sure: Nasrallah had 'read' his enemy better than it read him. If *he* had made a fundamental mistake in provoking the war in the first place, Israel made an even greater one in overestimating its ability to prosecute it. There might have been some ground for its leaders' 'combination of arrogance, boastfulness, euphoria and contempt for the enemy' – as one Israeli critic put it[57] – had it been facing one or more of the regular Arab armies; it had, after all, been its repeated, crushing and humiliating defeats of those inglorious institutions that largely accounted for the arrogance in the first place. But this was out of place in the case of Hizbullah. Perhaps it was the obtuseness that arrogance is apt to breed; in any case the fact was that, in spite of the two decades of very serious pain which Hizbullah had already inflicted on them, the Israelis evidently had little inkling of what this highly motivated, Islamically inspired, non-state guerilla force, this popular insurgency well versed in the skills and techniques of the new-style, 'asymmetrical' warfare, might be capable of in an all-out war against themselves. With his brutal attitude and inflated ego, his rush to combat, his assumption that it would all be over within a matter of days, and his failure to prepare for any alternative should it not be, Chief of Staff Halutz was the incarnation of that overweening hubris.[58]

MILITARY FAILURE

Halutz was no less central to the other fundamental error that Israel made – the exclusive reliance on air power, both for 'getting' Hizbullah directly, and indirectly through the Lebanese. That was perhaps to be expected of a former pilot who – when asked what it would have felt like to drop a one-ton bomb on an apartment block and kill seventeen civilians, nine of them children – famously, or infamously, replied: 'a slight shuddering of the left wing'.[59] He had also master-minded Israel's aerial 'war on terror' in the occupied territories, its 'targeted killings' of Palestinian leaders and militants. But what was relatively simple and successful in the never-ending, low-intensity combat with Hamas or Islamic Jihad – the electronic intelligence or the tip-off from a collaborator followed by the single guided missile from on high – was far from being so in the periodic, high-intensity showdowns with Hizbullah. Besides, this singular faith in the efficacy of air power had been largely discredited not merely in universal experience – from the London Blitz to the jungles of Vietnam – but, with Accountability and Grapes of Wrath, in Israel's own as well.

In addition to its supposed intrinsic merit, it possessed another, perhaps even more important, virtue in Israeli politicians' and com-manders' eyes. It would spare them the need for a ground offensive and the cost in casualties it was liable to entail. Israel's earlier experience in

Lebanon had bred a deep-seated, obsessive fear of entering that murderous 'quagmire' again.[60]

But when things did go wrong and re-entry was forced upon it, that exposed the third great mistake – or, more precisely, the institutional deterioration – of its vaunted war machine, which suddenly discovered that 'it wasn't ready to fight … didn't know how to fight and … didn't even know what it was fighting for.'[61] It was, at bottom, arrogance – and another of its offspring, complacency – that accounted for this state of affairs as well. For over the years Israel had come to hold two basic, perhaps essentially intuitive, assumptions. One was that its armed forces would not in any foreseeable future be fighting a major war again, because, thanks to their awe-inspiring 'deterrent power', no Arab state would dare embark on one. The other was that their only serious role would continue to be the repression of the Palestinians. So, with the 'air force chasing the enemies of Israel in their bedrooms', and the army confined to being 'a sub-contractor for the intelligence or a substitute for the police', who needed tanks, artillery and large-scale infantry formations? Or, rather, who needed to train them for a real war that would never come to pass? Training of such a serious kind had therefore as good as ceased. No wonder, then, that the harvest which that eventual, exceedingly unwanted ground offensive yielded was a rich one – rich, that is to say, not in valour, though that was not lacking, but in its opposite, as well as 'glaring deficiencies in basic soldiering' of many kinds.[62]

And the rot went deeper yet. In the afternoon of 12 July, after the abduction of Goldwasser and Regev, and as more soldiers were dying in a futile bid to rescue them, Halutz found time to confer with his stockbroker and instruct him to dump a $36,000 investment portfolio liable to be adversely affected by the war into which, unbeknown to anyone else, he was about to send his nation. What more shameful and disturbing illustration, wailed the post-war Jeremiahs, of the *mores* of contemporary Israel, of the descent into materialism, hedonism, every-man-for-himself and their corrosive impact on that vital institution, the army, which had been traditionally revered above all others.

MISSILES WERE KING

The war which, in those first few hours of it, Halutz told Olmert that Israel had already won, Israel was in reality already losing – or very soon would be. The generals thought they knew where Hizbullah's missile arsenals were, that in a few days of 'shock and awe' they could destroy the bulk of them. But they didn't know, and if they did, they couldn't get them from the air in any case. Ever since the 2000 withdrawal, they had been amassing intelligence for precisely this eventuality, this 'second round' against the only Arab enemy which had ever driven the Israeli army, unconditionally, from Arab soil. It may have served them quite well for the 'night of the Fajrs'. But whatever the air force knocked out then, and in the two or three days and nights that followed, it represented a very small portion – perhaps 7 per cent – of Hizbullah's overall military assets.[63] Nor was it just a question of missiles, or weaponry in general. They did not manage the 'targeted killing' of a single Hizbullah leader, or even a temporary silencing of al-Manar, the Hizbullah television station, in spite of repeated strikes against relay towers and antennae across the land.

But missiles were king. The 12,000 of them to which Nasrallah had publicly laid claim – but of which he seems to have had many more – came in various forms. The most formidable was the Iranian-supplied Zelzal-2, which, with a warhead of up to 600 kilograms and a range of 200 kilometres, could reach every major Israeli city. If he did indeed possess a few of those – for there was some doubt about that – he never fired them. Of the medium-size ones – Iranian-built Fajr-3s and 5s or Syrian Ouragans, between 43 and 100 km in range – that survived the initial Israeli onslaught, he made only occasional and judicious use. It was those old workhorses of Palestinian, then Islamist, missile warfare – the Katyusha-107s and 122s, with a maximum range of 11 and 20 km respectively – on which he chiefly relied; they, and particularly the 122s, were by far his most plentiful, and, being small and easily transported, the hardest for the Israelis to hit.

Since Ben-Gurion's days, taking the war into enemy territory, tank-led *Blitzkrieg*-style, had been classic Israeli doctrine. And in all the wars that, since 1948, the Arab armies fought and lost they never, for all the ultra-modern, mainly Soviet-supplied weaponry at their disposal, penetrated Israel's interior, or even struck it from afar. But now, with the new, 'asymmetrical', Islamist way of war, with non-state actors like Hizbullah and Hamas taking those armies' place, the 'home front' became Israel's most vulnerable one, its new, and disturbingly unfamiliar, Achilles heel.

Nasrallah may have been surprised by the scale of the Israeli onslaught, but he was prepared – far better than Israel itself – for the kind of battle which Israel proceeded to impose on him. To be sure, from the outset, he declared himself ready for a ceasefire, and indirect negotiations for the exchange of prisoners which had been his objective in the first place. 'If', however, 'the enemy want[ed] total war' then he was 'ready for that too – without any "red lines".' For him, missiles had always had a retaliatory role; if Israel hit Lebanese civilians, Hizbullah would hit Israeli ones in response. And that, albeit on an unprecedented scale, was how it would be now – 'not only we who [would] pay the price ... our children killed, our people made homeless'.[64]

The first missiles came on 13 July, immediately after the first Israeli air raids: 150 of them. They killed two Israelis in reprisal for fifty-five dead Lebanese, establishing the basic ratio, about twenty-five to one, which held good for the rest of the war. Some of them reached places, including Haifa, deeper inside Israel than Israelis had been warned to expect. That was a shock. But in the days to come, perhaps as great a shock as the projectiles themselves was the way in which Nasrallah promised, and then unfailingly delivered, them. It was a great reversal. The emptiest threats and vainest boasts were now coming mainly from the Israeli, not the Arab, side; and the 'liar and braggart' enjoyed greater credibility, even in Israel itself, than Olmert or Halutz.

The next day, 14 July, saw the first 'surprises' of which Nasrallah had earlier spoken. 'They start now,' he announced in his first wartime address from his bunker. 'Now, at sea, the Israeli warship that attacked our infrastructure, homes and citizens – watch it burning and sink with dozens of Zionist soldiers aboard.' The Israeli navy's flagship, the *Hanit*, did not sink. But an Iranian-supplied C-802 shore-to-ship guided missile – which Israel had no idea Hizbullah possessed – did disable it, and kill four of its crew as it cruised 10 km offshore.

'Bomb the *Dahiya* and we'll bomb Haifa' was the warning he
delivered after Israel began its onslaught on the 'southern suburbs'. And
again, two days later, he kept his word with a barrage of Fajrs that killed
eight workers at the city's railway station.

Of course, the Israelis had expected quite a few missiles, but not for
very long and not like this. But not only did they keep on coming, some
150 to 180 a day, they did so in swiftly executed, impressively
coordinated, mass retaliatory salvos, clearly ordered from the top and
betraying no sign of the breakdown in centralized command and
control which Israeli officials kept forecasting or claiming to detect.
And they crept further and further south – from Haifa to Tiberias, from
Nazareth to Afoula and Beit Shean, and finally, on 4 August, to Hadera.
Ninety kilometres south of the border, this coastal town, one of the
earliest Zionist settlements, was struck by two or three Khaibar-1s –
Hizbullah's name for the Syrian-built Ouragan – in almost instant
response to an air raid that had killed twenty-three Syrian farm
workers loading fruit and vegetables into a refrigerated container in
the Beqa'a Valley. Towards the end of the war, Nasrallah said that if
Israel hit central Beirut, which it was threatening to do, he would bomb
Tel Aviv – a pledge which, by now, Israelis had every reason to believe
he would keep, probably with his unused Zelzal-2s.

Only after it was all over did the Israelis grasp the full, formidable
measure of what Hizbullah had arrayed against them, and especially
what they dubbed its 'nature reserves'. These were areas, usually in
secluded, rocky ravines or patches of dense vegetation, where
Hizbullah had established an extraordinary network of military
installations and placed them out of bounds to Lebanese and UNIFIL
alike. They consisted of scores, if not hundreds, of underground
bunkers and tunnels. They were all located south of the Litani river, in
what was formerly the Israeli 'security zone', and most were within
three or four kilometres of the border. One, in fact, lay a mere 300
metres from an Israeli position on the other side of it, and within a
mere 100 metres of a UNIFIL position on Lebanese territory; but such
was the stealth and secrecy in which it had been excavated and
furbished that neither even knew it was there. Forty metres below
ground, with reinforced concrete roofs a metre thick, dormitories,

bathrooms, hot and cold running water, medical facilities, ventilation and air conditioning, and stocks of food, it could comfortably sustain and accommodate large numbers of fighters for weeks on end.[65]

It was in subterranean lairs such as these that they stored the bulk of their weapons and ammunition, part of an on-the-spot self-sufficiency in almost everything that reduced the Israelis' frenetic bombardment of roads, bridges, homes and moving vehicles to a largely pointless exercise. And it was from the 'nature reserves' that they launched their short-range, steep-trajectory Katyushas to which the Israelis had no answer. They did so from cunningly devised firing positions, which might, for example, take the form of pneumatically powered retractable platforms. It took the Israeli air force a mere ninety seconds to detect an incoming missile and direct the planes to take out its launcher. But with years of practice, the firing teams had become too quick for them; they had learned to perform this whole operation – launching the rocket, lowering the platform back into the ground, covering it with a fire-retardant blanket to hide its tell-tale heat signature from the circling, unmanned surveillance drones, and taking cover themselves – in less than a minute.

NORTHERN ISRAEL SUFFERS TOO

What the Katyushas were doing to northern Israel hardly compared with what the F-16s and the Apache helicopters were doing to Lebanon as a whole. By the war's end, up to 1,000 Lebanese civilians,[66] a third of them children, had died; nearly a million, a quarter of the population, had been forced to flee; whole villages and city neighbourhoods had been reduced to rubble, 77 bridges demolished, 900 commercial enterprises hit, 30,000 residential properties, offices, shops – and two hospitals – destroyed, 31 major public utilities, from ports to sewage treatment plants, destroyed or damaged. The Lebanese government put total losses at $6 billion. But northern Israel paid a price too. Forty-three civilians died. Some 300 buildings were destroyed and hundreds, perhaps thousands more were damaged. Maybe half a million people fled. Those were mainly the better-off, who, though likely to have private, well-appointed air-raid shelters of their own, preferred to stay in hotels – safely distant, if often extortionate in their over-charging – or with friends and relatives prepared to take them in. The 300,000 who remained behind, mainly the poor, the old and infirm, had to make do with public shelters. In the worst-hit towns, like Kiryat Shmona, they did so almost round the clock for at least a month. Thanks to long years of official neglect, the conditions inside the shelters were appalling – very hot, unhygienic and overcrowded. 'I never imagined I'd witness scenes like this in Israel,' said a French philanthropist, clearly shocked as he watched the hungry and the indigent, including women with babes in arms, shouting and brawling over the basic necessities – food, oil and milk – which he had come to distribute.[67] The authorities made no effort to evacuate them, and little to help in other ways; that was a source of resentment and discontent which they directed not merely at Hizbullah but at their own government, a further sign – of a piece with Halutz's 'insider trading' – of the kind of society, less and less given to solidarity in war, which once idealist Israel was becoming.[68]

Nothing like Lebanon, then, but these vicissitudes on the home front were nonetheless a demoralizing shock to an Israeli public accustomed to witnessing such things on the 'other side', never on their own. As for the Israeli leadership, what they mainly impressed on it was the need to deliver a decisive, crushing blow to Hizbullah. But the more pressing that need, the more painful was the realization that, with the patent failure of the air force, the ground forces would have to be sent in to inflict it. And these were already in difficulties as it was.

'BY FAR THE GREATEST GUERILLA GROUP IN THE WORLD'

In fact, they had been in there almost from the beginning. This, in effect, was the outcome of a compromise, a genuflexion, on the part of Halutz and his political masters, in favour of those such as Meir Dagan, chief of the Mossad intelligence service, who had argued that air power could only be truly effective in conjunction with the troops on the ground, and that these should have gone in straight away. The compromise meant, however, that instead of a full-scale invasion of South Lebanon and the military resources required to accomplish it, only a few 'special forces' were to engage in 'limited' or 'pinpoint' operations, quick, in-and-out forays, to 'mop up' Hizbullah's strongholds or weapons sites[69] as the air force performed the principal task of 'degrading' and breaking the organization from above.

It did not take the Israeli leadership very long to realize that the air force, on its own, had *not* yet won the war, and, on 17 July, four days after Halutz assured Olmert that it had, it was the ground forces' turn to get a taste of what lay ahead for *them*. Eighteen men of the Maglan reconnaissance unit were the first to do so just a kilometre inside Lebanon, near a strategically located, hilltop village called Maroun al-Ras. They knew something – though not much – about the 'nature reserves'. But they soon realized that they were in the middle of one. 'We expected a tent and three Kalashnikovs,' said a soldier called Gad, 'that was the intelligence we were given.' Instead, among the under-growth, they found a hydraulic steel door and the network of tunnels behind it. 'We didn't know what hit us, in seconds we had two dead' – struck down by grenades hurled from beneath their feet. As daylight broke the Maglans, one of the army's finest units, came under attack from all sides by Hizbullah forces who startled them with their fire-power and tenacity. 'Evidently', Gad went on, 'they'd never heard that an Arab soldier is supposed to run away after a short engagement with the Israelis.' As reinforcements from another elite unit, the Egoz, were sent to the rescue of their retreating comrades, several more men fell into a second ambush. Hours of battle ensued before Maglan and Egoz succeeded in dragging their dead and wounded back to Israel. But one thing was already obvious to military headquarters in Tel Aviv: this was going to be a much tougher fight than Halutz had bargained for.[70] In fact, what Israel was up against, said General Guy Zur, who commanded an armoured division in the war, was quite simply 'by far the greatest guerilla group in the world'.[71]

Great, perhaps, but not very big. All told, if its volunteer reservists were taken into account, Hizbullah was said to number between 15,000 and 30,000 men. But it was apparently a force of only some 3,000, or even a good deal less, who confronted the Israelis in the 33-day war, without need of reinforcement throughout.[72] They were split into two wings. One, the Nasr Brigade, was a full-time, uniformed group of experienced, highly disciplined fighters, a few hundred strong, who were deployed in the 'nature reserves' and other locations, and broken down into companies of fifteen to twenty men. The other was the 'village guards'; part-timers, many of them veterans of the 'liberation' war of the 1990s, they stayed behind to defend their villages after most of the inhabitants had fled.

In addition to keeping the Katyushas coming, they had one main goal; this was not, Nasrallah explained, to 'go in and conquer northern Palestine', but to make the Israeli army bleed, 'to inflict maximum casualties and damage to its capabilities'. To this end, they never tried to confront their vastly superior enemy head on, but to seek out its vulnerable points,[73] not to hold ground but to draw it forward and take it by surprise at times and places of their choosing. Everywhere they engaged it they were able to do so largely on their own terms. One reason for this, common to guerillas everywhere, was that, fighting on their own ground and among their own people, they knew every inch of the natural terrain, every nook and cranny of built-up areas. But another, special to Hizbullah, was those 'nature reserves' that were as invaluable for this kind of combat as for the firing of missiles. They correctly surmised that, with the failure of the air force, it would become the Israeli special forces' task to take them and other targets out. They laid their mines and booby traps and prepared their ambushes accordingly. They had CCTV cameras to watch the advancing army's every step.[74]

And more than that – they had intelligence. Together with the 'nature reserves', their ability to crack the sophisticated, 'frequency hopping' system through which Israeli commanders communicated with one another was one of the great – and for the Israelis very unpleasant – surprises of the war. On the strength of it, they could divine the Israelis' intentions in advance, an ability which, depriving them of the element of surprise, had a crucial impact on the war's whole course. There was a wider, psychological dividend too: the Hizbullahi code-breakers managed to get word of Israeli casualties and announce them on al-Manar television even before the Israeli authorities did so themselves.[75]

Not the least of Hizbullah's assets was the one which they themselves most prized: their intense Islamic faith, and the readiness for 'martyrdom' it engendered. It was in close combat that this showed to greatest advantage. In best guerilla practice, they did not seek these face-to-face encounters,[76] and, when they happened, their losses were usually greater than the Israelis'. On the other hand, they also proved themselves their equal or their better, sometimes defeating them in the field, forcing them into sudden retreat – or rescue, *in extremis*, by inter-vention from the air. If, in asymmetrical warfare, personal courage was a characteristic strength by which guerillas could offset the firepower and technological superiority of the conventional armies they were fighting against, mastery of such low- or medium-tech weapons as they did possess was obviously no bad thing either. And, in that department, it was with their anti-tank missiles, above all, that Hizbullah excelled. They had a whole range of these, from the antique, Russian-built Sagger-3s they had so often used before to the latest, laser-guided Kornet-Es which they had just acquired. The Nasr Brigade's hunter-killer missile teams made versatile use of them all, and not just against the latest Merkava-3s and 4s, and other armoured vehicles, of which they knocked out at least forty. They also used them on buildings in which enemy infantry had taken shelter – once killing nine in a single strike – as well as helicopters, bringing down a troop-carrying Sikorsky CH-53 and its five-man crew just moments after it had dropped off a thirty-man platoon. In all, they accounted for at least fifty of Israel's 119 military fatalities of the war.[77]

THE BATTLE OF BINT JBEIL

Eventually the Maglans and Egoz conquered Maroun al-Ras, or so at least, on 22 July, the Israelis claimed. They had killed quite a lot of Hizbullahis in the process. But the Hizbullahis had killed seven of *them*. Those were losses on a scale to which they were not accustomed; yet if that was already a steep price for the taking of a single village, how much more so when it turned out, as it shortly did, that it had not really been taken at all?

Nor did it augur well for what Maroun al-Ras was supposed to be: launching pad for a series of similar attacks on enemy positions just across the border, for a 'ground-force pressure' which, supplementary to the aerial and artillery blitz, was going to 'push Hizbullah out without arriving at the point where we have to invade and occupy'.[78] And, sure enough, the name of this otherwise unremarkable Shiite frontier village was soon to be seared into Israeli consciousness, along with that of Bint Jbeil, the 'capital' of the South, as painful emblems of Israel's war now going wrong on the ground as it already had in the air.

As it did so, Israeli generals, active or retired, developed a host of disparaging terms – the semi-war, half-pregnant war, or luxury-war-without-casualties – for the strategy which had brought this about.[79] 'Our brass', said an infantry reserve major, 'stupidly fell into the Hizbullah traps, [sending] us to attack as many villages as possible for no obvious reason.'[80] It made for a series of small campaigns that dissipated all the inherent advantages of a regular army – manpower, weaponry and technology – in favour of those of the other side.[81]

The complete elimination of Hizbullah would have been the only possible objective, clear to all, of the full-scale invasion that Halutz continued systematically to reject. But the objectives of these lesser incursions, as officially formulated, seemed anything but clear to the soldiers called upon to accomplish them.[82] The demolishing of so-called 'symbols' – with the objective of demoralizing the enemy – was the key, well-nigh obsessive, notion that inspired them.

Chief of symbols was Bint Jbeil. 'Nasrallah delivered his victory speech [after Israel's withdrawal in 2000] in Bint Jbeil,' General Benny Gantz, one of his staff, told Halutz. 'We're going to have to take that place apart. I would even consider a limited ground offensive in the area ... I'd place a film unit there to describe the speech and its current results, that is to say – to record the story to the end.'[83]

Halutz liked the idea, and the day after the fall of Maroun al-Ras, he ordered special forces to take Bint Jbeil in an operation – called Web of Steel in answer to Nasrallah's contemptuous 'spider's web' – that was to be completed within forty-eight hours, with the killing and capture of as many Hizbullahis as possible. Paratroopers were to attack the town from the west, the elite Golani Brigade from the east. Even as, on 24 July, they prepared to advance, they learned that Maroun al-Ras had not fallen after all; fighting for its possession had resumed; an Israeli tank had been set on fire. By nightfall of 25 July, however, Bint Jbeil *was* 'in [Israeli] hands'.[84] Or so at least a general of the Northern Command proclaimed.

And yet it *wasn't* – any more than Maroun al-Ras had been. With their superior intelligence, the Hizbullahis had read the signs well, and duly reinforced their presence in and around the town.[85] There were three times as many of them as the Israelis thought there were.[86] Apparently they had not actively sought the frontal confrontation which, in the early hours of 26 July, broke out between them and the Golanis occupying houses on the eastern edge of the town, but, once engaged in it, they were well placed to minimize their enemy's technological advantages in a battle of 'rifles, teeth and fingernails'. They lost a lot of men, but that was little consolation to the Israelis, who lost a further eight of their own.[87] On 28 July, the Hizbullahis staged a counter-offensive against paratroopers to the west. Again they suffered heavy casualties, but, on 30 July, the Israelis ended up by ceding what little of the town they had ever actually taken. For the rest of the war they rained down aerial destruction on Bint Jbeil, Maroun al-Ras, and a string of other places just across the border in which they suffered many dead – twenty-six in the village of Aita al-Shaab alone[88] – for very little, or even zero, territorial gain. But though they tried again and again, the army which had gone to Beirut in the 1982 war, and some had even forecast that it might do so again,[89] never truly conquered and occupied a single one of them.

For the post-war Winograd commission, the 'battle of Bint Jbeil' was one of the army's two colossal failures of the war.[90] Web of Steel, and the other 'limited operations' of the kind, revealed just what corroded metal that once all-conquering military machine was now made from. There were the confused and contradictory orders from on high, which discontented commanders sought to annul or circumvent; the troops who, between battles, had to scavenge for food and water by breaking into village shops or the canteens of fallen Hizbullahis far better supplied than themselves; the reservists who either headed to the front with hardly any of their combat gear because of shortages in the quartermasters' stores, or bought what they needed with their own money; the senior officers who did not cross the border with their soldiers, preferring to run their campaigns from secluded bunkers

inside Israel instead; the signal lack of discipline among even the best-
trained regulars, and reservists who were so much worse that
commanders hesitated to put them into battle at all. There was the
virtual mutiny on the outskirts of Bint Jbeil, when a certain Lieutenant
Adam Kima, a combat engineer, was ordered to clear the way into the
town. He refused, on grounds of unreasonable risk. He and his men
were arrested by military police and sentenced to fourteen days in gaol.
The men were very grateful: they said that Kima had saved their lives.[91]

Bint Jbeil shook the military and political leadership to the core.
There were fierce recriminations. The deputy head of the Northern
Command shouted at the chief of staff: 'The dead at Bint Jbeil are down
to you.'[92] As for Halutz himself, with the failure of his air force, and
now these losses on the ground, his self-confidence appeared to crack,
and twice he had to be briefly hospitalized.[93] For their part, the
politicians lost faith in the promises of the military. In fact, quite early
on in the war Olmert, while still exuding confidence in public, had
already lamented in private: 'I don't see how the army is going to get me
the victory I need.'[94]

THE NATION RALLIES TO HIZBULLAH

If it was Hizbullah up, and Israel down, on the military front, so it was
on others too.

Getting the Lebanese to 'get' Hizbullah, by bombing *them* as well,
was the first and most important of these. This soon turned into the
kind of fiasco, on a larger scale, that Accountability and Grapes of
Wrath had clearly portended that it would.

The main target of Israel's onslaught was of course the Shiites, in
part deliberately, in part because it was they who, physically, stood most
plainly in its way. But other communities, Sunnis, Druzes, Christians,
were not spared either – and that, plus the attacks on 'national' assets,
the army and the infrastructure, made it clear that everyone was to pay
for what a special few had done.

Those others could not forget their initial grudge against Hizbullah,
but, for the time being at least, they could, and did, subordinate it to
another one. In place of anger against the party that provoked the war

came a greater rage against Israel for the way it waged it. The more Israel bombed, the more savage and widespread its onslaught grew, the more the nation rallied to the only quarter that was not merely fighting back, but giving almost as good as it got. Public opinion polls demonstrated it. Before the war, with Hizbullah's status increasingly challenged, only a 58 per cent – and overwhelmingly Shiite – segment of the populace considered that Hizbullah had the right to retain its arms. Now, a full 87 per cent supported its 'resistance to Israeli aggression'; 96 per cent of the Shiites took that position, but other communities – 89 per cent of Sunnis, 80 per cent of Christians and Druzes – where anti-Hizbullah sentiment had formerly been strongest were not so far behind.[95] Street talk showed it too. 'A week ago', said one young man, 'I would have told you I hated Nasrallah. But now I pray for victory.' In Beirut's staunchly Sunni quarter of Tarik Jadideh a group of card-playing youngsters likewise agreed that there was no longer any contradiction between supporting their own community chieftain, Saad Hariri, and Nasrallah: 'We are all with the resistance now.'[96]

For Nasrallah, such voices were the voices of the 'good people', of the 'silent majority', of those 'who in hard times reveal their chivalry, honour, and patriotism'. And that, he could plausibly claim, was just what they were doing now, in Hizbullah's favour and at the expense of a government on which, with its 'illusory majority', the Americans and Israelis had been counting to join them in dealing it the *coup de grâce*. Before the war, America had actually enjoyed very considerable good-will in Lebanon; 38 per cent – a lot for an Arab country in these very anti-American times – deemed that it had played a constructive role on its behalf. But a Bush Administration which had leapt to the support of the 'Cedar Revolution' – and the new, '14 March' regime it spawned – when Syria was Lebanon's chief tormentor, was shamelessly abandoning it, fifteen months later, when Israel became its much greater one. With its tolerance, indeed active encouragement, of an onslaught that smote friends of the government and friends of Hizbullah alike, America threw all that goodwill away. Now, when asked whether it was being an 'honest mediator' in the conflict, 96 per cent of Shiites flatly asserted that it was not, an overwhelming verdict in which – more importantly – Sunnis and Christians, at 87 per cent, and Druzes at 81 per cent, were not so far behind. Furthermore, if the government had secretly hoped – as the Israelis *said*, and Nasrallah strongly *suspected*, it had – that Hizbullah would lose the war, then that had become a hope that not many people either shared, or expected to be fulfilled. Already, barely half-way through the war, 93 per cent of the Shiites thought that Hizbullah was on the way to winning it; and so did 72 per cent of the Sunnis, 54 per cent of the Druzes and 38 per cent of the Christians.[97]

'YOU AND THE WORLD DESCRIBED US AS INSANE – BUT WE THINK WE ARE WISE'

The prospect of a Hizbullah victory was perhaps less alarming to the Lebanese government than it was to the Sunni-dominated Arab estab-lishment, and especially those 'moderate' friends of America – Jordan, Egypt and Saudi Arabia – which had so incautiously taxed it with 'uncalculated adventurism' for starting it. For them, who had 'participated in shedding the blood of the victim and covered the crimes of the executioner', Nasrallah did not hide his disdain. Yes, he told them, 'we *are* adventurous' but in ways that 'brought us nothing but pride, freedom, honour and the head held high.' Yes, 'you and the world described us as insane – but we think we [are] wise.'[98]

And the 'good people' of the Arab world seemed to think so too. In every country but Lebanon, the Arab masses, unscathed themselves, could thrill almost unreservedly to the spectacle before them: a chubby, bespectacled, black-turbaned priest, in his bunker beneath the rubble, and his little band of *mujahideen* who were achieving what no Arab state, or combination of states, had come close to achieving before. And, in addition, they were wiping out at last those shaming images – of 'Arab soldiers hurriedly taking off their shoes, dropping their weapons, and fleeing to the nearest refuge'[99]– which repeated defeat had bequeathed.

Hizbullah deemed that it was fighting the '*Umma*'s battle'. And much of the *Umma* seemed to see it that way too. Demonstrators, mainly Islamist but substantially secular too, took to the streets in almost every Arab capital. In Cairo they chanted 'Nasrallah, our friend, hit and destroy Tel Aviv' and 'Khaybar, Khaybar,[100] Jews, the army of Muhammad will return.' In Sudan, they called on the *Umma to* join Hizbullah in pan-Islamic *jihad*. In Yemen, they linked Hizbullah to Hamas with shouts of 'no to the shameful official Arab stance towards the Palestinians and Lebanese'. An Iraq in the thick of its own civil war took time off to stage the largest rally of all; that was after their prime minister, Nouri Maliki, whom America had placed in power, so infuriated Congressmen during a visit to Washington that some of them demanded to know which side – America and Israel's, or Hizbullah's – he was on in 'the war on terror'. And one of them, former presidential hopeful Howard Dean, called him an 'anti-Semite' pure and simple.

In Nasrallah, the Arabs found themselves a new icon, who – said Rasha Salti, a Lebanese writer – 'displayed a persona, and a public behaviour, that were exactly opposite to those of Arab heads of states'. 'There is the most powerful man in the Middle East,' sighed an Arab deputy prime minister as, spell-bound like countless millions of others, he watched him address the *Umma* from his bomb-proof lair.[101] He was the most trusted too. Three young Egyptians in a Cairo street were keen to make their views known. 'He said he was going to bomb Haifa, and he did bomb Haifa,' said one of them in a voice loud enough for passers-by to hear. 'Nasrallah is a man of his word', agreed his companion, 'God protect him.'[102] In Syria, the three-million Christian minority were as enthusiastic about him as their Muslim compatriots. Priests led prayers for him, and women lit candles. 'I love him', said seventy-year-old Mona Muzaber, 'he is a patriot who doesn't seek personal gain.'[103]

For a while at least, Hizbullah transcended the great sectarian schism. The Sunni leader of Egypt's Muslim Brothers called for 10,000 Egyptian *mujahideen* to join their Shiite brethren in Lebanon; Sunni masses took to Cairo's streets on their behalf. 'We are all Shiites now,' said a radio station in Gaza. In vain did the pro-American 'moderate' regimes seek to mobilize their Sunni publics against Hizbullah's sponsor, Shiite Iran. Their publics did not respond; for them the real enemy was Israel – and America – and nothing was going to impress them more than this Shiite stedfastness and willingness to fight and die in righteous combat against them. In Saudi Arabia arch-conservative Wahhabi scholars condemned the anti-Hizbullah *fatwas* of their colleagues. Even al-Qaeda, steeped in doctrinal antipathy for the 'apostates' and sponsor, in Iraq, of many a ghastly suicide attack against them, got into the act, with at least an implicit appeal for Sunni–Shiite unity against the 'Zionist–Crusader' alliance.

And, of course, all this adulation of Hizbullah was inextricably intertwined with hostility to the regimes. In Cairo, the weekly newspaper *al-Dustur* likened the Arab 'kings and presidents' to the medieval princes who had let the Crusaders eat away at Muslim lands until they controlled them all. In Palestine, these 'helpless, pathetic, rotten Arab leaders' were as virulently, as daily, reviled as the pristine new champion was glorified.[104] The position taken by Saudi Arabia, Egypt and Jordan, it was everywhere being said, was worse than mere weakness and pusillanimity: it was a stab in the back by servile Arabs of valiant ones.

EVEN UNTO THE LANDS OF BUSH AND BLAIR

On the international front, that European discomfiture with Israel, which had manifested itself in the wake of its first, indiscriminate air strikes, had only deepened since. The rot was spreading even to the Britain of Tony Blair, steadfast still in his adherence to the American contention that Israel should be permitted to go on bombing till the 'terrorists' and 'extremists', the enemies of 'freedom and democracy', were sufficiently chastised, 'root causes' could be addressed, and Condoleezza Rice's 'new Middle East' begin to see the light of day. This servility of Bush's 'poodle', as the prime minister was frequently portrayed, on matters Middle Eastern was causing such unrest in the ranks of his ruling Labour Party that one MP would shortly publish an 'open letter' to him denouncing it as 'stupid' and 'morally indefensible'.[105] Even a member of his cabinet, Deputy Foreign Minister Kim Howell, was moved to declare, during a visit to Beirut, that it was 'very, very difficult to understand the kind of military tactics that have been used ... You know, if [you're] chasing Hizbullah, then go for Hizbullah. You don't go for the entire Lebanese nation ... I very

much hope the Americans understand what's happening to Lebanon
... the death of so many children and so many people.'

But the Bush Administration did not yet understand, or, if it did, did
not yet care enough to try to stop it. Yet even it was getting seriously
upset with its Israeli protégé – albeit mainly for military and strategic,
rather than moral, reasons. It was not simply that Israel had failed to
expand the war on Hizbullah by attacking Syria too. For that is what
'many parts' of the Bush Administration, led by the passionately pro-
Israeli neoconservative, National Security Adviser Elliot Abrams, had
been urging it to do, and there was a 'lot of anger' in the White House
that it hadn't.[106] But never mind Syria – more disturbing was Israel's
poor performance against Hizbullah itself. This Administration, more
even than others before it, set great store by Israel as a strategic asset,
and, confident of its military prowess, it had assumed that it would
easily accomplish the task which it had undertaken on America's behalf
as well as its own. But it was not long before the doubts, about both its
strategy and capabilities, set in. These only deepened when, ten days
into the war, the White House received a request for the emergency
supply of large amounts of precision-guided munitions. Though
immediately granted, the request dismayed top Pentagon officials
because it seemed to indicate that, having failed – despite an already
extravagant use of firepower – to do significant damage to Hizbullah
itself, Israel was now gearing up for a yet greater onslaught on what
remained of Lebanon's infrastructure. They interpreted a first, small-
scale call-up of reserves as another sign of things going wrong, and the
adverse impression this made was only compounded by what one
former US commander called the 'unprepared, sloppy and demoralized' air with which the reserves went about it.[107]

None of these misgivings were made public, however. Outwardly at
least, America was still as determined as ever to give Israel the time it
needed 'to finish the job', as the president of AIPAC, with fulsome
expressions of gratitude, put it.[108] And at a White House press
conference on 28 July Bush and Blair stood shoulder to shoulder in
their continued rejection of a ceasefire for which the rest of the world
was clamouring. But two days later came Qana.

QANA-II

In the second massacre within a decade to befall the place where Christ is said to have performed his first miracle, the Israeli air force unleashed two bombs, American-made, 2,000-pound, precision-guided Mk 84s, on a three-storey building soon after midnight on 30/31 July. Twenty-eight people – at first it was thought that fifty-seven had died – were exhumed the following morning from the basement where they had been sleeping, in the tragic belief that this would be their safest refuge in their largely deserted village. Most of them were women and children, and most had died slow and agonizing deaths, screaming for help as they suffocated in the smoke, dirt and debris from the structure that had collapsed above them.

As after Qana-I, the Israeli government immediately claimed that Hizbullah was to blame, because it had been firing Katyushas from the village, and it distributed pictures of its fighters purportedly doing so. At the same time, *The Israel Insider*, a self-styled 'independent, non-partisan online publication', said it 'looked like [the babies] had been dead for days'; Hizbullah operatives must have planted them there. A host of like-minded websites, mainly Israeli and American, instantly chimed in. It was all nothing but 'a most revolting Hizbullah fraud', in which – said *The American Thinker*, a popular conservative site – major media photographers had acted as 'willing' tools.[109] Such lurid conspiracy theories, widespread in the blogosphere, were apparently too outlandish for the mainstream Israeli media,[110] hardly temperate though they were in the contempt for Nasrallah and his motives to which they nonetheless gave voice. For him, they contended, this tragedy inflicted on his own people was a 'godsend'; he had been 'praying for a victory of this kind, for pictures of dead children, so much so that, had it not happened, he would have had to invent it.'[111]

> It was appalling [said the *Jerusalem Post*] that Hizbullah would deliberately target Israel's cities, and do so from civilian areas, hoping that Israel would kill greater numbers of Lebanese civilians ... appalling that this barbaric tactic – after some 5,000 Israeli bombing sorties – has proved 'effective', with tragic consequences for innocent Lebanese people, and producing

the expected international fallout: not against Hizbullah, but against Israel. Are we powerless to overturn the bizarre moral calculus by which Israel is held accountable for the barbaric tactics of its enemies?[112]

Arguments like these were of a piece with Israel's perception of itself as superior to its enemies not only in military prowess but in the altogether higher moral code – its 'purity of arms' – it observed in fighting them. If it hit civilians, it only did so by accident. By contrast, Hizbullah used its own people as a 'human shield'; and, even as it exploited Israeli scruples about harming Lebanese civilians, it deliberately targeted Israeli ones.

But it could be argued that the ethical balance was really quite otherwise, that it was actually Hizbullah which, in effect if not perhaps intent, ended up showing a greater respect for the rules of war than the Israelis.[113] For if, in fact, it did deliberately target those forty-three Israeli civilians who died in the course of the war, it did so in retaliation for the twenty-five times as many Lebanese civilians who 'accidentally' died at Israeli hands. But that was not all. There was plenty of evidence – which Israel's wartime media restrictions prevented from being reported contemporaneously – that on many occasions Hizbullah was actually aiming at Israeli military targets, and that the civilians who died in consequence constituted precisely the same kind of 'collateral' damage, caused by notoriously inaccurate Katyusha fire, as did their Lebanese counterparts who died in Israel's 'surgical' air strikes on Hizbullah's bases and personnel. For Israel was no less given to locating its military installations near to population centres than Hizbullah was. If Hizbullah had its headquarters in Beirut's populous southern suburbs, the Israeli army had its in the heart of Tel Aviv. Furthermore, it placed many of its temporary artillery positions close to, or even inside, civilian communities in the north. And most of these were Arab; in consequence, it was Arabs, only a fifth of Israel's total population, who, with eighteen dead, accounted for more than a third of its civilian fatalities.[114] In point of fact, as journalists and researchers on the spot reported, there was no sign that Hizbullah had used Qana as a firing point. Insofar as it did employ such tactics, that was very much the exception, not the rule. 'In the overwhelming majority of destroyed or damaged buildings it examined', reported Amnesty International, 'there was no evidence to indicate that [they] were being used by Hizbullah fighters as hide-outs or to store weapons.'[115] Similarly, Human Rights Watch reported that in the twenty-four cases of civilian casualties, covering about a third of the total, which it examined in detail, it found no evidence that 'Hizbullah deliberately used civilians as shields to protect them from retaliatory [Israeli] attack'.[116] It had little need of them in any case; for it had its 'nature reserves'.

The only 'accidental' thing about Qana-II was that it happened in exactly the same place as Qana-I. For something like this was inherently likely in any case. What really made it all but inevitable was that the Israelis were getting the worst of the war. And this was such an unexpected, unaccustomed state of affairs that it drove them, in their anger and perplexity, to extreme responses. A mere four days after the war began, when it was becoming obvious that Halutz's aerial onslaught had done very little to 'degrade' Hizbullah's missile capability, the Northern Command confessed that it had already exhausted its list of targets for attack. 'Something' had to be done, the commanders agreed, and they began a process of 'target stretching'. What this meant in practice was the systematic hitting of schools, community centres, mosques and houses on the fringes of Southern villages in the hope that, since they had failed to find Hizbullah's assets anywhere else, they would find them there.[117]

Qana was a direct consequence of this – as well as of the ground forces' adversities in Bint Jbeil. The loss of eight soldiers in that town was such a shock that, coming on top of the missiles, it generated calls for the kind of massive, indiscriminate retaliation of which non-combatants were bound to be the main victims. Defence Minister Peretz issued a directive absolving the army of responsibility for the safety of civilians in South Lebanon.[118] Trade and Industry Minister Eli Yishai, of the Shas religious party, proposed the 'flattening' of any villages from which Hizbullah fired on Israeli soldiers. 'What do you need infantry for?', asked a senior reserve air force officer, 'when four F-16s and cheap, old-fashioned bombs [can] eliminate Bint Jbeil completely?'[119] 'What's more correct,' asked columnist Amnon

Dankner, 'to suffer the slaughter of our best sons ... so as to be the most moral army in the world, or to erase villages that serve as warehouses for Hizbollah terror, save our sons, and be considered less moral?'[120] As for the frequently outspoken Minister of Justice Haim Ramon, it was his opinion that 'everyone in southern Lebanon is a terrorist' and that 'we are allowed to have another Qana, we are allowed to destroy everything'.[121]

TURNING-POINT

Qana-II was the same great turning point in the war as Qana-I had been in Grapes of Wrath, and for very similar reasons. It was the point at which, failure looming, Israel began to seek as decent, as face-saving an exit from it as it could, and America, going into reverse too, helped it find one.

As it floundered around, with its penny-packet ground incursions and its futile air campaign, and as its intelligence agencies opined that, at the rate things were going, Hizbullah's missiles would still be hitting the 'home front' for months to come,[122] Israel's leaders had already begun to scale down their original war aims. Sophistry had taken charge. It was less and less a victory, pure and simple, of which they now talked, merely the 'narrative', the 'image', or the 'perception' of one. It was no longer a question of securing the immediate, unconditional hand-over of sergeants Goldwasser and Regev. 'That will take time,' said Olmert; and it came to be understood that their freedom could only be secured through the negotiated exchange of prisoners that Nasrallah had asked for in the first place. Nor was it any longer a question of 'destroying', 'obliterating' or 'smashing' Hizbullah, but rather of 'crippling' and 'weakening' it, or, as one general put it, 'disrupting [its] military logic'. A foreign ministry spokesman was more modest still. Israel's 'main objective today', he said, was 'neither the defeat of Hizbullah nor the depletion of its firepower.' It was to 'dissuade Hizbullah from renewing its attacks on the border'.[123]

In the confusion of this retreat, different leaders said different things, but, in general, what were now termed 'realistic' objectives seemed to mean no more than pushing Hizbullah from the southern regions lying

mainly between the Litani river and the border. This would put Israel
beyond the reach of its short-range Katyushas – though not of its
longer-range Fajrs and Zelzal-2s. But it was no longer Israel itself that
would be doing this. Its only contribution would be to prepare the way,
by occupying a small strip of territory along the border, for an international force to take its place.[124] At the beginning of the war, it had
poured scorn on such an idea. But now, duly chastened, it was for the
first time in its history signalling a readiness to place some, at least, of
its defences in the hands of foreigners. They would, of course, have to
be reliable foreigners, a good 20,000 of them, heavily armed, preferably
from NATO countries; and unlike UNIFIL, which Israel held to be a
feeble, pusillanimous if not frankly hostile lot, they would have to have
a mandate, and a will, seriously to confront and fight Hizbullah. The
force would also lend backing – and backbone – to the Lebanese army,
as, for the first time in three decades, it deployed in strength in the
southern regions to be evacuated by Hizbullah.

FROM STRATEGIC ASSET TO STRATEGIC LIABILITY

Qana-II might not have been so manifestly deliberate as Qana-I, and
its casualty toll was substantially less, but, for America, the circumstances in which it happened rendered it a greater source of
embarrassment and exasperation. Condoleezza Rice, who was meeting
the Israeli defence minister in Jerusalem when her aides burst in to tell
her about it, was furious, in part because the minister had not already
told her, in part because of the thing itself. Wholly complicit in Israel's
military and strategic aims though the Americans were, they had
repeatedly impressed on it the importance of keeping civilian casualties
to a minimum.[125] Such massacres of innocents played very badly in the
Arab world, at American expense of course, but also at that of their
'moderate' friends, such as Jordan. There, with his public already up in
arms, King Abdullah rushed to excoriate this 'ugly crime'. Meanwhile,
in rare criticism of the United States, King Abdullah of Saudi Arabia
and other high officials urged it not to be 'led by Israel's ambitions', to
put a stop to the 'massacres and war crimes' it was committing 'against
the people, infrastructure and institutions of Lebanon'. Its veteran

foreign minister, Prince Saud al-Faisal, told Rice that if this was her 'new Middle East ... we would rather go back to the old'.[126]

That was one thing. The other was the conclusion the Americans now emphatically drew that Israel was not even going to 'deliver the goods' on the all-important military and strategic front either.[127] At first Rice and her entourage suspected that it had knowingly bombed an inhabited building, but then, deeply sceptical about its performance as they already were, they put it down to something else – 'the incredibly sloppy way [it] was handling the war'. 'Qana', said an American analyst, 'convinced Washington that the Israeli Defense Forces could not succeed in Lebanon – and that America's war by proxy there against Iran was doomed to failure.'[128] It was therefore time to bring this whole ill-fated enterprise to a close, to 'cut and bolt' before the going got worse. America's interest shifted from the military to the diplomatic arena – and to working actively for the ceasefire it had hitherto spurned.

SEARCH FOR A CEASEFIRE

What kind of ceasefire was it to be? That now became the question. Israel, America and Tony Blair's Britain still wanted it to be a 'sustainable' one, reflecting so far as possible the military and strategic gains Israel had gone to war to achieve; Lebanon, the Arabs and most of the rest of the world wanted it to be an 'immediate', and essentially unconditional, one. In the scramble to bring the war to a close, it was once again, as it had been after Qana-I, France which found itself as the counterweight to and chief interlocutor of the Americans. The 'front line' in this diplomatic contest was the office of the French ambassador to the UN, Jean-Marc de la Sablière, and the daily meetings he held there with his American counterpart, the rumbustious, militantly pro-Israeli neoconservative, John Bolton, who considered his boss, Condoleezza Rice, too well-disposed towards the Arabs.

Ceasefires generally have to reflect the balance of power on the ground in order to work. But, as with Grapes of Wrath, the United States, in its partisanship, began by seeking a diplomatic outcome out of all proportion to what Israel had achieved there. 'Condoleezza Rice needs military cards', said Israel's leading military correspondent Zeev Schiff at the time, 'but all that these now consist of is two villages the Israel Defence Forces have captured near the border.'[129] Nonetheless, the US persisted: the job of the international force in which Israel had acquiesced should be to complete what Israel had failed to accomplish itself. To this end it should go in under Chapter 7 of the UN Charter, which, authorizing 'military action' to 'restore international peace and security', would, in principle at least, have given it the right to use force both to disarm Hizbullah and prevent its re-armament with weapons smuggled across the border from Syria.

This was something which the other side simply could not countenance. To do so, it was said, would have re-ignited the Lebanese civil war. Formally speaking, this 'other side' meant the Lebanese state, embodied in Fuad Siniora's '14 March majority' government. But in practice it also – and mainly – meant Hizbullah, the state within that state, and the regional powers, Syria and Iran, which stood behind it. It was not that Hizbullah, in the pride of battlefield achievements, was wholly intransigent. On the contrary, it had paid heavily for those achievements – and caused the Lebanese state and people to pay heavily too – and, though ready to carry on the struggle, it was readier still to bring it to an end. Originally, it had objected to the very idea of the Lebanese army deploying in its place in the South; it had objected, too, to the deployment of an international force to help the army in its task, especially if it was to fall under the auspices of NATO and therefore, by extension, of America itself. But now, anxious to stem its losses, Hizbullah relented. It only did so, however, after receiving assurances, from UN officials who dealt directly with it, that the force would come in the form of an expanded UNIFIL, and operate under Chapter 6 of the UN Charter, which only authorizes the peaceful resolution of international conflicts.[130] That, in turn, enabled Hizbullah to agree to the deployment of the Lebanese army. For it knew that, though the army was supposed to be the country's sole, legitimate military force, it did not have the will or means to disarm it on its own. Hizbullah would therefore have no difficulty in preserving itself as the independent militia-cum-political party which it had always been, albeit without any formal, visibly armed and organized presence in the buffer zone between the Litani river and the border.

Reduced though Israel's war aims now were, however, it still had no assurance that diplomacy could achieve them in war's stead. Moreover, making matters worse, Rice was so publicly angry with it, both on account of Qana itself and its violating of the 48-hour bombing pause she had arranged in its wake, that she urged President Bush to defy his neoconservative advisers and bring the war to a swift end, even at the price of 'giving in to the French approach that we've been opposed to'.[131] So at first – post-Qana – Israel not merely continued the war, it defiantly stepped it up.

'THE WRITHING OF AN INJURED BEAST'

With the call-up of more reserves, Israel now had 10,000 men in action on its northern front. But all that these reinforcements yielded, in the first ten days of August, was more of the same, just more and greater floundering, or – to cite Israeli journalists Amos Harel and Avi Issacharoff in their book *34 Days* – the 'writh[ing]' of that 'injured beast', the Israeli army, in a war that 'seemed to be going nowhere'.[132]

Yet even as the beast was writhing, indeed precisely because it was, pressure had been building up inside it – and outside too – for that full-scale ground offensive which should have been undertaken from the beginning. True, there was opposition still, but most generals now wanted it 'at almost any cost'. Defence Minister Peretz had come to see it as the only possible solution. On a visit to the Northern Command, Olmert had insisted that 'we're not going to stop, we have to end the Katyusha fire', and, banging on the table, shouted at his commanders: 'Hit them, destroy them.' Even Halutz, the great procrastinator himself, had changed his mind as well, and, addressing the remaining doubters, warned them that 'if you don't want it carried out, then say so loud and clear. No half-way measures: we're not going to go half-way, a quarter or a third [of the way].'[133] Told that the casualties might be heavy, he replied that – though well of aware of that – this war now ranked as Israel's most important since the 'War of Independence', and if it ended 'with the current whine, without a ground operation, with Nasrallah alive and kicking, it could lead to a process that [would] threaten the existence of the state'.[134]

Two main reasons were now adduced for this belated, but fundamental, change of strategy. One was that, as Halutz said, the threat which Israel faced really was, in its ultimate dimensions, an existential one, that its army really did have to prove its mettle, and restore that 'deterrent power' which its dismal performance so far had brought to its lowest ever point.

> The entire Arab world [said the *Jerusalem Post*] is watching to
> see whether Hizbullah is a match for the mighty Israeli army ...
> Hizbullah's survival in the face of the best Israel can throw at it
> is the equivalent of throwing blood into a tank full of sharks.
> It would embolden the *jihadis* of the region and deal a terrible
> blow to those nascent forces that believe the Arab world ... must
> advance down the path of democracy and freedom rather than
> death and dictatorship.[135]

The other reason was that a full-scale ground offensive should deal the 'qualitative blow' to Hizbullah that would enable Israel to dictate the terms of a ceasefire.

With 30,000 men now under arms, and their commanders raring to go, it became a race between what came first, the invasion itself, or a ceasefire resolution pleasing enough for Israel to call it off. In the event, there came both.

By 10 August, after a week of hectic diplomatic to and fro, the Americans and the French were still arguing, on the forty-fourth floor of a New York office block, about such things as whether Chapter 6 or 7 of the UN Charter should govern the mandate of the international force, and whether or not an arms embargo along the Lebanese–Syrian frontier could be forcibly imposed. While the French seemed to be getting the upper hand in that venue, in another one, Jerusalem itself, it seemed to be the other way round; there the Israelis had won the acquiescence of Rice's envoy, David Welch, Assistant Secretary of State for Near East Affairs, to the altogether more 'pro-Israeli' draft of an eventual ceasefire resolution. But then, later in the day, the instructions which Rice sent to UN ambassador Bolton for further negotiations in

New York seemed to be a far cry from what had been agreed in Jerusalem. And when, at five o'clock (Jerusalem time) in the morning of the following day, Friday, 11 August, Olmert and his staff perused the latest Franco-American draft, hot from New York, they called it a 'disaster'. The French, they concluded, had won outright – a conclusion which could only have been reinforced when Bolton told the Israeli ambassador to the UN, Dan Gillerman, to tell his masters that 'Condi has sold out you guys to the French.'[136]

They were actually wrong in this conclusion. However, on the strength of it, Olmert and Peretz decided that it was no longer enough simply to threaten the great ground offensive, as their government had already repeatedly been doing, it was time actually to embark on it. A few minutes before five o'clock that Friday afternoon Olmert ordered the army to move. Three and a half hours later his office received the final Franco-American draft; a blend of chapters 6 and 7 of the UN Charter, or 'six-and-a-half' as some wit dubbed it, it was both 'good for Israel' – in Olmert and his foreign minister Tzipi Livni's words – yet acceptable to Lebanon and Hizbullah too. In its main provision, the 15,000 men of a greatly expanded, robuster UNIFIL would, by 'forceful means' if necessary, establish a buffer zone between the Litani river and the Israeli frontier; and this zone would be 'free of any armed personnel, assets and weapons' – Hizbullah's – other than UNIFIL's own, and the 15,000 men of the Lebanese army it would help to deploy there. Some six hours after that, about 3 o'clock in the morning (Jerusalem time) of Saturday, 12 August, the Security Council, meeting in emergency session, unanimously approved it in the form of Resolution 1701. It was, however, too late for Olmert to halt his military juggernaut. Or so at least he and his cohorts contended. Their argument? Maybe the Lebanese or Hizbullah would go back on their acceptance. In truth, however, neither he – nor Peretz or Halutz – wanted to call their operation off. They wanted to redeem themselves, to end the war with a demonstrable accomplishment to their names. So 'our sensitive prime minister decided that the army needed to push deep into enemy territory, to hoist the Israeli flag and to cry "Victory!" before bringing the troops back home; some of them safe and sound; others – as he could have predicted – in coffins.'[137]

'THE REAL WAR, WAR WITH A CAPITAL W'

Thirty-three of them did come back that way. It would have been twice that number had the Hizbullah anti-tank missile team which shot down that Sikorsky helicopter done so when it was landing with its thirty-odd soldiers aboard, instead of seconds later, when it was taking off with only its crew of five. But, in any case, those thirty-three, more than a quarter of the total for the whole war, were the entirely gratuitous victims of a 'final, fruitless and extremely costly' offensive, in which both political and military leaders had been 'willing to risk soldiers' lives for a goal whose benefit and chances of attainment were negligible from the start'.[138]

For the army, this was at last the real war, 'war with a capital W, war in all the meanings of the term'.[139] Its objective – insofar as it had a clear one at all – was to 'cleanse' Hizbullah and its missile-firing capability from southern Lebanon. But this real war was beginning just as Israel was agreeing that war of any kind was about to stop. Only a day before, the army had been asking for a full month or more to do the job properly;[140] now it had just sixty-three hours, from the time it had moved on Friday afternoon till the ceasefire set for 8.00 in the morning of Monday, 14 August.

In the event, it hardly even got to the Litani, let alone drove out Hizbullah, or knocked out any of its 'nature reserves' and missile launching sites. The downing of the helicopter was but one of a series of mishaps, generally as attributable to Israeli incompetence as to Hizbullah's proficiency, which, on top of the great offensive's inherent unfeasibility, compounded the fiasco into which it swiftly degenerated. The greatest mishap took place in the Wadi Salouqi, a ravine which a column of tanks had to traverse on its way to team up with Nahal infantrymen already airlifted to the village of Ghandouriyah on high ground not far from the Litani river. Together they were then supposed to have pushed westwards, linking up, around the port city of Tyre, with tank and infantry columns advancing up the coast. Hidden among the dense undergrowth of the wadi's steep slopes, Hizbullah fighters destroyed the commander's tank with a roadside bomb, and poured anti-tank missiles, rocket-propelled grenades and mortars into the rest of the column, hitting eleven tanks and killing eight crewmen. Altogether, seventeen men died, and fifty were wounded, in incidents directly or indirectly related to the Salouqi crossing, more than half the fatalities for the whole offensive.[141] For the Northern Command headquarters, it seemed for a while as though everything that could go wrong did go wrong. 'This was the Black Sabbath, a goddamned Sabbath', said an officer in the war room, 'every minute the teleprinter spat out another report ... a tank detonated, an IED [improvised explosive device], four killed. Casualties in Salouqi. Another soldier killed by friendly fire. Every line like this pushed us deeper into the ground.'[142]

A GRAND FINALE OF CLUSTER BOMBS

But as the ground forces flailed and floundered, in this, their grand finale, just as they had in its lesser precursors, there was one department, the long-range, high-tech onslaught from land, sea and air, in which the Israeli war machine did not falter. It had made enormous efforts down the years to acquire and develop technologies for destroying an enemy from afar while keeping its own casualties to a minimum, and it was only to be expected that it would make copious use of them now. But it did more than that – it ran riot. Israel's air force made as many combat sorties – 15,000, hitting 7,000 targets – as it had done in the whole of the 1973 war. But whereas in that ferocious, life-and-death struggle, the enemy had been the two most formidable and well-equipped of Arab armies launching all-out, simultaneous, surprise attacks on two broad fronts, this time it was a just a group of guerillas in the narrow strip of territory from which they lobbed their 4,228 missiles of the war. As for Israel's ground artillery, whereas, over 24 days of October 1973, it had fired some 53,000 shells, the tally exceeded 180,000 in the 33 days of July and August 2006.[143] If, for the Palestinians, and later for Hizbullah, the Katyusha had always been the signature weapon of south Lebanese cross-border warfare, for Israel it was cluster bombs. It had turned to these wantonly inaccurate, but viciously effective, little devils in all its wars; after the 1982 invasion the Reagan Administration withheld any further supplies of them for six years because, in violation of express commitments, Israel had used them against populated areas.[144] But there were no such constraints this time. 'What we did was insane and monstrous,' said the head of a rocket unit,[145] referring to an estimated 4.6 million of them with which both army and air force had carpeted southern Lebanon, mostly in one last, wild, non-stop cannonade during the final ground offensive. The bomblets are supposed to explode just before they hit the ground. But since the old, outdated type which Israel used – mainly American and apparently part of the Bush Administration's emergency, mid-war airlift of munitions – had an extraordinarily high failure rate, at least a million of them still lay about, unexploded, after the war was over – on roads and rooftops, in fields and orchards, around schools and hospitals, suspended from olive or banana trees. Innocuous-looking canisters, often enticingly similar to toys, they maimed or killed 200 people, mostly children, in the following eighteen months.[146]

It was not clear what the artillery blitz was meant to achieve – some thought it was just vengeance and spite, some that it was part of a plan to depopulate the South of its Shiites – but it certainly did not help the ground offensive. In fact, under the demoralizing impact of the downed helicopter and the Wadi Salouqi casualties, this just faded away virtually of its own accord. By Sunday morning the political and military leadership had lost any appetite for further gains. If the advance to the Litani had proceeded, it obviously would not have achieved much in the time remaining and might easily have ended up incurring even greater losses. So a few hours before the ceasefire the men who had risked their lives to get nowhere in particular were ordered to go no further. Meanwhile, dramatizing the futility of it all, Hizbullah, for its last hurrah, fired 250 missiles into northern Israel, its largest single-day barrage of the war. As relieved but resentful reservists made their way back across the border with the Monday morning ceasefire taking hold, the Deputy Chief of Staff, Moshe Kaplinsky, managed to contact one of them, his son Or, who asked him: 'What shall I tell the guys, dad?' 'Tell 'em we won,' came the reply.[147]

CHAPTER FOURTEEN

Who Won?

2006–2008

'A VICTORY TOO GREAT TO BE COMPREHENDED'

Who, in fact, did win? There was no question that, in terms of anticipated outcomes, the laurels of the 2006 war went to Hizbullah.[1] Still, this unusual, 'asymmetrical' conflict which, in any immediate, physical sense, changed very little on the ground, lent itself to opposing claims about what its outcome really meant. On 22 September, in his first post-war public appearance, Nasrallah staked his. The victory they were celebrating, he told the immense, euphoric throng, had been 'great, strategic, historic and divine' – so much so, indeed, that it was simply 'too great to be comprehended by us'. However, about one thing he was sure, and this was that it had transformed Lebanon from a 'small' state of the Middle East into a 'great' one.[2] It was an audacious proposition, yet not a wildly extravagant one. Lebanon certainly remained, in Bakunin's sense, the battleground of greater states than itself. Indeed, amid very serious fears that it might now disintegrate altogether, it was if anything more that battlefield than ever, more than ever a potential flashpoint in the course of the 'Great Arab Unravelling',[3] the decline and possible break-up of the whole existing Middle Eastern order. Yet, in spite of that, though in a very real sense *because* of it as well, it had become more, much more, than just the hapless object of others' actions; it was an agent, a prime mover, in its own right too. Lebanon, or perhaps one should say a very important segment of it, was now exerting at least as powerful an influence on the region as the region had always exerted on it. In their 'legendary resistance', proclaimed Nasrallah, 'the people of Lebanon' were offering a 'model' and a 'strong proof that it is not only Gaza, the West Bank and Jerusalem which Arab armies and peoples are capable of liberating, but – with one small decision and a bit of determination – [the whole of] Palestine too, from the river to the sea'.[4]

What Hizbullah had wrought did indeed have a great resonance around the Arab and Muslim worlds. Not for nothing had it been quickly baptized the Sixth Arab–Israeli War, the most important, many said, since the first, which had produced *al-Nakba* – the Calamity – and whose consequences the whole Arab 'nation' had at the time pledged itself to reverse. The effect, at this stage, was essentially psychological. But that did not prevent Arab commentators from speaking of 'earth-shaking regional consequences', of a 'contagion' that would inexorably spread, of 'a model of dignity, steadfastness and defiance' that would 'revive a frustrated Arab spirit burdened with the accumulations of pain and defeat', 'renew noble hopes and aspirations' that had been 'buried beneath the ruins of submission, injustice, repression, and humiliation'.[5]

Ever since Israel came into being, it had put its trust in the doctrine of the Iron Wall, the notion that force – and yet more force – was the only way to preserve and strengthen itself against Palestinians and Arabs who viscerally rejected its presence in their midst. It certainly had not won their acceptance by such means; what it had done was so to cow and intimidate them that they – or rather their regimes – no longer even considered the use, or threat, of force in response, and generally speaking comported themselves with a demeaning complaisance, not to say servility, towards both it and, above all, the American superpower which stood behind it. But here, at last, had come these 'combatants of Islam' to change all that. The Arab media had no doubt about their achievement: they had demonstrated, for the first time, that force could be met with successful counter-force. They had 'smashed the myth of Israel's invincibility', 'broken the barrier of fear', imparted great impetus to the rising popular demand for 'resistance' in place of acquiescence, appeasement and surrender. The plain fact was that Israel, even if not the 'spider's web' Nasrallah always said it was, *could* be defeated. That was his electrifying message. The Arabs had the resources: all they needed was the will and skills to use them.

'DE FACTO CALIPH OF THE ARABS AND THE MUSLIMS'

That they were not being used was a fault Nasrallah laid at the door of the Arab 'kings and presidents'. Whenever, he lamented, they found themselves 'torn between two choices – between Jerusalem, their people and the dignity of their homeland on the one hand and their thrones on the other – they always chose their thrones'.[6] Thus was Hizbullah's struggle with Israel inextricably bound up with another one, between itself – and other non-state actors like it – and the whole official Arab order. Whatever their virtues or vices, these non-state actors, a prime manifestation of the Great Unravelling, had broadly speaking arisen in those places where the official order was most eroded, or most glaringly deficient in its ability to promote and defend the basic interests and expectations of its people – in Lebanon with Hizbullah, in Palestine with Hamas, in Iraq with that maelstrom of ethnic and sectarian militias that foreign invasion had unleashed. Hizbullah was much the most advanced of them, and, at the hub of the world's most implacable conflict, the most significant, most destiny-shaping, for the whole region. The more successfully it confronted Israel, the greater the threat it presented to the Arab regimes, to the so-called 'Arab system' in which they were collectively represented, and to the strategy which that system had adopted for dealing with the historic Arab foe.

It was an accident, no doubt, but a richly symbolic one that, even as the non-state actor was confounding Israel on the battlefield, the 'system' was all but formally confessing to its own bankruptcy. 'Peace with Israel' – via the American-sponsored 'peace process' – had for decades been its strategic choice, a few mavericks excepted. But at a meeting of the Arab League a few days into the war, its secretary-general, Amr Moussa, formally pronounced the whole process 'dead': Arab governments, he said, could do no more. This was such a shocking admission of failure that Arab journalists, in an extraordinary violation of decorum, did not merely report on it, they barracked it. Hizbullah's achievement was therefore a double one, a military one against the Israelis, a moral, political and psychological one against virtually all the Arab regimes, but especially against the 'moderates', led by Egypt, Saudi Arabia and Jordan. These it were who dominated the 'system', yet despite the abject failure of the 'peace option' and their possession of large conventional armies of their own, they persisted in rejecting the military alternative, and when Hizbullah adopted it in their stead, they desperately sought to thwart it, virtually siding with the enemy to do so. With the success of his new, Islamist way of war, Nasrallah became more than just a role model, he became – for one commentator – nothing less than a '*de facto* caliph, a spiritual and political leader of the Arabs and Muslims'.[7]

In the event, he did not, as some even thought possible at the time, 'light the prairie fire' of wider Arab revolution and bring the whole, despised and decadent order down – but his 'victory' clearly changed the balance of power within it. It strengthened the Islamo-nationalist camp at the expense of the 'moderate' one. Of its non-state members, Hizbullah's Palestinian counterpart, Hamas, was a notable beneficiary. So was Syria, its only state member. It is true that when government-encouraged demonstrators paraded through Damascus shouting 'Oh Nasrallah, hit Tel Aviv too', many of their compatriots cannot but have wondered why the ruling Baathists, in charge of their self-styled 'citadel of Arabism', had failed yet again to lift a finger on sister-Lebanon's behalf, perhaps by striking into the occupied Golan. Indeed, no less a personage than the Grand Mufti himself vainly suggested such a course. But in a fiery speech he safely made *after* the ceasefire, President Asad had no compunction about virtually appropriating Hizbullah's victory as Syria's own. For this had, he said, vindicated his conviction that 'resistance and liberation go hand in hand', and 'unmasked' those other Arab leaders who, mere 'half-men' that they were, had only brought defeat and humiliation to their peoples. 'Resistance' – not 'subjugation' to America – would now be 'the core of "the new Middle East"'. Syria would 'liberate the Golan with [its] own hands, will and determination'. And it would do so, apparently, not merely by following the non-state actor's example, but even adopting some of its Islamist, 'asymmetrical' way of war as well.

But it was non-Arab Iran, linchpin of the Islamo-nationalist camp, that had the most cause to rejoice. And within hours of the ceasefire young men, on motorbikes or in cars and parading the yellow emblem of Hizbullah, were careering around central Tehran in celebration of this latest 'victory of Islam'. Citizens mounted to their rooftops to cry 'God is Great', just as they do, on II February every year, to celebrate the victory of the Islamic Revolution itself.

For the US and Israel, the mullahs were the great and growing enemy of all their purposes in the Middle East, and their defeat or downfall – and termination of their nuclear programme – was to have been the ultimate objective of a campaign in which the violent suppression of Hizbullah would have been only the start. But instead, they had only strengthened them. As the mullahs saw it, the US had posed a grave, even existential, military threat to themselves with its invasion of Afghanistan and Iraq. But now, with their counter-offensive in Lebanon, they were turning the tables on it, demonstrating their ability, by proxy, to retaliate against its Israeli partner and protégé[8] – and that was only an earnest of what they could do with all the other assets, no less formidable than Hizbullah itself, which they disposed of across the region, should any situation require it. No wonder that, amid the rejoicing, President Ahmadinejad, Holocaust-doubter and champion of a nuclear Iran, was moved to proclaim that if, as a result of the Sixth Arab–Israeli War, there was going to be a 'new Middle East', it would not be Condoleezza Rice's; it would be that of 'the Iranian people', and 'a Middle East without America and the usurper Zionist regime'.

NO, OUR SIDE WON

No, it was we who won, promptly claimed the other side. For President Bush, Lebanon was another front in the 'global war on terror' and, equating Israel's campaign there with the US-led ones in Iraq and Afghanistan, he pronounced Hizbullah the loser. Not that he had been surprised by its claims to the contrary; after all, he said, the 'terror' organization had a 'fantastic propaganda machine'. 'But how', he asked, 'can you claim victory, when, at one time you were a state-within-a-state, and now you're going to be replaced by a Lebanese army and an international force?' Resolution 1701, added his State Department, constituted a 'strategic reverse' for Hizbullah's Syrian and Iranian backers too. As for Shimon Peres, the Israeli elder statesman and deputy premier, the victory had been both 'military and political'. But he also went so far as to say that Hizbullah had come out of the war 'with its tail between its legs',[9] and this was so startling an assertion, so patently at odds with the evidence, as to suggest that there was something suspect, even deeply flawed, about these triumphal claims of the Israeli–American camp. And it soon became clear that there was.

To be sure, the balance sheet was not wholly in Hizbullah's favour. The Israelis did have one achievement to their credit. This was the deployment of the much expanded, robuster, European-led, 13,300-man UNIFIL, as well as 15,000 soldiers of the Lebanese army, throughout the territory between the Litani river and the southern border, where Hizbullah had enjoyed a virtually unimpeded presence before the war. And this did cause it a problem. It was very like the one which it had faced after its first great triumph of arms, the enforced Israeli withdrawal of 2000, but it was more serious. After 2000, it will be recalled, Hizbullah had been hard put to it, having successfully liberated virtually the whole of Lebanese territory, to find a means of justifying and perpetuating its basic *raison d'être*, its *jihad* and 'Islamic resistance' against the Zionist enemy. It had managed it, however, by going into its 'gradualist-pragmatic' mode of occasional 'reminder' operations – until the last of them, going too far, provoked the full-scale war it never wanted. But the loss of this southern sanctuary, and the network of 'nature reserves' and fortified positions it had patiently built up there, constituted a serious weakening of its whole *modus operandi*. It might not have completely eliminated its ability to renew such cross-border attacks, but it certainly rendered them more difficult. And after the war they completely ceased.

Moreover, the reasons for this were not merely technical and military, more importantly, they were political too: Hizbullah simply could not afford the risk of provoking more hostilities in any foreseeable future. Less than ever would its own Shiite constituency, let alone the Lebanese people at large, now stand for that. And the clear fact was that, as a result of the war, Lebanon's internal politics had become a more critical arena for Hizbullah's future than before. For ironically, the glory which it had garnered through the length and breadth of the Arab and Muslim worlds was never going to be matched in the place – its very own, diminutive, Lebanese backyard – where it needed it most. For there, political and sectarian animosities always ensured that what might become an object of passionate adulation for some was all too apt to become the object of fear and loathing for others. The great national schism, with Hizbullah's arms at its heart, not merely manifested itself again, it did so more dangerously than before. The government and its supporters accused Hizbullah of having brought catastrophe on the country. Hizbullah retorted that, on the contrary, it alone had done what any government, any self-respecting state, should have done itself – defend the nation against its enemies – and that its accusers were mere 'traitors' and 'backstabbers' in time of war. In such a climate, not surprisingly, sectarian tensions took a sharp turn for the worse, mainly between Shiites and Sunnis. And Hizbullah's feat of arms, a source of widespread, trans-sectarian pride during the war, became a source of great apprehension after it. If it could so humble the mightiest army in the Middle East, what might it do against its fellow Lebanese if, as many now feared, the internal conflict degenerated into violence, or even, heaven forbid, into renewed civil war?

Gains of a sort, actual or potential, these doubtless were, but they did very little to sustain the 'victory' claims of Israeli leaders. Indeed, hardly had the guns fallen silent than 'the war between the Jews' began, the 'all-out war' of recrimination about all that had gone wrong in the real one.[10] Within hours of their exit from Lebanon, reservists – outraged at the gap between their own experience there and the version of it propagated by the high command – took the lead with public protests against the military and political leadership, and with a petition demanding – and soon getting – a commission of inquiry into the whole conduct of the war. Within a few months Chief of Staff Halutz and key commanders had resigned in disgust or disgrace; the reputation of the Israeli army, most sacrosanct of institutions, fell to an unprecedented low. Prime Minister Olmert clung mulishly to office in spite of an approval rating which, at a mere 2 per cent, fell far below even that of his war-making accomplice, President Bush. Eventually the Winograd commission delivered its damning verdict on 'the worst kind of mistakes' the political and military leadership had made in 'initiating' the war, and the 'failure of the ground forces – and thus the whole Israeli Defence Forces – to carry out the missions assigned to them'.

Soldiers, strategists and politicians were saying things about the future of the Jewish state which had much in common, albeit from a diametrically opposing standpoint, with what their nemesis, Nasrallah himself, was saying. Israel had gone to war for one supreme goal: less to smash Hizbullah as such than to re-establish its 'deterrent power' throughout the region. But it had only succeeded in further undermining it. And this, said one, was not 'a mere military defeat'; it was a 'strategic failure ... eroding our national security's most important asset – the belligerent image of this country led by a vast, strong and advanced army capable of dealing our enemies a decisive blow if they even try so much as to bother us'.[11]

It would not be the first time that Israel had sought to redress the adverse consequences of one war with the waging of another, but this time the generals all but leapt to proclaim the necessity and inevitability of the 'second round', and even to predict when it would happen. One of them was Moshe Kaplinsky, the former Deputy Chief of Staff who had told his reservist son that Israel had actually won the last war. He now assured a Washington think tank that, by sending in its ground forces from the very outset, it really would win the next one.[12]

SELLING FISH IN THE SEA

The great flaw, the fly in the ointment of the Israeli–American 'victory' lay in its being a blatant case of counting one's chickens before they were hatched, or, as the Arab saying goes, 'selling fish in the sea'. It depended for its accomplishment not on the mere adoption of Resolution 1701, but on its implementation. And that, as its framers surely knew, had always been most unlikely to come to pass. For Hizbullah had never had any intention of disarming. And no one could make it do so, certainly not a weak and divided Lebanese government

on which the international powers-that-be had disingenuously conferred a responsibility which they were unwilling or afraid to assume
themselves.

Within six week of the ceasefire, Nasrallah was declaring, in *his*
'victory' speech, that Hizbullah was already stronger, in the weapons at
its disposal, than it had been at the outset of the war. On 12 July it had
boasted a mere 13,000 rockets, now it had 'more than 20,000' – and he
laid the stress on the 'more'.

He effectively declared something else as well. Hizbullah was not
merely re-arming militarily, it was arming politically too. In its early
days it had spurned politics altogether. Gradually, however, it had been
drawn into them, a process of 'Lebanonization' which had bred hopes
in many quarters that, with so little Lebanese territory left to liberate,
it would eventually shed its jihadist mission altogether and become just
a political party like any other. For Hizbullah, however, there never
had been such an either–or. For it, politics were not an end in
themselves; they were simply the means, whenever the need arose, to
preserve the 'Islamic resistance', the weapons, the will and ability to
pursue it. Now, after the war, both the need – and the opportunity –
were greater than before. And so were the goals that Nasrallah set
himself.

'GIVE ME THE STATE AND TO THE STATE I SHALL SURRENDER MY WEAPONS'

The Western-backed, '14 March majority' government, he now proclaimed, had to go. It was unfit to rule. A 'national unity government'
should take its place, a government that would rebuild Lebanon as 'a
just, strong, capable, honourable and resisting state' which could 'truly
protect' its citizens 'with arms, power, reason, unity, organization,
planning and national will'; a 'proud and noble' state which rejected
'foreign tutelage or hegemony', and a 'clean' state that banished 'theft
and waste'.[13]

Under such a state, he went on, the problem of Hizbullah's arms
would 'not even require a negotiating table' for its resolution. It would
wither away of its own accord:

[But] under *this* state, *this* authority, *this* regime ... any talk of
surrendering the resistance weapons means keeping Lebanon
exposed to an Israel that can bomb, kill and kidnap as it wants,
and plunder our land and waters ... We don't want to keep the
weapons forever. They will never be used inside Lebanon. They
are not Shiite weapons, but weapons for all the Lebanese.[14]

For many in the government, and the non-Shiite communities from
which it drew its main support, Nasrallah's 'just state' would have been
the end of Lebanon – model of inter-communal co-existence, meeting
place of East and West, bastion of a freedom, democracy and tolerance
unique to the Arab world – as they deemed it, ideally, to be. It would
have ushered in a totalitarian, theocratic regime, and the dominion of
one ideology, one sect, over all the others. It would have institutionalized the ascendancy of the Islamic Republic of Iran in Lebanon's
internal affairs, and it would have done this not only at the expense of
the West, but of all those Arab states with which Iran, and its Syrian
ally, did not agree. It would, so to speak, have rendered *de jure* what
Lebanon already was *de facto*: the only place where the Arabs could
fight the good fight against the historic Zionist foe – fight it, that is to
say, to the last Lebanese. And it was a kind of blackmail. 'The essence
of his speech', said Marwan Hamade, the minister of telecommunications, 'was: "Give me the state, and [to it] I shall surrender my
weapons."'[15]

Whether Nasrallah, who had always said that turning multi-
confessional Lebanon into an 'Islamic state' was impossible, really
entertained such maximalist ambitions was very much open to
question. Of one thing, however, there could be no doubt: he was not
prepared to live with the actively hostile state which, in the hands of
Prime Minister Fuad Siniora's government, he considered it to be.
'What has happened since the end of the war', Nasrallah said, 'is an
extension of Israel's war against Lebanon. And just as we fought in July
and August, so we will fight today, but with other weapons and other
rules.'[16] And by that he meant that Hizbullah would now seek a real
share in the running of the country. In his opinion, in fact, Hizbullah
and the '8 March' opposition of which it was the backbone should

already have been doing that in any case, because it was they, not the current government, who represented the true majority of the people. Meanwhile, however, he would be satisfied with the formation of a national unity government in which Hizbullah was strongly enough represented, either directly or via its allies, to enjoy 'veto power' over any decisions he did not like, especially those threatening Hizbullah's weapons, its right to 'resistance', and its determination to thwart any kind of American or Israeli tutelage over Lebanon.

So it was that Hizbullah launched a bold and escalating campaign to secure such a government. It began with the resignation of six ministers, five of them Shiites. This supposedly rendered the Siniora government 'illegitimate', on the grounds that, lacking any representation for one of the country's major sects, it violated the principle of inter-communal consensus. But the government did not see it that way. Nasrallah therefore resorted to direct action in the streets. First he ordered an indefinite sit-in in the heart of Beirut; his followers camped out day and night beneath the Grand Serail, the seat of government, from where the besieged prime minister denounced this action as tantamount to an attempted *coup d'état*. Then, in January 2007, with the government still standing firm, he ordered a one-day general strike. But this degenerated into ugly sectarian clashes, mainly between Shiites and Sunnis, leaving seven dead and 250 injured. Fearful that matters could get out of hand in a way that would be as ruinous for Hizbullah as everyone else, he took the exceptional step of issuing a *fatwa* urging the withdrawal from the streets of all Shiites – not just his party members – who, in sectarian solidarity, had spontaneously joined the fray. In the opposing camp, Saad Hariri and the Future Movement, the mainstream Sunni organization he had inherited from his father, appeared to have no more scruples than Nasrallah about exploiting sectarian solidarity for political ends, even cultivating support among the most extreme of anti-Shiite fundamentalist groups, especially in the northern city of Tripoli and the Beqa'a Valley.

Hizbullah's campaign coincided – though many did not believe it was a coincidence at all – with renewed assassinations of anti-Syrian personalities, including two MPs and a minister. These were widely presumed to be the handiwork of a Syria resolved to destroy a government that was no less resolved to get it tried, by international tribunal, for the murder of Rafiq Hariri. Hizbullah's open hostility to such a course, seen as blind adherence to Damascus, further alienated a great many Lebanese, especially Sunnis, who might have applauded it during the war. The purpose of the assassinations was apparently not merely to terrorize, but to deprive the government of the ministerial quorum it constitutionally required to stay in office, or of the majority in parliament it required to elect a president of its choice. For the term of the widely despised Emile Lahoud was now coming to an end, and who was to succeed him was becoming the fiercely contested question on which Lebanon's destiny increasingly seemed to hinge. Institutional collapse; the emergence of two governments; chaos, partition, a new civil war; a failed state, an Iraq or Somalia, in the making. These were the kind of worst-case scenarios now conjured up by people, pundits and politicians alike should parliament elect a divisive president, or, more likely, fail to elect one at all.

Petty and parochial in its strictly Lebanese dimension, the presidential crisis inevitably, like anything else in the 'small state' of the Middle East, had its regional and international dimension too. Foreign powers were engaged in such a multitude of 'mediations, initiatives, interventions and interferences', said Issa Ghorayeb of Beirut's *L'Orient Le Jour*, that it seemed to have become their veritable *cause célèbre*.[17] Indeed, those flimsy ribbons of barbed wire that separated the Grand Serail from the protesters permanently encamped outside it were actually the new front-line in the continuing battle of wills between the Islamo-nationalist camp on the one hand, America and the Arab 'moderates' on the other. Iran and Syria's determination to secure a president to their liking was only matched, if not outdone, by the Americans' to secure one to theirs. At one point, President Bush, more royalist than the king, was publicly urging his 'allies' in the '14 March' coalition to use what they deemed to be their constitutional right to elect a president of their choice by a simple majority vote. But that would have been a step too far for the Siniora government, all too well aware that, for the '8 March' opposition which insisted that only a two-thirds majority vote was constitutionally valid, it would have amounted to a 'declaration of war'. At another critical moment, Bush dispatched two warships to Lebanese coastal waters in a show of strength at which, again taking fright, Siniora himself had to protest.

Whatever the pressures their respective backers exerted on them, neither side wanted to push matters to another civil war, and, eventually, they got so far as to agree on the need for a neutral candidate, in the person of army commander General Michel Suleiman. But still the loyalist camp, deeming itself to have already made the main concessions, simply would not bend to the further conditions on which the opposition also insisted, and in particular a guarantee of their veto power in a 'national unity government' to come. Election day, 24 November 2007, came and went without a new president. Even then, however, the final break was averted: the '14 March' government ceded what it considered to be its right to elect a candidate by simple majority, and in return, as the outgoing Lahoud stepped down, the opposition did not challenge the automatic transfer of his powers to the Siniora cabinet, illegitimate though it considered it to be. But, against an ominous background of more inter-communal violence, car-bombs and assassinations, the deadlock persisted. A full seventeen times the speaker of parliament, Nabih Berri, set a new date for the crucial election, a full seventeen times he postponed it – until finally, in April 2008, he refused to set another. The stage was set for a Hizbullah coup.

THE TENTH GREATEST 'MISSILE POWER' IN THE WORLD

As Hizbullah was thus striving to secure itself politically, it was doing so militarily too. It was not the only one. Amid fears on all hands about where the domestic turmoil was leading, each camp accused the other of resuscitating old civil-war militias or creating new ones. The loyalists claimed that, as well as Shiites, Hizbullah was arming and training allied factions among Christians, Druzes and even Sunnis. The opposition said that a vast increase in the number of private security personnel guarding buildings in central Beirut masked a whole new Sunni militia – arm of Saad Hariri's Future Movement – in the making. Arms dealers were back in business; one, called 'Jaafar', boasted of his clients on both sides of the divide, of the 'untainted reputation' he enjoyed among them all.[18]

But Hizbullah's arming had less to do with the prospect of *fitna* – the internecine feuding of the Lebanese – than with the higher cause of anti-Zionist *jihad*. It was less small arms that it was after – though it was far from uninterested in those too – than the heavy stuff, missiles especially, with which it had humbled Israel in the 33-day war.[19] This could only come from Syria or Iran, smuggled across the rugged, mountainous march lands that separate Lebanon from its only Arab neighbour. But that was precisely what Security Council Resolution 1701 was supposed to put an end to, with its call on 'all states' to supply no 'arms and related materiel' to any other 'entity or individual' than the Lebanese government.

Although President Asad had officially welcomed 1701, personally assuring UN Secretary-General Kofi Annan that he would deploy additional troops to police the notoriously porous frontier, it quickly proved that he actually had no more intention of stopping the supply of weaponry than Hizbullah had of forgoing it. And no one could do anything about that either, as Syria issued dire warnings about 'the enmity' it would arouse between itself and Lebanon should anyone so much as try.[20] Theoretically, the enlarged, post-war UNIFIL could or should have done so. But, in practice, it had no such desire; no desire to expand its mandate – territorially – beyond the southern buffer zone where, thanks mainly to Hizbullah's consent, it was quite comfortably installed, or – functionally – to engage in coercive military action against which its contributing nations, alarmed by the inevitable casualties, would have soon rebelled.

Besides – decreed 1701 – UNIFIL could only have undertaken this task 'at the request' of a Lebanese government to which the international powers-that-be had left the ultimate responsibility for securing its frontiers just as they had the disarming of Hizbullah. But the government was never actually going to make such a request; for that would automatically have drawn it into a collision with both Hizbullah and Syria which, politically, it could not have withstood. It did make a show of sealing its border – at one time it had 8,000 troops stationed along it – and a couple of times, probably more by accident than design, it did intercept weapons destined for Hizbullah. But when it did so, Hizbullah, far from disowning them, unashamedly laid claim to them. It deemed it had the right to do so – and, in a sense, it actually did. For the fact of the matter was that the schizoid Lebanese state had contracted two obligations, one – international – to 1701, and the other – domestic – to the 'resistance' as 'the natural, honest expression of the Lebanese people's national right to liberate their land'. Inevitably, the domestic obligation won hands down, so much so that the regular 'progress' reports which the UN Secretary-General commissioned from his special envoys to the region became little more than international testimonials to the failure of 1701 – and the fiasco to which the Israeli–American 'victory' was being steadily reduced.

As the months passed precise Israeli estimates – broadly corroborated by the UN and Nasrallah himself – of the number of missiles in Hizbullah's possession steadily rose, from 20,000 to 30,000, and finally, in early 2008, to 42,000, making it the tenth largest 'missile power' in the world. They included a much higher proportion of the longer-range ones, like the Iranian-built Zelzal-2 which it had apparently refrained from using in the war, as well as three times its former stock of C-802s, those Chinese-made shore-to-ship rockets, one of which, it will be recalled, had nearly sunk the Israeli flagship *Hanit*. They could reach almost anywhere in Israel, from Tel Aviv to the Dimona nuclear plant in the far south.[21] Perhaps the Israelis' greatest worry was that the mysterious 'big surprise' which Nasrallah kept promising them would turn out to be precisely what they feared it was: the latest and most sophisticated of Russian anti-aircraft systems. For nearly thirty years, Israeli fighter-bombers had had Lebanese air space entirely to themselves; and with reconnaissance flights they were still violating it virtually every day. Such a system in Hizbullah's hands, the Israelis said, could fundamentally alter the aerial balance of power over Lebanon and western Syria.[22] All in all, the *Jerusalem Post* estimated, Hizbullah was now four times stronger than it was before the 33-day war.[23]

No longer able to engage in military activities in the UNIFIL/ Lebanese army buffer zone, and having renounced 'resistance' operations across the Israeli border, deterrence now became Hizbullah's principal role – the role, that is to say, which it deemed the Lebanese state incapable of undertaking and which it, the state-within-the-state, was assuming in its stead.

This did not mean that it retained no military capability in the buffer zone, only that it had to be a relatively modest and discreet one. After all, when things were quiet, most of its fighters in the region were just civilian residents of it like anyone else. There was an informal, but well-observed, understanding between them and the Lebanese army, and by extension with UNIFIL, that neither of these two would take any action against what, without actively looking for it, they could not actually 'see'. And it appears that, on this congenial basis, Hizbullah was able to do quite a lot – by way of infiltrating, stockpiling, and readying for immediate use large numbers of those short-range Katyushas, as well as anti-tank weapons, which had exacted such a toll in the war.[24]

But it did mean that Hizbullah's second, albeit main line of defence now lay further to the rear, north of the Litani, around the town of Nabatiyah and up into the lower Beqa'a Valley. There Hizbullah more or less replicated what it had formerly done right up to the Israeli border. It assembled a vast military infrastructure, complete with 'nature reserves' and all manner of other installations designed, with the rugged terrain aiding, to give an invading Israeli army as hard a time as it could possibly imagine. To this end, as before, it declared large tracts of territory 'off-limits' to everyone, representatives of the Lebanese state included, built new access roads to them, bought up swathes of mainly non-Shiite land and property in the vicinity, and peopled them where possible with poor, resistance-friendly members of its own community; it also enrolled new recruits in very great numbers, thousands of whom went to Iran for training.[25]

For all its secrecy and security precautions, Hizbullah did not, rather uncharacteristically, disguise what it was up to in general. After Israeli manoeuvres along its Lebanese border, it did not fail to advertise the counter-manoeuvres of unprecedented scale that it conducted itself as a supplementary means of dissuading its enemy from launching the war it did not want. But, like the Israelis, it clearly deemed one inevitable in the end.

In the event, however, it soon did get a war of sorts, a war in which it did what it had vowed it never would: it turned its arms, not on Israelis, but on its Lebanese fellow citizens.

THE HIZBULLAH STATE OF LEBANON

On 5 May 2008, the Siniora government took two fateful decisions. One was to declare an independent telecommunications network owned by Hizbullah to be 'illegal and illegitimate', an 'aggression against the state'. The other was to dismiss the chief of security at Beirut airport, a Shiite army officer, for failing to take action against unauthorized surveillance cameras which Hizbullah had installed there. Their purpose, the loyalist camp believed, was to record its leaders' incognito movements in and out of the country, rendering them vulnerable to assassination.[26] The government had known about the fibre optic landlines, immune to Israeli eavesdropping, for a long time and done nothing about them. There was much to suggest that it had been put up to this sudden, highly provocative action by the US, in conjunction with its 'moderate' allies, Saudi Arabia and Egypt. They were apparently raising the stakes in the presidential crisis in a bid to clinch the election of a partisan figure to their own liking. The US had made vague assurances about the help it would extend if help were needed.[27]

The decisions looked like the opening shot in an all-out campaign by the state to bring to heel the state-within-a-state and its militia, which had been relentlessly chipping away at its authority. For Nasrallah, it was tantamount to treason, a 'declaration of war against the resistance on behalf of America and Israel'. The telephone network, an integral part of Hizbullah's military infrastructure, had been of critical importance in the 33-day war. Having always vowed to 'cut off the hands' of anyone who sought to harm the resistance, Nasrallah was now, as it was said, going to 'use his weapons to defend his weapons'. His men took to the streets under cover of a general strike, besieging and blocking access to the international airport.

Then, even as he warned, in a television address from his bunker somewhere in the *Dahiya*, that if the decisions were not reversed greater conflict would ensue, fighters of Hizbullah and its allies Amal and the Syrian Socialist Nationalist Party, armed with assault rifles and rocket-propelled grenades, invaded the predominantly Sunni Muslim heart of West Beirut. With the army, which the government had been counting on to intervene, basically standing aside for fear that this last functioning national institution, a composite of all sects, would fall apart under the pressure of conflicting loyalties, Hizbullah routed the Future Movement's ill-trained, inexperienced militia. Within a day, its men had surrendered or fled. The marauders also briefly seized government buildings, and sacked Future Movement premises and media outlets. The two main '14 March' leaders, Hariri and Jumblat, were reduced to prisoners in their own homes. It was profoundly humiliating, especially for the Sunnis. But the fighting was not all one way; those doughty warriors, the Druzes, of whom a pro-Hizbullah faction went over to the loyalist mainstream, did inflict a very serious reverse on the Hizbullahis, at least eleven of whom were killed as columns of their heavily armed, mechanized infantry sought to carve a strategic pathway through the Druzes' ancestral mountain homeland. In all at least eighty people died in nearly a week of fighting that dragged on even after Jumblat, said to have been main architect of those ill-fated decisions, formally admitted defeat.[28]

Atrocities were committed on both sides. The demons of sectarianism stirred anew, most menacingly among the outraged, defeated Sunnis. Their community was already witnessing an upsurge of Islamist fundamentalists, extremists cast in the same Saudi Wahhabite mould from which al-Qaeda had sprung, and these, though generally supporters of the mainstream Sunni leadership, now deplored the 'moderation' and weakness it had shown; in the northern city of Tripoli, where they were strongest, one Khalid al-Daher, a former deputy, launched a 'national Islamic Resistance' to confront Hizbullah, that 'Persian army in Lebanon'.[29] Uncontested victor though Hizbullah was in this miniature civil war, morally and politically it had done further damage, not just in Lebanon but the whole Arab world, to the glorious image it had earned itself in the 33-day war.

But whatever Hizbullah's long-term profit-or-loss might be, in the short term there was no question about the shift in Lebanon's internal balance of power which its coup had wrought. The loyalists' political capitulation followed hard on the heels of its military one. The government unconditionally rescinded its decisions. Then the Arab League invited all the country's political leaders to Doha, Qatar, for make-or-break talks on a general settlement. Except for a Nasrallah under constant threat of Israeli assassination, most attended. As they left, banners raised along the airport road reflected the Lebanese people's disgust with the whole race of politicians: 'Reach an agreement', one read, 'or don't come back.' After five days of negotiations, reach one they finally, all but miraculously, did. Basically, Hizbullah and the opposition had got just about everything they wanted: a consensual president; a national unity government in which, with eleven seats out of thirty, they would enjoy 'veto power' to block decisions, though not to press an agenda of their own; a new and – in their judgement – much fairer electoral law through which, in forthcoming general elections, they hoped to prove that they, not the government, represented the true majority of the people. The critical question of Hizbullah's weapons – to be dealt with in a future 'national dialogue' under the auspices of the new president – was effectively relegated to the never-never.

Among the regional and international losers, the chief of them, the Bush Administration, sought to put a brave face on this defeat in the one arena where, with the Cedar Revolution and the expulsion of the Syrians, it had actually chalked up an achievement of sorts amid all its otherwise disastrous Middle Eastern misadventures. It continued to offer its 'unwavering support' for the Siniora government and the army even as Beirut was falling into Hizbullah's lap. But an exasperated Siniora did not return the admiration which Bush bestowed on him, telling him that if he had really wanted to help Lebanon he should have reined in Israel, ended its occupation of the 'Sheba'a Farms', and found a solution for the 'Palestine problem', which was the root cause of all his country's woes.[30]

As for the Israelis, they decided that the neighbour which, under Maronite stewardship, they once looked upon as their 'natural ally', had now, as a 'Hizbullah state' and 'Iranian satellite', turned into the very antithesis of that – into one of its most implacable and dangerous foes.[31]

'THE DAHIYA DOCTRINE'

Siniora was right. In the end, everything did come down to the 'Palestine problem', crux of the region's politics, pan-Arab, pan-Islamic cause *par excellence*, abiding grievance against America and the West. Historian Albert Hourani had said it half a century ago.[32] James Baker, George Bush *père*'s secretary of state, and a group of distinguished colleagues said it in a policy paper in late 2006: 'all key issues in the Middle East are inextricably linked', and none could be 'addressed effectively in isolation from other major regional issues, interests and unresolved conflicts'.[33] Although they said this in connection with Iraq, and America's deepening predicament there, what applied to so large, rich, and once so powerful and self-reliant an Arab country clearly applied even more forcefully to one, the 'small state' of Lebanon, that was so preternaturally prey to the influence of external forces. On nowhere else, other than Palestine itself, had the unresolved Arab–Israeli conflict impinged so deeply and disruptively.

But the Israelis, and the 'friends of Israel' in America, strenuously rejected this whole idea of intrinsic Middle Eastern 'linkages', of the 'Palestine problem' as the key to all the others. On the contrary, they insisted, it was actually peripheral to them. 'All told', said Amir Taheri in *Commentary*, the influential neoconservative mouthpiece, 'in the past six decades, this region has witnessed no fewer than 22 full-scale wars over territory and resources, not one of them having anything to do with Israel and the Palestinians.'[34] Whether they actually believed this argument or not was beside the point. For the real source of their alarm lay elsewhere, in their belief – a correct one – that Baker's 'linkages' were merely portents of the concessions Israel would be expected to make for the sake of an Arab–Israeli peace now held to be so important for the region and the world.

So the Israelis were, in effect, notifying any would-be international peace-makers that no concessions would be wrung from them which, in their opinion, ran counter to their own interests, be it on ideological or security grounds. If that meant no Middle East settlement, so be it. They would continue to secure their future in the same way – with their strong right arm – they always had. And, so far as Lebanon was concerned, that meant readying themselves for the 'next war' they deemed to be all but inevitable. This time they were going to win it, however cruel and costly that might be, and they spelled out two ways in which they would ensure that.

In 2006, they had made at least a theoretical distinction between Hizbullah and the rest of Lebanon; in principle, they only hit Lebanon – army, infrastructure, people – by mistake, or, to the extent that they did so on purpose, as part of their time-honoured, but ever-failing strategy of turning it against Hizbullah. This time they would go after both equally. And they would have all the more justification for doing so because Lebanon in all its component parts – not just its Shiites, but its Sunnis, Druzes and even its Maronites too – had made itself contemptible in their sight. As a postscript to the war which, by now, most Israelis recognized that they had lost, there was one last humiliation they had had to endure. They had had to hand over the five remaining Lebanese prisoners in their hands in exchange for the remains of sergeants Goldwasser and Regev, the two soldiers whose cross-border seizure had triggered the war in the first place. By Israeli accounts, the longest-serving and most important of them, Samir Quntar, was a terrorist of an exceptionally barbarous kind. When, soon after the Hizbullah coup, the deal was struck that enabled him and his comrades to return, free men, to their native land, it was not Hizbullah alone that staged the triumphal homecoming; the newly elected President Suleiman, the prime minister, speaker of parliament and entire cabinet, as well as several of the country's most representative political leaders, Christian or Muslim, loyalist or opposition, turned out to greet and praise them. Whatever atrocity Quntar might have perpetrated – and it turned out that, in all probability, the standard Israeli version was actually wrong[35] – the Lebanese were collectively in no mood, after all they had endured at Israel's hand, to pay it the heed which, in other circumstances, they might have. Symbolism was all; and the prisoners' return was bound to have been a source of national pride for them, just as the return of *their* dead had been one of grief for Israel. Obviously, however, the Israelis couldn't see it that way. 'Woe betide the people', said Prime Minister Olmert, 'who celebrate the release of a beastly man who bludgeoned the skull of a four-year-old toddler.' For the *Jerusalem Post*, this was the 'new Lebanon'. No longer, it said, could there be a 'good Lebanon' that Israel spared or a 'bad Hizbullah' it hit. Such 'artificial distinctions' had been 'swept away by this nauseating display of perverted unity: Lebanon and Hizbullah are one.' In the event of another war, 'the Israeli Defence Forces must wage it with ferocity – not on Hizbullah's terms, but across the Lebanese battlefield'.[36]

The second way they would make sure of winning the next war would be to eliminate another distinction which, in principle at least, they had also observed in the last: between civilian and military targets. Already under discussion in military circles, it was, appropriately enough, the commander of the northern front who, in October 2008, openly and authoritatively announced it. General Gadi Eisenkot called it the '*Dahiya* Doctrine' – after the name of the populous Beirut suburb where Hizbullah had its headquarters, and large swathes of which the air force had reduced to rubble in 2006.

What had happened there, he said, would 'happen in every village from which shots are fired in the direction of Israel. We will wield disproportionate power against [them] and cause immense damage and destruction. From our perspective, these are military bases. This isn't a suggestion. This is a plan that has already been authorized … Harming the population is the only means for restraining Nasrallah.' 'It was', said Michael Sfard, an expert in international law, 'as if Eisenkot … was standing on a hilltop, declaring his intention to commit war crimes. Straight and to the point, without the usual lip service about "the Israeli Defence Forces expressing condolences", or "in every war civilians get harmed." Now, in two short sentences, one of the IDF's senior commanders stated … his intention to violate the two central tenets of the international laws of war': that attacks may be directed only at enemy combatants not enemy civilians, and that even in attacks against enemy combatants disproportionate force is forbidden.[37]

For its part, Hizbullah, in scrupulously 'gradualist-pragmatic' mode, did very little that might have provoked a new war. Most remarkably, it did not reply in kind to the great provocation which Israel itself, the undoubted culprit, offered with the assassination in February 2008 of Imad Mughniyah, most venerated of Hizbullah 'martyrs'. Everyone, Arabs and Israelis alike, had expected Hizbullah to wreak spectacular revenge for that. Surely, on past form, it was a point of honour for it to have done so? And, in his funeral oration, had not Nasrallah himself told the Israelis that if they wanted this kind of 'open war' then they should have it – and it would be the beginning of their end? For 'the blood of Haj Imad, in its purity, [would] wash away this cancerous usurping entity planted in the heart of the Arab and Islamic nation'. But, despite the great significance he attached to the killing and the consequences it would bring in its wake, nothing actually happened.

And then, when all of a sudden a war did break out in which he had no part, his restraint took an even more impressive, one might almost say heroic, turn.

CHAPTER FIFTEEN

Gaza

2009

SHOCK AND AWE, ISRAELI-STYLE

Shortly after 11.30 on 27 December 2008, on the Jewish Sabbath itself, and at the height of the first working day of the Muslim week, with crowds of children returning home from morning school, some 90 Israeli war planes unleashed over 100 tons of explosives on some 100 targets throughout the 139 square kilometres of the Gaza Strip. In a little less than four minutes they killed more than 225 people and wounded at least 700. Some were doubtless what Israel calls 'terrorists', but scores of them were ordinary policemen, mainly new recruits at a passing-out parade with their families in attendance; the rest were just a random cross-section of Gazan society. This was 'shock and awe' Israeli-style – and the start of Operation Cast Lead.

It was supposed to deal an initial, crippling blow to that other non-state Islamist militia, the one based on Palestinian soil itself, that was becoming an increasingly coherent, disciplined and effective fighting force – and, though still lagging way behind it, more and more like the Hizbullah which it sought to emulate, and which, together with Iran, had helped to arm and train it. The missile was Hamas's trademark weapon too. For years it had been lobbing the primitive, home-made, short-range Qassam into the Israeli border town of Sderot. But of late it had introduced longer-range types that could reach such major southern towns as Ashkelon, Ashdod or Beersheba. The idea behind the inaugural onslaught, said an Israeli defence analyst, had been 'to kill as many people connected to Hamas as possible' in the hope of persuading its leaders to 'surrender or plead for a ceasefire'. That was why, 'in planning to attack buildings and sites populated by hundreds of people, the Israeli Defence Forces didn't warn them in advance to leave' – even though it must have known that, for a great many of them, any connection they might have had with Hamas's military wing was a tenuous one, or simply non-existent.[1]

Israel had been planning it for nearly two years, in accordance with a 'chosen war' strategy that bore a striking resemblance to the one which, in 1982, General Sharon used to invade Lebanon in his bid to destroy the Islamists' predecessor, Yasser Arafat's Palestine Liberation Organization. The plan became operational during the flimsy, six-month truce which Egypt had negotiated between the two sides. From the moment this so-called *tahdi'a*, or 'lull', had gone into effect Israel ignored the most important item on its side of the bargain. Far from lifting the suffocating blockade it had been imposing on Gaza, itself akin to an act of war, it systematically maintained and – towards the end – intensified it, rendering yet more extreme what, months before, a UN official had already called the 'subhuman' conditions in which Gaza's inhabitants were living.[2] Then, on 4 November, it launched an unprovoked raid into the Strip, killing six members of Hamas's Qassam Brigades. This very deliberate violation of the truce was the critical ruse that goaded Hamas into stepping up its retaliatory missile fire, and thereby furnishing an internationally serviceable pretext for the long-planned assault.

In the event, then, it was not Lebanon to which the '*Dahiya* Doctrine' was to be first applied. It was to be Gaza, and the 1,500,000 inhabitants of this most densely populated piece of territory on earth. And it soon emerged that the *Dahiya* Doctrine dovetailed very nicely with another, hardly less lethal sub-doctrine – and lesson from Lebanon too – which had been developed for Operation Cast Lead. 'We are very violent, we are not shying away from any method of preventing casualties among our troops', said one of several senior commanders who, perhaps inadvertently, revealed it. They called it 'urban warfare without gloves … You do not come close to a suspicious house without firing on it first, with a missile, with a tank, then tear off one of its walls with an armored

D9 [a huge tractor], and only then look to see who is inside, if anyone is still alive.'[3] Or, as Uri Avnery, the well-known peace activist, put it, it was 'the total destruction of everything in [the soldiers'] path', a 'readiness to kill eighty Palestinians to save one Israeli soldier'.[4] And particularly prominent in this campaign were the military rabbis of a once overwhelmingly secular army in which religious, kippah-wearing Jews now accounted for a good 40 per cent of newly graduated officers and 30 per cent of the men. More like medieval Christian warrior-priests than traditional Jewish sages, steeped in the extremist ethos of the religious settlers from whose ranks they were substantially drawn, they were bent on improving the army's 'combat values' in the wake of its failure at the hands of Hizbullah. With the educational brochures of the Army Rabbinate as their guide, they taught that present-day Palestinians were no different from the Philistines slain by the Israelites of yore, that it was mere immorality to be anything but cruel to the 'cruel' enemy, and mortal sin to relinquish to 'the gentiles' a 'single millimetre, finger or fingernail of the Land of Israel'.[5]

Indeed, in this, and many other ways, the shadow of Lebanon, 2006, fell over Gaza, 2009.

Thus, the Israelis' war aim, in its broadest terms, was to create in the south a whole 'new order', or 'security situation', like they had tried to do two and a half years before in the north. At its minimum, this meant neutralizing the missiles, either by imposing a new and truly effective ceasefire or by destroying them physically. And, just as in 2006 it had meant preventing Hizbullah's rearmament by blocking the flow of weapons overland from Syria, so now it meant achieving the same in the south, first by smashing the hundreds of tunnels beneath the Egyptian–Gazan border that were the last stage of the missiles' journey into the hands of the Hamas fighters, and secondly by securing the establishment of a *cordon sanitaire* around the Strip's borders. The maximum goal – and this looked more and more like the real one as the campaign unfolded – meant 'toppling' Hamas and restoring the rule of President Mahmoud Abbas's 'legitimate', internationally recognized Palestinian Authority, which, in response to an American-backed coup against its democratically elected regime, Hamas had driven out of Gaza the year before.[6] This was to be achieved, first, by attacking the 'infrastructure of terror', destroying it or at least so debilitating it that Hamas could no longer keep physical control of its militant fiefdom; and, secondly, by attacking the 'infrastructure of the [would-be] Palestine state', not merely its governmental and administrative institutions, but pretty much anything, industry, agriculture, commerce, that would contribute to the basic livelihood of its citizens.[7] Any such war on so densely packed a territory was bound to imperil virtually anyone who lived there. But that did not matter, because 'to harm civilians until we achieve political goals' was what the *Dahiya* Doctrine was basically about in any case.[8] Commanders were assigned a very generous range of 'pre-planned targets', 600 of them reportedly, compared with the mere 150 in Lebanon 2006.[9] 'There are many aspects of Hamas', a senior officer explained, 'and we're trying to hit the whole spectrum, because everything is connected and everything supports terrorism against Israel.'[10] These targets, advised another, should include 'decision-makers and the power elite, economic interests and the centres of civilian power that support the [enemy] organization'; the 'damage inflicted' on them, and the 'punishment meted out', should be such as to 'demand long and expensive reconstruction processes'.[11] The ultimate goal was to inflict such pain on the Gazans that they would turn against the regime which had brought this mayhem down on their heads, driving it from power.[12]

All these particular objectives underlay a larger, if less tangible one, directed at all the states and non-state forces in the region. This was to restore Israel's badly battered 'deterrent power', the threat and periodic use of which it deemed to be its only sure guarantee of survival. 'People didn't mess with Israel', said a researcher at the Institute for National Security Studies, 'because they were afraid of the consequences. Now the region is filled with provocative rhetoric about Israel the paper tiger. This operation is an attempt to re-establish the perception that if you provoke or attack you are going to pay a disproportionate price.'[13] Apart from the creation of the UNIFIL buffer zone between themselves and Hizbullah, the Israelis had achieved virtually none of their loudly proclaimed aims in the north. So now they were going to war against a much weaker, if fanatically determined, Hamas in the knowledge that they simply had to achieve them in the south – or the

Arabs would come to believe, as a Beirut columnist said, that this really did mark 'the beginning of the end for Israel'.[14]

After 'shock and awe' the Israel Defence Forces set about the task, 'sending Gaza decades into the past',[15] which General Yoav Galant, head of the Southern Command, assigned them, and giving Gaza a taste of the *'shoah'* – Hebrew for holocaust – which the deputy defence minister, Matan Vilnai, had earlier threatened it with.[16] In a campaign seemingly replete with war crimes and atrocities, the F-16s and Apache helicopters, the tanks, artillery and gunboats offshore bombarded schools and universities, mosques and clinics, premises of the United Nations Relief and Works Agency, the parliament and most government buildings, roads, bridges, generating stations, sewage lines, 21,000 residential apartment buildings, 1,500 factories and shops, and 80 per cent of the Strip's agricultural infrastructure;[17] ground forces shot at ambulance men and aid workers; and in one episode which prompted even that most taciturn of organizations, the International Red Cross, to issue a public condemnation, soldiers herded a hundred terrified civilians into a building, apparently for their own safety, later killed thirty of them by shelling the building, and then, over four days, prevented rescue workers from trying to reach the survivors, who included four emaciated children, too weak to stand, crouched at their dead mother's side.[18] In the 22-day war, some 1,330 Gazans died, at least half of them civilians, including 410 children, compared with 13 Israelis, 3 of them civilians hit by Hamas rockets, and 10 soldiers. In a letter to the London *Guardian*, twelve persons 'of Jewish origin' said that what the Israelis had done reminded them of the Warsaw Ghetto in Nazi-occupied Poland, and the 'death by hunger' promised them by the city's governor-general, Hans Frank.[19]

FOR HIZBULLAH – ONLY A POLITICAL, NOT A SHOOTING, WAR

Yet, throughout all this, what so many people, Lebanese and Arabs, greatly feared, and perhaps a lesser number devoutly hoped, that Hassan Nasrallah would do – he did not.

Champion of 'resistance' and hero of 2006, he might have stepped in to turn the struggle into a much larger and less unequal one – possibly drawing in other Middle Eastern states – in which Israel would probably have prevailed in the end, but at vastly greater cost to itself. He had powerful reasons for doing so. Like countless millions of Arabs, he had surely been following the terror and the agony of Gaza as it unfolded, in all its gruesome and enraging detail, on the Arab world's most popular television station, al-Jazeera. His anger, like theirs, must have been great and the desire to mete out retribution hardly less so. Ideologically, *jihad* was still his basic *raison d'être*, and Palestine still the only arena where, practically speaking, he had the means and opportunity to pursue it. Solidarity with the Gazans had, after all, been an important reason for the cross-border abduction of Israeli soldiers that led to the 33-day war. If the Israeli pounding of Gaza, then, had been motive enough for that, immeasurably more so should have been the devastation being visited on it now. There was also the moral obligation he owed a fellow-Islamist organization which he deemed part of a 'single movement with a single course, destiny and goal'.[20] The pressure on him to act would have reached its critical height if and when he, and Iran behind him, had felt that their 'little brother' was weakening to the point of collapse – and the grievous blow which that would have represented for Hizbullah and the whole Islamo-nationalist camp.

But he also had powerful reasons *not* to step in. He who had publicly admitted never even to have dreamt that the soldiers' abduction would have provoked an Israeli response of the magnitude that it did, was not going to provoke yet another one, knowing, as this diligent student of Israeli affairs surely did, that it would very likely have been carried out in accordance with the prescriptions of General Giora Eiland. In 'the Third Lebanon War', this strategist had written, Israel should 'eliminate' the country's military, 'destroy' its national infrastructure, including homes, and inflict 'intense suffering among the population'. Since 'the only good thing that [had] happened in the last war [had been] the relative damage caused to Lebanon's population', next time 'Lebanon [might] be razed to the ground'.[21] Nasrallah's own Shiite constituency would have had little or no stomach for that. And the outrage of the rest of the population would have very likely been so great as to ignite the kind of full-scale civil war that had only narrowly been averted, the previous May, by the '14 March' coalition's capitulation to Hizbullah's political *diktat*-by-arms.

To be sure, Nasrallah put his forces on alert, issued grim warnings, and told the Israelis that if 'you come to our villages, our lands, our neighbourhoods, you will discover that the July War was nothing, a walk in the park, compared with what you'll face this time'. But the subliminal message was clear enough. Hizbullah would only respond if attacked itself. For since the 2006 war 'resistance' no longer meant raids into enemy territory, but 'deterrence' and the defence of Lebanon's own.

So, instead of shooting war, Nasrallah went over to the offensive in that other war, the political one, which had so often accompanied it in the past. This was the struggle to change in Hizbullah's favour the whole political and strategic environment in which it had to operate. It could never defeat Israel on its own; that was axiomatic; only when others, states or non-state actors like itself, joined the 'Islamic resistance' which it had pioneered would the ultimate jihadist goal, the 'liberation of Jerusalem', come into the realm of the possible.[22] Meanwhile, there were forces in the region which, along with their external backers, would always stand in the 'resistance's' path; indeed, it seemed that the more headway the 'resistance' made and the more support and admiration it garnered among the Arab and Muslim masses, the more they would press their counter-offensive against it. For Islamists or secular nationalists, and others too, these forces were chiefly embodied, at state level, in the 'moderate', pro-American regimes of Egypt, Jordan, Saudi Arabia, and their protégé, Hamas's rival, the West Bank regime of President Mahmoud Abbas. Given the unique centrality and emotional import of the 'Palestine problem', this was another 'little war' in which, being fought on Palestine soil itself, the regional and international stakes were even higher than they had been in Lebanon 2006. It would, said Nasrallah, 'have repercussions not only for Gaza alone, or Palestine, but for the whole *Umma*'.

Just as in 2006, the 'moderates' had blamed Hizbullah for starting the war, so now did they blame Hamas. It was a standpoint all the more suggestive of their genuine alarm because Hamas was as true-blue, orthodox Sunni as themselves, whereas with Hizbullah sectarian fear of rising, militant Shiism had largely motivated them. The 'Arab system'

immediately fell into new depths of impotence and disarray; for the
first time since the foundation, sixty-eight years before, of its key
institution, the Arab League, the two sides of the great divide held
what, in effect, were two rival Arab summit conferences, with Hamas
– and non-Arab Iran – attending the pre-eminently Islamo-nationalists'
one, and Mahmoud Abbas representing the Palestinian Authority at
that of the 'moderates'. The general Arab perception was that, this time,
the latter were aligning themselves more overtly than ever before with
the historic Arab foe in wishing defeat on fellow Arabs doing valiant,
but unequal, battle against it, and that what, in 2006, might have been
no more than suspect 'silence' or 'concealed collaboration' had become
open 'co-operation' and 'partnership' now.[23] On them Nasrallah turned
his wrath. Hizbullah, he said, had not made enemies of those who had
betrayed it in 2006; but now it would of those 'who collaborate against
Gaza and its people'. And he singled out President Mubarak's Egypt as
the chief and most dishonourable of them.

It was no secret that, as the purveyor of a militant, Iranian-backed
fundamentalism arising on his very doorstep, Mubarak intensely
disliked Hamas and its ideological and organizational links with Egypt's
Muslim Brotherhood, the movement which constituted perhaps the
greatest challenge to the legitimacy, or even survival, of his ossified
regime. Nor was it much of a secret either that he wanted it cut down
to size, and expected Israel to do the job for him; what more shockingly
flaunted intimation of that than his very public handshake with Israeli
Foreign Minister Tzipi Livni, who, on the eve of the onslaught, had
gone to Cairo to apprise him of what was afoot?[24] It was the Rafah
crossing point, the Gazans' only access to the Arab world, on which
Nasrallah concentrated his incendiary accusations. Here, in Gaza's
hour of supreme adversity, was the ruler of the greatest Arab state, with
the greatest power to help or hinder Hamas in its struggle, keeping its
borders as hermetically sealed, bar a few ambulances and a trickle of
aid, as the Israelis did theirs. For many in the Arab world, it was Egypt's
ultimate shame, the betrayal of everything that it had once stood for
under Nasser and pan-Arabism. It was also, in the eyes of Hizbullah
and its allies, the key to the outcome of the conflict, the means by which
'the epic victory of Lebanon [would] be repeated' on Palestinian soil

itself. 'Egyptian officials', Nasrallah thundered, 'if you don't open this crossing, then you are partners to the crime, to the murders and the siege.' And he urged the Egyptian people 'to take to the streets' in their 'millions' and 'open the crossing' with their 'bare chests'. He appealed to the Egyptian army to move as well. And assert as he might that 'I am not calling for a coup', a coup, or rather a revolution, was surely what he really would have liked. It had, after all, been Palestine, and the Egyptian army's humiliation in the First Arab–Israeli War of 1948, which did so much to trigger the mother of all Arab revolutions, the overthrow of King Farouk in 1952.

Countless Egyptians, Muslim Brothers to the fore, clearly shared Nasrallah's outrage at the weakness and 'treachery' of the mildewed travesty of itself into which, nearly sixty years on, that bright new order had degenerated. It was not unreasonable for them to hope that, coming on top of all their other, more mundane woes, Palestine could once again rouse a long-suffering people to long-overdue revolt – and thereby wreak the kind of fundamental change in the whole geopolitical landscape of the Middle East of which organizations like Hizbullah and Hamas must dream.

WHO WON THIS TIME?

Such upheavals were not to be, not this time at least.

But neither, on the other hand, was that rout of his Palestinian ally which might have forced Nasrallah's hand. On 17 January Israel abruptly declared a unilateral ceasefire, and within a few days all its forces had withdrawn from the Strip. Hamas had weathered the onslaught, not so masterfully as Hizbullah two years before, but convincingly enough for everyone to pose the question once again: who had actually won? Of course, Israeli leaders said that Israel had. But Ismail Haniyah, the Hamas prime minister, thought otherwise; after Hizbullah's, he said, this was yet another 'divine victory' bestowed by God on the combatants of Islam. In reality, the 22-day war was even more inconclusive than its 33-day predecessor had been, with both sides seeking to achieve by diplomacy – though not a little continued violence too – what they had failed to achieve in all-out combat.

The Israelis did not even secure their minimum aims. They didn't destroy all of Hamas's rockets. Between their unilateral ceasefire and its own, Hamas launched a final, symbolic barrage, not the largest of its whole campaign as Hizbullah had so infuriatingly contrived to do, but what, in the circumstances, was a quite respectable tally of them. According to Israeli defence officials, it still had a good thousand out of an original 3,000 missiles left.[25] And in the absence of an agreed truce of the kind that had preceded the war, the Israelis had won no reasonable guarantee that Hamas would stop firing them in the future. In fact, the first lone, taunting projectile came in within a week. But had Hamas been deprived of the means to replenish its depleted arsenal? Therein lay the really important question. Achieving that in tiny, encircled Gaza should in principle have been a good deal easier than in Lebanon where, in 2006, failure had been immediate and complete. The US and several European states consulted one another about the dispatch of warships to police the Mediterranean approaches to Egypt and Gaza as well as the shipping lanes from Iran around the Arabian Peninsula to the Red Sea. The US signed a security agreement with Israel for the joint monitoring, with state-of-the-art equipment, of Egypt's border with Gaza. Egypt itself, while rejecting US or any other foreign forces on its soil, doubled its own contingent there. Yet hardly had the fighting stopped than the Palestinian smugglers were back in business, re-activating those tunnels that the Israelis had failed to damage or destroy, and repairing those that they had. 'We will continue to get weapons into Gaza – and the West Bank,' said a Hamas leader, 'those who think sea, air or satellite monitoring can detect weapons flow through tunnels are deluded.' And a tunnel owner agreed. 'The money is too good,' he said. Too good – that is to say – not just for him, but for all the owners' Egyptian confederates, be they the Bedouin tribes of northern Sinai, time-honoured smugglers beyond government control, or the lowly-paid officers and soldiers they had no difficulty bribing to look the other way.[26]

As for its maximum aims, if anything the Israelis only achieved the reverse of those. Perhaps, as they said, they had given Hamas quite a beating. It could hardly have been otherwise, so immense was the gulf between the sides: a few thousand guerillas, lightly armed and with very little of the physical room for manoeuvre on which guerilla warfare classically relies, pitted against the overwhelming might and firepower of the Israeli army and the savage, indiscriminate manner in which it was prepared to use them. Nor had the Israelis been taken unawares as they had been against Hizbullah; this time it was they who had the advantage of complete surprise, they who had all the time in the world to plan their assault down to its smallest detail and, with their long and deep penetration of Gazan society, all the means to compile intelligence of a sophistication they could never have managed against the famously secretive and impenetrable Hizbullah. All in all, as some Israelis put it, it was a 'war de luxe' from the outset, 'child's play' compared with previous ones. Pilots bombed unimpeded 'as if on practice runs' and ground forces bore down on an enemy who, whenever serious clashes occurred, simply retreated deeper and deeper into the labyrinth of concrete that was Gaza City. Though urban terrain generally favours the defender, the low-risk 'methodical crawl', blitzing all before them, at which the invaders advanced helped ensure a remarkable disparity in casualties – a mere ten Israeli soldiers killed, as against an unknown number of Hamas fighters, but very possibly up in the hundreds that the Israelis claimed.[27] As the army tightened the siege, and drew closer to the central strongholds and symbols of Hamas power, Prime Minister Olmert rejoiced at what he called the 'unprecedented blow' the organization had been dealt; military intelligence said that its leadership was in dire straits and its forces on the verge of collapse; one last push would finish it off.

For whatever reason – the great increase in casualties that an all-out, final offensive would almost certainly have caused, the advent of the Obama Administration, international outrage, the wild, anarchic Gazan 'Somalia' to which a complete Hamas defeat might have given birth – the Israelis never made that push. But it is questionable whether they would have succeeded even if they had. In any case, whatever beating Hamas might have taken, it had clearly survived – with much of its apparatus still intact. And for non-state militias like it and Hizbullah, survival – not to be defeated, not to lose possession and control of the territory on which they had fought – was 'victory', and if, in addition, they managed to keep the arms flowing too, the promise of more 'victories' to come.

Hamas might – for the time being – have been militarily weakened, but it had been politically strengthened. That was what happened with Hizbullah after *its* 'victory', and what Hamas, bathed in its aura of heroism and martyrdom, would now seek to emulate in its turn. State within the Lebanese state though Hizbullah had remained, it had also, by both constitutional and not-so-constitutional means, procured itself a powerful place as part of that state itself. Hamas, and particularly its 'external', Damascus-based leaders, seemed to harbour greater ambitions than that, nothing less, in fact, than the official leadership of the Palestinian people, or at least the dominant place within it. They felt they had surely earned it, that, in addition to the legitimacy of the ballot box, through their performance on the battlefield they had now acquired a new 'revolutionary' legitimacy as well.[28]

The Palestine Liberation Organization, whose creation in 1964 had marked the beginning of the Palestinian national struggle, was still, in principle, the 'sole legitimate representative of the Palestinian people' and its most important institution, the Palestine National Council, still their supreme legislature. But with the Oslo accord of 1993, the PLO had renounced violence, Yasser Arafat had moved into the occupied territories, and the Palestinian Authority which he established there, though *de jure* subordinate to it, became the real, *de facto* centre of Palestinian power; and although the PLO continued to perform routine administrative functions, it had otherwise fallen into institutional, moral and political irrelevance and decay.

It was by revitalizing this inert body, or perhaps even creating a new one, that Hamas now seemed bent on staking its leadership claim. *Its* PLO would formally reinstate 'armed struggle' as its chief mode of action, in place of the diplomacy and negotiation on which the PA had long since exclusively relied. For diplomacy had not merely failed to yield what it was supposed to, a 'Palestine state', co-existent with Israel, on the little that remained of original Palestine. What with Israel's continued Judaization of Jerusalem, its ever-expanding settlements, its monstrous 'security wall' and its whole, apartheid-like structure of separation and control which even South Africans deemed worse than their own had ever been[29] – what with all of that, the seemingly futile and interminable 'peace process' was well on the way to placing such a state forever beyond reach. In all probability, Hamas's PLO could only come into being at the price of intensified internecine strife, not merely among Palestinians, but across the region at large, with the Islamo-nationalist camp, led by an increasingly interventionist Iran, working for the emasculation or overthrow of the Fatah-based Palestinian regime, and the 'moderates' fighting to preserve it. But it didn't look to be an impossible goal.

To be sure, it was hard, after Gaza, to gauge Hamas's true standing among ordinary Palestinians. Like Hizbullah among the Lebanese, admiration for its military prowess was offset, for many, by anger and resentment at the calamity which, by falling into Israel's trap, it had brought down upon them; indeed, like Nasrallah himself, Khalid al-Mesha'al, its exile leader, reportedly admitted to underestimating the scale and fury of what Israel had been planning to unleash.[30] And, like Hizbullah again, the polls suggested that the honour it had won away from home – among Palestinians and Arabs outside its own, Gazan domain – was greater than its gains inside it.[31] One thing, however, was clear: Hamas had now supplanted Fatah and the PA in public esteem. Their standing, already low before Gaza, fell to a new nadir after it. Not merely, in their extreme distaste for their upstart rival, had they hoped for the defeat of fellow Palestinians at enemy hands, they had been even more indiscreet about it than the 'moderate' Arab camp to which they belonged. One official went so far as to say that Hamas leaders should be tried as 'war criminals' for causing the death of hundreds of innocent Palestinians, another that the Israelis had made a 'big mistake' in not finishing them altogether.[32] Worse still, the conviction grew that what an Israeli newspaper had reported months before[33] was actually true. This was that, in September, eight PA security chiefs, all Fatah veterans, had met with their Israeli counter-parts, and told them that they were preparing to fight an 'all-out' battle 'to the end' with the 'common enemy' Hamas; this would be 'the last chance for [their] generation to retain their grip on power before Hamas took over and devoured everything'. They had asked Israel to help with planning, training and the supply of weapons. The operation had been scheduled to take place before President Abbas's term of office expired on 9 January 2009 – a remarkable coincidence, falling as that day did two weeks into Israel's own, long-planned war on Hamas. Coming on top of the PA's other well-known vices – notably its corruption – such outright collaboration, not to say treason, sent a wave of anger through a West Bank population mostly in passionate sympathy with their Gazan compatriots. It badly rattled the PA, whose new, US-subsidized, Jordanian-trained police forces, armed with clubs and tear gas, had to break up a series of demonstrations, arresting Hamas supporters, confiscating Hamas flags and ripping up pro-Hamas placards.[34]

'After the Fatah putschists failed to return to Gaza aboard Zionist tanks, they tried to do so on concrete mixers and tons of cast iron.'[35] Thus did an Egyptian Islamist website mock the PA's post-war strategy to regain at least a token authority over its lost, rebellious province. For, as in Lebanon in 2006, after destruction came *re*construction – and an Arab and international community, European-led, ready, once more, to step in with funds, materials and technical expertise to meet this urgent need. The trouble was, however, that though willing to accept such help, Hamas, like Hizbullah, was resolved to take charge of it. It – not the PA – was the electorally legitimate authority in Gaza; it was clean, the PA was not. But, however popular, however representative of its own people Hamas might have been, for Europe, let alone the US, it was still a 'terrorist' organization that did not 'recognize' Israel's 'right to exist'; so Europe could not even 'talk' to it until it did. The most it would consider doing was to deal with a 'national unity' government – Hamas and Fatah combined – under the *pro forma* aegis of the PA. As for Israel, it wouldn't allow in a single bag of cement – or glass or steel – until it was satisfied that Hamas could not use them to rebuild its defences or manufacture new missiles.

In March 2009, 'national unity' talks began under Egyptian auspices. But, after so much vicious contention, and bloodshed too, could such rivals be reconciled ever again? And supposing Hamas, wearying of all these boycotts and blockades, decided to seize the main chance, and don the mantle of Palestinian leadership for itself? It was, after all, in the wake of its first and most famous military exploit, the 'battle of Karameh',[36] that, forty-one years before – and on a great wave of popular support – Fatah had wrested control of the PLO from the pliant, old-school politicians, creatures of the Arab regimes, who then ran it. Supposing what Fatah had thus done to others in its prime, Hamas now did to Fatah in its degeneracy? How would Israel and the world react to that?

'GOING CRAZY'

As for that other, most important of Israel's aims, restoring its 'deterrent power', only time might tell whether it had succeeded or not, but the first post-war indications did not look promising.

True, in strictly military terms, Israel had learned some lessons from 2006, introduced new tactics in the light of them, and, generally speaking, fought 'with far greater efficiency' than it had against Hizbullah.[37] But, more important – and another such lesson – was the far greater brutality with which it also fought. Indeed, it is no exaggeration to say that, with Gaza 2009, the hitting of civilian targets finally graduated as the very essence, and principal measure, of this sacrosanct 'deterrence' – this invincibility against all comers – now supposedly restored.

The fact was, as Hamas leaders pointed out, that ever since, in 1973, Israel ceased fighting wars against regular Arab armies, and found itself confronted with non-state militias instead – Fatah and company first, Hizbullah and Hamas thereafter – it never truly won any of them, and its 'deterrent power' had been declining accordingly. For sure Israel's priority might originally have been to find and hit enemy combatants rather than the civilians among whom they moved, as well as the missiles that were their weapon of choice. But it grew less and less successful in this even as its enemy grew in proficiency. As a result, along with new military tactics, it came up with new ethical codes to match. Their basic thrust was that the whole body of international law which governs the conduct of conventional warfare was no longer applicable to these new forms of unconventional, 'asymmetrical' or Islamist warfare; as far as Israel was concerned, to continue to abide by the old moralities was effectively to deny one side, the legitimate state, the right and ability to defeat the other, the 'terrorists' who would destroy it.[38] In response to international criticism, Defence Minister

Ehud Barak, like most of 'official' Israel, took indignant refuge in those time-honoured, ritual protestations about an Israeli army still 'unsurpassed in its moral traditions'. The truth was, however, that never before had that army travelled so very far from the 'purity of arms' which, since pre-state days, it had always claimed to observe. Perhaps at least as telling, in this respect, as the army's actual deeds were the words that came with them – in the dissertations and debates of the planners and the strategists before the war, and the indiscretions of commanders during it. And hardly less so was the wholesale re-surfacing of a venerable strain of politico-military thinking known in Israel as 'going crazy'.

The threatening of wild, irrational violence in response to political or military adversity had been a recurrent impulse ever since the formation of the state. It was first authoritatively documented, in the 1950s, by the doveish Prime Minister Moshe Sharett (earlier encoun-tered in these pages as the strong opponent of Ben-Gurion's dreams of violent geopolitical engineering in Lebanon)[39] who wrote of his defence minister, Pinhas Lavon, that he 'constantly preached for acts of madness' if ever Israel were crossed.[40] Never – half a century on – had generals, politicians and commentators been so forceful and concordant, whether approving or condemning, in the perception of their military deliberately 'going crazy', or, as Uri Avnery put it, 'behaving like madmen, going on the rampage, killing or destroying mercilessly' in their belief that 'the [success] of the war planners [depends on] the very barbarity of their plan' and that 'the atrocities will have ... a deterrent effect that holds for a very long time'.[41]

Actually, it held for about a week. And that first post-war missile was followed by a steady, if sporadic, succession of Qassams, Grads and mortars in the weeks to come. Not much deterrence there. But perhaps this reversion to the practice that which had driven the Israelis to war in the first place was essentially short-term and tactical, a judicious admixture of violence to the post-war diplomatic quest for the new and more durable truce which both sides seemed to want, or could live with, if the conditions were right. Hizbullah, after all, had immediately ceased all fire the moment Security Council Resolution 1701 had gone into effect, and has continued to do so ever since; and, for all their

dismal performance in that war, the Israelis claimed that this did indeed
amount to 'deterrence' restored, and working. Very likely Hamas will
eventually emulate its Lebanese mentor. But what about 'deterrence' in
its largest, long-term, strategic sense? What about Israel's security,
indeed its very survival, in that hostile environment in which it seems
forever condemned to have its being? For ultimately, that was what, in
the Israeli mind, 'deterrence' – or permanent military supremacy, the
Iron Wall, 200 nuclear warheads – was all about.

In this sense, the Gaza war was yet another self-inflicted injury. For
it made that environment more fundamentally, more viscerally hostile
than ever. Movements like Hizbullah and Hamas might indeed have
embodied much that a great many Arabs and Muslims, observant as
well as non-observant, feared, disliked and opposed – the illiberal,
retrogressive, totalitarian tendencies of the militant, 'political' Islam
they espoused, their proxy role in the hegemonic ambitions of non-
Arab Iran, their disruptive impact on the whole existing social and
political order, and threat of more of it, and worse, to come. Indeed,
these were things that made no small contribution to the great Arab
schism, over Palestine, which the Gaza war only served to deepen. But
there was one thing they embodied to which more and more Arabs did
subscribe – and did so, moreover, whichever of the rival camps their
particular regime happened to belong to, or whatever their religious
or political persuasions might be: Muslim or Christian, Islamist or
secular, right or left, conservative or liberal. And that was 'rejectionism',
the conviction that peace-through-negotiation with such an enemy was
impossible, and – as it habitually said of them – that force was the only
language it *might* understand. All the post-war opinion polls showed it.
And nothing implanted and intensified this negativity like the
'barbarism' – the 'killing of us like insects'[42] – which restoring Israel's
'deterrent power' so manifestly appeared to require.

Naturally, not just Hamas, but the whole Islamo-nationalist camp,
profited from this at the expense of the 'moderate', pro-American one.
Indeed, so central, so heated, did the 'Palestine question' become that,
for one analyst, a whole new pan-Arab 'narrative' – simple, dominant,
compelling – was in the making, the narrative of the 'Martyrs', who
were led by the Islamists, and the 'Traitors', who included most if not

all the Arab regimes, but especially Egypt, Saudi Arabia, Jordan and Lebanon's, and the Palestinian Authority.[43] In this scheme of things, the pressures on would-be 'Traitors' to look more like 'Martyrs' was very apparent in the *cri de coeur* from one of the Arab world's most prominent and respected champions of 'moderation', of inter-faith 'dialogue', and of a just and reasonable peace with Israel. Denouncing the Bush Administration's Middle Eastern legacy as a 'sickening' one, and its attitude to Gaza as a 'contribution to the slaughter of innocents', Prince Turki bin Faisal, former Saudi ambassador to Washington and London, said that his country, as 'the leader of the Arab and Muslim worlds', had so far resisted calls to lead a global *jihad* against Israel, but that such restraint was becoming increasingly difficult to maintain:

> Today every Saudi is a Gazan, and we remember well the words of our late King Faisal: 'I hope you will forgive my outpouring of emotions, but when I think that our holy Mosque in Jerusalem is being invaded and desecrated, I ask God that if I am unable to undertake holy *jihad*, then I should not live a moment more.'[44]

And, in years to come, there can be nothing like this 'barbarism' to undermine Israel's 'deterrent power' from another, less familiar, but ultimately, perhaps, far more important quarter. Unlike Lebanon, Gaza had no 'Qana', no single, outstanding massacre, and, in consequence, no clear-cut turning point at which, instead of urging its protégé on, the US, in its embarrassment, began quite suddenly pressuring it to end the war before it could achieve its goals. But, actually, at a deeper level, there was very much worse than Qana; there was day upon day of that nonchalant, remorseless, high-tech 'slaughter of innocents', especially children, and its raw, real-time projection on to all the television screens of the world. It did Israel's reputation – already lower than that of any other country but its arch-enemy Iran[45] – greater damage than anything, even the massacre of Sabra and Shatila, with which it had ever been associated before.

Nor was it just the war itself. It was a whole gamut of other things about the 'only democracy in the Middle East' on which the war threw a sudden, glaring and unflattering light; things that, by any other reckoning than its own, surely disqualified it for that membership of

the 'civilized world' by which it – and the 'friends of Israel' in the West
– had always set enormous store. There was the disdain for such
bedrock democratic notions as a 'free press' and 'freedom of information'. It barely even tried to hide it. For it was not merely on the usual,
convenient, catch-all 'security' grounds that it denied the foreign media
entry into the Gaza war zone; it did so, its officials asserted, because
they were 'biased, unethical and unprofessional' in their reporting.[46]
There was the Knesset vote, supported by all the major Jewish parties
from right to left, to ban Israel's only three Arab parties from par-
ticipating in forthcoming general elections because of the 'incitement'
and 'support for terrorism' supposedly implicit in their strong
opposition to the war.[47] Then there were the elections themselves and
'the true face of Israel' – as so many a dissident Israeli, not just Arabs,
put it – 'which they exposed'. That is to say, the 'face' of a whole society
lunging towards the extreme right, turning 'racism and nationalism into
accepted values', and embracing 'ideas that no one would have dared
let cross their lips ten or twenty years ago, lest they be thought utter
fascists';[48] of the triumph of the Yisrael Beitenu party, whose fifteen
seats made it the third largest in the country, and whose leader, Avigdor
Lieberman, a former Moldavian nightclub bouncer, once told the
Knesset, among other such lurid pronouncements, that any of its Arab
members who talked to Hamas should be executed for the same reason
that Nazi leaders, 'along with their collaborators', had been executed
after the Second World War.[49]

There was still, of course, a civic culture, associated with the left and
the so-called 'peace camp', that stood against this general trend. This
had no place in the traditional, establishment left, certainly not in
mainstream Labour, which, rhetoric aside, had long been barely
distinguishable from the mainstream nationalist right when it came to
issues of war and peace, and dealing with Arabs and Palestinians,[50] and
it is questionable whether it had one even in smaller, further-left
groups, such as Meretz, which had also made it into the Knesset. But
outside parliament, Peace Now, the original activist movement of the
kind, had long made it its business to challenge the militarism and
intransigence of Israeli governments, to combat the settler movement
and bring the occupation of the West Bank and Gaza to an end in a

final, 'land-for-peace' settlement. A more militant organization, Uri Avnery's Gush Shalom, or Peace Bloc, split off from Peace Now in 1993, and can be said to have set the moral and political agenda for the whole 'peace camp' ever since. A host of other organizations devoted themselves to combating specific aspects of the occupation – human rights abuses or the demolition of houses. A small band of journalists – often cited in this book – performed a similar role in the press. But, in the end, more remarkable than the existence of the 'peace camp', however dedicated and determined it might be, has been its marginality, and the meagreness of its influence on the general public – an influence which, if anything, has in recent times only seemed to decline.

And for all its activism on certain issues, Peace Now has often shown a tendency to fall in with mainstream opinion at critical junctures. Thus, like Meretz, it initially supported the Gaza war – as it had the Lebanese one – only backtracking when it began to look as if the army risked getting stuck in the 'Gazan mud'. Among the leading personalities associated with the organization, novelist Amos Oz – likewise replaying his stand on Lebanon – headed a long list of authors and intellectuals who, just before the war, had called on Israel to end its 'restraint' over Gaza.[51] Yet compromises of this kind appeared to win Peace Now little respect from society at large, which generally considered it to be 'unrealistic', too trusting of the Palestinians' intentions and too little concerned about Israel's own vital security interests. Only Gush Shalom held firm, denouncing Gaza from the outset, and, with a few others, staging demonstrations against it. But that only served to confirm the mainstream in its view of it as an unpatriotic 'lunatic fringe', or – with its loneliness in the field – to dramatize what a leading left-wing journalist called the 'frightening indifference, awful state of apathy and inaction' in Israel today, 'the emptiness of the town square … devoid of demonstrations and protests either for or against – completely empty'. 'Where', he asked, 'are the days when a massacre that we did not directly commit [Sabra and Shatila] was enough to bring hundreds of thousands on to the streets?'[52]

Despairing of their ability ever to change things from within, many in the 'peace camp' have long been arguing that only through some powerful external agency can Israel be saved from itself.[53] The Gaza war, and the world's reaction to it, intensified this feeling. But that, in turn, merely exacerbated the hostility towards them of the most right-wing government in Israel's history, as well as that of the electorate that put it there. All these 'peace-makers' wanted, said one of their bitterest critics, was to 'bring Israel to its knees and force a Pax Americana on it', or, as another put it, 'to fan the flames of anti-Semitism in the world and create a new blood libel against the Israeli Defence Forces and the State of Israel'. Was it not time, this latter asked, for the government to take legal action against them?[54] In fact the government was already planning to do just that, with a new campaign, reportedly the brain-child of Foreign Minister Lieberman, to rein in all non-government organizations, local or foreign, who were trying 'to de-legitimize Israel'.[55]

The further Israel went down this path – wrote Israeli 'new historian' Avi Shlaim in the London *Guardian* – the more it would look like the 'gangster state' headed by 'an utterly unscrupulous set of leaders' which, at its birth, Sir John Troutbeck, head of the British Middle East Office in Cairo, had long since said that it already was; or, in contemporary parlance, like the 'rogue states' which successive US administrations have habitually descried in the likes of the ayatollahs' Iran, Saddam's Iraq or Colonel Gadafi's Libya.[56] With such adverse perceptions of Israel gaining ground in respectable, mainstream Western discourse, could any American president, and least of all, perhaps, a Barack Obama, lend it much indulgence in 'deterrent' wars to come? Apparently even the Hamas prime minister, Ismail Haniyah, had serious doubts about that. It was not, he admitted, just the bravery of its fighters to which Hamas owed its 'victory', it was to the 'free peoples of the world, to the mammoth demonstrations in Europe and the Americas which forced Israel to retreat without realizing any of its objectives – besides the killing of children, women and the elderly'.[57]

Obaman Peace – Or Seventh War?

Coming hard on the heels of Lebanon 2006, Gaza 2009 was yet another and yet more dramatic episode, not merely in the Arab–Israeli conflict but in that interconnected, multi-faceted Middle Eastern mega-crisis of which it is the heart. Could anyone doubt that without some new and truly serious diplomatic action to stop the rot, not only would things get worse, they would do so at a quickening pace? If there was any quarter in the world that might – and after decades of *un*serious-ness it is as well to stress the *might* – possess the means, and above all the will, to undertake one it had to be the new American administration.

This is not the place for an armchair contribution to the 'peace process', or rather to that industry – of debates and seminars, policy papers and punditry, the outpourings of think tanks and academia – which, in addition to the practical exertions of governments and inter-national officialdom, it endlessly engenders. Suffice it to say that there has long been a broad international consensus about what a 'just, lasting and comprehensive' settlement in the Middle East should entail: namely, the 'two-state solution' under which, side by side with Israel, the Palestinians would establish a state of their own in the occupied territories, with East Jerusalem as its capital.

It is true that, for many, this has begun to look more and more improbable, rendered increasingly unviable as it has been by the vast expansion of Jewish settlements in East Jerusalem and the West Bank on which Israel has been engaged ever since the idea won serious international consideration, but more especially since 1993 and the Oslo agreement which effectively embodied it. The argument has been growing that only a 'one-state solution' is now possible, the creation of a bi-national entity in which Arabs and Jews cohabit on an equal footing. But – as former prime minister Ehud Olmert has famously said – the day the struggle for a 'South African-style' solution got going 'the state of Israel is finished.'[1] No American president could so much as think of adopting so radical a course.

President Obama, then, was from the start firmly wedded to 'two states for two peoples'. But of course, in principle at least, all his predecessors had been too. So the real question was just how seriously he would seek to bring it about. If, as many believed, his Administration represented the positively last chance for such a solution, to make it good he was going to have to summon up two virtues, and in very large, if not heroic, measure: impartiality – and the determination to apply it. 'Western purblindness', Walid Khalidi, doyen of Palestinian scholars, once wrote, 'is itself a hallmark of the Palestine problem'[2] – and the partiality of Western leaders, their inveterate favouring of one side over the other, to which the purblindness gave rise has been a *leitmotif* of this book. Indeed, it is no exaggeration to say that, more than any other single factor except the Zionist movement itself, their partiality virtually created *ab nihilo* this 'Palestine problem' which they have ever after been vainly trying to solve.

True impartiality can only be founded on at least an implicit acknowledgement of errors past. Thus, in and of itself, national self-determination and statehood for the Jewish people might have been a perfectly legitimate aim, just as it has been for any other people, and, in the light of Jewish history, it might even have been an indispensable, inspiring and supremely moral one. But it can hardly be gainsaid that in choosing Palestine as the place in which to enact it, the Zionists – and of course their Western sponsors – were all but automatically ensuring that this empowerment of an historically persecuted race entailed the *Nakba*, the Catastrophe, of another one. For Arabs and Palestinians, Jewish nationhood could only have materialized as another form of Western settler-colonialism, and a more extreme and repugnant one than usual in that it did not confine itself to political domination, economic exploitation and more or less racist attitudes towards an indigenous population, but sought to drive this population out of its ancestral homeland altogether. It very largely did so, and not in some haphazard, gradual or incremental way, not, famously, in some 'fit of absence of mind', but in a campaign of ethnic cleansing that was as brutally executed as it was long premeditated and minutely planned. The outcome, so far, of what is by now an almost centennial conflict is one of pure Zionist gain versus pure Arab/Palestinian loss. Mindful, no doubt, of the overwhelming moral debt it owed the Jews, the Christian West supported, or acquiesced in, this wholly one-sided gain as well as the aberrant methods by which it was achieved. As for the one-sided loss, that was sustained by a people who, in no way responsible for the historic persecution of the Jews, were in effect called upon to foot the bill for the sins of those who were. And then, on top of all that, they were constantly reproached, or even vilified, in the court of Western opinion for their persistent refusal – admittedly with sometimes aberrant methods of their own – to accept a wrong that no Western country would ever have accepted for itself.

There can be no serious peace-seeking diplomacy that fails to address this historical imbalance. That requires the adoption of what, from the standpoint of the currently dominant Western orthodoxy, would be seen as an egregiously 'pro-Arab' partisanship, but which, in any true historical reckoning, would be nothing of the sort. Quite the contrary. For it is not as if the Palestinians are demanding anything like the full redress that almost all such other colonially subject peoples have demanded – and largely secured. To be sure, that used to be their aim. But since 1988 they – or their internationally recognized, representative institutions, the Palestine Liberation Organization and the Palestine National Council – have formally renounced what, from both the standpoint of international jurisprudence and established anti-colonial norms, they were entitled to claim as their right: the recovery of their usurped homeland, the return of the refugees and the dismantling of the whole Zionist-colonial apparatus of immigration, settlement and political control. It was only their 'recognition' of the Jewish state, and its 'right to exist' on some 78 per cent of the territory they considered to be rightfully theirs, which enabled a 'peace process' to get going at all, or at least a peace process that had any prospect of eventual success. It is essentially Israel, disdaining any remotely comparable spirit of compromise in reply, which now impedes all further progress. For having secured so very much, it wants yet more. And *what* it wants – a greater share of original Palestine than the 78 per cent it has already has, the Judaization, through settlement, of much of the remaining 22 per cent, full-scale sovereignty over Arab, East Jerusalem, and various other things – is precisely what any serious American administration will be bending itself to combat. There can be no such thing as 'reciprocity' in the sense that Israel and 'the friends of Israel' in the US interpret it; giving up settlements is not a 'concession', it is a disgorging of what never belonged to Israel in the first place, either under international law or the requirements of a two-state solution. And, if Israel continues to kick against the pricks, any serious administration would need to resort to economic and diplomatic penalties of the kind that America has slapped on so many a miscreant down the years; and finally, if that does not work, *impose* a settlement with the aid of an international military force that will simultaneously guarantee the security of all the parties to it.

No sooner was he sworn into office than Obama designated peace in the Middle East as a key foreign policy interest of the United States. With his swift appointment of a special Middle East envoy – and with the reputation for integrity, perseverance and, above all, impartiality which George Mitchell enjoyed – he seemed to move in the right direction. But, right from the start too, it was clear that the obstacles in his path would be daunting. They were not merely the traditional ones, chief among them the fierce opposition that any president who 'gets tough' with Israel is bound to face, from Congress, 'the Lobby' and all those institutions in which the 'friends of Israel' hold such potent sway. For them, the very notion of impartiality, or 'even-handedness' as it is usually called in the United States, has always been a suspect one. Abraham Foxman, the president of the Anti-Defamation League, was quick to remind everyone of that with his remark, upon learning of Mitchell's appointment, that there could be 'no moral equivalence' between such adversaries as Israelis and Palestinians; in their case, he

said, even-handedness 'could only lead to the distortion of what' –
shared values – 'American–Israeli relations are all about'.[3] Newer – or,
rather, higher – obstacles had also been thrown up by that further right-
ward shift of a whole society which the Israeli elections registered and
duly mediated into official government policy. Obama's immense
popularity, combined with a first, perceptible tarnishing of Israel's
exalted reputation even among America's pro-Israeli political elite, was
doubtless going to help him. Yet, from the first, Arabs could not but
notice the continuities too. The America which under Bush had
condemned, and conspired to overturn, the results – in the shape of
Hamas rule – of the freest and fairest Palestinian elections ever held,
was quick, under Obama, to assure the Israelis that it would work with
whatever government their 'thriving democracy' threw up. It was
improbable, Arabs lost no time in concluding, that the new
Administration was going to stop the rot if it failed to abjure attitudes
like that.

In the event, Obama certainly went further than any of his predecessors – and especially the last two – in making it clear that the
major contribution to an eventual peace would have to come from
Israel. That was apparent, in the first place, from his rhetoric, from – for
example – the tone and substance, carefully pitched to the Arab ear, of
the 'address to the Muslim world' which he made from Cairo
University five months into his presidency. Rarely had words like
'occupation' ever fallen from the lips of a Bill Clinton or a George
Bush, and certainly never any mention of the Palestinian 'resistance' to
it which Obama all but likened to the American civil rights movement
or South Africa's struggle against apartheid. He dwelt on the Holocaust
as an irrefutable *raison d'être* of Israel's very existence, but, in the same
breath, he all but ascribed to the *Nakba* a comparable place in the
tragedy of the Palestinians. While condemning Hamas's violence
against civilians, he did not call it a 'terrorist organization', and even
accorded it a certain legitimacy as an authentic representative of the
Palestinian people and their aspirations. But, practically and most
importantly, he said it was high time that the Israelis ceased their
building of settlements in the West Bank and Jerusalem; this was both
'illegitimate' in itself and – he intimated – no less a violation of

previous agreements or obstacle to peace than anything that Hamas was doing.

Ever since Israel conquered the West Bank and Gaza in 1967, it has of course been the official position of every US administration that the settlements are illegal; but in practice, and despite periodic *pro-forma* protests, they effectively tolerated or even connived in them. But Obama and his Middle East envoys were immediately different. They appeared to take this official US position seriously at last, demanding a complete 'freeze' of all further settlement construction, and dismissing all the subterfuges, such as the disingenuous claim of 'natural growth', with which the Israelis had successfully inveigled their predecessors. In consequence settlements became the source of unprecedented tension between America and an Israel increasingly dismayed at the prospect of losing the very special status as America's ally, friend and protégé, and the automatic involvement in, and strong influence over, its Middle East decision-making, which it had come to look upon as part of the natural order. Settlements, and the way Obama handled the issue, were seen as a key, initial measure of just how resolute in facing Israel down Arabs and Palestinians could expect him to be. But they would also constitute a vital component of an eventual peace agreement itself. And herein lay the yet greater test to come. For it would have been one thing to put a genuine 'freeze' on further settlement construction. The dismantling of already existing settlements – and dispersing the nearly half a million Israelis who inhabit them – which the two-state solution at least implicitly requires, would be quite another. Would Obama really go on to insist on that too? Could he ever induce an Israeli government to take on the settlers, and their powerful accomplices within the whole Israeli body politic, in a monumental, destiny-shaping showdown like this? Though generally impressed with Obama's debut, most Arabs remained very sceptical about that. And by the summer of 2009, they were already noting signs of America's retreat from such positions as it had been bold enough to stake out, chiefly evident in new calls on Arab countries to 'normalize' relations with Israel in return for as yet vague and unspecified curbs on its settlement activities. Two of America's closest allies in the Arab world, Saudi Arabia and Jordan, mindful of a long history of unreciprocated Arab concessions, flatly rejected any such new ones, pointing out that, under the existing, Saudi-sponsored, collective Arab peace offer, 'normalization' would come at the end, not the beginning, of its implementation.

By autumn, Arab scepticism had turned into full-blown disenchantment, as the retreat looked more and more like abject surrender. It was, Obama said, no longer a total freeze on settlement construction that he required, simply a measure of 'restraint'; and soon after that – and even as settlement construction resumed with no less vigour than before – Secretary of State Hillary Clinton praised Netanyahu for making 'unprecedented' concessions that entirely escaped the attention of most observers. In any case – she proceeded even more astonishingly to assert – a settlement freeze never *had* been a precondition for the renewal of talks. So, rhetoric aside, just what, Arabs, Palestinians and despairing Israeli doves now asked, was the difference between Obama's policies in the Middle East and those of his predecessor, Bush? Even President Mahmoud Abbas, most patient and pliant of Palestinian leaders, threw down a gauntlet of sorts. He had banked his all on America and its pledges; and now he had been personally betrayed. He threatened to resign. Within less than a year of Obama's taking office, the 'peace process' looked sicker – just about terminal in fact – than it had almost ever looked before.

In the absence of a final Arab–Israeli peace, or even any sense of progress towards one, there will be war, or large-scale violence. It was ever thus in the Middle East. How much more so, then, if, after all the hopes vested in him, so promising and popular a new American president as Obama fails to solve the everlasting 'Palestine problem' in his turn. King Abdullah of Jordan even put a firm date on it: 'another conflict between Arabs or Muslims and Israel in the next twelve to eighteen months'.[4]

And doubtless, in due course, yet another one after that. This book didn't start out as a history of the Arab–Israeli struggle. Yet, at every stage of its writing, the struggle kept intruding on it as so inseparable, intrinsic and formative a part of its titular subject that that is what, in great measure, it actually turned out to be – a history in which Lebanon, the author's country of half a century's residence, nonetheless always remained to the fore as the lens through which he viewed it. And if, upon its completion, there was one main prognosis which it seemed to embody it was surely that a seemingly interminable conflict which began with the sword the sword will end; but it may have to administer many a bloody and painful, yet inconclusive blow, before it finally does so.

Of the forms which, in the absence of peace, further hostilities will likely take, the likeliest, for the first of them at least, will be the one that Gaza pre-empted – Israel's much-predicted 'second round' with Hizbullah, still very much the formidable foe which, Israel keeps threatening, it will sooner or later have to deal with. It is true that Lebanon did not quite turn into the fully-fledged 'Hizbullah state' which – with the parliamentary elections of June 2009 – Israel had feared it would. For in those the ruling '14 March' coalition came out on top again, with seventy-one seats against only fifty-seven for the '8 March' opposition. But even if Hizbullah and its friends did not secure the parliamentary majority which they had expected, they still – Nasrallah insisted – represented the 'popular' one; and in point of fact they did actually take the greater number of individual votes. In any case, continuing to re-arm, recruit and train on an unprecedented scale, this 'most technically-capable terrorist organization in the world' – as a new State Department report called it – remained the most powerful military and political organization in the country.[5]

Before long Israel was sounding new alarms about Russian-built, vehicle-mounted SA-8 missiles, capable of shooting down aircraft up to a height of 35,000 feet, on which Hizbullah personnel were reportedly being trained in Syria. These, it said, were 'destabilizing weapons', capable of posing such a threat to its mastery of the skies over Lebanon that their introduction into that country would constitute a 'red line' they could not permit Hizbullah to cross. Defence Minister Ehud Barak warned that, in another war – unlike the last – Israel would 'use its full force' against this Lebanese state of which a 'terror organization' had become an integral part.[6]

Then, in August, the whole internal Lebanese balance of power shifted in Hizbullah's favour when the great 'prestidigitator' himself, Druze chieftain Walid Jumblat, announced that he was distancing himself from the '14 March majority', of which he had been the most important and outspoken leader, if not the glue that really held its disparate elements together. The 'Cedar Revolution' it spawned had now exhausted itself, he said, and his continued association with right-wing, pro-American, 'isolationist' members of it was at odds with the basically Arab nationalist, pro-Palestinian and 'leftist' principles which he and his Druze-based Progressive Socialist Party purportedly stood for. He who had been most virulent in his denunciations of Baathist Syria now said that, with its 'occupation' of Lebanon over, it was time to rebuild the 'special relationship' with it. But his main, if discreeter, motives were altogether more local and pragmatic. Ever since Hizbullah's armed 'coup' of the year before, he had been growing more afraid for the future of his small and increasingly vulnerable community, and he now sought an accommodation with the Shiites, the rising power on Lebanon's sectarian chequerboard who represented potentially the greatest threat to it. He was not, he said, planning to join the '8 March' opposition, or even quit '14 March' altogether; rather he was finding his way into a centrist 'third force' appearing to take shape under the auspices of President Michel Suleiman. But whatever he was actually doing, it was clearly another significant political gain for Hizbullah — and a vexation to the Israelis.[7]

But not a few people in the region believe that while the next resort to arms might thus — and for the umpteenth time — *begin* on the Israeli–Lebanese front, for thirty-six years the only militarily active one outside Palestine itself, it might not, this time, remain confined to it. This time, in what would undoubtedly qualify as the 'Seventh Middle Eastern War', other members of the Islamo-nationalist camp might join in: Hamas; Syria; and even, most formidably, the rising regional hegemon and Israeli–American *bête noire*, the ayatollahs' Iran. Together, they would wage a Hizbullah-style 'missile war' writ large.

And in this case, the 'small state' of the Middle East would no longer be its battleground, or, at least, no longer its only one. For what was always well-nigh bound to happen sooner or later finally would have done so — and the battle would have come to the entire Middle East.

Notes

CHAPTER ONE: *The Seeds of Conflict*

1 Dershowitz, Alan, *The Israel–Hezbollah War*, An Amazon Short, 2006.
2 9 August 2006.
3 Bakunin, Mikhail, *L'Empire Knouto-Germanique et la Révolution Sociale*, Geneva, Imprimerie Coopérative, 1871, p. 50.
4 *Middle East Reporter*, Beirut, 23 September 2006.
5 Hadawi, Sami, *Bitter Harvest*, The New World Press, New York, 1967, p. 11.
6 Picard, Elizabeth, *Lebanon, A Shattered Country: Myths and Realities of the Wars in Lebanon*, Holmes & Meier, New York, London, 2002, p. 28.
7 Salibi, Kamal, *The Modern History of Lebanon*, Caravan Books, New York, 1977, p. 79.
8 Schulze, Kirsten, *Israel's Covert Diplomacy in Lebanon*, St Antony's College, Oxford, 1998, p. 152.
9 Hitti, Philip, *Lebanon in History: From the Earliest Times Until the Present*, Macmillan, London, New York, 1957, p. 244; Khalidi, Walid, *Conflict and Violence in Lebanon: Confrontation in the Middle East*, Harvard University Press, 1979, p. 34.
10 Harris, William, *The New Face of Lebanon*, Markus Wiener Publishers, Princeton, 2005, p. 41.
11 *The Daily Star*, Beirut, 30 August 2007.
12 Ibid.
13 Hamzeh, Ahmad Nizar, *In the Path of Hizbullah*, Syracuse University Press, New York, 2004, p. 11.
14 Sayigh, Rosemary, *Too Many Enemies: The Palestine Experience in Lebanon*, Zed Books, London, 1994, p. 159.
15 Hamzeh, op. cit., p. 12.
16 Eisenberg, Laura Zittrain, *My Enemy's Enemy, Lebanon in the Early Zionist Imagination, 1900–1948*, Wayne State University Press, Detroit, 1994, p. 48.
17 See Jeffreys, J. N. M., *Palestine: The Reality*, Longmans, Green and Co., London, 1939, Chapter II.

18 Lenczowski, George, *The Middle East in World Affairs*, Cornell University Press, New York, 1960, p. 80.

19 Davidson, Lawrence, 'The Past as Preludes: Zionism and the Betrayal of American Democratic Principles, 1917–48', *Journal of Palestine Studies*, No. 123, Spring 2002, p. 24.

20 Barbour, Neville, *Nisi Dominus*, Harrap, London, 1946, p. 52.

21 Khalidi, Walid, *From Haven to Conquest*, Institute for Palestine Studies, Beirut, 1971, p. 115.

22 Weizmann, Chaim, *Excerpts from his Historic Statements, Writings and Addresses*, The Jewish Agency for Palestine, New York, 1952, p. 48.

23 Ibid.

24 Eisenberg, op. cit., p. 22.

25 Litvinoff, Barnet, ed., *The Letters and Papers of Chaim Weizmann*, Vol. I, Series B, Paper 24, Jerusalem University Press, 1983, pp. 115–16, cited in Masalha, Nur, *Expulsion of the Palestinians*, Institute for Palestine Studies, Washington, 1992, p. 6.

26 Heller, Yosef, *The Struggle for the State: The Zionist Policy 1936–1948* [Hebrew], Jerusalem, 1984, p. 140, cited in ibid., p. 6.

27 Flapan, Simha, *Zionism and the Palestinians, 1917–1947*, Croom Helm, London, 1979, p. 56, cited in ibid., p. 17.

28 Ibid., p. 13.

29 Zangwill, Israel, *The Voice of Jerusalem*, London, Heinemann, 1920, pp. 93, 103, cited in ibid., pp. 13–14.

30 Ibid., pp. 8–38.

31 Ibid., p. 22.

32 Schechtman, Joseph B., *Rebel and Statesman: The Vladimir Jabotinsky Story, The Early Years*, New York, T. Yoseloff, 1956, p. 54, cited in ibid., p. 29.

33 Michael, George, 'Deciphering Ahmadinejad's Holocaust Revisionism', *Middle East Quarterly*, Summer 2008.

34 Antonius, George, *The Arab Awakening: The Story of the Arab National Movement*, Khayat's, Beirut, 1960, reprint of original, 1938 edition, p. 269; Shlaim, Avi, *The Politics of Partition: King Abdullah, The Zionists, and Palestine 1921–1951*, Oxford University Press, 1988, p. 40.

35 Antonius, op. cit., p. 285.

36 Ibid., pp. 243–324.

37 Flapan, Simha, p. 131, cited in Masalha, op. cit., p. 19.

38 Ibid., p. 20.

39 Eisenberg, op. cit., p. 21.

40 Gerber, Haim, 'Zionism, Orientalism and the Palestinians', *Journal of Palestine Studies*, No. 129, Autumn 2003, pp. 5–23; see Khalidi, Rashid, *Palestinian Identity: The Construction of Modern National Consciousness*, Columbia University Press, New York, 1997.

41 Schulze, op. cit., p. 199.

CHAPTER TWO: *Zionists and Maronites*

1   Leader of the 'Lovers of Zion'; see Eisenberg, op. cit., p. 41.
2   Ibid.
3   Fromkin, David, *A Peace to End All Peace: The Fall of the Ottoman Empire and the Creation of the Modern Middle East*, Avon Books, New York, 1989, pp. 441-2.
4   Eisenberg, op. cit., pp. 51-2.
5   Ibid., p. 52.
6   Ibid., p. 14.
7   Ibid., p. 31.
8   Ibid., p. 50.
9   Schulze, op. cit., p. 15.
10 Eisenberg, op. cit., p. 14.
11 Ibid., p. 56.
12 Ibid., p. 59.
13 Jabotinsky, Ze'ev, *Writings: On the Road to Statehood* [Hebrew], Jerusalem, pp. 51-66, cited in Shlaim, Avi, *The Iron Wall: Israel and the Arab World*, Penguin Books, London, 2000, pp. 13-14.
14 Brenner, Lenni, *Zionism in the Age of the Dictators*, Lawrence Hill, Chicago, 1983, chapter 10.
15 Davidson, op. cit., p. 26.
16 Ibid.
17 Eisenberg, op. cit., pp. 27, 59.
18 Ibid., p. 42.
19 Ibid., p. 71.
20 Ibid., p. 74.
21 Ibid., p. 75.
22 Ibid., p. 67.
23 Ibid., p. 69.
24 Ibid., p. 66.
25 John, Robert, and Hadawi, Sami, *The Palestine Diary:* Vol. One, *1914-1948*, The Palestine Research Centre, Beirut, 1970, p. 256.
26 15 July 1938.
27 John and Hadawi, op. cit., p. 289.
28 Davidson, op. cit., p. 33.
29 Segev, Tom, *One Palestine, Complete*, Little Brown and Co., New York, 2001, p. 422.
30 Niv, David, *The Campaign of the National Military Organization, 1931-1937*, Tel Aviv, cited in Halevi, Ilan, *De la Terreur au Massacre d'Etat*, Imprimerie Boudin, Paris, 1984, p. 98.
31 *National Bulletin,* No. 3, cited in ibid., p. 101.
32 John and Hadawi, op. cit., p. 274.
33 Eisenberg, op. cit., Chapter 4, pp. 88-116.
34 John and Hadawi, op. cit., p. 280.
35 Pappe, Ilan, *The Ethnic Cleansing of Palestine*, Oneworld Publications, Oxford, 2006, p. 16.

36 Weizmann, Chaim, *Trial and Error*, Harper and Brothers, New York, 1949, p. 367.
37 Eisenberg, op. cit., p. 96.
38 Ibid.
39 Ibid., p. 106.
40 Ibid., p. 97.
41 Ibid., p. 109.
42 Ibid., p. 149.
43 Ibid., p. 13.
44 Ibid., p. 109.
45 Ibid., p. 104.
46 Ibid., p. 107.
47 Ibid., p. 93.
48 Ibid., p. 100.
49 Ibid., p. 79.
50 Ibid., p. 117.
51 Ibid., p. 144.
52 Ibid., p. 125.
53 Ibid., p. 127.
54 Ibid., p. 125.
55 Ibid., p. 128.
56 Ibid., p. 129.
57 Schulze, op. cit., p. 21.
58 Eisenberg, op. cit., pp. 138, 140.
59 Ibid., pp. 139–40.
60 Ibid., pp. 35, 84.
61 Ibid., p. 80.

CHAPTER THREE: *The Reckoning Delayed*

1 McDonald, James, *My Mission to Israel*, Simon & Schuster, New York, 1952, p. 176.
2 Pappe, Ilan, 'Erasing the Palestinians' Past', *Journal of Palestine Studies*, No. 118, Winter 2001, pp. 108–9.
3 Pappe, *The Ethnic Cleansing of Palestine*.
4 Morris, Benny, *The Birth of the Palestinian Refugee Problem, 1947–49*, Cambridge University Press, Cambridge and New York, 1988.
5 Pappe, Ilan, 'The 1948 Ethnic Cleansing of Palestine', *Journal of Palestine Studies*, No. 141, Autumn 2006, p. 17.
6 Masalha, op. cit., pp. 131–2.
7 Ibid., pp. 17–22; Pappe, 'The 1948 Ethnic Cleansing', p. 12.
8 Pappe, *The Ethnic Cleansing of Palestine*, p. 23.
9 Ibid., p. 26.
10 Hirst, David, *The Gun and the Olive Branch: The Roots of Violence in the Middle East*, Faber and Faber, London, 2003, p. 255.
11 Pappe, *The Ethnic Cleansing of Palestine*, p. 28.

12 Pappe, 'The 1948 Ethnic Cleansing', pp. 16–17.

13 Ibid., p. 16; Pappe, *The Ethnic Cleansing of Palestine*, p. 26.

14 Soueid, Mahmoud, 'Israel au Liban, la Fin de 30 Ans d'Occupation?', *Revue d'Études Palestiniennes*, Beirut, 2000, p. 7.

15 Nazzal, Nafez, *The Palestinian Exodus from Galilee 1948*, The Institute for Palestine Studies, Beirut, 1978, pp. 91–2.

16 Hughes, Matthew, 'Lebanon's Armed Forces and the Arab–Israeli War, 1948–49', *Journal of Palestine Studies*, No. 134, Winter 2005, pp. 23–41.

17 Pappe, *The Ethnic Cleansing of Palestine*, p. 144.

18 Eisenberg, op. cit., p. 158.

19 Schulze, op. cit., pp. 30–2, 40.

20 Ibid., p. 162.

21 Shlaim, *The Iron Wall*, p. 116.

22 Rokach, Livia, *Israel's Sacred Terrorism: A Study Based on Moshe Sharett's 'Personal Diary' and Other Documents*, Association of Arab-American University Graduates, Belmont, Massachusetts, 1980, p. 8.

23 Shlaim, *The Iron Wall*, pp. 76–81, 119–22.

24 Nasser, Gamal Abdul, *Philosophy of the Revolution*, Government Printing Office, Cairo, n.d., p. 59.

25 Ben-Gurion, David, *Rebirth and Destiny*, Philosophical Library, New York, 1954, pp. 419, 446.

26 Protocol of the Jewish Agency Executive meeting, 7 June 1938, Vol. 28, No. 51, Central Zionist Archives, cited in Masalha, *Imperial Israel and the Palestinians*, Pluto Press, London, 2000, p. 7.

27 Eisenberg, op. cit., p. 17; Schulze, op. cit., p. 40.

28 Morris, Benny, *Israel's Border Wars 1949–1956: Arab Infiltration, Israeli Retaliation, and the Countdown to the Suez War*, Clarendon Press, Oxford, 1993, p. 12.

29 Lilienthal, Alfred, *What Price Israel*, Henry Regnery, Chicago, 1953, pp. 109–47, 155; Lilienthal, Alfred, *The Other Side of the Coin*, Devin-Adair, New York, 1965, pp. 89–163.

30 *Haaretz*, 11 August 2005, cited in *Journal of Palestine Studies*, No. 137, Autumn 2005, p. 120.

31 Shlaim, *The Iron Wall*, p. 49.

32 Ibid., pp. 45–6, 52–3; Shlaim, Avi, 'Husni Zaim and the Plan to Resettle Palestinian Refugees in Syria', *Journal of Palestine Studies*, No. 60, Summer 1986, pp. 69–80.

33 Ben-Gurion's diary, 13 February 1949, cited in Shlaim, *The Iron Wall*, p. 67.

34 Rokach, op. cit., p. 14.

35 Benziman, Uzi, *Sharon: An Israeli Caesar*, Adama Books, New York, 1985, pp. 50, 56.

36 Morris, *Israel's Border Wars*, p. 173.

37 Jiryis, Sabri, 'Secret of State: An Analysis of the Diaries of Moshe Sharett', *Journal of Palestine Studies*, No. 37, Autumn 1980, p. 51.

38 Shlaim, *The Iron Wall*, p. 144; Menuhin, Moshe, *The Decadence of Judaism in Our Time*, The Institute for Palestine Studies, Beirut, 1969, p. 176; Caplan, Neil, 'The New Historians', *Journal of Palestine Studies*, No. 96, Autumn 1995, p. 101.

39 Burns, General E. L. N., *Between Arab and Israeli*, Harrap, London, 1962, p. 18.
40 Shlaim, *The Iron Wall*, p. 164.
41 Ibid., p. 136.
42 Hirst, *The Gun and the Olive Branch*, p. 326.
43 Shlaim, *The Iron Wall*, p. 175.
44 Ibid., p. 175.
45 Ibid., p. 172; Shlaim, Avi, 'Israel, the Great Powers, and the Middle East Crisis of 1958', *Journal of Imperial and Commonwealth History*, No. 2, May 1999, p. 178.
46 Menuhin, op. cit., p. 182.
47 Shlaim, *The Iron Wall*, p. 204.
48 Schulze, op. cit., p. 42.
49 Morris, *Israel's Border Wars*, pp. 63, 92–5.
50 Rokach, op. cit., p. 18.
51 Ibid., p. 19.
52 Ibid., p. 20.
53 Ibid., p. 24.
54 Ibid., p. 24.
55 Ibid., p. 25.
56 Ibid., p. 28.
57 Schulze, op. cit., p. 48.
58 Shlaim, *The Iron Wall*, p. 171.
59 See Schulze, op. cit., pp. 45–6, citing Ben-Gurion's diary, as quoted in Moshe Shemesh, and Selwyn Ilan Troen, *The Suez–Sinai Crisis 1956: Retrospective and Reappraisal*, Frank Cass, London, 1990, p. 181; Masalha, op. cit., pp. 13–14, citing Moshe Dayan, *Milestones: An Autobiography* [Hebrew], Edanin and Dvir, Jerusalem and Tel Aviv, 1976, p. 255.
60 Shlaim, *The Iron Wall*, p. 202.
61 Schulze, op. cit., p. 53.
62 Harris, op. cit., p. 143.
63 Schulze, op. cit., p. 64.
64 Salibi, Kamal, *Crossroads to Civil War: Lebanon 1958–1976*, Caravan, New York, 1976, p. 18.
65 Schulze, op. cit., p. 70.
66 Christison, Kathleen, 'Bound By A Frame of Reference, Part II: US Policy and the Palestinians, 1948–88', *Journal of Palestine Studies*, No. 107, Spring 1998, pp. 20–34.
67 See Hirst, *The Gun and the Olive Branch*, pp. 332–44.
68 Picard, op. cit., p. 80.

CHAPTER FOUR: *Lebanon and the Palestinians*

1 Tibawi, A. L., 'Visions of the Return: The Palestine Arab Refugees in Arabic Poetry and Art', *Mideast Journal*, XVII, 1963, p. 523.
2 Al-Hout, Bayan Nuwayhed, *Sabra and Shatila, September 1982*, Pluto Press, London/Ann Arbor, p. 22.

3 Sayigh, Rosemary, *Palestinians: From Peasants to Revolutionaries*, Zed Press, London, 1978, p. 104.

4 Ibid., pp. 107, 125.

5 Ibid., p. 127.

6 Al-Hout, op. cit., p. 25.

7 Sayigh, *From Peasants to Revolutionaries*, p. 131.

8 Al-Hout, op. cit., p. 24.

9 Kazziha, Walid, *Revolutionary Transformation in the Arab World*, Charles Knight, London, 1975, p. 53.

10 Sayigh, Rosemary, *From Peasants to Revolutionaries*, pp. 131–2.

11 Hirst, *The Gun and the Olive Branch*, pp. 396–403.

12 Ibid., p. 404.

13 Sayigh, Yezid, *Armed Struggle and the Search for a State: The Palestine National Movement 1949–1993*, Oxford University Press, 2000, p. 124.

14 There was actually a more successful one the next day.

15 Hirst, *The Gun and the Olive Branch*, p. 406.

16 Sayigh, Rosemary, *From Peasants to Revolutionaries.*, p. 151.

17 Ibid., p. 147.

18 The English translation of the Arabic word for this concept is usually 'regionalism'; but since this book frequently uses that word in a rather different sense, 'localism' has been adopted in order to avoid confusion.

19 Hirst, *The Gun and the Olive Branch*, p. 425.

20 Ibid., pp. 424–5.

21 Ibid., p. 428.

22 Al-Hout, op. cit., p. 27.

23 Picard, op. cit., p. 81.

24 Sayigh, Yezid, 'Palestinian Military Performance in the 1982 War', *Journal of Palestine Studies*, No. 48, Summer 1983, pp. 3–24.

25 Hirst, *The Gun and the Olive Branch*, p. 413.

26 Sayigh, Yezid, *Armed Struggle*, p. 188.

27 Salibi, *Crossroads*, p. 54.

28 Khalidi, Walid, *Conflict*, p. 40.

29 Ibid., p. 69.

30 Muir, Jim, 'Lebanon: Arena of Conflict, Crucible of Peace', *The Middle East Journal*, Vol 38, No. 2, Spring 1984, p. 203.

31 Sayigh, Rosemary, *From Peasants to Revolutionaries*, pp. 150–1.

32 Sayigh, Yezid, *Armed Struggle*, p. 189.

33 See p. 48.

34 Sayigh, Rosemary, *From Peasants to Revolutionaries*, pp. 156–8; Abisaab, Rula Jurdi, 'The Cleric as Organic Intellectual: Revolutionary Shiism in the Lebanese Hawzas', in *Distant Relations, Iran and Lebanon in the Last 500 years*, [Chehabi, H. E., ed.], I. B. Tauris, London, New York, 2006, p. 239.

35 Sayigh, Rosemary, *From Peasants to Revolutionaries*, pp. 158–60; Sayigh, Rosemary, *Too Many Enemies*, p. 87.

36 Sayigh, Rosemary, *From Peasants to Revolutionaries*, pp. 160–1.

37 Ibid., p. 162.

38 Sayigh, Yezid, *Armed Struggle*, p. 191; *Arab Report and Record*, London, Swale Press, 1969, p. 434.
39 Khalidi, Walid, *Conflict and Violence*, p. 41.
40 Schulze, op. cit., pp. 72–9.
41 Sayigh, Yezid, *Armed Struggle.*, p. 194.

CHAPTER FIVE: *Civil War in Lebanon*

1 Salibi, *Crossraods*, p. 97; *Arab Report and Record*, 1975, p. 222.
2 Khalidi, Walid, *Conflict and Violence*, p. 47.
3 *Arab Report and Record*, Statement by Chief of Staff, General David Elazar, op. cit., 1972, p. 318.
4 Schulze, op. cit., p. 77.
5 Ibid., pp. 76–7.
6 *Arab Report and Record*, op. cit., 1973, p. 158.
7 Sayigh, Yezid, *Armed Struggle*, p. 317.
8 Ibid., p. 358.
9 Pakradouni, Karim, *La Paix Manquée: Le Mandat d'Elias Sarkis, 1976–1982*, Editions Fiches du Monde Arabe, Beirut, 1984, p. 106.
10 Khalidi, Walid, *Conflict and Violence*, p. 75.
11 Salibi, op. cit., p. 78.
12 Sayigh, Rosemary, *Too Many Enemies*, p. 178.
13 Hourani, Albert, *A Vision of History*, Beirut, 1961, p. 137.
14 See p. 61.
15 Schulze, op. cit., pp. 95, 111.
16 Christison, 'Bound By', p. 27.
17 Sayigh, Yezid, *Armed Struggle*, p. 453.
18 Trabulsi, Fawwaz, *A Modern History of Lebanon*, Pluto Press, London, 2007, p. 189.
19 Ibid., p. 191.
20 Sayigh, Yezid, *Armed Struggle*, p. 362.
21 Khalidi, Walid, *Conflict and Violence.*, p. 48.
22 Sayigh, Yezid, *Armed Struggle*, p. 365.
23 Ibid, p. 363.
24 Ibid., p. 383.
25 Harris, op. cit., p. 164.
26 Kissinger, Henry, *Years of Renewal*, Diane Publishing Company, New York, 1999, p. 1042.
27 Sayigh, Yezid, *Armed Struggle*, p. 389.
28 Ibid., p. 401.
29 Khalidi, Walid, *Conflict and Violence*, 109.
30 Hirst, *The Gun and the Olive Branch*, p. 533.

CHAPTER SIX: *Imperial Hubris*

1 MacBride, Sean, *Israel in Lebanon, Report of the International Commission*, Ithaca Press, London, 1982, p. 19.

2 Letter from Ben-Gurion to Haim Guri, 15 May 1963, cited in Michael Bar
   Zohar, *Ben Gurion*, Vol. III, p. 1547; see *Middle East International*, London,
   August 1977; Kapeliouk, Amnon, *Le Monde Diplomatique*, June 1977.

3 Hirst, *The Gun and the Olive Branch*, p. 476.

4 Schulze, op. cit., p. 95.

5 As it popularly came to be known, though its official designation was
   Operation Wisdom.

6 Tveit, Karsten, *A Pattern for Defeat*, pp. 47–50, private translation from the
   Norwegian [*Nederlag: Israels Krig i Libanon*, Cappelan, Oslo, 1985] by Peter
   Scott-Hansen; see also Khalidi, Walid, *Conflict and Violence*, pp. 124–9,
   Schulze, op. cit., pp. 96–8.

7 Ibid., p. 96; Hirst, David and Beeson, Irene, *Sadat*, Faber and Faber, London,
   1981, p. 299.

8 Tveit, op. cit., p. 1.

9 Schulze, op. cit., p. 107; Khalidi, Walid, *Conflict and Violence*, p. 126.

10 Schulze, op. cit., p. 153.

11 Black, Ian and Morris, Benny, *Israel's Secret Wars: A History of Israel's
   Intelligence Services*, Grove Press, London, 1991, p. 365.

12 Rabinovich, Itamar, *The War for Lebanon, 1970–1983*, Cornell University Press,
   New York, p. 97.

13 Schulze, op. cit., pp. 104–5.

14 Ibid., p. 112.

15 Ibid., p. 108.

16 Hirst, *The Gun and the Olive Branch*, pp. 529–30.

17 Boykin, John, *Cursed Is The Peacemaker: The American Diplomat Versus the Israeli
   General, Beirut, 1982*, Applegate Press, Belmont, California, 2002, p. 48; Hirst,
   The Gun and the Olive Branch, p. 516; Schulze, op. cit., pp. 112–13.

18 Black and Morris, op. cit., p. 171.

19 Hirst, *The Gun and the Olive Branch*, pp. 522, 534.

20 *Kivunim (A Journal for Judaism and Zionism)*, Jerusalem, February 1982.

21 Khalidi, Walid, *Conflict and Violence*, p. 112.

22 Tveit, op. cit., p. 97.

23 Ibid., p. 114.

24 Hirst, *The Gun and the Olive Branch*, p. 390.

25 Ibid., p. 245.

26 Tveit, op. cit.

27 Ibid., p. 97.

28 Ibid., p. 108.

29 Ibid., p. 109.

30 Ibid., p. 112.

31 Dean, John Gunther, *Danger Zones: A Diplomat's Fight for America's Interests*,
   New Academia Publishing, Washington, 2009, pp. 131–4, 136, 192; Dean, John,
   Statement on his 80th birthday, Middle East Policy Council, Washington, June
   2006; Killgore, Andrew [retired US ambassador], 'American Ambassador
   Recalls Israeli Assassination Attempt – With US Weapons', *Washington Report
   on Middle East Affairs*, November 2002; Killgore, Andrew, 'Israel's Failed

Assassination Attempt on US Ambassador Documented', *Washington Report on Middle East Affairs*, May 2004; *Inventory of Documents on Lebanon Presented by John Gunther Dean to US National Archives*, File 34, Carter Center, Atlanta; Randal, Jonathan, *The Tragedy of Lebanon: Christian Warlords, Israeli Adventurers and American Bunglers*, Chatto and Windus, London, 1983, p. 207.

32 Hamzeh, op. cit., p. 16.
33 Tveit, op. cit., p. 119; Hirst, David, *The Guardian*, London, 1 August 1979.
34 Hirst, David, *The Guardian*, 11 June 1980.
35 See p. 95.
36 Ibid.
37 Sayigh, Rosemary, *Too Many Enemies*, p. 113.
38 *The Financial Times*, London, 3 July 1982.
39 Tveit, op. cit., p. 121.
40 Ibid., p. 123.
41 Sayigh, Yezid, *Armed Struggle*, p. 506.
42 *Haaretz*, 25 June 1982.
43 Avner, Yariv, *Dilemmas of Security: Politics, Strategy, and the Israeli Experience in Lebanon*, Oxford University Press, 1987, p. 89, cited in Sayigh, Yezid, *Armed Struggle.*, p. 508.
44 Boykin, op. cit., p. 55.
45 Israel Radio, 12 May 1982.
46 *Yediot Aharonot, Maariv*, 6 February 1982.
47 *Yediot Aharonot*, 14 May 1982.
48 See Seale, Patrick, *Abu Nidal: A Gun for Hire*, Hutchinson, London, 1992.
49 Hirst, *The Gun and the Olive Branch*, p. 539.
50 Creveld, Martin van, *The Sword and the Olive: A Critical History of the Israeli Defense Force*, Public Affairs, New York, 1998, p. 288.
51 See ibid., p. 291; Sayigh, Yezid, *Armed Struggle.*, p. 524; Wright, Clifford, 'The Israeli War Machine in Lebanon', *Journal of Palestine Studies*, No. 46, Winter 1983, p. 39.
52 Creveld, op. cit., p. 302.
53 Shlaim, *The Iron Wall*, p. 405; Benziman, op. cit., p. 241.
54 Mansur, Camille, *Beyond Alliance: Israel in US Foreign Policy*, Columbia University Press, New York, 1994, p. xvi.
55 Boykin, op. cit., p. 57.
56 Benziman, op. cit., p. 239.
57 Seale, Patrick, *Asad*, I. B. Tauris, London, 1988, p. 394.
58 Boykin, op. cit., p. 70.
59 *Al-Hamishmar*, 5 August 1982.
60 See Sayigh, Yezid, *Armed Struggle*, p. 535.
61 *Jerusalem Post*, 24 June 1982.
62 *Nekudah*, journal of the Gush Emunim, 12 November 1982, cited in Masalha, *Imperial Israel and the Palestinians*, p. 108.
63 *Middle East International*, London, 16 July 1982.
64 Boykin, op. cit., p. 87.
65 *Maariv*, 20 August 1982.

66 Khalidi, Rashid, *Under Siege: P.L.O. Decisionmaking During the 1982 War*, Columbia University Press, New York, 1986, p. 47.
67 Boykin, op. cit., p. 99; Hirst, *The Gun and the Olive Branch*, p. 544.
68 Sayigh, Yezid, *Armed Struggle*, p. 531.
69 Boykin, op. cit., pp. 79, 279.
70 Randal, op. cit., p. 266.
71 Sayigh, Yezid, *Armed Struggle*, p. 530.
72 Boykin., op. cit., p. 234; Sayigh, Yezid, *Armed Struggle*, pp. 536–7; Randal, op. cit., p. 270.
73 *Jerusalem Post*, 3 August 1982.
74 Shlaim, *The Iron Wall*, p. 413.
75 Hirst, *The Gun and the Olive Branch*, p. 545.
76 Randal, op. cit., p. 244.
77 Hirst, *The Gun and the Olive Branch*, p. 545.
78 Khalidi, Rashid, *Under Siege*, pp. 98, 148.
79 Hirst, *The Gun and the Olive Branch*, pp. 547–8.

CHAPTER SEVEN: *The Massacre of Sabra and Shatila*

1 Schiff, Ze'ev and Ya'ari, Ehud, *Israel's Lebanon War*, Simon & Schuster, New York, 1984, p. 230.
2 Speech at a pro-government rally in Tel Aviv, 17 July 1982.
3 Schiff and Ya'ari, op. cit., p. 231.
4 Ibid., p. 233.
5 See Chapter Two.
6 Schulze, op. cit., p. 130.
7 Randal, op. cit., p. 273.
8 Schiff and Ya'ari, op. cit., pp. 233–6, Shlaim, *The Iron Wall*, p. 415.
9 Randal, op. cit., p. 258; Schulze, op. cit., p. 132.
10 Schiff and Ya'ari, op. cit., p. 255.
11 MacBride, op. cit., p. x.
12 Kapeliouk, Amnon, *Enquête sur un massacre: Sabra et Chatila*, Seuil, Paris, 1982, p. 30; MacBride, op. cit., p. 166; Cockburn, Alexander, *Village Voice*, 9 November 1982.
13 Boykin, op. cit., p. 239.
14 Ibid., p. 266.
15 See pp. 118–19.
16 Al-Hout, op. cit., p. 304.
17 Kapeliouk, op. cit., p. 26.
18 Ibid., p. 29.
19 Boykin, op. cit., p. 268; Schiff and Ya'ari, op. cit., p. 255.
20 Schiff and Ya'ari, op. cit., p. 253.
21 Ibid., p. 41.
22 *Nouvel Observateur*, Paris, 19–25 June 1982.
23 The Kahan Report, *Jerusalem Post*, Supplement, 9 February 1983.
24 Hirst, *The Gun and the Olive Branch*, p. 557.

25 Kapeliouk, op. cit., p 41.
26 The Kahan Report, op. cit.
27 Kapeliouk, op. cit., p. 70.
28 Randal, op. cit., p. 281.
29 Ibid., p. 14.
30 The Kahan Report, op. cit.
31 Kapeliouk, op. cit., p. 38.
32 Schiff and Ya'ari, op. cit., p. 261.
33 Kapeliouk, op. cit., pp. 47–51, 64–7; MacBride, op. cit., pp. 162–83, 268–80.
34 Kapeliouk, op. cit., p. 47.
35 Schiff and Ya'ari, op. cit., p. 261; The Kahan Report, op. cit.
36 Kapeliouk, op. cit., p. 54.
37 Ibid., p. 59.
38 Ibid., p. 60.
39 Ibid, p. 60; Schiff and Ya'ari, op. cit., p. 267.
40 Kapeliouk, op. cit., p. 64.
41 Schiff and Ya'ari, op. cit., p. 272.
42 Kapeliouk, op. cit., p. 74.
43 Schiff and Ya'ari, op. cit., p. 275.
44 MacBride, op. cit., p. 170.
45 Randal, op. cit., p. 16.
46 Ibid., p. 15; Kapeliouk, op. cit., p. 92; MacBride, op. cit., p. 176.
47 Excerpts from interview with Begin on Israeli Defence Force radio; see Schulze, op. cit., pp. 107, 114.
48 Kapeliouk, op. cit., p. 101.
49 Hirst, *The Gun and the Olive Branch*, p. 562.
50 Ibid., p. 562.
51 Davidson, Lawrence, 'Lebanon and the Jewish Conscience', *Journal of Palestine Studies*, No. 46, Winter 1983, p. 59.
52 24 September 1982.
53 Kapeliouk, op. cit., p. 103.
54 Al-Hout, op. cit., p. 298.
55 Davidson, 'Lebanon and the Jewish Conscience', p. 57.
56 Al-Hout, op. cit., p. 318; Schiff and Ya'ari, op. cit., p. 278.
57 Arens, Richard, 'Israel's Responsibility in Lebanon', *Journal of Palestine Studies*, No. 49, Autumn 1983, p. 83.
58 Hirst, *The Gun and the Olive Branch*, p. 565.
59 *New York Times*, 9 February 1983.
60 Ahmad, Eqbal, 'The Public Relations of Ethnocide', *Journal of Palestine Studies*, No. 47, Spring 1983, p. 33.
61 The Kahan Report, op. cit.
62 Ahmad, op. cit., p. 32.
63 Al-Hout, op. cit., p. 308; Kapeliouk, Amnon, *Le Monde Diplomatique*, July 1983.
64 *Al-Hamishmar*, 10 May 1978.
65 Kapeliouk, *Enquête*, p. 100.
66 Davidson, 'Lebanon and the Jewish Conscience', pp. 56–7.

67   See p. 34.
68   Gilmour, Ian and Andrew, 'Terrorism', *London Review of Books*, No. 18, 21 October 1986.
69   Kapeliouk, *Le Monde Diplomatique*, July 1982.
70   Avnery, Uri, *Ha'olam Hazeh*, 4 August 1982.
71   Fisk, Robert, *The Times*, London, 17 June 1982.
72   Davidson, 'Lebanon and the Jewish Conscience', p. 58.
73   Ahmad, op. cit., p. 36.
74   Kapeliouk, *Enquête*, p. III.
75   *Jerusalem Post*, 13 February 1983.
76   *Jerusalem Post*, 1 April 1983.
77   *Haaretz*, 19 November 1982.
78   Creveld, op. cit., pp. 351, 356.
79   Trabulsi, op. cit., pp. 220–1.
80   Boykin, op. cit., p. 277.
81   See Norton, Augustus Richard, '(In)security Zones in South Lebanon, *Journal of Palestine Studies*, No. 89, Autumn 1993, p. 68.
82   Sayigh, Rosemary, *Too Many Enemies*, p. 128.

CHAPTER EIGHT: *Khomeini, Islamists and the Shiite Uprising*

1   Hamzeh, op. cit., p. 8.
2   See pp. 12, 36.
3   See p. 114.
4   Chehabi, H. E., 'The Anti-Shah Opposition and Lebanon', 'Iran and Lebanon in the Revolutionary Decade', *Distant Relations*, pp. 194, 204.
5   Ibid. p. 193.
6   Ibid, p. 216.
7   Ibid., pp. 190, 197.
8   Hamzeh, op. cit., p. 28.
9   Hamzeh, op. cit., p. 40; Jaber, Hala, *Hezbollah: Born With A Vengeance*, Columbia University Press, New York, p. 64.
10   *Bayan*, July–September 1991, cited in Chehabi, op. cit., p. 36.
11   Goodarzi, Jubin M., *Syria And Iran: Diplomatic Alliance and Power Politics in the Middle East*, I. B. Tauris, London, New York, p. 138.
12   Ramazani. R. K, 'Khumayni's Islam in Iran's Foreign Policy', in *Islam in Foreign Policy* [A. Dawisha, ed.], Cambridge University Press, p, 181, cited in Goodarzi, op. cit., p. 60.
13   Goodarzi, op. cit., p. 46.
14   See pp. 112–14.
15   Goodarzi, op. cit., p. 87.
16   Ibid., p. 75.
17   Saad-Ghorayeb, Amal, *Hizbullah, Politics and Religion*, Pluto Press, London, 2002, p. II.
18   Hamzeh, op. cit., p. 24.
19   Harik, Judith, 'Hizballah's Public and Social Services and Iran', in Chehabi, *Distant Relations*, p. 271.

20 See, for example, Trabulsi, op. cit., p. 229.
21 Norton, Augustus Richard, *Hezbollah, A Short History*, Princeton University Press, 2007, p. 23; Sayigh, Rosemary, *Too Many Enemies*, p. 145.
22 Saad-Ghorayeb, op. cit., p. 14.
23 Goodarzi, op. cit., pp. 64, 71.
24 Ibid., pp. 61–2.
25 Chehabi, op. cit., p. 215.
26 Goodarzi, op. cit., pp. 62–69.
27 Ibid., p. 64; Chehabi, op. cit., p. 214.
28 Ibid., p. 215.
29 Chehabi, op. cit., p. 216; Hamzeh, op. cit., p. 24; Saad-Ghorayeb, op. cit., p. 14; Goodarzi, op. cit., p. 77.
30 Chehabi, op. cit., p. 216; Jaber, op. cit., p. 110.
31 Goodarzi, op. cit., p. 77.
32 Chehabi, op. cit., pp. 216–17.
33 Hamzeh, op. cit., p. 24.
34 Chehabi, op. cit., p. 265.
35 Ibid., p. 216.
36 Hamzeh, op. cit., p. 24.
37 Norton, Augustus Richard, *Amal and the Shi'a, Struggle for the Soul of Lebanon*, University of Texas Press, Austin, 1987, pp. 167–87.
38 Hamzeh, op. cit., pp. 34, 36; Saad-Ghorayeb, *Hizbullah, Politics and Religion*, p. 72.
39 Ibid., p. 67.
40 Ibid., p. 77.
41 Norton, *Hezbollah*, pp. 37, 40; Goodarzi, op. cit., p. 77; Saad-Ghorayeb, op. cit., p. 115.
42 Saad-Ghorayeb, op. cit., pp. 112, 114.
43 Ibid., pp. 134–5.
44 Ibid., pp. 40, 74, 112, 114, 162.
45 Hamzeh, op. cit., p. 25; Chehabi, H. E. and Mneimneh, Hassan, 'Five Centuries of Lebanese-Iranian Encounters', in Chehabi, ed., *Distant Relations*, p. 25.
46 Jaber, op. cit., p. 108; Chehabi, op. cit., p. 218.
47 Hirst, David *The Guardian*, London, 17 November 1983.
48 Jaber, op. cit., p. 47.
49 Goodarzi, op. cit., pp. 94–5.
50 Harris, op. cit., p. 180.
51 Goodarzi, op. cit., p. 88.
52 Saad-Ghorayeb, op. cit., p. 100.
53 *Middle East Reporter*, Beirut, 17 May 2008; Trabulsi, op. cit., p. 221; *Middle East International*, 22 July 1983, 15 June 1984.
54 Hirst, David, *The Guardian*, 28 December 1983.
55 Wright, Robin, *Sacred Rage: The Crusade of Modern Islam*, Simon & Schuster, New York, 1985, p. 74.

56 Thrall, Nathan, 'How the Reagan Administration Taught Iran the Wrong Lessons', *MERIA Journal*, Vol. 11, No. 2, Tel Aviv, June 2007.

57 Wright, Robin, *Sacred Rage.*, p. 71.

58 Lamberth, Judge Royce C., Memorandum Opinion, Peterson v. Islamic Republic of Iran (US District Court for the District of Columbia, 2003), p. 8.

59 Neff, Donald, *Middle East International*, London, 5 March 1988.

60 *Middle East International*, 9, 23 December 1983.

61 Jaber, op. cit., p. 75; various other, generally lesser, figures, are cited by other sources.

62 Saad-Ghorayeb, op. cit., p. 67.

63 Wright, Robin, *Sacred Rage*, p. 37.

64 Jaber, op. cit., p. 88.

65 Saad-Ghorayeb, op. cit., p. 131.

66 Jaber, op. cit., p. 75.

67 Sayigh, Rosemary, *Too Many Enemies*, pp. 145–6.

68 Hirst, David, *The Guardian*, 15 August 1984.

69 Sayigh, Rosemary, *Too Many Enemies*, pp. 129, 147.

70 Hirst, David, *The Guardian*, 15 August 1984; Tveit, op. cit., p. 257.

71 Saad-Ghorayeb, op. cit., p. 11.

72 Tveit, op. cit., pp. 241, 256.

73 Norton, *Amal*, p. 111.

74 Ibid., p. 112; Hamzeh, op. cit., p. 17.

75 Hamzeh, op. cit., p. 24.

76 Ibid., p. 87.

77 Sayigh, Rosemary, *Too Many Enemies*, p. 150.

78 Norton, *Hezbollah*, p. 66.

79 Sayigh, Rosemary, *Too Many Enemies*, p. 147; Hirst, David, *The Guardian*, 15 August 1984.

80 Tveit, op. cit., pp. 260–3.

81 Sayigh, Rosemary, *Too Many Enemies*, p. 131.

82 Wright, Robin, *Sacred Rage*, p. 217.

83 Norton, *Amal*, p. 120; Kidron, Peretz, *Middle East International*, 19 April 1985.

84 Sayigh, Rosemary, *Too Many Enemies.*, p., 148, citing *MERIP Reports*, No. 133, June 1985.

85 Tveit, op. cit., pp. 265, 268.

86 Sayigh, Rosemary, *Too Many Enemies*, p. 131.

87 Tveit, op. cit., p. 273.

88 Hirst, David, *The Guardian*, 5 March 1985.

89 Wright, Robin, *Sacred Rage*, p. 238.

90 Ibid.

91 Harris, op. cit., p. 211.

92 Norton, *Hezbollah*, p. 33.

93 Norton, *Amal*, p. 180.

94 Wright, Robin, *Sacred Rage*, p. 235.

CHAPTER NINE: *The Civil War Closes*

1 Muir, Jim, *Middle East International*, London, 13 September and 22 November 1985.
2 Trabulsi, op. cit., p. 234.
3 Hirst, David *The Guardian*, 26, 27, 28, 29 August 1985.
4 Harris, op. cit., p. 225.
5 Ibid., p. 270.
6 Ibid., p. 209.
7 Ibid., pp. 229, 263.
8 Ibid., pp. 266–7.
9 Ibid., p. 277.
10 Ibid., p. 278.
11 Butt, Gerald, 11 September 1992; Nasrallah, Fida, *Middle East International*, 11 September 1992.
12 Harris, op. cit., p. 288.
13 Hamzeh, op. cit., pp. 4, 28, 80.
14 Saad-Ghorayeb, op. cit., p. 112.
15 Hamzeh, op. cit., p. 51.
16 Saad-Ghorayeb, op. cit., p. 120.
17 Hamzeh, op. cit., p. 41.
18 Wright, Robin, *Sacred Rage*, p. 228.
19 Jaber, op. cit., pp. 26, 29.
20 Muir, Jim, *Middle East International*, 25 July 1985.
21 Jaber, op. cit., p. 28.
22 Hassan Nasrallah, cited in 'Chronologie', *Revue d'Études Palestiniennes*, No. 25, Autumn 1987, pp. 208, 213.
23 Jansen, Godfrey, *Middle East International*, 26 September 1986; Norton, *Amal*, p. 182.
24 'Chronologie', *Revue d'Études Palestiniennes*, No. 26, Winter 1987, pp. 141, 142–3.
25 'Chronologie', *Revue d'Études Palestiniennes*, No. 25, Autumn 1987, p. 230.
26 Norton, *Hezbollah*, p. 80.
27 Jaber, op. cit., p. 92.
28 Soueid, op. cit., p. 21.
29 'Chronologie', *Revue d'Études Palestiniennes*, No. 27, Spring 1988, p. 214.
30 Muir, Jim, *Middle East International*, 17 March 1989.
31 *Revue*, op. cit., No. 25, Autumn 1987, p. 225.
32 Hirst, *The Gun and the Olive Branch*, p. 19; Tamimi, Azzam, *Hamas, A History From Within*, Olive Branch Press, Massachusetts, 2007, p. 52.
33 Tamimi, op. cit., p. 53.
34 Haeri, Safa, *Middle East International*, 25 October 1991.
35 Haeri, Safa, *Middle East International*, 7 December 1990.
36 Haeri, Safa, *Middle East International*, 26 July 1991.
37 Haeri, Safa, *Middle East International*, 8 November 1991; Rekhess, Elie, 'The Terrorist Connection, Iran, the Islamic Jihad and Hamas', *Justice*, Vol. 5, Jerusalem, May 1995.

38 Norton, Augustus Richard, 'Lebanon's Condundrum', *Arab Studies Quarterly*, Winter 1999, p. 48.
39 Chehabi, op. cit., p. 214.
40 Jaber, op. cit., pp. 100–7.
41 Hamzeh, op. cit., pp. 74, 86; citing interview with *al-Wasat* newspaper, London, 3 March 1996.
42 Jaber, op. cit., pp. 115–20, 136.
43 Neff, Donald, *Middle East International*, 5 December 1986; Muir, Jim, *Middle East International*, 5 December 1986.
44 Hirst, David, *The Guardian*, 24 November 1986.
45 Fisk, Robert, *Pity the Nation: Lebanon at War*, Oxford University Press, 2001, p. 656.
46 Jaber, op. cit., pp. 117–18.
47 Ibid., p. 121.
48 'Chronologie', *Revue d'Études Palestiniennes*, No. 25, Autumn 1987, pp. 204, 230.
49 Memopack, *The Foreign Hostages in Lebanon*, Nicosia, 1991; *New York Times*, 27 November 1988.
50 Jaber, op. cit., p. 99.
51 Ibid., p. 99.
52 Ibid., pp. 115, 136, 139–40.
53 Saad-Ghorayeb, op. cit., p. 97.
54 Hamzeh, op. cit., p. 74.
55 Saad-Ghorayeb, op. cit., pp. 97–9.
56 Harik, Judith Palmer, *Hezbollah: The Changing Face of Terrorism*, I. B. Tauris, London, New York, 2007, p. 173.
57 Hirst, David, *The Guardian*, 9 August 1989; Muir, Jim, *Middle East International*, 16 March 1990.
58 Hamzeh, op. cit., p. 63.
59 Ibid., p. 102.
60 Norton, *Amal*, pp. 172–3.
61 Sayigh, Rosemary, *Too Many Enemies*, p. 242.
62 Ibid., pp. 231–61; *Middle East International*, 19 August 1985.
63 Goodarzi, op. cit., p. 199.
64 Ibid, pp. 149–50.
65 Chehabi, op. cit., p. 226; Norton, *Hezbollah*, p. 72.
66 Goodarzi, op. cit., p. 199.
67 Ibid., pp. 202–4; Harris, op. cit., p. 216.
68 Goodarzi, op. cit., p. 259.
69 Ibid., p. 264.
70 Ibid., p. 265.
71 Chehabi, op. cit., p. 227.
72 'Chronologie', *Revue d'Études Palestiniennes*, No. 30, Winter 1988, p. 145.
73 Goodarzi, op. cit., p. 277.
74 Ibid., pp. 275–6.
75 Harris, op. cit., p. 219.
76 Ibid., p. 196; Goodarzi, op. cit., p. 277.

77 Jaber, op. cit., p 35; Muir, Jim, *Middle East International*, 3 February 1989.
78 Picard, op. cit., p. 136.
79 Goodarzi, op. cit., p. 271.
80 Ibid., pp. 277, 284.
81 Ibid., pp. 287–8.
82 Saad-Ghorayeb, op. cit., p. 35.
83 See p. 188.
84 Norton, *Amal*, pp. 173–7.
85 Goodarzi, op. cit., pp. 146–7.
86 Chehabi, op. cit., p. 227.
87 See Qassem, Naim, *Hizbullah, The Story from Within*, Saqi, London, 2005, p. 17; Goodarzi, op. cit., p. 94.
88 Woodward, Bob, *Veil: The Secret Wars of the CIA 1981–1987*, Simon & Schuster, New York, 2005, p. 397; Oakley, Robert, Interview with PBS Frontline, September 2001, www.pbs.org/wgbh/pages/frontline/shows/target/interviews/oakley.html; Thrall, op. cit.; Jaber, op. cit., p. 69.
89 Hamzeh, op. cit., p. 104; Jaber, op. cit., p. 69.
90 Chehabi, op. cit., p. 226; Goksel, Timur, '"Mr UNIFIL" Reflects on a Quarter Century of Peacekeeping in South Lebanon', *Journal of Palestine Studies*, No. 14, Spring 2007, p. 71.
91 Jansen, Godfrey, *Middle East International*, 18 April 1986.
92 Harik, Judith, 'Hizballah's Public and Social Services and Iran', in Chehabi, *Distant Relations*, p. 280.
93 Ibid., p. 277.
94 Ibid., p. 275.
95 Jaber, op. cit., p. 149.
96 Harik, 'Hizballah's Public and Social Services', p. 281.
97 Hamzeh, op. cit., p. 10.
98 Saad-Ghorayeb, op. cit., p. 35.
99 Ibid., pp. 48–50.
100 Saad-Ghorayeb, op. cit., p. 38.
101 Ibid., p. 50.
102 Ibid., pp. 53, 82–7.
103 Butt, Gerald, *Middle East International*, 9 October 1992.

CHAPTER TEN: *Triumph of the Warrior-Priest*

1 'Chronologie', *Revue d'Études Palestiniennes*, No. 44, Summer 1992, p. 171; Muir, Jim, *Middle East International*, 21 February 1992.
2 Blanford, Nicholas, *Voice of Hizbullah, The Statements of Sayyed Hassan Nasrallah* [Noe, Nicholas, ed.], Verso, London, New York, 2007, p. 3.
3 See p. 111.
4 *From al-Sadr to Nasrallah, The March of the Resistance and the Lives of Two Men*, al-Rida Publications, Beirut, 2007, frontispiece.
5 Blanford, op. cit., pp. 1–7.
6 Harik, *Hezbollah*, p. 73; Hamzeh, op. cit., p. 132.
7 Ibid., p. 78.

8 Noe, op. cit., pp. 137–8.
9 Hamzeh, op. cit., p. 74.
10 Norton, 'Lebanon's Conundrum', p. 45; Jaber, op. cit., p. 212.
11 Hamzeh, op. cit., pp. 122–35.
12 Picard, op. cit., p. 176.
13 Norton, Augustus Richard, 'Lebanon End-Game', *Middle East Insight*, March/April 2000, p. 27.
14 Jaber, op. cit., pp. 210–11.
15 Blanford, op. cit., p. 9.
16 Harik, *Hezbollah*, p. 111.
17 Hirst, David, *al-Ahram Weekly*, Cairo, 19–25 April 2001.
18 Noe, op. cit., p. 174.
19 Harris, op. cit., p. 282.
20 Jansen, Godfrey, *Middle East International*, 29 May 1992.
21 Harik, *Hezbollah.*, pp. 50, 107.
22 Personal interview.
23 See, for example, Norton, Augustus Richard, 'Hizballah and the Israeli Withdrawal from Southern Lebanon', *Journal of Palestine Studies*, No. 117, Autumn 2000, p. 26.
24 Goksel, op. cit., p. 65.
25 Noe, op. cit., p. 148.
26 Blanford, op. cit., p. 8.
27 Norton, 'Hizballah and the Israeli Withdrawal', p. 29.
28 Shahak, Israel, *Middle East International*, 18 December 1992.
29 Hamzeh, op. cit., p. 90.
30 Shahak, op. cit.; Jansen, Godfrey, *Middle East International*, 29 May 1992.
31 Norton, *Hezbollah*, p. 87.
32 Personal interview.
33 Kidron, Peretz, *Middle East International*, 18 November 1994.
34 Creveld, op. cit., p. 305.
35 'Chronologie', *Revue d'Études Palestiniennes*, No. 50, Winter 1994, pp. 167, 168.
36 Ibid., p. 169.
37 Ibid., 170.
38 Ibid., p. 173; Muir, Jim, *Middle East International*, 6 August 1993.
39 Norton, '(In)security', p. 71.
40 'Chronologie', *Revue d'Études Palestiniennes*, p. 173.
41 Muir, *Middle East International*, 6 August 1993; Jaber, op. cit., p 173; 'Chronologie', *Revue d'Études Palestiniennes*, p. 177.
42 Harris, op. cit., p. 281; Norton, '(In)security', p. 71.
43 Ibid., p. 75.
44 Jaber, op. cit., p. 173; Norton, 'Lebanon's Conundrum', p. 51.
45 Hirst, David, *The Guardian*, London, 10 November 1994.
46 Ibid.
47 Ibid.
48 Ibid.

49 Ibid.

50 Hamzeh, op. cit., p. 59.

51 See pp. 20–1.

52 Parsi, Trita, *Treacherous Alliance: The Secret Dealings of Israel, Iran, and the United States*, Yale University Press, New Haven and London, 2007, pp. 101, 175.

53 Ibid., p. 110.

54 Ibid., pp. 113–15.

55 Ibid., pp. 104, 128.

56 Ibid., p. 139.

57 Ibid.

58 Ibid., pp. 162, 192.

59 Mearsheimer, John, and Walt, Stephen, *The Israel Lobby and US Foreign Policy*, Farrar, Straus and Giroux, New York, 2007, p. 291.

60 Neff, Donald, *Middle East International*, 26 April 1996.

61 Mearsheimer and Walt, op. cit., p. 289.

62 Neff, Donald, *Middle East International*, 2 February 1996.

63 Hirst, *The Gun and the Olive Branch*, p. 86.

64 Shahak, Israel and Mezvinsky, Norton, *Jewish Fundamentalism in Israel*, Pluto Press, London and Sterling, Virginia, 1999, p. 111; four years later, in 1998, under pressure from secular Jews, the Knesset passed a law against the erection of monuments to mass murderers.

65 Shlaim, *The Iron Wall*, p. 559.

66 Jaber, op. cit., p. 174.

67 Shlaim, *The Iron Wall*, p. 560.

68 'Chronology', *Journal of Palestine Studies*, No. 100, Summer 1996, p. 179.

69 Jaber, op. cit., p. 182; Norton, 'Hizballah and the Israeli Withdrawal', p. 27.

70 'Chronologie', *Revue d'Études Palestiniennes*, Autumn 1996, p. 140.

71 'Chronology', op. cit., p. 179.

72 Ibid., pp. 177, 179; Jaber, op. cit., pp. 178, 202–3.

73 Hirst, David, *The Guardian*, 1 May 1996.

74 Fisk, op. cit., pp. 670, 683.

75 Amnesty International, 'Unlawful Killings During Operation "Grapes of Wrath"', London, July 1996.

76 Timur Goksel, in interview with Agence France Presse, cited in 'Chronologie', *Revue d'Études Palestiniennes*, p. 147.

77 Letter from the UN Secretary General to the President of the UN Security Council, UN document S/1996/337, 7 May 1996.

78 Jaber, op. cit., pp. 196–8.

79 Norton, 'Hizballah and the Israeli Withdrawal', p. 27.

80 Hirst, David, *The Guardian*, 10 May 1996.

81 'Chronology', op. cit., p. 174.

82 Gambill, Gary, 'The Balance of Terror: War by Other Means in the Contemporary Middle East', *Journal of Palestine Studies*, No. 109, Autumn 1998, p. 64.

83 Neff, Donald, *Middle East International*, 10 May 1996; 'Chronologie', *Revue d'Études Palestiniennes*, p. 142.
84 'Chronologie', op. cit., p. 148.
85 'Chronology', op. cit., p. 181.
86 *Kol Ha'ir*, 10 May 1996.
87 *Newsweek*, 6 May 1996, cited in Jaber, op. cit., p. 176.
88 Noe, op. cit., pp. 146, 167.
89 Harik, *Hezbollah.*, p. 124.
90 Hamzeh, op. cit., p. 89.
91 Ibid., p. 94.
92 *Haaretz*, 16 July 1999, cited in Picard, op. cit., p. 183.
93 Jansen, Michael, *Middle East International*, 16 January 1998.
94 Hirst, David, 'South Lebanon: The War that Never Ends', *Journal of Palestine Studies*, No. 111, Spring 1999, p. 11.
95 Harik, *Hezbollah*, p. 132.
96 Hirst, *The Gun and the Olive Branch*, p 11; Norton, 'Hizballah and the Israeli Withdrawal', p. 30; Jansen, Michael, *Middle East International*, 24 October 1997.
97 Norton, 'Lebanon End-Game', p. 23.
98 Ibid., p. 31.
99 Hirst, David, *The Guardian*, 9, 10, 11 February 2000; Jansen, Michael, *Middle East International*, 25 February 2000.
100 Hirst, David, *The Guardian*, 8 February and 25 June 1999.
101 Norton, 'Hizballah and the Israeli Withdrawal', p. 31.
102 Hirst, David, *The Guardian*, 9, 10 February 2000.
103 Hirst, David, *The Observer*, London, 27 May 2000.
104 Norton, Augustus Richard, 'Lebanon's Malaise', *Survival*, Vol. 42, No. 4, Winter 2000–1, International Institute for Strategic Studies, London, p. 42.
105 Hirst, David, *The Guardian*, 4 March 1997.
106 Hirst, David, *The Guardian*, 29 February 2000; Margalit, Dan, *Haaretz*, 8 May 2000.
107 Noe, op. cit., p. 233.
108 Norton, *Survival*, p. 41.
109 Ibid.
110 Norton, 'Lebanon End-Game', p. 31.
111 Norton, *Survival*, p. 40; Harris, op. cit., p. 291; Hamzeh, op. cit., p. 96.
112 Norton, *Survival*, p. 39; Picard, op. cit., pp. 184–5.
113 Chronology, *Journal of Palestine Studies*, No. 117, Autumn 2000, p. 166.
114 Norton, *Hezbollah*, p. 90.
115 Norton, *Survival*, p. 39.
116 Noe, op. cit., p. 242.
117 Norton, *Hezbollah*, p. 93.
118 'Chronology', op. cit., p. 167.
119 Hirst, David, *The Guardian*, 17 July 2004.
120 Norton, *Hezbollah*, pp. 92–3.
121 *The Daily Star*, Beirut, 13 March 2000.

122 Noe, op. cit., p. 247; Hirst, David, *The Guardian*, 12 October 2000.

123 Hamzeh, op. cit., p. 97.

124 Harik, *Hezbollah*, p. 160.

125 Ibid., p. 160.

126 Hamzeh, op. cit., p. 60; Norton, *Hezbollah*, p. 93.

127 Hamzeh, op. cit., p. 148.

128 Ibid, p. 149; Harik, *Hezbollah.*, p. 189.

129 Hamzeh, op. cit., p. 148; Harik, *Hezbollah*, p. 200.

130 Hamzeh, op. cit., p. 149; Saad-Ghorayeb, *Hizbullah, Politics and Religion*, p. 165.

131 Ibid., p. 167.

132 Parsi, op. cit., p. 219.

133 Hamzeh, op. cit., p. 146.

134 Blanford, Nicholas, *Killing Mr Lebanon: The Assassination of Rafik Hariri and Its Impact on the Middle East*, I. B. Tauris, London, New York, 2006, p. 189.

135 *The Daily Star*, Beirut, 18 February 2007.

CHAPTER ELEVEN: *Redrawing the Map of the Middle East*

1 *Clean Break: A New Strategy for Securing the Realm*, Institute for Advanced Strategic and Political Studies, Washington, 1996.

2 Vest, Jason, 'The Men from JINSA and CSP', *The Nation*, New York, 2 September 2002.

3 Stauffer, Thomas, *Middle East International*, London, 21 March 2003.

4 Wurmser, David, *Middle East War*, American Enterprise Institute, 1 January 2001.

5 Halper, Stefan and Clarke, Jonathan, *America Alone: The Neo-Conservatives and the Global Order*, Cambridge University Press, Cambridge, New York, 2004, p. 139; see also Chernus, Ira, *Monsters to Destroy: The Neo-conservative War on Terror and Sin*, Paradigm Publishers, Boulder and London, 2006, p. 146.

6 5 January 2001.

7 9 February 2003.

8 Risen, James, *State of War: The Secret History of the CIA and the Bush Administration*, Free Press, New York, 2006, p. 222.

9 Lieven, Anatole, *America Right or Wrong: An Anatomy of American Nationalism*, Oxford University Press, New York, 2004, p. 187.

10 Mearsheimer and Walt, op. cit., pp. 255–6.

11 *The American Conservative*, 29 September 2002.

12 Bamford, James, *A Pretext for War*, Anchor Books, New York, 2004, p. 285.

13 Halper and Clarke, op. cit., p. 204.

14 Clarke, Richard, *Against All Enemies: Inside America's War on Terror*, Free Press, London, 204, pp. 30–1.

15 Chernus, op. cit., pp. 124–6, 153.

16 Bamford, op. cit., pp. 287–331; Chernus, op. cit., p. 157.

17 Mearsheimer and Walt, op. cit., pp. 232–3.

18 *Washington Post*, 13 February 2002.

19 Halper and Clarke, op. cit., p. 218.

20 *Washington Post*, 6 August 2002.

21 *Washington Post*, 11 October 2001.

22 Hirst, *The Gun and the Olive Branch*, pp. 68–74.

23 *Middle East International*, 28 September 2001.

24 Parsi, op. cit., p. 234.

25 *Middle East International*, 8 February 2002.

26 Hirst, *The Gun and the Olive Branch*, p. 39.

27 *The Times*, London, 5 November 2002.

28 Parsi, op. cit., p. 241.

29 Baram, Haim, *Middle East International*, 28 September 2001.

30 Project for the New American Century, *Letter to President Bush*, 20 September 2001.

31 Parsi, op. cit., p. 240.

32 Ibid., pp. 243–9.

33 Harik, *Hezbollah*, p. 184.

34 'Quarterly Update on Conflict and Diplomacy', *Journal of Palestine Studies*, No. 128, Summer 2003, p. 142; No. 130, Winter 2004, p. 131.

35 Mearsheimer and Walt, op. cit., p. 275.

36 *Jane's Intelligence Digest*, London, 23 January 2004.

37 Hirst, David, *The Guardian*, 6 October 2003.

38 Gambill, Gary, 'Lebanon Ambivalent Towards US War on Terror', *Middle East Intelligence Bulletin*, October 2001.

39 *Yediot Aharonot*, cited in 'Quarterly Update of Conflict and Diplomacy', *Journal of Palestine Studies*, No. 123, Spring 2002, p. 136.

40 *Middle East International*, 7 March 2003.

41 *Remarks at the United States Institute of Peace Conference*, Washington, 5 September 2002.

42 See p. 194.

43 Blanford, Nicholas, *Christian Science Monitor*, 31 July 2003; www.tinyrevolution.com/mt/archives/000416.html, 10 March 2005; Roger Morris, http://warincontext.org/2008/02/24/guest-contributor-roger-morris-americas-shadow-in-the-middle-east/, 24 February 2008.

44 Baer, Robert, *See No Evil: The True Story of a Ground Soldier in the CIA's War on Terrorism*, Three Rivers Press, New York, 2002, p 127; Blanford, Nicholas, *Christian Science Monitor*, 31 July 2003.

45 *New York Times*, 4 April 2002.

46 Reuters, 2 November 2001.

47 'Quarterly Update on Conflict and Diplomacy', *Journal of Palestine Studies*, No. 130, Winter 2004, p. 142.

48 Strindberg, Anders, *Middle East International*, 7 March 2003.

49 *Middle East International*, 28 September 2001.

50 Hamzeh, op. cit., p. 137.

51 Blanford, Nicholas, *Christian Science Monitor*, 31 July 2003.

52 Hamzeh, op. cit., p. 137.

53 Gambill, Gary, *Middle East Intelligence Bulletin*, December 2001.

54 Blanford, *Christian Science Monitor*, 31 July 2003

55 Gambill, *Middle East Intelligence Bulletin*, December 2001.

56 'Quarterly Update of Conflict and Diplomacy', *Journal of Palestine Studies*, No. 127, Spring 2003, p. 131.

57 Agence France Presse, 19 September 2001.

58 *Middle East International*, 23 November 2001.

59 *Middle East Reporter*, 10 November 2001.

60 Harik, *Hezbollah*, p. 189.

61 See pp. 69–74.

CHAPTER TWELVE: *Getting Syria Out of Lebanon*

1 Blanford, *Killing Mr Lebanon*, p. 64.

2 Ibid., p. 81.

3 Ibid., pp. 94, 122.

4 Ibid., p. 85.

5 *Middle East International*, London, 30 May 2003.

6 Mearsheimer and Walt, op. cit., p. 167.

7 Harris, op. cit., p. 298.

8 Blanford, *Killing Mr Lebanon*, p. 99.

9 Ibid., pp. 106–7.

10 Ibid., pp. 92–3.

11 Ibid., pp. 96, 103, Harris, op. cit., p. 299.

12 *Report of the International Independent Investigation Commission established pursuant to Security Council Resolution 1595, 2005* ['Mehlis Report'], 21 October 2005, paragraph 27; see also Blanford, *Killing Mr Lebanon*, p. 100.

13 Harris, op. cit., p. 298; Blanford, *Killing Mr Lebanon*, p. 102.

14 Blanford, *Killing Mr Lebanon*, p. 101.

15 Ibid., p. 102.

16 Ibid., p. 107.

17 Ibid., pp. 118–19.

18 Harris, op. cit., p. 299.

19 Blanford, *Killing Mr Lebanon*, p. 108.

20 Ibid., p. 113.

21 Ibid., pp. 114–15.

22 Ibid., p. 116.

23 Harris, op. cit., p. 301.

24 Blanford, *Killing Mr Lebanon*, p. 119.

25 Ibid., p. 123.

26 Ibid., p. 115.

27 Ibid., p. 123.

28 Mehlis Report, paragraph 2003.

29 *Middle East Reporter*, Beirut, 5 March 2005.

30 Cited in Hirst, David, *The Nation*, New York, 15 April 2005.

31 Ibid., p. 156.

32 Weisman, Steven, *New York Times*, 15 February 2005.

33 *The Daily Star*, Beirut, 30 August 2007.

34 See Harris, op. cit., p. 312; Leenders, Reinoud, 'How UN Pressure on Hizballah Impedes Lebanese Reform', *Middle East Report Online*, 23 May 2006.

35 *Middle East Reporter*, 11 March 2005.

36 Harris, op. cit., p. 303; Usher, Graham, *Middle East International*, 1 April 2005.

37 Blanford, *Killing Mr Lebanon*, p. 160.

38 *Jerusalem Post*, 30 March 2005.

39 Blanford, *Killing Mr Lebanon*, pp. 166, 172.

40 Rami Khouri and Gharida Dergham, cited in Hirst, David, *The Guardian*, 28 September 2005.

41 Mehlis Report, 'Introduction'.

42 *Der Spiegel*, 14 January 2006.

43 Hirst, David, *The Guardian*, 28 September 2005.

44 See p. 89.

45 'Hezbullah's Other War', *New York Times*, 4 August 2006.

46 Harris, op. cit., p. 306; *Middle East International*, 1 and 29 April, 13 May, 24 June 2005.

47 See p. 246.

48 *Al-Mahar*, 14 June 2005.

49 *Middle East Reporter*, 5 August 2005.

50 Ibid., 26 July & 29 August 2005.

51 'Hezbullah's Other War', *New York Times*, 4 August 2006.

52 *Middle East Reporter*, 15 February, 14 and 18 March 2006.

53 Noe, op. cit., p. 349.

54 *Middle East Reporter*, 17 February and 4 March 2006.

55 Blanford, *Killing Mr Lebanon*, p. 168.

56 *Al-Manar* television, 23 May 2006; *Middle East Reporter*, 17 February and 24 May 2006.

57 *Middle East International*, 29 April 2005.

58 See Leenders, Reinoud, 'How the Rebel Regained His Cause: Hizbullah & the Sixth Arab–Israeli War', *MIT Electronic Journal of Middle East Studies*, Vol. 6, Summer 2006.

59 Interview with *al-Jazeera* television, 21 July 2006; speech on *al-Manar* television, 14 August 2006.

60 *Middle East Reporter*, 25 February 2006.

61 Noe, op. cit., pp. 357, 361.

62 *Middle East Reporter*, 13, 14 November 2006.

63 Harris, op. cit., p. 309.

64 Blanford, *Killing Mr Lebanon*, p. 176.

65 This is what – before the killing – intelligence officials had told a Syrian dissident and former political prisoner of my acquaintance.

66 Blanford, *Killing Mr Lebanon*, p. 181.

67 Ibid., p. 176.

68 *Second Report of the Independent Investigation Commission*, 10 December 2005.
69 Blanford, *Killing Mr Lebanon*, p. 171.
70 Ibid., p. 180.
71 Ibid., p. 179.
72 Landis, Joshua, *syriacomment.com*, 8 November 2005.
73 Waldman, Peter, *The Wall Street Journal*, 4 August 2006.
74 See Hirst, David, *The Guardian*, 27 January 2005.
75 Saudi–US Relations Information Service, 25 September 2005.
76 General William Odom.
77 Taheri, Amir, *Newsweek*, 2 September 2005.
78 Khalaji, Mehdi, 'Apocalyptic Politics', Washington Institute for Near East Policy, January 2008.
79 Naji, Kasra, *Ahmadinejad: The Secret History of Iran's Radical Leader*, I. B. Tauris, London, New York, 2008, pp. 140, 144.
80 See pp. 253–6; Parsi, op. cit., p. 2.
81 Khalaji, op. cit.
82 Naji, op. cit., pp. 134–5.
83 Kohr, Howard, Executive Director of AIPAC, cited in Parsi, op. cit., p. 268.
84 El-Feki, Mustafa, *al-Ahram Weekly*, 16–22 February 2006.
85 Khamenei, Ali, Associated Press, 20 February 2006.
86 Dan Gillerman, *Israel News*, 21 February 2006.
87 'Chronology', *Journal of Palestine Studies*, No. 140, Summer 2006, p. 128; see also Naji, op. cit., p. 125.
88 *Washington Post*, 9 April 2006.
89 Ritter, Scott, *Target Iran: The Truth About the White House's Plans for Regime Change*, Nation Books, New York, 2006, p. 211; see also Mearsheimer and Walt, op. cit., p. 302.
90 See Hersh, Seymour, 'Last Stand – The Military's Problem with the President's Iran Policy', *New Yorker*, 10 July 2006.
91 Fallows, James, 'Will Iran be Next?', *Atlantic Monthly*, December 2004.
92 Gaffney, Mark, 'Iran: A Bridge Too Far?', www.informationclearinghouse.info/article7147.htm, 26 October 2004.
93 *Middle East Reporter*, 30 April 2006.
94 Mearsheimer and Walt, op. cit., p. 310.
95 Halliday, Fred, in *The War on Lebanon: A Reader* [Hovsepian, Nubar, ed.], Olive Branch Press, Massachusetts, 2008, p. 375.
96 Kalman, Matthew, *San Francisco Chronicle*, 21 July 2006.
97 Ibid.; Mearsheimer and Walt, op. cit., p. 309.
98 Hersh, Seymour, 'Watching Lebanon', *New Yorker*, 21 August 2006.
99 Ibid.
100 Zunes, Stephen, in Hovsepian, op. cit., p. 94.
101 Hersh, 'Watching Lebanon'.
102 Mearsheimer and Walt, op. cit., p. 308.
103 *New York Sun*, 13 July 2006.

CHAPTER THIRTEEN: *The Sixth War*

1 Harel, Amos, and Issacharoff, Avi, *34 Days: Israel, Hezbollah and the War in Lebanon*, Palgrave Macmillan, New York, 2008, pp. 8–15.
2 Noe, op. cit., p. 371.
3 Shadid, Anthony, *Washington Post*, 8 October 2006.
4 Noe, op. cit., p. 394.
5 Shadid, op. cit.
6 Shelah, Ofer, *Yediot Aharonot*, 26 June 2006.
7 'Quarterly Update on Conflict and Diplomacy', *Journal of Palestine Studies*, No. 141, Autumn 2006, p. 119.
8 13 July 2006.
9 *Al-Safir*, 3 and 5 July 2006.
10 Hersh, Seymour, *New Yorker*, 21 August 2006.
11 See Fishman, Alex, *Yediot Aharonot*, 16 July 2006; *Haaretz*, 30 April 2007.
12 Schiffer, Shimon, *Yediot Aharonot*, 14 July 2006.
13 Harel and Issacharoff, *34 Days*, p. 114.
14 Schiffer, Shimon, *Yediot Aharonot*, 14 July 2006.
15 14 July 2006.
16 Cobban, Helen, *The Boston Review*, November/December 2006.
17 Harel and Issacharoff, *34 Days*, pp. 78, 82.
18 Avnery, Uri, 'Israel's Self-Delusion after Defeat in Lebanon', *Redress Information & Analysis*, 3 September 2006.
19 Shtrasler, Nehemia, *Haaretz*, 1 September 2006.
20 Marcus, Yoel, *Haaretz*, 12 September 2007.
21 *Haaretz*, 13 July 2006.
22 Harel and Issacharoff, *34 Days*, p. 76.
23 Ibid., p. 177.
24 Ibid., p. 84.
25 *Maariv*, 14 July 2006.
26 *Yediot Aharonot*, 14 July 2006.
27 Flint, Julie, *The Daily Star*, Beirut, 24 July 2006.
28 'Chronology', *Journal of Palestine Studies*, No. 141, Autumn 2006, p. 213.
29 Harel and Issacharoff, *34 Days*, p. 91.
30 Mahnaimi, Uzi, *Sunday Times*, London, 27 August 2006.
31 Harel and Issacharoff, *34 Days*, pp. 96, 107.
32 Ploetzker, Daniel, *Yediot Aharonot*, 17 July 2006.
33 *The Guardian*, London, 19 July 2006; Cook, Jonathan, *al-Ahram Weekly*, 3–9 August 2006.
34 *The Guardian*, 20 July 2006; *Maariv*, 21 July 2006.
35 Neslen, Arthur, 'Diary From Tel Aviv', *Red Pepper*, July/August 2006.
36 *Middle East Reporter*, Beirut, 19 and 22 July 2006.
37 Harel and Issacharoff, *34 Days*, p. 98.
38 *Inter Press Service*, 19 August 2006.
39 Abedin, Mahan, *Saudi Debate*, 28 July 2006; Associated Press, 5 August 2006.
40 Harel and Issacharoff, *34 Days*, p. 104.

41 Kadmon, Sima, *Yediot Aharonot*, 17 July 2006.
42 See Chapter Twelve, p. 327.
43 *Weekly Standard*, 24 July 2006.
44 *National Review Online*, 16 July 2006.
45 www.humanevents.com. 17 July 2006.
46 Wright, Robin, *Washington Post*, 16 July 2006.
47 Kapeliouk, Amnon, *Le Monde Diplomatique*, September 2006.
48 Boot, Max, *Los Angeles Times*, 16 July 2006; CNN Online, 16 July 2006; *Yediot Aharonot*, 16 December 2006.
49 Zunes, Stephen, in Hovsepian, op. cit., p. 109.
50 See pp. 251–61.
51 Agence France Presse, 17 July; CNN, 23 July 2006.
52 Zunes, Stephen, *Foreign Policy in Focus*, 22 July 2006.
53 Buchanan, Patrick, *The Creators Syndicate*, 1 August 2006.
54 *Washington Post*, 25 July 2006.
55 Gumbel, Andrew, *The Independent*, London, 15 August 2006.
56 *Asia Times*, 12 October 2006.
57 Pedatzur, Reuven, *Haaretz*, 16 August 2006.
58 Avnery, Uri, 'What the Hell Has Happened to the Army?', *Redress Information & Analysis*, 14 August 2006.
59 *Yediot Aharonot*, 27 August 2002.
60 Harel and Issacharoff, *34 Days*, p. 172.
61 Atzmon, Gilad, *Redress Information & Analysis*, 14 August 2006.
62 Harel and Issacharoff, *34 Days*, pp. 226, 229, 253–4; Atzmon, op. cit.; *Haaretz*, 25 August 2006.
63 Crooke, Alistair, and Perry, Mark, 'Winning the Intelligence War' and 'Winning the Ground War', *Asia Times*, 12, 13 October 2006.
64 Speech of 14 July.
65 Blanford, Nicholas, 'Deconstructing Hizbullah's Surprise Military Prowess', *Jane's Intelligence Review*, 1 November 2006.
66 Virtually all reports put the total number of Lebanese killed at about 1,180, with at least 180 – Crooke, op. cit. – but probably a good deal more, being combatants.
67 Agence France Presse, 4 August 2006.
68 See, for example, Amnesty International, 'Israel/Lebanon: Deliberate Destruction or "Collateral Damage"? Israeli Attacks on Civilian Infrastructure', 23 August 2006; 'Israel/Lebanon, "Out of All Proportion –Civilians Bear the Brunt of War"', 21 November 2006; BBC News [online], 'The Middle East Crisis: Facts and Figures', 31 August 2006; UN Experts' Report on Special Fact-Finding Mission to Lebanon and Israel, 2 October 2006; *Le Monde*, 19 August 2006.
69 'Chronology', *Journal of Palestine Studies*, No. 141, Autumn 2006, p. 132.
70 Mahnaimi, op. cit.
71 *USA Today*, 14 September 2006.
72 Blanford, Nicholas, *Middle East Reporter*, 22 July 2006, *The Daily Star*, Beirut, 29 July 2006; Crooke, op. cit.

73 Harel and Issacharoff, *34 Days*, p. 128.

74 Mahnaimi, op. cit.

75 Crooke, op. cit.

76 Harel and Issacharoff, *34 Days*, p. 128.

77 Harel and Issacharoff, *34 Days*, p. 233; Crooke, op. cit., Blanford, 'Deconstructing'; Ben Yishai, Ron, *Yediot Aharonot*; Rapaport, Amir, *Maariv*, 21 July 2006.

78 Avi Pazner, a senior government spokesman, cited in Crooke, op. cit.

79 See Harel, op. cit., pp. 125–43.

80 Mahnaimi, op. cit.

81 Harel and Issacharoff, *34 Days*, pp. 128, 135.

82 Ibid., pp. 127, 137.

83 Ibid., p. 138.

84 Ibid., p. 140.

85 Ibid., p. 139.

86 *McClatchy Newspapers*, 30 July 2006.

87 Harel and Issacharoff, *34 Days*, pp. 140–1.

88 Blanford, 'Deconstructing'.

89 Rapaport, Amir, *Maariv*, 10 August 2006.

90 Harel, Amos, *Haaretz*, 1 February 2008.

91 Crooke, op. cit.; Atzmon, op. cit.; Harel, *34 Days*, pp. 127–43, 178–80.

92 Harel, *34 Days*, p. 143.

93 Ibid., p. 152.

94 Harel, *Haaretz*, 1 February 2006.

95 *The Daily Star*, Beirut, 29 July 2006.

96 Fielder, Lucy, *al-Ahram Weekly*, 20–26 July and 3–9 August 2006.

97 *The Daily Star*, Beirut, 29 July 2006.

98 Speech, 15 July 2006; interview with al-Jazeera, 20 July 2006.

99 Atwan, Abd al-Bari, *al-Quds al-Arabi*, London, 8 August 2006.

100 A reference to an Arabian town from which the Jewish population was expelled in the seventh century.

101 Macfarquhar, Neil, *New York Times*, 7 August 2006.

102 Howeidi, Amira, *al-Ahram Weekly*, 20–26 July 2006.

103 Reuters, 4 August 2006.

104 Rubinstein, Danny, *Haaretz*, 8 August 2006.

105 Dai Havard, representative for the district of Merthyr Tydfil.

106 Zunes, Stephen, in Hovsepian, op. cit., p. 98; Meyrav Wurmser, *Ynet*, 16 December 2006.

107 Crooke, op. cit.

108 Mearsheimer and Walt, op. cit., p. 329.

109 Morley, Jefferson, *Washington Post*, 2 August 2006.

110 See Harel and Issacharoff, *34 Days*, p. 162.

111 Ibid., p. 167; *Yediot Aharonot*, 31 July 2006.

112 31 July 2006.

113 Cook, Jonathan, 'Nearly All the War Crimes Were Israel's', *Counterpunch*, 16 August 2007.

114 Ibid.

115 Amnesty International, 'Israel/Lebanon: Deliberate Destruction'..

116 *Human Rights Watch*, 'Fatal Strikes: Israel's Indiscriminate Attacks Against Civilians in Lebanon', August 2006.

117 Harel and Issacharoff, *34 Days*, pp. 122, 161; Crooke, op. cit.

118 Barnea, Nahum, *Yediot Aharonot*, 31 July 2006.

119 Margalit, Dan, *Maariv*, 28 July 2006.

120 *Yediot Aharonot*, 30 July 2006.

121 *Daily Telegraph*, 28 July 2006; Levy, Gideon, *Haaretz*, 10 June 2007.

122 *Haaretz*, 28 July 2006.

123 Usher, Graham, *al-Ahram Weekly*, 27 July–2 August 2006.

124 Historically, Israel had never trusted international forces, except the American-backed multi-national force in Sinai, there by virtue of the Egyptian–Israeli peace treaty.

125 Harel and Issacharoff, *34 Days*, p. 163.

126 *Middle East Reporter*, 2, 3 August 2006.

127 Harel and Issacharoff, *34 Days*, p. 254.

128 Ibid., p. 165.

129 Cited in Cobban, op. cit.

130 Harel and Issacharoff, *34 Days*, p. 157.

131 Ibid., pp. 166–7.

132 Ibid., p. 191.

133 Ibid., pp. 183–4, 196.

134 Kaspit, Ben, *Maariv*, 10 August 2006.

135 *Jerusalem Post*, 11 August 2006.

136 Harel and Issacharoff, *34 Days*, p. 208.

137 Gilat, Mordechai, *Yediot Aharonot*, 29 January 2008.

138 Harel and Issacharoff, *34 Days*, pp. 229, 252.

139 Rapaport, Amir, *Maariv*, 10 August 2006.

140 Harel and Issacharoff, *34 Days*, pp. 209, 237.

141 Ibid., p. 224.

142 Ibid., p. 231.

143 Ibid., p. 236; Atzmon, op. cit.; Petras, James, *The Arab News*, 5 September 2006; 'Quarterly Update of Conflict and Diplomacy', *Journal of Palestine Studies*, No. 141, Autumn 2006, p. 138; Shelah, Ofer, *Maariv*, 26 August 2008.

144 Mearsheimer and Walt, op. cit., p. 322.

145 *Haaretz*, 8 September 2006.

146 *Human Rights Watch*, 'Flooding South Lebanon: Israel's Use of Cluster Munitions in Lebanon in July and August 2006', February 2008.

147 Harel and Issacharoff, *34 Days*, p 237.

CHAPTER FOURTEEN: *Who Won?*

1 See pp. 343–4.

2 www.mideastwire.com, 25 September 2006.

3 See p. 276.

4 www.mideastwire.com, 25 September 2006.

5 Abu Nimah, Hassan, *al-Ghad*, Amman, 10 August 2006.

6 www.mideastwire.com, 25 September 2006; this is a condensation of his actual, somewhat repetitive, words.

7 Barghouti, Tamim, *al-Ahram Weekly*, 3–9 August 2006.

8 Zibakalam, Sadegh, *Bitter Lemons*, 12 June 2008.

9 Agence France Presse, 13 August 2006.

10 Barnea, Nahum, *Yediot Aharonot*, 14 August 2006.

11 Pedatzur, Reuven, *Haaretz*, 16 August 2006.

12 Blanford, Nicholas, *Time*, 4 November 2007.

13 www.mideastwire.com, 25 September 2006.

14 Ibid.

15 *L'Orient Le Jour*, Beirut, 5 September 2006.

16 'Hizbullah and the Lebanese Crisis', International Crisis Group, Middle East Report No. 69, 10 October 2007.

17 *L'Orient Le Jour*, 7 November 2006.

18 *Middle East Reporter*, Beirut, 7 June 2008.

19 Badran, Tony, 'Lebanon's Militia Wars', *MERIA Journal*, June 2008.

20 *Middle East Reporter*, 30 April 2007.

21 *Yediot Aharonot*, 7 November 2007; *Middle East Reporter*, 1 December 2007; *Haaretz*, 18 May and 25 November 2008.

22 *Yediot Aharonot*, 5 August 2008; International Crisis Group, op. cit.; Exum, Andrew, 'Hizbullah's "Big Surprise" and the Litani Line', Washington Institute for Near East Policy, 29 August 2007.

23 7 November 2008.

24 *Haaretz*, 10 February 2008.

25 Exum, op. cit.; Blanford, Nicholas, 'UN Resolution 1701: A View from Lebanon', Washington Institute for Near East Policy, 21 October 2008.

26 'Quarterly Update on Conflict and Diplomacy', *Journal of Palestine Studies*, No. 148, Summer 2008, p. 136.

27 Ibid., p. 135.

28 *The Guardian*, 12 May 2008.

29 *Al-Nahar*, Beirut, 12 May 2008.

30 *Al-Nahar*, 19 May 2008.

31 *Haaretz*, 10, 12 May 2008.

32 See p. 103.

33 Baker, James, *Iraq Study Group Report*, Vintage Books, New York, 2006, p. 44.

34 *Commentary*, February 2007.

35 Dr Zvi Sela, a professional psychologist and one-time intelligence chief of the Israeli Prison Service, who spent long hours with Quntar, calls the standard Israeli version of the affair a 'fairy-tale'. 'He told me he didn't do it' – i.e. smash in the skull of a four-year-old girl – 'and I believe him.' According to Sela, it was the Israeli rescue team that accidentally shot both her and her father. *Haaretz*, 17 April 2009.

36 *Jerusalem Post*, 18 July 2008.

37 Sfard, Michael, *Haaretz*, 6 October 2008.

CHAPTER FIFTEEN: *Gaza*

1 Pedatzur, Reuven, *Haaretz*, 8 January 2009.
2 Makdisi, Saree, *American Task Force on Palestine*, 7 January 2009.
3 Ophir, Adi, *ZSpace*, 9 January 2009.
4 Avnery, Uri, 'How Many Divisions? The Moral Insanity Behind the Lies and Crimes', *Redress Information & Analysis*, 11 January 2009.
5 Harel, Amos, *Haaretz*, 26 January 2009; Avnery, Uri, *Redress Information & Analysis*, 1 February 2009; Cook, Jonathan, *Redress Information & Analysis*, 5 February 2009.
6 Oren, Amir, *Haaretz*, 5 January 2009.
7 See Ging, John, Director of UNRWA in Gaza, Agence France Presse, 23 January 2009.
8 Sfard, Michael, *Haaretz*, 6 October 2008.
9 'The Gaza War: A Strategic Analysis', Center for Strategic and International Studies, Washington, cited in *The Daily Star*, Beirut, 6 February 2009.
10 *Washington Post*, 30 December 2008.
11 Siboni, Gabriel, 'Disproportionate Force: Israel's Concept of Response in Light of the Second Lebanon War', *Insight*, No. 74, Institute for National Strategic Studies, 2 October 2008.
12 *Washington Post*, 14 January 2009.
13 Bonner, Ethan, *New York Times*, 28 December 2008.
14 al-Shahhal, Nahla, *al-Akhbar*, Beirut, 6 January 2009.
15 Cook, Jonathan, *Redress Information & Analysis*, 12 January 2009.
16 BBC News, 29 February 2008.
17 Cook, Jonathan, *American Task Force on Palestine*, 21 January 2009.
18 cnn.com/world, *New York Times*, 9 January 2009.
19 *The Guardian*, London, 10 January 2009.
20 Saad-Ghorayeb, Amal, *The Daily Star*, Beirut, 1 January 2009.
21 Eiland, Giora, 'Who's the Real Enemy', *Israel Opinion*, 24 July 2008; Eiland, Giora, *Strategic Assessment*, Vol. 11, No. 2, November 2008.
22 See p. 274.
23 Saad-Ghorayeb, *The Daily Star*, Beirut, 1 January 2009.
24 *Haaretz*, 1 December 2008.
25 Levy, Gideon, *Haaretz*, 22 January 2008.
26 *Jerusalem Post*, 22 January 2009; *Washington Post*, 25 January 2009.
27 Harel, Amos, and Issacharoff, Avi, *Haaretz*, 12, 17 January 2009; Levy, Gideon, *Haaretz*, 15 January 2009.
28 Yaghi, Mohamad, *al-Ayyam*, Ramallah, 30 January 2009.
29 Levy, Gideon, *Haaretz*, 20 July 2008.
30 *Al-Ahram*, Cairo, 20 January 2009.
31 Karon, Tony, *Time*, 12 February 2009.
32 Amayreh, Khalid, *al-Ahram Weekly*, 15–21 January 2009; *Jerusalem Post*, 23 January 2009.

33 *Yediot Aharonot*, 19 September 2008.

34 Erlanger, Steven, *New York Times*, 5 January 2009.

35 www.ikhwanonline.com, 28 January 2009.

36 See p. 84.

37 'The Gaza War: A Strategic Analysis', op. cit.

38 Harel, Amos, *Haaretz*, 6 February 2009; 'Did Israel Commit War Crimes in Gaza?', *Spiegel International*, 26 January 2009.

39 See pp. 62–6.

40 Rokach, op. cit., p. 38.

41 Melman, Yossi, *Haaretz*, 10 January 2009; Golden, Shai, *Haaretz*, 21 January 2009; Avnery, Uri, 'The Boss Has Gone Mad', *Redress Information & Analysis*, 19 January 2009; 'The Gaza War: A Strategic Analysis', op. cit.

42 www.syriacomment.com, 2 February 2009.

43 Ibish, Hussein, *Chicago Tribune*, 25 January 2009.

44 *The Financial Times*, 23 January 2009.

45 BBC World Service poll, 11 February 2009.

46 O'Loughlin, Toni, *The Guardian*, 6 January 2009.

47 The ban was subsequently overruled by the Supreme Court.

48 *Haaretz*, editorial, 23 January 2009; Levy, Gideon, *Haaretz*, 8 February 2009.

49 *Jerusalem Post*, 5 May 2006.

50 See, for example, Sternhell, Zeev, *Haaretz*, 5 April 2009; Shelah, Ofer, *Maariv*, 13 March 2009.

51 Adiv, Assaf, *Challenge*, Tel Aviv, 3 February 2009.

52 Levy, Gideon, *Haaretz*, 24 May 2009.

53 Gabay, Zvi, *Israel Hayom*, 16 April 2009.

54 Harel, Israel, *Haaretz*, 21 May 2009; Lord, Amnon, *Makor Rishon*, 17 July 2009.

55 Cook, Jonathan, www.redress.cc, August 2009.

56 Shlaim, Avi, *The Guardian*, 7 January 2009.

57 Al-Jazeera television, 1 February 2009.

EPILOGUE: *Obaman Peace – Or Seventh War?*

1 *Haaretz*, 29 November 2007.

2 *From Haven to Conquest: Readings in Zionism and the Palestine Problem Until 1948*, Institute for Palestine Studies, Beirut, 1971, pp. xxi–xxiv.

3 Foxman Abraham, 'Beyond Evenhandedness', *Forward Forum*, 20 February 2009.

4 Reuters, 11 May 2009.

5 Blanford, Nicholas, www.bitterlemons-international.org, 11 June 2009; *Country Reports on Terrorism*, US State Department, April 2009.

6 Beeston, Richard and Blanford, Nicholas, *The Times*, London, 4 August 2009; Harel, Amos, *Haaretz*, 6 August 2009; Weiss, Mark, *Irish Times*, 7 August 2009.

7 *The Daily Star*, Beirut, 3 and 4 August 2009, *Middle East Reporter*, Beirut, 3–7 August 2009.

Index

reputation after Gaza (2009), 415–16;
responses to Sabra and Shatila
massacres, 161–5, 167–8; 'right to
exist', 106; settlements, 419, 423–5;
strategy against Hizbullah, 243,
248–9; territorial expansion policy,
55–6; territory proposed, 14–15; US
relations, 137, 171–2, 195, 260–1, 280–1,
334, 340–1, 361, 367–9, 415, 423–5;
weaponry, 264
Israel Defence Forces (IDF): attacks
on civilians, 396, 399; ethics, 162, 164,
418; Gaza (2009), 402; Lebanon
(2006), 336; name, 57, 104–5; role,
104–5; Sabra and Shatila, 162, 164
Israel Insider, The, 362
Issacharoff, Avi, 369

Jaber, Ali, 203
Jabotinsky, Vladimir, 16, 28–9, 52, 116
Jamal, Khalil al-, 87, 100
Japanese Red Army, 100
Javits, Jacob, Senator, 61
Jawad, Wahib, 87
Jazeera, al-, 403
Jazira plain, 58
Jebel Amil, 12, 36, 176, 177, 187–8, 199
Jerusalem, East, Jewish settlements,
419, 423–5
Jerusalem, liberation: as common
Muslim cause, 217; Hizbullah aim,
204, 216, 217, 218, 241, 268, 376, 404
Jerusalem Day, 197, 217
Jerusalem Post: on 9/11, 280–1; on
Grunzweig's death, 168; on
Hizbullah, 252, 370, 389, 395; on Israeli
army, 370; on Lebanon invasion
(1982), 136; on Qana-II, 362–3; on
Sabra and Shatila, 161, 163
Jewish Agency, 37, 42, 46
Jewish Council, 230
Jezzin, resort, 204, 235
Jibril, Ahmad, 220
Jibsheet, village, 199, 201, 235
jihad: goals, 269, 274; Hizbullah
activities, 232, 233, 236, 274–5, 292, 314,

388; Hizbullah aim, 189, 204, 215–16,
241–2, 268–9, 309, 331–2, 380, 403; Iran
policy, 178, 179, 182, 199; Saudi policy,
415; Sudan call for, 359; volunteers
from Syria, 289
Jihad al-Bina (Jihad for Construction
Foundation), 240
Johnson, Lyndon, President, 72
Jordan (earlier Transjordan): army, 55;
Ben-Gurion's partition plan, 67;
'Black September' (1970), 85–6;
expulsion of Arafat, 97; Fatah base,
84–5; Hashemite monarchy, 55, 68–9;
Israel relations, 55, 424–5; Israeli
peace treaty, 246; Palestinian
refugees, 78, 124, 156; response to
Israeli war with Lebanon (2006), 339;
US ally, 150
Jordan river, 23, 72, 82
Jumblat, Kemal, 90, 91, 101, 112, 121
Jumblat, Walid: Hizbullah relations,
312–13, 314, 317, 339, 392; imprisonment,
392; Iran relations, 339; Lebanese
opposition leadership, 298, 304–5; on
Lebanese situation, 246; political
manoeuvring, 312–13, 314, 426–7; Syria
relations, 298, 299, 301, 303, 317–18, 339,
427
Junieh, port, 170, 234

Kaddoum, West Bank settlement, 117
Kahan, Itzhak, 163
Kahan Commission and Report, 163–4,
167–8
Kahhaleh, 87, 100
Kaouk, Nabil, Sheikh, 252, 268
Kaplinsky, Moshe, 374, 382
Kaplinsky, Or, 374, 382
Karameh, battle of, 84, 87, 92, 411
Karami, Omar, 309–10
Karami, Rashid, 110
Karine-A affair, 272–3, 285
Kaspit, Ben, 333
Kassir, Samir, 306
Katyusha missiles: Beirut artillery
duels, 207; firing positions, 349;